The Facts On File
DICTIONARY OF
PERSONNEL
MANAGEMENT
AND
LABOR RELATIONS

SECOND EDITION, REVISED AND EXPANDED

The Facts On File

DICTIONARY OF PERSONNEL MANAGEMENT AND LABOR RELATIONS

SECOND EDITION, REVISED AND EXPANDED

JAY M. SHAFRITZ

University of Colorado at Denver

The Facts On File
DICTIONARY OF PERSONNEL MANAGEMENT AND LABOR RELATIONS,
2ND EDITION

Library of Congress Cataloging in Publication Data
Shafritz, Jay M.
   The Facts On File dictionary of personnel management and labor relations.

   Rev. ed. of: Dictionary of personnel management and labor relations. 1st ed. c1980.
   1. Personnel management—Dictionaries.   2. Industrial relations—Dictionaries. I. Shafritz, Jay M.
Dictionary of personnel management and labor relations.
II. Facts on File, Inc.   III. Title.   IV. Title:
Dictionary of personnel management and labor relations.
HF5549.A23S52   1985   658.3′003′21   85-20823
ISBN 0-8160-1234-2

Printed in the United States of America

10 9 8 7 6 5 4 3 2 1

PREFACE

This dictionary is a tool for all those who must be knowledgeable about the theory, concepts, practices, laws, institutions, literature, and people of the academic disciplines and professional practices of personnel management and labor relations. In short, it is a tool—a source of expertise—for all those who are faced with, or concerned about, the managing of people in organizations.

A dictionary is inherently a "work in progress." Unless a subject is a dead language or an expired technology, its terminology is constantly changing and evolving into its future state. This is certainly true of personnel management and labor relations. Each year, for example, new Supreme Court decisions, new labor legislation, new advances in examination validation, and new personnel management processes change the language of personnel management and labor relations and advance (or impede depending upon one's perspective) the professional practice. This dictionary seeks to capture and codify the language of personnel management and labor relations fully aware that when finished it will be incomplete. A living language does not wait on publisher's deadlines.

While this effort may be incomplete by its nature, it is nevertheless comprehensive by design. Contained herein are all of the words, terms, phrases, processes, names, laws, and court cases with which personnel management and labor relations specialists should be familiar. And then some. Some because they are historically important. Some just for fun. The criteria for including definitions had to be rather loosely defined because the boundaries of personnel management and labor relations, both as academic disciplines and professional practices, are so wide that they overlap many other fields. It was the author's judgment that determined just how far to go into related fields such as law, economics, psychology, statistics, management, history, and medicine, among others. As a rule of thumb, if a term was found in any of several score personnel management or labor relations textbooks, it is included here. Generally excluded were any terms whose meaning in the context of personnel management and labor relations did not differ from definitions to be found in any standard dictionary of the English language.

This dictionary is generic. It neither favors nor discriminates against the private or public sector. Everything that the author found relevant to either sector was included. In the end, it turned out that 95 percent of the definitions were relevant to the private sector and 95 percent were relevant to the public sector. This seems to be a mathematical impossibility until you consider that 90 percent of the definitions are relevant to both sectors. Each sector can then claim 5 percent of the definitions as uniquely its own. The differences between personnel management and labor relations in the private sector and public personnel management and labor relations continue to grow less significant with the passing of each year and with the passing of each new wave of federal legislation.

In general, those items which are more central to the concerns of personnel management and labor relations tend to be given more detailed coverage than those that are more on the periphery of the subject. The references given at the end of most entries serve to give an example of the usage of the term as well as to provide sources for further information. Because such references have been given as often as is possible or practical, they are in their totality a comprehensive bibliography. In order to find all of the entries in any given subset of personnel management or labor relations, you need only find a logical large entry—bureaucracy, collective bargaining, strike, etc.—and follow the cross references.

In addition to the entries that the reader might expect to find in a dictionary concerned with personnel management and labor relations, there are some special kinds of entries that warrant a word of explanation:

- **BIOGRAPHICAL ENTRIES.** There are hundreds of identifications of individuals, both living and dead, who have been significant in the history, writing, and practice of personnel management and labor relations. Such entries are designed to merely identify an individual; that being the purpose of a dictionary. The author readily concedes that some notable individuals may have been excluded or that other individuals may have been described in words too brief to do them justice. Remember, the object was identification, not justice.

- **COURT CASES.** There are hundreds of legal decisions on issues relevant to personnel management and labor relations, including *every* major U.S. Supreme Court ruling in this area. Such judicial decisions are usually many pages long for good reason. So be cautious! A brief summary of a case, no matter how succinct, may not be sufficient information upon which to base formal action. These summaries were written to identify the case and its significance, not necessarily to make less work for lawyers. The full legal citation is given with each entry of this type so that the reader may readily locate the full text of any of these court cases.

- **JOURNALS.** A list of *all* of the journals and magazines that bear upon personnel management and labor relations would be almost as large as this entire dictionary. So the author included only those periodicals that most consistently address the concerns of personnel and labor relations specialists. Each periodical entry contains a statement of purpose as well as an appropriate address. A master list of all journal entries is found under the entry "personnel journals."

- **LAWS.** All federal laws that directly impact upon personnel and labor relations practices are summarized. The reader should be aware that these entries are necessarily brief summaries of complicated laws that are constantly subject to amendment.

- **ORGANIZATIONS.** All of the major governmental agencies, private organizations, and professional societies that bear upon personnel management and labor relations have been included. All such entries contain a statement of the purposes of the organization as well as its address and phone number.

- **TESTS.** Included are descriptions of the most commonly used commercial tests used in personnel selection and employee counseling. A master list of all commercial test entries is found under the entry for "personnel tests."

No one writes a dictionary alone. My various intellectual debts are acknowledged throughout this book by the bibliographic references that follow many of the entries. I am also indebted to the legions of anonymous Federal bureaucrats who prepared many of the manuals, regulations, and pamphlets that provided much of the raw material for so many entries. I am especially grateful to John W. Moore of the Moore Publishing Company, who did so much to inspire the first edition of this book and then graciously allowed me to do this second edition with Facts On File, Inc. On a more personal level many individuals encouraged me along the way. Albert C. Hyde, Daniel Oran, and David H. Rosenbloom (all sometime coauthors) were the most helpful. I am also indebted to Joseph D. Atkinson, Jr., Harry A. Bailey, Jr., Albert Bowman, Sarah Bowman, Patricia Breivik, Kay Smith Cormier, Stanley Goldstein, Mary Lou Goodyear, Robert W. Gage, Marshall Kaplan, William Kent, John W. Moore, Dail A. Neugarten, J. Steven Ott, E. Sam Overman, Thomas H. Patten, Jr., Raymond Pomerleau, Robert E. Quinn, Frank J. Thompson, Nobotoshi Umeda, and E. C. Wakham.

Finally some domestic acknowledgements. My wife, Luise, was my most severe critic, ever reminding me that the dictionary would get done sooner if I would turn off the television. At such times I always assured her that I was in fact diligently thinking about a complex definition. My sons, Todd and Noah, assisted me enormously by advising me of when I violated the laws of alphabetical order, by telling me to "hurry up and finish," and by ever reminding me of how difficult it is to manage the personnel of even a single household.

JAY M. SHAFRITZ

CONTENTS

The Facts On File

DICTIONARY OF PERSONNEL MANAGEMENT AND LABOR RELATIONS

SECOND EDITION, REVISED AND EXPANDED

A

AA: *see* AFFIRMATIVE ACTION.

AAA: *see* AMERICAN ARBITRATION ASSOCIATION.

AACSB: *see* AMERICAN ASSEMBLY OF COLLEGIATE SCHOOLS OF BUSINESS.

AAG: *see* AFFIRMATIVE ACTION GROUPS.

AAO: *see* AFFIRMATIVE ACTION OFFICER.

AAP: *see* AFFIRMATIVE ACTION PLAN or AFFIRMATIVE ACTION PROGRAM.

abandonment of position, quitting a job without formally resigning.

abdication, giving up a public office by ceasing to perform its function rather than by formally resigning.

Abel, I. W. (1908-   ), full name IORWITH WILBER ABEL, president of the United Steel Workers of America from 1965 to 1977. For biographical information, *see:* John Herling, *Right to Challenge: People and Power in the Steelworkers Union* (N.Y.: Harper & Row, 1972).

ability, the present power to perform a physical or mental function. *See* Stephen Dakin and A. John Arrowood, "The Social Comparison of Ability," *Human Relations* (February 1981).

ability test, performance test designed to reveal a measure of present ability (*e.g.,* a typing test).

ability to pay, concept from collective bargaining referring to an employer's ability to tolerate the costs of requested wage and benefit increases. Factfinders and arbitrators frequently use the "ability to pay" concept in justifying their decisions.

See also NATIONAL LABOR RELATIONS BOARD V. TRUITT MANUFACTURING.

Abood v. Detroit Board of Education, 431 U.S. 209 (1977), U.S. Supreme Court case, which held that public sector agency shops requiring nonunion employees to pay a service fee equivalent to union dues were constitutional. The court declared unconstitutional a union's use of such service fees for political and ideological purposes unrelated to collective bargaining. *See* Charles M. Rehmus and Benjamin A. Kerner, "The Agency Shop After *Abood:* No Free Ride, But What's the Fare?" *Industrial and Labor Relations Review* (October 1980).

abrogation of agreement, formal cancellation of a collective bargaining agreement or portion thereof.

absence, short-term unavailability for work, lasting at least one day or normal tour of duty. If an employee is absent from the job for a lesser period, it is usually considered a lateness. For an analysis of the relationship between absence and job satisfaction, *see* Nigel Nicholson, Colin A. Brow, and J. K. Chadwick-Jones, "Absence From Work and Job Satisfaction," *Journal of Applied Psychology* (December 1976). *See also* Donald L. Hawk, "Absenteeism and Turnover," *Personnel Journal* (June 1976). For some comparative statistics, *see* Janice Neipert Hedges, "Absence from Work—A Look at Some National Data," *Monthly Labor Review* (July 1973); Carol Boyd Leon, "Employed But Not At Work: A Review of Unpaid Absences," *Monthly Labor Review* (November 1981).

absence rate, amount of absence, calculated by the U.S. Bureau of Labor Statistics using the following formula:

$$absence\ rate = \frac{work\ days\ lost\ (per\ month)}{days\ worked\ plus\ days\ lost} \times 100$$

1

absence without leave, absence without prior approval.

absentee, any worker not present for one or more scheduled days of work. *See* John Scherba and Lyle Smith, "Computerization of Absentee Control Programs," *Personnel Journal* (May 1973); Steve Markham and Dow Scott, "Controlling Absenteeism: Union and Nonunion Differences," *Personnel Administrator* (February 1985).

absenteeism, as defined by the U.S. Bureau of Labor Statistics:

> the failure of workers to appear on the job when they are scheduled to work. It is a broad term which is applied to time lost because sickness or accident prevents a worker from being on the job, as well as unauthorized time away from the job for other reasons. Workers who quit without notice are also counted as absentees until they are officially removed from the payroll.

Generally, "absenteeism" is associated with unnecessary, unexcused, or habitual absences from work. For academic analyses of the problem, *see* R. Oliver Gibson, "Toward a Conceptualization of Absence Behavior of Personnel in Organizations," *Administrative Science Quarterly* (June 1966); J. K. Chadwick-Jones, Nigel Nicholson and Colin Brown, *Social Psychology of Absenteeism* (New York, Praeger Publishers, 1982). For "nuts-and-bolts" presentations of the problem, *see* Frederick J. Gaudet, *Solving the Problem of Employee Absence* (N.Y.: American Management Associations, 1963); Dan R. Dalton and James L. Perry, "Absenteeism and the Collective Bargaining Agreement: An Empirical Test," *Academy of Management Journal* (June 1981); Ronald J. Bula, "Absenteeism Control," *Personnel Journal* (June 1984). For a bibliography, *see* Paul M. Muchinsky, "Employee Absenteeism: A Review of the Literature," *Journal of Vocational Behavior* (June 1977). For the "no-fault" perspective, *see*: Darrell Olson and Ruth Bangs, "No-Fault Attendance Control: A Real World Application," *Personnel Administrator* (June 1984); Frank E. Kuzmits, "Is Your Organization Ready for No-Fault Absenteeism?" *Personnel Administrator* (December 1984).

See also REINFORCEMENT.

absolute advantage, an international trade concept formulated by Adam Smith which holds that one nation has an *absolute advantage* over another when it can produce more of a product using the same amount of resources than the other can.

See also ADAM SMITH, COMPARATIVE ADVANTAGE.

Academic Collective Bargaining Information Service, a clearinghouse and research center for information on all aspects of labor relations in higher education.

Academic Collective Bargaining Information Service,
Labor Studies Center
724 Ninth Street, N.W.
University of the District of Columbia
Washington, D.C. 20001
(202) 727-2903

Academy of Management, nonprofit organization with primary objectives of advancing research, learning, teaching, and practice in the field of management and encouraging the extension and unification of knowledge pertaining to management. The Academy, most of whose members are college teachers, views itself as America's academic "voice" in U.S. management.

Academy of Management Journal, quarterly that publishes articles in the fields of business policy and planning, international management, management consulting, management education and development, management history, manpower management, organizational behavior, organization and management theory, organization development, production-operations management, social issues in management, organizational communication, and health care administration.

The *Journal* publishes original research of an empirical nature either in the form of articles or as research notes. Although studies which serve to test either theoretical propositions or hypotheses derived from practice are of particular interest, exploratory work and survey research findings are also included. The *Journal* does not publish purely conceptual papers which do not contain any original data. Conceptual articles of this kind are published in the *Academy of Management Journal.*

Academy of Management Journal
P.O. Box KZ
Mississippi State University
Mississippi State, MS 39762

Academy of Management Review, quarterly that publishes articles in the field of business policy and planning, international management, management consulting, management education and development, management history, personnel/human resources, organizational behavior, organization and management theory, organization development, production-operations management, social issues in management, organizational communication, and health care administration.

The *Review* seeks distinguished original manuscripts which (a) move theoretical conceptualization forward in the field of management, and/or (b) indicate new theoretical linkages that have rich potential for theory and research in management, and (c) provide clear implications of theory for problem-solving in administrative and organizational situations.

Academy of Management Review
P.O. Box KZ
Mississippi State University
Mississippi State, MS 39762

accelerating premium pay, bonus incentive system in which pay rates rise as production standards are exceeded. For example, an employee who exceeds standard production by two percent may get just a two percent bonus, while an employee who exceeds by five percent may get a ten percent bonus.

acceptable level of unemployment, an acceptable level of unemployment means that the individual to whom it is acceptable still has a job.

acceptance theory of authority: *see* ZONE OF ACCEPTANCE.

accession, any addition to the workforce of an organization.

accession rate, also called HIRING RATE, number of employees added to a payroll during a given time period, usually expressed as a percentage of total employment. The accession rate is a significant indicator of economic growth—an increase (decrease) tends to indicate economic recovery (recession). Statistics on the accession rates of major industries are gathered monthly by the Bureau of Labor Statistics of the U.S. Department of Labor. Accession rates can be computed using the following formula:

$$accession\ rate = \frac{total\ accessions \times 100}{total\ number\ of\ workers}$$

accidental death benefit, feature found in some life insurance policies that provides for payment of additional amounts to the beneficiary if the insured party dies as a result of an accident. When such provisions allow for an accidental death benefit that is twice the normal value of the policy, they are known as "double-indemnity" provisions.

accident and sickness benefits, variety of regular payments made to employees who lose time from work due to off-the-job disabilities occasioned by accidents or sickness.

accident frequency rate, as computed by the Bureau of Labor Statistics, the accident frequency rate is the total number of disabling injuries per million hours worked. *See* Paul C. Rohan and Bernard Brody, "Frequency and Costs of Work Accidents in North America, 1971-80," *Labour and Society* (April-June 1984).

accident prevention, total planned effort

on the part of labor, management, and government regulators to eliminate the causes and severity of industrial injuries and accidents. For a text, *see* Willie Hammer, *Occupational Safety Management and Engineering* (Englewood Cliffs, N.J.: Prentice-Hall, 1976). *Also see* Robert A. Reber, Jerry A. Wallin, and Jagdeep S. Chhokar, "Reducing Industrial Accidents: A Behavioral Experiment," *Industrial Relations* (Winter 1984).

accident-proneness, concept that implies that certain kinds of personalities are more likely to have accidents than others. However, psychological research supports the assertion that accident-proneness is more related to situational factors than personality factors. For the classic analysis on the subject, *see* A. G. Arbous and J. E. Kerrich, "The Phenomenon of Accident-Proneness," *Industrial Medicine and Surgery* (April 1953). Nevertheless, Joseph T. Kunce established a relationship between "Vocational Interest and Accident Proneness," in the *Journal of Applied Psychology* (June 1967).

accident severity rate, generally computed as the number of work days lost because of accidents per thousand hours worked.

accountability, extent to which one is responsible to higher authority—legal or organizational—for one's actions in society at large or within one's particular organizational position. For discussion in a public administration context, *see* Jerome B. McKinney and Lawrence C. Howard, *Public Administration: Balancing Power and Accountability* (Oak Park, Ill.: Moore Publishing Co., 1979). For a private sector context, *see* Robert Albanese, *Managing: Toward Accountability for Performance,* 3rd ed. (Homewood, Ill.: Richard D. Irwin, rev. ed., 1981).

accreditation, the process by which an agency or organization evaluates and recognizes a program of study or an institution as meeting certain predetermined standards. The recognition is called accreditation. Similar assessment of individ-

uals is called *certification. See* PERSONNEL ACCREDITATION INSTITUTE.

achievement battery: *see* ACHIEVEMENT TEST.

achievement drive, also called ACHIEVEMENT NEED, motivation to strive for high standards of performance in a given area of endeavor. For the classic work on achievement motivation, *see* David C. McClelland, *The Achieving Society* (Princeton, N.J.: Van Nostrand Rinehold Co., 1961). *Also see* David C. McClelland, "Achievement Motivation Can be Developed," *Harvard Business Review* (November–December 1965); Perry Pascarella, *The New Achievers* (New York, The Free Press, 1984).

achievement need: *see* ACHIEVEMENT DRIVE.

achievement test, test designed to measure an individual's level of proficiency in a specific subject or task. A collection of achievement tests designed to measure levels of skill or knowledge in a variety of areas is called an achievement battery. *See* Norman E. Gronlund, *Constructing Achievement Tests* (Englewood Cliffs, N.J.: Prentice-Hall, 2nd ed., 1977).

ACIPP: *see* ADVISORY COUNCIL ON INTER-GOVERNMENTAL PERSONNEL POLICY.

across-the-board increase, increase in wages, whether expressed in dollars or percentage of salary, given to an entire workforce.

act, written bill formally passed by a legislature, such as the U.S. Congress. An act is a "bill" from its introduction until its passage by a legislature. An act becomes a law when it is signed, by a chief executive, such as the U.S. President.

actionable, an act or occurrence is actionable if it provides adequate reason for a grievance or lawsuit.

action plan, a description of the specific steps involved in achieving a goal. *See*

Waldron Berry, "An Action Planning Process for All," *Supervisory Management* (April 1984).

action research, in its broadest context, the application of the scientific method to practical problems. As the basic model underlying organization development, action research, according to Wendell L. French and Cecil H. Bell, Jr., in *Organization Development: Behavioral Science Interventions for Organization Improvement* (Englewood Cliffs, N.J.: Prentice-Hall, 1973), is:

the process of systematically collecting research data about an ongoing system relative to some objective, goal, or need of that system; feeding these data back into the system; taking actions by altering selected variables within the system

based both on the data and on hypotheses; and evaluating the results of actions by collecting more data. This definition characterizes action research in terms of the activities comprising the process: first a static picture is taken of an organization; on the basis of "what exists," hunches and hypotheses suggest actions; these actions typically entail manipulating some variable in the system that is under the control of the action researcher (this often means doing something differently from the way it has always been done); later, a second static picture is taken of the system to examine the effects of the actions taken. For a book-length study of action research in action, *see* William F. Whyte and Edith L. Hamilton, Action *Research for Management* (Homewood, Ill.: Irwin-Dorsey

---

AN ACTION RESEARCH MODEL FOR ORGANIZATION DEVELOPMENT

etc.

Joint action planning (Objectives of OD program and means of attaining goals, e.g., "team building")

Feedback to key client or client group

Further data gathering

Data gathering and diagnosis by consultant

Consultation with behavioral scientist consultant

Key executive perception of problems

Action (new behavior)

Action planning (determination of objectives and how to get there)

Discussion and work on data feedback and data by client group (new attitudes, new perspectives emerge)

Feedback to client group (e.g., in team building sessions, summary feedback by consultant: elaboration by group)

Data gathering

Action

Action planning

Discussion and work on feedback and emerging data

Feedback

Data gathering (reassessment of state of the system)

SOURCE: Wendell French, "Organization Development: Objectives, Assumptions and Strategies," *California Management Review* Vol. 12, No. 2 (Winter 1969), p. 26. © 1969 by the Regents of the University of California. Reprinted by permission of the Regents.

Press, 1964). *See also* Mark A. Frohman, Marshall Sashkin, and Michael J. Kavanagh, "Action Research As Applied to Organization Development," *Organization and Administrative Sciences* (Spring/Summer 1976); Melvin Blumberg and Charles D. Pringle, "How Control Groups Can Cause Loss of Control in Action Research: The Case of Rushton Coal Mine," *The Journal of Applied Behavioral Science,* Vol. 19, No. 4 (1983); Michael Peters and Viviane Robinson, "The Origins and Status of Action Research," *The Journal of Applied Behavioral Science,* Vol. 20, No. 2 (1984).

active listening, counseling technique in which the counselor listens to both the facts and the feelings of the speaker. Such listening is called "active" because the counselor has the specific responsibilities of showing interest, of not passing judgment, and of helping the speaker to work out his or her problems. For a discussion, *see* Carl R. Rogers and Richard E. Farson, "Active listening," *Readings in Management: An Organizational Perspective,* edited by C. R. Anderson and M. J. Gannon (Boston: Little, Brown and Co., 1977).

actuarial projections, mathematical calculations involving the rate of mortality for a given group of people. *See* Robert W. Batten, *Mortality Table Construction* (Englewood Cliffs, N.J.: Prentice-Hall, 1978) and Howard E. Winklevoss, *Pension Mathematics with Numerical Illustrations* (Homewood, Ill.: Richard D. Irwin, 1977).

actuary, specialist in the mathematics of insurance. *See* John H. Flittie and Andrea Feshbach, "Ten Questions to Ask Your Actuary," *Governmental Finance* (June 1981).

Adair v. United States: *see* ERDMAN ACT OF 1898.

Adamson Act of 1916, federal law that provided the eight-hour day for interstate railroad employees. Its constitutionality was upheld by the U.S. Supreme Court in *Wilson v. New,* 243 U.S. 332 (1917).

Adams v. Tanner, 224 U.S. 590 (1917), U.S. Supreme Court case that held private employment agencies could be regulated by the states but could not be prohibited.

Adaptability Test, The, mental ability test designed specifically for use in industrial job placements. This 35-item, spiral-omnibus test is used primarily with clerical workers and first-line supervisors. TIME: 15 minutes; AUTHORS: Joseph Tiffin and C. H. Lawshe; PUBLISHER: Science Research Associates, Inc. (*see* TEST PUBLISHERS).

addiction: *see* DRUG ADDICTION.

ad hoc, Latin meaning: for this special purpose or for this one time.

ad hoc arbitrator, arbitrator selected by the parties involved to serve on one case. Nothing prevents the arbitrator from being used again if both parties agree. *Ad hoc* or temporary, single-case arbitration is distinguished from "permanent" arbitration where arbitrators are named in an agreement to help resolve disputes about the agreement that may arise during the life of the agreement.

ad hoc committee, committee created for a specific task or purpose, whose existence ceases with the attainment of its goal.

ad-hocracy, Alvin Toffler's term, in *Future Shock* (N.Y.: Random House, 1970), for "the fast-moving, information-rich, kinetic organization of the future, filled with transient cells and extremely mobile individuals." Ad-hocracy is obviously a contraction of ad hoc (Latin for "to this" or temporary) and bureaucracy.

Adkins v. Children's Hospital: *see* WEST COAST HOTEL V. PARRISH.

adjudication, the formal giving, pronouncing, or recording of a judgment for one side or the other in a legal case.

adjusted case, according to the National Labor Relations Board, cases are closed as "adjusted" when an informal settlement agreement is executed and compliance with its terms is secured. A central element in an "adjusted" case is the agreement of the parties to settle differences without recourse to litigation.

adjustment assistance, financial and technical assistance to firms, workers, and communities to help them adjust to rising import competition. While the benefits of increased trade to the importing country generally exceed the costs of adjustments, the benefits are widely shared while the adjustment costs are sometimes narrowly concentrated on a few domestic producers and communities. Both import restraints and adjustment assistance are designed to reduce these hardships. But adjustment assistance, unlike import restraints, allows the economy to enjoy the full benefits of trade expansion. Adjustment assistance is designed to facilitate structural shifts of resources from less productive to more productive industries, contributing further to improved standards of living. Under U.S. law qualified workers adversely affected by increased import competition can receive special unemployment compensation, retraining to develop new skills, and job search and relocation assistance; affected firms can receive technical assistance and loan guarantees to finance their modernization or shift to other product lines, and communities threatened by expanding imports can receive loans and other assistance to attract new industry or to enable existing plants to move into more competitive fields. *See:* Steve Charnovitz, "Trade Adjustment Assistance: What Went Wrong?" *The Journal of the Institute for Socioeconomic Studies* (Spring 1984).

administrative agency, any impartial private or governmental organization that oversees or facilitates the labor relations process. The contemporary pattern of labor relations in both the public and private sectors relies on administrative agencies to provide on-going supervision of the collective bargaining process. While generally headed by a board of from three to five members, these agencies make rulings on unfair labor practices, on the appropriateness of bargaining units, and, sometimes, on the proper interpretation of a contract or the legitimacy of a scope of bargaining. They also oversee representation elections and certify the winners as the exclusive bargaining agents for all of the employees in a bargaining unit. The National Labor Relations Board is the prototype of administrative agencies dealing with labor relations. The NLRB model has been adapted to the public sector by the federal government and several states. The equivalent agency for federal employees is the Federal Labor Relations Authority. In the states such agencies are generally called Public Employment Relations Boards (or PERBs). Typically, their functions parallel those of the NLRB, as does the methods by which they are appointed, their terms of office, and their administrative procedures. One important difference in the public sector is that binding arbitration over interests may be used instead of strikes as the final means of resolving disputes. When this is the case, the PERB may have a role in overseeing the use of arbitration and even the substance of the arbitrators' rulings when they raise serious issues about the scope of bargaining or public policy.

administrative analysis, totality of the approaches and techniques that allow an organization to assess its present condition in order to make adjustments that further enhance the organization's ability to achieve its goals.

See also SYSTEMS ANALYSIS and STRATEGIC MANAGEMENT.

administrative behavior, human behavior in an organizational context. While administrative behavior tends to be used interchangeably with organizational behavior, the latter by implication restricts itself to work organizations while the former is rightly concerned with all of the organizations of society. The classic work on this subject is Herbert A. Simon, *Administrative Behavior: A Study of Decision-Making Processes in Administrative Organizations* (New York: Macmillan, 3rd ed., 1947,

1976). *See also* Herbert Kaufman, *The Forest Ranger: A Study in Administrative Behavior* (Baltimore: Johns Hopkins Press, 1960) and Sidney Malick and Edward H. Van Ness, eds., *Concepts and Issues in Administrative Behavior* (Englewood Cliffs, N.J.: Prentice-Hall, 1962).

See also BUREAUCRACY and ORGANIZATIONAL BEHAVIOR.

Administrative Conference of the United States, a permanent independent agency established by the Administrative Conference Act of 1964. The purpose of the Administrative Conference is to develop improvements in the legal procedures by which federal agencies administer regulatory, benefit, and other government programs. As members of the Conference, agency heads, other federal officials, private lawyers, university professors, and other experts in administrative law and government are provided with a forum in which they can conduct continuing studies of selected problems involving administrative procedures and combine their experience and judgment in cooperative efforts toward improving the fairness and effectiveness of such procedures.

Administrative Conference of the United States
2120 L Street, N.W.
Washington, D.C. 20037
(202) 254-7020

administrative due process, term encompassing a number of points in administrative law which require that the administrative procedures of government agencies and regulatory commissions, as they affect private parties, be based upon written guidelines that safeguard individual rights and protect against the arbitrary or inequitable exercise of bureaucratic power.

See also DUE PROCESS.

administrative law, as defined by the man who has written the standard texts on the subject, Kenneth Culp Davis:

Administrative law is the law concerning the powers and procedures of administrative agencies, including especially the law governing judicial review of administrative action. An administrative agency is a governmental authority, other than a court and other than a legislative body, which affects the rights of private parties through either adjudication, rulemaking, investigating, prosecuting, negotiating, settling, or informally acting. An administrative agency may be called a commission, board, authority, bureau, office, officer, administrator, department, corporation, administration, division or agency. Nothing of substance hinges on the choice of name, and usually the choices have been entirely haphazard. When the President, or a governor, or a municipal governing body exercises powers of adjudication or rulemaking, he or it is to that extent an administrative agency.

See Kenneth Culp Davis, *Administrative Law Text,* 3rd ed. (St. Paul, Minn.: West Publishing Co., 1972). *Also see* Bernard Schwartz and H. W. R. Wade, *Legal Control of Government: Administrative Law in Britain and the United States* (New York: Oxford-Clarendon Press, 1972); Donald P. Rothschild and Charles H. Koch, Jr., *Fundamentals of Administrative Practice and Procedure: Cases and Procedure* (Charlottesville, Va.: Michie Bobbs-Merrill Law Publishing, 1981); Kenneth F. Warren, *Administrative Law in the American Political System* (St. Paul, Minn.: West Publishing, 1982); Richard C. Cortner, *The Bureaucracy in Court: Commentaries and Case Studies in Administrative Law* (Port Washington, N.Y.: Kennikat Press, 1982).

administrative law judge, also called HEARING EXAMINER and HEARING OFFICER, governmental official who conducts hearings in the place of and in behalf of a more formal body, such as the National Labor Relations Board or the Merit Systems Protection Board. *See* Paul N. Pfeiffer, "Hearing Cases Before Several Agencies —Odyssey of an Administrative Law Judge," *Administrative Law Review* (Summer 1975).

administrative morality, use of religious, political, or social precepts to create standards by which the quality of public administration may be judged; in the main, the standards of honesty, responsiveness, efficiency, effectiveness, competence, effect on individual rights, adherence to democratic procedures, and social equity. *See* Paul H. Appleby, *Morality and Administration in American Government* (Louisiana State University Press, 1952); Robert T. Golembiewski, *Men, Management, and Morality: Toward A New Organizational Ethic* (New York: McGraw-Hill, 1965); Dwight Waldo, "Reflections on Public Morality:" *Administration and Society* (November 1974); Joel L. Fleishman, Lance Liebman and Mark H. Moore, eds., *Public Duties: The Moral Obligations of Government Officials* (Cambridge, Mass.: Harvard University Press, 1981); Gregory D. Foster, "Legalism, Moralism and the Bureaucratic Mentality," *Public Personnel Management,* Vol. 10, No. 1 (1981).

administrative order, a directive carrying the force of law issued by an administrative agency.

Administrative Procedure Act of 1946, basic law of how U.S. Government agencies must operate in order to provide adequate safeguards for agency clients and the general public.

administrative process, according to Stephen P. Robbins, *The Administrative Process: Integrating Theory and Practice* (Englewood Cliffs, N.J.: Prentice-Hall, 1976), the "planning, organizing, leading, and evaluating of others so as to achieve a specific end." However, in the context of public administration, the administrative process also involves exercising the formal authority of the state. *See* Louis C. Gawthrop, ed., *The Administrative Process and Democratic Theory* (Boston: Houghton Mifflin Co., 1970).

administrative reform, according to Gerald Caiden, *Administration Reform* (Chicago: Aldine, 1969), "administrative reform—the artificial inducement of administrative transformation against resistance—has existed ever since men conceived better ways of organizing their social activities. . . . Administrative reform is power politics in action; it contains ideological rationalizations, fights for control of areas, services, and people, political participants and institutions, power drives, campaign strategies and obstructive tactics, compromises and concessions."

administrative remedy, a means of enforcing a right by going to an administrative agency either for help or for a decision. People are often required to "exhaust all administrative remedies" by submitting their problems to the proper agency before taking their case to court.

Administrative Science Quarterly, this quarterly, the premier scholarly journal of its kind, is dedicated to advancing the understanding of administration through empirical investigation and theoretical analysis. Articles cover all phases of management, human relations, organizational behavior, and organizational communications.

Administrative Science Quarterly
Graduate School of Management
Cornell University
Malott Hall
Ithaca, NY 14853

administrative workweek, period of seven consecutive calendar days designated in advance by the head of the agency. Usually an administrative workweek coincides with a calendar week.

administrator, any manager; the head of a government agency; or someone appointed by a court to handle a deceased person's estate.
See also MANAGEMENT.

admonition, simple reproval of an employee by a supervisor.
See also REPRIMAND.

ADO: *see* ALLEGED DISCRIMINATORY OFFICIAL.

Advanced Personnel Test (APT), test of verbal reasoning ability used by business and industry for employment and upgrading of management and research personnel. TIME: Untimed. AUTHOR: W. S. Miller. PUBLISHER: Psychological Corporation (*see* TEST PUBLISHERS).

advance on wages, wages/salaries drawn in advance of work performance or earned commissions. Also applies to payments in advance of the regular pay day for sums already earned.

adverse action, personnel action considered unfavorable to an employee, such as discharge, suspension, demotion, etc.
See also DISCIPLINARY ACTION.

adverse effect, differential rate of selection (for hire, promotion, etc.) that works to the disadvantage of an applicant subgroup, particularly subgroups classified by race, sex, and other characteristics on the basis of which discrimination is prohibited by law.
See also WASHINGTON V. DAVIS.

adverse impact, when a selection process for a particular job or group of jobs results in the selection of members of any racial, ethnic, or sex group at a lower rate than members of other groups, that process is said to have adverse impact. Federal EEO enforcement agencies generally regard a selection rate for any group that is less than four-fifths (4/5) or eighty percent of the rate for other groups as constituting evidence of adverse impact. *See* John Klinefelter and James Thompkins, "Adverse Impact in Employment Selection," *Public Personnel Management* (May–June 1976); Irwin Greenberg, "An Analysis of the EEOC 'Four-Fifths' Rule," *Management Science* (August 1979); Gail F. Jones, "Usefulness of Different Statistical Techniques for Determining Adverse Impact in Small Jurisdictions," *Review of Public Personnel Personnel Administration* (Fall 1981); Robert J. Haertel, "The Statistical Procedures for Calculating Adverse Impact," *Personnel Administrator* (February 1984).

See also SYSTEMIC DISCRIMINATION and WASHINGTON V. DAVIS.

adverse-inference rule, an analytical tool used by the Equal Employment Opportunity Commission (EEOC) in its investigations. The EEOC holds that when relevant evidence is withheld by an organization when the EEOC feels that there is no valid reason for such a withholding, the EEOC may presume that the evidence in question is adverse to the organization being investigated. The EEOC Compliance Manual permits use of the adverse-inference rule only if "the requested evidence is relevant," the evidence was requested "with ample time to produce it and with notice that failure to produce it would result in an adverse inference," and the "respondent produced neither the evidence nor an acceptable explanation."

advisory arbitration, arbitration that recommends a solution of a dispute but is not binding upon either party.

Advisory Council on Intergovernmental Personnel Policy (ACIPP), organization created to advise the President on intergovernmental personnel matters. It was established on January 5, 1971 by President Nixon's Executive Order 11607, in accordance with the requirements of the Intergovernmental Personnel Act of 1970 (Public Law 91-648). The Council was abolished June, 25, 1974 by Executive 11792.

affected class, according to the U.S. Department of Labor's Office of Federal Contract Compliance:
persons who continue to suffer the present effects of past discrimination. An employee or group of employees may be members of an affected class when, because of discrimination based on race, religion, sex, or national origin, such employees, for example, were assigned initially to less desirable or lower paying jobs, were denied equal opportunity to advance to better paying or more desirable jobs, or were subject to layoff

or displacement from their jobs.

Employees may continue to be members of an "affected class" even though they may have been transferred or advanced into more desirable positions if the effects of past discrimination have not been remedied. For example, if an employee who was hired into a lower paying job because of past discriminatory practices has been subsequently promoted, further relief may be required if the employee has not found his or her "rightful place" in the employment structure of a federal government contractor.

affidavit, written statement made under oath before a person permitted by law to administer such an oath (e.g., a notary public). Such statements are frequently used in labor arbitration and other formal hearings.

affirmative action, when the term first gained currency in the 1960s, it meant the removal of "artificial barriers" to the employment of women and minority group members. Toward the end of that decade, however, the term got lost in a fog of semantics and came out meaning the provision of compensatory opportunities for hitherto disadvantaged groups. In a formal, legal sense, affirmative action now refers to specific efforts to recruit, hire, and promote disadvantaged groups for the purpose of eliminating the present effects of past discrimination. For an official treatment, see U.S. Equal Employment Opportunity Commission, *Affirmative Action and Equal Employment: A Guidebook for Employers* (Washington, D.C., U.S. Government Printing Office, 1974). For a hostile critique, see Nathan Glazer, *Affirmative Discrimination: Ethnic Inequality and Public Policy* (N.Y.: Basic Books, 1975). *Also see* Margery M. Milnick, "Equal Employment Opportunity and Affirmative Action: A Managerial Training Guide," *Personnel Journal* (October 1977); Diane P. Jackson, "Affirmative Action for the Handicapped and Veterans: Interpretative and Operational Guidelines," *Labor Law Journal* (February 1978); Carl J. Bellone and Douglas H.

Darling, "Implementing Affirmative Action Programs: Problems and Strategies," *Public Personnel Management,* Vol. 9, No. 3 (1980); Michael A. Hitt and Barbara W. Keats, "Empirical Identification on the Criteria for Effective Affirmative Action Programs," *The Journal of Applied Behavioral Science,* Vol. 20, No. 3 (1984); David H. Rosenbloom, "The Declining Salience of Affirmative Action in Federal Personnel Management," *Review of Public Personnel Administration* (Summer 1984).

See also the following entries:
DEFUNIS V. ODEGAARD
EQUAL EMPLOYMENT OPPORTUNITY
PHILADELPHIA PLAN
REGENTS OF THE UNIVERSITY OF CALIFORNIA V. ALLAN BAKKE
REVERSE DISCRIMINATION
RIGHTFUL PLACE
TITLE VII
TOKENISM
UNITED STEELWORKERS OF AMERICA V. WEBER ET AL.
UPWARD-MOBILITY PROGRAM
VOCATIONAL REHABILITATION ACT OF 1973

Affirmative Action Compliance Manual for Federal Contractors, publication of the Bureau of National Affairs, Inc., which includes a "News and Developments" report, plus the manual used by the Office of Federal Contract Compliance Programs (OFCCP), the OFCCP Construction Compliance Program Operations Manual, and material taken from the official compliance manuals used by the Department of Defense, the Department of the Treasury, the Department of Housing and Urban Development, and the Department of Health and Human Services—with appropriate excerpts from other official compliance manuals.

affirmative action groups, also called PROTECTED GROUPS, segments of the population that have been identified by federal, state, or local laws to be specifically protected from employment discrimination. Such groups include women, identified minorities, the elderly, and the handicapped.

affirmative action officer, individual in an organization who has the primary responsibility for the development, installation, and maintenance of the organization's affirmative action program.

affirmative action plan, an organization's written plan to remedy past discrimination against, or underutilization of, women and minorities. The plan itself usually consists of a statement of goals, timetables for achieving milestones, and specific program efforts.

affirmative action program, formal course of action undertaken by employers to hire and promote women and minorities in order to remedy past abuses or maintain present equity. The most basic tool of an affirmative action program is the affirmative action plan.

affirmative discrimination: see AFFIRMATIVE ACTION.

affirmative order, order issued by the National Labor Relations Board (NLRB) or similar state agency demanding that an employer or union take specific action to cease performing and/or undo the effects of an unfair labor practice. For example, the NLRB might issue an affirmative order to a company to "make whole" a wrongfully discharged employee by reinstating the employee with full back pay and reestablishing the employee's seniority and other rights.

affirmative recruitment, recruiting efforts undertaken to assure that adequate numbers of women and minorities are represented in applicant pools for positions in which they have been historically underutilized.

AFL: see AMERICAN FEDERATION OF LABOR.

AFL-CIO: see AMERICAN FEDERATION OF LABOR-CONGRESS OF INDUSTRIAL ORGANIZATIONS.

African-American Labor Center, AFL-CIO sponsored organization whose goal is to help the free trade union movement in Africa.

African-American Labor Center
1125 15th Street, N.W. Suite 404
Washington, D.C. 20005
(202) 429-0050

age certificate, a paper authorizing the employment of a minor. *See* WORKING PAPERS.

age discrimination, disparate or unfavorable treatment of an individual in an employment situation because of age. The Age Discrimination in Employment Act of 1967 makes most age discrimination illegal, except where a bona fide occupational qualification (BFOQ) is involved. Executive Order 11141 prohibits age discrimination in the federal government. *See* W. L. Kendig, *Age Discrimination in Employment* (N.Y.: American Management Associations, 1978); Frank P. Doyle, "Age Discrimination and Organizational Life," *Industrial Gerontology* (Summer 1973); Donald P. Schwab and Herbert G. Heneman III, "Age Stereotyping in Performance Appraisal," *Journal of Applied Psychology* (October 1978); James W. Walker and Daniel E. Lupton, "Performance Appraisal Programs and Age Discrimination Law," *Aging and Work*, Vol. 1, No. 2 (1978); Paul S. Greenlaw and John P. Kohl, "Age Discrimination in Employment Guidelines," *Personnel Journal* (March 1982); Robert H. Faley, Lawrence S. Kleiman and Mark L. Lengnick-Hall, "Age Discrimination and Personnel Psychology: A Review and Synthesis of the Legal Literature with Implications for Future Research," *Personnel Psychology* (Summer 1984).

Age Discrimination in Employment Act of 1967 (ADEA), as amended, prohibits discrimination on the basis of age against any person between the ages of 40 and 70. There is no upper age limit with respect to employment in the Federal Government. The law applies to all public employers, private employers of 20 or more employees, employment agencies serving covered employers, and labor unions of more than 25 members. Employers may not fail or refuse to hire, discharge, or otherwise discriminate against any individual with respect to compensation or terms or conditions of employment because of age. Employment agencies may not fail or refuse to refer an individual because of age, and labor unions may not exclude or expel a person because of age, or otherwise discriminate regarding terms or conditions of employment. The ADEA prohibits help-wanted advertisements which indicate preference, limitation, specification or discrimination based on age. For example, terms such as "girl" and "35-55," may not be used because they indicate the exclusion of qualified applicants based on age. The law does not prohibit discharge or discipline of an employee for good cause.

The ADEA does not cover situations in which age is a bona fide occupational qualification, such as modeling "junior miss" fashions; differences which are based on reasonable factors other than age, such as the use of physical examinations where heavy physical demands are made upon the worker; registered apprenticeship programs; and differences based on bona fide seniority systems or employee benefit plans such as retirement, pension, or insurance plans. However, the act prohibits using employee benefit plans as a basis for refusing to hire older applicants or retiring older employees. The law does not permit the involuntary retirement of workers under age 70, except for certain senior executive and high-level policymaking employees.

In addition to the Federal law, many States have age discrimination laws, or provisions in their fair employment practices law that prohibit discrimination based on age. Some of these laws have no upper limit in protections against age discrimination in employment, others protect workers until they reach 60, 65, or 70 years of age. See Cynthia E. Gitt, "The 1978 Amendments to the Age Discrimination in Employment Act—A Legal Overview," *Marquette Law Review* (Summer 1981); Michael H. Schuster and Christopher S. Miller, "Performance Ap-

praisal and the Age Discrimination in Employment Act," *Personnel Administrator* (March 1984); Michael Schuster and Christopher S. Miller, "An Empirical Assessment of the Age Discrimination in Employment Act," *Industrial and Labor Relations Review* (October 1984).

See also the following entries:
EQUAL EMPLOYMENT OPPORTUNITY COMMISSION V. WYOMING
OSCAR MAYER & CO. V. EVANS
RETIREMENT AGE
UNITED AIRLINES V. MCMANN

ageism, in the tradition of racism and sexism, ageism is discrimination against those who are considered old.

agency, employment: *see* EMPLOYMENT AGENCY.

agency shop, union security provision, found in some collective bargaining agreements, which requires that non-union employees of the bargaining unit must pay the union a sum equal to union dues as a condition of continuing employment. The agency shop was designed as a compromise between the union's desire to eliminate "free riders" by means of compulsory membership and management's wish that union membership be voluntary. Its constitutionality was upheld by the U.S. Supreme Court in *Abood* v. *Detroit Board of Education*. For legal analyses, see Norman E. Jones, "Agency Shop," *Labor Law Journal* (November 1959); Raymond N. Palombo, "The Agency Shop in a Public Service Merit System," *Labor Law Journal* (July 1975).

See also ABOOD V. DETROIT BOARD OF EDUCATION, ELLIS V. BROTHERHOOD OF RAILWAY CLERKS, and NATIONAL LABOR RELATIONS BOARD V. GENERAL MOTORS.

agent, person who is formally designated to act on behalf of either an employee or a union.

See also BARGAINING AGENT and BUSINESS AGENT.

agent provocateur, individual who is specifically hired by an organization to create trouble for a rival organization by inducing its members to perform acts that are in the best interest of the opposition.

aggregate cost method, also called AG-GREGATE METHOD, projected funding technique that computes pension benefits and costs for an entire plan rather than for its individual participants.

AGPA: *see* AMERICAN GROUP PSYCHO-THERAPY ASSOCIATION.

agreement: *see* the following entries:
BLANKET AGREEMENT
FAIR-SHARE AGREEMENT
GENTLEMEN'S AGREEMENT
INDEX OF AGREEMENT
INDIVIDUAL AGREEMENT
INTERIM AGREEMENT
LABOR AGREEMENT
MASTER AGREEMENT
MODEL AGREEMENT
OPEN-END AGREEMENT
SWEETHEART AGREEMENT

AIM: *see* AMERICAN INSTITUTE OF MANAGEMENT.

Air Traffic Controllers Strike, 1981 strike of the Professional Air Traffic Controllers Organization (PATCO) that resulted in the complete destruction of the union and the dismissal of 11,000 air traffic controllers. On July 29, 1981, 95 percent of PATCO's 13,000 members voted to reject the government's final offer. As one striking controller put it: "Where are they going to get 13,000 controllers and train them before the economy sinks? The reality is, we are it. They have to deal with us." The government was equally determined in its resolve to keep the planes flying. First, it cut back scheduled flights and reduced staff at smaller airports. Then, it brought supervisors and retired controllers back to service and ordered military controllers to civilian stations. Finally, President Reagan addressed the nation on television. After reminding viewers that it is illegal for federal government employees to strike and that each controller signed an oath asserting that he or she would never strike,

he proclaimed: "They are in violation of the law, and if they do not report for work within 48 hours, they have forfeited their jobs and will be terminated." Just over one thousand controllers reported back. Most thought that the president was bluffing. But he wasn't. Over 11,000 former controllers received formal letters of dismissal. The union's assets were frozen by the courts, some PATCO leaders were literally hauled away to jail in chains, and the Department of Transportation started formal proceedings to decertify the union. In late October the Federal Labor Relations Authority formally decertified PATCO— the first time that it had ever done so to any union of government workers. In December PATCO filed for bankruptcy. In the end over 11,000 controllers who stayed on strike permanently lost their jobs. *See* David B. Bowers, "What Would Make 11,500 People Quit Their Jobs?" *Organizational Dynamics* (Winter 1983); Herbert R. Northrup, "The Rise and Demise of PATCO," *Industrial and Labor Relations Review* (January 1984).

Alabama Power Co. v. *Davis,* 431 U.S. 581 (1977), U.S. Supreme Court case, which held that employers who rehire a returning veteran are required to credit the employee's military service toward the calculation of pension benefits. A unanimous court concluded that "pension payments are predominantly rewards for continuous employment with the same employer," rather than deferred compensation for services rendered. Thus, the purpose of Section 9 of the Selective Service Act, as explained by Justice Thurgood Marshall for the Court, is to protect veterans "from the loss of such rewards when the break in their employment resulted from their response to the country's military needs."

Albemarle Paper Co. v. *Moody,* 422 U.S. 405 (1975), U.S. Supreme Court case that established the principle that once discrimination has been proven in a Title VII (of the Civil Rights Act of 1964) case, the trial judge ordinarily does not have discretion to deny back pay. For analyses, see William H. Warren, *"Albemarle* v. *Moody:* Where It All Began," *Labor Law Journal* (October 1976); Thaddeus Holt, "A View from Albemarle," *Personnel Psychology* (Spring 1977); James Ledvinka and Lyle F. Schoenfeldt, "Legal Developments in Employment Testing: Albemarle and Beyond," *Personnel Psychology* (Spring 1978).

alcoholism, detrimental dependency on alcoholic beverages. It was only in 1956 that the American Medical Association first recognized alcoholism as a disease. However, it is still not universally recognized as such. Almost all large organizations have some program to deal with alcoholic employees. For a comprehensive reference on employee alcoholism, see Joseph F. Follman, Jr., *Alcoholics and Business: Problems, Costs, Solutions* (N.Y.: Amacom, 1976). *Also see* Marilyn C. Regier, *Social Policy in Action: Perspectives on the Implementation of Alcoholism Reforms* (Lexington, Mass.: Lexington Books, 1979); Tia Schneider Denenberg and R. V. Denenberg, *Alcohol and Drugs: Issues in the Workplace* (Washington, D.C.: The Bureau of National Affairs, Inc., 1983); Joseph Madonia, "Managerial Responses to Alcohol and Drug Abuse Among Employees," *Personnel Administrator* (June 1984); Tim Bornstein, "Drug and Alcohol Issues in the Workplace: An Arbitrator's Perspective," *Arbitration Journal* (September 1984).

Major national organizations offering information on alcoholism include:
1. *Alcoholics Anonymous*
   P.O. Box 459
   Grand Central Station
   New York, NY 10017
2. *National Clearinghouse for Alcohol Information*
   Box 2345
   Rockville, MD 20852
3. *National Council on Alcoholism*
   1100 17th Street, N.W.
   Washington, D.C. 20036
4. *National Institute on Alcohol Abuse and Alcoholism*

5600 Fishers Lane
Rockville, MD 20857

Alexander v. *Gardner-Denver Company,* 415 U.S. 36 (1974), U.S. Supreme Court case, that held the prior submission of a claim to arbitration under the non-discrimination clause of a collective bargaining agreement does not foreclose an employee from subsequently exercising his right to a trial *de novo* under title VII of the Civil Rights Act of 1964. For analyses, see Gary R. Siniscalco, "Effect of the Gardner-Denver Case on Title VII Disputes," *Monthly Labor Review* (March 1975); Sanford Cohen and Christian Eaby, "The Gardner-Denver Decision and Labor Arbitration," *Labor Law Journal* (January 1976); M. M. Hoyman and L. E. Stallworth, "Arbitrating Discrimination Cases After *Gardner-Denver,"* *Monthly Labor Review* (October 1983); Karen Elwell and Peter Feuille, "Arbitration Awards and *Gardner-Denver* Lawsuits: One Bite or Two?" *Industrial Relations* (Spring 1984); Michele Hoyman and Lamont E. Stallworth, "The Arbitration of Discrimination Grievances in the Aftermath of *Gardner-Denver,"* *Arbitration Journal* (September 1984); Aubrey R. Fowler, Jr., "Arbitration, the Trilogy, and Individual Rights: Developments Since *Alexander* v. *Gardner-Denver,"* *Labor Law Journal* (March 1985).

alienation, a concept originally from Marxism which held that industrial workers would experience feelings of disassociation because they lacked control of their work (and thus be ripe for revolution). The word has lost its Marxist taint and now refers to any feelings of estrangement from one's work, family, society, etc. *See* Michael P. Smith, "Alienation and Bureaucracy: The Role of Participatory Administration," *Public Administration Review* (November–December 1971); Robert P. Vecchio, "Worker Alienation as a Moderator of the Job Quality-Job Satisfaction Relationship: The Case of Racial Differences," *Academy of Management Journal* (September 1980); John F. Witte, *Democracy, Authority, and Alienation in Work* (University of Chicago Press, 1980); Abraham K. Korman, Ursula Wittig-Berman, and Dorothy Lang, "Career Success and Personal Failure: Alienation in Professionals and Managers," *Academy of Management Journal* (June 1981); Beverly H. Burris, *No Room at the Top: Underemployment and Alienation in the Corporation* (New York: Praeger Publishers, 1983).

aliens: *see* the following entries:
AMBACH V. NORWICK
CITIZENSHIP, U.S.
ESPINOZA V. FARAH MANUFACTURING COMPANY
EXAMINING BOARD V. FLORES DeOTERO
FOLEY V. CONNELIE
HAMPTON V. MOW SUN WONG
SUGARMAN V. DOUGALL

Alien Registration Act of 1940, also called the SMITH ACT, U.S. law that requires the annual registration of aliens. It also prohibits advocating the violent overthrow of the U.S. government.

allies, generally speaking, unions may engage in concerted activity against secondary employers if such an employer is deemed to be the "ally" of the primary employer. The ally relationship is complicated and subject to a number of tests. Frequently, one employer will be viewed as the ally of another if they are substantially owned and managed by the same group of people or corporation. Additionally, where one employer agrees to perform work for another employer who has been struck, and this agreement is a result of the strike itself rather than a normal business arrangement, the employer performing the work becomes the ally of the other. *See* Paul A. Brinker, "The Ally Doctrine," *Labor Law Journal* (September 1972).

alleged discriminatory official (ADO), individual charged in a formal equal employment opportunity complaint with having caused or tolerated discriminatory actions. For an analysis of the due process procedures to which ADOs are entitled, *see* Glenn E. Schweitzer, "The Rights of

Federal Employees Named as Alleged Discriminatory Officials," *Public Administration Review* (January-February 1977).

Alliance for Labor Action, title given to the United Auto Workers' efforts from 1969 to 1972 to organize workers in industries where the AFL-CIO was only slightly represented.

Allied Chemical Workers v. *Pittsburgh Plate Glass Co.,* 404 U.S. 157 (1971), case in which the U.S. Supreme Court held that unions have no right to bargain over retirees' benefits because retired persons are neither employees nor members of a bargaining unit.

allied health personnel, specially trained and licensed (when necessary) health workers other than physicians, dentists, podiatrists and nurses. The term has no constant or agreed upon detailed meaning, sometimes being used synonymously with para-medical personnel; sometimes meaning all health workers who perform tasks which must otherwise be performed by a physician; and sometimes referring to health workers who do not usually engage in independent practice.

Allis-Chalmers **decision:** *see* NATIONAL LABOR RELATIONS BOARD V. ALLIS-CHALMERS.

allocate, also REALLOCATE, to assign a position or class to a particular salary grade in the salary schedule, based on an evaluation of its relative worth. To reallocate is to change the existing allocation of a position or class to a different salary grade in the schedule.

allowable charge, generic term referring to the maximum fee that a third party will use in reimbursing a provider for a given service. An allowable charge may not be the same as either a reasonable, customary or prevailing charge as the terms are used under the Medicare program.

allowance, financial payment to compensate an employee for the extra expense of living at a hardship post, for special clothing (such as uniforms), or for some other benefit that personnel policy allows.

See also the following entries:
CLOTHING ALLOWANCE
COST-OF-LIVING ALLOWANCE
FAMILY ALLOWANCE
FATIGUE ALLOWANCE
HARDSHIP ALLOWANCE
HOUSING ALLOWANCE
MILEAGE ALLOWANCE
RELOCATION ALLOWANCE
SUBSISTENCE ALLOWANCE
TAX-REIMBURSEMENT ALLOWANCE

allowed time, also called NORMAL TIME, time given an employee to perform a task. Normally includes an allowance for fatigue and personal and/or unavoidable delays.

alphabetism, discrimination against those whose names begin with letters at the end of the alphabet.

alternate form, also called EQUIVALENT FORM or COMPARABLE FORM, any of two or more versions of a test that are the same with respect to the nature, number, and difficulty of the test items and that are designed to yield essentially the same scores and measures of variability for a given group.

alternate-form reliability, measure of the extent to which two parallel or equivalent forms of a test are consistent in measuring what they purport to measure.

alternation ranking, technique, used in job evaluation and performance appraisal, that ranks the highest and the lowest, then the next highest and the next lowest, etc., until all jobs have been ranked.

Amalgamated Association of Street, Electric Railway, and Motor Coach Employees of America v. Lockridge, 403 U.S. 274 (1971), case in which the U.S. Supreme Court held that a complaint from a union member that his union had wrongfully interfered with his employment (he was suspended from his union because of

dues arrearage) was a matter within the exclusive jurisdiction of the National Labor Relations Board.

Ambach v. Norwick, 441 U.S. 68 (1979), U.S. Supreme Court decision, which held that barring aliens from permanent certification as public school teachers did not violate the 14th Amendment's equal protection clause. The ruling upheld the New York Education Law's citizenship requirement for public (but not private) school teachers.

See also the following entries:
CITIZENSHIP, U.S.
FOLEY V. CONNELIE
HAMPTON V. MOW SUN WONG
SUGARMAN V. DOUGALL

American Arbitration Association (AAA), formed in 1926, a public service, nonprofit organization dedicated to the resolution of disputes of all kinds through the use of arbitration, mediation, democratic election and other voluntary methods. The AAA does not act as arbitrator. Its function is to submit to parties selected lists from which disputants may make their own choices and to provide impartial administration of arbitration. The association's National Panel of Arbitrators consists of some 40,000 men and women, each an expert in some field or profession, who have been nominated for their knowledge and reputation for impartiality. In nonlabor cases, these arbitrators serve without compensation except under unusual circumstances. They offer their time and skill as a public service. AAA's panels also include impartial experts in labor-management relations for arbitrating disputes arising out of the application and interpretation of collective bargaining agreements.

The AAA's access to impartial experts, its reputation for impartiality, and its experience in dispute-settling techniques of all kinds are put at the disposal of the public in ways other than the administration of arbitrations. Its Community Dispute Services division applies the techniques of arbitration, mediation, and factfinding to the solution of conflicts of all kinds in urban areas. AAA's Election Department conducts impartial polls to choose union officers, to determine the appropriate representatives for school teachers, to select committee members in local anti-poverty programs, and for many other purposes.

The AAA is the most important single center of information, education and research on arbitration. Among the association's periodicals are three monthly publications summarizing labor arbitration awards in private industry, in schools, and in other agencies of government; a monthly news bulletin for members and arbitrators; a quarterly journal, *The Arbitration Journal*, containing reports of arbitration court cases and authoritative articles on arbitration; a bimonthly report of no-fault automobile arbitration awards; a quarterly law letter on arbitration; various specialized pamphlets on arbitration practice and procedure; and outlines for teaching labor-management arbitration and arbitration law courses. The AAA's library serves other educational institutions as a clearing house of information and answers the research inquiries of AAA members and of students.

Although headquartered in New York, the AAA has regional offices throughout the United States. For further information, *see* Robert Coulson, *Labor Arbitration — What You Need To Know* (N.Y.: American Arbitration Association, 2nd ed., 1978).

American Arbitration Association
140 West 51st Street
New York, NY 10020
(212) 484-4000
See also NATIONAL ACADEMY OF ARBITRATORS.

American Assembly of Collegiate Schools of Business (AACSB), an organization of institutions devoted to higher education for business and administration, formally established in 1916. Its membership has grown to encompass not only educational institutions but business, government, and professional organizations as well, all seeking to improve and promote higher education for business and working to solve problems of mutual concern. Through its accrediting function, the AACSB provides guidelines to educational institutions in program, resource, and faculty planning. The Accreditation Council of AACSB is recognized by the Council on Postsecondary Accreditation and by the U.S. Department of Education as the sole accrediting agency for bachelors and masters programs in business administration.

AACSB
605 Old Ballas Road
Suite 220
St. Louis, Missouri 63141
(314) 872-8481

1755 Massachusetts Avenue, N.W.
Suite 320
Washington, D.C. 20036
(202) 483-0400

The following colleges and universities have masters or undergraduate baccalaureate programs that have been accredited by the AACSB as of 1984.

University of Akron
University of Alabama
University of Alabama in Birmingham
University of Alberta
Appalachian State University
University of Arizona
Arizona State University
University of Arkansas
University of Arkansas at Little Rock
Arkansas State University
Atlanta University
Auburn University
Babson College
Ball State University
University of Baltimore
Baruch College—The City University of New York
Baylor University
Boise State University
Boston College
Boston University
Bowling Green State University
Bradley University
University of Bridgeport
Brigham Young University
University of California
University of California, Los Angeles
California Polytechnic State University,

San Luis Obispo
California State College, Bakersfield
California State University, Chico
California State University, Fresno
California State University, Fullerton
California State University, Hayward
California State University, Long Beach
California State University, Los Angeles
California State University, Northridge
California State University, Sacramento
Canisius College
Carnegie-Mellon University
Case Western Reserve University
University of Central Arkansas
University of Central Florida
Central Michigan University
University of Chicago
University of Cincinnati
Clarkson College
Clemson University
Cleveland State University
University of Colorado at Denver
Colorado State University
Columbia University
University of Connecticut
Cornell University
Creighton University
Dartmouth College
University of Dayton
University of Delaware
University of Denver
DePaul University
University of Detroit
Drake University
Drexel University
Duke University
Duquesne University
East Carolina University
East Texas State University
Eastern Michigan University
Eastern Washington University
Emory University
University of Florida
Florida Atlantic University
Florida International University
Florida State University
Fordham University
Fort Lewis College
George Washington University
Georgetown University
University of Georgia
Georgia Institute of Technology
Georgia Southern College

Georgia State University
Harvard University
University of Hawaii
Hofstra University
University of Houston
University of Houston at Clear Lake City
Howard University
Idaho State University
University of Illinois at Chicago
University of Illinois at Urbana-Champaign
Illinois State University
Indiana State University
Indiana University
University of Iowa
James Madison University
University of Kansas
Kansas State University
Kent State University
University of Kentucky
Lamar University
Lehigh University
Louisiana State University
Louisiana Tech University
University of Louisville
Loyola Marymount University
Loyola University, Chicago
Loyola University, New Orleans
University of Maine at Orono
Marquette University
University of Maryland
University of Massachusetts
Massachusetts Institute of Technology
Memphis State University
University of Miami
Miami University
The University of Michigan
The University of Michigan-Flint
Michigan State University
Middle Tennessee State University
University of Minnesota
University of Mississippi
Mississippi State University
University of Missouri-Columbia
University of Missouri-Kansas City
University of Missouri-St. Louis
University of Montana
Montana State University
Murray State University
University of Nebraska-Lincoln
University of Nebraska at Omaha
University of Nevada-Reno
University of New Mexico
New Mexico State University

University of New Orleans
New York University
Nicholls State University
The University of North Carolina at Chapel Hill
University of North Carolina at Charlotte
University of North Carolina at Greensboro
North Carolina A & T State University
University of North Dakota
University of North Florida
North Texas State University
Northeast Louisiana University
Northeastern University
Northern Arizona University
Northern Illinois University
Northwestern University
University of Notre Dame
Ohio University
The Ohio State University
University of Oklahoma
Oklahoma State University
Old Dominion University
University of Oregon
Oregon State University
University of the Pacific
Pacific Lutheran University
Pan American University
University of Pennsylvania
The Pennsylvania State University
University of Pittsburgh
University of Portland
Portland State University
Purdue University
Rensselaer Polytechnic Institute
University of Rhode Island
University of Richmond
University of Rochester
Rutgers-The State University of New Jersey
Saint Cloud State University
St. John's University
St. Louis University
University of San Diego
San Diego State University
University of San Francisco
San Francisco State University
University of Santa Clara
Seattle University
Seton Hall University
Shippensburg University
University of South Alabama
University of South Carolina
University of South Dakota

University of South Florida
University of Southern California
Southern Illinois University at Carbondale
Southern Illinois University at Edwardsville
Southern Methodist University
University of Southern Mississippi
Stanford University
State University of New York at Albany
State University of New York at Buffalo
Stephen F. Austin State University
Syracuse University
Temple University
University of Tennessee at Chattanooga
University of Tennessee, Knoxville
Tennessee Technological University
The University of Texas at Arlington
University of Texas at Austin
The University of Texas at San Antonio
Texas A & M University
Texas Christian University
Texas Southern University
Texas Tech University
University of Toledo
Tulane University
University of Tulsa
University of Utah
Utah State University
Valdosta State College
Vanderbilt University
Villanova University
University of Virginia
Virginia Commonwealth University
Virginia Polytechnic Institute and State University
University of Washington
Washington University
Washington and Lee University
Washington State University
Wayne State University
West Georgia College
West Virginia University
Western Carolina University
Western Illinois University
Western Kentucky University
Western Michigan University
Wichita State University
College of William and Mary
Winthrop College
University of Wisconsin-Eau Claire
University of Wisconsin-La Crosse
University of Wisconsin-Madison
University of Wisconsin-Milwaukee
University of Wisconsin-Oshkosh

University of Wisconsin-Whitewater
Wright State University
University of Wyoming

American Association for Counseling and Development, a professional association of 40,000 members concerned with personnel and guidance work at all educational levels from kindergarten through higher education, in community agencies, correction agencies, rehabilitation programs, government, business/industry and research facilities. Formerly (until 1983) the American Personnel and Guidance Association.

> American Association for Counseling
> and Development
> 5999 Stevenson Ave.
> Alexandria, VA 22304
> (703) 823-9800

American Center for Quality of Work Life, promotes greater workforce involvement in quality of work and safety issues through training and research.

> American Center for Quality of
> Work Life
> 1411 K Street, N. W., Suite 930
> Washington, D.C. 20005
> (202) 338-2933

American Enterprise Institute for Public Policy Research (AEI), independent, nonprofit, nonpartisan research and educational organization whose basic purpose is to promote the competition of ideas. AEI, which tends to favor deregulation, decentralization, and a market-economy, provided the Reagan administration with a fair share of both ideas and advisors.

> AEI
> 1150 17th Street, N.E.
> Washington, D.C. 20036
> (202) 862-5800

American Federation of Labor (AFL), organized in 1881 as a federation of craft unions, the Federation of Organized Trade and Labor Unions, it changed its name to the American Federation of Labor in 1886 after merging with those craft unions that had become disenchanted with the Knights of Labor.

The AFL was not immediately noted for its size. But it endured. It rode out the political and economic turmoil of the 1890s. When major strikes of industrially organized workers, such as the Homestead Strike and the Pullman Strike, failed so badly that they cast doubt on the viability of industrial unionism itself, the AFL and its craft workers remained relatively secure. When more radical unions such as the Industrial Workers of the World failed to achieve the overthrow of the capitalistic system, the AFL was content in its conservatism. In 1898 it had 275,000 members. By 1904 in the wake of the Spanish-American War, it had 1.7 million. During World War I, its membership increased to 4.1 million. Wartime demand for skilled labor was an important factor in the AFL's growth. But the AFL also endured because of its emphasis on collective bargaining by skilled employees. While its achievements were not spectacular, it negotiated enough agreements and displayed enough conservatism to convince many in the business community of the legitimacy of the collective bargaining process. The AFL would remain the most comprehensive American labor organization until the 1930s, when the rise of industrial, as opposed to craft, unionism posed a serious threat to its structure and organizational pattern. In 1955, the AFL merged with the Congress of Industrial Organizations to become the AFL-CIO (see AMERICAN FEDERATION OF LABOR—CONGRESS OF INDUSTRIAL ORGANIZATIONS).

See Philip Taft, *The A. F. of L. in the Time of Gompers* (New York: Harper, 1957); James Oliver Morris, *Conflict Within the AFL: A Study of Craft Versus Industrial Unionism, 1901-1938* (Ithaca: Cornell University, Cornell Studies in Industrial Relations, vol. 10, 1958); Philip Taft, *The A. F. of L. From the Death of Gompers to the Merger* (New York: Harper, 1959); Frank L. Grubbs, *The Struggle for Labor Loyalty: Gompers, the A. F. of L., and the Pacifists* (Durham: Duke University Press, 1968); Simon Larson, *Labor and Foreign Policy: Gompers,*

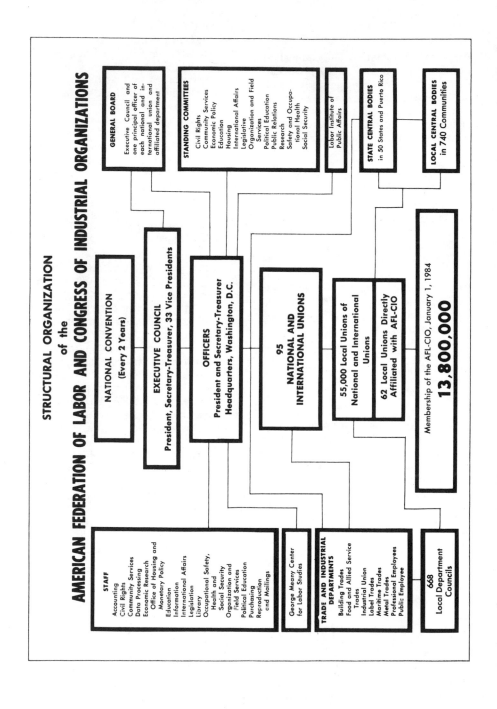

STRUCTURAL ORGANIZATION
of the
AMERICAN FEDERATION OF LABOR AND CONGRESS OF INDUSTRIAL ORGANIZATIONS

NATIONAL CONVENTION
(Every 2 Years)

EXECUTIVE COUNCIL
President, Secretary-Treasurer, 33 Vice Presidents

OFFICERS
President and Secretary-Treasurer
Headquarters, Washington, D.C.

GENERAL BOARD
Executive Council and one principal officer of each national and international union and affiliated department

STANDING COMMITTEES
Civil Rights
Community Services
Economic Policy
Education
Housing
International Affairs
Legislative
Organization and Field Services
Political Education
Public Relations
Research
Safety and Occupational Health
Social Security

Labor Institute of Public Affairs

STATE CENTRAL BODIES
in 50 States and Puerto Rico

LOCAL CENTRAL BODIES
in 740 Communities

95
NATIONAL AND
INTERNATIONAL UNIONS

55,000 Local Unions of National and International Unions

62 Local Unions Directly Affiliated with AFL-CIO

Membership of the AFL-CIO, January 1, 1984
13,800,000

STAFF
Accounting
Civil Rights
Community Services
Data Processing
Economic Research
Office of Housing and Monetary Policy
Education
Information
International Affairs
Legislation
Library
Occupational Safety, Health and Social Security
Organization and Field Services
Political Education
Purchasing
Reproduction and Mailings

George Meany Center for Labor Studies

TRADE AND INDUSTRIAL DEPARTMENTS
Building Trades
Food and Allied Service Trades
Industrial Union
Label Trades
Maritime Trades
Metal Trades
Professional Employees
Public Employee

668
Local Department Councils

the AFL, and the First World War (Rutherford, N.J.: Fairleigh Dickinson University Press, 1975); Philip S. Foner. *The AFL in the Progressive Era, 1910-1915* (New York: International Publishers, 1980); Stuart Bruce Kaufman, "Birth of a Federation: Gompers Strives 'Not to Build a Bubble'," *Monthly Labor Review* (November 1981).

American Federation of Labor-Congress of Industrial Organizations (AFL-CIO), a voluntary federation of over 100 national and international unions operating in the United States. The AFL-CIO is itself not a union; it does no bargaining. It is perhaps best thought of as a union of unions. The affiliated unions created the AFL-CIO to represent them in the creation and execution of broad national and international policies and in coordinating a wide range of joint activities.

Each member union of the AFL-CIO remains autonomous, conducting its own affairs in the manner determined by its own members. Each has its own headquarters, officers and staff. Each decides its own economic policies, carries on its own contract negotiations, sets its own dues and provides its own membership services. Each of the affiliated unions is free to withdraw at any time. But through its voluntary participation, it plays a role in establishing over-all policies for the U.S. labor movement, which in turn advance the interests of every union.

The AFL-CIO serves its constituent unions by:

1. Speaking for the whole labor movement before Congress and other branches of government.
2. Representing U.S. labor in world affairs, through its participation in international labor bodies and through direct contact with the central labor organizations of free countries throughout the world.
3. Helping to organize the unorganized workers of the United States.
4. Coordinating such activities as community services, political education and voter registration for greater effectiveness.

While retaining control over their own affairs member unions have ceded a degree of authority to the AFL-CIO in certain matters. These include:

1. *Ethical practices.* Every affiliated union must comply with the AFL-CIO Ethical Practices Codes, which established basic standards of union democracy and financial integrity.
2. *Totalitarian domination.* No union controlled by Communists, fascists or other totalitarians can remain in the AFL-CIO.
3. *Internal disputes.* Each union has agreed to submit certain types of disputes with other affiliated unions to the mediating and judicial processes of the AFL-CIO.

AFL-CIO
815 16th Street, N.W.
Washington, D.C. 20006
(202) 637-5000

American Federation of Labor v. National Labor Relations Board, 308 U.S. 401 (1940), U.S. Supreme Court case, which held that the National Labor Relations Board under Section 9 (d) of the National Labor Relations (Wagner) Act of 1935 had the discretion to determine appropriate bargaining units and that such a certification is not subject to review by federal appellate courts.

American Federation of Labor v. Swing, 312 U.S. 321 (1941), U.S. Supreme Court case, which held that stranger picketing is lawful. Justice Felix Frankfurter wrote that "a State cannot exclude working men from peacefully exercising the right of free communication by drawing the circle of economic competition between employers and workers so small as to contain only an employer and those directly employed by him."

American Federation of Musicians v. Wittstein, 379 U.S. 171 (1964), U.S. Supreme Court case, which held that Section 101 (a) (3) (B) of the Labor-Management Reporting and Disclosure (Landrum-Griffin) Act of 1959 permits a weighted-voting system under which

23

delegates cast a number of votes equal to the membership of their local union.

American Group Psychotherapy Association (AGPA), professional association organized in 1942 to provide a forum for the exchange of ideas among qualified professional persons interested in group psychotherapy; to publish and to make publication available on all subjects relating to group psychotherapy; to encourage the development of sound training programs in group psychotherapy for qualified mental health professionals; to establish and maintain high standards of ethical, professional group psychotherapy practice; and to encourage and promote research in group psychotherapy.

American Group Psychotherapy Association
1995 Broadway
New York, NY 10023
(212) 787-2618

American Institute for Free Labor Development, an AFL-CIO-sponsored organization dedicated to promoting free and democratic unions throughout Latin America and the Caribbean.

American Institute for Free Labor Development
1015 20th Street, N.W.
Washington, D.C. 20036
(202) 659-6300

American Institute of Management (AIM), founded in 1948 to conduct studies in management research and to enhance the development of the managerial sciences as an educational discipline, AIM serves as a professional association for managers. Its purpose is to improve management thinking, practices, performance, and results through pertinent comments, studies, meetings, and publications that contribute to managerial knowledge, skill, and theory.

American Institute of Management
45 Willard Street
Quincy, MA 02169
(617) 472-0277

American Management Associations

(AMA), with over 85,000 members the AMA is by far the largest organization for professional managers. AMA programs operate principally through its divisions: Finance, General Management, Information Systems and Technology, Insurance & Employee Benefits, Manufacturing, Marketing, Management Systems, Research and Development, Human Resources, Packaging, International Management, Purchasing, Transportation and Physical Distribution, and General Administrative Services. AMACOM is its in-house publishing division.

American Management Associations
135 West 50th Street
New York, N.Y. 10020
(212) 586-8100

American Municipal Association: *see* NATIONAL LEAGUE OF CITIES.

American Newspaper Publishers Association v. National Labor Relations Board, 345 U.S. 100 (1953), U.S. Supreme Court case, in which it was held that requiring employers to pay printers for setting "bogus" type was not an unfair labor practice on the part of the union under Section 8(b) (6) of the National Labor Relations Act. The court said that Section 8(b) (6) "condemned only the exactment by a union of pay from an employer in return for services not performed and not to be performed, but not the exactment of pay for work done by an employee with the employer's consent."
See also FEATHERBEDDING.

American Personnel and Guidance Association: *see* AMERICAN ASSOCIATION FOR COUNSELING AND DEVELOPMENT

American Plan, term used by employers in the early part of this century to encourage open or non-union shops. By implication, the closed or union shop was portrayed as alien to the nation's individualistic spirit, restrictive of industrial efficiency, and generally "un-American."

American Productivity Center, Inc., created in 1977, a privately funded, nonprofit organization dedicated to strengthening the free enterprise system by developing practical programs to improve productivity and the quality of working life in the United States.

American Productivity Center, Inc.
123 North Post Oak Lane
Houston, TX 77024
(713) 681-4020

American Psychological Association (APA), founded in 1892 and incorporated in 1925, the APA is the major psychological organization in the United States. With more than 58,000 members, it includes most of the qualified psychologists in the country.

The purpose of the APA is to advance psychology as a science and a profession and as a means of promoting human welfare by the encouragement of psychology in all its branches in the broadest and most liberal manner. It does so by the promotion of research in psychology and the improvement of research methods and conditions; by the continual improvement of the qualifications; and competence of psychologists through high standards of ethical conduct, education, and achievement; and by the dissemination of psychological knowledge through meetings, psychological journals, and special reports.

American Psychological Association
1200 Seventeenth Street, N.W.
Washington, D.C. 20036
(202) 955-7600

American Shipbuilding Co. v. National Labor Relations Board, 380 U.S. 300 (1965), U.S. Supreme Court case, which held that an employer, in the face of a bargaining impasse, could temporarily shut down his plant and lay off his employees for the sole purpose of bringing pressure to bear in support of his bargaining position.

See also LOCKOUT.

American Society for Personnel Administration (ASPA), a nonprofit, professional association of personnel and industrial relations managers. Founded in 1948, ASPA today serves over 33,000 members with 380 chapters in the United States and 37 other countries. It is the largest professional association devoted exclusively to human resource management.

ASPA's purpose is (1) to provide assistance for the professional development of members, (2) to provide international leadership in establishing and supporting standards of excellence in human resource management, (3) to provide the impetus for research to improve management techniques, (4) to serve as a focal point for the exchange of authoritative information, and (5) to publicize the human resource management field to create a better understanding of its functions and importance.

American Society for Personnel
  Administration
606 N. Washington Street
Alexandria, VA 22314
(703) 548-3440

American Society for Personnel Administration Accreditation Institute: *see* PERSONNEL ACCREDITATION INSTITUTE.

American Society for Personnel Administration Code of Ethics: *see* CODE OF ETHICS.

American Society for Public Administration (ASPA), a nationwide, nonprofit educational and professional organization dedicated to improved management in the public service through exchange, development, and dissemination of information about public administration. ASPA has over 18,000 members and subscribers representative of all governmental levels, program responsibilities, and administrative interests. Its membership includes government administrators, teachers, researchers, consultants, students, and civic leaders. Since its inception in 1939, ASPA has provided national leadership in advancing the "science, processes, and art" of public administration. It is the only organization of its kind in the U.S. aiming broadly to improve administration of the public service at all levels of government and in all functional and program fields. Society members are located in every state as well as overseas. Many activities are carried out through more than 113 chapters in major governmental and educational centers. The ASPA program includes publications, meetings, education, research, and various special services, all aimed at improved understanding and strengthened administration of the public service.

> *American Society for Public*
> *Administration*
> 1120 G Street, N. W.
> Washington, D.C. 20005
> (202) 393-7878

American Society for Training and Development (ASTD), a national professional society of 22,000 members for persons with training and development responsibilities in business, industry, government, public service organizations, and educational institutions. Founded in 1944 ASTD is the only organization devoted exclusively to the comprehensive education, development, and expansion of the skills and standards of professionals in training and human resource development. Formerly (until 1964) the American Society of Training Directors.

> *American Society for Training and*
> *Development*
> P.O. Box 5307
> Madison, WI 53705
> (608) 274-3440

American Steel Foundries v. Tri-City Central Trades Council, 257 U.S. 184 (1921), U.S. Supreme Court case, which held that the rights of pickets are restricted to "observation, communication and persuasion"; and required that strikebreakers be given "clear passage."

amicus curiae, literally, "friend of the court"; any person or organization allowed to participate in a lawsuit who would not otherwise have a right to do so. Participation is usually limited to filing a brief on behalf of one side or the other. *See* Samuel Krislov, "The *Amicus Curiae* Brief: From Friendship to Advocacy," *Yale Law Journal* (March 1963).

analogies test, test that asks a whole series of questions such as: a foot is to a man as a paw is to what? The examinee is usually given four or five answers to choose from.

analogue, individual's counterpart or opposite number in another organization.

analysis of variance, statistical procedure for determining whether the change noted in a variable that has been exposed to other variables exceeds what may be expected by chance.

analytical estimating, work measurement technique whereby the time required to perform a job is estimated on the basis of prior experience.

Anderson v. Mt. Clemens Pottery, 328 U.S. 680 (1946), U.S. Supreme Court case, which held that employers were liable for "portal-to-portal" pay claims under the provisions of the Fair Labor Standards Act. This decision led to the passage of the Portal-to-Portal Pay Act of 1947, which established a cutoff date for back claims.

> *See also* PORTAL-TO-PORTAL PAY ACT OF 1947.

andragogy, science of adult learning. For books by the leading authority on the theory and process of andragogy, *see* Malcolm S. Knowles, *The Modern Practice of Adult Education* (N.Y.: Association Press, 1969): Malcolm S. Knowles, *The Adult Learner: A Neglected Species,* 3rd ed. (Houston: Gulf Publishing, 1984); Malcolm S. Knowles and Associates, *Andragogy In Action: Applying Modern Principles of Adult Learning* (San Francisco: Jossey-Bass, 1984).

annual earnings, employee's total compensation during a calendar year—includes basic salary or wages, all overtime and premium pay, vacation pay, bonuses, etc.

annualized cost, cost of something for a 12-month period. Annualized costs may be figured on the calendar year, the fiscal year, the date a contract becomes effective, etc.

annuitant, one who is the recipient of annuity benefit payments.
See also RE-EMPLOYED ANNUITANT.

annuity, annual sum payable to a former employee who has retired.
See also the following entries:
DEFERRED ANNUITY
DEFERRED LIFE ANNUITY
FIXED ANNUITY
GROUP ANNUITY
TAX-DEFERRED ANNUITY

Anti-Kickback Act of 1934: see KICKBACK.

anti-labor legislation, any law at any level of government that organized labor perceives to be to its disadvantage and to the disadvantage of prime union interests—better hours, wages, and working conditions. Leading examples would be "right-to-work" laws and "anti-strike" laws.

Anti-Racketeering Act of 1934, also called the HOBBS ACT, a federal law that, as amended, prohibits the use of extortion or violence that in any way obstructs, delays, or affects interstate commerce. Thus, it is a federal crime for union leaders to either blackmail employers or accept bribes for not calling strikes.
See also LABOR RACKETEER.

Anti-Strikebreaker Act of 1936, also called the BYRNES ACT, federal statute that prohibits employers from transporting strikebreakers across state lines. As amended in 1938, it also forbids the interstate transportation of persons for the purpose of interfering with peaceful picketing (common carriers excluded).

Anti-Trust Act of 1914: see CLAYTON ACT.

antitrust laws, those federal and state statutes which limit the ability of businesses and unions to exercise monopoly control and cause the restraint of trade. See William J. Bigoness, Richard A. Mann, Barry S. Roberts, "Does Your Collective Bargaining Agreement Violate Anti-trust Law?" *Personnel Administrator* (October 1981); James P. Watson, "Antitrust Claims in Labor Disputes After Associated General Contractors: A Prognosis," *Labor Law Journal* (June 1983); Edward B. Miller, *Antitrust Laws and Employee Relations: An Analysis of Their Impact on Management and Union Policies* (Philadelphia, PA: The Wharton School's Industrial Research Unit, University of Pennsylvania, 1984).

APA: see AMERICAN PSYCHOLOGICAL ASSOCIATION.

Apex Hosiery Company v. Leader, 310 U.S. 469 (1940), U.S. Supreme Court case, which held that strikes did not constitute a restraint of interstate commerce merely because a strike caused a decline in the volume of goods moving in interstate commerce.

APGA: see AMERICAN PERSONNEL AND GUIDANCE ASSOCIATION.

apparatchik, Russian word for a bureaucrat, now used colloquially to refer to any administrative functionary. The word as used in English seems to have no political connotations; it merely implies that the individual referred to mindlessly follows orders.

appeal, any proceeding or request to a higher authority that a lower authority's decision be reviewed.

appellant, one who appeals a case to a higher authority.

appellate jurisdiction, power of a tribunal to review cases that have previously been decided by a lower authority.

apple polishers, as defined in Edward M. Cook, "The High Cost of Promoting Apple Polishers," *Personnel Administration* (May–June 1966):

There are two major categories of apple polishers: (a) *Hard-Core Apple Polisher* — The compulsive yes man; never known to disagree with a superior; seldom supports his subordinates if conflict develops; pleasant personality; has many good qualities but close study of performance reveals the apple polishing syndrome. He seldom seeks real responsibility, contributes little that is creative, has seldom actually fought for his ideas or grasped a nettlesome problem with his bare hands; he may be valuable on the lower rungs of the corporate ladder, dangerous as he ascends, murder if allowed to select, cultivate, and proliferate subordinates in his own image. (2) *Skin-Deep Apple Polisher* — This category includes many younger people who are ambitious and have been led to believe that polishing is somehow almost as important as performance; many of these individuals are salvageable if the right kind of supervisor influences them in time. Unfortunately, some may become hard-core eventually, depending on organization climate; included in this group are many good, creative men of integrity who don't enjoy polishing and eventually move on to organizations which don't require it.

applicant, an individual seeking initial employment or an in-house promotional opportunity.

applicant pool, all those individuals who have applied for a particular job over a given period.

applicant population, the set of individuals within a geographical area, with identifiable characteristics or a mix of such characteristics, from which applicants for employment are obtained. Changes in recruiting practices may change certain characteristics of those who apply for work and therefore may change the nature of the applicant population.

applicant tally, tally system by which the EEO status of applicants is recorded at the time of application or interview. By periodically comparing applicant tally rates with rates of appointment and/or rejection, the progress of affirmative action recruitment efforts can be measured.

application blank, frequently the first phase of the selection process. Properly completed it can serve three purposes: (1) it is a formal request for employment; (2) it provides information that indicates the applicant's fitness for the position; and (3) it can become the basic personnel record for those applicants who are hired. Application blanks must conform to all EEOC guidelines; requested information must be a valid predictor of performance. For additional information, *see* C. C. Kessler and G. J. Gibbs, "Getting the Most from Application Blanks and References," *Personnel* (January-February 1975); Ernest C. Miller, "An EEO Examination of Employment Applications," *The Personnel Administrator* (March 1980); Debra D. Purrington, "A Review of State Government Employment Application Forms for Suspect Inquiries," *Public Personnel Management* (Spring 1982).

See also WEIGHTED APPLICATION BLANK.

applied psychology, generally, the practical use of the discoveries and principles of psychology. *See* Harry W. Hepner, *Psychology Applied to Life and Work* (Englewood Cliffs, N.J.: Prentice-Hall, 6th ed., 1979); Wayne F. Casio, *Applied Psychology in Personnel Management,* second edition (Reston, VA: Reston/Prentice-Hall, 1982).

appointing authority: *see* APPOINTING OFFICER.

appointing officer, also APPOINTING AUTHORITY, person having power by law, or by lawfully delegated authority, to make appointments to positions in an organization.

appointment, non-elective government job. Most jurisdictions offer several different kinds of appointments. For example, the federal government offers the following four varieties in its merit system:

1. *Temporary appointment* — does not ordinarily last more than 1 year. A temporary worker can't be promoted and can't transfer to another job. Temporary employees are not under the retirement system. Persons over 70 can be given only temporary appointments, but the appointments can be renewed.
2. *Term appointment* — made for work on a specific project that will last more than 1 year but less than 4 years. A term employee can be promoted or reassigned to other positions within the project for which that employee was hired. He is not under the retirement system. If you accept a temporary or term appointment, your name will stay on the list of eligibles from which you were appointed. This means that you will remain eligible for permanent jobs that are normally filled by career-conditional or career appointments.
3. *Career-conditional appointment* — leads after 3 years' continuous service to a career appointment. For the first year, the employee serves a probationary period. During this time, it must be demonstrated that the employee can do a satisfactory job and he or she may be dismissed for failure to do so. Career-conditional employees have promotion and transfer privileges. After career-conditional employees complete their probation, they cannot be removed except for cause. However, in reduction-in-force (layoff) actions, career-conditional employees are dismissed ahead of career employees.
4. *Career appointment* — employee serves a probationary period, as described above, and has promotion and transfer privileges. After completion of the probation, this type of employee is in the last group to be affected in layoffs.

See also NONCOMPETITIVE APPOINTMENT and PROVISIONAL APPOINTMENT.

apportionment, the formal allocation of the number of representatives that a political sub-division (such as a state) or an organizational unit (such as a local union) may elect to represent them in another political forum.

apprentice, according to the U.S. Department of Labor's *Dictionary of Occupational Titles* (Fourth Edition, 1977):

. . . a worker who learns, according to written or oral contractual agreement, a recognized skilled craft or trade requiring one or more years of on-the-job training through job experience supplemented by related instruction, prior to being considered a qualified skilled worker. High school or vocational school education is often a prerequisite for entry into an apprenticeship program. Provisions of apprenticeship agreement regularly include length of apprenticeship; a progressive scale of wages; work processes to be taught; and amount of instruction in subjects related to the craft or trade, such as characteristics of materials used, physics, mathematics, estimating, and blueprint reading. Apprenticeability of a particular craft or trade is best evidenced by its acceptability for registration as a trade by a State apprenticeship agency or the Federal Bureau of Apprenticeship and Training. Generally, where employees are represented by a union, apprenticeship programs come under the guidance of joint apprenticeship committees composed of representatives of the employers or the employer association and representatives of the employees. These committees may determine need for apprentices in a locality and establish minimum apprenticeship standards of education, experience, and training. In instances where Committees do not exist, apprenticeship agreement is made between apprentice and employer, or an employer group.

While the title, "apprentice," is often loosely used as a synonym for any beginner, helper, or trainee, this is technically incorrect. For an evaluation of current practices, *see* Norman Parkin, "Apprenticeships: Outmoded or Undervalued?" *Personnel Management* (May 1978).

apprentice rate, also APPRENTICE SCALE, usually a schedule of rates for workers in formal apprenticeship programs that gradually permits the attainment of the minimum journeyman rate.

apprentice scale: *see* APPRENTICE RATE.

Apprenticeship Act of 1937, also called the FITZGERALD ACT, Public Law 77-308, law that authorized the Secretary of Labor to formulate and promote the furtherance of labor standards necessary to safeguard the welfare of apprentices and to cooperate with the states in the promotion of such standards.

apprenticeship system, a Federal-State partnership established by the National Apprenticeship Act to encourage high standards for apprenticeship training and to promote the apprenticeship concept among business and industry. Apprenticeship is a system for teaching skilled trades and crafts through a combination of on-the-job training and classroom instruction. National standards approved by the Bureau of Apprenticeship and Training or State apprenticeship agencies govern the scope of work, courses of instruction, length of training, and amount of pay. A great advantage to apprenticeship training is that apprentices are paid while they learn. Typically an entering apprentice earns about half of the wage rate of a highly skilled fully qualified worker (journeyworker), and receives an increase about every 6 months. Upon completion of the program, the apprentice receives a certificate or card which shows that she or he has become a journeyworker in a specific occupation.

Department of Labor regulations published in May 1978 require sponsors of apprenticeship programs with more than five apprentices to take affirmative action to recruit women, as well as minorities, when these groups do not have a reasonable share of training opportunities.

A number of States provide information about apprenticeship programs through Apprenticeship Information Centers, which are generally operated by the State employment service. The Bureau of Apprenticeship and Training of the U.S. Department of Labor, State apprenticeship agencies, unions, and employers who operate apprenticeship programs can provide more information about apprenticeship opportunities. *See* Vernon M. Briggs, Jr., and Felician F. Foltman, eds., *Apprenticeship Research: Emerging Findings and Future Trends* (Ithaca, N.Y.: Cornell University, New York State School of Industrial and Labor Relations, 1981).

Apprentice Information Centers: *see* UNITED STATES EMPLOYMENT SERVICE.

apprentice training: *see* APPRENTICE.

appropriate unit, also known as BARGAINING UNIT and APPROPRIATE BARGAINING UNIT, group of employees that a labor organization seeks to represent for the purpose of negotiating agreements; an aggregation of employees that has a clear and identifiable community of interest and that promotes effective dealings and efficiency of operations. It may be established on a plant or installation, craft, functional or other basis.

aptitude, capacity to acquire knowledge, skill, or ability with experience and/or a given amount of formal or informal education or training.

Aptitude Classification Test, Flanagan: *see* FLANAGAN APTITUDE CLASSIFICATION TEST.

aptitude test, usually a battery of separate tests designed to measure an individual's overall ability to learn. A large variety of specialized aptitude tests have been developed to predict an applicant's performance on a particular job or in a particular course of study. *See* Edwin E. Ghiselli, *The Validity of Occupational Aptitude Tests* (N.Y.: John Wiley & Sons, 1966).

arbiter, also arbitrator, one chosen to

decide a disagreement. In a formal sense an *arbiter* is one who has the power to decide while an *arbitrator* is one who is chosen to decide by the parties to the dispute; but the words tend to be used interchangeably. *See:* Murray Greenberg and Philip Harris, "The Arbitrator's Employment Status as a Factor in the Decision Making Process," *Human Resource Management* (Winter 1981); John Smith Herrick, "Labor Arbitration as Viewed by Labor Arbitrators," *The Arbitration Journal* (March 1983); Orley Ashenfelter and David E. Bloom, "Models of Arbitrator Behavior: Theory and Evidence," *The American Economic Review* (March 1984).

arbitrability, whether or not an issue is covered by a collective bargaining agreement and can be heard and resolved in arbitration. The U.S. Supreme Court held, in *United Steelworkers* v. *Warrior & Gulf Navigation Co.,* 363 U.S. 574 (1960), that any grievance is arbitrable unless there is an express contract provision excluding the issue from arbitration; doubts "should be resolved in favor of coverage." *See* Mark M. Grossman, *The Question of Arbitrability: Challenges to the Arbitrator's Jurisdiction and Authority* (Ithaca, N.Y., Cornell University, New York State School of Industrial and Labor Relations, 1984).

See also UNITED STEELWORKERS OF AMERICA V. WARRIOR AND GULF NAVIGATION CO.

arbitrary, an action decided by personal whim that was not guided by general principles or rules.

arbitration, means of settling a labor dispute by having an impartial third party (the arbitrator) hold a formal hearing and render a decision that may or may not be binding on both sides. The arbitrator may be a single individual or a board of three, five, or more. When boards are used, they may include, in addition to impartial members, representatives from both of the disputants. Arbitrators may be selected jointly by labor and management or recommended by the Federal Mediation and

Conciliation Service, by a state or local agency offering similar referrals, or by the private American Arbitration Association. *See* Henry S. Farber, "Role of Arbitration in Dispute Settlement," *Monthly Labor Review* (May 1981); Harry Graham, "Arbitration Results in the Public Sector," *Public Personnel Management* (Summer 1982); Owen Fairweather, *Practice and Procedure in Labor Arbitration,* second edition (Washington, D.C.: BNA Books, 1983); Aubrey R. Fowler, Jr., "Responsibilities in Arbitration: A Tripartite View," *Personnel Administrator* (November 1984); Richard L. Kanner, "The Dynamics of the Arbitration Process," *Arbitration Journal* (June 1984); Frank Elkouri and Edna Asper Elkouri, *How Arbitration Works* (Washington, D.C.: Bureau of National Affairs, Inc., 4th ed., 1985).

See also the following entries:
BINDING ARBITRATION
COMPULSORY ARBITRATION
EXPEDITED ARBITRATION
FINAL OFFER ARBITRATION
GRIEVANCE ARBITRATION
INTEREST ARBITRATION
OBLIGATORY ARBITRATION
TERMINAL ARBITRATION
TEXTILE WORKERS V. LINCOLN MILLS
UNITED STEELWORKERS OF AMERICA V. AMERICAN MANUFACTURING CO.
UNITED STEELWORKERS OF AMERICA V. ENTERPRISE WHEEL AND CAR CORP.
VOLUNTARY ARBITRATION
WAGE ARBITRATION
ZIPPER CLAUSE

arbitration acts, laws that help (and sometimes require) the submission of certain types of problems (often labor disputes) to an arbitrator.

arbitration clause, provision of a collective bargaining agreement stipulating that disputes arising during the life of the contract over its interpretation are subject to arbitration. The clause may be broad enough to include "any dispute" or restricted to specific concerns.

Arbitration Journal, quarterly journal of the American Arbitration Association, Inc., includes articles written by practitioners and academics on all phases of arbitration and labor relations as well as reviews of related legal decisions.

Arbitration Journal
American Arbitration Association, Inc.
140 West 51st Street
New York, NY 10020

arbitration standards, the four fundamental criteria that arbitrators must be concerned with in making their judgments: acceptability, equity, the public interest, and ability to pay. The mix of these factors that will be applied in any particular case of arbitration will depend upon the arbitrator's proclivities, the nature of the dispute, and, if it is in the public sector, the standards, if any, set forth in the pertinent legislation.

arbitration tribunal, panel created to decide a dispute that has been submitted to arbitration.

arbitrator, one who conducts an arbitration.
See also NATIONAL ACADEMY OF ARBITRATORS and PERMANENT ARBITRATOR.

architectural barriers, physical aspects of a building that might hinder or prevent the employment of a physically handicapped person. The lack of a ramp, for example, may prevent a person in a wheelchair from entering a building having only stairways for access. The Architectural Barriers Act of 1968 (Public Law 90-480), as amended, requires that buildings constructed with federal funds be accessible to and usable by the physically handicapped.

Architectural Barriers Act of 1968: *see* ARCHITECTURAL BARRIERS.

archives, permanently available records created or received by an organization for its formal/official purposes.

area agreement, collective bargaining agreement that covers a variety of employers and their workers in a large geographical area.

area labor-management committees, groups of local labor and business leaders who seek to solve problems affecting the economic well-being of an entire community, rather than just a particular worksite or industry. *See:* Richard D. Leone and Michael F. Eleey, "The Origins and Operations of Area Labor-Management Committees," *Monthly Labor Review* (May 1983).

area of consideration, geographic area within which all candidates who meet the basic requirements for promotion to a position are given the opportunity to be considered.

area standards picketing, picketing to demand that the primary employer pay "area standards" wages; that is, wages that are paid to union labor by other employers in the same geographic area.

area wage differences, differing pay rates for various occupations in differing geographic areas.

area wage survey: *see* WAGE SURVEY.

area-wide bargaining, collective bargaining between a union and the representatives of an industry in the same city or locality.

Argyris, Chris (1923-   ), one of the most influential advocates of the use of organization development (OD) techniques. His writings have provided the theoretical foundations for innumerable empirical research efforts dealing with the inherent conflict between the personality of a mature adult and the needs of modern organizations. Major works include: *Personality and Organization* (N.Y.: Harper & Row, 1957); *Understanding Organizational Behavior* (Homewood, Ill.: Dorsey, 1960); *Interpersonal Competence And Organization Effectiveness* (Homewood, Ill.: Dorsey, 1962); *Integrating the Individual and the Organization* (N.Y.:

Wiley, 1964); *Intervention Theory and Method* (Reading, Mass.: Addison-Wesley, 1970); *Management and Organizational Development* (N.Y.: McGraw-Hill, 1971); *Organization Learning: A Theory of Action Perspective,* with Donald A. Schon (Reading, Mass.: Addison-Wesley, 1978).
See also PSEUDO-EFFECTIVENESS.

arithmetic mean: *see* MEAN.

Arizona v. *Norris,* U.S. Supreme Court case, 77 L. Ed. 2d 1236 (1983), which held that employers may not require female employees to make the same contributions to a pension plan as men while giving the males a larger benefit. The Court limited its ruling to plan contributions made after July 31, 1983, and did not specify how equalization of benefits must be achieved, which meant that it could be attained by raising women's benefits, lowering men's benefits, or a combination of the two approaches.

Army Alpha and Beta Tests, in 1917 a special committee of the American Psychological Association was convened to develop tests that would help the U.S. Army classify the abilities of its recruits. The committee developed the Army Alpha Intelligence Test (a verbal test for literate recruits) and the Army Beta Intelligence Test (a nonverbal test suited for illiterate and foreign-born recruits). After World War I, the tests were released for civilian use and became the progenitors of modern industrial and educational group intelligence/aptitude testing.

Arnett v. *Kennedy,* 416 U.S. 134 (1974), U.S. Supreme Court case, which held that the administrative procedures afforded federal employees discharged "for such cause as will promote the efficiency of the service" neither violated the due process rights of such employees nor were unconstitutionally vague.

Arnold Co. v. *Carpenters District Council of Jacksonville: see* WILLIAM E. AR-NOLD CO. V. CARPENTERS DISTRICT OF JACKSONVILLE.

artificial barriers to employment, limitations (such as age, sex, race, national origin, parental status, credential requirements, criminal record, lack of child care, and absence of part-time or alternative working patterns/schedules) in hiring, firing, promotion, licensing, and conditions of employment which are not directly related to an individual's fitness or ability to perform the tasks required by the job.

artisan, skilled craft worker.

Ashurst-Sumners Act of 1935, federal law that forbids the interstate shipping of goods produced by convict labor into states that prohibit convict labor.

ASPA: *see* AMERICAN SOCIETY FOR PERSONNEL ADMINISTRATION or AMERICAN SOCIETY FOR PUBLIC ADMINISTRATION.

ASQ: *see* ADMINISTRATIVE SCIENCE QUARTERLY.

assembly line, production method requiring workers to perform a repetitive task on a product as it moves along on a conveyor belt or tract. Although much has been written about the "inhuman" demands of machine-paced work, the classic study remains Charles R. Walker and Robert H. Guest's *The Man on the Assembly Line* (Cambridge, Mass.: Harvard University Press, 1952).

Assembly of Governmental Employees, state and local public employees dedicated to the maintenance of merit principles and the extension of collective bargaining.
Assembly of Governmental Employees
1730 Rhode Island Ave., N.W.
Washington, D.C. 20036
(202) 347-5628

assertiveness training, training program designed to help less assertive people communicate and express their ideas and feelings more effectively. The ideal level of assertiveness lies somewhere between passivity and aggressiveness and is contingent upon circumstances. The concept was pioneered by J. Wolpe in his *Psychotherapy by Reciprocal Inhibition* (Stanford, Calif.: Stanford University Press, 1958). For a general discussion, *see* Harold H. Dawley, Jr., and W. W. Wenrich, *Achieving Assertive Behavior: A Guide to Assertive Training* (Belmont, Calif.: Wadsworth Publishing Co., 1976). For the obverse, *see* Michael D. Ames, "Non-Assertion Training Has Value Too," *Personnel Journal* (July 1977). *Also see* Madelyn Burley-Allen, *Managing Assertively: How to Improve Your People Skills* (New York: John Wiley, 1983).

assessment center, the term "assessment center" does not refer to a particular place. Rather, it is a process consisting of the intense observation of a subject undergoing a variety of simulations and stress situations over a period of several days. Assessment centers have proven to be an increasingly popular way of identifying individuals with future executive potential so that they may be given the appropriate training and development assignments.

As the assessment center concept is more widely adopted, one question will become more and more commonplace: If the door to management development and advancement goes through the assessment center, who will be the gatekeeper? Unless the organization can afford to process its entire management cadre through assessment centers, those individuals not selected for attendance might justifiably conclude they have been negatively evaluated. The decision, or nondecision, not to send an individual to an assessment center while peers are being sent could even have considerable legal ramifications. Because management development funds will continue to be a scarce resource, any organization implementing an assessment center program must also be concerned with designing an equitable nomination process.

For accounts of assessment center methodologies, *see* Douglas W. Bray, "The Assessment Center Method," *Training and Development Handbook,* Robert L. Craig,

ed. (N.Y.: McGraw-Hill, 2nd ed., 1976); William C. Byham and Carl Wettengel, "Assessment Centers for Supervisors and Managers: An Introduction and Overview," *Public Personnel Management* (September–October 1974); Wayne F. Cascio and Val Silbey, "Utility of the Assessment Center as a Selection Device," *Journal of Applied Psychology* (April 1979); William C. Byham, "Starting an Assessment Center the Correct Way," *Personnel Administrator* (February 1980); Task Force on Assessment Center Standards, "Standards and Ethical Considerations for Assessment Center Operations," *Personnel Administrator* (February 1980); Paul R. Sackett, "A Critical Look at Some Common Beliefs About Assessment Centers," *Public Personnel Management* (Summer 1982); Linda L. Kolb, "Use of Assessment Center Methodology for Appraising Performance," *Personnel Administrator* (October 1984).

See also IN-BASKET EXERCISE.

assessments, amounts paid, by union members in addition to their regular dues when a union needs funds urgently in order to support a strike or some other union endorsed cause. The amount of these assessments are usually limited by a union's constitution and/or bylaws.

asset-linked annuity: *see* VARIABLE ANNUITY.

Asian American Free Labor Institute, AFL–CIO sponsored organization whose goal is to help the free union movement in Asia and the Middle East.

Asian American Free Labor Institute
1125 15th Street, N.W.
Washington, D.C. 20005
(202) 737-3000

assignment of wages, also called AT-TACHMENT OF WAGES, procedure that has an employer, upon the authorization of the employee, automatically deduct a portion of the employee's wages and pay it to a third party, usually a creditor. When this is ordered by a court, the process is known as garnishment.

See also GARNISHMENT.

association, employer: *see* EMPLOYERS' ASSOCIATION.

Association for Union Democracy, an organization seeking to advance democratic practices within unions through research, publications and training.

Association for Union Democracy
30 Third Ave.
Brooklyn, N.Y. 11217
(212) 855-6650

association agreement, model or standardized collective bargaining agreement put forth by an employer's association.

assumption-of-risk doctrine, common-law concept that an employer should not be held responsible for an accident to an employee if the employer can show that the injured employee had voluntarily accepted the hazards associated with a given job.

ASTD: *see* AMERICAN SOCIETY FOR TRAINING AND DEVELOPMENT.

Atkins v. **Kansas,** 191 U.S. 207 (1903), U.S. Supreme Court decision that established the right of government to regulate the hours of private contractors working for the government.

attachment of wages: *see* ASSIGNMENT OF WAGES.

attendance bonus, also called ATTENDANCE MONEY, possible payment to an employee that serves as inducement to regular attendance.

attitude, learned predisposition to act in a consistent way toward particular persons, objects, or conditions. *See* John M. Ivancevich, "Predicting Absenteeism From Prior Absence and Work Attitudes," *Academy of Management Journal* (March 1985).

attitude scale, any series of attitude indices that have given quantitative values relative to each other.

attitude survey, questionnaire, usually anonymous, that elicits the opinion of employees. Once completed they are summarized and analyzed to determine compliance with and attitudes toward current personnel management policies. *See* Martin Fishbein (ed.), *Readings in Attitude Theory and Measurement* (N.Y.: John Wiley, 1967); Price Pritchett, "Employee Attitude Surveys: A Natural Starting Point for Organization Development," *Personnel Journal* (April 1975); Stuart M. Klein, Allen I. Kraut, and Alan Wolfson, "Employee Reactions to Attitude Survey Feedback: A Study of the Impact of Structure and Process," *Administrative Science Quarterly* (December 1971); Randall B. Dunham and Frank J. Smith, *Organizational Surveys* (Glenview, Ill.: Scott, Foresman and Co., 1979); Wallace Martin, "What Management Can Expect From an Employee Attitude Survey," *Personnel Administrator* (July 1981); Mitchell Lee Marks, "Conducting an Employment Attitude Survey," *Personnel Journal* (September 1982).

attrition, reduction in the size of a workforce through normal processes, such as voluntary resignations, retirements, discharges for cause, transfers, and deaths. *See* Jack Frye, "Attrition in Job Elimination," *Labor Law Journal* (September 1963); James A. Feldt and David F. Andersen, "Attrition Versus Layoffs: How to Estimate the Costs of Holding Employees on Payroll When Savings are Needed," *Public Administration Review* (May–June 1982).

audio-visual media, those things that communicate information through human sight or sound sensors—films, slides, recordings, maps, etc. *See* James E. Holbrook, "Here's How to Sell Your Ideas for Audio-Visual Training Programs to Top Management," *Personnel Administrator* (July 1981).

audit, desk/job: *see* DESK AUDIT.

au pair, British term which usually refers to a foreign girl who does light domestic chores for a family in exchange for room and board.

authoritarian theory: *see* THEORY X.

authority, power inherent in a specific position or function that allows an incumbent to perform assigned duties and assume assigned responsibilities. *See* Richard Bendix, *Work and Authority in Industry: Ideologies of Management in the Course of Industrialization* (New York: Wiley, 1956); Robert L. Peabody, *Organizational Authority: Superior-Subordinate Relationships in Three Public Service Organizations* (New York: Atherton, 1964); Richard Sennett, *Authority* (New York: Knopf, 1980); and Richard E. Flathman, *The Practice of Political Authority* (University of Chicago Press, 1980).

authorization card, form signed by a worker to authorize a union to represent the worker for purposes of collective bargaining. The U.S. Supreme Court held, in *National Labor Relations Board* v. *Gissel Packing Co.,* 395 U.S. 575 (1969), that the National Labor Relations Board had the power to require an employer to bargain with a union which had obtained signed authorization cards from a majority of the employees. In such circumstances a secret ballot election is considered unnecessary. *See* Daniel F. Gruender and Philip M. Prince, "Union Authorization Cards: Why Not Laboratory Conditions?" *Labor Law Journal* (January 1981).

See also SHOWING OF INTEREST.

authorization election, or REPRESENTATION ELECTION, polls conducted by the National Labor Relations Board (or other administrative agency) to determine if a particular group of employees will be represented by a particular union or not. *See* Dean S. Ellis, Laurence Jacobs, and Cary Mills, "A Union Authorization Election: The Key to Winning," *Personnel Journal* (April 1972); Julius G. Getman, Stephen B. Goldberg, and Jeanne B. Herman, *Union Representation Elections: Law and*

Reality (N.Y.: Russell Sage Foundation, 1976); Edward L. Harrison, Douglas Johnson, and Frank M. Rachel, "The Role of the Supervisor in Representation Elections," *Personnel Administrator* (September 1981); Marvin J. Levine and David C. Martin, "The *Gissel* Doctrine Revisited: Should NLRB Bargaining Orders or Representation Elections Determine Union Status?" *Labor Law Journal* (June 1983); Ronald L. Seeber and William N. Cooke, "The Decline in Union Success in NLRB Representation Elections," *Industrial Relations* (Winter 1982); Gary L. Tidwell, "The Supervisor's Role in a Union Election," *Personnel Journal* (August 1983); John J. Lawler, "The Influence of Management Consultants on the Outcome of Union Certification Elections," *Industrial and Labor Relations Review* (October 1984).

See also the following entries:

CERTIFICATION
JOY SILK MILLS V. NATIONAL LABOR RELATIONS BOARD
NATIONAL LABOR RELATIONS BOARD V. EXCHANGE PARTS
RUN-OFF ELECTION
SHOWING OF INTEREST

automatic checkoff, also called COMPULSORY CHECKOFF, illegal procedure whereby the employer deducts union dues and assessments from the pay of all employees in the bargaining unit without the prior consent of each individual employee. Section 302 of the Labor-Management Relations (Taft-Hartley) Act of 1947 provides that checkoffs must be voluntary and initiated only upon the written authorization of each employee on whose account such deductions would be made.

automatic renewal, a collective bargaining contract clause which extends the agreement automatically in the absence of notice by either party to negotiate a new contract.

automatic stabilizer, also called BUILT-IN STABILIZER, a mechanism having a countercyclical effect that automatically moderates changes in incomes and outputs in the economy without specific decisions to change government policy. Unemployment insurance and the income tax are among the most important of the automatic stabilizers in the United States.

See also COUNTERCYCLICAL.

automatic wage adjustment, raising or lowering of wage rates in direct response to previously determined factors such as an increase/decrease in the Consumer Price Index or the company's profits.

automatic wage progression, the increasing of wages premised on length of service.

automation, sometimes called MECHANIZATION, use of machines to do work that would otherwise have to be done by humans. While examples of automation go back to ancient times, the term itself was only coined in the mid 1930s by D. S. Harder, then of General Motors. As a word, automation has a considerable emotional charge since its manifestations have tended to create technological unemployment.

Automation tends to be popularly used interchangeably with mechanization—the use of machines. However, a production system is not truly automated unless the machinery is to some degree self-regulated—that is, capable of adjusting itself in response to feedback from its earlier outputs. This attribute lessens the need for human attendants. According to Herbert A. Simon, in *The Shape of Automation for Men and Management* (N.Y.: Harper & Row, 1965),

the term "mechanization" has nearly been replaced by its newer synonym, "automation." Automation is nothing new; it is simply the continuation of that trend toward the use of capital in production that has been a central characteristic of the whole Industrial Revolution. What is possibly new, if anything, is the extension of mechanization to wider and wider ranges of productive processes, and the growing prospect of complete mechanization— that is, the technical feasibility of productive processes that do not require human participation.

See George E. Biles and Richard A. Bassler, "Low-Priced Automation for Personnel Management Functions, *Personnel Administrator* (August 1984); Zane Quible and Jane N. Hammer, "Office Automation's Impact on Personnel," *Personnel Administrator* (September 1984); David F. Noble, *Forces of Production: A Social History of Industrial Automation* (New York: Knopf, 1984).

automaton, person acting mechanically in a monotonous routine without the need to use any intellectual capacities. The thrust of the scientific management movement was to make workers the most efficient possible automatons. A significant portion of modern industrial unrest is directly related to the workforce's resentment at being treated in such a manner.

auxiliary agency, also called HOUSEKEEPING AGENCY or OVERHEAD AGENCY, administrative unit whose prime responsibility is to serve other agencies of the greater organization. Personnel agencies are usually auxiliary, housekeeping, or overhead agencies.

average deviation, also called MEAN DEVIATION, measure of dispersion that provides information on the extent of scatter, or the degree of clustering, in a set of data.

average earned rate, total earnings for a given time period divided by the number of hours worked during the period.

average hourly earnings, wages earned by an employee per hour of work during a specific time period. The average hourly earnings are computed by dividing total pay received by the total hours worked. *See* Richard Esposito and Kenneth Shipp, "Industry Diffusion Indexes for Average Weekly Hours," *Monthly Labor Review* (May 1983).

average incumbents, average workforce strength figure found by adding the workforce strengths at the beginning and end of a specified report period and dividing this sum by two. This type of computation is widely used in turnover analysis.

average straight-time hourly earnings, average wages earned per hour exclusive of premium payments and shift differentials.

award, at the end of the arbitration process, the final decision of the arbitrator(s) when such arbitration is binding on both parties.

award, incentive: *see* INCENTIVE AWARD.

AWOL, absent without official leave. This term is usually restricted to the military.

B

Babbage, Charles (1792-1871), English mathematician and inventor. Best known as the "father" of the modern computer, he is also acclaimed for building upon the assembly line concepts of Adam Smith and anticipating the scientific management techniques of Frederick W. Taylor. Major works include: *On the Economy of Machinery and Manufactures* (London: Charles Knight, 1832); *Passages from the Life of a Philosopher* (London: Longman & Green, 1864). For modern biographies, *see* Maboth Moseley, *Irascible Genius: A Life of Charles Babbage, Inventor* (London: Hutchinson & Co., 1964); Philip and Emily Morrison, eds., *Charles Babbage and His Calculating Engines* (N.Y.: Dover Publications, 1961); Anthony Hyman, *Charles Babbage, Pioneer of the Computer* (Princeton University Press, 1982).

Babbitt v. United Farm Workers, 60 L. Ed. 2d 895 (1979), U.S. Supreme Court case, which held that a state's regulation of union election procedures did not violate First Amendment rights.

Babcock and Wilcox decision: *see* NA-TIONAL LABOR RELATIONS BOARD V. BABCOCK AND WILCOX.

Baby Wagner Acts, state labor laws that parallel the federal Wagner-Connery Act of 1935.

back loaded, a labor agreement providing for a greater wage increase in its later years; for example, a three-year contract that provides for a two-percent increase in the first year and six percent in each of the remaining two years.
Also see FRONT LOADED.

back pay, delayed payment of wages for a particular time period.

back-to-work movement, striking employees returning to their jobs before their union has formally ended the strike.

backward bending supply curve, the graphic depiction of the assumption that as wages increase, workers will continue to offer to work only to a point; thereafter the amount of offered labor will decline as the demand for more leisure increases relative to the demand for more income.

Baer, Fred William (1884-1946), president of the International Association of Fire Fighters from 1919 to 1946.

Baggett v. Bullitt, 377 U.S. 360 (1960), U.S. Supreme Court case that held two sections of a State of Washington loyalty oath unconstitutional on the grounds that the oath was too broad and too vague.
See also LOYALTY.

Bailey v. Richardson, 182 F. 2d 46 (1950), affirmed by an equally divided Supreme Court, 341 U.S. 918 (1951), U.S. Court of Appeals (District of Columbia Circuit) case that upheld the constitutionality of the loyalty program in the federal government. The majority decision held that there is no prohibition against dismissal of government employees because of their political beliefs, activities, or affiliation and that "the First Amendment guarantees free speech and assembly, but it does not guarantee governmental employ. . . ." The case became a *cause celebre* when it became known that during a hearing on Ms. Bailey's loyalty she was asked "did you ever write a letter to the Red Cross about the segregation of blood?" Traditional notions of due process were also violated in hearings not providing for confrontation and cross examination. Eventually, the "doctrine of privilege" upon which the court's reasoning was based was abandoned by the judiciary. *See* David H. Rosenbloom, *Federal Service and the Constitution* (Ithaca: Cornell University Press, 1971) and William Van Alstyne, "The Demise of the Right-Privilege Distinction in Constitutional Law," *Harvard Law Review*, Vol. 81 (1968).

Bakke, E. Wight (1903–1971), social scientist most noted for his pioneering empirical research on the problemsolving behavior of groups in organizations. Major works include: *Bonds of Organization* (N.Y.: Harper & Row, 1950); *The Fusion Process* (New Haven, Conn.: Labor and Management Center, Yale University, 1953).

Bakke **decision:** *see* REGENTS OF THE UNIVERSITY OF CALIFORNIA V. ALLAN BAKKE.

band curve chart or CUMULATIVE BAND CHART, chart on which the bands of a graph are plotted one above the other.

bank holiday, any of the traditional legal holidays or other special occasions when banks as well as most, but not all, other businesses remain closed. The six essentially "standard" paid holidays are: Christmas Day, Thanksgiving Day, New Year's Day, Independence Day, Labor Day, and Memorial Day. Many business and government jurisdictions offer as many as twice this number of paid holidays for their employees, but the specific days vary with local customs. In addition to the six listed above, all federal employees have paid holidays for Washington's Birthday, Columbus Day, and Veteran's Day.

Bankruptcy Act: *see* CHAPTER ELEVEN and WAGE EARNER PLAN.

bar examination, written test that new lawyers must pass in order to practice law.

bargaining: *see* the following entries:
BLUE SKY BARGAINING
COALITION BARGAINING
COLLECTIVE BARGAINING
CRISIS BARGAINING
GOOD-FAITH BARGAINING
INDIVIDUAL BARGAINING
INDUSTRY-WIDE BARGAINING
JOINT BARGAINING
MULTIEMPLOYER BARGAINING
PATTERN BARGAINING
PRODUCTIVITY BARGAINING
REGIONAL BARGAINING
SUNSHINE BARGAINING

bargaining agent, the union organization (not an individual) that is the exclusive representative of all the workers, union as well as non-union, in a bargaining unit. Employers may voluntarily agree that a particular union will serve as the bargaining agent for their employees, or the decision on representation can be settled by secret ballot election conducted by the federal National Labor Relations Board or a counterpart state agency.

bargaining agreement: *see* LABOR AGREEMENT.

bargaining item, illegal: *see* ILLEGAL BARGAINING ITEM.

bargaining rights, legal rights that all workers have to bargain collectively with their employers.
See also EXCLUSIVE BARGAINING RIGHTS.

bargaining strength, relative power that each of the parties holds during the negotiating process. The final settlement often reflects the bargaining power of each side. *See* Samuel B. Bacharach and Edward J. Lawler, "Power and Tactics in Bargaining," *Industrial and Labor Relations Review* (January 1981); Samuel B. Bacharach and Edward J. Lawler, *Bargaining: Power, Tactics, and Outcomes* (San Francisco, Calif., Jossey-Bass Inc., Publishers, 1981); Peter Navarro, "Union Bargaining Power in the Coal Industry,

1945-1981," *Industrial and Labor Relations Review* (January 1983).

bargaining theory, the sum of several approaches to the study of how people negotiate and how to negotiate successfully. These approaches include mathematical modeling, game theory, various schools of psychology, and the study of bargaining in many different settings.

bargaining theory of wages, theory that wages are based on the supply and demand for labor, that wages can never be higher than a company's break-even point or lower than bare subsistence for the workers, and that the actual "price" of labor is determined by the relative strengths—the bargaining power—of employers and workers. While the bargaining theory does not explain wage determination over the long run, it is generally accepted as the most pragmatic explanation of short-run wage determination. The beginnings of the bargaining theory are found in Adam Smith's *The Wealth of Nations* (1776), but its modern formulation dates from John Davidson's *The Bargaining Theory of Wages* (N.Y.: G.P. Putnam's Sons, 1898). *Also see* John T. Dunlop (ed.), *Theory of Wage Determination* (N.Y.: St. Martin's Press, 1957).

bargaining unit, or simply UNIT, group of employees, both union members as well as others, that an employer has recognized and/or an administrative agency has certified as appropriate for representation by a union for purposes of collective bargaining. All of the employees in a bargaining unit are subsequently covered in the labor contract that the union negotiates on their behalf. Bargaining units may be as small as the handful of workers in a local shop or as large as the workforce of an entire industry. The size of a bargaining unit is important in that it significantly affects the relative bargaining strength of both labor and management. *See* James L. Perry and Harold L. Angle, "Bargaining Unit Structure and Organizational Outcomes," *Industrial Relations* (Winter 1981); John E. Abodeely, Randi C. Hammer and Andrew L. Sandler, *The NLRB and the*

Appropriate Bargaining Unit, revised edition (Philadelphia: Wharton School, University of Pennsylvania, 1981); Berton B. Subrin, "Conserving Energy at the Labor Board: The Case for Making Rules on Collective Bargaining Units," *Labor Law Journal* (February 1981); Kathryn A. Gellens, "Determining Supervisory Status and Bargaining Unit Composition in the Nursing Profession," *Labor Law Journal* (June 1982).

See also the following entries:
 AMERICAN FEDERATION OF LABOR V.
  NATIONAL LABOR RELATIONS BOARD
 APPROPRIATE UNIT
 NATIONAL LABOR RELATIONS BOARD V.
  MAGNAVOX
 UNION SECURITY

Barnard, Chester I. (1886-1961), a Bell System executive closely associated with the Harvard Business School, best known for his sociological analyses of organizations that encouraged and foreshadowed the post World War II behavioral revolution. Barnard viewed organizations as cooperative systems where "the function of the executive" was to maintain the dynamic equilibrium between the needs of the organization and the needs of its employees. In order to do this, management had to be aware of the interdependent nature of the formal and informal organization. Barnard's analysis of the significance and role of informal organizations provided the theoretical foundations for a whole generation of empirical research. Major works include: *The Functions of the Executive* (Cambridge, Mass.: Harvard University Press, 1938); *Organization and Management: Selected Papers* (Cambridge, Mass.: Harvard University Press, 1948). For biography, *see* William B. Wolf, *How to Understand Management: An Introduction to Chester I. Barnard* (Los Angeles: Lucus Brothers Publishers, 1968); William B. Wolf, *The Basic Barnard: An Introduction to Chester I. Barnard and His Theories of Organization and Management* (Ithaca, N.Y.: New York State School of Industrial and Labor Relations, Cornell University, 1974).

Barr v. Matteo, 360 U.S. 564 (1959), U.S. Supreme Court case concerning the immunity of federal administrators from civil suits for damages in connection with their official duties. The court, without majority opinion, held that the acting director of the Office of Rent Stabilization had such an immunity. By implication, other federal employees would be immune from civil suits depending upon the nature of their responsibilities and duties.

See also the following entries:
BUTZ V. ECONOMOU
SPALDING V. VILAS
WOOD V. STRICKLAND

Barry, Leonora (Marie Kearney) (1849-1930), also known as MOTHER LAKE, led the women's division of the Knights of Labor from 1886 to 1890. Acquired her nickname following her marriage to O. R. Lake in 1890.

BARS: see BEHAVIORALLY ANCHORED RATING SCALES.

base period, time that an employee must work before becoming eligible for state unemployment insurance benefits.

base points, minimum point values given to the factors in a job evaluation system.

base rate: see BASE SALARY.

base salary, or BASE RATE, standard earnings before the addition of overtime or premium pay.

base time, time required for an employee to perform an operation while working normally with no allowance for personal/unavoidable delays or fatigue.

basic rate of pay, employee's hourly wage. The regular rate of pay upon which overtime and other wage supplements would be computed.

basic workday, number of hours in a normal workday, as established by collective bargaining agreements or statutory law. Premium payments must usually be paid

for time worked in excess of the basic workday. The eight-hour day is widely accepted as the standard basic workday.

basic workweek, number of hours in a normal workweek, as established by collective bargaining agreements or statutory law. Premium payments must usually be paid for time worked in excess of the basic workweek. The 40-hour week is widely accepted as the standard basic workweek.

See also FAIR LABOR STANDARDS ACT.

Batterton v. Francis, 432 U.S. 416 (1977), U.S. Supreme Court case, which held that a state could deny welfare benefits for families of unemployed fathers if the father is unemployed as a result of a strike.

battery, or TEST BATTERY, two or more tests administered together and standardized on the same population so that the results on the various tests are comparable. The term battery is also used to refer to any tests administered as a group. See W. Considine, *et al.,* "Developing a Physical Performance Test Battery for Screening Chicago Fire Fighter Applicants," *Public Personnel Management* (January–February 1976).

Bay Ridge Company v. Aaron, 334 U.S. 446 (1948), U.S. Supreme Court case, which held that premium payments provided for in collective bargaining agreements had to be considered in computing the "regular rate" of pay for overtime computations.

Beck, Dave (1894-   ), president of the International Brotherhood of Teamsters (1952-1957) who was sentenced to prison in 1958 because of income tax evasion. Under Beck's leadership, the Teamsters grew so corrupt that they were expelled from the AFL–CIO in 1958. As a direct result of the notoriety of the Beck case, the U.S. Congress passed the Labor-Management Reporting and Disclosure (Landrum-Griffin) Act of 1959, which created safeguards against irresponsible and corrupt union leadership.

Bedaux Plan also BEDAUX POINT SYSTEM, wage incentive plan introduced in 1916 by Charles E. Bedaux, which provided that the bonus earned for incentive effort be divided between the employee and management.

Bedford Cut Stone Company v. Journeymen Stone Cutters' Association, 174 U.S. 37 (1927), U.S. Supreme Court case, which held that union members cannot, without being in violation of the Sherman Anti-Trust Act of 1890, refuse to work on work that had previously been worked on by non-union labor.

beggar-thy-neighbor policy, a course of action through which a country tries to reduce unemployment and increase domestic output by raising tariffs and instituting non-tariff measures that impede imports. Countries that pursued such policies in the early 1930s found that other countries retaliated by raising barriers against the first country's exports, which tended to worsen the economic difficulties that precipitated the initial protectionist action.

beginner's rate, or TRAINEE RATE, wage rate for an inexperienced employee. Once a previously established training period is completed, an employee is entitled to the regular rate of pay for the job.

behaviorally anchored rating scales (BARS), performance evaluation technique that is premised upon the scaling of critical incidents of work performance. For the methodology, see Donald Schwab, Herbert Heneman III, and Thomas DeCotiis, "Behaviorally Anchored Scales: A Review of the Literature," *Personnel Psychology,* Vol. 28 (1975); Frank J. Landy, *et al.,* "Behaviorally Anchored Scales for Rating the Performance of Police Officers," *Journal of Applied Psychology* (December 1976); Michael Loar, Susan Mohrman and John R. Stock, "Development of a Behaviorally Based Performance Appraisal System," *Personnel Psychology* (Spring 1982).

behavior modeling, training, usually for first or second line supervisors, that uses videotapes and/or roleplaying sessions to give supervisors an opportunity to improve their supervisory abilities by imitating "models" who have already mastered such skills. For summaries of the technique, *see* Bernard L. Rosenbaum, "New Uses for Behavior Modeling," *The Personnel Administrator* (July 1978); Scott B. Parry and Leah R. Reich, "An Uneasy Look at Behavior Modeling," *Training and Development Journal* (March 1984); John T. Clifford, Frank Petrock and James Davisson, "Behavior Modeling for Quality Assurance," *SAM Advanced Management Journal* (Summer 1984).

behavior models, diagrams used by social scientists to better explain their theories of human behavior. For examples see JOHARI WINDOW and MANAGERIAL GRID.

behavior modification (B Mod), use of positive or negative reinforcements to change the behavior of individuals or groups. *See* C. E. Schneider, "Behavior Modification: Training the Hard Core Unemployed," *Personnel* (May-June 1973); C. Ray Gullett and Robert Reisen, "Behavior Modification: A Contingency Approach to Employee Performance," *Personnel Journal* (April 1975); W. Clay Hamner and Ellen P. Hamner, "Behavior Modification on the Bottom Line," *Organizational Dynamics* (Spring 1976); Jerry L. Gray, "The Myths of the Myths About Behavior Mod in Organizations," *Academy of Management Review* (January 1979); James C. Robinson, "Will Behavior Modeling Survive the '80s?" *Training and Development Journal* (January 1980); Donald T. Tosti, "Behavior Modeling: A Process," *Training and Development Journal* (August 1980).

behavioral sciences, general term for all of the academic disciplines that study human and animal behavior by means of experimental research.
See also NATIONAL TRAINING LABORATORIES INSTITUTE FOR APPLIED BEHAVIORAL SCIENCE.

behavioral technology, emerging discipline that seeks to meld together both the technical and human aspects of the workplace. It places equal emphasis on the social as well as the technological sciences in order to foster the individual's fullest use as both a human and technical resource. *See* James G. Brianas, "Behavioral Technology: A Challenge to Modern Management," *Public Personnel Management* (July–August 1973).

behaviorism, school of psychology which holds that only overt behavior is the proper subject matter for the entire discipline. According to the foremost exponent of behaviorism, B. F. Skinner, "behaviorism is not the science of human behavior; it is the philosophy of that science." *About Behaviorism* (N.Y.: Alfred A. Knopf, 1974).

Bell, Daniel (1919-), sociologist whose critiques of modern industrial societies have touched upon their politics and their management. Bell is considered to be both a major critic of the "machine civilization" of the scientific management era and a pioneer in social forecasting. Major works include: *Work and Its Discontents: The Cult of Efficiency in America* (Boston: Beacon Press, 1956); *The End of Ideology* (Glencoe, Ill.: The Free Press, 1960); *The Coming of Post-Industrial Society* (N.Y.: Basic Books, 1973).
   See also POST-INDUSTRIAL SOCIETY.

benchmark, any standard that is identified with sufficient detail so that other similar classifications can be compared as being above, below, or comparable to the "benchmark" standard.

benchmark position, position used as a frame of reference in the evaluation of other positions.

beneficiary, person, group, or organization to whom an insurance policy is payable.

benefit, a sum of money provided in an insurance policy payable for certain types of loss, or for covered services, under the terms of the policy. The benefits may be paid to the insured or on his behalf to others.

benefit, death: *see* DEATH BENEFIT.

benefit-cost analysis: *see* COST-BENEFIT ANALYSIS.

benefit period, the period of time for which payments for benefits covered by an insurance policy are available. The availability of certain benefits may be limited over a specified time period, for example two well-baby visits during a one-year period. While the benefit period is usually defined by a set unit of time, such as a year, benefits may also be tied to a spell of illness.

benefit plans, welfare programs administered by a union for its members and paid for out of dues, voluntary contributions, or special assessments.
   See also the following entries:
     CAFETERIA BENEFITS PLAN
     FLAT-BENEFIT PLAN
     FRINGE BENEFITS
     HEALTH BENEFITS

benefit seniority, use of seniority in computing an employee's economic fringe benefits such as pensions, vacations, bonuses, etc.

Benge, Eugene J. (1896-), generally credited with having "invented" the factor-comparison method of job evaluation in the 1920s. Major works include: *Manual of Job Evaluation* with S. Burk and E. N. Hay (N.Y.: Harper Bros., 1941); *How to Manage for Tomorrow* (Homewood, Ill.: Dow Jones-Irwin, 1975); *Elements of Modern Management* (N.Y.: AMACOM, 1976).

Bennett Mechanical Comprehension Test (BMCT), paper-and-pencil test that uses pictures to test the individual on basic understanding of mechanical principles and facts. TIME: 30/35 minutes. AUTHOR: George K. Bennett. PUBLISHER:

Psychological Corporation (*see* TEST PUBLISHERS).

Bennis, Warren G. (1925-   ), a leading proponent of organization development, is perhaps best known for his continuous sounding of the death knell of bureaucratic institutions. Bennis has indicted most present organizational formats as inadequate for a future that will demand rapid organizational and technological changes, participatory management, and the growth of a more professionalized workforce. Organizations of the future, Bennis maintains, will be more responsive to these needs and in consequence, decidedly less bureaucratic, less structured, and less rigid. Major works include: *Changing Organizations* (N.Y.: Mc-Graw-Hill, 1966); *The Temporary Society*, with Philip E. Slater (N.Y.: Harper & Row, 1968); *Organization Development: Its Nature, Origins, and Prospects* (Reading, Mass.: Addison-Wesley, 1969); *The Leaning Ivory Tower*, with P. W. Biederman (N.Y.: Jossey-Bass, 1973).

See also POSTBUREAUCRATIC ORGANIZATIONS:

Bentham, Jeremy (1748-1832), a utilitarian philosopher who held that self-interest was the prime motivator and that a government should strive to do the greatest good for the greatest numbers.

bereavement leave: *see* FUNERAL LEAVE.

Berne, Eric (1910-1970), the psychoanalyst who founded the field of transactional analysis. Major works include: *Games People Play: The Psychology of Human Relationship* (N.Y.: Grove Press, 1964); *Principles of Group Treatment* (N.Y.: Oxford University Press, 1966); *What Do You Say After You Say Hello?* (N.Y.: Grove Press, 1972); *Intuition & Ego States: The Origins of Transactional Analysis* (N.Y.: Harper & Row, 1977). For biography, *see* Warren D. Cheney, "Eric Berne: Biographical Sketch," in Eric Berne, *Beyond Games and Scripts* (N.Y.: Grove Press, 1976).

Bernreuter Personality Inventory (BPI), personality inventory commonly used in business and industry to measure six personality traits (neurotic tendency, self-sufficiency, intro-extroversion, dominance/submission, self confidence, and sociability). TIME: 25-30 minutes. AUTHOR: Robert G. Bernreuter. PUBLISHER: Consulting Psychologists Press, Inc. (*see* TEST PUBLISHERS).

Bertalanffy, Ludwig von (1901-1972), Austrian-Canadian biologist considered to be the "father of general systems theory." His basic statement on the subject is: *General System Theory: Foundations, Development, Applications* (N.Y.: George Braziller, rev. ed., 1968). For a biography, *see* Mark Davidson, *Uncommon Sense: The Life and Thought of Ludwig von Bertalanffy (1901-1972), Father of General Systems Theory* (Boston: Houghton Mifflin, 1983).

bespoke work, archaic term for special orders. In the olden days master craftsmen would produce products either on speculation (hoping that they would later find a buyer for them) or in response to a specific order. These latter products were bespoke work—they had literally been spoken for.

Beth Israel Hosptial v. National Labor Relations Board, 57 L. Ed. 2d 370 (1978), U.S. Supreme Court case, which upheld a National Labor Relations Board determination that employees seeking to organize a bargaining unit of hospital employees could not be prohibited from distributing leaflets in a hospital cafeteria patronized predominantly by hospital employees. To a limited extent, the court gave its approval to the NLRB's attempt to permit a substantial range for union communication to actual and potential members, provided such communication does not disrupt employer's business activities.

BFOQ: *see* BONA FIDE OCCUPATIONAL QUALIFICATION.

bias, tendency of a selection device to err

in a particular direction.
See also CULTURAL BIAS.

biased sample, sample that does not truly represent the total population from which it was selected.

bidding, means by which an employee of an organization makes known his or her interest in a vacant position in that same organization. *See* Elaine Gale Wrong, "Arbitrators, the Law, and Women's Job Bids," *Labor Law Journal* (December 1982).

Bieber, Owen (1939-), became president of the United Auto Workers in 1983.

Big Blue, the International Business Machines Corporation (IBM).

Big Eight, slang term for the eight largest public accounting firms: Arthur Anderson and Co.; Coopers and Lybrand; Ernst and Ernst; Haskins and Sells; Peat, Marwick, Mitchell and Company; Price Waterhouse and Company; Touche Ross and Company, and Arthur Young and Company. *See* Mark Stevens, *The Big Eight: An Inside View of America's Eight Most Powerful and Influential Accounting Firms* (New York: Macmillan, 1981).

bigotry: *see* DISCRIMINATION.

big labor, organized labor in general or the AFL-CIO. *See* Marilyn Wilson, "Big Labor Faces Reality," *Dun's Business Month* (February 1982).

Big Steel, and LITTLE STEEL, historically "big steel" has referred to just the United States Steel Corporation, and "little steel" was all others. More recently, "big steel" has been used to refer collectively to all of the largest steel makers.

Big Three, the largest American auto makers: General Motors, Ford, and Chrysler.

Bildisco case, *see* NATIONAL LABOR RELATIONS BOARD V. BILDISCO & BILDISCO.

bill: *see* ACT.

bill of rights, *the* "bill of rights" was the first ten amendments to the U.S. Constitution. Nowadays the term is also used for any important listing of rights and/or privileges. For the "bill of rights" of union members, see the Labor-Management Reporting and Disclosure Act of 1959.

bimodal distribution, frequency distribution in which there are two modes—two most frequently occurring scores. A graphic presentation would show two peaks.

binding arbitration, actually a redundancy! Arbitration, unless it is advisory, is by its nature binding upon the parties.

Binet, Alfred (1857-1911), French psychologist who originated the first modern intelligence test. For a biography, see Theta Holmes Wolf, *Alfred Binet* (University of Chicago Press, 1973).

bi-partite board, labor-management committee established as part of a grievance process in order to resolve a dispute short of arbitration.

birth leave, paid time off upon the birth of a child. This is generally available only to men. Women, should the occasion warrant, would necessarily take maternity leave. See Nancy Norman and James T. Tedeschi, "Paternity Leave: The Unpopular Benefit Option," *Personnel Administrator* (February 1984).
See also MATERNITY LEAVE.

biserial correlation, correlation between the score on a particular item and the total test score.

Bishop v. Wood, 426 U.S. 341 (1976), U.S. Supreme Court case, which held that an employee's discharge did not deprive him of a property interest protected by the Due Process Clause of the U.S. Constitution's 14th Amendment. The court further asserted that even assuming a false explanation for the employee's discharge, he was still not deprived of an interest in liberty protected by the clause if the reasons for his discharge were not made public.

Bituminous Coal Act of 1937, federal law that regulates the sale of bituminous coal in interstate commerce and provides collective bargaining rights for coal miners.

black leg: *see* SCAB.

black list, originally lists prepared by merchants containing the names of men who had gone bankrupt. The early union movement found that employers were using "don't hire" lists of men who joined unions. But the National Labor Relations (Wagner) Act of 1935 made such blacklisting illegal. In the 1950's, many in the entertainment industry were "blacklisted" and thus denied employment for alleged "un-American" activities. For a history of this period, *see* David Caute, *The Great Fear: The Anti-Communist Purge Under Truman and Eisenhower* (N.Y.: Simon & Schuster, 1978).

black-lung disease, scientific name PNEUMOCONIOSIS, chronic and disabling occupational disease (mostly of miners) resulting from the inhalation of dusts over a long period of time. Its popular name results from the tendency of the inhaled dusts to blacken lung tissue. *See* Carvin Cook, "The 1977 Amendments to the Black Lung Benefits Law," *Monthly Labor Review* (May 1978).

See also USERY V. TURNER ELKHORN MINING CO.

Blake, Robert R. (1918-   ) **and Jane S. Mouton** (1930-   ), industrial psychologists best known for their conceptualization of the "managerial grid"—a graphic description of the various managerial approaches. The grid itself represents leadership styles that reflect two prime dimensions, "concern for people" on the vertical axis, and "concern for production" on the horizontal axis. For a complete presentation of the grid concept, *see* any of their books: *The Managerial Grid* (Houston, Texas: Gulf Publishing, 1964);

Corporate Excellence Through Grid Organization Development (Houston, Texas; Gulf Publishing, 1968); *Building a Dynamic Organization Through Grid Organization Development* (Reading, Mass.: Addison-Wesley, 1969).

blanket agreement, collective bargaining agreement that is based on industrywide negotiations or negotiations covering a large geographic area within an industry.

blanketing-in, term for largescale importation of previously noncareer jobs into the regular civil service. In the short run, "blanketing-in" can be (and has been) used to protect political favorites from the next administration. In the long run, blanketing-in is one of the major means through which the career civil service has been enlarged. For a comprehensive discussion of the process, *see* Hugh Heclo, *A Government of Strangers: Executive Politics in Washington* (Washington, D.C.: The Brookings Institution, 1977), pp. 41-46.

Blau, Peter M. (1918-   ), sociologist who has specialized in the study of formal organizations and bureaucracies and produced pioneering empirical as well as theoretical analyses of organizational behavior. Major works include: *The Dynamics of Bureaucracy* (Chicago: University of Chicago Press, 1955, revised 1963); *Bureaucracy in Modern Society* (N.Y.: Random House, 1956); *Formal Organizations,* with W. Richard Scott (San Francisco: Chandler Publishing, 1962); *Exchange and Power in Social Life* (N.Y.: Wiley, 1964); *The American Occupational Structure* (N.Y.: Wiley, 1967); *The Structure of Organizations* (N.Y.: Basic Books, 1971); *The Organization of Academic Work* (N.Y.: Wiley, 1973).

Blaylock, Kenneth T. (1935-   ), became president of the American Federation of Government Employees in 1976.

bleeding shark, an employee in trouble at work who is attacked by others instead of helped.

BLS: *see* BUREAU OF LABOR STATISTICS.

blue-circle rate: *see* GREEN-CIRCLE RATE.

blue-collar workers, those workers, both skilled and unskilled, engaged primarily in physical labor. For example, the U.S. Bureau of the Census considers all craftsmen, construction workers, machine operators, farm workers, transportation equipment operators, factory production and maintenance workers to fit into the blue-collar category. For an analysis of blue-collar angst, *see* Irving Howe (ed.), *The World of the Blue-Collar Worker* (N.Y.: Quadrangle Books, 1972). *Also see* Nancy R. Brunner, "Blue-Collar Women," *Personnel Journal* (April 1981); Robert Schrank, "Horse-Collar Blue-Collar Blues," *Harvard Business Review* (May–June 1981); Mary Russell, "Career Planning in a Blue Collar Company," *Training and Development Journal* (January 1984); Loren M. Solnick, "The Effect of Blue-Collar Unions on White Collar Wages and Fringe Benefits," *Industrial & Labor Relations Review* (January 1985).

Blue Cross and Blue Shield, non-profit group health insurance plans for, respectively, hospital and physician's fees.

Blue Eagle: *see* NATIONAL INDUSTRIAL RECOVERY ACT OF 1933.

blue flu, when police officers informally strike by calling in sick, they are said to be suffering from a disease so unique that it affects only police—the blue flu. *See* Casey Ichniowski, "Arbitration and Police Bargaining: Prescriptions for the Blue Flu," *Industrial Relations* (Spring 1982).

blue laws, state and local legislation banning commercial and related activities on particular days, usually Sunday.

Blue Shield: *see* BLUE CROSS AND BLUE SHIELD.

blue sky bargaining, unreasonable and unrealistic negotiating demands by either side, made usually at the beginning of the negotiating process. The only "useful" purposes of such bargaining are to (1) satisfy an outside audience that their concerns are being attended to, (2) delay the "real" negotiations because such a delay is thought to hold a tactical advantage, and (3) provide a basis for compromise as the negotiations progress.

BMCT: *see* BENNETT MECHANICAL COMPREHENSION TEST.

BMod: *see* BEHAVIOR MODIFICATION.

BNA: *see* BUREAU OF NATIONAL AFFAIRS, INC.

BNA Pension Reporter, Bureau of National Affairs, Inc., information service that provides weekly notification of developments under the Employee Retirement Income Security Act of 1974, including enforcement actions, court decisions, labor and industry activities, and employee benefit trust fund regulation; activities of the Department of Labor, the Internal Revenue Service, the Pension Benefit Guaranty Corporation, and Congress; and state and local government actions.

BNA Policy and Practice Series, "common-sense" guide on the handling of employer-employee relations published by the Bureau of National Affairs, Inc. Covers personnel management, labor relations, fair employment practices, wages and hours, and compensation.

Board of Regents v. Roth, 408 U.S. 564 (1972), U.S. Supreme Court case, which established the principle that a dismissed or nonrenewed public employee had no general constitutional right to either a statement of reasons or a hearing. However, both of these might be constitutionally required, the court ruled, in individual instances where any of the following four conditions existed:
1. Where the removal or nonrenewal was in retaliation for the exercise of constitutional rights such as freedom of speech or association.
2. Where the adverse action impaired

the individual's reputation.
3. Perhaps not fully distinguishable from the above, where a dismissal or nonrenewal placed a stigma or other disability upon the employee which foreclosed his or her freedom to take advantage of other employment opportunities.
4. Where one had a property right or interest in the position, as in the case of tenured or contracted public employees.

bod biz, slang term for sensitivity training programs.

body chemistry, nebulous concept that refers to the fact that strangers, upon meeting, react to a variety of irrational and subliminal signals, which, in turn, determine whether they like each other or not.

***Boeing* decision:** *see* NATIONAL LABOR RELATIONS BOARD V. BOEING.

bogey, easily exceeded informal standard that employees may establish in order to restrict production.

bona fide occupational qualification (BFOQ or BOQ), *bona fide* is a Latin term meaning "in good faith," honest, or genuine. A BFOQ, therefore, is a *necessary* occupational qualification. Title VII of the Civil Rights Act of 1964 allows employers to discriminate against applicants on the basis of religion, sex, or national origin, when being considered for certain jobs if they lack a BFOQ. However, what constitutes a BFOQ has been interpreted very narrowly by the EEOC and the federal courts. Legitimate BFOQ's include female sex for a position as an actress or male sex for a sperm donor. There are no generally recognized BFOQ's with respect to race or color. Overall, a BFOQ is a job requirement that would be discriminatory and illegal were it not for its necessity for the performance of a particular job. For analyses, *see* Jeffery M. Shaman, "Toward Defining and Abolishing the Bona Fide Occupational Qualification Based on Class Status," *Labor Law Jour-*

nal (June 1971); Thomas Stephen Neuberger, "Sex as a Bona Fide Occupational Qualification Under Title VII," *Labor Law Journal* (July 1978).
See also DOTHARD V. RAWLINSON.

bona fide union, union that was freely chosen by employees and that is not unreasonably or illegally influenced by their employer.

bonus, also called SUPPLEMENTAL COMPENSATION, any compensation that is in addition to regular wages and salary. Because "bonus" has a mildly paternalistic connotation, it has been replaced in some organizations by "supplemental compensation."
See also the following entries:
DANGER-ZONE BONUS
NONPRODUCTION BONUS
PRODUCTION BONUS
STEP BONUS

boondoggle, slang term for any wasteful and/or unproductive program.

Booster Lodge No. 405, Machinists* v. *National Labor Relations Board, 412 U.S. 84 (1973), U.S. Supreme Court case, which held that a union's attempt to collect fines from strikers who had resigned from the union before crossing picket lines was an unfair labor practice.

bootleg wages, wages above union scale that an employer might pay in a tight labor market in order to retain and attract employees, as well as wages below union scale that an employee might accept in lieu of unemployment.

BOQ: *see* BONA FIDE OCCUPATIONAL QUALIFICATION.

Boren, James H.: *see* INTERNATIONAL ASSOCIATION OF PROFESSIONAL BUREAUCRATS.

***Borg-Warner* case:** *see* NATIONAL LABOR RELATIONS BOARD V. WOOSTER DIVISION OF BORG-WARNER CORP.

boss, slang term used by subordinates to refer to anyone from whom they are willing to take orders. *See* John J. Gabarro and John P. Kotter, "Managing Your Boss," *Harvard Business Review* (January-February 1980); William P. Anthony, *Managing Your Boss* (New York: AMACOM, 1983).

Boston Police Strike of 1919, the nation's first taste of large-scale municipal labor problems. While the patrolmen struck for a variety of reasons including the right to form a union and affiliate with the AFL, the strike brought chaos to the city. Samuel Gompers protested the police commissioner's refusal to allow the union to affiliate with the AFL. Calvin Coolidge, then Governor of Massachusetts, responded with his famous assertion that "there is no right to strike against the public safety by anybody, anywhere, anytime." These words so captured the public's imagination that a tidal wave of support gained him the Republican vice-presidential nomination in 1920 (when Harding died in 1923, Coolidge became president). The failure of the Boston Police Strike was a lesson that would inhibit municipal unionization for many decades.

For a history, see Francis Russell, *A City in Terror—1919—The Boston Police Strike* (New York: The Viking Press, 1975).

bottom line, the profit or loss for an activity; the final result of an activity, a final conclusion; or responsibility. *See* Michael O'Keefe, "The Link to Bottom-Line Results," *Training and Development Journal* (January 1981).

bottom-line concept, in the context of equal employment opportunity, the bottom-line concept suggests that an employer whose total selection process has no adverse impact can be assured that EEO enforcement agencies will not examine the individual components of that process for evidence of adverse impact. However, not all EEO enforcement agencies subscribe to the concept.

bottom-up management, catch-phrase describing a philosophy of participative management designed "to release the thinking and encourage the initiative of all those down from the bottom up." For the original presentation, *see* W. B. Given, Jr., *Bottom Up Management* (N.Y.: Harper & Row, 1949).

Boulwareism, approach to collective bargaining in which management makes a final "take-it-or-leave-it" offer that it believes is both fair and is the best it can do. The concept is named for Lemuel R. Boulware, a vice president of the General Electric Company, who pioneered the tactic in the 1950s. If the final offer is rejected by the union, management grants the benefits of the offer to all non-union workers and assures the union that there will be no retroactive benefits when the union finally accepts the "final" offer. Because this tactic called for management to communicate directly to the workers, circumventing the union, it was challenged as an unfair practice. Boulwareism, as used by General Electric, was found in violation of the National Labor Relations Act in a 1969 ruling of the U.S. Circuit Court of Appeals in New York. The company's appeal to the U.S. Supreme Court was denied. The major defense of Boulwareism is: Lemuel R. Boulware, *The Truth About Boulwareism: Trying To Do Right Voluntarily* (Washington, D.C.: Bureau of National Affairs, 1969).

bounded rationality: *see* SATISFICING.

bourgeois, in the context of Marxism a member of the ruling class in capitalistic societies; one of the owners of the means of production. The plural is *bourgeoisie*. Marx distinguished between the *haute bourgeoisie*, the real leaders of industry; and the *petite bourgeoisie*, the small businessmen, whom he felt really belonged with the proletariat.

boycott, during the mid-19th century, Charles C. Boycott, a retired English army captain, was in Ireland managing the estate of an absentee owner. His methods were so severe and oppressive that the local citizens as a group refused to deal with him in any manner. When Captain Boycott was forced to flee home to England, the first boycott or nonviolent intimidation through ostracism was a success.

In the context of labor relations, a boycott is any refusal to deal with or buy the products of a business as a means of exerting pressure in a labor dispute. The U.S. Supreme Court has consistently held that boycotts are an illegal "restraint of trade" under the Sherman Antitrust Act of 1890.

See also the following entries:
LAWLOR V. LOEWE
NATIONAL WOODWORK MANUFACTURES ASSOCIATION V. NATIONAL LABOR RELATIONS BOARD
PRIMARY BOYCOTT
SECONDARY BOYCOTT
UNITED STATES V. HUTCHESON

Boyle, (W.A.) "Tony" (1904-1985), John L. Lewis' handpicked successor, president of the United Mine Workers from 1963 to 1972. After conspiring to kill "Jock" Yablonski, a union rival, he was convicted on three counts of first degree murder for the 1969 deaths of Yablonski, his wife, and daughter.

Boys Market v. Retail Clerks' Local 770, 398 U.S. 235 (1970), U.S. Supreme Court case, which held that when a labor contract has a no-strike provision and provides an arbitration procedure, a federal court may, upon the request of an employer, issue an injunction to terminate a strike by employees covered by such a contract. This reversed an earlier decision, *Sinclair Refining* v. *Atkinson,* 370 U.S. 195 (1962), that forbade federal courts from issuing injunctions to stop a strike in violation of a no-strike clause. For an analysis, *see* John A. Relias, "The Developing Law Under Boys Markets," *Labor Law Journal* (December 1972).

BPI: *see* BERNREUTER PERSONALITY INVENTORY.

bracero program, or BRACERO SYSTEM,

during World War II, the farm manpower shortage was so great that Mexican field hands or braceros were imported as seasonal farm workers. The practice, sanctioned by law in 1951, was long opposed by organized labor and was terminated by Congress in 1964. Since that time, however, an informal and unofficial bracero program has evolved from the large numbers of illegal aliens coming into the United States from Mexico.

See also UNDOCUMENTED WORKERS.

Bradford, Leland P. (1905-   ), director of the National Training Laboratories from 1947 to 1967, who pioneered the development of "sensitivity" training. Major works include: *T-Group Theory and Laboratory Method: Innovation in Re-Education,* co-editor (N.Y.: John Wiley, 1964); *Making Meetings Work: A Guide for Leaders & Group Members* (San Diego, Calif.: University Associates, 1976).

brain drain, pejorative term referring to the unfortunate flow of human capital—talent—from a country or an organization. While historically used to describe the exodus of doctors, scientists, and other professionals from a particular country, it is colloquially used to refer to the departure of any valued employee or group of employees. *See* Walter Adams (ed.), *The Brain Drain* (N.Y.: Macmillan, 1968).

brainstorming, frequently used to describe any group effort to generate ideas. It has a more formal definition—a creative conference for the sole purpose of producing suggestions or ideas that can serve as leads to problem solving. The concept has been most developed by Alex Osborn. See his *Applied Imagination* (N.Y.: Charles Scribner's Sons, 1963). For a how-to-do-it account, *see* Ronald H. Gorman and H. Kent Baker, "Brainstorming Your Way to Problem-Solving Ideas," *Personnel Journal* (August 1978). *Also see* Toby Katz, "Brainstorming Updated," *Training and Development Journal* (February 1984).

Branti v. Finkel, 445 U.S. 507 (1980), Supreme Court case expanding on the Court's earlier ruling in *Elrod* v. *Burns* (1976) that the dismissal of nonpolicymaking, nonconfidential public employees for their partisan affiliation violates the First and/or Fourteenth Amendments. The burden is on the hiring authority to demonstrate that partisan affiliation is an appropriate requirement for effective performance in office, which could not be done in this instance involving the position of assistant public defender.

brass, slang term of military origin which now refers to the key executives in an organization.

breach of contract, violation of a collective bargaining agreement by either party. If established grievance machinery is not adequate to deal with the dispute, traditional lawsuits remain as a remedy.

bread-and-butter unions: *see* BUSINESS UNIONS.

breakdown: *see* NERVOUS BREAKDOWN.

Brennen, Peter J. (1918–   ), Secretary of Labor from 1973 to 1975.

bridge job, position specifically designed to facilitate the movement of individuals from one classification and/or job category to another classification and/or category. Such bridge jobs are an integral part of many career ladders and upward mobility programs.

Bridges, Harry (1901–   ), full name ALFRED BRYANT RENTON BRIDGES, president of the International Longshoremen's and Warehousemen's Union from 1937 to 1977, who has, because of suggested Communist leanings, been one of the most controversial of U.S. labor leaders. For a biography, *see* Charles P. Larrowe, *Harry Bridges: The Rise and Fall of Radical Labor in the U.S.* (N.Y.: Lawrence Hill and Co., 2nd ed. rev., 1977).

brief, a written statement prepared by each side in a formal lawsuit or hearing which summarizes the facts of the situation and makes arguments about how the law should be applied.

Brock William E. (1930–   ), became Secretary of Labor in 1985.

Brookings Institution, nonprofit organization devoted to research, education, and publication in economics, government, foreign policy, and the social sciences generally. In its research, it functions as an independent analyst and critic, committed to publishing its findings for the information of the public. In its conferences and other activities, it serves as a bridge between scholarship and public policy, bringing new knowledge to the attention of decision makers and affording scholars a better insight into policy issues. The Institution's Advanced Study Program is devoted to public policy education of leaders in both government and business.

Brookings Institution
1775 Massachusetts Avenue, N.W.
Washington, D.C. 20036
(202) 797-6000

broken time, or SPLIT SHIFT, daily work schedule that is divided by a length of time considerably in excess of the time required for a normal meal break. For example, a school bus driver may work from 6 to 10 a.m. and then from 2 to 6 p.m.

brotherhood, term used by some of the older unions as an indication of solidarity and common interests. For example, the Brotherhood of Railroad Signalmen.

Brown v. General Services Administration, 425 U.S. 820 (1976), U.S. Supreme Court case, which held that Congress intended Title VII of the Civil Rights Act of 1964 to provide the sole statutory protection against employment discrimination for federal employees—even though it is not the sole protection for workers in the private sector.

brown lung disease, scientific name BYSSINOSIS, chronic and disabling lung disease that affects workers in cotton mills. *See* Mary Lee Gosney, "Whatever Happened to Brown Lung? Compensation for Difficult to Diagnose Occupational Diseases," *Industrial Relations Law Journal,* Vol. 3, No. 1 (1979).

brownie points, a pejorative term for presumed credits earned for acts done for your organizational superiors that your organizational peers would consider demeaning or servile; in other words, sucking up to the boss.

buckology, basic technique for evading responsibility. *See* R. C. Burkholder, "Buckology: The Art and Science of Passing the Buck," *Supervision* (March 1978).

buddy system, on-the-job training technique that has a trainee assigned to work closely with an experienced worker until the trainee has gained enough experience to work alone.

budget, financial plan serving as a pattern for and control over future operations—hence, any estimate of future costs or any systematic plan for the utilization of the workforce, material, or other resources. Budgets are short-range segments of action programs that set out planned accomplishments and estimate the resources to be applied for the budget periods in order to attain those accomplishments.

budgeting, the process of translating planning and programming decisions into specific projected financial plans for relatively short periods of time.

Buffalo Forge Co.* v. *United Steelworkers, 423 U.S. 911 (1976), U.S. Supreme Court case, which held that federal courts were permitted to enjoin a strike over a nonarbitrable issue pending an arbitrator's decision on whether the strike violates a no-strike pledge in a collective bargaining contract.

buggin's turn, British phrase for promotion based on seniority rather than merit.

built-in stabilizers, features of the economy (such as unemployment benefits, welfare payments, etc.) that automatically act to modify the severity of economic downturns.

See also AUTOMATIC STABILIZER.

bump, or BUMPING, layoff procedure that gives an employee with greater seniority the right to displace or "bump" another employee. Sometimes bumping rights are restricted to one plant, office, or department. Because of legally guaranteed bumping rights, the laying off of a single worker can lead to the sequential transfers of a dozen others. *See* Wilbur C. Rich, "Bumping, Blocking and Bargaining: The Effect of Layoffs on Employees and Unions," *Review of Public Personnel Administration* (Fall 1983).

burden of proof, requirement that a party to an issue show that the weight of evidence is on his or her side in order to have the issue decided in his or her favor.

Burdine* v. *Texas Department of Community Affairs, U.S. Supreme Court case, 450 U.S. 248 (1980), which held that employers charged with discrimination do not have to prove that a person hired or promoted was better qualified than the person passed over. Instead, the employer need only provide adequate evidence that race or sex was not a factor in the decision.

The unanimous opinion of the Supreme Court, written by Justice Lewis F. Powell, Jr., said that although Federal law prohibits discrimination, it does not demand that an employer give preferential treatment to minorities or women; that an employer does not have to prove that its action is lawful, rather the employer need only produce evidence which would allow a judge to conclude that the decision had not been motivated by discriminatory animus.

bureau, government department, agency or subdivision of same.

bureaucracy, while bureaucracy is used as a general invective to refer to any inefficient organization, its more formal usage has it referring to a specific set of structural arrangements. The dominant structural definition of bureaucracy, indeed the point of departure for all further analyses on the subject, is that of the German sociologist, Max Weber. Drawing upon studies of ancient bureaucracies in Egypt, Rome, China, and the Byzantine Empire, as well as on the more modern ones emerging in Europe during the 19th and early part of the 20th centuries, Weber used an "ideal type" approach to extrapolate from the real world the central core of features that would characterize the most fully developed bureaucratic form of organization. This "ideal type" is neither a description of reality nor a statement of normative preference. It is merely an identification of the major variables or features that characterize bureaucracy. The fact that such features might not be fully present in a given organization does not necessarily imply that the organization is "non-bureaucratic." It may be an immature rather than a fully developed bureaucracy. At some point, however, it may be necessary to conclude that the characteristics of bureaucracy are so lacking in an organization that it could neither reasonably be termed bureaucratic nor be expected to produce patterns of bureaucratic behavior.

Weber's "ideal type" bureaucracy possesses the following characteristics:

1. The bureaucrats must be personally free and subject to authority only with respect to the impersonal duties of their offices.
2. They are arranged in a clearly defined hierarchy of offices.
3. The functions of each office are clearly specified.
4. Officials accept and maintain their appointments freely—without duress.
5. Appointments are made on the basis of technical qualifications which ideally are substantiated by examinations—administered by the appointing authority, a university, or both.
6. Officials should have a money salary as well as pension rights. Such salaries must reflect the vary-

ing levels of positions in the hierarchy. While officials are always free to leave the organization, they can be removed from their offices only under previously stated specific circumstances.
7. An incumbent's post must be his sole or at least his major occupation.
8. A career system is essential. While promotion may be the result of either seniority or merit, it must be premised on the judgment of hierarchical superiors.
9. The official may not have a property right to his position nor any personal claim to the resources which go with it.
10. An official's conduct must be subject to systematic control and strict discipline.

While Weber's structural identification of bureaucratic organization (first published in 1922) is perhaps the most comprehensive statement on the subject in the literature of the social sciences, it is not always considered satisfactory as an intellectual construct. For example, Anthony Downs, in *Inside Bureaucracy* (Boston: Little, Brown, 1967), argues that at least two elements should be added to Weber's definition. First, the organization must be large. According to Downs, "any organization in which the highest ranking members know less than half of the other members can be considered large." Second, most of the organization's output cannot be "directly or indirectly evaluated in any markets external to the organization by means of voluntary *quid pro quo* transactions."

Definitions of bureaucracy apply equally to organizations in the public as well as the private sector. However, public sector bureaucracies tend to operate in a somewhat different climate from those in the private sector. What has come to be known as the "third sector"—not-for-profit organizations such as hospitals, universities, and foundations—would analytically be classed with public organizations because of the lack of free-market forces upon them. In short, bureaucracy is best conceptualized as a specific form or organization, and public bureaucracy should be considered a special variant of bureaucratic organization.

The literature on bureaucracy is immense. The following is a representative sample: Alan A. Altshuler and Norman C. Thomas, *The Politics of the Federal Bureaucracy* (New York: Harper & Row, 2nd ed., 1977); Peter Blau and Marshall Meyer, *Bureaucracy in Modern Society* (New York: Random House, 1971); Michel Crozier, *The Bureaucratic Phenomenon* (Chicago: University of Chicago Press, 1964); Michael T. Dalby and Michael S. Werthman, *Bureaucracy in Historical Perspective* (Glenview, Ill.: Scott, Foresman & Co., 1971); Virginia B. Ermer and John H. Strange (eds.), *Blacks and Bureaucracy* (New York: Crowell, 1972); Douglas M. Fox, *The Politics of City and State Bureaucracy* (Pacific Palisades, Calif.: Goodyear Publishing Co., 1974); Wolf V. Heydebrand, *Hospital Bureaucracy: A Comparative Study of Organizations* (New York: Dunellen, 1973); Ralph P. Hummel, *The Bureaucratic Experience* (New York: St. Martin's, 2nd ed., 1982); Henry Jacoby, *The Bureaucratization of the World* (Berkeley: University of California Press, 1973); Herbert Kaufman, "Fear of Bureaucracy: A Raging Pandemic," *Public Administration Review* (January–February 1981); Daniel Katz, *et al., Bureaucratic Encounters* (Ann Arbor, Mich.: Institute for Social Research, 1975); Fred A. Kramer, *Perspectives on Public Bureaucracy: A Reader on Organization* (Cambridge, Mass.: Winthrop Publishers, 2nd ed., 1977); Lewis C. Mainzer, *Political Bureaucracy* (Glenview, Ill.: Scott, Foresman, 1973); Robert K. Merton, *et al., Reader in Bureaucracy* (New York: Free Press, 1952); Marshall W. Meyer, *Change in Public Bureaucracies* (New York: Cambridge University Press, 1979); Nicos P. Mouzelis, *Organization and Bureaucracy* (Chicago: Aldine, 1973); B. Guy Peters, *The Politics of Bureaucracy: A Comparative Approach* (New York: Longman, 1978); Francis E. Rourke, *Bureaucracy, Politics and Public Policy* (Boston: Little, Brown, 1969); Francis E.

Rourke (ed.), *Bureaucracy, Politics, and the Public Interest* (Boston: Little, Brown and Co., 1972); Francis E. Rourke (ed.), *Bureaucratic Power in National Politics* (Boston: Little, Brown and Co., 1972); Victor A. Thompson, *Bureaucracy and Innovation* (University: University of Alabama Press, 1969); Victor A. Thompson, *Bureaucracy and the Modern World* (Morristown, N.J.: General Learning Press, 1976); Ludwig Von Mises, *Bureaucracy* (New Haven, Conn.: Yale University Press, 1944); Carol H. Weiss and Allen H. Barton, eds., *Making Bureaucracies Work* (Beverly Hills, Calif.: Sage Publications, 1980); James Q. Wilson, "The Bureaucracy Problem," *Public Interest* (Winter 1967); and Peter Woll, *American Bureaucracy* (New York: W. W. Norton & Co., Inc., 1963).

See also the following entries:
CROZIER, MICHEL J.
INTERNATIONAL ASSOCIATION OF PROFESSIONAL BUREAUCRATS
LAW OF BUREAUCRATIC ASSIMILATION
POSTBUREAUCRATIC ORGANIZATIONS
REALPOLITIK
RED TAPE
REPRESENTATIVE BUREAUCRACY
WEBER, MAX

bureaucrat, denizen of a bureaucracy.
See also APPARATCHIK.

Bureau of International Labor Affairs, agency of the Department of Labor that assists in formulating international economic and trade policies affecting U.S. workers. It administers the trade adjustment assistance program under the Trade Act of 1974, which provides special benefits for workers adversely affected by import competition. It helps represent the U.S. in multilateral and bilateral trade negotiations and on such international bodies as the General Agreement on Tariffs and Trade, the International Labor Organization and the Organization for Economic Cooperation and Development. The Bureau also helps provide direction to U.S. labor attaches at embassies abroad, carries out technical assistance projects overseas, and arranges trade union exchange and other programs for foreign visitors to the U.S.

Bureau of International Labor Affairs
Department of Labor
200 Constitution Ave. N.W.
Washington, D.C. 20210
(202) 523-8165

Bureau of Labor Statistics (BLS), agency responsible for the economic and statistical research activities of the Department of Labor. The BLS is the government's principal factfinding agency in the field of labor economics, particularly with respect to the collection and analysis of data on manpower and labor requirements, labor force, employment, unemployment, hours of work, wages and employee compensation, prices, living conditions, labor-management relations, productivity and technological developments, occupational safety and health, structure and growth of the economy, urban conditions and related socio-economic issues, and international aspects of certain of these subjects.

It has no enforcement or administrative functions. Practically all of the basic data it collects from workers, businesses, and from other governmental agencies are supplied by voluntary cooperation based on their interest in and need for the analyses and summaries that result. The research and statistical projects planned grow out of the needs of these groups, as well as the needs of Congress and the federal and state governments. The information collected is issued in monthly press releases, in special publications, and in its official publication, the *Monthly Labor Review*. Other major BLS periodicals include: *The Consumer Price Index, Wholesale Prices and Price Indexes, Employment and Earnings, Current Wage Developments, Occupational Outlook Handbook,* and *Occupational Outlook Quarterly.* For histories, *see* Jonathan Grossman and Judson MacLaury, "The Creation of the Bureau of Labor Statistics," *Monthly Labor Review* (February 1975); J. P. Goldberg and W. T. Moye, "The AFL and a National BLS: Labor's Role is Crystalized," *Monthly Labor Review* (March 1982); H.

M. Douty, "A Century of Wage Statistics: The BLS Contributions," *Monthly Labor Review* (November 1984).

Bureau of Labor Statistics
200 Constitution Avenue N.W.
Washington, D.C. 20210
(202) 523-1327

Bureau of National Affairs, Inc. (BNA), the largest private employer of information specialists in the nation's capital. Its function is to report, analyze, and explain the activities of the federal government and the courts to those persons who are directly affected—educators, attorneys, labor relations practitioners, business executives, accountants, union officials, personnel administrators, and scores of others. The BNA organization is universally recognized as a leading source of authoritative information services. Its labor information reports and services include:

Affirmative Action Compliance Manual
for Federal Contractors
BNA Pension Reporter
BNA Policy and Practice Series
Collective Bargaining Negotiations &
Contracts
Construction Labor Report
Daily Labor Report
EEOC Compliance Manual
Employment and Training Reporter
Fair Employment Practice Service
Government Employee Relations
Report
Government Manager, The
Labor Arbitration Reports
Labor Relations Reporter
Retail/Services Labor Report
Union Labor Report
White Collar Report

BNA Communications, Inc., produces employee communication, motivational, and supervisory and sales training films, case studies for management development, and related instructional materials.

Bureau of National Affairs, Inc.
1231 25th Street, N.W.
Washington, D.C. 20037
(202) 452-4500

bureaupathology, term used by Victor A. Thompson, in *Modern Organization*

(N.Y.: Knopf, 1960), to describe the pathological or dysfunctional aspects of bureaucracy. According to Thompson, the bureaupathic official usually exaggerates the official, non-technical aspects of relationships and suppresses the technical and the informal. He stresses rights, not abilities. Since his behavior stems from insecurity, he may be expected to insist on petty rights and prerogatives, on protocol, on procedure—in short, on those things least likely to affect directly the goal accomplishment of the organization. For example, a rather functionless reviewing officer will often insist most violently on his right of review and scream like an injured animal if he is bypassed. He will often insist on petty changes, such as minor changes in the wording of a document. If he has a counterpart at a higher organizational level, he will probably insist on exclusive contact with that higher clearance point. By controlling this particular communication channel he protects his authority and influence.

Also see George West, "Bureaupathology and the Failure of MBO," *Human Resource Management* (Summer 1977).

burnout, worker's feeling of mental and physical fatigue that causes indifference and emotional disengagement from his or her job. *See* Harry Levinson, "When Executives Burn Out," *Harvard Business Review* (May-June 1981); Oliver L. Niehouse, "Burnout: A Real Threat to Human Resources Managers," *Personnel* (September-October 1981); Whiton Stewart Paine, ed., *Job Stress and Burnout: Research, Theory, and Intervention Perspectives* (Beverly Hills, Calif.: Sage Publications, Inc., 1982); Morley D. Glicken and Katherine Janka, "Executives Under Fire: The Burnout Syndrome," *California Management Review* (Spring 1982).

Burns decision: *see* NATIONAL LABOR RELATIONS BOARD V. BURNS INTERNATIONAL SECURITY SERVICES.

business agent, full-time officer of a local union, elected or appointed, who handles grievances, helps enforce agreements, and otherwise deals with the union's financial, administrative, or labor-management problems.

See also FINNEGAN V. LEU.

business cycles, the recurrent phases of expansion and contraction in overall business activity. Although no two business cycles are alike, they are all thought to follow a pattern of prosperity, recession (or depression), and recovery. *See* Donald A. Larson, "Labor Supply Adjustment Over the Business Cycle," *Industrial and Labor Relations Review* (July 1981); George Sayers Bain and Farouk Elsheikh, "Union Growth and the Business Cycle: A Disaggregated Study," *British Journal of Industrial Relations* (March 1982).

business games: *see* MANAGEMENT GAMES.

business necessity, the major legal defense for using an employment practice that effectively excludes women and/or minorities. The leading court case, *Robinson v. Lorrilard Corp.,* 444 F.2d 791 (4th Cir. 1971); *cert. denied,* 404 U.S. 1006 (1971), holds that the test of the business necessity defense

is whether there exists an overriding legitimate business purpose such that the practice is necessary to the safe and efficient operation of the business. Thus, the business purpose must be sufficiently compelling to override any racial impact; the challenged practice must effectively carry out the business purpose it is alleged to serve; and there must be available no acceptable alternative policies or practices which would better accomplish the business purpose advanced, or accomplish it equally well with a lesser differential racial impact.

business unions also called BREAD-AND-BUTTER UNIONS, the conservative U.S. trade unions have been called "bread-and-butter" or "business" unions because they have tended to concentrate on gaining better wages and working conditions for their members rather than devote significant efforts on political action as many European unions have done. The classic description of business unionism was given by Adolph Strasser (1871-1910), president of the Cigar Makers Union and one of the founders of the AFL, when he told a congressional committee: "We have no ultimate ends. We are going from day to day. We fight only for immediate objectives—objectives that will be realized in a few years. —we are all practical men." For a historical analysis, see Philip Taft, "On the Origins of Business Unionism," *Industrial and Labor Relations Review* (October 1963).

Butz v. Economou, 438 U.S. 478 (1978), Supreme Court case that provided an immunity from suit for civil damages to federal administrative officials exercising adjudicatory functions. *See* Gerald J. Miller, "Administrative Malpractice before and after *Butz v. Economou,*" *Bureaucrat* (Winter 1980-81); Michael W. Dolan, "Government Employee Accountability and the Federal Tort Claims Act," *Bureaucrat* (Fall 1980); Robert G. Vaughn, "The Personal Accountability of Civil Servants," *Bureaucrat* (Fall 1980).

buzz group, device that seeks to give all the individuals at a large meeting an equal opportunity to participate by breaking the larger meeting into small groups of from six to eight persons each. These "buzz groups" then designate one person each to report on their consensus (and dissents if any) when the total group reconvenes.

buzzwords, Robert Kirk Mueller, in *Buzzwords: A Guide to the Language of Leaderships* (N.Y.: Van Nostrand Reinhold Co., 1974), credits the late Professor Ralph Hower of Harvard for first using "buzzwords" to mean "those phrases that have a pleasant buzzing sound in your ears while you roll them on your tongue and that may overwhelm you into believing you know what you're talking about when you don't." In spite of this "formal" definition, the technical vocabularies of any occupational specialty are often referred to as buzzwords.

Byrnes Act: *see* ANTI-STRIKEBREAKER ACT OF 1936.

C

cafeteria benefits plan, also called SMORGASBORD BENEFITS PLAN, any program that allows employees to choose their fringe benefits within the limits of the total benefit dollars for which they are eligible. This allows each employee to have, in effect, his own individualized benefit program. Because such programs cost more to administer, they tend to exist mainly as part of high-level, managerial compensation packages. However, increasing computer capabilities will make it increasingly likely that such plans will be more widely offered. *See* George W. Hettenhouse, "Compensation Cafeteria for Top Executives," *Harvard Business Review* (September-October 1971); Robert V. Goode, "Complications at the Cafeteria Checkout Line," *Personnel* (November-December 1974); Berwyn N. Fragner, "Employees' 'Cafeteria' Offers Insurance Options," *Harvard Business Review* (November-December 1975); David J. Thomsen, "Introducing Cafeteria Compensation in Your Company," *Compensation Review*, Vol. 10 (First Quarter 1978); Peter W. Stonebraker, "A Three-Tier Plan for Cafeteria Benefits," *Personnel Journal* (December 1984).

Cahan, Abraham (1860-1951), journalist, novelist, and socialist, who was one of the most powerful voices for the union movement during the early part of this century. *See* Jules Chametzky, *From the Ghetto: The Fiction of Abraham Cahan* (Amherst: University of Massachusetts Press, 1977).

California Management Review (CMR), quarterly that seeks to serve as a bridge between creative thought about management and executive action. An authoritative source of information and ideas contributing to the advancement of management science, it is directed to active managers, scholars, teachers, and others concerned with management.

> *California Management Review*
> Graduate School of Business
>   Administration
> 350 Barrows Hall
> University of California
> Berkeley, CA 94720

COPSystem: *see* CALIFORNIA OCCUPATIONAL PREFERENCE SURVEY.

California Occupational Preference Survey, also called COPSYSTEM, self-report inventory of job activity interest. Scores used in vocational guidance and counseling. Areas of interest measured include science, technology, business, outdoors, clerical, arts, communication, and service-oriented professions. TIME: 30/40 minutes. AUTHORS: R. R. Knopp, Bruce Grant, G. D. Demos, PUBLISHER: Educational and Industrial Testing Service (*see* TEST PUBLISHERS).

California Psychological Inventory (CPI), 480-item true/false questionnaire that measures the personality characteristics of normal (non-psychiatrically disturbed) individuals. TIME: 45/60 minutes. AUTHOR: Harrison G. Gough. PUBLISHER: Consulting Psychologists Press, Inc.

California Short Form Test of Mental Maturity (CTMM/SF), intelligence test that measures functional capacities basic to learning, problemsolving, and responding to new situations. It is a shortened version of the California Test of Mental Maturity (CTMM) and omits the measure of spatial relationships. TIME: 45 minutes. AUTHORS: Elizabeth Sullivan, Willis W. Clark, and Ernest Tiegs. PUBLISHER: California Test Bureau/McGraw-Hill (*see* TEST PUBLISHERS).

California Test of Mental Maturity (CTMM), intelligence test that measures functional capacities basic to learning, problemsolving, and responding to new situations (*i.e.*, logical reasoning, spatial relationships, numerical reasoning, verbal concepts, and memory). TIME: 90 minutes. AUTHORS: Elizabeth Sullivan, Willis W. Clark, and Ernest W. Tiegs. PUBLISHER: California Test Bureau/McGraw-Hill.

call-back pay, compensation, often at premium rates, paid to workers called back on the job after completing their normal shift. Contract provisions often provide for a minimum number of hours of call-back pay regardless of the number of hours actually worked.

call-in pay, wages or hours of pay guaranteed to workers (usually by contract provision) who, upon reporting to work, find no work to do.

Campbell, Alan K. (1923–   ), nickname SCOTTY, the last chairman of the U.S. Civil Service Commission, who became the first director of the Office of Personnel Management in 1979.

Canadian Labour Congress (CLC), Canadian counterpart of the AFL-CIO.

candidate, applicant for a position.

candidate population, all of the individuals who apply for a particular position.

Cannon v. *Guste,* 423 U.S. 918 (1975), U.S. Supreme Court case, which held that a Louisiana statute requiring state civil service employees to retire at age 65 violated neither the due process nor the equal protection clause of the 14th Amendment.

capacity utilization rate, the percentage of plant and equipment actually being used for productive purposes during a given time period. Statistical data on capacity utilization is available each month from the Department of Commerce and is an important leading indicator.

CAPE: *see* COALITION OF AMERICAN PUBLIC EMPLOYEES.

capital, the designation applied in economic theory to one of the three traditional factors of production, the others being land and labor. Capital can refer either to physical capital, such as plant and equipment, or to financial resources in general.

capital intensive, any production process requiring a large proportion of capital relative to labor.

capitalism, private ownership of most means of production and trade combined with a generally unrestricted marketplace of goods and services.

captive shop, any production unit whose output is used almost entirely by the company owning it.

career, total work history of an individual. Harold L. Wilensky has defined career in structural terms as "a succession of related jobs, arranged in a hierarchy of prestige, through which persons move in an ordered (more-or-less predictable) sequence," in his article, "Orderly Careers and Social Participation: The Impact of Work History on Social Integration in the Middle Mass" from the *American Sociological Review* (August 1961). For an analysis of the career interactions between individuals and their organizations, *see* Edgar H. Schein, "The Individual, the Organization, and the Career: A Conceptual Scheme," *Journal of Applied Behavioral Science* (July–August 1971).

career appointment: *see* APPOINTMENT.

career change, occurs when individuals break with their present careers in order to enter other fields. For analyses, *see* Marie R. Haug and Marvin B. Sussman, "The Second Career—Variant of a Sociological Concept," *Journal of Gerontology,* Vol. 23 (1967); Dale L. Hiestand, *Changing Careers after Thirty-five* (New York: Columbia University Press, 1971); Riman-

tas Vaitenas and Yoash Weiner, "Developmental, Emotional, and Interest Factors in Voluntary Mid-Career Change," *Journal of Vocational Behavior,* Vol. 11 (1977); Harry Levinson, "A Second Career: The Possible Dream," *Harvard Business Review* (May–June 1983).

career-conditional appointment: *see* APPOINTMENT.

career counseling, guidance provided to employees in order to assist them in achieving occupational training, education, and career goals. *See* Ted R. Gambill, "Career Counseling: Too Little, Too Late?" *Training and Development Journal* (February 1979); Andre G. Beaumont, Alva C. Cooper and Raymond H. Stockard, *A Model Career Counseling and Placement Program,* 3d ed. (Bethlehem, Pa.: College Placement Services, Inc., 1980); Russell B. Flanders and Neale Baxter, "The Sweat of Their Brows: A Look Back Over Occupational Information and Career Counseling," *Occupational Outlook Quarterly* (Fall 1981); Karen Raskin-Young, "Career Counseling in a Large Organization," *Training and Development Journal* (August 1984).

career curve: *see* MATURITY CURVE.

career decisionmaking, or OCCUPATIONAL DECISIONMAKING, evaluation process that leads to a choice of an occupation for an individual to pursue. *See* Martin Katz, "A Model of Guidance for Career Decision-Making," *Vocational Guidance Quarterly* (September 1966); Donald R. Kaldor and Donald G. Zytowski, "A Maximizing Model of Occupational Decision-Making," *Personnel and Guidance Journal* (April 1969).

career development, systematic development designed to increase an employee's potential for advancement and career change. It may include classroom training, reading, work experience, etc. *See* Meryl R. Louis, "Managing Career Transition: A Missing Link in Career Development," *Organizational Dynamics* (Spring 1982);

I. Marlene Thorn, Francis X. Fee and Jane O'Hara Carter, "Career Development: A Collaborative Approach," *Management Review* (September 1982); Beverly L. Kaye, "Performance Appraisal and Career Development: A Shotgun Marriage," *Personnel* (March–April 1984); Caela Farren and Beverly Kaye, "The Principles of Program Design: A Successful Career Development Model," *Personnel Administrator* (June 1984); Kathy E. Kram and Lynn A. Isabella, "Alternatives to Mentoring: The Role of Peer Relationships in Career Development," *Academy of Management Journal* (March 1985).

career earnings formula, a formula which bases pension benefits on average earnings in all years of credited service.

career ladder, series of classifications in which an employee may advance through training and/or on-the-job experience into successively higher levels of responsibility and salary. *See* Russ Smith and Margret Waldie, "Multi-Track Career Ladders: Maximizing Opportunities," *Review of Public Personnel Administration* (Spring 1984).

career lattice, a term that identifies horizontal and/or diagonal paths of occupational mobility leading from the entry level. Most often these paths link parallel paths of vertical or upward occupational mobility. A horizontal path of occupational mobility is often called a job transfer while a diagonal path is often referred to as a transfer-promotional path. This "lateral" mobility usually occurs within an occupational field (*i.e.*, engineering, accounting) but usually not within the same specific occupational classification.

career management, aspect of personnel management that is concerned with the occupational growth of individuals within an organization. *See* Marion S. Kellogg, *Career Management* (N.Y.: American Management Association, Inc., 1972); Douglas T. Hall and Francine S. Hall, "What's New in Career Management," *Organizational Dynamics* (Summer 1976);

Edward O. Joslin, "Career Management: How to Make it Work," *Personnel* (July–August 1977).

career mobility, also called JOB MOBILITY, degree to which an individual is able to move or advance from one position to another. *See* Yoav Vardi, "Organizational Career Mobility: An Integrative Model," *Academy of Management Review* (July 1980); Terry A. Beehr, Thomas D. Taber, and Jeffrey T. Walsh, "Perceived Mobility Channels: Criteria for Intraorganizational Job Mobility," *Organizational Behavior and Human Performance* (October 1980); George J. Borjas, "Job Mobility and Earnings Over the Life Cycle," *Industrial and Labor Relations Review* (April 1981); Sheldon E. Haber, "The Mobility of Professional Workers and Fair Hiring," *Industrial and Labor Relations Review* (January 1981); Sue Estler, "Evolving Jobs as a Form of Career Mobility: Some Policy Implications," *Public Personnel Management,* Vol. 10, No. 4 (Winter 1981).

career negotiation, that aspect of career planning that has both the individual employee and the organization, in the light of their respective interests and needs, develop (negotiate) a career plan that serves both parties. *See* James F. Wolf and Robert N. Bacher, "Career Negotiation: Trading Off Employee and Organizational Needs," *Personnel* (March–April 1981).

career path, direction of an individual's career as indicated by career milestones. An employee following a career path may proceed up a single career ladder and then beyond it into supervisory or executive positions, or an employee may move from one career ladder to another. *See* Joseph J. Wnuk, Jr., "Career Paths," *Training and Development Journal* (May 1970); James W. Walker, "Let's Get Realistic About Career Paths," *Human Resource Management* (Fall 1976); Donald Grass, "A Guide to R & D Career Pathing," *Personnel Journal* (April 1979).

career pattern, sequence of occupations of an individual or group of individuals. The study of career patterns has spawned the theory that an individual's work history is good predictor of future vocational behavior. For the pioneering research, *see* William H. Form and Delbert C. Miller, "Occupational Career Pattern as a Sociological Instrument," *American Journal of Sociology* (January 1949); Donald E. Super, "Career Patterns as a Basis for Vocational Counseling," *Journal of Counseling Psychology,* Vol. 1, No. 1 (1954).

career planning, according to James W. Walker, "Does Career Planning Rock the Boat," *Human Resources Management* (Spring 1978), career planning

is the personal process of planning one's life work. It entails evaluating abilities and interests, considering alternative career opportunities, establishing career goals and planning practical development activities. The process results in decisions to enter a certain occupation, join a particular company; accept or decline job opportunities (relocations, promotions or transfers, etc.) and ultimately leave a company for another job or for retirement.

Also see Charles E. Okosky, "Career Planning," *Personnel Journal* (November 1973); Sam Gould, "Career Planning in the Organization," *Human Resource Management* (Spring 1978); John J. Leach, "The Career Planning Process," *Personnel Journal* (April 1981); Jonathan P. West, *Career Planning, Development, and Management: An Annotated Bibliography* (New York: Garland Publishing Co., 1983).

career promotion, promotion made on the basis of merit, but without competition with other employees. An example is the promotion of an employee who, as he or she learns more about the job, can do more difficult kinds of work and assume greater responsibility, so that he or she is performing duties classified at a higher grade level.

career reserved position, position within the U.S. federal Senior Executive Service that has a specific requirement for political impartiality; may be filled only by career appointment.

career system, sequence of progressively more responsible positions in the same general occupation that an organization makes available to qualified individuals.

Carter v. *United States,* 407 F. 2d 1238 (1968), U.S. Court of Appeals, District of Columbia Circuit case, which held that a Federal Bureau of Investigation employee, whose job tenure was within the ambit of the Universal Military Training and Service Act (1964), could not be dismissed for allegedly "sleeping with young girls and carrying on" without a trial to determine whether such activities, to the extent that they occurred, presented sufficient "cause" within the meaning of that statute.

Cary v. *Westinghouse Electric Corp.,* 375 U.S. 261 (1964), U.S. Supreme Court case, which held that disputes involving work assignments were arbitrable.

Case Co. v. *National Labor Relations Board: see* J. I. CASE CO. V. NATIONAL LABOR RELATIONS BOARD.

case law, all recorded judicial and administrative agency decisions.

casual labor, employees that are (1) essentially unskilled, (2) used only a few days at a time, or (3) needed seasonally.

catalyst: *see* CHANGE AGENT.

catastrophic health insurance, health insurance which provides protection against the high cost of treating severe or lengthy illnesses or disabilities. Generally such policies cover all or a specified percentage of medical expenses above an amount that is the responsibility of the insured himself (or the responsibility of another insurance policy up to a maximum limit of liability).

Cattell Culture Fair Intelligence Test, basic general intelligence test. Scores are relatively free of educational and cultural influences, desirable where environmental factors may unduly influence conventional test scores. Particularly useful for relating intelligence to achievement, educational, and vocational guidance, testing of foreign-speaking/bilingual subjects, immigrant testing and cross-cultural studies. TIME: 30/60 minutes. AUTHORS: Raymond B. and A. K. S. Cattell. PUBLISHER: Bobbs-Merrill Company, Inc. (see TEST PUBLISHERS).

cause, short form of "just cause," reason given for removing someone from an office or job. The cause cited may or may not be the real reason for the removal.

C case, an unfair labor practice case before the NLRB.

CCH: see COMMERCE CLEARING HOUSE, INC.

CEA: see COUNCIL OF ECONOMIC ADVISERS.

cease-and-desist order, ruling, frequently issued in unfair labor practice cases, which requires the charged party to stop conduct held to be illegal and take specific action to remedy the unfair labor practice.

ceiling, upper limit of ability measured by a test. A test has a low ceiling for a given population if many examinees obtained perfect scores; it has a high ceiling if there are few or no perfect scores.

ceiling, job or position: see JOB CEILING.

Census, Bureau of the, general purpose statistical agency of the U.S. federal government that collects, tabulates, and publishes a wide variety of statistical data about the people and the economy of the nation. These data are utilized by the Congress, by the executive branch, and by the public generally in the development and evaluation of economic and social programs.

Bureau of the Census
Department of Commerce
Washington, D.C. 20233
(301) 763-4051

Center for Political Studies: see INSTITUTE FOR SOCIAL RESEARCH.

Center for Research on Utilization of Scientific Knowledge: see INSTITUTE FOR SOCIAL RESEARCH.

central clearance, the Office of Management and Budget's (OMB) coordination and assessment of recommendations and positions taken by the various federal departments and agencies on legislative matters as they relate to a president's program. For the classic account of the development of central clearance, see Richard E. Neustadt, "Presidency and Legislation: The Growth of Central Clearance," *American Political Science Review* (September 1954). For an update, see Robert S. Gilmour, "Central Legislative Clearance: A Revised Perspective," *Public Administration Review* (March–April 1971).

Central Hardware Co. v. *National Labor Relations Board,* 407 U.S. 539 (1972), U.S. Supreme Court case, which held that non-employee organizers seeking to solicit on an employer's private property must show that the property has assumed some of the characteristics of public property and that no reasonable alternative means of reaching the employees is available.

central hiring hall: see HIRING HALL.

centralization, also DECENTRALIZATION, any process by which the power and authority in an organization or polity are concentrated. *Decentralization* is the reverse—power and authority are distributed more widely in an organization or polity. See James Fesler, "Approaches to Understanding Decentralization," *The Journal of Politics* (August 1965); Irving Kristol, "Decentralization for What?" *The Public Interest* (Spring 1968); Herbert Kaufman, "Administrative Decentralization and Political Power," *Public Administration Review* (January-February 1969); Dwight Ink and Alan L. Dean, "A Concept of Decentralization," *Public Administration Review* (January-February 1970); Adam W.

Herbert, "Management Under Conditions of Decentralization and Citizen Participation," *Public Administration Review* (October 1972); Henry J. Schmandt, "Municipal Decentralization: An Overview," *Public Administration Review* (October 1972); Mario Fantini and Marilyn Gittel, *Decentralization: Achieving Reform* (New York: Praeger Publishers, 1973); Norman Furniss, "The Practical Significance of Decentralization," *The Journal of Politics* (November 1974); David O. Porter and Eugene A. Olsen, "Some Critical Issues in Government Centralization and Decentralization," *Public Administration Review* (January-February 1976); and Allen Barton *et al.*, *Decentralizing City Government: An Evaluation of the New York City Manager Experiment* (Lexington, Mass.: Lexington Books, 1977).

central labor union, association of local labor unions in a specific geographic region.

central tendency, series of statistical measures that provide a representative value for a distribution, or, more simply, refer to how scores tend to cluster in a distribution. The most common measures of central tendency are the mean, median, and the mode.

CEO: *see* CHIEF EXECUTIVE OFFICER.

certificate, list of eligibles ranked, according to regulations, for appointment or promotion consideration. A more useful term is "candidate list."

certification, formal determination by the National Labor Relations Board or other administrative agency that a particular union is the majority choice, and thus the exclusive bargaining agent, for a group of employees in a given bargaining unit. *Decertification* is the opposite process where an administrative agency withdraws a union's official designation as the exclusive bargaining agent. In both cases, these actions are usually preceded by a formal polling of the union membership. *See* Arthur P. Brief and Dale E. Rude, "Voting

in Union Certification Elections: A Conceptual Analysis," *Academy of Management Review* (April 1981); William E. Fulmer and Tamara A. Gilman, "Why Do Workers Vote for Union Decertification?" *Personnel* (March-April 1981); William E. Fulmer, "Decertification: Is the Current Trend a Threat to Collective Bargaining?" *California Management Review* (Fall 1981); John C. Anderson, Gloria Busman, Charles A. O'Reilly, III, "The Decertification Process: Evidence from California," *Industrial Relations* (Spring 1982); Richard Block and Myron Roomkin, "Determinants of Voter Participation in Union Certification Elections," *Monthly Labor Review* (April 1982); William N. Cook, "Determinants of the Outcomes of Union Certification Elections," *Industrial and Labor Relations Review* (April 1983); James P. Swann, Jr., "The Decertification of a Union," *Personnel Administrator* (January 1983).

See also ACCREDITATION and OCCUPATIONAL CERTIFICATION.

certification, selective, certifying only the names of eligibles who have special qualifications required to fill particular vacant positions.

certification of eligibles, procedure whereby those who have passed competitive civil service examinations have their names ranked in order of score and placed on a list of those eligible for appointment. When a government agency has a vacancy, it requests its personnel arm to provide a list of eligibles for the class to which the vacant position has been allocated. The personnel agency then "certifies" the names of the highest ranking eligibles to the appointing authority for possible selection. Usually, only a limited number of the qualified eligibles are certified. When a jurisdiction requires that three eligibles be certified to the appointing authority, this is referred to as the "rule of three." For an overview, *see* Carmen D. Saso and Earl P. Tanis, *Selection and Certification of Eligibles: A Survey of Policies and Practices* (Chicago: International Personnel Management Association, 1974).

certification proceeding, process by which the National Labor Relations Board discovers whether or not the employees of an organization want a particular union to represent them.

certified employee organization, union that an administrative agency has certified as the official representative of the employees in a bargaining unit for the purpose of collective negotiations. Such certification is usually the direct result of a representation election.

Certified Public Accountant (CPA), accountant certified by a state government as having met specific educational and experience requirements.

certiorari, order or writ from a higher court demanding that a lower court send up the record of a case for review. Except for a few instances of original jurisdiction, most cases that reach the U.S. Supreme Court do so because the Supreme Court itself has issued such a writ or "granted certiorari." If certiorari is denied by the Supreme Court, it means that the justices are content to let the lower-court decision stand.

CETA: *see* COMPREHENSIVE EMPLOYMENT AND TRAINING ACT OF 1973.

CFI: *see* WLW CULTURE FAIR INVENTORY.

CFR: *see* CODE OF FEDERAL REGULATIONS.

Chaikin, Sol C. (1918-   ), became president of the International Ladies' Garment Workers' Union in 1975.

chain picketing, continuous, moving human chain sometimes formed by striking workers to prevent anyone from crossing their picket line.

chance score, score that has a significant probability of occurring on the basis of random selection of answers.

Chandler v. Roudebush, 425 U.S. 840 (1976), U.S. Supreme Court case, which held federal employees, after exhausting all administrative remedies concerning a claim of sexual and/or racial discrimination, have the same right to a trial *de novo* in the federal courts as is enjoyed by other employees under the Civil Rights Act of 1964 as amended.

change agent, or CATALYST, descriptive ways of referring to organization development consultants or facilitators. *See* Lee Grossman, *The Change Agent* (N.Y.: AMACOM, 1974); Stephen R. Michael and others, *Techniques of Organizational Change* (New York: McGraw Hill Book Co., 1981); Stephen R. Michael, "Organizational Change Techniques: Their Present, Their Future," *Organizational Dynamics* (Summer 1982).

Chapter 11, that portion of the Bankruptcy Reform Act of 1978 which allows insolvent corporations to undergo a reorganization which transfers ownership to a new corporation made up of old owners and creditors. This procedure, supervised by a federal bankruptcy court, also allowed the business to continue operating during the process. While it was not intended at the time of the Act's passage, Chapter 11 has turned out to be a way by which companies in financial difficulty can evade their union contracts. Companies are increasingly using Chapter 11 to technically become different legal entities that are not bound to the union contract of the original company. The best known instance of this is Continental Air Lines. In September of 1983 it filed for bankruptcy under Chapter 11, dismissed its 12,000 employees, and offered "new" non-union jobs to about one-third of them at about one-half of their previous pay. *See* Ralph S. Berger, "The Collective Bargaining Agreement in Bankruptcy: Does the Duty to Arbitrate Survive?" *Labor Law Journal* (November 1984).

Also see *NATIONAL LABOR RELATIONS BOARD V. BILDISCO & BILDISCO.*

charging party, any individual who formally asserts that he or she is aggrieved because of an unlawful employment practice.

charismatic leadership, leadership that is based on the compelling personality of the leader rather than upon formal position. *See* Robert J. House, "A 1976 Theory of Charismatic Leadership," in James G. Hunt and Lars L. Larson, eds., *Leadership: The Cutting Edge* (Carbondale, Ill.: Southern Illinois University Press, 1977); Ann Ruth Willner, *The Spellbinders: Charismatic Political Leadership* (New Haven, CT: Yale University Press, 1984).

Chavez, Cesar (Estrada) (1927-   ), leader of the United Farm Workers' Union and its predecessor organization (the National Farm Workers Association) since 1962, who is nationally known for his tactic of calling for grape and lettuce boycotts. For biographies, *see* Joan London and Henry Anderson, *So Shall Ye Reap: The Story of Cesar Chavez and the Farm Workers Movement* (N.Y.: Crowell, 1970); George D. Horwitz, *La Causa: The California Grape Strike* (N.Y.: Macmillan, 1970); Ronald B. Taylor, *Chavez and the Farm Workers* (Boston: Beacon Press, 1975).

checkoff, union security provision, commonly provided for in the collective bargaining agreement, that allows the employer to deduct union dues, assessments, and initiation fees from the pay of all union members. The deducted amounts are delivered to the union on a prearranged schedule. The Labor-Management Relations (Taft-Hartley) Act of 1947 requires that union members must give written permission for these fees to be deducted.

checkoff, compulsory: *see* AUTOMATIC CHECKOFF.

chief executive officer (CEO), individual who is personally accountable to the board of directors or the electorate for the activities of the organization or the jurisdiction. *See* Chris Argyris, "The CEO's Behavior: Key to Organizational Development," *Harvard Business Review* (March-April 1973); Robert H. Rock, *The Chief Executive Officer* (N.Y.: D.C. Heath-Lexington Books, 1977); Harry Levinson, "Criteria for Choosing Chief Executives," *Harvard Business Review* (July-August 1980); John F. Rockart and Michael E. Treacy, "The CEO Goes On-Line," *Harvard Business Review* (January-February 1982).

See also GENERAL MANAGER.

chief steward, union representative who supervises the activities of a group of shop stewards.

chi-square, statistical procedure that estimates whether the observed values in a distribution differ from the expected distribution and thus may be attributed to the operation of factors other than chance. Particular values of chi-square are usually identified by the symbol x^2.

childbirth: *see* PREGNANCY.

child care: *see* DAY CARE.

child labor, originally this meant employing children in a manner that was detrimental to their health and social development; but now that the law contains strong child labor prohibitions, the term refers to the employment of children below the legal age limit.

Efforts by the labor movement and social reformers to prevent the exploitation of children in the workplace date back well into the nineteenth century. As early as 1842, some states (Connecticut and Massachusetts) legislated a maximum ten hour work day for children. In 1848, Pennsylvania established a minimum working age of twelve for factory jobs. But it would be twenty years more before any state had inspectors to enforce child labor laws. And it would not be until the late 1930s that federal laws would outlaw child labor (mainly through the Fair Labor Standards Act). The practice was so entrenched that earlier federal attempts to outlaw child labor were construed by the

Supreme Court as being unconstitutional infringements on the power of the states to regulate conditions in the workplace. For histories of the horrendous conditions that led to the passage of federal and state child labor prohibitions, see Jeremy P. Felt, *Hostages of Fortune: Child Labor Reform in New York State* (Syracuse, N.Y.: Syracuse University Press, 1965); Walter I. Trattner, *Crusade for the Children: A History of the National Child Labor Committee and Child Labor Reform in America* (Chicago: Quadrangel Books, 1970); Ronald B. Taylor, *Sweatshops in the Sun: Child Labor on the Farm* (Boston: Beacon Press, 1973). For present day impact, see Daniel J. B. Mitchell and John Clapp, "The Impact of Child-Labor Laws on the Kinds of Jobs Held by Young School-Leavers," *The Journal of Human Resources* (Summer 1980); Lee Swepston, "Child Labour: Its Regulation by ILO Standards and National Legislation," *International Labour Review* (September–October 1982); Thomas A. Coens, "Child Labor Laws: A Viable Legacy for the 1980s," *Labor Law Journal* (October 1982).

See also FAIR LABOR STANDARDS ACT and WORKING PAPERS.

chilling effect, employment practices, government regulations, court decisions, or legislation (or the threat of these) may create an inhibiting atmosphere or chilling effect that prevents the free exercise of individual employment rights. A "chilling" effect tends to keep minorities and women from seeking employment and advancement in an organization even in the absence of formal bars. Other chilling effects may be positive or negative, depending upon the "chillee's" perspective. For example, even discussion of proposed regulations can "chill" employers or unions into compliance.

Christmas bonus: *see* NONPRODUCTION BONUS.

chronic unemployment, unemployment lasting longer than six months.

CIO: *see* (1) CONGRESS OF INDUSTRIAL ORGANIZATIONS and (2) AMERICAN FEDERATION OF LABOR-CONGRESS OF INDUSTRIAL ORGANIZATIONS.

circuit court of appeals: *see* COURT OF APPEALS.

citizenship, U.S., a requirement for public employment in some jurisdictions. For a discussion of recent court rulings, *see* Arnold L. Steigman, "Public Administration by Litigation: The Impact of Court Decisions Concerning Citizenship on Public Personnel Management," *Public Personnel Management* (March–April 1979); Charles O. Agege, "Employment Discrimination Against Aliens: The Constitutional Implications," *Labor Law Journal* (February 1985).

See also the following entries:
    AMBACH V. NORWICK
    FOLEY V. CONNELIE
    HAMPTON V. MOW SUN WONG
    SUGARMAN V. DOUGALL

City of Los Angeles, Department of Water & Power v. Manhart, 55 L.Ed.2d 657 (1978), U.S. Supreme Court case, which held that a pension plan requiring female employees to contribute more from their wages to gain the same pension benefits as male employees was in violation of Title VII of the Civil Rights Act 1964. While the actual statistics were undisputed (women live longer than men), the court reasoned that Title VII prohibits treating individuals "as simply components of a racial, religious, sexual or national class." See Linda H. Kistler and Richard C. Healy, "Sex Discrimination in Pension Plans Since *Manhart,*" *Labor Law Journal* (April 1981).

civilian labor force: *see* LABOR FORCE.

civil rights, generally, the protections and privileges given to all citizens by the U.S. Constitution. However, "civil rights" frequently is used to refer to those positive acts of government that seek to make constitutional guarantees a reality for all citizens.

Civil Rights Act of 1964, the most far-reaching regulation of labor relations since the National Labor Relations Act of 1935. Designed to eliminate racial and sexual discrimination in most areas of U.S. life, it affected employers of 15 or more employees engaged in interstate commerce by providing for the withholding of federal funds from programs administered in a discriminatory manner and establishing a right to equal employment opportunity without regard to race, color, religion, sex or national origin. It also created the Equal Employment Opportunity Commission (EEOC) to assist in implementing this right. Its provisions were extended to public sector employers in 1972 (*see* EQUAL EMPLOYMENT OPPORTUNITY ACT OF 1972).

See also EQUAL EMPLOYMENT OPPORTUNITY COMMISSION and TITLE VII.

Civil Rights Acts of 1866, 1870, and 1971, insure equality before the law in a variety of functional areas (ability to enter into contracts, sue, give evidence, and secure equal protection of persons and property) and establish that individuals or governments denying any rights or privileges shall be liable for legal action. These acts are often used in conjunction with, but are not replaced by, the Civil Rights Act of 1964 as the basis for suits.

Civil Rights Acts of 1957 and 1960, the Civil Rights Act of 1957 (Public Law 85-135) is generally considered to be the beginning of contemporary civil rights legislation. It established the U.S. Commission on Civil Rights and strengthened the judiciary's ability to protect civil rights. The Civil Rights Act of 1960 (Public Law 86-449) served mainly to plug legal loopholes in the 1957 law. For a broad history of the civil rights movement, *see* Richard Bardolph (ed.), *The Civil Rights Record: Black Americans and the Law, 1849-1970* (N.Y.: Thomas Y. Crowell Co., 1970).

Civil Rights Commission: *see* COMMISSION ON CIVIL RIGHTS.

civil service, collective term for all of those employees of a government who are not members of the military services. For histories of the U.S. civil service, *see* Paul P. Van Riper, *History of the United States Civil Service* (Evanston, Ill.: Row, Peterson, 1958); Jay M. Shafritz, *Public Personnel Management: The Heritage of Civil Service Reform* (N.Y.: Praeger, 1975). *Also see* W. D. Heisel, "Alternatives to Traditional Civil Service," *Public Personnel Management Journal* (Fall 1983).

See also INTERNATIONAL CIVIL SERVICE.

Civil Service Assembly of the United States and Canada: *see* INTERNATIONAL PERSONNEL MANAGEMENT ASSOCIATION.

civil service commission, government agency charged with the responsibility of promulgating the rules and regulations of the civilian personnel management system. Depending upon its legal mandate, a civil service commission may hear employee appeals and take a more active (or passive) role in the personnel management process. *See* Donald R. Harvey, *The Civil Service Commission* (N.Y.: Praeger, 1970); Winston W. Crouch, *A Guide for Modern Personnel Commissions* (Chicago: International Personnel Management Association, 1973).

See also GRANT'S CIVIL SERVICE COMMISSION.

Civil Service Commission, U.S.: *see* GRANT'S CIVIL SERVICE COMMISSION, MERIT SYSTEMS PROTECTION BOARD, OFFICE OF PERSONNEL MANAGEMENT, and UNITED STATES CIVIL SERVICE COMMISSION.

Civil Service Commission v. National Association of Letter Carriers: *see* UNITED STATES CIVIL SERVICE COMMISSION V. NATIONAL ASSOCIATION OF LETTER CARRIERS.

Civil Service Journal, official quarterly of the U.S. Civil Service Commission. It ceased publication in 1979.

Civil Service Reform Act of 1978, on March 2, 1978, President Carter, with the enthusiastic support of his Civil Service

Commission leadership, submitted his civil service reform proposals to Congress. On that same day, before the National Press Club, he further called his proposals to Congress' attention by charging that the present federal personnel system had become a "bureaucratic maze which neglects merit, tolerates poor performance, and permits abuse of legitimate employee rights, and mires every personnel action in red tape, delay, and confusion."

The reform bill faced considerable opposition from federal employee unions (who thought the bill was too management-oriented) and from veterans' groups (who were aghast at the bill's curtailment of veterans' preferences). The unions lost. The veterans won. The bill passed almost totally intact. The major exception was the deletion of strong veterans' preference curtailments. The Senate passed the bill by voice vote and the House endorsed it with the wide margin of 365 to 8. On October 13, 1978—only six months after he had submitted it to the Congress—President Carter signed the Civil Service Reform Act of 1978 into law.

The act mandated that (in January of 1979) the U.S. Civil Service Commission would be divided into two agencies—an Office of Personnel Management (OPM) to serve as the personnel arm of the chief executive and an independent Merit Systems Protection Board (MSPB) to provide recourse for aggrieved employees. In addition, the act created a Federal Labor Relations Authority (FLRA) to oversee federal labor-management policies.

While the act includes provisions for new performance appraisal systems, mandates new adverse action and appeals procedures, and requires a trial period for new managers and supervisors, probably its greatest management innovation is the creation of the Senior Executive Service (SES). The SES will pool the most senior-level managers (GS 16 and up) into an elite 11,000-member executive corps that the Office of Personnel Management will have wide latitude in rewarding and punishing. Unfortunately, this elite group is bound to be known, perhaps with some affection, as the "SES pool." See Kenneth W. Kramer, "Seeds of Success and Failure: Policy Development and Implementation of the 1978 Civil Service Reform Act," *Review of Public Personnel Administration* (Spring 1982); Carl J. Bellone, "Structural vs. Behavioral Change: The Civil Service Reform Act of 1978," *Review of Public Personnel Administration* (Spring 1982); Ellen M. Bussey, ed., *Federal Civil Service Law and Procedures: A Basic Guide* (Washington, D.C.: Bureau of National Affairs, Inc., 1985).

See also (1) FEDERAL LABOR RELATION AUTHORITY, (2) MERIT SYSTEMS PROTECTION BOARD, (3) OFFICE OF PERSONNEL MANAGEMENT, and (4) SENIOR EXECUTIVE SERVICE.

Civil Service Retirement and Disability Fund, the accumulation of money held in trust by the U.S. Treasury for the purpose of paying annuity, refund, and death benefits to persons entitled to them. The Fund's funds come from five main sources: (1) deductions from the pay of employees who are members of the Civil Service Retirement System; (2) contributions by the employing agencies in amounts which match the deductions from their employees'; (3) payments from the U.S. Treasury for interest on the existing unfunded liability of the system and for the cost of allowing credit for military service; (4) appropriations to meet liabilities that result from changes in the system; and (5) interest earned through investment of money received from the first four sources. How is the money invested? It is invested by the U.S. Treasury in government securities.

class, unique position or a group of positions sufficiently similar in respect to duties and responsibilities that the same title may be used to designate each position in the group, the same salary may be equitably applied, the same qualifications required, and the same examination used to select qualified employees.

See also the following entries:
GROUP OF CLASSES
SERIES OF CLASSES

SPECIFICATION
TITLE

class action, search for judicial remedy that one or more individuals may undertake on behalf of themselves and all others in similar situations. Rule 23(b) of the Federal Rules of Civil Procedure establishes the technical legal requirements for the definition of a class in federal court proceedings:

One or more members of a class may sue or be sued as representative parties on behalf of all only if (1) the class is so numerous that joinder of all members is impractical, (2) there are questions of law or facts common to the class, (3) the claims or defenses of the representative parties are typical of the claims or defenses of the class, and (4) the representative parties will fairly and adequately protect the interests of the class.

See James W. Loewen, *Social Science in the Courtroom: Statistical Techniques and Research Methods for Winning Class-Action Suits* (Lexington, Mass.: Lexington Books, 1982).

classical organization theory: *see* ORGANIZATION THEORY.

classification: *see* POSITION CLASSIFICATION.

Classification Acts: *see* POSITION CLASSIFICATION.

Classification and Compensation Society, founded in 1969 to promote and improve classification and compensation as a professional field. The Society's goals are to provide for the exchange of ideas, information, and experiences for the benefit of members and employing organizations; provide perspective on events and problems; and stimulate creative efforts to improve or develop concepts, techniques, programs, and systems. Advancement of these objectives is accomplished through work study groups; open forums such as seminars and conferences; and publication of articles, studies, reports and technical papers.

Classification and Compensation Society
810 18th Street, NW
Washington, D.C. 20006
(202) 783-4847

classification standards, descriptions of classes of positions that distinguish one class from another in a series. They are, in effect, the yardstick or benchmark against which positions are measured to determine the proper level within a series of titles to which a position should be assigned.

classified service, all those positions in a governmental jurisdiction that are included in a formal merit system. Excluded from the classified service are all exempt appointments. Classified service is a term that predates the concept of position classification and has no immediate bearing on position classification concepts or practices.

classify, group positions according to their duties and responsibilities and assign a class title. To reclassify is to reassign a position to a different class, based on a re-examination of the duties and responsibilities of the position.

Clayton Act, also called the ANTI-TRUST ACT OF 1914, hailed at the time as labor's "Magna Carta," the Clayton Act sought to exempt labor unions from antitrust laws and to limit the jurisdiction of courts in issuing injunctions against labor organizations. Subsequent judicial construction limited its effectiveness and new laws were necessary to achieve its original intent.

See also LAWLOR V. LOEWE.

CLC: *see* CANADIAN LABOUR CONGRESS.

clean-up time, time during the normal work day when employees are allowed to cease production in order to clean themselves, their clothing, or their workplace. Clean-up-time allowances are frequently written into union contracts.

cleansing period, the Labor-Management Reporting and Disclosure (Landrum-

Griffin) Act of 1959 required, under Section 504, that a person previously a member of the Communist party or convicted of criminal acts must undergo a "cleansing period" of five years before he can hold a union office. However, the U.S. Supreme Court, in *United States* v. *Archie Brown*, 381 U.S. 437 (1965), declared Section 504 unconstitutional as a bill of attainder.

Clear it with Sidney, "Sidney" was Sidney Hillman (1887–1946), President of the Amalgamated Clothing Workers from its creation in 1913 until his death. Because he was a close political advisor to President Franklin D. Roosevelt, the president was reported to have said "clear everything with Sidney" in connection with the selection of his vice-presidential running mate in 1944. Because "clear it with Sidney" was widely publicized and criticized, it became symbolic of the labor movement's "pervasive" influence in government.

Cleveland Board of Education v. *Lafleur,* 414 U.S. 632 (1974), U.S. Supreme Court case, which held that arbitrary mandatory maternity leaves were unconstitutional. The court held that requiring pregnant teachers to take unpaid maternity leave five months before expected childbirth was in violation of the due process clause of the 14th Amendment.

clique, organizational sub-group whose members prefer to associate with each other on the basis of common interests. Melville Dalton, in *Men Who Manage* (N.Y.: Wiley, 1959), offers an extensive analysis of organizational cliques and concludes that they

> are both an outgrowth and instrument of planning and change. They fall into recognizable types shaped by, and related to, the official pattern of executive positions. Cliques are the indispensable promoters and stabilizers— as well as resisters—of change; they are essential, both to cement the organization and to accelerate action. They pre-

serve the formalities vital for moving to the goal, and they provoke but control the turmoil and adjustment that play about the emerging organization.

clock card, form designed to be used with a time clock.

closed anti-union shop, work organization that will not hire current or prospective union members. Such a tactic is illegal if the organization is engaged in interstate commerce.

closed shop, union security provision that would require an employer to only hire and retain union members in good standing. The Labor-Management Relations (Taft-Hartley) Act of 1947 made closed shops illegal. *See* Charles G. Goring and others, *The Closed Shop: A Comparative Study of Public Policy and Trade Union Security in Britain, the USA, and West Germany* (New York: St. Martin's Press, 1981).

closed union, union that formally bars new members or makes becoming a member practically impossible in order to protect the job opportunities of its present members.

closing date, when a civil service examination is announced, applications are accepted as long as the announcement is "open." The closing date is the deadline for submitting applications and is usually stated on the announcement.

clothing allowance, funds provided by employers to employees so that they can buy special clothing, such as uniforms or safety garments.

cluster laboratory, laboratory training experience for a group of people from the same organization. The group consists of several subgroups of individuals whose work in the larger organization is related.

CMR: *see* CALIFORNIA MANAGEMENT REVIEW.

CMT: *see* CONCEPT MASTERY TEST.

coaching, also COACHING ANALYSIS, face-to-face discussions with a subordinate in order to effect a change in his or her behavior. *Coaching analysis* consists of analyzing the reasons why unsatisfactory performance is occurring. According to Ferdinand F. Fournies, in *Coaching for Improved Work Performance* (N.Y.: Van Nostrand Reinhold, 1979), there are five steps in the coaching technique:

1. Getting the employee's agreement that a problem exists.
2. A mutual discussion of alternative solutions.
3. Mutual agreement on the action to be taken to solve the problem.
4. Measuring the results of subsequent performance.
5. Recognize achievement and improved performance when it occurs.

Also see Neil Rackham,"The Coaching Controversy," *Training and Development Journal* (November 1979); Jack Kondrasuk, "The Coaching Controversy Revisited," *Training and Development Journal* (February 1980); James F. Wolf and Frank P. Sherwood, "Coaching: Supporting Public Executives on the Job," *Public Administration Review* (January–February 1980).

coalition bargaining, also COORDINATED BARGAINING, in coalition bargaining an employer negotiates with a group of unions whose goal is to gain one agreement covering all or identical agreements for each. *Coordinated bargaining* differs only in that bargaining sessions take place simultaneously at differing locations. *See* George H. Hildebrand, "Cloudy Future for Coalition Bargaining," *Harvard Business Review* (November–December 1968); Stephen B. Goldberg, "Coordinated Bargaining: Some Unresolved Questions," *Monthly Labor Review* (April 1969); David Lewin and Mary McCormick, "Coalition Bargaining in Municipal Government: The New York City Experience," *Industrial and Labor Relations Review* (January 1981).

Coalition of American Public Employees (CAPE), formed in 1972 by leaders of public employees organizations in an effort to coordinate programs of political, legal, and legislation action and public education at the national and state level. Members included the American Federation of State, County and Municipal Employees (AFSCME); the National Education Association (NEA); the American Nurses Association (ANA); the Physicians National Housestaff Association (PNHA); and the National Association of Social Workers (NAWS). Representing nearly 4 million workers, CAPE was the largest organization of public employees in the nation. It ceased to exist on August 31, 1982.

Coalition of Black Trade Unionists, an organization of unionists united to advance the interests of blacks and other minorities in the union movement.
Coalition of Black Trade Unionists
P.O. Box 13055
Washington, D.C. 20009
(202) 429-1203

Coalition of Labor Union Women, a group dedicated to advancing the interests of women in the union movement.
Coalition of Labor Union Women
15 Union Square
New York, N.Y. 10003
(212) 277-5330

Coal Mine Health and Safety Act of 1969: *see* USERY V. TURNER ELKHORN MINING CO.

Codd* v. *Velger, 429 U.S. 624 (1977), Supreme Court case, which held that public employees are not constitutionally entitled to a hearing in dismissals where no issue of fact is at stake.

Code of Ethical Practices, the code of union ethics adopted by the AFL–CIO that sets standards of union morality, financial responsibility, democratic practices, etc.

code of ethics, statement of professional standards of conduct to which the practitioners of many professions say they subscribe. For example, the Code of Ethics of the American Society for Personnel Administration offers the following nice thoughts:

As a member of the American Society for Personnel Administration, I acknowledge my responsibility to strive for personal growth in my chosen career field and commit myself to observe the following ethical practices:

- I will respect the dignity of the individual as one of the essential elements of success in any enterprise.
- I will demonstrate and promote a spirit of cooperative effort between owners, managers, employees and the general public, directly or indirectly connected with the enterprise.
- I will advance those ethical employee relations concepts in personnel administration and labor relations which contribute to the objectives of the enterprise.
- I will reveal the facts in any situation where my private interests are in conflict with those of my employer or other principals.
- I will not permit considerations of religion, nationality, race, sex, age, party politics, or social standing to influence my professional activities.
- I will strive to attain and demonstrate a professional level of competence within the body of knowledge comprising the management field.
- I will encourage and participate in research to develop and advance new and improved management methods, skills and practices, sharing the productive results of such research with others.
- I will never use the Society or its membership for purposes other than those for which they were designed.

See Donald R. Cressey and Charles A. Moore, "Managerial Values and Corporate Codes of Ethics," *California Management Review* (Summer 1983).

See also ETHICS and STANDARDS OF CONDUCT.

Code of Federal Regulations (CFR), annual cumulation of executive agency regulations published in the daily *Federal Register,* combined with regulations issued previously that are still in effect. Divided into 50 titles, each representing a broad subject area, individual volumes of the CFR are revised at least once each calendar year and issued on a staggered quarterly basis. An alphabetical listing by agency of subtitle and chapter assignments in the CFR is provided in the back of each volume under the heading "Finding Aids" and is accurate for the revision date of that volume.

codetermination, in German MITBESTIMMUNGSRECHT, union participation in all aspects of management even to the extent of having union representatives share equal membership on an organization's board of directors. In Germany, where codetermination is often legally required, the process is called *Mitbestimmungsrecht,* literally meaning "the right of codetermination." *See* Svetozar Pejovich (ed.), *The Codetermination Movement in the West: Labor Participation in the Management of Business Firms* (Lexington, Mass.: Lexington Books, 1978); Robert J. Kuhne, *Co-Determination in Business: Workers' Representatives in the Boardroom* (New York: Praeger, 1980); Alfred L. Thimm, *The False Promise of Codetermination: The Changing Nature of European Workers' Participation* (Lexington, Mass.: Lexington Books, 1980).

coefficient of correlation: *see* CORRELATION COEFFICIENT.

coffee break, also called TEA BREAK, popular term for any brief rest period for workers. While work breaks for refreshments and socializing go back to ancient times, it wasn't until after World War II that coffee breaks became a national institution: first, because millions of workers brought the custom with them from World War II military service and, second, because by this time considerable research on worker fatigue had consistently shown that beverage breaks reduce fatigue while improving alertness and productivity. The

British, of course, have tea breaks. For a brief history of the coffee break, *see* William J. Tandy, "Tempest in a Coffee Pot," *Public Personnel Review* (October 1953). *See also* Steven Habbe, "Coffee, Anyone?" *The Conference Board Record* (July 1965).

cognitive dissonance, theory first postulated by Leon Festinger, in *A Theory of Cognitive Dissonance* (Evanston, Ill.: Row, Peterson Co., 1957), which holds that when an individual finds himself in a situation where he is expected to believe two mutually exclusive things, the subsequent tension and discomfort generates activity designed to reduce the dissonance or disharmony. For example, an employee who sees himself in an inequitable wage situation could experience cognitive dissonance. The theory of cognitive dissonance assumes that a worker performing the same work as another but being paid significantly less will do something to relieve his dissonance. Among his options are asking for a raise, restricting output, or seeking another job. For studies on wage inequity, *see* J. Stacy Adams, "Wage Inequities, Productivity and Work Quality," *Industrial Relations* (October 1963); William M. Evan and Roberta G. Simmons, "Organizational Effects of Inequitable Rewards in Two Experiments in Status Inconsistency," *Administrative Science Quarterly* (June 1969). For further studies in cognitive dissonance, *see* J. W. Brehm and A. R. Cohn, *Explorations in Cognitive Dissonance* (N.Y.: John Wiley, 1962):

See also INEQUITY THEORY.

COLA: *see* COST-OF-LIVING ADJUSTMENT.

cold-storage training, the preparation of employees for jobs in advance of the need for them in these particular jobs.

Cole v. Richardson, 405 U.S. 676 (1971), U.S. Supreme Court case, which upheld the right of Massachusetts to exact from its employees a promise to "oppose the overthrow of the government of the United States of America or of this Commonwealth by force, violence or by any illegal or unconstitutional method." A public employer may legitimately require employees to swear or affirm their allegiance to the Constitution of the United States and of a particular state. Beyond that, the limits of constitutional loyalty oaths are unclear.

See also LOYALTY OATH.

collective bargaining, a comprehensive term that encompasses the negotiating process that leads to a contract between labor and management on wages, hours, and other conditions of employment as well as the subsequent administration and interpretation of the signed contract. Collective bargaining is, in effect, the continuous relationship that exists between union representatives and employers. The four basic states of collective bargaining are: (1) the establishment of organizations for bargaining, (2) the formulation of demands, (3) the negotiation of demands, and (4) the administration of the labor agreement.

Collective bargaining is one of the keystones of the National Labor Relations Act, which declares that the policy of the United States is to be carried out

by encouraging the practice and procedure of collective bargaining and by protecting the exercise by workers of full freedom of association, self-organization, and designation of representatives of their own choosing, for the purpose of negotiating the terms and conditions of their employment or other mutual aid or protection.

See: Meyer S. Ryder, Charles M. Rehmus and Sanford Cohen, *Management Preparation for Collective Bargaining* (Homewood, Ill.: Dow Jones-Irwin, 1976), Edwin F. Beal and James P. Begin, *The Practice of Collective Bargaining*, sixth edition (Homewood, Ill.: Richard D. Irwin, 1982); Harold W. Davey, Mario F. Bognanno and David L. Estenson, *Contemporary Collective Bargaining*, 4th ed. (Englewood Cliffs, N.J.: Prentice-Hall, 1982); Charles S. Loughran, *Negotiating a Labor Contract: A Management Handbook* (Washington, D.C.: Bureau of National Affairs, Inc., 1984).

For the public sector perspective, *see:* Joyce M. Najita and Helene S. Tanimoto, *Guide to Statutory Provisions in Public Sector Collective Bargaining: Characteristics, Functions, and Powers of Administrative Agencies* (Honolulu: Industrial Relations Center, University of Hawaii, 1981); Charles A. Salerno, *Police at the Bargaining Table* (Springfield, Ill.: Charles C. Thomas, 1981); Randell W. Eberts and Joe A. Stone, *Unions and Public Schools: The Effects of Collective Bargaining on American Education* (Lexington, Mass.: Lexington Books, 1984).

See also the following entries:

H. J. HEINZ CO. V. NATIONAL LABOR
  RELATIONS BOARD
INLAND STEEL CO. V. NATIONAL LABOR
  RELATIONS BOARD
PORTER CO. V. NATIONAL LABOR
  RELATIONS BOARD
PRODUCTIVITY BARGAINING
REGIONAL BARGAINING
REOPENER CLAUSE
RETIREMENT AGE
REVERSE COLLECTIVE BARGAINING
SPLIT-THE-DIFFERENCE
SUNSHINE BARGAINING
TEXTILE WORKERS V. LINCOLN MILLS
UNFAIR LABOR PRACTICES (EMPLOYERS)
UNFAIR LABOR PRACTICES (UNIONS)
UNION SECURITY CLAUSE
WELFARE FUNDS
ZIPPER CLAUSE

Collective Bargaining Negotiations & Contracts, biweekly reference service published by the Bureau of National Affairs, Inc., which presents comprehensive coverage of wage rates and data, and cost-of-living figures; bargaining issues, demands, counterproposals, and significant settlements; strategy, techniques, industry facts and figures; equal employment opportunity activities as they affect collective bargaining.

collective negotiations, in the public sector "collective bargaining" may sometimes be legally and/or semantically unacceptable; so "collective negotiations" is available as an alternative. *See* Robert T.

Woodworth and Richard B. Peterson. *Collective Negotiation for Public and Professional Employees* (Glenview, Ill.: Scott, Foresman, 1969).

College Placement Annual: see COLLEGE PLACEMENT COUNCIL, INC.

College Placement Council, Inc., nonprofit corporation that provides professional services to career planning and placement directors at four-year and two-year colleges and universities in the United States, as well as to employers who hire graduates of these institutions. Each year the Council publishes the *College Placement Annual* which includes the occupational needs anticipated by approximately 1,300 corporate and governmental employers who normally recruit college graduates.

College Placement Council, Inc.
P.O. Box 2236
Bethlehem, PA 18001

College and University Personnel Association (CUPA), international organization dedicated to providing current methodology, models, studies, and other references to human resource professionals associated with higher education around the world.

College and University Personnel
  Association
11 Dupont Circle
Washington, D.C. 20036
(202) 462-1038

Collyer **doctrine,** the predisposition of the National Labor Relations Board to defer to arbitral awards in disputes involving unfair labor practices if certain conditions are met—one of them being that the arbitrator must have considered and resolved the statutory issues, if any, present in the case. This was first enunciated in the case of *Collyer Insulated Wire,* 192 NLRB 837 (1971). *See* Dennis K. Reischl, "Applying *Collyer* in the Federal Sector: Past Due Remedy," *Labor Law Journal* (June 1982).

comer, slang term for younger managers

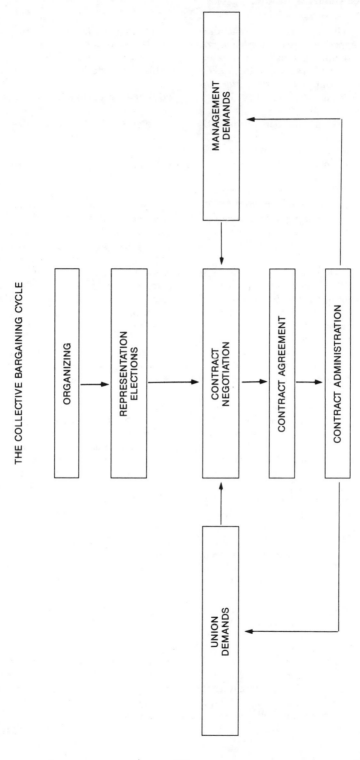

THE COLLECTIVE BARGAINING CYCLE

ORGANIZING

REPRESENTATION ELECTIONS

CONTRACT NEGOTIATION

CONTRACT AGREEMENT

CONTRACT ADMINISTRATION

MANAGEMENT DEMANDS

UNION DEMANDS

who seem to have the potential of assuming top management responsibilities. For how to find and best use your organization's "comers," *see* Robert A. Pitts, "Unshackle Your 'Comers,'" *Harvard Business Review* (May-June 1977).

Commerce clause, the part of the U.S. Constitution that allows Congress to control trade with foreign countries and from state to state. This is called the *commerce power* (Article One, Section Eight of the Constitution). If anything "affects interstate commerce" (such as labor unions, product safety, etc.), it is fair game for the federal government to regulate what goes on or even to take over all regulation.

Commerce, Department of, created in 1913 when the Congress split the Department of Commerce and Labor (founded in 1903) into two cabinet level departments; encourages, serves, and promotes the nation's economic development and technological advancement. It offers assistance and information to domestic and international business; provides social and economic statistics and analyses for business and government planners; assists in the development and maintenance of the U.S. merchant marine; provides research for and promotes the increased use of science and technology in the development of the economy; provides assistance to speed the development of the economically underdeveloped areas of the nation; seeks to improve understanding of the earth's physical environment and oceanic life; promotes travel to the United States by residents of foreign countries; assists in the growth of minority businesses; and seeks to prevent the loss of life and property from fire.
Department of Commerce
14th St. Between Constitution Ave.
and E Street N.W.
Washington, D.C. 20230
(202) 377-2000

Commerce Clearing House, Inc. (CCH), publishers of a variety of loose leaf information services concerned with law, taxes, business, urban affairs, etc.

Commerce Clearing House, Inc.
4025 W. Peterson Ave.
Chicago, IL 60646
(312) 583-8500

commission earnings, compensation to sales personnel that is based on a percentage of the value of the sales for which they are individually credited.

Commissioners of Conciliation: *see* CONCILIATION.

Commission on Civil Rights, also called CIVIL RIGHTS COMMISSION, the role of the Commission on Civil Rights is to encourage constructive steps toward equal opportunity for minority groups and women. The Commission investigates complaints, holds public hearings, and collects and studies information on denials of equal protection of the laws because of race, color, religion, sex, or national origin. Voting rights, administration of justice, and equality of opportunity in education, employment, and housing are among the many topics of specific Commission interest.

The Commission on Civil Rights, created by the Civil Rights Act of 1957, makes findings of fact but has no enforcement authority. Findings and recommendations are submitted to both the President and the Congress. More than 60 percent of the Commission's recommendations have been enacted, either by statute, executive order, or regulation. The Commission evaluates federal laws and the effectiveness of government equal opportunity programs. It also serves as a national clearinghouse for civil rights information.
Commission on Civil Rights
1121 Vermont Avenue N.W.
Washington, D.C. 20425
(202) 376-8177

commission plan, any of a variety of compensation programs for sales employees where wages or salary are established totally or in part as a percentage of the total dollar value of sales made over a given period of time. *See* John P. Steinbrink, "How to Pay Your Sales Force,"

Harvard Business Review (July-August 1978).

Committee for Industrial Organization, committee established within the American Federation of Labor in 1935 that grew to be the Congress of Industrial Organizations in 1938. *See* (1) CONGRESS OF INDUSTRIAL ORGANIZATIONS and (2) AMERICAN FEDERATION OF LABOR-CONGRESS OF INDUSTRIAL ORGANIZATIONS.

committeeman, or COMMITTEEWOMAN, worker (usually) elected by co-workers to represent the union membership in the handling of grievances and the recruitment of new union members among other duties.

Committee on Political Education (COPE), nonpartisan organization of the AFL-CIO, made up of members of the AFL-CIO's Executive Council, has the responsibility spelled out in the AFL-CIO Constitution of "encouraging workers to register and vote, to exercise their full rights and responsibilities of citizenship, and to perform their rightful part in the political life of the city, state and national communities."

COPE is not a political party, nor is it committed to the support of any particular party. From the first convention of the AFL-CIO (in 1955) to the most recent, COPE has been instructed to work in support of candidates who support issues of concern to the AFL-CIO regardless of the party affiliation of the candidate. The policies of COPE are determined by its national committee in line with the policies and programs adopted by the AFL-CIO conventions.

COPE reports facts about issues and candidates. It publishes voting records of elected officials to help AFL-CIO members inform themselves in order to vote intelligently. Candidates for political offices are recommended to the membership in the appropriate area by state and local COPE bodies, representing affiliated unions at the local and state level. The basis for the endorsement is the record and the program of the candidates compared to the policies of the AFL-CIO.

For a critical review of COPE's activities, see: Terry Catchpole, *How to Cope with COPE: The Political Operations of Organized Labor* (New Rochelle, N.Y.: Arlington House, 1968).
Committee on Political Education
815 16th Street, N.W.
Washington, D.C. 20006
(202) 637-5101

Committee on the Civil Services: *see* FULTON COMMITTEE.

common labor rate, wage rate for the least skilled physical or manual labor in an organization. This is usually an organization's lowest rate of pay.

common law of the shop, or INDUSTRIAL RELATIONS COMMON LAW, common law is the total body of law established by judicial precedent. The *common law of the shop* or *industrial relations common law* is that portion of the common law that applies to the workplace. *See* Brian Heshizer, "The New Common Law of Employment: Changes in the Concept of Employment at Will," *Labor Law Journal* (February 1985).

common situs picketing, picketing of an entire construction site by members of a single union to increase their strike's impact and to publicize a dispute with one or more contractors or subcontractors. In 1976, President Ford vetoed a bill that would have made common situs picketing legal. See Paul A. Brinker, "Common Situs Picketing in Construction Unions Since 1958," *Labor Law Journal* (June 1972); Stephen J. Cabot and Robert J. Simmons, "The Future of Common Situs Picketing," *Labor Law Journal* (December 1976).

Commonwealth* v. *Hunt: *see* SHAW, LEMUEL.

Commonwealth* v. *Pullis: *see* CORDWAINERS OF PHILADELPHIA.

communication, process of exchanging information, ideas, and feelings between

Community Dispute Services:

two or more individuals or groups. *Horizontal communication* refers to such an exchange among peers or people at the same organizational level. *Vertical communication* refers to such an exchange between individuals at differing levels of the organization. For a text, *see* William V. Haney, *Communications and Interpersonal Relations* (Homewood, Ill.: Richard D. Irwin, 4th ed., 1979). *Also see* Roger D'Aprix, "The Oldest (and Best) Way to Communicate With Employees," *Harvard Business Review* (September–October 1982).

See also NONVERBAL COMMUNICATIONS.

Community Dispute Services: *see* AMERICAN ARBITRATION ASSOCIATION.

community of interest, criterion used to determine if a group of employees make up an appropriate bargaining unit.

community wage survey, any survey whose purpose is to ascertain the structure and level of wages among employees in a local area.

company doctor, slang term for an expert brought in to save a company or organization from severe difficulties. The "doctor" could be a new chief executive, a consultant, a lawyer, an accountant, or other person with special expertise.

company fellowship plan, formal arrangement under which a particular company provides one or more graduate students with nonrepayable monetary allowances to help them attend universities, on a full-time basis, in pursuit of a master's or a doctoral degree. The specific details of such plans vary widely. *Company scholarship plans* differ in that they are restricted to undergraduate study. For a survey of company fellowship/scholarship plans, *see* J. Roger O'Meara, *Combating Knowledge Obsolescence: Company Fellowship Plans* (New York: The Conference Board, 1968).

company loans, loans made to employees by a company. Such loans are usually in response to an emergency, usually of short duration, and usually without interest.

company scholarship plan: *see* COMPANY FELLOWSHIP PLAN.

company spy, also called LABOR SPY, someone hired by an employer to report on what is happening within a union.

company store, store operated by an organization for the exclusive use of employees and their families. The largest company store in the world is the U.S. military's PX (Post Exchange) system.

company town, slang term for any community whose economy is dominated by one employer. True company towns, where the company literally owned all of the land, buildings, and stores are practically nonexistent in the modern U.S.— with the possible exception of remote areas of Alaska. For history, *see* James B. Allen, *The Company Town in the American West* (Norman, Okla.: University of Oklahoma Press, 1966); Christopher Norwood, "The Bittersweet Story of the First Company Town," *Business and Society Review* (Summer 1976).

company union, an historical term that described unions organized, financed, or otherwise dominated by an employer. The National Labor Relations (Wagner) Act of 1935 outlawed employer interference with unions, thus relegating company unions to history.

See also TEXAS AND NEW ORLEANS RAILWAY V. BROTHERHOOD OF RAILWAY AND STEAMSHIP CLERKS and UNFAIR LABOR PRACTICES (EMPLOYERS).

comparable form test: *see* ALTERNATE FORM.

comparable worth, providing equitable compensation for performing work of a comparable value as determined by the relative worth of a given job to an organization. The basic issue of comparable worth is whether Title VII of the Civil Rights Act of 1964 makes it unlawful for an employer to pay one sex at a lesser rate than the other when job performance is of comparable worth or value. For example, should graduate nurses be paid less than gardeners; or should beginning librarians with a master's degree be paid less than beginning managers with a master's degree? Historically, nurses and librarians have been paid less than occupations of "comparable worth" because they were considered "female" jobs. Comparable worth as a legal concept and as a social issue directly challenges traditional and market assumptions about the worth of a job. *See* Bruce A. Nelson, *et al.*, "Wage Discrimination and the 'Comparable Worth' in Perspective," *University of Michigan Journal of Law Reform* (Winter 1980); Donald J. Treiman and Heidi I. Hartmann, eds., *Women, Work and Wages: Equal Pay for Jobs of Equal Value* (Washington, D.C.: National Academy Press, 1981); Helen Remick, "The Comparable Worth Controversy," *Public Personnel Management,* Vol. 10, No. 4 (Winter 1981); Mary Helen Doherty and Ann Harriman, "Comparable Worth: The Equal Employment Issue of the 1980s," *Review of Public Personnel Administration* (Summer 1981); John R. Schnebly, "Comparable Worth: A Legal Overview," *Personnel Administrator* (April 1982); Stanley C. Wisniewski, "Achieving Equal Pay for Comparable Worth Through Arbitration," *Employee Relations Law Journal* (Autumn 1982); Clarence Thomas, "Pay Equity and Comparable Worth," *Labor Law Journal* (January 1983); Elaine Johansen, "Managing the Revolution: The Case for Comparable Worth," *Review of Public Personnel Administration* (Spring 1984); Sean DeForrest, "How Can Comparable Worth Be Achieved?" *Personnel* (September–October 1984); Helen Remick, ed., *Comparable Worth and Wage Discrimination: Technical Possibilities and Political Realities* (Philadelphia, Pa.: Temple University Press, 1984).

See also EQUAL PAY FOR EQUAL WORK and COUNTY OF WASHINGTON V. GUNTHER.

compa-ratio, a person's current salary as a percentage of the midpoint of his or her salary range.

comparative-norm principle, as defined in Arthur A. Sloane and Fred Witney, *Labor Relations* (Englewood Cliffs, N.J.: Prentice-Hall, 3rd ed., 1977):

To a great extent, company and union negotiators make use of the "comparative-norm principle" in wage negotiations. The basic idea behind this concept is the presumption that the economics of a particular collective bargaining relationship should neither fall substantially behind nor be greatly superior to that of other employer-union relationships; that, in short, it is generally a good practice to keep up with the crowd, but not necessarily to lead it.

compassionate leave, any leave granted for urgent family reasons. This term, which is mainly used by the military, is sometimes informally abbreviated to "passionate leave."

compensable factors, various elements of a job that, when put together, both define the job and determine its value to the organization.

compensable injury, work injury that qualifies an injured worker for workers' compensation benefits.

compensation, *also* PAY *or* REMUNERATION, generic terms that encompass all forms of organizational payments and rewards. For general discussions, *see* Patrick R. Pinto and Benjamin H. Lowenberg, "Pay: A Unitary View," *Personnel Journal* (June 1973); Edward E. Lawler III, "New Approaches To Pay: Innovations That Work," *Personnel* (September–October 1973); Thomas A. Mahoney (ed.), *Compensation and Reward Perspectives* (Homewood, Ill.: Richard D. Irwin, Inc., 1979); Sara M. Freedman, Robert T. Keller and John R. Montanari, "The Compensation Program: Balancing Organizational and Employee Needs," *Compensation Review,* Vol. 14,

No. 4 (1982); Benson Rosen and Sara Rynes, "Compensation, Jobs and Gender," *Harvard Business Review* (July-August 1983).
> *See also* the following entries:
> BONUS
> DEFERRED COMPENSATION
> EXECUTIVE COMPENSATION
> INDIRECT WAGES
> UNEMPLOYMENT BENEFITS

compensation management, the facet of management concerned with the selection, development, and direction of the programs that implement an organization's financial reward system. For surveys of the subject, *see* Richard I. Henderson, *Compensation Management: Rewarding Performance in the Modern Organization* (Reston, Va.: Reston Publishing Co., 1976); Thomas H. Patten, Jr., *Pay: Employee Compensation and Incentive Plans* (N.Y.: The Free Press, 1977); George T. Milkovich and Jerry M. Newman, *Compensation* (Plano, Tex.: Business Publications, Inc., 1984).

Compensation Review, quarterly journal covering all aspects of employee compensation. Also contains "condensations of noteworthy articles" from other business and professional publications that relate to compensation.
> *Compensation Review*
> **Editorial Adress:**
> *AMACOM*
> Division of American Management
>   Associations
> 135 West 50th Street
> New York, NY 10020
> **Subscriptions:**
> *Compensation Review*
> Trudeau Road
> Saranac Lake, NY 12983

compensatory time, time off in lieu of overtime pay.

competence, ability to consistently perform a task or job to an acceptable standard.
> *See also* INTERPERSONAL COMPETENCE.

competitive area, during layoffs or reductions-in-force employees of large organizations are sometimes restricted to competing for retention in their competitive area—the commuting area to which they are assigned.

competitive level, all positions of the same grade within a competitive area which are sufficiently alike in duties, responsibilities, pay systems, terms of appointment, requirements for experience, training, skills, and aptitudes that the incumbent of any of them could readily be shifted to any of the other positions without significant training or undue interruption to the work program. In the federal government, the job to which an employee is officially assigned determines his competitive level.

competitive promotion, selection for promotion made from the employees rated *best* qualified in competition with others, all of whom have the *minimum* qualifications required by the position.

competitive seniority, use of seniority in determining an employee's right, relative to other employees, to job related "rights" that cannot be supplied equally to any two employees.

competitive service, a general term for those civilian positions in a governmental jurisdiction that are not specifically excepted from merit system regulations.

competitive wages, rates of pay that an employer, in competition with other employers, must offer if he or she is to recruit and retain employees.

complaint examiner, official designated to conduct discrimination complaint hearings.

completion item, test question that calls for the examinee to complete or fill in the missing parts of a phrase, sentence, etc.

compliance agency, generally, any government agency that administers laws and/or regulations relating to equal employment opportunity. Specifically, a federal agency delegated enforcement responsibilities by the U.S. Department of Labor's Office of Federal Contract Compliance Programs (OFCCP) to ensure that federal contractors adhere to EEO regulations and policies. See Kenneth C. Marino, "Conducting an Internal Compliance Review of Affirmative Action," Personnel (March-April 1980).

complimentary interview, according to Joseph P. Cangemi and Jeffrey C. Claypool, "Complimentary Interviews: A System for Rewarding Outstanding Employees," Personnel Journal (February 1978),

the general purpose of a complimentary interview is to positively evaluate personnel and to give them performance feedback, recognition and praise, to highlight potential, and to enhance organizational planning.

composite score, score derived by combining scores obtained by an applicant on two or more tests or other measures.

Comprehensive Employment and Training Act of 1973 (CETA), as amended, CETA established a program of financial assistance to state and local governments to provide job training and employment opportunities for economically disadvantaged, unemployed, and underemployed persons. CETA provided funds for state and local jurisdictions to hire unemployed and underemployed persons in public service jobs. The CETA reauthorization legislation expired in September 1982. It was replaced by the Job Training Partnership Act of 1982, which was signed into law in October 1982. The legislation provides for job training programs which are planned and implemented under the joint control of local elected government officials and private industry councils in service delivery areas designated by the Governor of each State. The new law took effect October 1, 1983, providing for a 1-year transition period under the CETA system. See William Mirengoff and Lester

Rindler, The Comprehensive Employment and Training Act: Impact on People, Places, Programs-An Interim Report (Washington, D.C.: National Academy of Sciences, 1976): William Mirengoff and others, CETA: Accomplishments, Problems, Solutions (Kalamazoo, Mich.: The W.E. Upjohn Institute for Employment Research, 1982); Pawan K. Sawhney, Robert H. Jantzen and Irwin L. Herrnstadt, "The Differential Impact of CETA Training," Industrial and Labor Relations Review (January 1982); Laurie J. Bassi, "The Effect of CETA on the Postprogram Earnings of Participants," The Journal of Human Resources (Fall 1983); Royal S. Dellinger, "Implementing the Job Training Partnership Act," Labor Law Journal (April 1984).

compressed time, the same number of hours worked in a week spread over fewer days than normal.

comp time: see COMPENSATORY TIME.

compulsory arbitration, negotiating process whereby the parties are required by law to arbitrate their dispute. Some state statutes concerning collective bargaining impasses in the public sector mandate that parties who have exhausted all other means of achieving a settlement must submit their dispute to an arbitrator. The intent of such requirements for compulsory arbitration is to induce the parties to reach agreement by presenting them with an alternative that is both certain and unpleasant. See Carl M. Stevens, "Is Compulsory Arbitration Compatible with Bargaining," Industrial Relations (February 1966); Mollie H. Bowers, "Legislated Arbitration: Legality, Enforceability, and Face-Saving," Public Personnel Management (July August 1974).

See also LOCAL 174, TEAMSTERS V. LUCAS FLOUR CO.

compulsory checkoff: see AUTOMATIC CHECKOFF.

compulsory retirement, cessation of employment at an age specified by a union contract or company policy.

81

Concept Mastery Test (CMT), intelligence test that measures ability to deal with ideas or concepts by sampling two kinds of verbal problems: synonyms-antonyms and the completion of analogies. Questions draw on concepts from physical and biological sciences, mathematics, history, geography, literature, music, etc. Measures power or capacity rather than speed. TIME: 35/40 minutes. AUTHOR: L. M. Terman. PUBLISHER: Psychological Corporation (*see* TEST PUBLISHERS).

concerted activity, any organized activity, such as striking or picketing, by a union to further some collective purpose. This has five main categories:

1. *Economic*—activity which seeks to protect or enhance the economic status of the employees represented by the union. It can involve efforts to gain higher wages, fringe benefits, or the like.
2. *Recognitional*—activity undertaken by a union to gain the right to exclusively represent a group of employees in a collective bargaining relationship with their employer.
3. *Unfair Labor Practices*—unions may protest unfair labor practices by engaging in concerted activity, such as strikes, picketing, and handbilling to force the employer to abandon practices that the union believes are both unfair and illegal.
4. *Information Dissemination*—unions may also engage in concerted activity to publicize information about an employer's practices or products.
5. *Contract Interpretation*—unions can engage in concerted activity to force an employer to adhere to the union's interpretation of a contract, if there is no clause in the contract prohibiting such activity.

concession, something given by one party in a negotiating process in order to gain something else; for example, a union may agree to lower wages in order to get greater employment security. *See* Paul Bosanac, "Concession Bargaining, Work Transfers, and Midcontract Modification: *Los Angeles Marine Hardware Company*," *Labor Law Journal* (February 1983); D. Quinn Mills, "When Employees Make Concessions," *Harvard Business Review* (May–June 1983); James W. (Mike) Heller, "Unilateral Action in a Concession Bargain Context," *Labor Law Journal* (December 1984).

conciliation: *see* MEDIATION.

Conciliation, Commissioners of: *see* MEDIATION.

conciliator, individual who is assigned or who assumes the responsibility for maintaining disputing parties in negotiations until they reach a voluntary settlement. The Federal Mediation and Conciliation Service (FMCS) has Commissioners of Conciliation located in its various regional offices available to assist parties in the settlement of labor-management disputes.

concurrent validity, to assess the concurrent validity of a prospective employment examination, it must be given to individuals already performing successfully on the job. Each incumbent must also be independently rated by supervisors on actual job performance. Then the test scores and the ratings are correlated. If the better workers also obtain the better test scores, then the examination can be said to have concurrent validity. *See* Bruce A. Fournier and Paul Stager, "Concurrent Validation of a Dual-Task Selection Test," *Journal of Applied Psychology* (October 1976); Marvin H. Trattner, "Task Analysis in the Design of Three Concurrent Validity Studies of the Professional and Administrative Career Examination," *Personnel Psychology* (Spring 1979).

Conference Board, Inc., The, independent, nonprofit business research organization. Since 1916 it has continuously served as an institution for scientific research in the fields of business economics and business management. Its sole purpose is to promote prosperity and security by assisting in the effective operation and sound development of voluntary productive enterprise. The Board has more than 4,000 associates and serves 40,000 individuals throughout the world. It does continuing research in the fields of economic conditions, marketing, finance, personnel administration, international activities, public affairs, antitrust, and various other related areas.

The Conference Board, Inc.
845 Third Ave.
New York, NY 10022
(212) 759-0900

confidence testing, testing approach that allows the subject to express his or her attraction to or confidence in possible answers in percentage terms. See Ernest S. Selig, "Confidence Testing Comes of Age," *Training and Development Journal* (July 1972).

conflict of interest, any situation where a decision that may be made (or influenced) by an office holder may (or may appear to) be to that office holder's personal benefit. See Common Cause, *Serving Two Masters: A Common Cause Study of Conflicts of Interest in the Executive Branch* (Washington, D.C.: Common Cause, 1976) and Robert G. Vaughn, *Conflict-of-Interest Regulation in the Federal Executive Branch* (Lexington, Mass.: Lexington Books, 1979).

conflict resolution, according to Kenneth E. Boulding, in *Conflict and Defense: A General Theory* (N.Y.: Harper & Bros., 1962), the objective of conflict resolution is to see that conflicts, which are inevitable, remain constructive rather than destructive. Traditional administrative theory, having been based on the models provided by the military and the Catholic Church, viewed organizational conflict as deviancy. But the growing recognition that reasonable conflict can produce organizational benefits is leading to changes in administrative structure that will permit and control conflict. Since it has been the hierarchical structure of organizations that has commonly suppressed the potential value of conflict, that hierarchical structure must

be altered before conflict can come into its full beneficent flower. The implications of this for the future of personnel management are awesome. See A. C. Filley, "Some Normative Issues in Conflict Management," *California Management Review* (Winter 1978); Eleanor Phillips and Ric Cheston, "Conflict Resolution: What Works?" *California Management Review* (Summer 1979); Michele Stimac, "Strategies for Resolving Conflict: Their Functional and Dysfunctional Sides," *Personnel* (November-December 1982); Paul Joyce and Adrian Woods, "The Management of Conflict: A Quantitative Analysis," *British Journal of Industrial Relations* (March 1984); Dean Tjosvold, "Making Conflict Productive," *Personnel Administrator* (June 1984); Vincent L. Ferraro and Sheila A. Adams, "Interdepartmental Conflict: Practical Ways to Prevent and Reduce It," *Personnel* (July-August 1984); M. Afzalur Rahim, "A Strategy for Managing Conflict in Complex Organizations," *Human Relations* (January 1985).

confrontation meeting, organization development technique that has an organizational group (usually the management corps) meet for a one-day effort to assay their organizational health. See Richard Beckhard, "The Confrontation Meeting," *Harvard Business Review* (March-April 1967).

congressional exemption, exclusion of the approximately 18,000 congressional staff employees from coverage of the large variety of laws regulating working conditions that the U.S. Congress has passed throughout the years. Each member of Congress has complete autonomy over the pay and working conditions of his or her staff and need not comply with laws on labor relations, equal pay, civil rights, occupational safety, etc.

See also DAVIS V. PASSMAN.

Congress of Industrial Organizations (CIO), labor organization that originated in 1935, when the Committee for Industrial Organization was formed within the American Federation of Labor (AFL) to foster the organization of workers in mass production industries. The activities of the Committee precipitated a split in the AFL because many of the older union leaders refused to depart from the craft union concept. In 1937, those unions associated with the committee were formally expelled from the AFL. One year later, those unions formed their own federation—the Congress of Industrial Organizations—with John L. Lewis as its first president. In 1955, the CIO formally merged with the AFL to form the present AFL-CIO. For histories of the split, *see* Walter Galenson, *The CIO Challenge to the AFL: A History of the American Labor Movement, 1935-1941* (Cambridge, Mass.: Harvard University Press, 1960); Nelson Lichtenstein, *Labor's War at Home: The CIO in World War II* (New York, Cambridge University Press, 1982).

See also AMERICAN FEDERATION OF LABOR-CONGRESS OF INDUSTRIAL ORGANIZATIONS.

Connell v. Higginbotham, 403 U.S. 207 (1971), U.S. Supreme Court case, which held that it was unconstitutional to require public employees to swear that they "do not believe in the overthrow of the Government of the United States or of the State of Florida by force or violence." The court reasoned that at the very least, the Constitution required that a hearing or inquiry be held to determine the reasons for refusal.

See also LOYALTY OATH.

consensual validation, procedure of using mutual agreement as the criterion for validity.

consent decree, approach to enforcing equal employment opportunity involving a negotiated settlement that allows an employer to not admit to any acts of discrimination yet agree to greater EEO efforts in the future. Consent decrees are usually negotiated with the Equal Employment Opportunity Commission or a federal court. *See* Lewis J. Ringler, "EEO Agreements and Consent Decrees may be Booby-Traps," *The Personnel Admini-*

strator (February 1977); Ichniowski Casey, "Have Angels Done More? The Steel Industry Consent Decree," *Industrial and Labor Relations Review* (January 1983).

constant dollar, a dollar value adjusted for changes in prices. Constant dollars are derived by dividing current dollar amounts by an appropriate price index, a process generally known as deflating. The result is a constant dollar series as it would presumably exist if prices and transactions were the same in all subsequent years as in the base year. Any changes in such a series would reflect only changes in the real volume of goods and services. Constant dollar figures are commonly used for computing the gross national product and its components and for estimating total budget outlays.

See also CURRENT DOLLAR.

constituency, individuals or groups having an interest in the activities of a public official or agency.

constitutional rights, rights guaranteed to all citizens by the U.S. Constitution or rights guaranteed to all union members by the union's constitution.

conspiracy doctrine: *see* SHAW, LEMUEL.

construct, an idea or concept created or synthesized ("constructed") from available information and refined through scientific investigation. In psychological testing, a construct is usually dimensional, an attribute of people that varies in degree from one person to another. Tests are usually intended to be measures of intellectual, perceptual, psychomotor, or personality constructs (*e.g.,* a clerical test may measure the construct known as "perceptual speed and accuracy" or the performance of invoice clerks may be measured in terms of "ability to recognize errors").

construct validity, measure of how adequate a test is for assessing the possession of particular psychological traits or qualities.

Construction Labor Report, weekly report on union-management developments in the construction labor field published by the Bureau of National Affairs, Inc. Covers bargaining issues, settlements, job-safety and health developments under the Occupational Safety and Health Administration, equal employment opportunity activities, union policies and activities, agency and court decisions, arbitration awards, and state and federal legislative developments. Also supplies economic data, such as industry earnings, hours of work, cost of living, and employment figures.

constructive discharge theory, if an employer makes conditions of continued employment so intolerable that it results in a "constructive discharge" whereby the employee "voluntarily" leaves, the employer may still be subject to charges that the employer violated Title VII of the Civil Rights Act of 1964, which generally prohibits employers from discharging employees because of their race, color, sex, or national origin.

consultant, individual or organization temporarily employed by other individuals or organizations because of some presumed expertise. *Internal consultants* are often employed by large organizations to provide consulting services to its various units. *See* Arthur N. Turner, "Consulting is More Than Giving Advice," *Harvard Business Review* (September–October 1982); Danielle B. Nees and Larry E. Greiner, "Seeing Behind the Look-Alike Management Consultants," *Organizational Dynamics* (Winter 1985).

Consumer Credit Protection Act of 1970, limits the amount of an employee's disposable income which may be garnished and protects employees from discharge because of one garnishment.

Consumer Price Index (CPI), also called COST-OF-LIVING INDEX, monthly statistical measure of the average change in prices over time in a fixed market basket of goods and services. Effective with the January 1978 index, the Bureau of Labor Statistics began publishing CPI's for two population groups: (1) a new CPI for all Urban Consumers (CPI-U) which covers approximately 80 percent of the total noninstitutional civilian population; and (2) a revised CPI for Urban Wage Earners and Clerical Workers (CPI-W) which represents about half the population covered by the CPI-U. The CPI-U includes, in addition to wage earners and clerical workers, groups which historically have been excluded from CPI coverage, such as professional, managerial, and technical workers, the self-employed, short-term workers, the unemployed, and retirees and others not in the labor force.

BLS introduced an important improvement in the CPI-U with release of the January 1983 data. The Bureau changed the homeownership component from an "asset" approach to a "flow-of services" approach. The change was implemented by a rental equivalence technique. The CPI-W will continue to use the old home-ownership method until January 1985, when it also will be changed to incorporate a rental equivalence measure of home-ownership costs.

The CPI is based on prices of food, clothing, shelter, and fuels, transportation fares, charges for doctors' and dentists' services, drugs, and other goods and services that people buy for day-to-day living. Prices are collected in 85 urban areas across the country from over 18,000 tenants, 18,000 housing units for property taxes, and about 24,000 establishments—grocery and department stores, hospitals, filling stations, and other types of stores and service establishments. All taxes directly associated with the purchase and use of items are included in the index. Prices of food, fuels, and a few other items are obtained every month in all 85 locations. Prices of most other commodities and services are collected every month in the five largest geographic areas and every other month in other areas. Prices of most goods and services are obtained by personal visits of the Bureau's trained representatives. Mail questionnaires are used to obtain public utility rates, some fuel prices, and certain other items.

In calculating the index, price changes for the various items in each location are averaged together with weights which represent their importance in the spending of the appropriate population group. Local data are then combined to obtain a U.S. city average. Separate indexes are also published for 28 local areas. Area indexes do not measure differences in the level of prices among cities; they only measure the average change in prices for each area since the base period.

The index measures price changes from a designated reference date—1967—which equals 100.0. An increase of 22 percent, for example, is shown as 122.0. This change can be expressed in dollars as follows: The price of a base period "market basket" of goods and services in the CPI has risen from $10 in 1967 to $12.20. For a brief history, see Julius Shiskin, "Updating the Consumer Price Index—An Overview," Monthly Labor Review (July 1974). Also see Robert J. Gordon, "The Consumer Price Index: Measuring Inflation and Causing It," The Public Interest (Spring 1981); P. Cagan and G. H. Moore, "Some Proposals to Improve the Consumer Price Index," Monthly Labor Review (September 1981); Daniel J. B. Mitchell, "Should The Consumer Price Index Determine Wages?" California Management Review (Fall 1982).

contact counseling, according to Len Sperry and Lee R. Hess, Contact Counseling: Communication Skills for People in Organizations (Reading, Mass.: Addison-Wesley, 1974), contact counseling "is the process by which the manager aids the employee to effectively problem-solve and develop."

contempt, a willful disobeying of a judge's command or official court order.

contact counseling, according to Len Sperry and Lee R. Hess, Contact Counseling: Communication Skills for People in Organizations (Reading, Mass.: Addison-Wesley, 1974), contact counseling "is the process by which the manager aids the employee to effectively problem-solve and develop."

contempt, a willful disobeying of a judge's command or official court order.

content validity, a selection device has content validity if it measures the specific abilities needed to perform the job. Examinations that require applicants to perform an actual, representative sample of the work done on the job would obviously have content validity. See Stephen Wollack, "Content Validity: Its Legal and Psychometric Basis," Public Personnel Management (November-December 1976); Lyle F. Shoenfeldt et al., "Content Validity Revisited," Journal of Applied

Consumer Price Index, 1880-1983
Note: Data before 1973 are estimated from several sources
Source: BLS.

Psychology (October 1976); Erich P. Prien, "The Function of Job Analysis in Content Validation," *Personnel Psychology* (Summer 1977); Stephen J. Mussio and Mary K. Smith, *Content Validity: A Procedural Manual* (Chicago: International Personnel Management Association, 1973); Robert M. Guion, " 'Content Validity' in Moderation," *Personnel Psychology* (Summer 1978); Lawrence S. Kleinman and Robert H. Faley, "Assessing Content Validity: Standards Set by the Court," *Personnel Psychology* (Winter 1978); Dwight R. Norris and James A. Buford, Jr., "A Content Valid Writing Test: A Case Study," *The Personnel Administrator* (January 1980).

contextual variable, a condition that may affect the validity of a test.

contingency management, also called SITUATIONAL MANAGEMENT, any management style that recognizes that the application of theory to practice must necessarily take into consideration, and be contingent upon, the given situation. *See* Henry L. Tosi and W. Clay Hamner, *Organizational Behavior and Management: A Contingency Approach* (Chicago, Ill.: St. Clair Press, 1974); Robert P. Vecchio, "A Dyadic Interpretation of the Contingency Model of Leadership Effectiveness," *Academy of Management Journal* (September 1979); Donald D. White and Bill Davis, "Behavioral Contingency Management: A Bottom-Line Alternative for Management Development," *The Personnel Administrator* (April 1980); John Prooslin Goodman and William R. Sandberg, "A Contingency Approach to Labor Relations Strategies," *Academy of Management Review* (January 1981).

contingency model of leadership effectiveness, Fred E. Fiedler's theory of leadership effectiveness. According to Fiedler, the appropriate leadership style is determined by three critical elements in the leader's situation: (1) the power position of the leader; (2) the task structure; (3) the leader-member personal relationships. The nature of these three factors determines

the "favorableness" of the situation for the leader, which in turn requires a particular leadership style. Fiedler views leader behavior as a single dimension ranging from "task-oriented" to "relationship-oriented." He contends that task-oriented leaders perform best in very favorable or very unfavorable situations, whereas relationship-oriented leaders are best in mixed situations. Fiedler suggests that it may be to an organization's advantage to try to design jobs to fit leaders' styles rather than attempting to change leaders' behavior to fit the situation. For the original presentation, *see* Fred E. Fiedler, *A Theory of Leadership Effectiveness* (N.Y.: McGraw-Hill, 1967). For a critique of Fiedler's concepts, *see* George Green, James Orris, and Kenneth M. Alvares, "Contingency Model of Leadership Effectiveness: Some Methodological Issues," *Journal of Applied Psychology* (June 1971).

contingent, something that is possible, but not assured, because it depends on future events or actions (known as contingencies) that may or may not occur.

continuing education, general term that usually refers to graduate or undergraduate course work undertaken on a part-time basis in order to keep up to date on new developments in one's occupational field, learn a new field, or contribute to one's general education. *See* Irwin M. Rubin and Homer G. Morgan, "A Projective Study of Attitudes Toward Continuing Education," *Journal of Applied Psychology*, Vol. 51, No. 6 (1967); Philip T. Crotty, "Continuing Education and the Experienced Manager," *California Management Review* (Fall, 1974); Richard Morano, "Continuing Education in Industry," *Personnel Journal* (February 1973).

continuous negotiating committee, labor-management committee established to review a collective bargaining agreement on a continuous basis.

contract: *see* the following entries:
BREACH OF CONTRACT

EMPLOYMENT CONTRACT
INCENTIVE CONTRACT
INDIVIDUAL CONTRACT
IRON-CLAD OATH
LABOR AGREEMENT
MASTER AGREEMENT
SWEETHEART CONTRACT
TERMINATION CONTRACT
YELLOW-DOG CONTRACT

contract bar, an existing collective bargaining agreement that bars a representative election sought by a competing union.

contracting-out, having work performed outside an organization's own work force. Contracting-out has often been an area of union-management disagreement. While many unions recognize management's right to occasionally subcontract a job requiring specialized skills and equipment not possessed by the company or its employees, they oppose the letting of work that could be done by the organization's own work force. In particular, unions are concerned if work normally performed by its members is contracted to firms having inferior wages or working conditions or if such action may result in reduced earnings or layoffs of regular employees. See Daniel D. Brener and Danial W. Fitzpatrick, "An Experience in Contracting Out for Services," *Governmental Finance* (March 1980); Ronald Donovan and Marsha J. Orr, *Subcontracting in the Public Sector: The New York State Experience* (Ithaca, N.Y.: Cornell University, New York State School of Industrial and Labor Relations, 1982).
See also FIBREBOARD PAPER PRODUCTS CORPORATION V. NATIONAL LABOR RELATIONS BOARD.

contract labor, workers imported from a foreign country for employment with a specific employer.

contributory pension plan, any pension program that has employees contributing a portion of the cost.

control group, in a research design this is a group of similar characteristics to the experimental or subject group which is not exposed to the experimental treatment and which is used for comparative purposes.

convalescent leave, federal government agencies have the right to grant convalescent leave to civilian employees on duty abroad who are injured as a result of "war, insurgency, mob violence, or other similar hostile action." Such leave with pay is completely separate from an employee's sickleave benefits.

convergent validity, in testing, evidence that different measures of a construct will produce similar results.

converted score, general term referring to any of a variety of "transformed" scores, in terms of which raw scores on a test may be expressed for such reasons as facilitating interpretation and permitting comparison with scores on other tests' forms. For example, the raw scores obtained by candidates on the various College Board tests are converted to scores on a common scale that ranges from 200 to 800.

convict labor: see ASHURST-SUMNERS ACT OF 1935.

coolie labor, originally a term for unskilled Asian labor in the 19th-century U.S., the phrase is now applied—typically in a jocular or derisive manner—to any cheap labor.

cooling-off period, any legal provision that postpones a strike or lockout for a specific period of time in order to give the parties an additional opportunity to mediate their differences. While the device has great popular appeal, it has proven to be of doubtful value because "more time" will not necessarily resolve a labor dispute. The first federal requirements for a cooling-off period were set forth in the War Labor Disputes (Smith-Connally) Act of 1943. This was superseded by the national emergency provisions of the Labor Management Relations (Taft-Hartley) Act of 1947, which called for an 80-day cooling-off period in the event of a "national emergency."

cooperative education, an educational process wherein students alternate formal studies with actual work experiences. It is distinguished from other part-time employment in that successful completion of the off-campus experiences becomes a prerequisite for graduation. For an account of one company's experiences over twenty years, *see* Jack J. Phillips, "Is Cooperative Education Worth It? One Company's Answer," *Personnel Journal* (October 1977). For a text, *see* Ronald W. Stadt and Bill G. Gooch, *Cooperative Education* (Indianapolis: Bobbs-Merrill Co., Inc., 1977).

Cooperative School and College Ability Test (SCAT), test designed to measure basic verbal and mathematical abilities. Most commonly used to yield an estimate of academic potential in college, this test is also used by manager assessment centers. TIME: 40/50 minutes. PUBLISHER: Cooperative Tests and Services, Educational Testing Service (*see* TEST PUBLISHERS).

Cooperative School Program: *see* UNITED STATES EMPLOYMENT SERVICE.

Cooper v. Delta Airlines, 274 F.Supp. 781 (1967), case in which a U.S. District Court invalidated the practice of firing women stewardesses who were either married or more than 32 years old.

cooptation, efforts of an organization to bring and subsume new elements into its policymaking process in order to prevent such elements from being a threat to the organization or its mission. The classic analysis of cooptation is found in Philip Selznick's *TVA and the Grass Roots* (Berkeley, Calif.: University of California Press, 1949). *Also see:* Ronald S. Burt, *Corporate Profits and Cooptation: Networks of Market Constraints and Directorate Ties in the American Economy* (New York: Academic Press, 1983).

coordinated bargaining: *see* COALITION BARGAINING.

coordination of benefits, provisions and procedures used by insurers to avoid duplicate payment for losses insured under more than one insurance policy. For example, some people have a duplication of benefits, for their medical costs arising from an automobile accident, in their automobile and health insurance policies. A coordination of benefits or antiduplication clause in one or the other policy will prevent double payment for the expenses by making one of the insurers the *primary payer,* and assuring that no more than 100 percent of the costs are covered.

COPE: *see* COMMITTEE ON POLITICAL EDUCATION.

Copeland Act: *see* KICKBACK.

Cordwainers of Philadelphia, the first American labor organization created specifically for collective bargaining. In 1792 the Philadelphia Cordwainers (shoemakers) formed a union. While it lasted only about a year, it was part of a more general trend. Other skilled craftsmen, including tailors, masons, cabinet makers, and printers soon organized as well. The cordwainers themselves later established the Federal Society of Journeymen Cordwainers which lasted from 1794 to 1806. One of the major problems unions faced throughout this early period was their dubious legal status. Here, again, the Philadelphia cordwainers were at the forefront, but at the forefront of a major setback. In the case of *Commonwealth v. Pullis* (1806), the Philadelphia Mayor's Court found them guilty of engaging in a criminal conspiracy when they went out on strike. The court upheld an indictment charging eight of the cordwainers with (1) conspiring that "none would work in the shoemaking trade except for higher wages that had customarily been paid," (2) conspiring to use "threats, menaces, and other unlawful means" to prevent other craftsmen from working at lower rates, and (3) seeking to control entry into the trade

89

through a strictly enforced apprenticeship program. The cordwainers were each fined a week's pay (eight dollars) plus court costs—and that was the end of their union.

Corning Glass Works v. Brennan, 417 U.S. 188 (1974), U.S. Supreme Court case, which held that it was a violation of the Equal Pay Act of 1963 to continue to pay some men at a higher rate ("red circle") than women for the same work even though all new hires for these same positions would receive the same salary regardless of sex.

Coronado Coal v. United Mine Workers, 268 U.S. 295 (1925), U.S. Supreme Court case, which held that unincorporated organizations such as labor unions could be sued and held liable for damages.

corporate culture: *see* ORGANIZATIONAL CLIMATE.

corporation headhunter: *see* HEADHUNTER.

corporation man, concept, developed by Anthony Jay, in *Corporation Man: Who He Is, What He Does, Why His Ancient Tribal Impulses Dominate the Life of the Modern Corporation* (N.Y.: Random House, 1971), which holds man's primitive instincts as a hunter prevail in the corporate world.

correction for guessing, reduction in a test score for wrong answers—sometimes applied in scoring multiple-choice questions—that is intended to discourage guessing and to yield more accurate ranking of examinees in terms of their true knowledge.

correlation, relationship or "going-togetherness" between two sets of scores or measures; the tendency of one score to vary concomitantly with the other.

correlation, biserial: *see* BISERIAL CORRELATION.

correlation coefficient, number express-

ing the degree to which two measures tend to vary together. A correlation coefficient can range from -1.00 (a perfect negative relationship) to $+1.00$ (a perfect positive relationship). When there is no correlation between two measures, the coefficient is 0. A correlation coefficient only indicates concomitance; it does not indicate causation.

The values of the correlation coefficient are easily misinterpreted since they do not fall along an ordinary, absolute scale. For example, a correlation coefficient of .20 does not signify twice as much relationship as does one of .10, nor can a correlation coefficient be interpreted as a percentage statement. A correlation coefficient is a mathematical index number, which requires for its interpretation some knowledge of that branch of mathematical statistics known as correlation theory. As a very rough guide to interpretation, however, a correlation between a single employment test and a measure of job performance of approximately .20 often is high enough to be useful (such correlations rarely exceed .50), a correlation of .40 is ordinarily considered very good, and most personnel research workers are usually pleased with a correlation of .30.

The mathematical symbol for the correlation coefficient is: r.

cosmic search, in the context of equal employment opportunity, the cosmic search refers to an endless search by an employer for an alternative selection procedure with less adverse impact.

cosmopolitan-local construct, two latent social roles that manifest themselves in organizational settings, according to Alvin W. Gouldner. The first role, *cosmopolitan,* tends to be adopted by true professionals. It assumes a small degree of loyalty to the employing organization, a high commitment to specialized skills, and an outer-reference group orientation. The second role, *local,* tends to be adopted by nonprofessionals. It assumes a high degree of loyalty to the employing organization, a low commitment to specialized skills, and an inner-reference group orientation.

These role models are extremes and represent the two ends of a continuum. *See* Alvin W. Gouldner, "Cosmopolitans and Locals: Toward an Analysis of Latent Social Roles—I," *Administrative Science Quarterly* (December 1957). While Gouldner's construct has received substantial empirical testing and criticisms, its value as a general model remains evident. For a critical examination of the construct, *see* Andrew J. Grimes and Philip K. Berger, "Cosmopolitan-Local: Evaluation of a Construct," *Administrative Science Quarterly* (December 1970). *See also* Timothy A. Almy, "Local-Cosmopolitanism and U.S. City Managers," *Urban Affairs Quarterly* (March 1975).

cost-benefit analysis, also BENEFIT-COST ANALYSIS, any process by which organizations seek to determine the effectiveness of their spending, in relation to costs, in meeting policy objectives. *See* E. J. Mishan, *Cost-Benefit Analysis*, new and expanded edition. (N.Y.: Praeger Publishers, 1976); Logan Cheek, "Cost Effectiveness Comes to the Personnel Function," *Harvard Business Review* (May–June 1973); P. G. Sassone and William Schaffer, *Cost-Benefit Analysis: A Handbook* (New York: Academic Press, 1978); Elizabeth David, "Benefit-Cost Analysis in State and Local Investment Decisions," *Public Administration Review* (January–February 1979); Edward M. Gramlich, *Benefit-Cost Analysis of Government Programs* (Englewood Cliffs, N.J.: Prentice-Hall, 1981).

cost center, accounting device whereby all related costs attributable to some "center" within an institution, such as an activity, department, or program (*e.g.*, a hospital burn center), are segregated for accounting or reimbursement purposes. Contrasts with segregating costs of different types, such as nursing, drugs or laundry, regardless of which "center" incurred them.

cost-effectiveness analysis, an analytical technique used to choose the most efficient method for achieving a program or policy goal. The costs of alternatives are measured by their requisite estimated dollar expenditures. Effectiveness is defined by the degree of goal attainment, and may also (but not necessarily) be measured in dollars. Either the net effectiveness (effectiveness minus costs) or the cost-effectiveness ratios of alternatives are compared. The most cost-effective method chosen may involve one or more alternatives. The limited view of costs and effectiveness distinguishes this technique from cost-benefit analysis, which encompasses society-wide impacts of alternatives.

See also COST-BENEFIT ANALYSIS.

costing-out, determining the actual cost of a contract proposal (wages and fringe benefits). *See* W. D. Heisel and Gordon S. Skinner, *Costing Union Demands* (Chicago: International Personnel Management Association, 1976); Robert E. Allen and Timothy J. Keaveny, "Costing Out a Wage and Benefit Package," *Compensation Review* (Second Quarter 1983).

cost of insurance, the amount which a policyholder pays to the insurer minus what he gets back from it. This should be distinguished from the rate for a given unit of insurance ($10 for a $1000 life insurance policy).

cost-of-living adjustment (COLA), also COST-OF-LIVING ALLOWANCE, a *cost-of-living adjustment* is an increase in compensation in response to increasing inflation. A *cost-of-living allowance* is additional compensation for accepting employment in high costs of living areas. *See* Robert J. Thorton, "A Problem with the 'COLA' Craze," *Compensation Review* (Second Quarter 1977); Rufus E. Runzheimer, Jr., "How Corporations are Handling Cost of Living Differentials," *Business Horizons* (August 1980); Clarence R. Deitsch and David A. Dilts, "The COLA Clause: An Employer Bargaining Weapon?" *Personnel Journal* (March 1982); Wallace E. Hendricks, and Lawrence M. Kahn, "Cost-of-Living Clauses in Union Contracts: Determinants and Effects," *Industrial and Labor Relations Review* (April 1983).

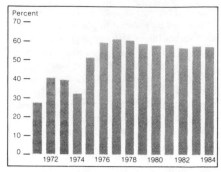

Percent of workers covered by COLA clauses in collective bargaining agreements covering 1,000 workers or more, 1971–84

Cost of Living Council, federal agency, authorized by the Economic Stabilization Act of 1970, which monitored inflation. Created by Executive Order 11615 in 1971, it was abolished by Executive Order 11788 in 1974.

cost-of-living escalator: *see* ESCALATOR CLAUSE.

Cost-of-Living Index: *see* CONSUMER PRICE INDEX.

cost-push inflation: *see* INFLATION, COST-PUSH.

Council of Economic Advisers (CEA), established in the Executive Office of the President by the Employment Act of 1946, the CEA consists of three economists (one designated chairman) appointed by the president with the advice and consent of the Senate who formulate proposals to "maintain employment, production and purchasing power." The CEA, as the president's primary source of economic advice, assists the president in preparing various economic reports. For a history, *see* Edward S. Flash, *Economic Advice and Presidential Leadership: The Council of Economic Advisors* (New York: Columbia University Press, 1965).

   Council of Economic Advisers
   Executive Office Building
   Washington, D.C. 20500
   (202) 395-5084

Council on Wage and Price Stability, established in 1974 within the Executive Office of the President, the Council monitored the economy as a whole with respect to key indicators such as wages, costs, productivity, profits, and prices. The council became inactive in 1981.

counseling, crisis: *see* CRISIS INTERVENTION.

counseling, employee: *see* EMPLOYEE COUNSELING.

countercyclical, actions aimed at smoothing out swings in economic activity. Countercyclical actions may take the form of monetary and fiscal policy (such as countercyclical revenue sharing or jobs programs). Automatic (built-in) stabilizers have a contercyclical effect without necessitating changes in governmental policy.
   See also AUTOMATIC STABILIZER.

counterproposal, offer made by a party in response to an earlier offer made by another party.

countervailing power concept developed by John Kenneth Galbraith which holds that large industries have an inherent tendency to generate the development of large buyers and unions which seek to *countervail* their power; in effect both buyers and sellers are prevented from abusing power by the development of *countervailing powers* in the economy. *See* his *American Capitalism: The Concept of Countervailing Power* (Boston: Houghton Mifflin, 1956).

County of Washington* v. *Gunther, 68 L. Ed. 2d 751 (1981), U.S. Supreme Court case which held that a claim of sex-based wage discrimination was not precluded by a failure to allege performance of work equal to that performed by male counterparts. This case involved female matrons of a county jail who performed substantially equal work to that performed by male guards, but were compensated less. Although they alleged in their complaint a violation of the equal pay standard of the

Equal Pay Act as between themselves and the male guards, they did not allege that job performance was "substantially equal" as required under the Act. Suing under Title VII, the matrons' argument was that even if their job content was not substantially equal to that of the male guards, some of the differences in compensation paid to them was because of sex discrimination. While the Court agreed with the matrons, it dodged the issue of comparable worth. Justice Brennan and his majority opinion wrote that, "respondent's claim is not based on the controversial concept of 'comparable worth'." See Laura N. Gasaway, "Comparable Worth: A Post *Gunther* Overview," *The Georgetown Law Journal* (June 1981); Barbara N. McLennan, "Sex Discrimination in Employment and Possible Liabilities of Labor Unions: Implications of *County of Washington* v. *Gunther*," *Labor Law Journal* (January 1982).

See also COMPARABLE WORTH.

court of appeals, also called FEDERAL COURT OF APPEALS and U.S. COURT OF APPEALS, appellate court below the U.S. Supreme Court, which hears appeals from cases tried in federal district courts. In most cases, a decision by a court of appeals is final since only a small fraction of their decisions are ever reviewed by the U.S. Supreme Court. Before 1948 the court of appeals was called the circuit court of appeals.

cousin laboratory, a laboratory training experience for people who have no direct working relationship with each other but come from the same organization.

Couturier, Jean J. (1927-), as executive director of the National Civil Service League, he was the individual most responsible for the League's promulgation of its 1970 "Model Public Personnel Administration Law," which called for the abolition of traditional civil service commissions. For an account of this abolition movement, see Jean J. Couturier, "The Quiet Revolution in Public Personnel

Law," *Public Personnel Management* (May-June 1976).

covered jobs, all those positions that are affected and protected by specific labor legislation.

cover your ass (CYA), any bureaucratic technique that serves to hold the individual bureaucrat harmless for policies or actions with which he or she was once associated.

Coxey's Army, originally a group of about 500 unemployed men who marched on Washington in 1894 in an effort to pressure the government into providing public works employment. The "army" led by a self-styled "general," Jacob S. Coxey, ended ignominiously when Coxey and a few of his followers were arrested for trespassing on White House grounds. For a history, see Donald L. McMurry, *Coxey's Army: A Study of the Industrial Army Movement of 1894* (Seattle, Wash.: University of Washington Press, 1929, 1968).

CPA: see CERTIFIED PUBLIC ACCOUNTANT.

CPI: see (1) CALIFORNIA PSYCHOLOGICAL INVENTORY and (2) CONSUMER PRICE INDEX.

CPI Detailed Report, U.S. Bureau of Labor Statistics' monthly publication featuring detailed data and charts on the Consumer Price Index.
   CPI Detailed Report
   Superintendent of Documents
   Government Printing Office
   Washington, D.C. 20402

CPM: see CRITICAL PATH METHOD.

craft, any occupation requiring specific skills that must be acquired by training.

craft guild: see GUILD.

craft union, also called HORIZONTAL UNION and TRADE UNION, labor organization that restricts its membership to skilled craft workers (such as plumbers, carpenters, etc.), in contrast to an industrial union that seeks to recruit all workers in a particular industry. The U.S. labor movement has its origins in small craft unions. For a history, *see* Lloyd Ulman, *The Rise of the National Trade Union* (Cambridge, Mass.: Harvard University Press, 1966). For an international perspective, *see:* E. Owen Smith, editor, *Trade Unions in the Developed Economies* (New York: St. Martin's Press, 1981).

craft unit, bargaining unit that consists only of workers with the same specific skill (such as electricians, plumbers, or carpenters).

Crawford Small Parts Dexterity Test, two-part, timed test of manual dexterity. Measures fine eye-hand coordination such as that used in clock repair, hearing aid repair, and in manipulation of small hand tools. TIME: 15/20 minutes. AUTHORS: John E. and Dorothea M. Crawford. PUBLISHER: Psychological Corporation (*see* TEST PUBLISHERS).

creativity test, test that stresses divergent thinking or the ability to create new or original answers; considered useful for examining the culturally disadvantaged and certain ethnic groups whose command of English is not highly developed. Such tests utilize common and familiar objects in order to sample the testee's originality, flexibility, and fluency of thinking. Tasks include suggesting improvements in familiar devices such as telephones or listing many possible uses for a broom handle. The tests are scored simply on the number of acceptable answers given by the subject. *See* John A. Hattie, "Conditions for Administering Creativity Tests," *Psychological Bulletin* (November 1977).

credentialism, an emphasis on paper manifestations, such as college degrees, instead of an actual ability to accomplish the tasks of a job. For two attacks on the value of the credentials offered by higher education, *see* John Keats, *The Sheepskin Psychosis* (Philadelphia: J. B. Lippincott,

1965); Caroline Bird, *The Case Against College* (N.Y.: David McKay Co., 1975). For how to avoid the problem, *see* H. Dudley Dewhirst, "It's Time to Put the Brakes on Credentialism," *Personnel Journal* (October 1973). For a history, *see* Randall Collins, *The Credential Society: An Historical Sociology of Education and Stratification* (New York: Academic Press, 1979).

See also RESTRICTIVE CREDENTIALISM.

credit check, reference check on a prospective employee's financial standing. Such checks are usually only conducted when financial status may bear upon the job, as with bank tellers, for example.

credit union, not a labor union, but a cooperative savings and loan association.

credited service, employment time that an employee has for benefit purposes.

crisis bargaining, collective bargaining negotiations conducted under the pressure of a strike deadline.

crisis intervention, a formal effort to help an individual experiencing a crisis to reestablish equilibrium. A crisis is a turning point in a person's life. It can be the death of a child, spouse, or parent. It can be a heart attack. It can be anything that tests the limits of an individual's ability to cope. *See* Mike Berger, "Crisis Intervention in Personnel Administration," *Personnel Journal* (November 1969); William Getz et al., *Fundamentals of Crisis Counseling: A Handbook* (Lexington, Mass.: Lexington Books, 1974); Romaine V. Edwards, *Crisis Intervention and How it Works* (Springfield, Ill.: Charles C. Thomas, 1977); Morley D. Glicken, "Managing a Crisis Intervention Program," *Personnel Journal* (April 1982).

criterion, plural CRITERIA, measure of job performance or other work-related behavior against which performance on a test or other predictor measure is compared.

criterion contamination, influence on

criterion measures of variables or factors not relevant to the work behavior being measured. If the criterion is, for example, a set of supervisory ratings of competence in job performance and if the ratings are correlated with the length of time the supervisor has known the individual people he/she rates, then the length of acquaintance is a contaminant of the criterion measure. Similarly, if the amount of production on a machine is counted as the criterion measure and if the amount of production depends in part on the age of the machine being used, then age of machinery is a contaminant of production counts.

criterion objective: see PERFORMANCE OBJECTIVE.

criterion-referenced test, test by which a candidate's performance is measured according to the degree a specified criterion has been met. See W. James Popham, *Criterion-Referenced Measurement* (Englewood Cliffs, N.J.: Prentice-Hall, 1978); Frank L. Schmidt and John E. Hunter, "The Future of Criterion-Related Validity," *Personnel Psychology* (Spring 1980); Leonard Berger, "The Promise of Criterion-Referenced Performance Appraisal (CRPA)," *Review of Public Personnel Administration* (Summer 1983).

criterion related validation: see STATISTICAL VALIDATION.

criterion relevance, judgment of the degree to which a criterion measure reflects the important aspects of job performance. Such a judgment is based on an understanding of the measurement process itself, of the job and worker requirements as revealed through careful job analysis, and of the needs of the organization.

critical-incident method, also called CRITICAL-INCIDENT TECHNIQUE, identifying, classifying and recording significant examples—critical incidents—of an employee's behavior for purposes of performance evaluation. The theory behind the critical-incidents approach holds that there are certain key acts of behavior that make the difference between success and failure. After the incidents are collected they can be ranked in order of frequency and importance and assigned numerical weights. Once scored, they can be equally as useful for employee development and counseling as for formal appraisals. For the pioneering work on the concept, see John C. Flanagan, "The Critical Incident Technique," *Psychological Bulletin* (July 1954); John C. Flanagan and Robert K. Burns, "The Employee Performance Record: A New Approach and Development Tool," *Harvard Business Review* (September–October 1957). *Also see* John M. Champion and John H. James, *Critical Incidents in Management* (Homewood, Ill.: Richard D. Irwin, Inc., 4th ed., 1980).

critical path method (CPM), network-analysis technique for planning and scheduling. The "critical path" is a sequence of activities that connect the beginning and end of events or program accomplishments. See J. D. Wiest and F. K. Levy, *A Management Guide to PERT/CPM* (Englewood Cliffs, N.J.: Prentice-Hall, 2nd ed., 1977).

critical score: see CUTTING SCORE.

cross-examine, to question the opposition witnesses during a trial or hearing.

cross-check, procedure by which the National Labor Relations Board or an appropriate state agency compares union authorization cards to an employer's payroll to determine whether a majority of the employees wish union representation. With the employer's consent, such a cross-check can bring union recognition and certification without a formal hearing and election.

cross picketing, picketing by more than one union when each claims to represent the workforce.

cross validation, process which seeks to apply the results of one validation study to another. As such, it is a check on the accuracy of the original validation study.

Crozier, Michel J. (1922–   ), French sociologist whose book, *The Bureaucratic Phenomenon* (Chicago: University of Chicago Press, 1964), is considered by Howard E. McCurdy to be "the best empirical study of bureaucratic behavior since the Hawthorne studies." *Also see The Stalled Society* (New York: Viking Press, 1973).

crude score: *see* RAW SCORE.

CTMM: *see* CALIFORNIA TEST OF MENTAL MATURITY.

CTMM/SF: *see* CALIFORNIA SHORT FORM TEST OF MENTAL MATURITY.

cultural bias, in the context of employee selection, cultural bias refers to the indirect and incidental (as opposed to direct and deliberate) bias of individuals and instruments making selection decisions. Also, the propensity of a test to reflect favorable or unfavorable effects of certain types of cultural backgrounds. *See* Ollie A. Jensen, "Cultural Bias in Selection," *Public Personnel Review* (April 1966).

culturally disadvantaged, groups that do not have full participation in U.S. society because of low incomes, substandard housing, poor education, and other "atypical" environmental experiences.

culture-fair test, also called CULTURE-FREE TEST, a test yielding results that are not culturally biased. For an analysis, *see* R. L. Thorndike, "Concepts of Culture-Fairness," *Journal of Educational Measurement* (Summer 1971).

cumulative band chart: *see* BAND CURVE CHART.

cumulative frequency, sum of successively added frequencies (usually) of test scores.

cumulative frequency chart, graphic presentation of a cumulative frequency distribution, which has the frequencies expressed in terms of the number of cases or as a percentage of all cases.

cumulative percentage, cumulative frequency expressed as a percentage.

CUPA: *see* COLLEGE AND UNIVERSITY PERSONNEL ASSOCIATION.

current dollar, the dollar value of a good or service in terms of prices current at the time the good or service was sold. This is in contrast to the value of the good or service in constant dollars.
   See also CONSTANT DOLLAR.

Current Wage Developments, U.S. Bureau of Labor Statistics' monthly report about collective bargaining settlements and unilateral management decisions about wages and benefits.
   Current Wage Developments
   Superintendent of Documents
   Government Printing Office
   Washington, D.C. 20402

curricular validity, degree to which an examination is representative of the body of knowledge for which it is testing.

curriculum vita: *see* RESUME.

cutback, workforce reduction that results in layoffs.

cutting score, also called CRITICAL SCORE, PASSING SCORE, or PASSING POINT, test score used as an employment requirement. Those at or above such a score are eligible for selection or promotion, whereas those below the score are not.
   There are many approaches to establishing the cutting score. Perhaps the most defensible is one of the job-related approaches (*e.g.*, using data from a criterion-related validity study). A common and practical approach is the *flexible passing score*, which is established for each test on the basis of a number of factors (some of which, such as the number of positions to be filled, may not be job-related). Arbitrari-

ly establishing a cutting score of 70 percent in an attempt to be certain all eligibles possess the traits desired for a job (the *70-percent syndrome*) is not defensible from a psychometric point of view and has resulted in the costly situation where no applicants are eligible after taking a difficult test. *See* Glenn G. McClung, *Considerations in Developing Test Passing Points* (Chicago: International Personnel Management Association, 1974).

See also MULTIPLE CUTTING SCORE.

cycle time: *see* JOB SCOPE.

cyclical unemployment, unemployment caused by a downward trend in the business cycle.

D

DAF: *see* DECISION-ANALYSIS FORECASTING.

Daily Labor Report, this Bureau of National Affairs, Inc., report gives Monday through Friday notification of all significant developments in the labor field. Covers congressional activities, court and NLRB decisions, arbitration, union developments, key contract negotiations, and settlements.

daily rate, basic pay earned by an employee for a standard work day.

Dale, Ernest (1917-), a leading authority on management and leadership who asserted that executive ability was not necessarily transferable among organizations and cultures. Major works include: *The Great Organizers* (N.Y.: McGraw-Hill, 1960); *Staff in Organization*, with L. F. Urwick (N.Y.: McGraw-Hill, 1960); *Management: Theory and Practice* (N.Y.: McGraw-Hill, 1965); *Modern Management Methods*, with C. C. Michelon (Cleveland: World Publishing, 1965).

Danbury Hatters' **case:** *see* LAWLOR V. LOEWE.

danger-zone bonus, bonus paid to employees as an inducement to get them to work in an area that is especially hazardous.

Darby Lumber **case:** *see* UNITED STATES V. DARBY LUMBER.

Darlington **case:** *see* TEXTILE WORKERS V. DARLINGTON MANUFACTURING COMPANY.

DAT: *see* DIFFERENTIAL APTITUDE TESTS.

data, *datum* is a single bit of information; *data* is the plural of datum.

data bank, also called DATA BASE, information stored in a computer system so that any particular item or set of items could be extracted or organized as needed. Data bank (or data base) is also used to refer to any data-storage system.

datum: *see* DATA.

Davis-Bacon Act of 1931, also called PREVAILING WAGE LAW, federal law passed in 1931, which requires contractors on federal construction projects to pay the rates of pay and fringe benefits that prevail in their geographic areas. Prevailing rates are determined by the Secretary of Labor and must be paid on all federal contracts and subcontracts of $2,000.00 or more. For an economic analysis of the impact of the act, *see* Armand J. Thieblot, Jr., *et al., The Davis-Bacon Act* (Phila.: The Wharton School of the University of Pennsylvania, 1975). *Also see* Robert S. Goldfarb and John F. Morrall III, "The Davis-Bacon Act: An Appraisal of Recent Studies," *Industrial and Labor Relations Review* (January 1981).

Davis, Keith (1918-), sometimes called "Mr. Human Relations" because his work marks the beginning of the modern view of human relations with its empirical approach to understanding organizational behavior. Major works include: *Human*

Relations in Business (N.Y.: McGraw-Hill, 1957); Human Relations at Work (N.Y.: McGraw-Hill, 1962); Business and Its Environment, with R. L. Blomstron (N.Y.: McGraw-Hill, 1966); Human Behavior at Work (N.Y.: McGraw-Hill, 1977).

Davis Reading Test, this test yields two scores measuring the level and speed of reading comprehension. Used by business and industry in employee training and development and in assessment centers. TIME: 40/55 minutes. AUTHORS: F. B. and C. C. Davis. PUBLISHER: Psychological Corporation (see TEST PUBLISHERS).

Davis v. Passman, 60 L.Ed. 2d 846 (1979), U.S. Supreme Court case, which held that a woman discharged from employment by a U.S. congressman had the 5th Amendment right to seek to recover damages from the congressman for alleged sex discrimination.
See also CONGRESSIONAL EXEMPTION.

day care, a newly emerging employee fringe benefit increasingly coming about because more than half of all mothers with children under six are now in the labor force. See Oscar Ornato and Carol Buckham, "Day Care: Still Waiting Its Turn as a Standard Benefit," Management Review (May 1983); Sheila B. Kamerman, "Child-Care Services: A National Picture," Monthly Labor Review (December 1983); Sandra L. Burud, Pamela R. Aschbacher and Jacquelyn McCroskey, Employer-Supported Child-Care: Investing in Human Resources (Dover, Mass.: Auburn House Publishing Co., 1984); Thomas I. Miller, "The Effects of Employer-Sponsored Child Care on Employee Absenteeism, Turnover, Productivity, Recruitment or Job Satisfaction: What is Claimed and What is Known," Personnel Psychology (Summer 1984).

day wage, earnings for a set number of hours per day.

daywork, regular day shift that is paid on the basis of time rather than output.

day worker, casual, usually unskilled, worker hired by the day.

dead time, time on the job lost by a worker through no fault of his own.

dead work, mining term that refers to required work (removing debris, rocks, etc.) that does not directly produce the material being mined.

deadheading, bypassing of more senior employees in order to promote a more qualified but more junior employee. In the transportation industry, deadheading refers to (1) the movement of empty vehicles to a place where they are needed and (2) the practice of providing free transportation for the company's employees.

Dean v. Gadsden Times Publishing Corp., 412 U.S. 543 (1973), Supreme Court case, which upheld an Alabama law providing that an employee called to serve on a jury "shall be entitled to his usual compensation received from such employment less the fee or compensation he received for serving" as a juror.

death benefit, benefit provided under a pension plan that is paid to an employee's survivors or estate. Payments may be made in monthly installments or in a lump sum.

Debs, Eugene V(ictor) (1855–1926), probably the most famous labor organizer of his time and Socialist Party candidate for president of the United States five times between 1900 and 1920. For biographies, see Ray Ginger, The Bending Cross: A Biography of Eugene Victor Debs (New Brunswick, N.J.: Rutgers University Press, 1949); Nick Salvatore, Eugene V. Debs: Citizen and Socialist (University of Illinois Press, 1982).

debugging, process of detecting, locating, and removing mistakes or imperfections from a computer program or any new system.

De Canas v. Bica, 424 U.S. 351 (1976),

U.S. Supreme Court case, which upheld a California statute penalizing those who employed illegal aliens when such employment decreased the employment of citizens and other aliens.

decertification petition, a formal request to the NLRB (or other appropriate administrative agency) that a decertification election be held. If the union loses, it will no longer have the right to represent workers in the bargaining unit where the election is held.

See CERTIFICATION.

decile, division that contains one tenth of whatever is being divided.

decision-analysis forecasting (DAF), variant of the Delphi Technique developed by the U.S. Civil Service Commission to assist senior management in forecasting manpower and organizational needs. It is specifically designed for use on problems where the experience and judgments of top-level policymakers comprise the basic and often the only information.

DAF develops its forecasts by: (1) "decomposing" each manpower planning problem into its relevant factors, (2) quantifying subjective preferences and probability judgments for each problem factor and (3) combining the available data plus these quantified judgments into a table of predictions. The methodology draws largely on decision-analysis theory, using "decision trees" and some simple mathematics from probability theory.

For the complete methodology, see Bureau of Executive Manpower, U.S. Civil Service Commission, *Decision Analysis Forecasting for Executive Manpower Planning* (Wash., D.C.: U.S. Government Printing Office, June 1974). *Also see* Jacob W. Uivila and Rex V. Brown, "Decision Analysis Comes of Age," *Harvard Business Review* (September–October 1982).

See also DELPHI TECHNIQUE.

decisionmaking, career or occupational: *see* CAREER DECISIONMAKING.

decision rule, any directive established to make decisions in the face of uncertainty. For example, a payroll office might be given a decision rule to deduct one hour's pay from an employee's wages for each lateness that exceeds ten minutes but is less than one hour.

decision table, a tabular presentation of the various factors associated with, as well as the decision options for, a given problem.

Grant level procedure									
Conditions	Rules								
	1	2	3	4	5	6	7	8	9
Live at home	Y	Y	Y	N	N	N	N	N	N
Married	Y	Y	N	Y	N	N	Y	–	N
Over 21	Y	N	–	–	Y	N	–	Y	N
Live in college	–	–	–	N	N	N	Y	Y	Y
Actions									
Grant level 1			X	X					
Grant level 2	X					X			X
Grant level 3				X	X				
Appeal possible if hardship	X	X							
Query procedure								X	X

Limited entry decision table

Source: D. Hawgood, Business Data Processing *(New York: Facts on File, 1984), p. 72.*

decision theory, a body of knowledge concerned with the nature and processes of decisionmaking. Decision theory abstracts given situations into a more structured problem which calls for the decisionmaker to deal with the situation by an objective judgment. Frequently dependent upon quantitative analysis, decision theory is also called *statistical decision theory* and *Bayesian decision theory.* Bayesian refers to Thomas Bayes (1702–1761) who provided a mathematical basis for probability inference. See John W. Boudreau, "Decision Theory Contributions to HRM Research and Practice," *Industrial Relations* (Spring 1984).

decision tree, graphic method of presenting various decisional alternatives so that the various risks, information needs and courses of action are visually available to

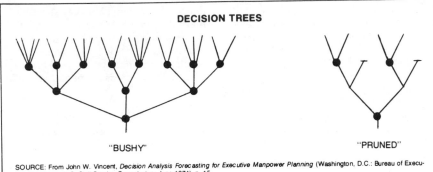

DECISION TREES

"BUSHY"

"PRUNED"

SOURCE: From John W. Vincent, *Decision Analysis Forecasting for Executive Manpower Planning* (Washington, D.C.: Bureau of Executive Manpower, U.S. Civil Service Commission, June 1974), p. 15.

the decisionmaker. The various decisional alternatives are displayed in the form of a tree with nodes and branches. Each branch represents an alternative course of action or decision, which leads to a node which represents an event. Thus, a decision tree shows both the different courses of action available as well as their possible outcomes. According to John F. Magee, in "Decision Trees for Decision Making," *Harvard Business Review* (July-August 1964), making a decision tree requires management to:

1. identify the points of decision and alternatives available at each point;
2. identify the points of uncertainty and the type or range of alternative outcomes at each point;
3. estimate the values needed to make the analysis, especially the probabilities of different events or results of action and the costs and gains of various events and actions; and
4. analyze the alternative values to choose a course.

decruitment, slang term for the process of recycling older middle- and top-level managers into lower-level, lower-paying positions. The concept was pioneered in Denmark, where some employers freeze promotions for managers at age 50 and start decruiting them at age 60. *See* Yitzchak M. Shkop and Esther M. Shkop, "Job Modification as An Alternative to Retirement," *Personnel Journal* (July 1982).

deduction, any amount for any reason that is withheld from an employee's pay and credited toward a legitimate purpose such as taxes, insurance, United Fund, etc.

deferred annuity, annuity that does not start until after a specified period or until the annuitant reaches a specified age.

deferred compensation, withholding of a portion of current earnings until a later time, usually retirement, when the receiver would likely be in a lower income-tax bracket. *See* George H. Cauble, "Deferred Compensation: An Employee Income and Tax Deferral Plan That is as Good as it Sounds," *Public Personnel Management* (Summer 1983).

deferred full vesting, pension plan that provides that an employee retains rights to accrued benefits if he or she is terminated after a specified age and/or after he or she completes a specified period of service in the organization.

deferred graded vesting, pension plan that provides that an employee acquires a right to a specified percentage of accrued benefits if and when he or she meets the participation requirements stipulated by the plan.

deferred life annuity, annuity that becomes effective at a specified future date. If death occurs before the specified date, no benefits are paid. Once the annuity has started, it continues only for the life of the insured.

deferred rating system, for most federal government positions at GS-9 and above, and for most scientific positions, vacancies are filled under a deferred rating system. There are no "standings" on one of these registers and no numerical score is assigned at time of application, since applications are not rated until specific vacancies become available. Candidates are rated and referred for appointment consideration on the basis of their relative qualifications for a particular position. The best-qualified applicants will be placed at the top of the list of eligibles and will be referred to the agency for employment consideration on the basis of their qualifications and according to the laws regarding veterans' preference and appointment. The names of all other applicants will be returned to the register for possible consideration at a later time.

deferred wage increase, negotiated pay increase that does not become effective until a specified future date.

defined benefit plan, a pension plan which includes a formula for calculating retirement benefits (such as a specified percent of earnings or flat dollar amount per year of service) and obligates the employer to provide the benefits so determined. Therefore, employer contributions are not fixed, but are whatever is needed, together with earnings of pension fund investments, to finance the required benefits.

defined contribution plan, a pension plan that obligates the employer to contribute money to a pension fund according to a formula (such as a specified percent of earnings). Benefits are not fixed, but depend on the amount of employer contributions and the earnings of pension fund investments.

DeFunis v. Odegaard, 416 U.S. 312 (1974), U.S. Supreme Court case, concerning a white male who was denied admission to law school at the same time minority applicants with lesser academic credentials were accepted. DeFunis challenged the school's action on the grounds that it denied him equal protection of the laws in violation of the fourteenth amendment. He was successful in local court and was admitted. On appeal, the school won a reversal in the state supreme court. Nevertheless, DeFunis remained in law school pending further action by the U.S. Supreme Court. As the nation awaited a definitive resolution of the issue of reverse discrimination, the Supreme Court sought to avoid the problem. Since DeFunis had completed all but his last quarter of law school and was not in danger of being denied his diploma no matter what was decided, a majority of the justices seized upon this fact and declared that the case was consequently "moot"—that it was beyond the court's power to render decisions on hypothetical matters of only potential constitutional substance. See Allan P. Sindler, *Bakke, DeFunis, and Minority Admissions: The Quest for Equal Opportunity* (New York: Longman, 1978).

See also the following entries:
REGENTS OF THE UNIVERSITY OF CALIFORNIA V. ALLEN BAKKE
REVERSE DISCRIMINATION
UNITED STEELWORKERS OF AMERICA V. WEBER, ET AL.

degrees, gradations used in the point-rating method of job evaluation to differentiate among job factors.

dehiring, generally, any means of encouraging a marginal or unsatisfactory employee to quit as an alternative to being fired. This face-saving technique allows an organization to: (1) avoid the distasteful aftermath of firing an employee, (2) avoid the implication that someone made a mistake in hiring the employee, (3) avoid the adverse effect of the public thinking that the company is not a secure place in which to be employed, and (4) protect the feelings of the employee involved. See Lawrence L. Steinmetz, *Managing the Marginal and Unsatisfactory Performer,* (Reading, Mass.: Addison-Wesley Publishing Company, 1969).

delegation, designating or appointing of a person with the power to act as one's representative or agent in specified matters. A delegation of authority in an organizational sense may be implied in statements of responsibility for functional entities or group endeavors but can also be documented by other methods. Certain delegations that are granted to a single individual may be restricted as to any further redelegations (*e.g.*, it could restrict a senior clerk from delegating some disagreeable task that clerk was responsible for to a junior clerk). Delegation of authority begins at the executive level and filters down through an organization to workers themselves who must have enough authority to make decisions called for in their daily tasks.

delphi method, a procedure for forecasting specific technological and social events. Experts are asked to give their best judgment as to the probability of a specific event occurring. The results are collated and then returned to the original experts for their perusal along with an opportunity to revise their own predictions. Revised estimates with supporting arguments are then recorded and recirculated again and again; in theory, the feedback always narrows the range of answers. In the end, a group prophecy will have been arrived at without the possibility of distortion from face-to-face contact, leadership influences, or the pressure of group dynamics. *See* Harold A. Linstone and Murray Turoff (eds.), *The Delphi Method: Techniques and Applications* (Reading, Mass.: Addison-Wesley Publishing Co., 1975); John Rohrbaugh, "Improving the Quality of Group Judgment: Social Judgment Analysis and the Delphi Technique," *Organizational Behavior and Human Performance* (August 1979); Gregory W. Fischer, "When Oracles Fail—A Comparison of Four Procedures for Aggregating Subjective Probability Forecasts." *Organizational Behavior and Human Performance* (August 1981).

demand, the strength of buyer desire for and willingness to pay for a product or service.

de minimus, short form of *de minimus non curat lex;* Latin for "the law does not bother with trifles."

demotion, reassignment of an employee to a job of lower status, responsibility, and pay. There are three basic kinds of demotions: (1) *voluntary demotion,* is usually the result of a reduction in force; the employee takes a job of lower status and pay rather than being laid off; (2) *involuntary demotion* results from a worker's inability to perform adequately on the job; (3) *disciplinary demotion* usually takes place after an employee has been repeatedly warned to stop some kind of misconduct or disruptive behavior. For the classic analysis of the problem, *see* F. H. Goldner, "Demotion in Industrial Management," *American Sociological Review* (October 1965). *Also see* Lynn Isabella and Douglas T. Hall, "Demotions and Career Growth," *Training and Development Journal* (April 1984).

dental plan, also called DENTAL INSURANCE, group insurance program, either contributory or noncontributory, that typically pays for some portion of the following dental services for an employee and his/her family:
1. diagnostic and preventive services (oral examinations and prophylaxis);
2. oral surgery;
3. restorative services (fillings and inlays);
4. endodontic treatment (root canal therapy);
5. periodontic treatment (treatment of gums);
6. prosthodontic services (dentures and bridgework); and
7. orthodontic services (straightening of teeth).

See Richard A. Harvey, "Designing a Corporate Dental Plan," *Compensation Review (Third Quarter 1975).*

See also SUPPLEMENTAL MEDICAL INSURANCE.

departmental seniority, also called UNIT SENIORITY, seniority based on years of service in a particular subsection of a larger organization as opposed to seniority based simply on total years of service to the larger organization, company, or governmental jurisdiction.

dependent variable, factor in an experimental relationship, which has or shows variation that is hypothesized to be caused by another independent factor or variable.

derivative violation: see UNFAIR LABOR PRACTICES (EMPLOYERS).

derived score, any test score that is obtained after some statistical treatment or manipulation of the raw score.

Derwent, Clarence (1884-1959), president of the Actor's Equity Association from 1946 to 1952. For an autobiography, see *The Derwent Story: My First Fifty Years in the Theatre in England and America* (N.Y.: H. Schuman, 1953).

descriptive average, estimate of a mean based upon incomplete data.

desk audit, also called JOB AUDIT, review of the duties and responsibilities of a position through an interview with the incumbent and/or the incumbent's supervisor made at the employee's desk or regular place of work.

detail, temporary assignment of an employee to a different position for a specified period with the assumption that the employee will return to "normal" duties at the end of the detail. Technically, a position cannot be "filled" by a detail, as the employee continues to be the incumbent of the position from which he was detailed.

Detroit Edison Company v. National Labor Relations Board, 59 L.Ed. 2d 333 (1979), U.S. Supreme Court case, which held that the NLRB could not order an employer to provide testing information to a union without the examinee's consent.

deviation, amount by which a score differs from a reference value such as the mean or the norm.

dexterity test, also called PSYCHOMOTOR TEST, any testing device that seeks to determine the motor/mechanical skills of an individual.

diagnostic test, any testing device that is primarily designed to identify the nature and/or source of an individual's disabilities.

Dickson, William J. (1904–   ), chief of the Employee Relations Research Department at the Hawthorne Works of the Western Electric Company during the famous Hawthorne experiments. As such, he collaborated with the Harvard research group led by Elton Mayo. He was co-author, with F.J. Roethlisberger, of the definitive account of the experiments, *Management and the Worker* (Cambridge, Mass.: Harvard University Press, 1939). He also wrote, again with Roethlisberger, *Counseling in An Organization* (Cambridge, Mass.: Harvard University Press, 1966).

dicta, in its most common usage, dicta is that portion of the opinion of a judge that is not the essence of the judge's decision. In the context of arbitration, dicta becomes any opinion or recommendation an arbitrator expresses in making an award that is not necessarily essential to the resolution of the dispute. According to Anthony V. Sinicropi and Peter A. Veglahn, in "Dicta in Arbitration Awards: An Aid or Hindrance?" *Labor Law Journal* (September 1972),

by using dicta, the arbitrator can clarify obligations of the parties in their collective bargaining relationship. Conversely, the arbitrator may upset a mutually acceptable understanding by the parties with his gratuitous advice on an issue. Dicta can either strengthen and stabilize a collective bargaining relationship or emasculate that relationship. Obviously, the parties are free to disregard the arbitrator's views as expressed in dicta.

Dictionary of Occupational Titles (DOT), the DOT is an outgrowth of the needs of the public employment service system for a comprehensive body of standardized occupational information for purposes of job placement, employment counseling and occupational career guidance. Now in its fourth edition, the DOT includes standardized and comprehensive descriptions of job duties and related information for 20,000 occupations, covers nearly all jobs in the U.S. economy, groups occupations into a systematic occupational classification structure based on interrelationships of job tasks and requirements, and is designed as a job-placement tool to facilitate matching job requirements and worker skills. *See* Employment and Training Administration, U.S. Department of Labor, *Dictionary of Occupational Titles* (Washington, D.C.: Government Printing Office, 4th ed., 1977). *Also see* Ann R. Miller and Others, *Work, Jobs, and Occupations: A Critical Review of the Dictionary of Occupational Titles* (Washington, D.C.: National Academy Press, 1980); Pamela S. Cain and Donald J. Treiman, "The Dictionary of Occupational Titles as a Source of Occupational Data," *American Sociological Review* (June 1981).

See also UNITED STATES EMPLOYMENT SERVICES.

Diemer, Hugo (1870-1939), a pioneer in the teaching of management at the college level and the author of a highly influential text, *Factory Organization and Administration* (New York: McGraw-Hill, 1910; fifth edition, 1935).

Diemer Plan, wage-incentive plan providing for normal day rates, plus an increase of 0.05 percent for each one percent of production above the standard, with a 10 percent bonus.

differential, displacement: *see* DISPLACEMENT DIFFERENTIAL.

Differential Aptitude Tests (DAT), battery of aptitude tests designed for educational and vocational guidance. Provides a profile of relative strengths and weaknesses in eight abilities (verbal reasoning, numerical ability, abstract reasoning, clerical speed and accuracy, mechanical reasoning, space relations, spelling, and language usage). TIME: Approximately 3 hours. AUTHORS: G.K. Bennett, H. G. Seashore, and A. G. Wesman. PUBLISHER: Psychological Corporation (*see* TEST PUBLISHERS).

differential piece work, also DIFFERENTIAL PIECE RATE, wage program in which the money rate per piece is determined by the total number of pieces produced over a time period—usually a day.

See also TAYLOR DIFFERENTIAL PIECE-RATE PLAN.

differentials, increases in wage rates because of shift work or other conditions generally considered to be undesirable. *See* Graef S. Crystal, "The Re-emergence of Industry Pay Differentials," *Compensation Review* (Third Quarter 1983). *See also* the following entries:

NIGHT DIFFERENTIAL
SKILL DIFFERENTIAL
WAGE DIFFERENTIAL

differential user charge, any user charge scaled to meet the requirements of different kinds of customers, levels of usage, time or season of use, etc.

differential validation, also called DIFFERENTIAL PREDICTION, the underlying assumption of differential validation/prediction holds that different tests or test scores might predict differently for different groups. Some social groups, because of a variety of sociological factors, tend to score lower (higher) than other groups on the same test.

difficulty index, any of a variety of indexes used to indicate the difficulty of a test question. The percent of some specified group, such as students of a given age or grade, who answer an item correctly is an example of such an index.

diffusion index, a statistical measure of the overall behavior of a group of economic time series. It indicates the percentage of series expanding in the selected group. If one-half of the series in the group are rising over a given time span, the diffusion index value equals 50. The limits of a diffusion index are 0 and 100. As an analytical measure, the diffusion index is helpful in indicating the spread of economic movements from one industry to another and from one economic process to another.

diminishing marginal utility of income, the principle that suggests that the marginal value of an additional dollar of income to a rich person is less than to a poor person. This concept is a mainstay of progressive taxation because it suggests that graduated income taxes will have less of a negative effect on wealthier members of the community than on those with less wealth. Proportionally larger tax payments by those with higher incomes recognizes the diminishing marginal utility of income.

directed interview, also NONDIRECTIVE INTERVIEW, the *directed interview* has the interviewer in full control of the interview content, typically soliciting answers to a variety of specific questions. In the *nondirective interview*, in contrast, it is more the responsibility of the interviewee to determine the subjects to be discussed.
See also INTERVIEW.

direct labor, also INDIRECT LABOR, *direct labor* consists of work performed on a product that is a specific contribution to its completion. *Indirect labor* consists of all overhead and support activities that do not contribute directly to the completion of a product. *See* Robert V. Penfield, "A Guide to the Computation and Evaluation of Direct Labor Costs," *Personnel Journal* (June 1976).

director of personnel: *see* PERSONNEL DIRECTOR.

direct relief: *see* RELIEF.

disability, also called WORK DISABILITY, according to Sar A. Levitan and Robert Taggart, *Jobs for the Disabled* (Baltimore: Johns Hopkins University Press, 1977), "there are essentially two interrelated dimensions of work disability: the presence or perception of physical or mental handicaps and a reduced work capacity." *See* Robert B. Nathanson, "The Disabled Employee: Separating Myth from Fact," *Harvard Business Review* (May–June 1977); Robert B. Nathanson and Jeffrey Lambert, "Integrating Disabled Employees into the Workplace," *Personnel Journal* (February 1981); Nancy J. Schweitzer and John Deely, "Interviewing the Disabled Job Applicant," *Personnel Journal* (March 1982).
Also see HANDICAPPED.

disability insurance, insurance designed to compensate individuals who lose wages because of illness or injuries.

disability retirement, retirement caused by a physical inability to perform on the job. *See* D. Bell and W. Wiatrowski, "Disability Benefits for Employees in Private Pension Plans," *Monthly Labor Review* (August 1982).

disabled veteran, veteran of the armed services who has a service-connected disability and is rated 10 percent or more disabled by the Veterans Administration. Disabled veterans generally have the right to a 10-point bonus on federal government entrance examinations. Many state and local governments offer similar advantages.
See also VETERANS PREFERENCE.

disadvantaged, culturally: *see* CULTURALLY DISADVANTAGED.

disadvantaged workers, usually unemployed or underemployed and either a member of a minority group, handicapped, or over 45 years of age. They tend to have lower education rates and higher criminal-arrest rates than the rest of the population. *See* Lloyd Zimpel (ed.), *The Disadvantaged Worker: Readings in*

Developing Minority Manpower (Reading, Mass.: Addison Wesley, 1971); James L. Koch, "Employing the Disadvantaged: Lessons from the Past Decade," *California Management Review* (Fall 1974); Daphne Williams Nitri, "Training the Economically Disadvantaged," *Training and Development Journal* (September 1980).

disaffiliation, withdrawal of a local union from its national or international union membership or the withdrawal of a national or international union from its federation membership. When a federation or national union initiates disaffiliation, the process is more properly called suspension or expulsion.

discharge: *see* DISMISSAL.

discharge, discriminatory: *see* DISCRIMINATORY DISCHARGE.

discharge warning, formal notice to an employee that he or she will be discharged if unsatisfactory work behavior continues.

disciplinary action, any action short of dismissal taken by an employer against an employee for a violation of company policy. *See* Walter E. Baer, *Discipline and Discharge Under the Labor Agreement* (N.Y.: American Management Associations, 1972); Edward L. Harrison, "Legal Restrictions on the Employer's Authority to Discipline," *Personnel Journal* (February 1982); Ira G. Asherman, "The Corrective Discipline Process," *Personnel Journal* (July 1982); Dan Cameron, "The When, Why and How of Discipline," *Personnel Journal* (July 1984).

See also ADVERSE ACTION and NATIONAL LABOR RELATIONS BOARD V. J. WEINGARTEN, INC.

disciplinary demotion: *see* DEMOTION.

disciplinary fine, fine that a union may levy against a member for violating a provision of the union's bylaws. *See* Dell Bush Johannesen, "Disciplinary Fines as Interference with Protected Rights: Section 8(6)(1) (A)," *Labor Law Journal* (May 1973).

disciplinary layoff, suspension of an employee as punishment for violating some rule or policy.

discipline: *see* the following entries:
ADMONITION
ADVERSE ACTION
DISCIPLINARY ACTION
PREVENTIVE DISCIPLINE
PROGRESSIVE DISCIPLINE
REPRIMAND
SLIDE-RULE DISCIPLINE

discipline clause, provision of a collective bargaining agreement that stipulates the means for disciplining workers who violate management or union rules.

discount, employee: *see* EMPLOYEE DISCOUNT.

discouraged workers, also called HIDDEN UNEMPLOYED, persons who want to work but are not seeking employment because of a belief that such an effort would be fruitless. For analyses, *see* Paul O. Flaim, "Discouraged Workers and Changes in Unemployment," *Monthly Labor Review* (March 1973); Joseph L. Gastwirth, "Estimating the Number of 'Hidden Unemployed'," *Monthly Labor Review* (March 1973); T. Aldrich Finegan, "Discouraged Workers and Economic Fluctuations," *Industrial and Labor Relations Review* (October 1981); Donald R. Williams, "Young Discouraged Workers: Racial Differences

Discouraged workers by when last worked and, for those who worked the previous year, reasons for leaving last job, 1979–83					
[Numbers in thousands]					
When last worked and reason for leaving last job	1979	1980	1981	1982	1983
Total	766	993	1 103	1 567	1 641
Never worked	101	155	141	223	229
Last worked more than 5 years ago	158	217	221	339	332
Last worked 1 to 5 years ago	251	288	366	536	625
Worked last year	255	334	375	469	454
Left job because of:					
School, family	40	54	63	62	57
Health	16	10	15	12	10
Retirement	8	8	11	17	16
Economic problems	125	180	202	268	280
Other reasons	67	82	83	109	92

Source: Paul O. Flaim, "Discouraged Workers: How Strong Are Their Links to the Job Market?" Monthly Labor Review *(August 1983).*

Explored," *Monthly Labor Review* (June 1984).

discriminant validity, evidence that a measure of a construct is indeed measuring that construct.

discrimination, in the context of employment, the failure to treat equals equally. Whether deliberate or unintentional, any action that has the effect of limiting employment and advancement opportunities because of an individual's sex, race, color, age, national origin, religion, physical handicap, or other irrelevant criteria is discrimination. Because of the EEO and civil rights legislation of recent years, individuals aggrieved by unlawful discrimination now have a variety of administrative and judicial remedies open to them. Employment discrimination has its origins in the less genteel concept of bigotry. For the standard history, *see* Gustavus Myers, *History of Bigotry in the United States,* edited and revised by Henry M. Christman (N.Y.: Capricorn Books, 1943, 1960). *Also see* William P. Murphy, Julius G. Getman and James E. Jones, Jr., *Discrimination in Employment,* 4th ed. (Washington, D.C.: Bureau of National Affairs, Inc., 1979).
　　See also the following entries:
　　AGE DISCRIMINATION
　　CIVIL RIGHTS ACT OF 1964
　　EQUAL EMPLOYMENT OPPORTUNITY
　　EQUAL EMPLOYMENT OPPORTUNITY
　　　ACT OF 1972
　　IMPACT THEORY OF DISCRIMINATION
　　INSTITUTIONAL DISCRIMINATION
　　INTERNATIONAL BROTHERHOOD OF
　　　TEAMSTERS V. UNITED STATES
　　MCDONNELL DOUGLAS CORP.
　　　V. GREEN
　　NATIONAL ORIGIN DISCRIMINATION
　　RELIGIOUS DISCRIMINATION
　　REVERSE DISCRIMINATION
　　RIGHTFUL PLACE
　　SEX DISCRIMINATION
　　SYSTEMIC DISCRIMINATION
　　THIRD-PARTY ALLEGATIONS OF
　　　DISCRIMINATION
　　UNFAIR LABOR PRACTICES
　　　(EMPLOYERS)
　　UNFAIR LABOR PRACTICES (UNIONS)
　　WASHINGTON V. DAVIS

discrimination index, any of a variety of indexes used to indicate the extent to which a test item differentiates among examinees with respect to some criterion (such as the test as a whole).

discriminatory discharge, dismissal of an employee for union activity. This is an unfair labor practice. *See* Joseph L. Gastwirth, "Statistical Methods for Analyzing Claims of Employment Discrimination," *Industrial and Labor Relations Review* (October 1984).

dishonest graft: *see* HONEST GRAFT.

dismissal, also called DISCHARGE, management's removal of an employee from employment. *See* Robert W. Fisher, "When Workers Are Discharged—An Overview: A Special Report on the Handling of Dismissal Cases in U.S. Law, Contract and Custom," *Monthly Labor Review* (June 1973); Erwin S. Stanton, "The Discharged Employee and the EEO Laws," *Personnel Journal* (March 1976); Clyde W. Summers, "Protecting *All* Employees Against Unjust Dismissal," *Harvard Business Review* (January-February 1980); Frederick Brown, "Limiting Your Risks in the New Russian Roulette—Discharging Employees," *Employee Relations Law Journal* (Winter 1982-83); Gail Frommer Brod, "The NLRB Changes Its Policy on the Legality of an Employer's Discharge of a Disloyal Supervisor," *Labor Law Journal* (January 1983); Larry D. Farley and Joseph J. Allotta, "Standards of Proof in Discharge Arbitration: A Practitioner's View," *Labor Law Journal* (July 1984).
　　See also the following entries:
　　BISHOP V. WOOD
　　BOARD OF REGENTS V. ROTH
　　HINES V. ANCHOR MOTOR FREIGHT
　　MCDONALD V. CITY OF WEST BRANCH,
　　　MICHIGAN
　　SAMPSON V. MURRAY
　　UNFAIR LABOR PRACTICES
　　　(EMPLOYERS)

dismissal pay: *see* SEVERANCE PAY.

disparate effect, tendency of an employment screening device or criteria to limit the appointment opportunities of women and minorities at a greater rate than for nonminority males.

displaced employee, employee of the federal government who is serving or who last served under career or career-conditional appointment or an employee with competitive status who is serving or who last served with Group I or Group II tenure in an excepted position, when: (1) the employee has received a reduction-in-force notice and the employing agency determines that he or she cannot be placed on another position in his or her competitive area; (2) the employee declines to transfer within his or her function, or to accept a new assignment, to another commuting area, and the employing agency determines that he or she will not be placed in another position in his or her own commuting area; (3) the employee is receiving compensation for injuries (under subchapter 1, chapter 81, of title 5, U.S. Code); or (4) the employee is under age 60 or is a recovered disability annuitant or a disability annuitant restored to earning capacity. Federal civil service regulations require agencies to have in operation a positive program of placement assistance for their displaced employees.

See also GROUP I TENURE/GROUP II TENURE/GROUP III TENTURE.

displaced homemaker, usually a woman who has been caring for a family and has lost her means of support through divorce, separation, death, or the disabling of a spouse and has only the briefest work experience outside the home. See Tish Sommers and Laurie Shields, "Displaced Homemakers: 'Forced Retirement' Leaves Many Penniless," Civil Rights Digest (Winter 1978); Nancy C. Baker, New Lives for Former Wives: Displaced Homemakers (Garden City, N.Y.: Doubleday, 1980); Laurie Shields, Displaced Homemakers: Organizing for a New Life (New York: McGraw-Hill, 1980); Eileen Applebaum, Back to Work: Determinants of Women's Successful Re-entry (Boston Mass.: Auburn House Publishing Co., 1981).

displacement differential, compensation equal to the difference between an employee's regular pay and the rate of a temporary assignment caused by layoff or technological displacement. Such differentials are usually available only for a limited time.

disposable personal income, see PERSONAL INCOME.

distractors, also called FOILS, in multiple-choice examinations, the incorrect alternatives serve the function of being, and are called, distractors or foils.

distribution, bimodal: see BIMODAL DISTRIBUTION.

district council, a level of labor organization below the national union but above the locals. The district council is composed of local unions in a particular industry within a limited geographic area.

district court, also called FEDERAL DISTRICT COURT and U.S. DISTRICT COURT, court of original jurisdiction for most federal cases. This is the only federal court that holds trials where juries and witnesses are used. Each state has at least one district court. When equal employment opportunity problems cannot be resolved within an organization, they frequently spill over into the local, federal district court.

division of labor, also called FACTORY SYSTEM, production process that has individual workers specializing in the varying aspects of a larger task. The most famous and influential statement on the economic rationale of the factory system is found in Adam Smith's The Wealth of Nations (1776). Smith discusses the optimum organization of a pin factory and finds that, while traditional pin makers could produce a few dozen pins a day, pin workers organized in a factory with each performing a limited operation could produce tens of thousands a day. See Charles F. Sabel, Work and Politics: The Division of Labor in Industry (New York, Cambridge University Press, 1982).

dock, deduct a part of an employee's wages as a penalty for tardiness, absenteeism, breakage, etc.

doctrine of mutuality, according to Julius Rezler and S. John Insalata, "Doctrine of Mutuality: A Driving Force in American Labor Legislation," *Labor Law Journal* (May 1967), the

doctrine of labor mutuality basically contends that whenever a legal burden or restriction is imposed by a legislative act on a party to industrial relations, either the same burden or restriction should be imposed upon the other party or the restriction should be removed from the first party, too. The doctrine also implies that whenever a right or privilege is conferred by a legislative act on one of the parties, the same right or privilege should be conferred on the other party or be withdrawn from the first party, too.

DOL: *see* LABOR, DEPARTMENT OF.

dollar devaluation adjustments, an adjustment made to expatriate workers to compensate for the loss of purchasing power in the host country which is a direct result of a lower rate of exchange between the dollar and the host currency.

domicile, an individual's permanent legal residence. While an individual can legally have many residences, he or she can have only one domicile. Some government jurisdictions have residency requirements that require employees to be domiciled within the bounds of the jurisdiction. *See* Stephen L. Hayford, "Local Government Residency Requirements and Labor Relations: Implications and Choices for Public Administrators," *Public Administration Review* (September-October 1978).

See also MCCARTHY V. PHILADELPHIA CIVIL SERVICE COMMISSION.

Donovan, Raymond J. (1930-   ), Secretary of Labor from 1981 to 1985.

Dorchy v. Kansas, 272 U.S. 306 (1926), U.S. Supreme Court case, which held that there is no constitutional right to strike.

DOT: *see* DICTIONARY OF OCCUPATIONAL TITLES.

Dothard v. Rawlinson, 433 U.S. 321 (1977), U.S. Supreme Court case, which upheld an Alabama regulation that prohibits the employment of women as prison guards in "contact positions" (requiring continual close physical proximity to inmates) within the state's correctional facilities.

See also BONA FIDE OCCUPATIONAL QUALIFICATION.

dotted-line responsibility, a customer's obligations after signing. Where? On the "dotted-line." Or an obligation that organizational members have to consult with, but not report to, each other. This is reflective of the "dotted-line" connections that exist on organization charts.

double-breasting, a practice whereby a single management operates two (or more) legally different companies; one union, the other non-union. This is particularly common in the construction industry.

double-dipper, about 100,000 retired military personnel are employed by the federal government as civilian workers. Because they draw two government incomes, they are colloquially called double-dippers. The term is sometimes applied, with an intentional or unintentional lack of precision, to state and local government employees—even to elected officials—who also hold private sector jobs while occupying what are or are held to be full-time positions. More recently the term has been applied to civil service pensioners who also become eligible for social security retirement benefits. *See* Robert Dalrymple, Susan Grad and Duke Wilson, "Civil Service Retirement System Annuitants and Social Security," *Social Security Bulletin* (February 1983).

double indemnity: *see* ACCIDENTAL DEATH BENEFIT.

double time, penalty or premium rate of

pay for overtime work, for holiday or Sunday work, etc., amounting to twice the employee's regular hourly wage.

dovetail seniority, the combining of two or more seniority lists (for example, when different companies merge) into a master seniority list. Each employee retains his previously earned seniority even though he may thereafter be employed by a new employer.

downgrading, reassignment of an employee to a position having a lower rate of pay and/or lesser responsibilities.

Downs, Anthony (1940-), economist and policy analyst whose classic book on bureaucracy, *Inside Bureaucracy* (Boston: Little, Brown, 1967), sought to justify bureaucratic government on economic grounds and develop laws and propositions that would aid in predicting the behavior of bureaus and bureaucrats.

See also BUREAUCRACY.

down time, periods of inactivity while waiting for the repair, setup or adjustment of equipment.

down-time pay, payments for time spent idle because of equipment failures (or routine maintenance) that are clearly beyond the responsibility of the employee.

dramaturgy, manner in which an individual acts out or theatrically stages his or her organizational role. All organization members are involved in such impression management, as Victor A. Thompson, in *Modern Organization* (N.Y.: Alfred A. Knopf, 1961), indicates:

We must try to control the information or cues imparted to others in order to protect our representations of self and to control the impressions others form about us. We are all involved, therefore, in dramaturgy.

drawing account, fixed sum advanced to sales personnel at regular time intervals (weekly or monthly) or a limited amount against which the sales person can draw as needed during a predetermined time period so long as the outstanding balance does not reach a predetermined limit. Amounts so drawn must be paid back to the company out of commission earnings during the same time period.

Drawing accounts may be guaranteed or nonguaranteed. According to William J. Standon and Richard H. Buskirk, *Management of the Sales Force* (Homewood, Ill.: Richard D. Irwin, rev. ed., 1964),

under a nonguaranteed plan the advance is strictly a loan. If a salesperson does not earn enough in commissions to pay back the advanced funds in one time period, then the balance of the debt is carried over to the next period . . . . A guaranteed drawing account is operated in much the same fashion, with one big exception. At the end of a stated period, if a salesman's commissions total less than his draw, the debt is canceled. It is not carried forward, he starts with a clean slate. Thus, a guaranteed draw is much like a salary. As a result, a compensation method consisting of a commission plus a guaranteed drawing account is classed as a combination plan while a commission plus a nonguaranteed draw is still considered a straight commission plan.

Drucker, Peter F. (1909-), the pre-eminent philosopher of management, the world's best-selling management author, and the man usually credited with having invented "management by objectives." Major works include: *The Concept of the Corporation* (N.Y.: John Day Co., 1946); *The New Society* (N.Y.: Harper & Row, 1950); *The Practice of Management* (N.Y.: Harper & Row, 1954); *Managing for Results* (N.Y.: Harper & Row, 1964); *The Effective Executive* (N.Y.: Harper & Row, 1967); *The Age of Discontinuity* (N.Y.: Harper & Row, 1969); *Management: Tasks, Responsibilities, Practices* (N.Y.: Harper & Row, 1974). For a biography, *see* John J. Tarrant, *Drucker: The Man Who Invented Corporate Society* (N.Y.: Warner Books, 1976). *Also see* Alan M. Kantrow, "Why Read Peter Drucker?" *Harvard Business Review* (January–February 1980).

See also the following entries:
KNOWLEDGE WORKER
MANAGEMENT BY OBJECTIVES
PENSION FUND SOCIALISM

drug addiction, also DRUG ABUSE, *drug addiction* is any habitual use of a substance which leads to psychological and/or physiological dependence. *Drug abuse* consists of using drugs to one's physical, emotional and/or social detriment without being "formally" addicted. For the dimensions of the problem, see Pasquale A. Carone and Leonard W. Krinsky (eds.), *Drug Abuse in Industry* (Springfield, Ill.: Charles C. Thomas Publishers, 1973); Rolf E. Rogers and John T. C. Colbert, "Drug Abuse and Organizational Response: A Review and Evaluation," *Personnel Journal* (May 1975); Ken Jennings, "The Problem of Employee Drug Use and Remedial Alternatives," *Personnel Journal* (November 1977). For how drug-abuse cases have been handled in arbitration, see Kenneth Jennings, "Arbitrators and Drugs," *Personnel Journal* (October 1976). For the public employer's perspective, see George W. Noblit, Paul H. Radtke, and James G. Ross, *Drug Use and Public Employment: A Personnel Manual* (Chicago: International Personnel Management Association, 1975). For a legal perspective, see Peter A. Susser, "Legal Issues Raised by Drugs in the Workplace," *Labor Law Journal* (January 1985)

dry promotion, slang term for a promotion that offers an increase in status but no monetary increase.

dual-career couple, a husband and wife pursuing professional careers that both feel are equally important. This has important implications for recruitment and transfer polices: for example, one spouse may be unwilling to accept a move unless an appropriate job is also found for the other. See Francine S. Hall and Douglas T. Hall, *The Two-Career Couple* (Reading, Mass.: Addison-Wesley, 1979); Carole K. Holahan and Lucia A. Gilbert, "Conflict Between Major Life Roles: Women and Men

in Dual-Career Couples," *Human Relations* (June 1979); Richad E. Kopelman, Lyn Rosenweig and Laura H. Lally, "Dual-Career Couples: The Organizational Response," *Personnel Administrator* (September 1982); Howard Hayghe, "Married Couples: Work and Income Patterns," *Monthly Labor Review* (December 1983); Maria Helene Sekas, "Dual-Career Couples—A Corporate Challenge," *Personnel Administrator* (April 1984); Patricia A. Mathews, "The Changing Work Force: Dual-Career Couples and Relocation," *Personnel Administrator* (April 1984).

Dual Compensation Act of 1964, (Public Law 88-448), provides that civilian employees of the federal government shall not be entitled to receive basic compensation from more than one civilian office for more than an aggregate of 40 hours of work in any one calendar week (Sunday through Saturday). The act also contains a variety of exemptions.

dual ladder, also called PARALLEL LADDER, a variant of a career ladder, provides dual or parallel career hierarchies so that both professional and managerial employees will be afforded appropriate career advancement. See Bertram Schoner and Thomas Harrell, "The Questionable Dual Ladder," *Personnel* (January–February 1965); Fred Goldner and R. R. Ritti, "Professionalism as Career Immobility," *American Journal of Sociology* (March 1967); Carl L. Bellas, "The Dual Track Career System within the Internal Revenue Service," *Public Personnel Management* (September–October 1972).

dual pay system, wage program that allows employees to select the more advantageous of alternative means of computing earnings. For example, transportation employees might have the option of being paid on the basis of miles traveled or on the basis of hours worked.

dual unionism, situation where two rival unions claim the right to organize workers in a particular industry or locality.

Dubinsky, David (1892-1982), president of the International Ladies' Garment Workers' Union from 1932 to 1966, one of the founders of the Liberal Party in New York State in 1944, and one of the founders of the Americans for Democratic Action in 1947. For an autobiography, *see* David Dubinsky and A. H. Raskin, *David Dubinsky: A Life with Labor* (N.Y.: Simon and Schuster, 1977).

due process, the due process clause of the U.S. Constitution requires that "no person shall be deprived of life, liberty, or property without due process of law." While the specific requirements of due process vary with new Supreme Court decisions, the essence of the idea is that individuals must be given adequate notice and a fair opportunity to present their side in a legal dispute and that no law or government procedure should be arbitrary or unfair. *See* Joseph Shane, "Due Process and Probationary Employees," *Public Personnel Management* (September-October 1974); Lewis R. Amis, "Due Process in Disciplinary Procedures," *Labor Law Journal* (February 1976); Deborah D. Goldman, "Due Process and Public Personnel Management," *Review of Public Personnel Personnel Administration* (Fall 1981); David W. Ewing, "Due Process: Will Business Default?" *Harvard Business Review* (November-December 1982); Raymond L. Hogler, "Employee Discipline and Due Process Rights: Is There an Appropriate Remedy?" *Labor Law Journal* (December 1982).

dues, fees that must be periodically paid by union members in order for them to remain in good standing with their union. The dues are used to finance all of the activities of the union and its affiliates. For a survey of who pays what, *see* Charles W. Hickman, "Labor Organizations' Fees and Dues," *Monthly Labor Review* (May 1977).

  See also UNFAIR LABOR PRACTICES (UNIONS).

dues checkoff: *see* CHECKOFF.

dues picket line, a common union practice before the checkoff was in widespread use was to have the union officers and their close supporters form a *dues picket line* at the factory gate on pay days in order to encourage union members to pay their dues. Any union member seeking to cross the line without paying might find himself in a situation with violent overtones.

dumping ground of management: *see* TRASHCAN HYPOTHESIS.

Dunlop, John T. (1914-   ), Secretary of Labor from 1975 to 1976.

Dunlop v. Bachowski, 421 U.S. 560 (1975), U.S. Supreme Court case, which held that, while a decision of the Secretary of Labor to initiate or not initiate civil action to set aside a union's election of officers is not excepted from judicial review, the reviewing court's review must be limited to determining whether the "Secretary's decision is so irrational as to be arbitrary and capricious, and the court's review may not extend to an adversary trial of a complaining union member's challenges to the factual basis for the Secretary's decision."

Dunnette, Marvin D. (1926-   ), industrial psychologist, one of the most prolific researchers and writers in the areas of personnel selection and organizational effectiveness. Major works include: *Psychology Applied to Business and Industry,* with W. K. Kirchner (N.Y.: Appleton-Century-Crofts, 1965); *Personnel Selection and Placement* (Belmont, Calif.: Wadsworth Publishing Company, 1966); *Managerial Behavior, Performance, and Effectiveness,* with J. P.Campbell, E. E. Lawler III, and K. E. Weick, Jr. (N.Y.: McGraw-Hill, 1970); *Handbook of Industrial and Organizational Psychology* (Chicago, Illinois: Rand McNally, 1976).

Durkin, Martin P. (1900-1964), Secretary of Labor during 1953.

duty, large segment of the work done by one individual. A job is made up of one or more duties.

duty station, the specific geographical area in which an employee is permanently assigned.

duty to bargain, positive obligation under various state and federal laws that employers and employees bargain with each other in good faith. Section 8 (d) of the Labor-Management Relations (Taft-Hartley) Act of 1947 holds that the duty to bargain collectively

is the performance of the mutual obligation of the employer and the representative of the employees to meet at reasonable times and confer in good faith with respect to wages, hours, and other terms and conditions of any employment, or the negotiation of an agreement, or any question arising thereunder, and the execution of a written contract incorporating any agreement reached if requested by either party, but such obligation does not compel either party to agree to a proposal or require the making of a concession.

For legal analyses, see Archibald Cox, "The Duty to Bargain in Good Faith," *Harvard Law Review* (June 1958); Stanley A. Gacek, "The Employer's Duty to Bargain on Termination of Unit Work," *Labor Law Journal* (October 1981).

See also GOOD FAITH BARGAINING.

duty of fair representation, obligation of a labor union to represent all of the members in a bargaining unit fairly and without discrimination. See Jean T. McKelvey (ed.), *The Duty of Fair Representation* (Ithaca, N.Y.: New York State School of Industrial and Labor Relations, Cornell University, 1977); George W. Bohlander, "Fair Representation: Not Just a Union Problem," *The Personnel Administrator* (March 1980); Stanley J. Schwartz, "Different Views of the Duty of Fair Representation," *Labor Law Journal* (July 1983); Stephen Allred, "The *Bowen* Decision: Mandate for Reexamination of Apportionment of Damages in Fair Representation Cases," *Labor Law Journal* (July 1983).

See also ELECTRICAL WORKERS V. FOUST and UNFAIR LABOR PRACTICES (UNIONS).

dyad, interpersonal encounter or relationship between two people or two groups. Dyads are frequently artificially (as opposed to spontaneously) created for sensitivity training purposes. See David M. Herold, "Two Way Influence Processes in Leader-Follower Dyads," *Academy of Management Journal* (June 1977).

dynamic psychology, school of psychology that is primarily concerned with motivation.

dynamic system, any system that has its parts interrelated in such a way that a change in one part necessarily affects other parts of the system. This is in contrast to a *static system* whose parts can be affected independently of the rest of its system.

E

EAP: see EMPLOYEE ASSISTANCE PROGRAM.

earmark, also RED CIRCLE, terms used to designate a position for restudy when vacant to determine its proper classification before being refilled.

earnings, total remuneration of an employee or group of employees for work performed, including wages, bonuses, commissions, etc.

See also GUARANTEED EARNINGS.

earthquake manager, one who shakes everything up.

Eastex, Inc.* v. *National Labor Relations Board, 57 L. Ed. 2d 428 (1978), U.S. Supreme Court case, which affirmed a National Labor Relations Board ruling that union members have the right to distribute, on their employers' property, leaflets containing articles pertaining to political issues (such as right-to-work laws and minimum wages) as well as those directly connected to the union-employer relationship.

econometric model, a set of related equations used to analyze economic data through mathematical and statistical techniques. Such models are devised in order to depict the essential quantitative relationships that determine the behavior of output, income, employment, and prices. Econometric models are used for forecasting, estimating the likely quantitative impact of alternative assumptions, including those pertaining to government policies, and for testing various propositions about the way the economy works.

econometrics, a subdiscipline of economics which is known by its use of mathematical techniques, such as regression analysis and modeling to test economic theories and forecast economic activity. *See* Brigitte H. Sellekaerts and Stephen W. Welch, "An Econometric Analysis of Minimum Wage Noncompliance," *Industrial Relations* (Spring 1984).

Economic Advisers, Council of: *see* COUNCIL OF ECONOMIC ADVISERS.

economic analysis, a systematic approach to the problem of choosing how to employ scarce resources and an investigation of the full implications of achieving a given objective in the most efficient and effective manner. The determination of efficiency and effectiveness is implicit in the assessment of the cost effectiveness of alternative approaches.
See also EFFECTIVENESS AND EFFICIENCY.

economic determinism, doctrine holding that economic concerns are the primary motivating factors of human behavior.

economic efficiency, the mix of alternative factors of production which results in maximum outputs, benefits, or utility for a given cost. Also, that mix of productive factors which represents the minimum cost at which a specified level of output can be obtained.

economic man, concept that finds humans motivated *solely* by economic factors—always seeking the greatest reward at the least possible cost. Any management philosophy assuming that workers are motivated by money and can be further motivated only by more money is premised on the "economic man" concept. *See* Harvey Leibenstein, *Beyond Economic Man: A New Foundation for Microeconomics* (Cambridge, Mass.: Harvard University Press, 1976).

economic goals, better wages, hours, or working conditions.

economic indicators, measurements of various economic and business movements and activities in a community, such as: employment, unemployment, hours worked, income, savings, volume of building permits, volume of sales, etc., whose fluctuations affect and may be used to determine overall economic trends. The economic time series can be segregated into leaders, laggers and coinciders in relation to movements in aggregate economic activity.

Economic Opportunity Act of 1964, this act, the keystone of the Johnson Administration's "war on poverty," created the Jobs Corps and other work-incentive programs. For histories, *see* Sar A. Levitan, *The Great Society's Poor Law* (Baltimore: The Johns Hopkins Press, 1969); Robert H. Haveman (ed.), *A Decade of Federal Anti-Poverty Programs: Achievements, Failures, and Lessons* (N.Y.: Academic Press, 1977); James T. Patterson, *America's Struggle Against Poverty, 1900-1980* (Cambridge, Mass.: Harvard University Press, 1981).
See also GREAT SOCIETY.

economic policy, process by which a government manages its economy. Economic policy generally consists of three dimensions—fiscal policy, monetary policy, and any other facet of public policy that has economic implications (*i.e.,* energy policy, farm policy, labor union policy, etc.). The interaction of these dimensions of economic policy becomes crucial since none can operate in a vacuum. While monetary policy basically exercises control over the quantity and cost (interest rates) of money and credit in the economy, fiscal policy deals with the size of budgets, deficits, and taxes. Other policy areas, such as housing policy (also dependent upon interest rates), and programs dependent upon deficit spending involve aspects of both monetary and fiscal policy and vice versa. However, their interrelationship does not exist with regard to implementation. Monetary policy, while receiving major inputs from the President and other executive agencies, is the responsibility of the Federal Reserve Board, an independent agency. Fiscal policy, while receiving similar inputs from the Federal Reserve Board, is primarily the responsibility of the president and Congress. The degree of equality and subsequent share of responsibility here varies within a stable range. While a president may wish to spend this or that amount, only Congress has the constitutional ability to levy taxes. See Charles Schultze, *The Politics and Economics of Public Spending* (Washington, D.C.: The Brookings Institution, 1968); Edward R. Tufte, *Political Control of the Economy* (Princeton, N.J.: Princeton University Press, 1979); and Robin W. Broadway, *Public Sector Economics* (Englewood Cliffs, N.J.: Prentice-Hall, 1979).

See also the following entries:
FISCAL POLICY
MACROECONOMICS
MICROECONOMICS
MONETARY POLICY
POLITICAL ECONOMY

Economic Policy Board, President Ford's cabinet-level committee on foreign and domestic economic policy. See Roger Porter, *Presidential Decision Making: The Economic Policy Board* (N.Y.: Cambridge University Press, 1980).

Economic Report of the President, economic assessment and forecast which is prepared by the Council of Economic Advisors for presentation to the Congress each January.

Economic Stabilization Program, federal program established to control wages and prices. On August 15, 1971, all wages and prices were frozen for a period of ninety days. During that period a system of wage and price controls administered through a Cost of Living Council was implemented. Controls continued, with periodic changes in the flexibility and the intensity with which they were enforced until their legislative authority ultimately expired in April, 1974.

economies of scale, cost savings resulting from aggregation of resources and/or mass production. In particular, it refers to decreases in average cost when all factors of production are expanded proportionately. For example, hospital costs for a unit of service are generally less in 300 than 30 bed hospitals.

economic strike, strike that is undertaken for economic gain; that is, for better wages, hours, and working conditions.
See also NATIONAL LABOR RELATIONS BOARD V. MACKAY RADIO & TELEGRAPH COMPANY.

economic time series, a set of quantitative data collected over regular time intervals (e.g., weekly, monthly, quarterly, annually) which measures some aspect of economic activity. The data may measure a broad aggregate such as the gross national product, or a narrow segment such as the sale of trucks or the price of labor.

economy and efficiency audits, audits that seek to determine (a) whether an organizational entity is managing and utilizing its resources (such as personnel, property, space) economically and efficiently, (b) the causes of inefficiencies or uneconomical practices, and (c) whether the entity has complied with laws and regulations concerning matters of economy and efficiency.

EDP: see ELECTRONIC DATA PROCESSING.

educable retarded person, individual who is only mildly retarded and thus employable in many simple jobs, usually requiring repetitive tasks.

education, cooperative: *see* COOPERATIVE EDUCATION.

Educational and Industrial Testing Service: *see* TEST PUBLISHERS.

Educational Testing Service (ETS), private, commercial test publisher that provides tests and related services for schools, colleges, government agencies and the professions.
Educational Testing Service
Rosedale Rd.
Princeton, NJ 08541
(609) 921-9000

Edwards Personal Preference Schedule (EPPS), inventory widely used in personal counseling and personality research that is designed to measure the relative importance of 15 key needs or motives (*i.e.*, achievement, deference, order, exhibition, autonomy, affiliation, intraception, succorance, dominance, abasement, nurturance, change, endurance, heterosexuality, and aggression). Time: Approximately 45 minutes. AUTHOR: A. L. Edwards. PUBLISHER: Psychological Corporation (*see* TEST PUBLISHERS). *See* Janet E. Helms, *A Practitioner's Guide to the Edwards Personnel Preference Schedule* (Springfield, Ill.: Charles C. Thomas, 1983).

EEO: *see* EQUAL EMPLOYMENT OPPORTUNITY.

EEO-1, the annual report on the sex and minority status of various workforce categories that is required of all employers with 100 or more employees. The report must be filed with the Joint Reporting Committee of the Equal Employment Opportunity Commission and the Office of Federal Contract Compliance.

EEO Act of 1972: *see* EQUAL EMPLOYMENT OPPORTUNITY ACT OF 1972.

EEOC: *see* EQUAL EMPLOYMENT OPPORTUNITY COMMISSION.

EEOC Compliance Manual, publication of the Bureau of National Affairs, Inc., which provides a summary of the latest Equal Employment Opportunity Commission (EEOC) developments and the photographic text of the official operations manual that is followed by the staff of the EEOC.

EEO Counselor: *see* EQUAL EMPLOYMENT OPPORTUNITY COUNSELOR.

EEO Officer: *see* EQUAL EMPLOYMENT OPPORTUNITY OFFICER.

effective labor market, labor market from which an employer actually draws applicants, as distinct from the labor market from which an employer attempts to draw applicants.

effectiveness, traditionally, the extent to which an organization accomplishes some predetermined goal or objective; more recently, the overall performance of an organization from the viewpoint of some strategic constituency. Effectiveness is not entirely dependent upon the efficiency of a program because program outputs may increase without necessarily increasing effectiveness. Effectiveness is increased by strategies which employ resources to take advantage of changes in unmanageable factors in such a way that the greatest possible advancement of whatever one is seeking is achieved. *See* P. S. Goodman and J. M. Pennings, *New Perspectives on Organizational Effectiveness* (San Francisco: Jossey-Bass, 1977); Philip B. Coulter, "Organizational Effectiveness in the Public Sector: The Example of Municipal Fire Protection," *Administrative Science Quarterly* (March 1979); Kim Cameron, "Critical Questions in Assessing Organizational Effectiveness," *Organizational Dynamics* (Autumn 1980); Leonard Greenhaigh, "Maintaining Organizational Effectiveness During Organizational Retrenchment," *The Journal of Applied Behavioral Science,* Vol. 18, No.

2 (1982); Raymond F. Zammuto, *Assessing Organizational Effectiveness* (Albany: State University of New York Press, 1982); Edward E. Lawler III, "Education, Management Style, and Organizational Effectiveness," *Personnel Psychology* (Spring 1985).

Also see PERSONNEL EFFECTIVENESS GRID.

efficacy, commonly used synonymously with effectiveness, but may usefully be distinguished from it by using efficacy for the results of actions undertaken under ideal circumstances and effectiveness for their results under usual or normal circumstances. Actions can thus be efficacious and effective, or efficacious and ineffective, but not the reverse.

efficiency, also EFFICIENCY RATIO, productive efficiency is generally determined by seeking the ratio of output to input, which is called the *efficiency ratio.*

$$\text{EFFICIENCY} = \frac{\text{OUTPUT}}{\text{INPUT}}$$

Generally speaking, efficiency refers to the promotion of administrative methods that will produce the largest store of results for a given objective at the least cost; the reduction of material and personnel costs while maximizing precision, speed, and simplicity in administration. According to the traditional view, efficiency is the primary aim of the administrative sciences. *See* Aaron Wildavsky, "The Political Economy of Efficiency: Cost-Benefit Analysis, Systems Analysis and Program Budgeting," *Public Administration Review* (December 1966); Selwyn W. Becker and Duncan Neuhauser, *The Efficient Organization* (New York: Elsevier, 1975); Joseph L. Bower, "Managing for Efficiency, Managing for Equity," *Harvard Business Review* (July-August 1983).

See also PRODUCTIVITY.

efficiency expert, mildly pejorative and decidedly dated term for a management or systems analyst.

efficiency rating, now dated term for performance appraisal. The Civil Service Reform Act of 1978 mandates that each federal agency will install employee "performance appraisal" systems. For an account of the old ways, *see* Mary S. Schinagl, *History of Efficiency Ratings in the Federal Government* (N.Y.: Bookman Associates, 1966).

See also PERFORMANCE APPRAISAL.

efficiency ratio: *see* EFFICIENCY.

80-percent rule: *see* ADVERSE IMPACT.

elasticity, a numerical measure of the responsiveness of one variable to changes in another. If greater than one, it indicates that the first variable is relatively elastic to changes in the second (i.e., when the second changes by one percent, the first changes by more than one percent). If the numerical value of elasticity is equal to or less than one (i.e., unitary elasticity or less) the first variable is said to be *inelastic* to changes in the second (a one percent change in the second variable will cause a one percent or less change in the first).

elasticity of demand, measure of the sensitivity of demand for a product or service to changes in its price (price elasticity) or the income of the people demanding the product or service (income elasticity). Price elasticity is the ratio of the resulting percentage change in demand to a given percentage change in price. *See* Kim B. Clark and Richard B. Freeman, "How Elastic Is the Demand for Labor?" *The Review of Economics and Statistics* (November 1980).

Electrical Workers v. Foust, 60 L.Ed. 2d 698 (1979), U.S. Supreme Court case, which held that an award of punitive damages for a union's breach of its duty of fair representation in processing an employee's grievance was prohibited by the Railway Labor Act.

See also DUTY OF FAIR REPRESENTATION.

electronic data processing (EDP), computer manipulation of data. The term is gradually being supplanted by "management information systems."

See also MANAGEMENT INFORMATION SYSTEM.

element, also called JOB ELEMENT, smallest unit into which a job can be divided without analyzing the physical and mental processes necessarily involved. *See* Ronald A. Ash, "Job Elements for Task Clusters," *Public Personnel Management* (Spring 1982).

Elfbrandt v. Russell, 384 U.S. 11 (1966), U.S. Supreme Court case holding an Arizona loyalty oath unconstitutional in violation of freedom of association since, coupled with a perjury statute, it proscribed membership in any organization having for one of its purposes the overthrow of the government of the State of Arizona. The Court reasoned that one might join such an organization without supporting its illegal purposes.
See also LOYALTY OATH.

Elgin, Joliet & Eastern Railway v. Burley, 325 U.S. 711 (1945), U.S. Supreme Court case, which upheld the right of employees to object to a compromise settlement of a grievance committee when they had not formally authorized the committee to act for them.

eligible, any applicant for appointment or promotion who meets the minimum qualification requirements.

eligible list, also called ELIGIBLE ROSTER and ELIGIBLE REGISTER, list of qualified applicants in rank order established from the test score results of competitive examinations.
See also RE-EMPLOYMENT LIST.

Ellis v. Brotherhood of Railway Clerks, 80 L. Ed. 2d 428 (1984), U.S. Supreme Court case, in which the Court restricted activities that unions in the railroad and airline transportation industries may finance using fees obtained from workers who object to the expenditures. The Court's interpretation of the Railway Labor Act applies only to workers who are represented by a union in collective bargaining but are not members of the union. The money at question is the so-called "agency shop fee" paid by "nonmembers" in lieu of the dues paid by fellow employees who are members of the union.

In the ruling, written by Justice Byron White, the Court said that if an employee objects, the employee's agency shop payments cannot be used for organizing other workers or for paying union legal expenses for lawsuits over issues not specifically related to the bargaining agreement covering the workers. See Jan W. Henkel and Normal J. Wood, "Limitations on the Use of Union Shop Funds After *Ellis:* What Activities Are 'Germane' to Collective Bargaining?" *Labor Law Journal* (December 1984).

Elrod v. Burns, 427 U.S. 347 (1976), U.S. Supreme Court case, which held that the 1st Amendment, which safeguards the rights of political beliefs and association, prevents political firings of state, county, and local workers below the policymaking level.

Emergency Employment Act of 1971, federal statute that authorized federal funds for state and local government public service jobs during times of high unemployment. It was superseded by the Comprehensive Employment and Training Act of 1973. For a history, *see* Howard W. Hallman, *Emergency Employment: A Study in Federalism* (University, Ala.: University of Alabama Press, 1977).

eminence grise, "gray eminence," the power behind the throne. Staff officers are sometimes accused of exercising such power.

Emerson, Harrington (1853-1931), one of the first management consultants in the U.S., known as the "high priest of efficiency" because of advocacy of eliminating "wanton, wicked waste." Major works include: *Efficiency as a Basis for Operation and Wages* (N.Y.: The Engineering Magazine Co., 1911) and *The Twelve Principles of Efficiency* (N.Y.: The Engineering Magazine Co., 1913). *Also see*

William F. Muhs, "Worker Participation in the Progressive Era: An Assessment by Harrington Emerson," *Academy of Management Review* (January 1982).

emolument, any monetary gain or other advantage achieved from employment; a more comprehensive term than wages and/or salaries.

emotionally handicapped employees, also EMOTIONAL REHABILITANTS, a polite way of referring to employees who have had or are having a problem with mental illness. *Emotional rehabilitant,* a more formal label, has been defined in Charles A. Burden and Russell Faulk, "The Employment Process for Rehabilitants: Two Studies of the Hiring of Emotional Rehabilitants," *Personnel Journal* (October 1975), as "a person who has suffered an emotional illness serious enough to require hospitalization, but has since recovered and has been judged by medical and social authorities to be ready to reenter the customary, competitive work situation."

empirical, findings or conclusions derived from direct and repeated observations of a phenomenon under study.

empirical validity, validity of a test according to how well the test actually measures what it was designed to measure. Most other kinds of validity are efforts to achieve empirical validity.

employ, hire the services of an individual and/or his or her equipment.

employee, general term for all those who let themselves for hire.
See also DISPLACED EMPLOYEE and PROBATIONARY EMPLOYEE.

employee assistance program (EAP), formal program designed to assist employees with personal problems through both (1) internal counseling and aid and (2) a referral service to outside counseling resources. The thrust of such programs is to increase productivity by correcting distracting outside personal prob-lems. *See* Richard T. Hellan and Carl R. Tisone, "Employee Assistance Programming: Personnel's Sobering Influence on the Bottom Line," *The Personnel Administrator* (May 1976); Paul M. Roman, "Employee Assistance Programs in Australia and the United States: Comparisons of Origin, Structure, and the Role of Behavioral Science Research," *The Journal of Applied Behavioral Science,* Vol. 19, No. 3 (1983); Harvey Shore, "Employee Assistance Programs—Reaping the Benefits," *Sloan Management Review* (Spring 1984); Dale A. Masi, *Designing Employee Assistance Programs* (New York: AMACOM, 1984).

Employee Assistance Quarterly, a journal of research on work-based alcoholism, drug, and mental health programs.
Employee Assistance Quarterly
The Howarth Press
28 East 22nd Street
New York, N.Y. 10010

employee benefits: *see* FRINGE BENEFITS.

employee counseling, formal efforts on the part of an organization to help its members deal with their personal and professional problems and concerns so that they will be more effective in both their personal and organizational lives. For the classic work on employee counseling, *see* William J. Dickson and F. J. Roethlisberger, *Counseling In An Organization: A Sequel to the Hawthorne Researches* (Boston: Graduate School of Business Administration, Harvard University, 1966).
Also see John H. Meyer and Teresa C. Meyer, "The Supervisor as Counselor—How to Help the Distressed Employee," *Management Review* (April 1982); Stephen J. Holoviak and Sharon Brookens Holoviak, "The Benefits of In-House Counseling," *Personnel* (July–August 1984).
See also PRE-RETIREMENT COUNSELING.

employee development, term that may include career development and upward mobility. It may be oriented toward development for better performance on an employee's current job, for learning a new policy or procedure, or for enhancing an employee's potential for advancement. *See* Donald B. Miller, "Training Managers to Stimulate Employee Development," *Training and Development Journal* (February 1981).

employee discount, reduction in the price of goods or services offered by an employer to employees as a benefit. For a survey of company discount policies, *see* Geneva Seybold, *Discount Privileges for Employees* (New York: The Conference Board, 1967).

employee relations, personnel function that centers upon the relationship between the supervisor and individual employees.

employee selection: *see* PERSONNEL SELECTION.

employees, exempt: *see* EXEMPT EMPLOYEES.

Employee Retirement Income Security Act of 1974 (ERISA), popularly known as PENSION REFORM ACT OF 1974, federal statute enacted to protect "the interest of participants in employee benefit plans and their beneficiaries . . . by establishing standards of conduct, responsibility, and obligations for fiduciaries of employee benefit plans, and by providing for appropriate remedies, sanctions, and ready access to the Federal courts." The basic intent of ERISA is to insure that employees will eventually gain appropriate benefits from the pension plans in which they participate. *See* Peter Henle and Raymond Schmitt, "Pension Reform: The Long Hard Road to Enactment," *Monthly Labor Review* (November 1974); Donald G. Carlson, "Responding to the Pension Reform Law," *Harvard Business Review* (November–December 1974); Bruce M. Stott, "How Will ERISA Affect Your Pension Plan?" *Personnel Journal* (June 1977); Raymond J. Donovan, "Effective Administration of ERISA," *Labor Law Journal* (March 1982); Kathleen D. Gill, ed., *ERISA: The Law and the Code*

(Washington, D.C.: Bureau of National Affairs, Inc., 1985).

See also LABOR-MANAGEMENT SERVICES ADMINISTRATION and RETIREMENT EQUALITY ACT OF 1984.

employee stock-ownership plan (ESOP), employee benefit plan that uses company stock to provide deferred compensation. For how-to-do-it, *see* Charles A. Scharf, *Guide to Employee Stock Ownership Plans: A Revolutionary Method for Increasing Corporate Profits* (Englewood Cliffs, N.J.: Prentice-Hall, 1976). For criticism, *see* Burton W. Teague, "In Review of the ESOP Fable," *The Conference Board Record* (February 1976). *Also see* Geoffrey W. Latta, *Profit Sharing, Employee Stock Ownership, Savings, and Asset Formation Plans in the Western World* (Philadelphia: Wharton School, University of Pennsylvania, 1979).

employer association: *see* EMPLOYERS' ASSOCIATION.

employer paternalism: *see* PATERNALISM.

employer strike insurance: *see* MUTUAL STRIKE AID.

employer unit, any bargaining unit that holds all of the eligible employees of a single employer.

employers' association, also called EMPLOYER ASSOCIATION, voluntary organization of employers whose purpose is to deal with problems common to the group. Such associations have frequently been formed primarily to present a united front in dealing with the representatives of their respective organized workers. *See* Jean-Jacques Oechslin, "Employers' Organizations: Current Trends and Social Responsibilities," *International Labour Review* (September–October 1982).

employment, occupational activity, usually, but not necessarily, for pay.

See also FULL EMPLOYMENT and SEASONAL EMPLOYMENT.

Employment Act of 1946, federal statute that created the Council of Economic Advisors in the Executive Office of the President and asserted that it was the federal government's responsibility to maintain economic stability and promote full employment. For a legislative history of the act, *see* Stephen K. Bailey, *Congress Makes A Law* (N.Y.: Columbia University Press, 1950). *See also* Hugh S. Norton, *The Employment Act and the Council of Economic Advisors, 1946-1976* (Columbia: University of South Carolina Press, 1977).

employment agency, private employment agencies provide brokerage services between employers and individuals seeking work. Fees or commission are charged the employer, the worker, or both. *See* Terry L. Dennis and David P. Gustafson, "College Campuses vs. Employment Agencies as Sources of Manpower," *Personnel Journal* (August 1973); John M. Malloy, "Employment Agency Fees: An Area of Continued Litigation?" *Taxes* (February 1974); Tomas Martinez, *The Human Marketplace: An Examination of Private Employment Agencies* (New Brunswick, N.J.: Transaction Books, 1976).

Employment and Earnings, U.S. Bureau of Labor Statistics' comprehensive monthly report on employment, hours, earnings, and labor turnover by industry, area, occupation, etc.

> Employment and Earnings
> Superintendent of Documents
> Government Printing Office
> Washington, D.C. 20402

Employment and Training Administration (ETA), agency of the Department of Labor that encompasses a group of offices and services. Major units include: the U.S. Employment Service; the Office of Employment Programs and Training; and the Bureau of Apprenticeship and Training.

> Employment and Training Administration
> Department of Labor
> 200 Constitution Ave., N.W.

Washington, D.C. 20210
(202) 376-7032

Employment and Training Reporter, weekly notification-and-reference service published by the Bureau of National Affairs, Inc. Provides technical assistance on the effective utilization of the nation's human resources, including where and how to apply for employment and training funds, and how to develop successful programs. Covers the Comprehensive Employment and Training Act. Gives program guides, plus complete listings of federally funded employment and training programs and full texts of noteworthy documents.

employment-at-will, the common law concept that an employment having no specific term may be terminated by either party with or without notice or cause. In recent years discharged employees have increasingly challenged what they consider to be wrongful discharges. They have based their court suits on claims of violation of public policy, the existence of an implied contract, and the covenant of good faith and fair dealing. Generally speaking, only those employees protected by collective bargaining, antidiscrimination laws, civil service, and teacher tenure laws are not subject to "at-will" discharges. *See:* Anthony T. Oliver, Jr., "The Disappearing Right to Terminate Employees at Will," *Personnel Journal* (December 1982); Marco L. Colosi, "Who's Pulling the Strings on Employment at Will?" *Personnel Journal* (May 1984); Lawrence Z. Lorber, "Basic Advice on Avoiding Employment-At-Will Troubles," *Personnel Administrator* (February 1984); Emily A. Joiner, "Erosion of the Employment-at-Will Doctrine," *Personnel* (September-October 1984).

employment contract, generally a contract is a promise or set of promises for which the law offers a remedy if the promise(s) is breached. According to John J. Villarreal, "Employment Contracts for Managers and Professionals," *Personnel Journal* (October 1974), an employment

contract specifically refers to
the agreed-upon contributions/induce-
ments between employer and employee
for the services of each. These promises must be legally enforceable and they
must be made by mature, knowledgeable and consenting individuals. . . .For
each employment contract there must
be agreements between the organization
and the individual on goals to be accomplished, units of measurement, performance targets and organizational
rewards.

Employment Cost Index (ECI), measures
the rate of change in employee compensation, which includes wages, salaries, and
employers' cost for employee benefits.
Several elements distinguish the ECI from
other surveys of employee compensation.
It is comprehensive in that it (1) includes
costs incurred by employers for employee
benefits in addition to wages and salaries;
and (2) covers all establishments and occupations in both the private nonfarm and
public sectors. It measures the change in
a fixed set of labor costs so that it is not
affected over time by changes in the composition of the labor force. *See* Beth Levin,
"The Employment Cost Index: Recent
Trends and Expansion," *Monthly Labor
Review* (May 1982).

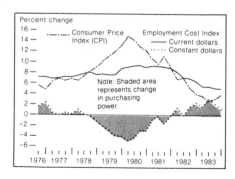

*Source: BLS. Percent change in the
Employment Cost Index for wages and
salaries of private industry workers and in
the Consumer Price Index for urban wage
earners and clerical workers, 1976-83.*

employment interview: *see* INTERVIEW.

employment manager, job title
sometimes given to managers who function as personnel directors.

employment-population ratio (E-P ratio),
also called EMPLOYMENT RATIO, ratio of
employment to working-age population.
Some economists think that the E-P ratio
is more useful for diagnosing the severity
of an economic slowdown than is the
unemployment rate. *See* Christopher
Green, "The Employment Ratio as an
Indicator of Aggregate Demand Pressure,"
Monthly Labor Review (April 1977); Carol
Boyd Leon, "The Employment-Popu-
lation Ratio: Its Value in Labor Force
Analysis," *Monthly Labor Review*
(February 1981).

employment practice, in the context of
equal employment opportunity, an
employment practice is any screening
device operating at any point in the
employment cycle. If an employment
practice is not related to job performance,
it will not be able to withstand a court
challenge.

employment ratio: *see* EMPLOYMENT-
POPULATION RATIO.

employment relations, general term for
all relationships that occur in a worker-
manager context. While used synonymously with labor relations and industrial
relations, it is often applied in non-union
situations in order to emphasize "non-
union."

employment standard, a specific requirement for employment. An employment
standard can be based on a wide variety
of things. For example, if assessment is
based on tests, the standard might be a
specific cutting score. If education is assessed, the standard might be a specific
class standing, or grades of B or better in
certain courses of study.

Employment Standards Administration
(ESA), agency of the Department of Labor
that administers laws and regulations setting employment standards, providing

workers' compensation to those injured on their jobs and requiring federal contractors to provide equal employment opportunity. Its major divisions include the Wage and Hour Division, the Office of Federal Contract Compliance, and the Office of Workers' Compensation.

Employment Standards Administration
Department of Labor
200 Constitution Ave., N.W.
Washington, D.C. 20210
(202) 523-8165

employment taxes, also called PAYROLL TAXES, any of a variety of taxes levied by governments on an employer's payroll. The most common employment tax is the employer's contribution to social security known as FICA taxes (after the Federal Insurance Contribution Act). There are also FUTA taxes (after the Federal Unemployment Tax Act) and sometimes other unemployment insurance contributions required by state law. *See* Samuel S. Ress, "Payroll Taxes and Controls," *CPA Journal* (April 1977); Julian Block, "How to Save on Employment Taxes," *Administrative Management* (February 1976).

employment testing, any means of measuring the qualifications of applicants for employment in specific positions. *See* Robert M. Guion, *Personnel Testing* (N.Y.: McGraw-Hill, 1965); J. M. Thyne, *Principles of Examining* (N.Y.: John Wiley, 1974); M. T. Matteson, "Employment Testing: Where Do We Stand?" *The Personnel Administrator* (January 1975).

Emporium Capwell Co. **v. *Western Addition Community Organization,*** 420 U.S. 50 (1975), U.S. Supreme Court case, which held that employees have no right to bypass union management grievance procedures in order to protest alleged racial discrimination.

encounter group, form of group psychotherapy in which body contact and/or emotional expression are the primary forms of interaction as opposed to traditional verbal interaction. Encounter groups seek to produce experiences which force individuals to examine themselves in new and different ways, aided by others. Part of the emphasis on body movement includes attention to nonverbal communications. An individual should learn to be more conscious of his/her own nonverbal communications, to read others' signs more adequately and to practice being more adept in his/her body language. *See* A. Burton (ed.), *Encounter* (San Francisco: Jossey-Bass, 1969); Dianna Hartley, Howard B. Roback, and Stephen I. Abramowitz, "Deterioration Effects on Encounter Groups," *American Psychologist*, (March 1976); Kurt W. Back, *Beyond Words: The Story of Sensitivity Training and the Encounter Movement* (New York: Russell Sage Foundation, 1972); Carl A. Bramlette and Jeffry H. Tucker, "Encounter Groups: Positive Change or Deterioration?" *Human Relations* (April 1981).

end-testing, examining individuals who have just completed a course of training on the subject in which they were trained in order to measure the individual's attainments and/or the effectiveness of the training.

enjoin, require or command. A court's injunction directs (enjoins) a person or persons to do or not do certain acts.

enterprise zone, also called URBAN ENTERPRISE ZONE, area of high unemployment and poverty which is granted business tax reductions by a state in order to lure industry and concomitant prosperity. *See* Neal R. Pierce, "Enterprise Zones Open Urban Opportunities," *Public Administration Times* (February 1, 1981).

entitlement program, any government program which pays benefits to individuals, organizations or other governments who meet eligibility requirements set by law. *See* Eleanor Chelimsky, "Reducing Fraud and Abuse in Entitlement Programs: An Evaluative Perspective," *The GAO Review* (Summer 1981).

entrance level position, position in an occupation at the beginning level grade.

entrance rate, also called PROBATIONARY RATE and HIRING RATE, hourly rate of pay at which new employees are hired.

entropy, term from thermodynamics that is applicable to all physical systems and sometimes applied to social systems. It refers to the inherent tendency of all closed systems, which do not interact with their environments, to move toward a chaotic state in which there is no further potential for work. According to James G. Miller, in "Living Systems: Basic Concepts," *Behavioral Science* (July 1965), "the disorder, disorganization, lack of patterning, or randomness of organization of a system is known as its *entropy.*"

Negative entropy, an arresting of the entropy process, can be acquired by an open system, according to Daniel Katz and Robert L. Kahn, in *The Social Psychology of Organizations* (N.Y.: John Wiley & Sons, 1966):

The open system, however, by importing more energy from its environment than it expends, can store energy and can acquire negative entropy.

For an expansive view of the concept, *see* Jeremy Rifkin, *Entropy: A New World View* (New York: Bantam, 1980).

entry level jobs, those jobs in which employers will accept and hire workers for which no work experience is required. Any job, even though training and/or educational requirements may be extensive, is considered entry level if there is no previous work experience requirement.

environmental differential, additional pay authorized for a duty involving unusually severe hazards or working conditions.

EPI: *see* EYSENCK PERSONALITY INVENTORY.

EPPS: *see* EDWARDS PERSONAL PREFERENCE SCHEDULE.

E-P ratio: *see* EMPLOYMENT-POPULATION RATIO

equal employment opportunity (EEO), concept fraught with political, cultural, and emotional overtones. Generally, it applies to a set of employment procedures and practices that effectively prevent any individual from being adversely excluded from employment opportunities on the basis of race, color, sex, religion, age, national origin, or other factors that cannot lawfully be used in employment efforts. While the ideal of EEO is an employment system that is devoid of both intentional and unintentional discrimination, achieving this ideal may be a political impossibility because of the problem of definition. One man's equal opportunity may be seen by another as tainted with institutional racism or by a woman as institutional sexism. Because of this problem of definition, only the courts have been able to say if, when, and where EEO exists. For the law of EEO, *see* Barbara Lindemann Schlei and Paul Frossman, *Employment Discrimination Law,* 2nd ed. (Washington, D.C.: Bureau of National Affairs, Inc., 1983); Charles A. Sullivan, Michael J. Zimmer, and Richard F. Richards, *Federal Statutory Law of Employment Discrimination* (Indianapolis, Indiana: Michie Bobbs-Merrill, 1980); Daniel B. Edelman, *EEO in the Judicial Branch: An Outline of Policy and Law* (Williamsburg, VA: National Center for State Courts, 1981). For the history of EEO in the federal government, *see* David H. Rosenbloom, *Federal Equal Employment Opportunity: Politics and Public Personnel Administration* (N.Y.: Praeger, 1977).

See also the following entries:
DISCRIMINATION
FAIR EMPLOYMENT PRACTICE COMMITTEE GOALS
HISHON V. KING AND SPALDING
NATIONAL ASSOCIATION FOR THE ADVANCEMENT OF COLORED PEOPLE V. FEDERAL POWER COMMISSION
REHABILITATED OFFENDER PROGRAM
RELIGIOUS DISCRIMINATION
REPRESENTATIVE BUREAUCRACY
REVERSE DISCRIMINATION
RIGHTFUL PLACE
SCHLESINGER V. BALLARD
SEX PLUS
THIRD PARTY
TITLE VII

Equal Employment Opportunity Act of 1972,

also called EEO ACT OF 1972, amends Title VII of the 1964 Civil Rights Act by strengthening the authority of the Equal Employment Opportunity Commission and extending anti-discrimination provisions to state and local governments and labor organizations with 15 or more employees and public and private employment agencies. *See* William Brown III, "The Equal Employment Opportunity Act of 1972—The Light at the Top of the Stairs," *Personnel Administration* (June 1972); Harry Grossman, "The Equal Employment Opportunity Act of 1972, Its Implications for the State and Local Government Manager," *Public Personnel Management* (September–October 1973).

See also HAZELWOOD SCHOOL DISTRICT V. UNITED STATES.

Equal Employment Opportunity Commission

(EEOC), created by Title VII of the Civil Rights Act of 1964, the EEOC is composed of five members (one designated chair) appointed for five-year terms by the president, subject to the advice and consent of the Senate. The EEOC's mission is to end discrimination based on race, color, religion, sex, or national origin in hiring, promotion, firing, wages, testing, training, apprenticeship, and all other conditions of employment and to promote voluntary action programs by employers, unions, and community organizations to make equal employment opportunity an actuality.

The EEOC's operations are decentralized to 48 field offices which receive written charges of discrimination against public and private employers, labor organizations, joint labor-management apprenticeship programs, and public and private employment agencies. EEOC members may also initiate charges alleging that a violation of Title VII has occurred. Charges of Title VII violation must be filed with the EEOC within 180 days of the alleged violation. The EEOC is responsible for notifying persons so charged within 10 days of the receipt of a new charge. Before investigation, a charge must be deferred for 60 days to a local, fair employment practices agency in states and municipalities where an enforceable, fair employment practices law is in effect. (The deferral period is 120 days for an agency which has been operating less than one year.) After an investigation, if there is reasonable cause to believe the charge is true, the district office attempts to remedy the alleged unlawful practices through the informal methods of conciliation, conference and persuasion.

Unless an acceptable conciliation agreement has been secured, the EEOC may, after 30 days from the date the charge was filed, bring suit in an appropriate federal district court. (The U.S. Attorney General brings suit when a state government, governmental agency, or a political subdivision is involved.) If the EEOC or the Attorney General does not proceed in this manner, at the conclusion of the administrative procedures, or earlier at the request of the charging party, a "Notice of Right to Sue" is issued, which allows the charging party to proceed within 90 days in a federal district court. In appropriate cases, the EEOC may intervene in such civil action if the case is of general public interest. The investigation and conciliation of charges having an industrywide or national impact are coordinated or conducted by the EEOC's Office of Systemic Programs.

If it is concluded after a preliminary investigation that prompt judicial action is necessary to carry out the purposes of the act, the EEOC or the Attorney General, in a case involving a state government, governmental agency, or political subdivision, may bring an action for appropriate temporary or preliminary relief pending final disposition of a charge.

The EEOC encourages and assists in voluntary action by employers, unions, and employment agencies through affirmative action programs, providing the EEOC's services in developing multiplant and industrywide programs and in identifying discriminatory systems and devising ways to change them. Such programs are designed to help those organizations achieve EEO goals through nondiscriminatory recruiting, fair employee selection procedures, expanded training programs, and job upgrading. Federal employees or applicants who want to file complaints of job discrimination based on race, color, national origin, sex, religion, age, or physical or mental handicap must first consult an equal employment opportunity counselor within their agency within 30 calendar days of the alleged act. If the complaint cannot be resolved informally, the person may file a formal complaint within 15 calendar days following the final interview with the counselor.

The EEOC has direct liaison with state and local governments, employer and union organizations, trade associations, civil rights organizations, and other agencies and organizations concerned with employment of minority-group members and women. The EEOC engages in and contributes to the cost of research and other mutual interest projects with state and local agencies charged with the administration of fair employment practices laws. Furthermore, the Commission enters into worksharing agreements with the State and local agencies in order to avoid duplication of effort by identifying specific charges to be investigated by the respective agencies. See William A. Webb, "The Mission of the Equal Employment Opportunity Commission," *Labor Law Journal* (July 1983); Frank J. Thompson, "Deregulation at the EEOC: Prospects and Implications," *Review of Public Personnel Administration* (Summer 1984).

> *Equal Employment Opportunity Commission*
> 2401 E St., N.W.
> Washington, D.C. 20507
> (202) 634-6922
> *See also* 706 AGENCY.

Equal Employment Opportunity Commission v. *Wyoming,* 75 L.Ed. 2d 18 (1983), U.S. Supreme Court case, which upheld the Federal Government's 1974 extenstion of the Age Discrimination in Employment Act to cover State and local government workers.

equal employment opportunity counselor, specifically designated individual within an organization who provides an open and systematic channel through which employees may raise questions, discuss real and imagined grievances, and obtain information on their procedural rights. Counseling is the first stage in the discrimination complaint process. The counselor through interviews and inquiries attempts to informally resolve problems related to equal employment opportunity. *See* U.S. Civil Service Commission, *Equal Employment Opportunity Counseling: A Guidebook* (Washington, D.C.: Government Printing Office, October 1975).

equal employment opportunity officer, official within an organization who is designated responsibility for monitoring EEO programs and assuring that both organizational and national EEO policies are being implemented.

equality, also EGALITARIANISM, philosophic disposition toward the greater political and social equality of the citizens within a state; this is, all citizens would have an equal claim on the political and economic rewards of the society. However, economists warn that "any insistence on carving the pie into equal slices would shrink the size of the pie." Arthur M. Okun, *Equality and Efficiency: The Big Tradeoff* (Washington, D.C.: The Brookings Institution, 1975).

Equal Pay Act of 1963, basically an amendment to the Fair Labor Standards Act of 1938, the Equal Pay Act of 1963 (Public Law 88-38) prohibits pay discrimination because of sex and provides that men and women working in the same establishment under similar conditions must receive the same pay if jobs require equal (similar) skill, effort, and responsibility. *See* John E. Burns and Catherine G. Burns, "An Analysis of the Equal Pay Act," *Labor Law Journal* (February 1973).

equal pay for equal work, principle that salary rates should not be dependent upon factors unrelated to the quantity or quality of work. In 1960, 20 states had laws applicable to private employment that prohibited discrimination based on sex in the rate of pay. Today, 37 states have equal pay provisions either in their minimum wage laws or in separate statutes. Moreover, another eight states, the District of Columbia, and Puerto Rico prohibit pay discrimination based on sex in their fair employment practices or civil rights laws.

States with equal pay laws which are applicable to most kinds of private employment are:

Arizona	Montana
Arkansas	Nebraska
California	Nevada
Colorado	New Hampshire
Connecticut	New Jersey
Florida	New York
Georgia	North Dakota
Hawaii	Ohio
Idaho	Oklahoma
Illinois	Oregon
Indiana	Pennsylvania
Kansas	Rhode Island
Kentucky	South Dakota
Maine	Tennessee
Maryland	Virginia
Massachusetts	Washington
Michigan	West Virginia
Minnesota	Wyoming
Missouri	

States that have no specific equal pay provision relating to private employment but that do prohibit pay discrimination based on sex:

Alaska	Puerto Rico
Delaware	South Carolina
District of Columbia	Utah
Iowa	Vermont
New Mexico	Wisconsin

Five States do not have an equal pay provision or law prohibiting sex discrimination in private employment; (however, four of these have acted in some way to eliminate such discrimination):

Alabama	Mississippi	Texas
Louisiana	North Carolina	

See Francine D. Blau, *Equal Pay in the Office* (Lexington, Mass.: Lexington Books, 1977); Barrie O. Pettman (ed.), *Equal Pay For Women: Progress and Problems in Seven Countries* (N.Y.: McGraw-Hill, 1977); Raymond L. Hogler, "Equal Pay, Equal Work, and the United States Supreme Court," *Labor Law Journal* (November 1981); Winn Newman, "Pay Equity Emerges as a Top Labor Issue in the 1980's," *Monthly Labor Review* (April 1982); Paul S. Greenlaw and John P. Kohl, "The EEOC's New Equal Pay Guidelines," *Personnel Journal* (July 1982); Judith A. Alexander, *Equal-Pay-for-Equal Work Legislation in Canada* (Ottawa, Ontario: Economic Council of Canada, 1984).

equal protection of laws, constitutional requirement that the government will in no way fail to treat equals equally, set up illegal categories to justify treating persons unfairly, or give unfair or unequal treatment to a person based on that person's race, religion, etc.

Equal Rights Amendment, in 1972 Congress passed the Equal Rights Amendment (ERA); but it never became law because not enough of the states ratified it. The proposed 27th Amendment read: "Equality of rights under the law shall not be denied or abridged by the United States or any state on account of sex."

equated scores, scores from different tests of the same variable which are reduced by weighting in order to have a common basis for comparison.

equating, process of adjusting the raw statistics obtained from a particular sample to corresponding statistics obtained for a base group or reference population.

equipercentile equating, process that treats as equivalent those raw scores that fall at the same percentile in different samples although the raw scores themselves may be different.

equity, external/internal: see EXTERNAL EQUITY.

equity theory: see INEQUITY THEORY.

equivalent form: see ALTERNATE FORM.

Erdman Act of 1898, the essence of this act, which banned interstate railroads from discriminating against union-member employees, was held unconstitutional by the U.S. Supreme Court, in *Adair* v. *United States,* 208 U.S. 161 (1908).

ergonomics: *see* HUMAN-FACTORS ENGINEERING.

ERISA: *see* EMPLOYEE RETIREMENT INCOME SECURITY ACT OF 1974.

ESA: *see* EMPLOYMENT STANDARDS ADMINISTRATION.

escalator clause, also called COST-OF-LIVING ESCALATOR, provision of a collective bargaining agreement which allows for periodic wage adjustments in response to changes in the cost of living usually as determined by the Consumer Price Index of the Bureau of Labor Statistics. *See* Francis S. Cunningham, "The Use of Price Indexes in Escalator Contracts," *Monthly Labor Review* (August 1963); Robert H. Ferguson, *Cost-of-Living Adjustments in Union-Management Agreements* (Ithaca, N.Y.: New York State School of Industrial and Labor Relations, Cornell University, 1976); Wayne Vroman, "Cost-of-Living Escalators and Price-Wage Linkages in the U.S. Economy, 1968–1980," *Industrial & Labor Relations Review* (January 1985).

escape clause, in a maintenance-of-membership shop, a union contract may provide for a period of time during which union members may withdraw (escape) from the union without affecting their employment.

ESOP: *see* EMPLOYEE STOCK-OWNERSHIP PLAN.

Espinoza* v. *Farah Manufacturing Company, 414 U.S. 86 (1973), U.S. Supreme Court case, which held that an employer who refused to hire a lawfully admitted resident alien because of a longstanding policy against the employment of aliens could not be held liable under Title VII of the Civil Rights Act of 1964 if the company already employed a significant percentage of other employees who were of the same national origin but were also U.S. citizens.

esprit de corps, strong feelings of unity and common purpose on the part of a group.

estate planning, also ESTATE BUILDING, *estate planning* is concerned with the distribution of one's assets—one's estate—at death. *Estate building,* usually part of an executive compensation program, is concerned with turning portions of an executive's salary and fringe benefits into assets that will benefit his heirs after the executive's death. According to Thomas H. Patten, Jr., in *Pay: Employee Compensation and Incentive Plans* (N.Y.: The Free Press, 1977),

an estate can be defined in the field of executive compensation as the sum and substance of the earnings and acquisitions a person has conserved for eventual transmission to others. In order to have such an estate one must take steps to create it, conserve it, and transmit it to one's heir's. To a very important extent, although it may seem flippant to put it this way, estate planning amounts to planning how to disinherit the Internal Revenue Service (but in a lawful way).

Also see: Robert J. Lynn, *Introduction to Estate Planning in a Nutshell,* 3rd edition (St. Paul, Minn.: West, 1983); Robert A. Esperti and Renno L. Peterson, *The Handbook of Estate Planning* (New York: McGraw-Hill, 1983).

ETA: *see* EMPLOYMENT AND TRAINING ADMINISTRATION.

Ethical Practices Committee, a committee within the AFL–CIO whose charge is to keep the AFL–CIO "free from any taint of corruption or communism."

ethics, a set of moral principles or values.

There are many ethical individuals working as personnel operatives. However, their ethical standards tend to reflect their personal background rather than some abstract standards of personnel management. While professional codes of conduct have been put forth by a variety of organizations—such as the American Society for Personnel Administration (*see* CODE OF ETHICS) and the International Personnel Management Association (*see below*)—their impact has been inconsequential.

Thomas H. Patten, Jr., in "Is Personnel Administration A Profession," *Personnel Administration* (March–April 1968), has succinctly summarized the dilemma of ethical codes for personnel managers.

In a showdown disagreement with higher management, the personnel administrator who cited his professional ethical code as a basis for a course of action (assuming he had also complied with the law) would be regarded as either a naive, high-minded idealist or simply a fool. He would also be brave to so jeopardize his mealticket and future employment status. In any event, if he were to stand firm and threaten quitting as a sanction for his convictions, the letter of resignation would probably be eagerly awaited by a disgusted management (but one well pleased to be rid of a cloud-nine character).

Charles R. Milton's book, *Ethics & Expediency in Personnel Management: A Critical History of Personnel Philosophy* (Columbia, S.C.: University of South Carolina Press, 1970), deals mainly with changing styles of personnel management and only in the most peripheral sense with the ethic dilemmas of the personnel manager. *Also see* Debra W. Stewart, "Managing Competing Claims: An Ethical Framework for Human Resources Decision Making," *Public Administration Review* (January–February 1984).

See also CODE OF ETHICS and STANDARDS OF CONDUCT.

CODE OF ETHICS
FOR THE
INTERNATIONAL PERSONNEL
MANAGEMENT ASSOCIATION

I pledge that, according to my ability and my judgment, I will pursue these goals and keep these commitments:

I will respect and protect the dignity of individuals, honoring their right to fair consideration in all aspects of employment and to the pursuit of a rewarding career without regard to race, sex, religion, age, or national origin.

I will foster and apply management practices and merit principles which motivate employees to develop their full capability as competent, productive members of their organization.

I will endeavor to insure that full and early consideration is given to the human aspects of management plans and decisions.

I will assist employees and management in understanding and fulfilling their mutual responsibilities and obligations.

I will give freely of my knowledge and my time in the counseling and development of those pursuing a career in personnel management and will contribute to the development and dissemination of professional knowledge for the improvement of the art.

I will treat as privileged, information accepted in trust.

I will not compromise, for personal gain or accommodation, my integrity or that of my employer, but will faithfully respect and apply this Code in the conduct of my professional duties and responsibilities.

Ethics in Government Act of 1978, federal statute that seeks to deal with possible conflicts of interest by former federal executive branch employees by imposing post-employment prohibitions on their activities. The restrictions in the law are concerned with the former government employees' representation or attempts to influence federal agencies, not with their employment by others. What is prohibited depends on how involved a former employee was with a matter while with the government and whether he or she was one of a specified group of senior employees. *See* J. Jackson Walter, "The Ethics in Government Act, Conflict of Interest Laws and Presidential Recruiting," *Public Administration Review* (November–December 1981).

ethnic categories: *see* RACE CATEGORIES.

ethnic group, social, biological or (sometimes) political division of humankind. *See* David Nachmias and David Rosenbloom, "Bureaucracy and Ethnicity," *American*

Journal of Sociology (January 1978);
Joseph Rothschild, *Ethnopolitics: A Conceptual Framework* (New York: Columbia University Press, 1981); Thomas Sowell, *Ethnic America: A History* (New York: Basic Books, 1981); Stephen Steinberg, *The Ethnic Myth: Race, Ethnicity, and Class in America* (New York: Atheneum, 1981).

Etzioni, Amitai W. (1929-   ), sociologist and author of a variety of books on international relations, best known to organizational analysts for his studies of how organizations interact with the larger society and how the various parts of organizations interact, change, and survive. Major works include: *A Comparative Analysis of Complex Organizations* (Glencoe, Ill.: The Free Press, 1961); *Modern Organizations* (Englewood Cliffs, N.J.: Prentice-Hall, 1964).

eupsychian management, term originated by Abraham H. Maslow, in *Eupsychian Management: A Journal* (Homewood, Ill.: Richard D. Irwin, Inc., 1965), to describe an ideal situation with respect to workers motivation, productivity, and mental health. Relating eupsychian management to his more famous "hierarchy of needs," Maslow defines it as "the culture that would be generated by 1000 self-actualizing people on some sheltered island."

examination: *see* EMPLOYMENT TESTING.

examination, assembled, examination that includes as one of its parts a written or performance test which applicants are required to take at appointed times and places.

examination, group oral: *see* GROUP ORAL INTERVIEW.

examination, unassembled, examination in which applicants are rated on their education, experience, and other qualifications as shown in the formal application and any supportive evidence that may be required, without assembling for a written or performance test.

Examining Board v. Flores de Otero, 426 U.S. 572 (1976), U.S. Supreme Court case, which held that a Puerto Rican statute permitting only U.S. citizens to practice privately as civil engineers was unconstitutional and that resident aliens could not be denied the same opportunity.

Excelsior rule, the National Labor Relations Board has held that an employer must provide a list of the names and addresses of all employees eligible to vote in a forthcoming representation election. While the list is given to the NLRB, it is made available to emloyee organizations. The U.S. Supreme Court, in NLRB v. *Wyman-Gordon Co.,* 394 U.S. 759 (1969), upheld the NLRB's right to demand such a list.

excepted positions, also called EXEMPTED POSITIONS, U.S. civil service positions that have been excepted or exempted from merit system requirements. Most of the excepted positions in the U.S. Civil Service are excluded by statute and are under merit systems administered by agencies such as the Tennessee Valley Authority, the Federal Bureau of Investigation, U.S. Foreign Service, and the U.S. Postal Service. Excepted position has the same meaning as *unclassified position,* or *position excepted by law,* or *position excepted by executive order,* or *position excepted by civil service rule,* or *position outside the competitive service* as used in existing statutes and executive orders.

excepting language, the Attorney General of the United States has held that language relied on to establish an exception from the competitive service must be so plain and unequivocal as to admit of no doubts. When acts are silent on how appointments shall be made, the civil service laws, rules, and regulations apply.

excess plan, an integrated pension plan which provides relatively higher pensions on earnings above a specified level than on earnings below that level. A pure excess plan calculates pensions only on earnings above the specified level, while a step-rate excess plan has separate calculation formulas for earnings above and below the specified level.

Exchange Parts decision: *see* NATIONAL LABOR RELATIONS BOARD V. EXCHANGE PARTS.

exclusionary clause, that part of a contract that tries to restrict the legal remedies available to one side if the contract is broken.

exclusive recognition, also called EXCLUSIVE BARGAINING RIGHTS, in the private sector the only form of recognition available to a union representing a specific bargaining unit. An employer is required to negotiate in good faith, to give exclusive bargaining rights, to a union holding such recognition. In fact, a private employer may not bargain or consult with a union that does not hold exclusive recognition without committing an unfair labor practice.

As a term, exclusive recognition has had its greatest usage in the federal service. The Civil Service Reform Act of 1978 provides that in order to obtain exclusive recognition, a union must: (1) qualify as a bona fide union, (2) submit to the agency a roster of its officers and representatives, a copy of its constitution and bylaws, and a statement of its objectives, and (3) show that it has majority support solely by means of a secret ballot election in which it receives a majority of the votes cast. Exclusive recognition entitles the union to act for, and to negotiate agreements covering, all the employees in the unit. It guarantees the union the opportunity to be represented at discussions between management and employees concerning grievances and personnel policies.

ex-con: *see* EX-OFFENDER.

executive, any of the highest managers in an organization.
See also GROUP EXECUTIVE and PLURAL EXECUTIVE.

executive compensation, totality of the benefits paid to the members of the upper levels of the organizational hierarchy. According to William H. Cash, "Executive Compensation," *The Personnel Administrator* (September 1977),

executive compensation programs are generally viewed as being made up of five basic elements—base salary, short-term (annual) incentives or bonuses, long-term incentives and capital appreciation plans, fringe benefits, and perquisites.

For a bibliography, *see* Karen B. Tracy, "On Executive Compensation," *Harvard Business Review* (January–February 1977).

executive development: *see* MANAGEMENT DEVELOPMENT.

Executive Interchange Program: *see* PRESIDENT'S EXECUTIVE INTERCHANGE PROGRAM.

executive order, any rule or regulation, issued by a chief administrative authority, that, because of precedent and existing legislative authorization, has the effect of law. Executive orders are the principal mode of administrative action on the part of the president of the United States.

The power of a president to issue executive orders emanates from the constitutional provision requiring him to "take care that the laws be faithfully executed," the Commander-in-Chief clause, and express powers vested in him by congressional statutes. *See* William D. Neighbors, "Presidential Legislation by Executive Order," *University of Colorado Law Review* (Fall 1964) and William Hebe, "Executive Orders and the Development of Presidential Power," *Villanova Law Review* (March 1972).

Executive Order 8802, presidential executive order of June 25, 1941, which (1) required that defense contractors not discriminate against any worker because of race, creed, or national origin and (2) established a Committee on Fair Employment Practice to investigate and remedy violations.

THE RECOGNITION PROCESS

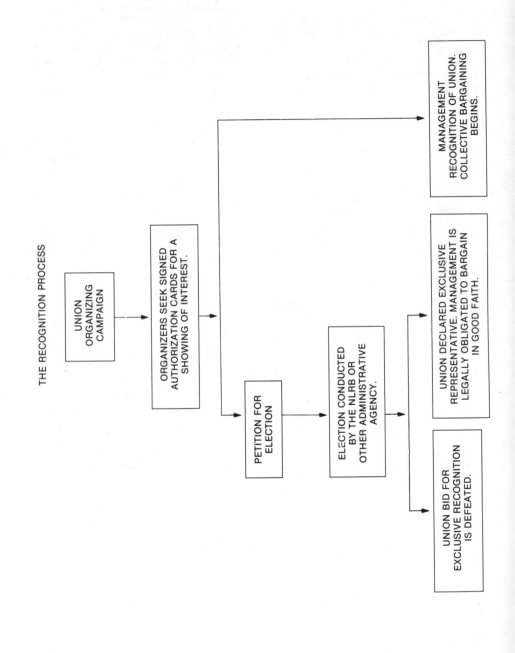

UNION ORGANIZING CAMPAIGN

ORGANIZERS SEEK SIGNED AUTHORIZATION CARDS FOR A SHOWING OF INTEREST.

MANAGEMENT RECOGNITION OF UNION. COLLECTIVE BARGAINING BEGINS.

PETITION FOR ELECTION

ELECTION CONDUCTED BY THE NLRB OR OTHER ADMINSTRATIVE AGENCY.

UNION DECLARED EXCLUSIVE REPRESENTATIVE. MANAGEMENT IS LEGALLY OBLIGATED TO BARGAIN IN GOOD FAITH.

UNION BID FOR EXCLUSIVE RECOGNITION IS DEFEATED.

Executive Order 10925, presidential executive order of March 6, 1961, which, for the first time, required that "affirmative action" be used to implement the policy of nondiscrimination in employment by the federal government and its contractors.

Executive Order 10988, presidential executive order of January 17, 1962, which first established the right of federal employees to bargain with management over certain limited issues. Considered the "Magna Carta" of labor relations in the federal government, it was superseded by Executive Order 11491.

Executive Order 11141, presidential executive order of February 12, 1964, which prohibits employment discrimination because of age by federal government contractors.

Executive Order 11246, presidential executive order of September 24, 1965, which requires federal government contracts to contain provisions against employment discrimination because of race, color, religion, or national origin.
See also PHILADELPHIA PLAN.

Executive Order 11375, presidential executive order of October 17, 1967, which requires federal government contracts to contain provisions against employment discrimination because of sex.

Executive Order 11451: *see* PRESIDENT'S EXECUTIVE INTERCHANGE PROGRAM.

Executive Order 11478, presidential executive order of August 8, 1969, which prohibits discrimination in federal government employment because of race, color, religion, sex, or national origin.

Executive Order 11491, presidential executive order of October 29, 1969, which granted each federal employee the right to join or not join a labor organization, created the Federal Labor Relations Council (which was superseded by the Federal Labor Relations Authority) and generally expanded the scope of bargaining for

federal employees. *See* Ed D. Roach and Frank W. McClain, "Executive Order 11491: Prospects and Problems," *Public Personnel Review* (July 1970).

Executive Order 11914, presidential executive order of April 28, 1976, which extends nondiscrimination with respect to the handicapped provisions of the Vocational Rehabilitation Act of 1973 to all federal departments and agencies.

Executive Order 11935: *see* HAMPTON V. MOW SUN WONG.

Executive Order 12008: *see* PRESIDENTIAL MANAGEMENT INTERN PROGRAM.

executive oversight, total process by which an executive attempts to exercise control over his organization and hold individual managers responsible for the implementation of their programs. *See* Lance T. LeLoup and William B. Moreland, "Agency Strategies and Executive Review: The Hidden Politics of Budgeting," *Public Administration Review* (May–June 1978).

executive recruiter: *see* HEADHUNTER.

Executive Schedule, key management and policymaking positions in the federal service are compensated under the Executive Schedule. Secretaries of cabinet departments, heads of agencies and their principal deputies, assistant secretaries, members of boards and commissions—a total of nearly 700 positions—are assigned to one of the five levels of the Executive Schedule, largely on the basis of protocol and interorganizational alignment. Virtually all the positions covered by the Executive Schedule are created by statute and carry specific statutory responsibilities and authorities.

executive session, any meeting of a legislative group or subgroup that is not open to the public.

Executive Stock Acquisition Plan, sanctioned under Section 423 of the Internal Revenue Code, the plan allows executives who are granted options to buy company stock at a price equal to the lessor of 85 percent of the market price on the date of the option grant or 85 percent of the market price at the time the option is exercised. Executives participating in such a plan authorize payroll deductions over a pre-determined period of time, usually a year or more, that pay for all or part of the optional stock at the end of the purchase period. James E. McKinney, "The Tax Reform Act of 1976 and Executive Stock Compensation Plan," *Personnel* (May–June 1977), discusses administration of the plan:

> During the purchase period, the executive is credited with any dividends paid on the stock or the interest accrued on his payments. The executive can withdraw from the plan at any time during the purchase period, and his payments will be returned to him along with either the dividend equivalents or interest accrued. If this kind of prefinancing arrangement is utilized, options should be granted at fairly frequent intervals (at least biannually and preferably annually) and for modest amounts of stock. The use of more frequent grants is analogous to dollar-averaging stock purchases and helps avoid another problem inherent in stock options—option price. If options are granted infrequently on a one-time basis at the market price of the stock on the particular day the option was granted, the price may or may not bear a relationship to the true value of the stock.

executive supplemental compensation, type of nonproduction bonus that is based upon an estimate of an executive's contribution to the profitability of the company over a given time period.

Exemplary Rehabilitation Certificates: *see* UNITED STATES EMPLOYMENT SERVICE.

exempted positions: *see* EXCEPTED POSITIONS.

exempt employees, employees who, because of their administrative, profes-

sional or executive status, are not covered by the overtime provisions of the Fair Labor Standards Act. In consequence, their employing organizations are not legally required to pay them for overtime work. For an analysis of the problem, *see* Robert A. Sbarra, "Exempt Employee Overtime," *Compensation Review* (First Quarter 1976).

exemption, deduction from gross income for income tax purposes allowed for the support of one's self and dependents.

exit interview, also called SEPARATION INTERVIEW, tool to monitor employee terminations that seeks information on why the employee is leaving and what he or she liked or disliked about his or her job, working conditions, company policy, etc. Exit interviews are usually, and most desirably, conducted by the personnel department and not by the supervisor of the exiting employee. When interviews are not possible, *exit questionnaires* seek to gather the same information. *See* Charles Bahn, "Expanded Use of the Exit Interview," *Personnel Journal* (December 1965); Martin Hilb, "The Standardized Exit Interview," *Personnel Journal* (June 1978); Laura Garrison and Jacqueline Ferguson, "Separation Interviews," *Personnel Journal* (September 1977); Wanda R. Embrey, R. Wayne Mondy, and Robert M. Noc, "Exit Interview: A Tool for Personnel Development," *Personnel Administrator* (May 1979); Pamela Garretson and Kenneth S. Teel, "The Exit Interview: Effective Tool or Meaningless Gesture?" *Personnel* (July–August 1982).

ex-offender, anyone who, having been convicted of a crime, served time in prison. For an analysis of the problem of employing ex-offenders, *see* Marvin A. Jolson, "Are Ex-Offenders Successful Employees?" *California Management Review* (Spring 1975); Frederick Englander, "Helping Ex-Offenders Enter the Labor Market," *Monthly Labor Review* (July 1983).

ex officio, Latin phrase ("by virtue of his

office"). Many individuals hold positions on boards, commissions, councils, etc., because of an office that they temporarily occupy. For example, the mayor of a city may be an *ex officio* member of the board of trustees of a university in his or her city.

expansion demand, the new job openings created by expansion or growth in a given occupation or industry.

ex parte, Latin meaning: with only one side present.

expectancy, probability of success on the job in terms of a specific criterion and associated with a known fact about an individual such as a test score, level of education, etc.

expectancy theory, also VALENCE, *expectancy theory* holds that individuals have cognitive "expectancies" regarding outcomes that are likely to occur as a result of what they do, and that individuals have preferences among these various outcomes. Consequently, motivation occurs on the basis of what the individual expects to occur as a result of what he chooses to do. An "expectancy" in this context refers to an employee's perceived probability that a given level of effort will result in a given outcome, such as a promotion or raise in salary. The value that an employee places on this outcome, the strength of the employee's preference for it, has been termed *valence* by Victor H. Vroom, *Work and Motivation* (N.Y.: John Wiley, 1964). Valence can be positive or negative, depending on whether an individual is attracted to or repelled by a possible outcome. See Robert J. House, H. Jack Shapiro, and Mahmoud A. Wahba, "Expectancy Theory as a Predictor of Work Behavior and Attitude: A Reevaluation of Empirical Evidence," *Decision Sciences* (July 1974); Daniel R. Ilgen, Delbert N. Nebeker and Robert D. Pritchard, "Expectancy Theory Measures: An Empirical Comparison in an Experimental Simulation," *Organizational Behavior and Human Performance* (October 1981); Gedaliahu H. Harel and Loretta K. Co-

nen, "Expectancy Theory Applied to the Process of Professional Obsolescence," *Public Personnel Management* (Spring 1982); Samuel B. Pond, III, Achilles A. Armenakis and Samuel B. Green, "The Importance of Employee Expectations in Organizational Diagnosis," *The Journal of Applied Behavioral Science,* Vol. 20, No. 2 (1984); Roger T. Kaufman and Geoffrey Woglom, "The Effects of Expectations on Union Wages," *The American Economic Review* (June 1984).

See also PSYCHOLOGICAL CONTRACT.

expedited arbitration, because conventional arbitration is frequently so time consuming and expensive, this new streamlined process is being increasingly incorporated into union contracts in an effort to cut down the backlog of grievance cases. In 1971, in response to the concern of parties over rising costs and delays in grievance arbitration, the Labor-Management Committee of the American Arbitration Association recommended the establishment of expedited procedures, under which cases could be scheduled promptly and awards rendered no later than five days after the hearings. In return for giving up certain features of traditional labor arbitration (such as transcripts, briefs, and extensive opinions), the parties utilizing simplified procedures can get quick decisions and realize certain cost savings. While the term expedited arbitration can be applied to any "fast" method of resolving disputes through the use of an arbitrator, it is usually characterized by on-site hearings and the minimal involvement of the hierarchies of both union and management. For details of the technique, see Lawrence Stessin, "Expedited Arbitration: Less Grief Over Grievances," *Harvard Business Review* (January-February 1977).

experience-based learning, *see* laboratory training.

experience rating, insurance term which refers to a review of a previous year's group-claims experience in order to establish premium rates for the following year.

See Joseph M. Becker, *Experience Rating in Unemployment Insurance: An Experiment in Competitive Socialism* (Baltimore: The Johns Hopkins University Press, 1972).

experienced unemployed, term from the U.S. Bureau of the Census that refers to "unemployed persons who have worked at any time in the past."

experimenter effect, any distortion in an experiment's findings because of the behavior or attitudes of the experimenters.
See also HAWTHORNE EFFECT.

expert, efficiency: *see* EFFICIENCY EXPERT.

expiration date, time established by a collective bargaining agreement for the agreement to terminate.

external alignment, relationship of positions within an organization to similar positions in the near environment. In theory, the most desirable external alignment calls for compensation programs similar to those provided by other employers in the local labor market.

external equity, also INTERNAL EQUITY, a measure of the justice of an employee's wages when the compensation for his/her position is compared to the labor market as a whole within a region, profession, or industry. *Internal equity* is a measure of the justice of an employee's wages when the compensation for his/her position is compared to similar positions within the same organization. *See* Thomas A. Mahoney, "Justice and Equity: A Recurring Theme in Compensation," *Personnel* (September-October 1975).

external house organ: *see* HOUSE ORGAN.

external labor market, geographic region from which employers reasonably expect to recruit new workers.

extrinsic motivation, motivation not an inherent part of the work itself. When one works solely for the monetary rewards, one is extrinsically motivated.

Eysenck Personality Inventory (EPI), measures two independent dimensions of personality, extraversion-introversion and neuroticism-stability. Consists of 57 yes-no items with falsification scale to reflect distortion. TIME: 10/15 minutes. AUTHORS: H. J. and S. B. G. Eysenck. PUBLISHER: Educational and Industrial Testing Service (*see* TEST PUBLISHERS).

F

Fabricant, Solomon (1906-　　), labor economist, best known for his work on productivity measurement. *See* his *A Primer on Productivity* (N.Y.: Random House, 1969).

face amount, in life insurance, this is the amount, stated on the front of the policy, that is payable upon the death of the insured. The actual amount payable to the beneficiary may differ according to the policy's specific provisions, such as double indemnity, or subsequent riders.

face validity, also called FAITH VALIDITY, measure of the degree to which a test *appears* to be valid. While this is the most superficial kind of validity, it may contribute significantly to the legitimacy of the test in the eyes of the candidates (an important consideration in avoiding legal challenges). However, it can also deceive employers who may be tempted to save the time and money required for genuine validation. According to Raymond B. Cattell, "Validity and Reliability: A Proposed More Basic Set of Concepts," *Journal of Educational Psychology* (February 1964),

in some trivial sense face or faith validity perhaps still has a role, but in diplomacy rather than psychology, as when an industrial psychologist is pressured to make tests which a chief executive will, from the depths of his ignorance commend or sanction as measuring what he conceives to be this or that trait.

facilitator, individual who serves as a catalyst, usually in a formal organization development effort, in order to improve the interactions and interpersonal relationships of a group.

FACT: *see* FLANAGAN APTITUDE CLASSIFICATION TEST.

factfinding, an impartial review of the issues in a labor dispute by a specially appointed third party, whether it be a single individual, panel, or board. The factfinder holds formal or informal hearings and submits a report to the administrative agency and/or the parties involved. The factfinder's report, usually considered advisory, may contain specific recommendations. According to Robert E. Doherty, "On Factfinding: A One-Eyed Man Lost Among the Eagles," *Public Personnel Management* (September–October 1976),

factfinding nowadays seems to be regarded as a way station in the onward march toward the strike, unilateral management determination or (in most instances) further haggling which eventually ends up in a settlement—a settlement which may or may not bear a relationship to the factfinder's report. The factfinder is only rarely treated with deference—and rightfully so. It takes considerable audacity to believe that after a few hours of testimony any individual whose talents are somewhat less than those of a Solomon can come to understand the issues well enough to render a report that is sufficiently clear and logical to impress both parties.

factor analysis, any of several methods of analyzing the intercorrelations among test scores or other sets of variables. *See* Wayne K. Kirchner and June A. Lucas, "Using Factor Analysis to Explore Employee Attitudes," *Personnel Journal* (June 1970); Richard L. Gorsuch, *Factor Analysis* (Phila.: W. B. Saunders, 1974); T. Gregory Morton, "Factor Analysis, Multicollinearity, and Regression Appraisal

Models," *The Appraisal Journal* (October 1977).

factor evaluation system, also called FACTOR COMPARISON SYSTEM, a hybrid of traditional duties or position classification systems. With traditional duties classification, different combinations of factors are used for different positions; the factor evaluation system uses the same factors for all positions. With traditional duties classification, grade levels are ascertained by the weight and eloquence of narrative descriptions; the factor evaluation system determines grade levels by comparing positions directly to one another. The main ingredient of a factor evaluation system is, obviously, the factor—any of the various key elements individually examined in the evaluation process. Once the factors of a position have been identified, they can be ranked—the factors of one position are compared to another. Such a factor comparison can have only three outcomes. Any given factor must be higher, lower, or equal to the factor of another position. When positions are ranked by factors, all of the factors of each position are compared and an overall ranking is achieved. *See* Lawrence L. Epperson, "The Dynamics of Factor Comparison/Point Evaluation," *Public Personnel Management* (January–February 1975).

factors: *see* JOB FACTORS.

factors of production, the resources used to produce goods and services. There are three traditional factors: land, labor, and capital. Recently, management or entrepreneurship has come to be considered a factor as well. *See* CAPITAL.

factory system: *see* DIVISION OF LABOR.

fair day's work, generally, the amount of work produced in a work day by a qualified employee of average skill exerting average effort.

Fair Employment Practice Commission (FEPC), generic term for any state or local government agency responsible for administrating/enforcing laws prohibiting employment discrimination because of race, color, sex, religion, national origin, or other factors.

Fair Employment Practice Committee, (FEPC), former federal committee. In 1941, President Franklin D. Roosevelt issued Executive Order 8802, which called for the elimination of discrimination based upon race, color, religion, or national origin within the defense production industries and the federal service. A newly created Fair Employment Practice Committee was charged with implementing the order. By almost all accounts, however, the committee was weak and even somewhat disinterested in combating discrimination in the federal service. In 1946, it met its demise through an amendment to an appropriations bill. For its history, *see* Louis C. Kesselman, *The Social Politics of FEPC* (Chapel Hill, N.C.: University of North Carolina Press, 1948); Will Maslow, "FEPC—A Case History in Parliamentary Maneuver," *University of Chicago Law Review*, Vol. 13 (June 1946).

fair employment practice laws, all government requirements designed to prohibit discrimination in the various aspects of employment. *See* James S. Russell, "A Review of Fair Employment Cases in the Field of Training," *Personnel Psychology* (Summer 1984).

Fair Employment Practice Service, reference service published by the Bureau of National Affairs, Inc., which covers federal and state laws dealing with equal opportunity in employment. Full texts of federal and state FEP laws, orders, and regulations, as well as federal, state, and local court opinions, and decisions of the Equal Employment Opportunity Commission.

Fair Labor Standards Act (FLSA), also called WAGES AND HOURS ACT, federal statute of 1938, which, as amended, establishes minimum-wage, overtime-pay, equal-pay, recordkeeping, and child-labor

standards affecting more than 50 million full-time and part-time workers.

Basic Wage Standards. Covered non-exempt workers are entitled to a minimum wage of not less than $3.35 an hour and overtime at not less than one and one-half times the employee's regular rate is due after 40 hours of work in the workweek. Wages required by FLSA are due on the regular pay day for the pay period covered. (Hospitals and residential care establishments may adopt, by agreement with the employees, a 14-day overtime period in lieu of the usual 7-day workweek, if the employees are paid at least time and a half their regular rate for hours worked over 8 in a day or 80 in a 14-day work period.)

Who is Covered? All employees of certain enterprises having workers engaged in interstate commerce, producing goods for interstate commerce, or handling, selling, or otherwise working on goods or materials that have been moved in or produced for such commerce by any person are covered by FLSA. A covered enterprise is the related activities performed through unified operation or common control by any person or persons for a common business purpose and is:

1. engaged in laundering or cleaning of clothing or fabrics; or
2. engaged in the business of construction or reconstruction; or
3. engaged in the operation of a hospital; an institution primarily engaged in the care of the sick, the aged, the mentally ill or defective who reside on the premises; a school for mentally or physically handicapped or gifted children; a preschool, an elementary or secondary school; or an institution of higher education (regardless of whether or not such hospital, institution or school is public or private or operated for profit or not for profit); or
4. comprised exclusively of one or more retail or service establishments whose annual gross volume of sales or business done is not less than $362,500; or

5. any other type of enterprise having an annual gross volume of sales or business done of not less than $250,000.

The dollar volume standard mentioned above in (4) and (5) excludes excise taxes at the retail level which are separately stated. Any establishment which has as its only regular employees the owner thereof or members of the owner's immediate family is not considered part of any enterprise.

Federal employees are subject to the minimum-wage, overtime, child-labor, and equal-pay provisions of FLSA. Employees of state and local governments are subject to the same provisions, unless they are engaged in traditional governmental activities, in which case they are subject to the child-labor and equal-pay provisions only. The Supreme Court has indicated that such traditional governmental activities include schools, hospitals, fire prevention, police protection, sanitation, public health parks and recreation.

Employees who are not employed in a covered enterprise may still be entitled to the act's minimum-wage, overtime-pay, equal-pay, and child-labor protections if they are individually engaged in interstate commerce. These employees include:

1. communication and transportation workers;
2. employees who handle, ship, or receive goods moving in interstate commerce;
3. clerical or other workers who regularly use the mails, telephone, or telegraph for interstate communication or who keep records on interstate transactions;
4. employees who regularly cross state lines in the course of their work; and
5. employees of independent employers who perform clerical, custodial, maintenance, or other work for firms engaged in commerce or in the production of goods for commerce.

Domestic service workers such as maids, day workers, housekeepers, chauffeurs, cooks, or full-time baby sitters are covered if they (1) receive at least $100 in cash wages in a calendar year from their em-

ployer or (2) work a total of more than 8 hours a week for one or more employers.

Tipped Employees. Tipped employees are those who customarily and regularly receive more than $30 a month in tips. The employer may consider tips as part of wages, but such a wage credit must not exceed 40 percent of the minimum wage.

The employer who elects to use the tip credit provision must inform the employee in advance and must be able to show that the employee receives at least the minimum wage when direct wages and the tip credit allowance are combined. Also, employees must retain all of their tips, except to the extent that they participate in a valid tip pooling or sharing arrangement.

Employer-Furnished Facilities. The reasonable cost or fair value of board, lodging, and other facilities provided by the employer may, as determined by the Wage and Hour Administrator, be considered part of wages.

Subminimum Wage Provisions. Learners, apprentices, and handicapped workers may, under certain circumstances, be paid less than the minimum wage, as well as full-time students in retail or service establishments, agriculture, or institutions of higher education. Special certificates issued by the Wage and Hour Administrator must be obtained by employers wishing to use these provisions.

Equal Pay Provisions. The equal-pay provisions of FLSA prohibit wage differentials based on sex, between men and women employed in the same establishment on jobs that require equal skills, effort, and responsibility and are performed under similar working conditions.

Exemptions from Both Minimum Wage and Overtime. Executive, administrative, and professional employees (including teachers and academic administrative personnel in elementary or secondary schools) and outside sales persons; employees of certain individually owned and operated small retail or service establishments not part of a covered enterprise; employees of certain small newspapers, switchboard operators of small telephone companies, seamen employed on foreign vessels, and employees engaged in fishing operations; farm workers employed by anyone who used no more than 500 mandays or farm labor in any calendar quarter of the preceding calendar year; casual baby sitters and persons employed as companions to the elderly or infirm.

Exemptions from Overtime Provisions Only. Certain highly-paid commission employees of retail or service establishments; auto, truck, trailer, farm implement, boat, or aircraft salesworkers, or partsmen and mechanics servicing autos, trucks or farm implements, and who are employed by nonmanufacturing establishments primarily engaged in selling these items to ultimate purchasers; employees of railroads and air carriers, taxi drivers, certain employees of motor carriers, seamen on U.S. vessels, and local delivery employees paid on approved trip rate plans; announcers, news editors, and chief engineers of certain nonmetropolitan broadcasting stations; domestic service workers residing in the employers' residences; employees of motion picture theaters, and farmworkers.

Child Labor Provisions. FLSA child-labor provisions are designed to protect the educational opportunities of minors and prohibit their employment in jobs and under conditions detrimental to their health or well-being. Regulations governing youth employment in nonfarm jobs differ somewhat from those pertaining to agricultural employment. In nonfarm work, the permissible kinds and hours of work, by age are:

1. *18 years or older:* any job, whether hazardous or not, for unlimited hours;
2. *16 and 17 years old:* any nonhazardous job, for unlimited hours;
3. *14 and 15 years old:* outside of school hours in various non-manufacturing, nonmining, nonhazardous jobs, under these conditions: no more than 3 hours on a school day, 18 hours in a school week, 8 hours on a non-school day or 40 hours in a non-school week. Also, work may not begin before 7 a.m. nor end after 7 p.m. except from June 1 through Labor Day, when evening hours are

extended to 9 p.m. Under a special provision, 14- and 15-year-olds enrolled in an approved Work Experience and Career Exploration Program may be employed for up to 23 hours in school weeks and 3 hours on school days (including during school hours).

Fourteen is the minimum age for most nonfarm work. However, at any age, youths may deliver newspapers, perform in radio, television, movie or theatrical productions, work for parents in their solely owned nonfarm business (except in manufacturing or on hazardous jobs), gather evergreens, and make evergreen wreaths.

Permissible kinds and hours of work for youths employed in agriculture are:

1. *16 years and older:* any job whether hazardous or not, for unlimited hours;
2. *14 and 15 years old:* any non-hazardous farm job outside of school hours;
3. *12 and 13 years old:* outside of school hours in nonhazardous jobs, either with parents' written consent or on the same farm as the parents;
4. *under 12 years old:* jobs on farms owned or operated by parents or, with parents' written consent, outside of school hours in nonhazardous jobs on farms not covered by minimum wage requirements.

Local minors 10 and 11 years of age may work for no more than 8 weeks between June 1 and October 15 for employers who receive approval from the Secretary of Labor. This work must be confined to hand-harvesting short season crops outside school hours under very limited and specified circumstances prescribed by the Secretary of Labor.

Minors of any age may be employed by their parents at any time in any occupation on a farm owned or operated by their parents.

Recordkeeping. Employers are required to keep records on wages, hours and other items. Most of the information is of the kind generally maintained by employers in ordinary business practice and in compliance with other laws and regulations.

The records do not have to be kept in any particular form and time clocks need not be used. With respect to an employee subject to both minimum wage and overtime pay provisions, the following records must be kept:

1. personal information, including employee's name, home address, occupation, sex, and birth date (if under 19 years of age);
2. hour and day when workweek begins;
3. total hours worked each workday and each workweek;
4. total daily or weekly straight-time earnings;
5. regular hourly pay rate for any week when overtime is worked;
6. total overtime pay for the workweek;
7. deductions from or additions to wages;
8. total wages paid each pay period; and
9. date of payment and pay period covered.

Records required for exempt employees differ from those for nonexempt workers and special information is required on employees working under uncommon pay arrangements or to whom lodging or other facilities are furnished. Employers who have homeworkers must make entries in handbooks supplied by the Division.

Enforcement. The Wage and Hour Division of the U.S. Department of Labor administers and enforces FLSA with respect to private employment, state and local government employment, and federal employees of the Library of Congress, U.S. Postal Service, Postal Rate Commission, and the Tennessee Valley Authority.

The Wage and Hour Division's enforcement of FLSA is carried out by compliance officers stationed across the U.S. As the division's authorized representatives, they have the authority to conduct investigations and gather data on wages, hours, and other employment conditions or practices, in order to determine compliance with the act. Where violations are found, they also may recommend changes in employment practices, in order to bring an employer into compliance with the law.

It is a violation of FLSA to fire or in any other manner discriminate against an employee for filing a complaint or participating in a legal proceeding under the law. Willful violations may be prosecuted criminally and the violater fined up to $10,000. A second conviction may result in imprisonment. Violators of the child labor provisions are subject to a civil money penalty of up to $1,000 for each violation.

For histories of FLSA, *see* Jonathan Grossman, "Fair Labor Standards Act of 1938: Maximum Struggle for a Minimum Wage," *Monthly Labor Review* (June 1978); P. K. Elder and H. D. Miller, "The Fair Labor Standards Act: Changes of Four Decades," *Monthly Labor Review* (July 1979); Horst Brand, "The Evolution of Fair Labor Standards: A Study in Class Conflict," *Monthly Labor Review* (August 1983).

See also the following entries:
    CHILD LABOR
    NATIONAL LEAGUE OF CITIES V. USERY
    OVERTIME
    UNITED STATES V. DARBY LUMBER

fair representation: *see* DUTY OF FAIR REPRESENTATION.

fair-share agreement, arrangement whereby both the employer and the union agree that employees are not obligated to join the union, but that all employees must pay the union a prorated share of bargaining costs as a condition of employment.

faith validity: *see* FACE VALIDITY.

Fall River system, an early factory system which employed men, women and children and made no special provision for their housing.

false negative, any incidence whereby an individual, who is in fact qualified, is excluded by a test or some other screening criteria.

false positive, any incidence whereby an individual, who is in fact unqualified, is selected because of a test or some other screening criteria.

family allowances, payments to workers, in addition to regular wages, based on the number of dependent children that a worker may have. Almost all of the major industrial countries, except the United States, have family-allowance programs financed by their governments. For an analysis, *see* George E. Rejda, "Family Allowances as a Program for Reducing Poverty," *The Journal of Risk and Insurance* (December 1970).

family-expense policy, health insurance policy that insures both the individual policyholder and his or her immediate dependents (usually spouse and children).

family T-group, work team that undertakes a T-group effort as a unit.
See also T-GROUP.

FAS: *see* FUNDAMENTAL ACHIEVEMENT SERIES.

fatigue, weariness caused by physical or mental exertion that lessens the capacity to, and the will for, work. For an analysis, *see* R. A. McFarland, "Fatigue In Industry: Understanding Fatigue in Modern Life" *Ergonomics,* Vol. 14, No. 1 (1971).

fatigue allowance, in production planning, this is that additional time added to "normal" work time to compensate for the factor of fatigue.

fatigue curve, also MONOTONY CURVE, graphic representation of productivity increases and decreases influenced by fatigue. As workers "warm up" or practice their tasks, productivity increases; thereafter fatigue sets in and productivity decreases. After lunch or coffee breaks, productivity should rise again slightly, but thereafter continuously decline until the end of the day. This pattern varies with differing kinds of work. Fatigue curve measurements are essential in establishing realistic work standards.

A *monotony curve* is characterized by a drop in productivity in the middle of the work period, great variability in the rate of productivity, and a tendency to "end

spurt"—show an increase in productivity at the end of the work period due to a feeling of relief that the work period is almost over.

The classic work on fatigue and monotony curves was done as part of the Hawthorne experiments. *See* F. J. Roethlisberger and William J. Dickson, *Management and the Worker* (Cambridge, Mass.: Harvard University Press, 1939). *See also* HAWTHORNE STUDIES.

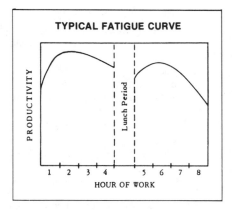

TYPICAL FATIGUE CURVE

fat work, slang term for work that offers more money for no more than normal effort; also work that offers regular wages but requires a less than normal effort.

favoritism, according to John E. Fisher in "Playing Favorites in Large Organizations," *Business Horizons* (June 1977),
> one way authoritarian executives control subordinates is by permitting favorites to enjoy opportunities for highly visible accomplishments while making it difficult, if not impossible, for those who are in disfavor to do so. Then when the favorite is promoted or meritoriously cited, his sponsor can point with pride to how impressive his achievements look on paper. If a nonfavorite has the temerity to complain about the choice, he is confronted with his own predictable paucity of accomplishments. Often the latter is puzzled by his lack of accomplishments despite his application of hard work, initiative and resourcefulness. If he reflects, however, he may recall that his soundest recom-

mendations have been turned down and his initiative curbed at every turn.

Fayol, Henri (1841-1925), French executive engineer who developed the first comprehensive theory of management. His *Administration Industrielle et Générale* (published in France in 1916), was almost ignored in the U.S. until Constance Storrs' English translation, *General and Industrial Management* (London: Pitman, 1949), appeared. Today his theoretical contributions are generally considered as significant as those of Frederick W. Taylor.

featherbedding, term, meaning an easy or superfluous job, which originated in the U.S. Army in the 1850s. Those frontier soldiers who had easy jobs at headquarters and could sleep in comfortable featherbeds were called "feathered soldiers." So featherbedding grew to mean any job that required little or no work.

Today featherbedding connotes any labor practice that requires an employer to pay for more workers than are truly needed for a job, or to pay for work that is not performed. Featherbedding provisions in labor contracts usually have their origin in work rules that were once efficient but have become obsolete due to newer technology. Union leaders often insist on maintaining the older practices in order to protect the jobs of those whose livelihoods are threatened by the new technology.

The Labor-Management Relations (Taft-Hartley) Act of 1947 makes it an unfair labor practice "to cause or attempt to cause an employer to pay or deliver or agree to pay or deliver any money or other thing of value in the nature of an exaction, for services which are not performed." This provision has not had much effect, however, because of the legal subtleties of defining featherbedding practices. *See* Robert D. Leiter, *Featherbedding and Job Security* (N.Y.: Twayne Publishers, 1964); Paul A. Weinstein (ed.), *Featherbedding and Technological Change* (Boston: D.C. Heath, 1965).

See also AMERICAN NEWSPAPER PUBLISHERS ASSOCIATION V. NATIONAL LABOR RELATIONS BOARD and UNFAIR LABOR PRACTICES (UNIONS).

Federal Bureau of Apprenticeship and Training: *see* APPRENTICE.

federal court of appeals: *see* COURT OF APPEALS.

federal district court: *see* DISTRICT COURT.

Federal Employee's Compensation Act of 1916, federal statute administered by the U.S. Department of Labor that provides compensation for disability and death, medical care, and rehabilitation services for all civilian employees and officers of the United States who suffer injuries while in the performance of their duties.

Federal Employees Part-Time Career Employment Act of 1978, federal statute that requires federal agencies to implement employment programs for part-timers (persons working between 16 and 32 hours per week).

Federal Executive Institute, The (FEI), established by Executive Order in 1968, this is the federal government's primary in-residence training facility for executive development.

Federal Executive Institute
Route 28 North
Charlottesville, VA 22903
(804) 296-0181

Federal Job Information Centers, a nationwide network of centers that provide information on federal employment. Administered by the Office of Personnel Management, the centers have for the most part been closed by the Reagan administration.

Federal Labor Relations Authority (FLRA), created by the Civil Service Reform Act of 1978 to oversee the creation of bargaining units, supervise elections, and otherwise deal with labor-management issues in federal agencies. The FLRA is headed by a chairman and two members, who are appointed on a bipartisan basis to staggered 5-year terms. The FLRA replaces the Federal

Federal Labor Relations Authority

Labor Relations Council (FLRC).

Within the FLRA, a general counsel, appointed to a 5-year term, will investigate alleged unfair labor practices and prosecute them before the FLRA. Also within the FLRA and acting as a separate body, the Federal Service Impasses Panel (FSIP) acts to resolve negotiation impasses.

Federal Labor Relations Authority
500 C Street, S.W.
Washington, D.C. 20424
(202) 382-0711

Federal Labor Relations Council (FLRC), established in 1969 by Executive Order 11491 and supplanted by the Federal Labor Relations Authority pursuant to provisions of the Civil Service Reform Act of 1978.

federal labor union, a local union affiliated directly with the AFL-CIO rather than with a national or international union.

Federal Mediation and Conciliation Service (FMCS), created by the Labor-Management Relations (Taft-Hartley) Act of 1947 as an independent agency of the federal government, FMCS helps prevent disruptions in the flow of interstate commerce caused by labor-management disputes by providing mediators to assist disputing parties in the resolution of their differences. FMCS can intervene on its own motion or by invitation of either side in a dispute. Mediators have no law enforcement authority and rely wholly on persuasive techniques. FMCS also helps provide qualified third-party neutrals as factfinders or arbitrators.

The mediator's efforts are directed toward the establishment of sound and stable labor-management relations on a continuing basis. FMCS mediators assist representatives of labor and management in settling disputes about wages, hours, and other aspects of the employment relationship that arise in the course of negotiations. In this work, the mediator has a more basic function—encouraging and promoting better day-to-day relations between labor and management. He/she

THE FEDERAL LABOR RELATIONS AUTHORITY (FLRA)

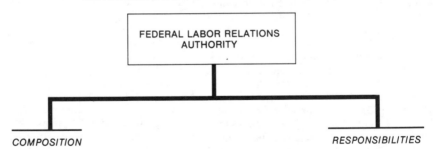

FEDERAL LABOR RELATIONS AUTHORITY

COMPOSITION

- THREE MEMBERS, FIVE YEAR TERMS
- APPOINTED BY PRESIDENT, ADVICE AND CONSENT OF SENATE
- REMOVAL ONLY FOR CAUSE

RESPONSIBILITIES

- ADMINISTERS AND INTERPRETS TITLE VII OF CIVIL SERVICE REFORM ACT OF 1978
- DETERMINES APPROPRIATENESS OF UNITS
- SUPERVISES OR CONDUCTS ELECTIONS
- DECIDES NEGOTIABILITY QUESTIONS
- RESOLVES CONSULTATION ISSUES
- COMPELLING NEED DETERMINATIONS
- DECIDES UNFAIR LABOR PRACTICE CASES
- CONSIDERS ARBITRATION AWARD EXCEPTIONS

thereby helps to reduce the incidence of work stoppages. Issues arising in negotiations may then be faced as problems to be settled through mutual effort rather than issues in dispute.

FMCS offers its facilities in labor-management disputes in any industry affecting interstate commerce, either upon its own motion or at the request of one or more of the parties to the dispute, whenever in its judgment such dispute threatens to cause a substantial interruption of commerce. Employers and unions are required to file with FMCS a notice of every dispute affecting commerce not settled within 30 days after prior service of a notice to terminate or modify an existing contract. FMCS is required to avoid the mediation of disputes that would have only a minor effect on interstate commerce if state or other conciliation services are available to the parties. FMCS is directed to make its mediation and conciliation facilities available only as a last resort and in exceptional cases in the settlement of grievance disputes arising over the application or interpretation of existing collective bargaining agreements.

On the joint request of employers and unions, FMCS will also assist in the selection of arbitrators from a roster of private citizens who are qualified as neutrals to adjudicate matters in dispute.

Regional Offices—Federal Mediation and Conciliation Service

Region	Address/Telephone
Eastern Region	Room 2937, 26 Federal Plaza, New York, NY 10278, 212-264-1000.
Southern Region	Suite 400, 1422 W. Peachtree St. NW., Atlanta, Ga. 30309, 404-881-2473.
Central Region	Room 1659, 175 W. Jackson Blvd., Chicago, Ill. 60604, 312-353-7350.
Western Region	Suite 235, 50 Francisco St., San Francisco, Calif. 94133, 415-556-4670.

FMCS has offices in 79 principal cities, with meeting facilities available for labor-management negotiations. *See* Jerome T. Barrett and Lucretia Dewey Tanner, "The FMCS Role in Age Discrimination Complaints: New Uses of Mediation," *Labor Law Journal* (November 1981); Kay McMurray, "The Federal Mediation and Conciliation Service: Serving Labor-Management Relations in the Eighties," *Labor Law Journal* (February 1983).

> *Federal Mediation and Conciliation Service*
> 2100 K Street N.W.
> Washington, D.C. 20427
> (202) 653-5290

Federal Pay Comparability Act of 1970, federal statute that placed the initiative for maintaining pay comparability for federal employees with the president rather than with the Congress. *See* Raymond Jacobson, "Pay Comparability," *Civil Service Journal* (April–June 1974); George L. Stelluto, "Federal Pay Comparability: Facts to Temper the Debate," *Monthly Labor Review* (June 1979).

Federal Personnel Manual (FPM), publication of the Office of Personnel Management (OPM) that contains all OPM personnel regulations and instructions to federal agencies.

Federal Register, daily publication that is the medium for making available to the public federal agency regulations and other legal documents of the executive branch. These documents cover a wide range of government activities—environmental protection, consumer product safety, food and drug standards, occupational health and safety, and many more areas of concern to the public. Perhaps more importantly, the *Federal Register* includes *proposed* changes in regulated areas. Each proposed change published carries an invitation for any citizen or group to participate in the consideration of the proposed regulation through the submission of written data, views, or arguments, and sometimes by oral presentations.

For further information on the *Federal Register*, write to the Office of the Federal Register, National Archives and Records Service, Washington, D.C. 20408.

Federal Salary Reform Act of 1962: *see* SALARY REFORM ACT OF 1962.

Federal Service Entrance Examination (FSEE), from 1955 through 1974, the U.S. Civil Service Commission's most basic means of selecting new college graduates for over 200 different occupational specialties. In the early 1970s, the FSEE came under increasing attack because of its adverse impact on equal employment opportunity. In 1975, it was replaced by the Professional and Administrative Careers Examination (PACE). *See* Robert Sadacca, *The Validity and Discriminatory Impact of the Federal Service Entrance Examination* (Washington, D.C.: The Urban Institute, 1971).

See also PROFESSIONAL AND ADMINISTRATIVE CAREERS EXAMINATION.

Federal Service Impasses Panel (FSIP), located within the Federal Labor Relations Authority, the Federal Service Impasses Panel has the responsibility of aiding federal agencies and their labor organizations in settling their negotiation impasses when voluntary efforts have failed. The FSIP may authorize binding arbitration, third-party factfinding, or other appropriate measures.

Federal Service Impasses Panel
500 C Street, S.W.
Washington, D.C. 20424
(202) 382-0711

Federal Supplemental Compensation, a program enacted in 1982 to provide benefits to individuals who exhaust all of their rights to benefits under the regular and extended Unemployment Insurance programs. In States where extended benefits are not in effect, exhaustees of regular unemployment insurance immediately become eligible for Federal Supplemental Compensation. In States on extended benefits, an individual must exhaust those benefits before collecting Federal Supplemental Compensation. *See:* Arlene Holen, "Federal Supplemental Compensation and Unemployment Insurance Recipients," *Monthly Labor Review* (April 1984).

Federal Times, weekly newspaper that covers pending civil service legislation, compensation problems, corruption, labor/management concerns, and other issues of interest to federal government employees.

Federal Times
475 School Street, S.W.
Washington, D.C. 20024
(202) 554-7131

Federal Wage System, established by Public Law 92-392, this is the basic pay system for the almost half a million trade, craft, and labor—blue-collar—employees of the federal government.

Rates of pay for Federal Wage System employees are maintained in line with prevailing levels of pay for comparable work within each local wage area. Within each local wage area there is a single set of wage schedules applicable to the blue-collar employees of all agencies in the area. Each nonsupervisory schedule consists of 15 grades. A single grade structure applies nationwide. Individual positions are graded on the basis of job evaluation in accordance with a uniform set of job-grading standards. There are separate leader and supervisory schedules for each area.

Uniform policies and procedures for the Federal Wage System are established by the Office of Personnel Management, but significant roles in policymaking and operation of the system are played by both agencies and employee unions.

The prevailing rate principle on which federal blue-collar pay rates are based dates from the 1860s. While there have been many changes in the determination of blue-collar pay since then, with respect to occupational and agency coverage, agency authorities, and administrative procedures, the basic principle is over 100 years old.

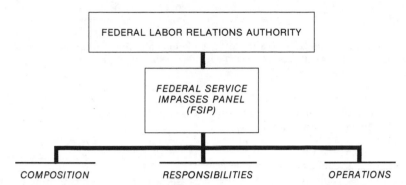

FEDERAL SERVICE IMPASSES PANEL (FSIP)

FEDERAL LABOR RELATIONS AUTHORITY

FEDERAL SERVICE
IMPASSES PANEL
(FSIP)

COMPOSITION	RESPONSIBILITIES	OPERATIONS
• AT LEAST SEVEN MEMBERS APPOINTED BY THE PRESIDENT, ONE OF WHOM IS DESIGNATED AS CHAIRMAN (PRESENTLY SEVEN MEMBERS)	• CONSIDERS NEGOTIATION IMPASSES • TAKES SUCH ACTION AS IT CONSIDERS NECESSARY TO SETTLE IMPASSE	• GENERATED BY REQUEST OF EITHER OR BOTH AGENCY AND LABOR ORGANIZATION, FMCS OR FSIP EXECUTIVE DIRECTOR FOLLOWING SUBMISSION OF REQUEST TO IMPASSES PANEL • DETERMINES WHETHER PARTIES HAVE NEGOTIATED TO THE POINT OF IMPASSE, WHETHER FURTHER NEGOTIATIONS MIGHT RESOLVE IMPASSE WHETHER VOLUNTARY ARRANGEMENTS FOR THIRD PARTY DISPUTES SETTLEMENTS MIGHT RESOLVE IMPASSE • CONSIDERS IMPASSES, RECOMMENDS PROCEDURES FOR RESOLVING IMPASSE (RETURN TO NEGOTIATIONS, MEDIATION OR OTHER VOLUNTARY ARRANGEMENTS) OR SETTLES IMPASSE BY APPROPRIATE ACTION

Federal Women's Program, established in 1967 by the U.S. Civil Service Commission to enhance the employment and the advancement of women. Executive Order 11478, signed by President Nixon on August 8, 1969, integrated the Federal Women's Program with other equal employment opportunity programs. Federal agencies must designate a Federal Women's Program coordinator to provide advice on special concerns of women and to insure that agency affirmative action plans are designed to eliminate barriers to the full employment of women at all levels and in all occupations. For a history, *see* Helene S. Markoff, "The Federal Women's Program," *Public Administration Review* (March–April 1972).

federation, national and/or international

unions joined together for common purposes. The AFL-CIO is the major U.S. union federation.

Federation of Organized Trade and Labor Unions: *see* AMERICAN FEDERATION OF LABOR.

feedback, information about the effect and/or results of the behavior of a person or system that is communicated back to that person or system so that human behavior or organization (mechanical) performance might be modified. For accounts of how to use organization feedback, *see* David A. Nadler, *Feedback and Organization Development: Using Data-Based Methods* (Reading, Mass.: Addison-Wesley Publishing Co., 1977); Robert T. Golembiewski and Richard J. Hilles, *Toward the Responsive Organization: The Theory and Practice of Survey/Feedback* (Salt Lake City: Brighton Publishing, 1979); David A. Nadler, Cortlandt Cammann and Philip H. Mirvis, "Developing a Feedback System for Work Units: A Field Experiment in Structural Change," *Journal of Applied Behavioral Science* (January–February–March 1980); Daniel R. Ilgen and William A. Knowlton, Jr., "Performance Attributional Effects on Feedback from Superiors," *Organizational Behavior and Human Performance* (June 1980); Alan Brown and Frank Heller, "Usefulness of Group Feedback Analysis as a Research Method: Its Application to a Questionnaire Study," *Human Relations* (February 1981). For how it relates to productivity, *see* Peter G. Kirby, "Productivity Increases Through Feedback Systems," *Personnel Journal* (October 1977). For information on handling negative feedback, *see* Thomas B. Wilson, "Making Negative Feedback Work," *Personnel Journal* (December 1978). *See also* Herbert Kaufman, *Administrative Feedback: Monitoring Subordinates' Behavior* (Washington, D.C.: Brookings Institution, 1973).

FEI: *see* FEDERAL EXECUTIVE INSTITUTE.

fellow servant doctrine, common-law concept that an employer should not be held responsible for an accident to an employee if the accident resulted from the negligence of another employee.

fellowship plan, company: *see* COMPANY FELLOWSHIP PLAN.

FEPC: *see* (1) FAIR EMPLOYMENT PRACTICE COMMITTEE and (2) FAIR EMPLOYMENT PRACTICE COMMISSION.

Fibreboard Paper Products Corporation v. National Labor Relations Board, 379 U.S. 203 (1965), U.S. Supreme Court case, which held that a company was obligated to bargain over an economically motivated decision to subcontract work previously performed by union members.

fiduciary, a person who manages money or property for others. Anyone who has discretionary authority or responsibility for the administration of a pension plan is a fiduciary.

Fiedler, Fred E. (1922–   ), psychologist most noted for his contingency theory of leadership effectiveness, which holds that leadership is a function both of the leader and the leadership situation. Major works include: *A Theory of Leadership Effectiveness* (N.Y.: McGraw-Hill, 1967); *Leadership and Effective Management,* with Martin Chemers (Glenview, Ill.: Scott, Foresman & Co., 1974).

field examiner, administrative agency employee who conducts certification elections and investigates charges of unfair labor practices.

field review, method of employee appraisal whereby a representative of the personnel department visits an employee's work site in order to gather the information necessary for a written evaluation.

field theory, developed by Kurt Lewin, field theory holds that an individual's behavior at any given time is the result of his/her basic personality interacting with the psychological forces of the environment. *See* Kurt Lewin, "Behavior and Development as a Function of the Total Situation," in Dorwin Cartwright (ed.), *Field Theory in Social Science* (N.Y.: Harper & Bros., 1951).

final offer arbitration, also called LAST OFFER ARBITRATION, negotiating stratagem that has an arbitrator choose from among the disputing parties' final or last offers. Peter Feuille, in *Final Offer Arbitration: Concepts, Development, Techniques* (Chicago: International Personnel Management Association, 1975), describes its intended role in the collective bargaining process:

> Since the arbitrator will not be free to compromise between the parties' positions, the parties will be induced to develop ever more reasonable positions prior to the arbitrator's decision in the hope of winning the award. And, the theory goes, these mutual attempts to win neutral approval should result in the parties being so close together that they will create their own settlement. In other words, the final offer procedure was purposefully designed to contain the seeds of its own destruction.

For a case study, *see* Gary Long and Peter Feuille, "Final Offer Arbitration: 'Sudden Death' in Eugene," *Industrial and Labor Relations Review* (January 1974). *Also see* Angelo S. DeNisi and James B. Dworkin, "Final-Offer Arbitration and the Naive Negotiator," *Industrial and Labor Relations Review* (October 1981).

financial core member, someone who pays a union's initiation fees and monthly dues, but does not actually join. Such employees are entitled to fair representation in collective bargaining and grievances by the union, but they have no right to political participation in its affairs. By the same token, however, the union has no disciplinary authority over them.

fink, slang term for a strikebreaker—any individual who hires out to help an employer break a strike. According to H. L. Mencken, "fink" is a perversion of "pink" for "Pinkerton." The Pinkertons were employees of the Pinkerton Detective Agen-

cy who were frequently hired to harass and otherwise oppose strikes in the latter part of the 19th century. As Pinkerton's, Inc., the agency is still in business selling guard and security services.

Finnegan v. Leu, 456 U.S. 431 (1982), U.S. Supreme Court case which upheld the right of a successful challenger for the leadership of a union to dismiss all the business agents who had supported the incumbent in the election. The Court reasoned that democracy itself would be served by enabling elected union leaders to carry out their programs and policies without resistance from business agents who were in opposition to them. The Court also maintained that the removal of a business agent on these grounds, which was allowed under the union's constitution, was not an act of discipline that interfered with the agent's rights of freedom of speech.

fire, discharge from employment. The word has such a rude connotation that it is hardly ever used for formal purposes. It seems so much more genteel and antiseptic to terminate, discharge, dismiss, sever, or lay off an employee. For two "self-help" books on firing, *see* John J. Tarrant, *Getting Fired: An American Ordeal* (N.Y.: Van Nostrand Reinhold Co., 1974); Auren Uris and Jack Tarrant, *How to Keep from Getting Fired* (Chicago: Henry Regnery Co., 1975). *See also* Stephen S. Kaagen, "Terminating People from Key Positions," *Personnel Journal* (February 1978); Frederic D. Homer and Garth Massey, "On Being Canned: Personnel Decisions in Democratic Bureaucracies," *Bureaucrat* (Spring 1979); Edward J. Mandt, "Employee Termination: Proceed with Care," *Management Review* (December 1980); Laurence J. Stybel, Robin Cooper and Maryanne Peabody, "Planning Executive Dismissals: How to Fire a Friend," *California Management Review* (Spring 1982); David W. Ewing, "Your Right to Fire," *Harvard Business Review* (March–April 1983); Daniel T. Kingsley, *How to Fire An Employee* (New York: Facts on File, 1984).

Fire Fighters Local Union No. 1784 v. Stotts, U.S. Supreme Court case, 81 L. Ed. 483 (1984), which held that courts may not interefere with seniority systems to protect newly hired black employees from layoff. The case began in 1977 when black firefighters charged that the Memphis, Tenn., fire department had violated Title VII of the Civil Rights Act of 1964 by engaging in racial discrimination in hiring and promotion of employees. In 1980, the city and the black employees agreed on an affirmative action plan that was approved by a federal district judge. In 1981, when the city was suffering from budget problems, some of the newly hired black firefighters were among those scheduled for layoff because the city's contract with the union contains a "last-hired, first-fired" provision. In response to a request from the threatened black workers, the district court ordered the city not to follow seniority in determining who was to be laid off "insofar as it will decrease the percentage" of black firefighters. The result was that 72 whites were laid off or demoted along with only 8 blacks. They were all rehired or promoted 6 months later.

The union and the city appealed the seniority ruling to the U.S. Court of Appeals but lost, leading to their appeal to the Supreme Court.

Writing for the majority, Justice Byron R. White said that the law permits remedies only for individuals who can prove they are "actual victims" of job discrimination, rather than groups of disadvantaged minorities who may not have suffered specific wrongs in a specific job situation. To back this holding, he cited a 1964 memorandum issued by sponsors of Title VII which said "Title VII does not permit the ordering of racial quotas in business or unions." Justice White also said that it is "inappropriate to deny an innocent employee the benefit of seniority." *See:* Louis P. Britt III, "Affirmative Action: Is There Life After Stotts?" *Personnel Administrator* (September 1984).

FIRO B, 54-item, self-report questionnaire designed to measure interpersonal needs of inclusion, control, and affection on six scales. It obtains information on both expressed and desired behaviors in various interpersonal situations. TIME: 8-15 minutes. AUTHOR: William C. Schutz. PUBLISHER: Consulting Psychologist Press, Inc. (*see* TEST PUBLISHERS).

first-dollar coverage, coverage under an insurance policy which begins with the first dollar of expense incurred by the insured for the covered benefits.

first-line management, level of management that is just above the workers (for example, a foreman). See W. Earl Sasser, Jr., and Frank S. Leonard, "Let First-Level Supervisors Do Their Job," *Harvard Business Review* (March-April 1980); Ernest A. Doud, Jr., and Edward J. Miller, "First-Line Supervisors: The Key to Improved Performance," *Management Review* (December 1980); Lawrence L. Steinmetz and H. Ralph Todd, Jr., *First-Line Management: Approaching Supervision Effectively,* 3rd edition (Plano, Texas: Business Publications, 1983).

fiscal policy, the manipulation of government finances, by raising or lowering taxes or levels of spending, to promote economic stability and growth.

FIT: *see* FLANAGAN INDUSTRIAL TEST.

Fitzgerald, A. Ernest (1926-   ), most famous "whistle blower."

Fitzgerald was the GS-17 Deputy for Management Systems in the Office of the Assistant Secretary of the Air Force who in 1968 first testified to cost overruns on the Air Force's giant C-5A military cargo plane. The Air Force, which had not acknowledged the cost overruns, stripped him of his primary duties of overseeing cost reports on the major weapons systems and assigned him to essentially clerical tasks. A year later the Air Force reorganized Fitzgerald's office and abolished his job. Fitzgerald appealed the Air Force action. After almost four years of litigation, Fitzgerald was reinstated to his original civil service position and given back pay.

The Fitzgerald affair triggered a great

deal of discussion in the media and the government about the need to protect "whistle-blowers." For Fitzgerald's own account, *see* A. Ernest Fitzgerald, *The High Priests of Waste* (New York: W. W. Norton, 1972).

See also WHISTLE BLOWER.

Fitzgerald Act: *see* APPRENTICESHIP ACT OF 1937.

Fitzpatrick v. Bitzer, 424 U.S. 953 (1976), U.S. Supreme Court case, which ruled that the Equal Employment Opportunity Act of 1972 amendments to Title VII of the Civil Rights Act of 1964 created an exception to the immunity of states to backpay suits. The court held that this exception was authorized by the 14th Amendment's grant of power to Congress to enforce that amendment's ban on state denials of equal protection.

Fitzsimmons, Frank (Edward) (1908–1981), succeeded Jimmy Hoffa as president of the International Brotherhood of Teamsters in 1967. For details of Fitzsimmons' career, *see* Walter Sheridan, *The Fall and Rise of Jimmy Hoffa* (N.Y.: Saturday Review Press, 1972); Steven Brill, *The Teamsters* (N.Y.: Simon & Schuster, 1978).

fixed annuity, annuity that provides constant, periodic dollar payments for its entire length.

fixed-benefit retirement plan, retirement plan whose benefits consist of a fixed amount or fixed percentage.

fixed shift, work shift to which an employee is assigned indefinitely.

flagged rate, also called OVERRATE, compensation rates paid to employees whose positions warrant lower rates.

Flanagan Aptitude Classification Test (FACT), battery of 19 tests that provide specific predictions of success in 37 occupations. Each FACT test corresponds to an aptitude or job element. Multiple-choice

(5 options) items that measure comprehension, expression, ingenuity, reasoning, coordination, vocabulary, alertness, etc. TIME: 10½ hours—of 3½ hours each. AUTHOR: John C. Flanagan. PUBLISHER: Science Research Associates, Inc. (*see* TEST PUBLISHERS).

For shortened version, *see* FLANAGAN INDUSTRIAL TEST.

Flanagan Industrial Test (FIT), 18 short aptitude tests designed for use in personnel selection and placement programs for a wide variety of jobs. Tests measure such items as arithmetic, coordination, electronics, ingenuity, math/reasoning, judgment/comprehension, vocabulary, memory, and planning. Shortened adaptation (for business use) of the Flanagan Aptitude Classification Test (FACT). TIME: 165/218 minutes. AUTHOR: John C. Flanagan. PUBLISHER: Science Research Associates, Inc. (*see* TEST PUBLISHERS).

flat-benefit plan, pension plan whose benefits are unrelated to earnings. Such a plan might provide a stipulated amount per month per year of service.

flat organization, also TALL ORGANIZATION, one whose structure has comparatively few levels. In contrast, a *tall organization* is one whose structure has many levels. *See* Rocco Carzo, Jr., and John N. Yanovzas, "Effects of Flat and Tall Organization Structure," *Administrative Science Quarterly* (June 1969); Edwin E. Ghiselli and Jacob P. Siegel, "Leadership and Managerial Success in Tall and Flat Organization Structures," *Personnel Psychology* (Winter 1972).

See also PYRAMID.

flat rate, also called STANDARD RATE and SINGLE RATE, pay structure offering only one rate of pay for each pay level.

***Fleetwood Trailer Co.* decision:** *see* NATIONAL LABOR RELATIONS BOARD V. MACKAY RADIO & TELEGRAPH COMPANY.

flexible passing score: *see* CUTTING SCORE.

flexible working hours: *see* FLEXI-TIME.

flexi-time, flexible work schedule in which workers can, within a prescribed band of time in the morning and again in the afternoon, start and finish work at their discretion as long as they complete the total number of hours required for a given period, usually a month. That is, the workday can vary from day to day in its length as well as in the time that it begins and ends. The morning and evening bands of time often are designated as "quiet time." Telephone calls and staff meetings are confined to "core time," which generally runs from midmorning to midafternoon. Time clocks or other mechanical controls for keeping track of the hours worked usually are a part of flexi-time systems.

For discussions of the concept, *see* Janice Neipert Hedges, "New Patterns for Working Time," *Monthly Labor Review* (February 1973); Alvar O. Elbing, Herman Gadon, and John R. M. Gordon, "Flexible Working Hours: It's About Time," *Harvard Business Review* (January–February 1974); Cary B. Barad, "Flexitime Under Scrutiny: Research on Work Adjustment and Organizational Performance," *The Personnel Administrator* (May 1980); Halcyone H. Bohen and Anamaria Viveros-Long, *Balancing Jobs and Family Life: Do Flexible Work Schedules Help?* (Philadelphia, Pa.: Temple University Press, 1981); William D. Hicks and Richard J. Klimoski, "The Impact of Flexitime on Employee Attitudes," *Academy of Management Journal* (June 1981); Richard A. Wheat, "The Federal Flexitime System: Comparison and Implementation," *Public Personnel Management* (Spring 1982); Glenn W. Rainey, Jr., and Lawrence Wolf, "The Organizationally Dysfunctional Consequences of Flexible Work Hours: A General Overview," *Public Personnel Management* (Summer 1982); Robert C. Wender and Ronald L. Sladky, "Flexible Plans Are Not Just For Large Firms," *Personnel Administrator* (December 1984). *See also* 4-DAY WORKWEEK.

Flore, Edward (1877–1945), president of the Hotel and Restaurant Employee's International Alliance and Bartenders' International League of America from 1911 to his death. For a biography, *see* Jay Rubin and M. J. Obermeier, *Growth of a Union: The Life and Times of Edward Flore* (N.Y.: The Historical Union Association, Inc., 1943).

Florida Power & Light Co. v. Brotherhood of Electrical Workers, 417 U.S. 790 (1974), U.S. Supreme Court case, which held that supervisors who are union members may be disciplined by their unions for performing nonsupervisory tasks, so long as the supervisors do not act as management bargainers or grievance adjusters.

flowchart, graphic representation of an analysis of, or solution to, a problem that uses symbols to indicate various operations, equipment, and data flow.

FLRA: *see* FEDERAL LABOR RELATIONS AUTHORITY.

FLRC: *see* FEDERAL LABOR RELATIONS COUNCIL.

FLSA: *see* FAIR LABOR STANDARDS ACT.

FLSA decision: *see* NATIONAL LEAGUE OF CITIES V. USERY.

FMCS: *see* FEDERAL MEDIATION AND CONCILIATION SERVICE.

focus job area, a unit of an establishment's work force (such as a seniority unit, job title, etc.) in which minorities or women are concentrated or underrepresented relative either to their overall representation in the relevant work force sector or to their availability for the jobs in question. This concept is more related to determining the existence of discrimination rather than to finding underutilization for the purpose of setting goals as part of an affirmative action program.

foils: *see* DISTRACTORS.

Foley v. Connelie, 435 U.S. 291 (1978),

U.S. Supreme Court case, which upheld a New York law requiring state police to be U.S. citizens. The court reasoned that because state police exercise considerable discretion in executing the laws, a state may exclude aliens from such positions without unconstitutionally denying them equal protection of the laws.

See also the following entries:
AMBACH V. NORWICK
CITIZENSHIP, U.S.
HAMPTON V. MOW SUN WONG
SUGARMAN V. DOUGALL

Follett, Mary Parker (1868–1933), early social psychologist who anticipated, in the 1920s, many of the conclusions of the Hawthorne experiments of the 1930s and the post-World War II behavioral movement. In calling for "power with," as opposed to "power over," she anticipated the movement toward more participatory management. Her "law of the situation" is contingency management in its humble origins. Major works include: *The New State* (N.Y.: Longmans, Green, 1918); *Creative Experience* (N.Y.: Longmans, Green, 1924). For her collected papers, see Henry C. Metcalf and Lyndall Urwick (eds.), *Dynamic Administration: The Collected Papers of Mary Parker Follett.* For an appreciation of her contributions, see Elliot M. Fox, "Mary Parker Follett: The Enduring Contribution," *Public Administration Review* (November–December 1968).

force-field analysis, procedure for determining what factors, or forces, seem to be contributing to a problem.

forced choice, testing technique that requires the subject to choose from among a given set of alternatives.

forced-distribution method, performance appraisal technique that predetermines the percentage of ratees to be placed in the various performance categories.

Foreign Service pay system, actually consists of four different pay schedules:
1. *Foreign Service Officer schedule*

consists of eight levels. Individual Foreign Service Officers are assigned to levels on a rank-in person basis similar to that of the military personnel system.
2. *Foreign Service Information Officer schedule* of the U.S. Information Agency is identical in structure and operation to the Foreign Service Officer schedule.
3. *Foreign Service Reserve schedule* also consists of eight levels, and is used for temporary appointments of people who are not part of the regular Foreign Service career system.
4. *Foreign Service Staff Officer schedule* covers the administrative and support employees of the Foreign Service. It consists of 10 grades.

foreman, first-line supervisor—the first level of management responsible for securing adequate production and the managerial employee who supervises the work of nonmanagerial employees. The extent to which the foreman is responsible for the traditional functions of management varies considerably from one organization to another. For a complete analysis, see Thomas H. Patten, Jr., *The Foreman: Forgotten Man of Management* (N.Y.: American Management Association, 1968). For a classic account of the role of the foreman, see F. J. Roethlisberger, "The Foreman: Master and Victim of Double Talk," *Harvard Business Review* (Spring 1945; reprinted September–October 1965).

Present day foremen work under a fading occupational title. It has fallen victim to the U.S. Department of Labor's effort to "de-sex" the nature of work and has been retired as an officially acceptable job title by the fourth edition of the *Dictionary of Occupational Titles* (1977).

formal organization: see INFORMAL ORGANIZATION.

Form 171: see STANDARD FORM 171.

formula score, raw score on a multiple-choice test after a correction for guessing has been applied. With five-choice items, for example, the formula score is the number of correct answers minus one-fourth the number of wrong answers. This makes zero the score that would most likely be obtained by random guessing.

Form W-2, also called W-2 FORM and WAGE AND TAX STATEMENT, by the end of January of each year, employers must provide each employee with at least two copies of his or her withholding statement, officially a Wage and Tax Statement or Internal Revenue Service Form W-2, showing earnings for the preceding year and various deductions. Employees must file one copy of their Form W-2 with their federal income-tax return.

Fortune, biweekly trade magazine covering all aspects of the business world. *Fortune* has long been considered the most prestigious of its kind.

Fortune
541 North Fairbanks Court
Chicago, IL 60611

Fortune 500, directory of the 500 largest U.S. industrial corporations published each year since 1955 by *Fortune.* These organizations are frequently described according to their rank in the directory, particularly in recruiting advertisements. For example, see Lloyd D. Elgart, "Women on *Fortune* 500 Boards," *California Management Review* (Summer 1983). A *Fortune* 500 company is any company on the list; a *Fortune* 100 company is one of the 100 largest. Listed below, in rank order, is the *Fortune* 100 for 1984. For the complete list and supporting statistical details, see *Fortune* (April 30, 1984).
Fortune 100 (1984)
1. Exxon
2. General Motors
3. Mobil
4. Ford Motor
5. International Business Machines
6. Texaco
7. E.I. du Pont de Nemours
8. Standard Oil (Indiana)
9. Standard Oil of California
10. General Electric
11. Gulf Oil
12. Atlantic Richfield
13. Shell Oil
14. Occidental Petroleum
15. U.S. Steel
16. Phillips Petroleum
17. Sun
18. United Technologies
19. Tenneco
20. ITT
21. Chrysler
22. Procter & Gamble
23. R.J. Reynolds Industries
24. Getty Oil
25. Standard Oil (Ohio)
26. AT&T Technologies
27. Boeing
28. Dow Chemical
29. Allied
30. Eastman Kodak
31. Unocal
32. Goodyear Tire & Rubber
33. Dart & Kraft
34. Westinghouse Electric
35. Phillip Morris
36. Beatrice Foods
37. Union Carbide
38. Xerox
39. Amerada Hess
40. Union Pacific
41. General Foods
42. McDonnell Douglas
43. Rockwell International
44. PepsiCo
45. Ashland Oil
46. General Dynamics
47. Minnesota Mining & Manufacturing
48. Coca-Cola
49. Consolidated Foods
50. Lockheed
51. Georgia-Pacific
52. Monsanto
53. W.R. Grace
54. Signal Companies
55. Anheuser-Busch
56. Nabisco Brands
57. Johnson & Johnson
58. Coastal
59. Raytheon
60. Honeywell

61. Charter
62. General Mills
63. TRW
64. Caterpillar Tractor
65. Aluminum Co. of America
66. Sperry
67. Gulf & Western Industries
68. Continental Group
69. Bethlehem Steel
70. Weyerhaeuser
71. Ralston Purina
72. Colgate Palmolive
73. American Home Products
74. Litton Industries
75. Hewlett-Packard
76. Control Data
77. Texas Instruments
78. LTV
79. American Brands
80. International Paper
81. Motorola
82. Burroughs
83. Archer-Daniels-Midland
84. Digital Equipment
85. Borden
86. Champion International
87. Armco
88. Esmark
89. Diamond Shamrock
90. CPC International
91. Time Inc.
92. Deere
93. Bristol-Meyers
94. Martin Marietta
95. Firestone Tire & Rubber
96. IC Industries
97. North American Philips
98. Agway
99. Pfizer
100. H.J. Heinz

Forty-Plus Club, organization of unemployed executives over 40 who band together to help each other find jobs.

Foster v. *Dravo Corp.,* 420 U.S. 92 (1975), U.S. Supreme Court case, which held that a veteran, upon being restored to his former civilian position under the Military Selective Service Act, is not entitled to full vacation benefits for the years he was in military service, if the vacation scheme was intended as a form of short-term deferred compensation for work performed and not as accruing automatically as a function of continued association with the company.

See also VETERANS REEMPLOYMENT RIGHTS.

Foster, William Z(ebulon) (1881–1961), labor organizer who became a leading figure in the American Communist Party, serving as its candidate for president of the United States in 1924, 1928, and 1932. For a biography, *see:* Arthur Zipser, *Workingclass Giant: The Life of William Z. Foster* (New York: International Publishers, 1981).

4-day workweek, reallocation of the standard 40-hour workweek over four days instead of five. By lengthening the workday, employees get a 3-day weekend every week with no loss of pay. This concept differs from the 4-day/32-hour workweek that some union leaders advocate. For the basic work on this subject, *see* Riva Roor (ed.), *4 Days, 40 hours and Other Forms of the Rearranged Workweek* (N.Y.: Mentor Books, 1973).

See also FLEXI-TIME.

four-fifths rule: *see* ADVERSE IMPACT.

FPM: *see* FEDERAL PERSONNEL MANUAL.

Franks v. *Bowman Transportation Co.:* *see* RETROACTIVE SENIORITY.

Fraser, Douglas (1916–   ), president of the United Auto Workers from 1977 to 1983. For a biographical sketch, *see* Ron Chernow, "Douglas Fraser: Labor's Courtly Rebel," *Saturday Review* (March 4, 1979).

Freedom of Information Act of 1966, (Public Law 89-487, as amended by Public Law 93-502), provides for making information held by federal agencies available to the public, unless it comes within one of the specific categories of matters exempt from public disclosure. The legislative history of the act (particularly the recent amendments) makes it clear that the primary purpose was to make information maintained by the executive branch of the federal government more available to the public. At the same time, the act recognized that records that cannot be disclosed without impairing rights of privacy or important government operations must be protected from disclosure.

Virtually all agencies of the executive branch of the federal government have issued regulations to implement the Freedom of Information Act. These regulations inform the public where certain types of information may be readily obtained, how other information may be obtained on request, and what internal agency appeals are available if a member of the public is refused requested information. To locate specific agency regulations pertaining to freedom of information, consult the *Code of Federal Regulations* index under "Information Availability." For an analysis of possible conflicts between the Freedom of Information Act and the National Labor Relations Act, *see* Stephen J. Cabot, " 'Freedom of Information' vs. the NLRB: Conflicts and Decisions," *Personnel Journal* (June 1977).

See also NATIONAL LABOR RELATIONS BOARD V. ROBBINS TIRE AND RUBBER CO. and NATIONAL TECHNICAL INFORMATION SERVICE.

free-response test, technique used in psychological testing that places no restriction on the kind of response an individual is to make (so long as it relates to the situation presented).

free rider, derogatory term for a person working in a bargaining unit and receiving substantially all of the benefits of union representation without belonging to the union.

frequency distribution, tabulation of scores (or other data) from high to low, or low to high, showing the number of individuals who obtain each score or fall in each score interval.

frictional unemployment, unemployment that is due to the inherent time lag involved with the re-employment of labor.

friend of the court: *see* AMICUS CURIAE.

friendly societies, early labor groups formed by workers for social and philanthropic purposes.

fringe benefits, also called EMPLOYEE BENEFITS, general term used to describe any of a variety of nonwage or supplemental benefits (such as pensions, insurance, vacations, paid holidays, etc.) that employees receive in addition to their regular wages. For an economic analysis, *see* Bevars Mabry, "The Economics of Fringe Benefits," *Industrial Relations* (February 1973). For discussions, *see* Ralph L. Harris, "Let's Take the 'Fringe' out of Fringe Benefits," *Personnel Journal* (February 1975); Richard C. Huseman, John D. Hatfield, and Richard B. Robinson, "The MBA and Fringe Benefits," *The Personnel Administrator* (July 1978); Richard B. Freeman, "The Effects of Unionism on Fringe Benefits," *Industrial and Labor Relations Review* (Ju-

Actual and projected distribution of total compensation between cash payroll and fringe benefits, selected years, 1950–2055		
(In percent)		
Year	Cash payroll	Fringe benefits
Actual:		
1950	95.0	5.0
1960	92.2	7.8
1970	89.7	10.3
1980	84.2	15.8
Projected:		
1990	80.6	19.4
2000	77.5	22.5
2020	71.5	28.5
2035	67.4	32.6
2055	62.2	37.8

Source: Yung-Ping Chen, "The Growth of Fringe Benefits: Implications for Social Security," Monthly Labor Review *(November 1981).*

ly 1981); R. Frumkin and W. Wistrowski, "BLS Takes a New Look at Employee Benefits," *Monthly Labor Review* (August 1982); Donald C. Platten, "The Employee Benefits—Does the Company Also?" *Harvard Business Review* (September-October 1983); Henry Saveth, "Benefit Programs After Tax Reform," *Personnel Journal* (October 1984); Kenneth Gagala and Gene Daniels, *Labor Guide to Negotiating Wages and Benefits* (Reston, VA: Reston/Prentice-Hall, 1985).

See also PERQUISITES.

front loaded, a labor agreement providing for a greater wage increase in its early period; for example, a three-year contract that provides for a ten-percent increase in the first year and four percent in each of the remaining two years. *See* John B. Beare, "Uncertainty and Front-End Loading of Labor Agreements," *Journal of Labor Research,* Vol. VI (1985).

front pay, compensation provided to an individual or group which begins when a remedy for alleged discrimination is agreed to and ends when the individual or group attains its "rightful place."

Fry v. United States, 421 U.S. 542 (1975), U.S. Supreme Court case, which held that state governments had to abide by federal wage and salary controls even though the enabling legislation did not expressly refer to the states. Such legislation was ruled constitutional because general raises to state employees, even though purely intrastate in character, could significantly affect interstate commerce, and thus could be validly regulated by Congress under the Constitution's Commerce Clause.

FSEE: *see* FEDERAL SERVICE ENTRANCE EXAMINATION.

FSIP: *see* FEDERAL SERVICE IMPASSES PANEL.

full-crew rule, safety regulation requiring a minimum number of workers for a given operation.

full employment, economic situation where all those who want to work are able to. In recent years, economists have been telling the public that "full" employment really means from 3 to 6 percent unemployment. *See* Marilyn Wilson, "What Is 'Full Employment'?" *Dun's Business Month* (February 1983).

Full Employment and Balanced Growth Act of 1977: *see* HUMPHREY-HAWKINS ACT OF 1977.

full field investigation, personal investigation of an applicant's background to determine whether he/she meets fitness standards for a critical-sensitive federal position.

Fullilove v. Klutznick, U.S. Supreme Court case, 448 U.S. 448 (1980), which held that Congress has the authority to use quotas to remedy past discrimination, reasoning that the 14th Amendment's requirement of equal protection means that groups historically denied this right may be given special treatment. *See* Peter G. Kilgore, "Racial Preferences in the Federal Grant Programs: Is There a Basis for Challenge After *Fullilove v. Klutznick?*" *Labor Law Journal* (May 1981).

full-time workers, also PART-TIME WORKERS, according to the Bureau of Labor Statistics, *full-time workers* are those employed at least 35 hours a week and *part-time workers* are those who work fewer hours. Workers on part-time schedules for economic reasons (such as slack work, terminating or starting a job during the week, material shortages, or inability to find full-time work) are among those counted as being on full-time status, under the assumption that they would be working full time if conditions permitted. The BLS classifies unemployed persons in full-time or part-time status by their reported preferences for full-time or part-time work. For a discussion of what the terms mean, *see* Janice Neipert Hedges and Stephen J. Gallogly, "Full and Part Time: A Review of Definitions," *Monthly Labor Review* (March 1977).

full-time-worker rate, wage rate of regular full-time employees, as distinguished from the wage rate of temporary or part-time employees performing the same job.

fully funded pension plan, pension plan whose assets are adequate to meet its obligations into the foreseeable future.

Fulton Committee, formally COMMITTEE ON THE CIVIL SERVICE, 1966-1968, British committee whose charge was to "examine the structure, recruitment and management, including training, of the Home Civil Service and to make recommendations." The committee, whose 1968 report recommended major reforms, was popularly known after its chairman, Lord Fulton. The Spring 1969 issue of *Public Administration* is devoted to summaries of the report's many volumes.

functional authority, authority inherent to a job or work assignment.

functional illiterate, individual whose reading and writing skills are so poor that he/she is incapable of functioning effectively in the most basic business, office, or factory situations. Because many functional illiterates are high school graduates, the value of such diplomas is being increasingly discounted by personnel offices.

functional job analysis, technology of work analysis that measures and describes a position's specific requirements. Functional job analysis can discard traditionally restrictive labels for positions. In their place, a variety of component descriptions are used to more accurately illustrate the specific and varied duties actually performed by an incumbent. Functional job analysis data readily lend themselves to computerized personnel management information systems. *See* Sidney A. Fine, "Functional Job Analysis: An Approach to a Technology for Manpower Planning," *Personnel Journal* (November 1974); Steven Spirn and Lanny Solomon, "A Key Element in EDP Personnel Management: Functional Job Analysis," *Personnel Journal* (November 1976).

functional leadership, concept holding that leadership emerges from the dynamics associated with the particular circumstances under which groups integrate and organize their activities, rather than from the personal characteristics or behavior of an individual. *See* Robert G. Lord, "Functional Leadership Behavior: Measurement and Relation to Social Power and Leadership Perceptions," *Administrative Science Quarterly* (March 1977).

functus officio, Latin term that can be applied to an officer who has fulfilled the duties of an office that has expired and who, in consequence, has no further formal authority. Arbitrators are said to be *functus officio* concerning a particular case after they have declared their awards on it. According to Israel Ben Scheiber, in "The Doctrine of Functus Officio with Particular Relation to Labor Arbitration," *Labor Law Journal* (October 1972),

the need to plead the doctrine of "functus officio" cannot be regarded as a major problem or one that occurs with any significant degree of regularity. However, to an arbitrator who is asked to interpret, modify or clarify the language of his award (usually by the losing party) because of a claim that he has overlooked some fact or, in any event, not worded his opinion and/or award with sufficient clarity, a request to reopen the case and to issue a supplemental award can be a source of considerable embarrassment. This is so, in part, because to the aggrieved party, being told that an arbitrator is "functus officio" often appears as a senseless refuge and a convenient and unsatisfactory excuse given by the arbitrator for refusing to correct or make clear something which he has written and therefore should be able to clarify to the satisfaction of the applicant.

Fundamental Achievement Series (FAS), verbal and numerical tests for educational and vocational placement of the disadvantaged individual. Can be used for assessment and placement into employment or training programs. TIME: 60 minutes. AUTHORS: G.K. Bennett and

J.E. Doppelt. PUBLISHER: Psychological Corporation (see TEST PUBLISHERS).

funded pension plan, pension plan that provides for the periodic accumulation of money to meet the pension plan's obligations in future years.

funding method, any of the procedures by which money is accumulated to pay for pensions under a pension plan.

funeral leave, also called BEREAVEMENT LEAVE, paid time off for an employee at the time of a death in his/her immediate family. The majority of all employers offer such time off, usually three or four days. The biggest problem with administering such a benefit is defining just what constitutes a member of the "immediate" family.

furlough, period of absence from work, initiated either by the employer as a layoff or the employee as a leave of absence.

Furnco Construction Corp. v. Waters, 57 L.Ed. 2d 957 (1978), U.S. Supreme Court case, which held that the initial burden of proving a case of employment discrimination rests upon the complainant.

Furuseth, Andrew (1854-1938), president of the International Seaman's Union from 1908 until his death. For a biography, see Hyman G. Weintraub, *Andrew Furuseth: Emancipator of the Seamen* (Berkeley, Calif.: University of California Press, 1959).

future shock, as defined in the leading work on future shock, Alvin Toffler's *Future Shock* (New York: Random House, 1970), "the distress, both physical and psychological, that arises from an overload of the human organism's physical adaptive systems and its decision making processes. Put more simply, future shock is the human response to overstimulation." Also see James M. Mitchell and Rolfe E. Schroeder, "Future Shock for Personnel Administration," *Public Personnel Management* (July-August 1974). For one man's antidote to the problem, see George S. Odiorne, "Management by Objectives: Antidote to Future Shock," *Personnel Journal* (April 1974).

futuristics, fledgling discipline that seeks to anticipate future societal developments and present alternative courses of action for the polity's consideration. Within this discipline, there is a growing literature on the future of work. For two examples, see Paul Dickson, *The Future of the Workplace: The Coming Revolution in Jobs* (N.Y.: Weybright and Talley, 1975); William T. Morris, *Work and Your Future: Living Poorer, Working Harder* (Reston, Va.: Reston Publishing Co., 1975); Barry O. Jones, *Sleepers, Wake! Technology and the Future of Work* (New York: Oxford University Press, 1982); Delores Hayden, *Redesigning the American Dream: The Future of Housing, Work, and Family Life* (New York: W.W. Norton, 1984).

G

gag rules, or GAG ORDERS, colloquial terms for any formal instructions from a competent authority, usually a judge, to refrain from discussing and/or advocating something. One of the most famous gag rules/orders is President Theodore Roosevelt's executive orders in 1902 and 1904, which forbade federal employees, on pain of dismissal, either as individuals or as members of organizations, to seek any pay increases or to attempt to influence legislation before Congress, except through the heads of their departments. Roosevelt's gag orders were repealed by the Lloyd-LaFollette Act of 1912, which granted public employees the right to organize unions.

gainsharing, any of a variety of wage payment methods in which the worker receives additional earnings due to increases in productivity. *See* PROFIT SHARING.

games: *see* MANAGEMENT GAMES.

game theory, a mathematical approach to decisionmaking in situations involving two or more players with presumably conflicting interests. Because the theory of games assumes rationality on the part of the players, the strategies and decisions of one player are heavily dependent upon the anticipated behavior of the opposition. The possible outcomes of a two person game are frequently presented in a *payoff matrix* consisting of numbers arranged in rows and columns with the degrees of preference that each player assigns to each outcome. Of course, a player's overall strategy is a *game plan*.

gaming simulation, a model of reality with dynamic parts that can be manipulated to teach the manipulator(s) how to better cope with the represented processes in real life. *See* John G. H. Carlson and Michael J. Misshauk, *Introduction to Gaming: Management Decision Simulations* (N.Y.: John Wiley, 1972); Gilbert B. Siegel, "Gaming Simulation in the Teaching of Public Personnel Administration," *Public Personnel Management* (July-August 1977).

Gantt, Henry L(awrence) (1861-1919), contemporary and protege of Frederick W. Taylor, was a pioneer in the scientific management movement and inventor of the "Gantt Chart." For a collection of his major works, *see* Alex W. Rathe (ed.), *Gantt on Management* (N.Y.: American Management Association, 1961). For a biography, *see* Leon R. Alford, *Henry Lawrence Gantt: Leader in Industry* (N.Y.: Harper & Bros., 1934).

Gantt Chart, developed during World War I by Henry L. Gantt, the Gantt Chart's distinguishing feature is that work planned and work done are shown in the same space in their relation to each other and in their relation to time. Today any chart which uses straight lines to compare planned and actual progress over time could be called a Gantt Chart.

GAO: *see* GENERAL ACCOUNTING OFFICE.

Garcia* v. *San Antonio Metropolitan Transit Authority, 83 L. Ed. 2nd 1016 (1985), U.S. Supreme Court case that held that the application of the minimum wage and overtime requirements of the Fair Labor Standards Act to public agency employment does not violate any Constitution provision. This reversed *National League of Cities* v. *Usery,* 426 U.S. 833 (1976).

***Gardner-Denver* case:** *see* ALEXANDER V. GARDNER-DENVER COMPANY.

Garfield, James A(bram) (1831-1881), 20th president of the United States, was assassinated on July 2, 1881, by Charles Guiteau, an insane attorney who had worked for Garfield's election and was angry about not receiving a patronage appointment. Garfield's death gave new life to the reform movement, culminating in the passage of the Pendelton or Civil Service Act of 1883.

Garner* v. *Board of Public Works of Los Angeles, 341 U.S. 716 (1951), Supreme Court case upholding the constitutionality of a municipal loyalty oath requiring its employees to disclose whether they were or ever had been a member of the Communist Party and to take an oath to the effect that for five years prior to the effective date of the ordinance they had not advocated the overthrow of the government by force or belonged to any organization so advocating.
See also LOYALTY.

garnishment, any legal or equitable procedure through which earnings of any individual are required to be withheld for the payment of any debt. Most garnishments are made by court order.

The Federal Wage Garnishment Act limits the amount of an employee's disposable earnings subject to garnishment in any one week and protects the employee from discharge because of garnishment for any one indebtedness. It does not change other matters related to garnishment, such as the right of a creditor to collect the full amount owed, and most garnishment procedures established by state laws or rules. The largest amount of total disposable earnings subject to garnishment in any workweek may not exceed the lesser of: (1) 25 percent of the disposable earnings for that week or (2) the amount by which disposable earnings for that week exceeds 30 times the federal minimum hourly wage.

No court of the United States, or any state, may make, execute, or enforce any order or process in violation of these restrictions.

The restrictions on the amount that may be garnished in a week do not apply to: (1) court orders for the support of any person, such as child support and alimony; (2) bankruptcy court orders under Chapter XIII of the Bankruptcy Act; and (3) debts due for state or federal taxes. A levy against wages for a federal tax debt by the Internal Revenue Service is not restricted by this law.

The Federal Wage Garnishment Act is enforced by the Secretary of Labor, acting through the Wage and Hour Division, U.S. Department of Labor.

Garrity v. New Jersey, 385 U.S. 493 (1967), Supreme Court case holding that a New Jersey practice of dismissing public employees who relied upon the Fifth Amendment privilege against self-incrimination was unconstitutional.

GATB: see GENERAL APTITUDE TEST BATTERY.

Gateway Coal Company v. United Mine Workers, 414 U.S. 368 (1974), U.S. Supreme Court case, which held that disputes over safety issues can be submitted to arbitration and that courts can issue injunctions against work stoppages provoked by such disputes.

GAW: see GUARANTEED ANNUAL WAGE.

Geduldig v. Aiello, 417 U.S. 484 (1974), U.S. Supreme Court case, which held that the State of California's temporary disability insurance programs, which denied benefits for pregnancy related disabilities was not in violation of the equal protection clause of the 14th Amendment.

Gellerman, Saul W. (1929-   ), industrial psychologist and an authority on the application of the behavioral sciences to management. Major works include: *Motivation and Productivity* (N.Y.: American Management Association, 1963); *The Management of Human Relations* (N.Y.: Holt, Rinehart & Winston, 1966); *Management by Motivation* (N.Y.: American Management Association, 1968); *Behavioral Science in Management* (Baltimore: Penguin Books, 1974).

General Accounting Office (GAO), independent agency created by the Budget and Accounting Act of 1921 to audit federal government expenditures and assist Congress with its legislative oversight responsibilities. The GAO is directed by the Comptroller General of the United States, who is appointed by the president with the advice and consent of the Senate for a term of 15 years.

General Accounting Office
441 G Street N.W.
Washington, D.C. 20548
(202) 275-2812

General Aptitude Test Battery (GATB), group of tests designed by the United States Employment Service and used extensively in state employment offices. The series of 12 tests measure nine aptitude areas: intelligence, verbal aptitude, numerical aptitude, spatial aptitude, form perception, clerical perception, motor coordination, finger dexterity, and manual dexterity. Scores from the tests are combined to create measures of individual aptitudes and general intelligence. The GATB has demonstrated impressive validity. *See* Stephen E. Bennis, "Occupational Validity of the General Aptitude Test Battery," *Journal of Applied Psychology* (June 1968).

See also NONREADING APTITUDE TEST BATTERY.

General Electric Co. v. Gilbert, 429 U.S. 125 (1976), U.S. Supreme Court case, which held that excluding pregnancies from sick-leave and disability benefit programs is not "discrimination based on sex" and so is not a violation of Title VII of the Civil Rights Act of 1964. This decision led to a Title VII amendment (the Pregnancy Discrimination Act of 1978) that reversed the court's decision. *See* Steven C. Kahn, "*General Electric Co. v. Gilbert:* Retreat from Rationality?" *Employee Relations Law Journal* (Summer 1977).

See also PREGNANCY and PREGNANCY DISCRIMINATION ACT OF 1978.

general increase, any upward salary adjustment governing the pay of most employees.

general labor union, any labor organization that accepts as members workers in every category of skill.

***General Motors* decision:** *see* NATIONAL LABOR RELATIONS BOARD V. GENERAL MOTORS.

General Schedule (GS), basic pay system for federal white-collar employees. It is the largest of the civilian pay systems, covering approximately 1.4 million of the total of 2.8 million civilian employees.

The General Schedule, established by the Classification Act of 1949, consists of eighteen grades or "levels of work" which are described broadly. Virtually any job can be accommodated within the schedule by evaluation of its level of duties, responsibilities, and qualification requirements. As befits its title, the General Schedule exhibits great occupational diversity: messengers, typists, secretaries, engineers, administrative personnel, research scientists, as well as occupations which are neither white-collar nor blue-collar in the traditional sense (police and fire fighters, for example).

A single pay table, nationwide in its applicability, sets forth the pay rates for the General Schedule. From 1949, when the General Schedule was enacted, until 1962, pay rates were adjusted by Congress on an irregular basis, largely in response to the pressures of inflation on employees' salaries. In 1962, Congress established the principle that pay rates would be maintained on the basis of comparability with rates paid in the private sector, as these rates were arrived at through the interplay of market forces. Authority to adjust the pay rates remained with the Congress, however, and full comparability was not achieved, in theory, until the passage of the Federal Pay Comparability Act of 1970, which delegated to the President authority for making annual adjustments of General Schedule pay rates under the principle of comparability.

general strike, work stoppage by a substantial portion of the total work force of a locality or country. Because general strikes have tended to be more political than pragmatic in their goals, they have historically been more popular in Europe than in the United States. General strikes have been decidedly infrequent since World War II. *See* Christopher Farman, *The General Strike, May, 1926* (London: Hart-Davis, 1972); David Jay Bercuson, *Confrontation at Winnipeg: Labour, Industrial Relations, and the General Strike* (Montreal: McGill-Queen's University Press, 1974); Gordon Ashton Phillips, *The General Strike: The Politics of Industrial Conflict* (London: Weidenfeld and Nicolson, 1976); Mick Jenkins, *The General Strike of 1842* (London: Lawrence and Wishart, 1980).

general systems theory, term that describes efforts to build theoretical models that are conceptually, as Kenneth E. Boulding, "General Systems Theory—The Skeleton of Science," *Management Science* (April 1956), puts it, "somewhere between the highly generalized constructions of pure mathematics and the specific theories of the specialized disciplines." For the work of the man who sought a unity of science by introducing this notion, *see* Ludwig von Bertalanffy, *General Systems Theory: Foundations, Development, Ap-*

GENERAL SCHEDULE
1985 Pay Schedule for Federal White-Collar Workers

GS	1	2	3	4	5	6	7	8	9	10
1	$ 9,339	$ 9,650	$ 9,961	$10,271	$10,582	$10,764	$11,071	$11,380	$11,393	$11,686
2	10,501	10,750	11,097	11,393	11,521	11,860	12,199	12,538	12,877	13,216
3	11,458	11,840	12,222	12,604	12,986	13,368	13,750	14,132	14,514	14,896
4	12,862	13,291	13,720	14,149	14,578	15,007	15,436	15,865	16,294	16,723
5	14,390	14,870	15,350	15,830	16,310	16,790	17,270	17,750	18,230	18,710
6	16,040	16,575	17,110	17,645	18,180	18,715	19,250	19,785	20,320	20,855
7	17,824	18,413	19,012	19,606	20,200	20,794	21,388	21,982	22,576	23,170
8	19,740	20,393	21,056	21,714	22,372	23,030	23,688	24,346	25,004	25,662
9	21,804	22,531	23,258	23,985	24,712	25,439	26,166	26,893	27,620	28,347
10	24,011	24,811	25,611	26,411	27,211	28,011	28,811	29,611	30,411	31,211
11	26,381	27,260	28,139	29,018	29,897	30,776	31,655	32,534	33,413	34,292
12	31,619	32,673	33,727	34,781	35,835	36,889	37,943	38,997	40,051	41,105
13	37,599	38,852	40,105	41,358	42,611	43,864	45,117	46,370	47,623	48,876
14	44,430	45,911	47,392	48,873	50,354	51,835	53,316	54,797	56,278	57,759
15	52,262	54,044	55,746	57,488	59,230	60,972	62,714	64,465	66,198	67,940
16	61,296	63,339	65,382	67,425	69,468*	71,511*	73,554*	75,597*	77,640*	
17	71,804*	74,197*	76,590*	78,983*	81,376*					
18	84,157*									

*In most cases, the maximum salary payable is $68,700.

163

plications (N.Y.: George Braziller, 1968).
See also SYSTEMS ANALYSIS and SYSTEMS APPROACH.

generic management, those areas and concerns of management that are of common concern to both the public and private sectors. See Myron D. Fottler, "Is Management Really Generic?" *Academy of Management Review* (January 1981).

gentlemen's agreement, any agreement or understanding based solely on oral communications. It is usually unenforceable if one party reneges.

geographical differential, also called IN-TERCITY DIFFERENTIAL, differences in wage rates for the same work in various regions or cities.

George, Leo E. (1888-1967), president of the National Federation of Post Office Clerks from 1923 until 1956. For early biography, see Karl Baarslag, *History of the National Federation of Post Office Clerks* (Washington, D.C.: National Federation of Post Office Clerks, 1945).

geriatrics, also GERONTOLOGY and IN-DUSTRIAL GERONTOLOGY, that branch of medicine concerned with the special medical problems of older people. *Gerontology* is that branch of biology which is concerned with the nature of the aging process. *Industrial gerontology* is a far more comprehensive term that summarizes all of those areas of study concerned with the employment and retirement problems of workers who are middle-aged and beyond. See Harold L. Sheppard (ed.), *Towards an Industrial Gerontology: An Introduction to a New Field of Applied Research and Service* (Cambridge, Mass.: Schenkman Publishing Company, 1970); Arthur N. Schwartz and James A. Peterson, *Introduction to Gerontology* (New York: Holt, Rinehart and Winston, 1979); Robert L. Kane *et al.*, *Geriatrics in the United States: Manpower Projections and Training Considerations* (Lexington, Mass.: Lexington Books, 1981); Louis Lowy, *Social Policies and Programs on*

Aging (Lexington, Mass.: Lexington Books, 1980); Mildred Doering, Susan R. Rhodes and Michael Schuster, *The Aging Worker: Research and Recommendations* (Beverly Hills, CA: Sage, 1983).

Germer, Adolph F. (1881-1966), prominent union organizer and socialist, was one of the Congress of Industrial Organizations' most active early leaders. See Lorin Lee Cary, "Institutionalized Conservatism in the Early C.I.O.: Adolph Germer, A Case Study," *Labor History* (Fall 1972).

gerontology: see GERIATRICS.

GERR: see GOVERNMENT EMPLOYEE RELATIONS REPORT.

GERT, acronym for GRAPHICAL EVALUATION AND REVIEW TECHNIQUE, process that provides a framework for modeling real-world research and development projects requiring many false starts, redoings, and multiple outcomes. For a text, see Lawrence J. Moore and Edward R. Clayton, *GERT Modeling and Simulation: Fundamentals and Applications* (N.Y.: Petrocelli-Charter, 1976). For a specific application to personnel, see T. W. Bonham, Edward R. Clayton, and Lawrence J. Moore, "A GERT Model to Meet Future Organizational Manpower Needs," *Personnel Journal* (July 1975).

Gestalt therapy, psychotherapy technique pioneered by Frederic S. Perls, which emphasizes the treatment of a person as a biological and perceptual whole. "Gestalt" is a German word for a configuration, pattern, or otherwise organized whole whose parts have different qualities than the whole. According to William R. Passons, "Gestalt Therapy Interventions for Group Counseling," *Personnel and Guidance Journal* (November 1972),

in Gestalt therapy the principal means for facilitating responsibility and integration is the enhancement of self-awareness. These changes, however, are not forced or programmed. Rather they are allowed. As Perls stated it: "This is the great thing to understand: that awareness per se—by and of itself—can be curative."

Necessarily, then, Gestalt interventions are designed to enhance awareness of the person's "now" experience—emotionally, cognitively, and bodily. As such, many of the interventions lend themselves to group counseling.

The classic work on this subject is F. S. Perls, R. F. Hefferling and P. Goodman, *Gestalt Therapy* (N.Y.: Julian Press, 1951).

GETA: *see* GOVERNMENT EMPLOYEES TRAINING ACT OF 1958.

get the sack, be fired. At the dawn of the Industrial revolution, factory workers had to use their own tools. When a worker was fired, he was given a sack in which to gather up his tools.

Gilbert **case:** *see* GENERAL ELECTRIC CO. V. GILBERT.

Gilbreth, Frank Bunker (1868-1924) **and Lillian Moller** (1878-1972), husband and wife team who were the pioneers of time-and-motion study.

Frank and Lillian Gilbreth's influence on the scientific management movement was rivaled only by that of Frederick W. Taylor. Frank Gilbreth became the archetypical "efficiency expert." Two of their twelve children illustrated his mania for efficiency in their memoir, *Cheaper By the Dozen*, Frank B. Gilbreth, Jr., and Ernestine Gilbreth Carey (N.Y.: Grosset & Dunlap, 1948):

> Yes, at home or on the job, Dad was always the efficiency expert. He buttoned his vest from the bottom up, instead of from the top down, because the bottom-to-top process took him only three seconds, while the top-to-bottom took seven. He even used two shaving brushes to lather his face, because he found that by so doing he could cut seventeen seconds off his shaving time. For a while he tried shaving with two razors, but he finally gave that up.

"I can save forty-four seconds," he grumbled, "but I wasted two minutes this morning putting this bandage on my throat."

It wasn't the slashed throat that really bothered him. It was the two minutes.

For more serious biographies, *see* Edna Yost, *Frank and Lillian Gilbreth: Partners for Life* (New Brunswick, N.J.: Rutgers University Press, 1949); Lillian Moller Gilbreth, *The Quest for the One Best Way: A Sketch of the Life of Frank Bunker Gilbreth* (Easton, Pa.: Hive Publishing, 1973). For their collected works, *see* William R. Spriegel and Clark E. Myers (eds.), *The Writings of the Gilbreths* (Homewood, Ill.: Richard D. Irwin, 1953).

See also SCIENTIFIC MANAGEMENT and THERBLIG.

Ginzberg, Eli (1911-   ), political economist, and the leading authority on manpower research and employment and training policy. Major works include: *Human Resources: The Wealth of a Nation* (N.Y.: Simon and Schuster, 1958); *The American Worker in the Twentieth Century*, with Hyman Berman (The Free Press of Glencoe, 1963); *The Development of Human Resources* (N.Y.: McGraw-Hill, 1966); *Manpower Agenda for America* (N.Y.: McGraw-Hill, 1968); *Manpower Strategy for the Metropolis* (N.Y.: Columbia University Press, 1968); *The Human Economy* (N.Y.: McGraw-Hill, 1976). For biographical sketch, *see* Gloria Stevenson, "Eli Ginzberg: Pioneer in Work Force Research," *Worklife* (May 1976).

girl Friday: *see* MAN FRIDAY.

giveback, any demand by management that a union accept a reduction in the present terms of employment. *See* The Bureau of National Affairs Editorial Staff, "Give-Backs Highlight Three Major Bargaining Agreements," *Personnel Administrator* (January 1983); Scott A. Kruse, "Giveback Bargaining: One Answer to Current Labor Problems," *Personnel Journal* (April 1983).

Gleason, Thomas W. (1900-   ), became president of the International Longshoremen's Association in 1963.

global plan, according to Kenneth E. Foster, Gerald F. Wajda, and Theodore R. Lawson, "Global Plan for Salary Administration," *Harvard Business Review* (September-October 1961), a global plan "is a survey technique by which data on salary schedules, representing all employees from similar firms, can be arranged in a form that lends itself to simple statistical measurements."

GNP: *see* GROSS NATIONAL PRODUCT.

goals, also QUOTAS and TIMETABLE, within the context of equal employment opportunity a *goal* is a realistic objective which an organization endeavors to achieve through affirmative action. A *quota*, in contrast, restricts employment or development opportunities to members of particular groups by establishing a required number or proportionate representation which managers are obligated to attain without regard to "equal" employment opportunity. To be meaningful any program of goals or quotas must be associated with a specific *timetable*—a schedule of when the goals or quotas are to be achieved. *See* Daniel Seligman, "How 'Equal Opportunity' turned into Employment Quotas," *Fortune* (March 1973); Neil C. Churchill and John K. Shank, "Affirmative Action and Guilt-Edged Goals," *Harvard Business Review* (March-April 1976). For a case study of how the nation's largest private employer met its government mandated goals and timetables, *see* Carol J. Loomis, "A.T. & T. in the Throes of 'Equal Employment,' " *Fortune* (January 15, 1979). *See also* David H. Rosenbloom, "The Civil Service Commission's Decision to Authorize the Use of Goals and Timetables in the Federal Equal Employment Opportunity Program," *Western Political Quarterly* (June 1973).
   See also FULLILOVE V. KLUTZNICK and KIRKLAND V. NEW YORK STATE DEPARTMENT OF CORRECTIONAL SERVICES.

GOCL: *see* GORDON OCCUPATIONAL CHECK LIST.

Goesaert v. Cleary, 335 U.S. 464 (1948), U.S. Supreme Court case, which found state laws denying women the right to practice certain occupations to be unconstitutional under the 14th Amendment's equal protection clause.

going rate, wage rate most commonly paid to workers in a given occupation.

Goldberg, Arthur Joseph (1908-   ), appointed Secretary of Labor by President John F. Kennedy in 1961, and associate justice of the U.S. Supreme Court in 1962. In 1965, he resigned from the court to be President Lyndon B. Johnson's ambassador to the United Nations until 1968. He has often been called the "architect" of the AFL-CIO because as legal counsel to the CIO he was a prime mover in the merger. *See* his *AFL-CIO: Labor United* (New York: McGraw-Hill, 1956). For a hostile biography, *see* Victor Lasky, *Arthur J. Goldberg: The Old and the New* (New Rochelle, N.Y.: Arlington House, 1970).

Goldberg v. Kelly, 397 U.S. 254 (1970), U.S. Supreme Court case, which held that the due process clause of the Constitution requires government agencies to provide welfare recipients with an opportunity for an evidentiary hearing before terminating their benefits.

goldbricking, a "goldbrick" was a slang term for something that had only a surface appearance of value well before it was adopted by the military to mean shirking or giving the appearance of working. The word has now come to imply industrial work slowdowns whether they be individual initiatives (or the lack of individual initiative) or group efforts (organized or otherwise).

gold-circle rate, pay rate that exceeds the maximum rate of an employee's evaluated pay level.

golden handcuffs, the feeling of being

bound to remain in a job because financial benefits would be forfeited upon resignation.

golden handshake, dismissing an employee while at the same time providing him/her with a large cash bonus.

golden parachute, either being able to leave a company with a substantial financial benefit; or a no-cut contract given to executives of a company facing a takeover bid. *See* Philip L. Cochran and Steven L. Wartick, "Golden Parachutes: A Closer Look," *California Management Review* (Summer 1984).

goldfish-bowl bargaining: *see* SUNSHINE BARGAINING.

Gompers, Samuel (1850-1924), one of the founders of the American Federation of Labor in 1886. He was the first president of the AFL and held that post, except for one year, until his death. For his autobiography, *see Seventy Years of Life and Labor: An Autobiography,* 2 volumes (N.Y.: E. P. Dutton, 1925). Other biographies include: Bernard Mandel, *Samuel Gompers: A Biography* (Yellow Springs, Ohio: The Antioch Press, 1963); Stuart Bruce Kaufman, *Samuel Gompers and the Origins of the American Federation of Labor: 1848-1896* (Westport, Conn.: Greenwood Press, 1973); Harold C. Livesay, *Samuel Gompers and Organized Labor in America* (Boston: Little, Brown, 1978).

good faith, in the context of equal employment opportunity, "good faith" is the absence of discriminating intent. The "good faith" of an employer is usually considered by the courts in fashioning an appropriate remedy to correct the wrongs of "unintentional" discrimination.

good-faith bargaining, Section 8(a) (5) of the National Labor Relations Act makes it illegal for an employer to refuse to bargain in good faith about wages, hours, and other conditions of employment with the representative selected by a majority of the employees in a unit appropriate for collective bargaining. A bargaining representative seeking to enforce its right concerning an employer under this section must show that it has been designated by a majority of the employees, that the unit is appropriate, and that there has been both a demand that the employer bargain and a refusal by the employer to do so.

The duty to bargain covers all matters concerning rates of pay, wages, hours of employment, or other conditions of employment. These are called "mandatory" subjects of bargaining about which the employer, as well as the employees' representative, must bargain in good faith, although the law does not require "either party to agree to a proposal or require the making of a concession." These mandatory subjects of bargaining include, but are not limited to, such matters as pensions for present and retired employees, bonuses, group insurance, grievance procedure, safety practices, seniority, procedures for discharge, layoff, recall, or discipline, and the union shop. On "nonmandatory" subjects—that is, matters that are lawful but not related to "wages, hours, and other conditions of employment"—the parties are free to bargain and to agree, but neither party may insist on bargaining on such subjects over the objection of the other party.

An employer who is required to bargain under this section must, as stated in Section 8(d), "meet at reasonable times and confer in good faith with respect to wages, hours, and other terms and conditions of employment, or the negotiation of an agreement, or any question arising thereunder, and the execution of a written contract incorporating any agreement reached if requested by either party."

An employer, therefore, will be found to have violated Section 8 (a) (5) if its conduct in bargaining, viewed in its entirety, indicates that the employer did not negotiate with a good-faith intention to reach agreement. However, the employer's good faith is not at issue where its conduct constitutes an out-and-out refusal to bargain on a mandatory subject. For example, it is a violation for an employer, regardless of good faith, to refuse to bargain about a subject it believes is not a mandatory subject of bargaining, when in fact it is.

See also the following entries:
DUTY TO BARGAIN
NATIONAL LABOR RELATIONS BOARD V. INSURANCE AGENTS' INTERNATIONAL UNION
NATIONAL LABOR RELATIONS BOARD V. TRUITT MANUFACTURING
UNFAIR LABOR PRACTICES (EMPLOYERS)
UNFAIR LABOR PRACTICES (UNIONS)

good standing, being in compliance. For example, a union member is in "good standing" with his union if he or she meets all of the requirements for membership and his or her dues and other fees are current.

goon, also GOON SQUAD, slang terms for a man or men hired to create or resist violence during a labor dispute.

gopher, while this is not formally listed as a job title on anybody's resume, many a successful manager will admit to having worked his way up from gopher—go for coffee, go for this, go for that, etc.

Gordon Occupational Check List (GOCL), test in checklist format, that includes 240 statements of job activities found in occupations with middle and lower degrees of skill and responsibility. Used in vocational counseling with non-college-bound students. TIME: 20/25 minutes. AUTHOR: Leonard Gordon. PUBLISHER: Harcourt, Brace, Jovanovich, Inc. (see TEST PUBLISHERS).

Gouldner, Alvin W. (1920-1981), a leading sociologist who has made some of the most significant contributions to the field of industrial sociology. Major works include: Patterns of Industrial Bureaucracy (Glencoe, Ill.: The Free Press, 1954); Wildcat Strikes, with R.A. Peterson (Yellow Springs, Ohio: Antioch Press, 1954); Notes on Technology and the Moral Order, with Richard A. Peterson (Indianapolis: Bobbs-Merrill, 1962); Enter Plato (N.Y.: Basic Books, 1965); The

Coming Crisis of Western Sociology (N.Y.: Basic Books, 1970).

See also COSMOPOLITAN-LOCAL CONSTRUCT.

Government Employee Relations Report (GERR) published by the Bureau of National Affairs, Inc., this is a weekly notification and reference service designed solely for the public sector. Provides comprehensive coverage of all significant developments affecting public employee relations on the federal, state, and local levels.

Government Employees Training Act of 1958, federal statute (Public Law 85-507), which held that

in order to promote efficiency and economy in the operation of the Government and provide means for the development of maximum proficiency in the performance of official duties by employees thereof, to establish and maintain the highest standards of performance in the transaction of the public business, and to install and utilize effectively the best modern practices and techniques which have been developed, tested, and proved within or outside of the Government, it is necessary and desirable in the public interest that self-education, self-improvement, and self-training by such employees be supplemented and extended by Government-sponsored programs, provided for by this Act, for the training of such employees in the performance of official duties and for the development of skills, knowledge, and abilities which will best qualify them for performance of official duties.

GETA (1) was a clear-cut mandate that the federal workforce should be trained to its most effective level, (2) authorized expenditures for training, (3) provided for both centralized training by the U.S. Civil Service Commission and departmental training programs, and (4) authorized agencies to buy training from existing educational and professional institutions.

grade, established level or zone of difficulty. Positions of the same difficulty and responsibility tend to be placed in the same grade even though the content of the work differs greatly.

grade creep, also called GRADE ESCALATION, long-term tendency for positions to be reallocated upward. For an analysis of the problem, *see* Seymour S. Berlin, "The Manager, the Classifier, and Unwarranted Grade Escalation," *Civil Service Journal* (July–September 1964).

gradual pressure strike, concerted effort by employees to influence management by gradually reducing production until their objectives are met. *See* Michael L. Broorshire and J. Fred Holly, "Resolving Bargaining Impasses Through Gradual Pressure Strikes," *Labor Law Journal* (October 1973).

graduated wages, wages adjusted on the basis of length of service and performance.

graft, honest/dishonest: *see* HONEST GRAFT.

Grand Canyon management, as described by William Thomas, in "Humor for Hurdling the Mystique in Management," *Management of Personnel Quarterly* (Winter 1970),

> Few sights in the world are like the Grand Canyon. It is one of nature's most splendid scenarios. To see it from close up one can take advantage of a certain kind of tour—renting a mule and riding through the canyon itself. Mules are used on these tours instead of horses because they are surefooted and the tourist can sit relaxed, concentrating on the surroundings, secure in the knowledge that his mount will miss nary a step. That accurately describes the Grand Canyon Manager. He sits on his (mule) and watches everything going on around him. Staff people, particularly those in areas like Personnel, are frequent practitioners of Grand Canyon Management.

grandfather clause, originally a device used by some states of the Old South to disenfranchise black voters. Grandfather clauses, written into seven state constitutions during the Reconstruction era, granted the right to vote only to persons whose ancestors, "grandfathers," had voted prior to 1867. The U.S. Supreme Court ruled, in *Guinn* v. *United States*, 238 U.S. 347 (1915), that all grandfather clauses were unconstitutional because of the 15th Amendment. Today, a grandfather clause is a colloquial expression for any provision or policy that exempts a category of individuals from meeting new standards. For example, if a company were to establish a policy that all managers had to have a master's degree as of a certain date, it would probably exempt managers without such degrees who were hired prior to that date. This statement of exemption would be a grandfather clause. *See* Christopher Leman, "How to Get There from Here: The Grandfather Effect and Public Policy," *Policy Analysis* (Winter 1980).

Grant's Civil Service Commission, on the last day of the legislative session of the 41st Congress in 1871, a rider was attached to an otherwise unrelated appropriations bill authorizing President Ulysses S. Grant to make rules and regulations for the civil service. The rider itself was only one sentence long and did not formally require the president to do anything. It certainly would not have passed had it been thought to be anything more than a symbolic sop to the reformers. The rider authorized the president "to prescribe such rules and regulations for the admission of persons into the civil service of the United States as will best promote the efficiency thereof, and ascertain the fitness of each candidate. . . ." To the surprise of almost everyone, Grant proceeded to appoint a civil service commission. He authorized them to establish and implement appropriate rules and regulations. The commission required boards of examiners in each department who worked under the commission's general supervision. All things considered a viable program existed during 1872 and 1873. Several thousand persons were examined and several hundred were actually appointed. But once the Congress realized that Grant was serious about reform and intent upon cutting into their patronage powers, the program was terminated. Congress simply refused to appropriate funds for the work of the commission and the president formally abolished it in 1875.

For an exhaustive history, see Lionel V. Murphy, "The First Federal Civil Service Commission: 1871-1875," *Public Personnel Review* (October 1942).

grapevine, informal means by which organizational members give or receive information. According to Keith Davis, in "The Care and Cultivation of the Corporate Grapevine," *Dun's* (July 1973),

wherever people congregate in groups, the grapevine is sure to grow. It may manifest itself in smoke rings, jungle tom-toms, taps on prison walls or just idle chitchat, but it will always be there. Indeed, the word grapevine has been part of our jargon ever since the Civil War, when telegraph lines were strung loosely from tree to tree in vine-like fashion and resulted in messages that were frequently garbled.

For a more scholarly analysis by Keith Davis, see "Management Communication and the Grapevine," *Harvard Business Review* (September-October 1953). *Also see* Roy Rowan, "Where Did *That* Rumor Come From?" *Fortune*, August 13, 1979.

graphical evaluation and review technique: *see* GERT.

graphic rating scale, performance appraisal chart that lists traits (such as promptness, knowledge, helpfulness, etc.) with a range of performance to be indicated with each (unsatisfactory, satisfactory, etc.).

graphology: *see* HANDWRITING ANALYSIS.

graveyard shift, also called LOBSTER SHIFT, slang terms for the tour of duty of employees who work from 11 p.m. or midnight until dawn.

Great Society, label for the 1960s domestic policies of the Johnson administration that were premised on the belief that social and/or economic problems could be solved by new federal programs. *See* Sar Levitan, *The Great Society's Poor Law* (Baltimore: The Johns Hopkins Press, 1969); Henry J. Aaron, *Politics and the Professors: The Great Society in Perspective* (Washington, D.C.: The Brookings Institution, 1978); Sar A. Levitan and Robert Taggart, "The Great Society Did Succeed," *Political Science Quarterly* (Winter 1977); Michael K. Brown and Stephen P. Erie, "Blacks and the Legacy of the Great Society: The Economic and Political Impact of Federal Social Policy," *Public Policy* (Summer 1981).

Green card, a small document which identifies an alien as a permanent resident of the U.S. The "green card" was originally green, but now is white and salmon.

Green, William (1873-1952), succeeded Samuel Gompers as president of the American Federation of Labor in 1924 and held that office until his death. For a biography, see Max Danish, *William Green: A Pictorial Biography* (N.Y.: Inter-Allied Publications, 1952).

green-circle rate, also called BLUE-CIRCLE RATE, pay rate that is below the minimum rate of an employee's evaluated pay level.

green hands, slang term for inexperienced workers.

grievance, while a grievance may be any dissatisfaction felt by an employee in connection with his/her employment, the word generally refers to a formal complaint initiated by an employee, by a union, or by management concerning the interpretation or application of a collective bargaining agreement or established employment practices. For a discussion of how to avoid grievances, see W. B. Werther, Jr., "Reducing Grievances Through Effective Contract Administration," *Labor Law Journal* (April 1974). *Also see* Stephen B. Goldberg and Jeanne M. Brett, "An Experiment in the Mediation of Grievances," *Monthly Labor Review* (March 1983); Donald S. McPherson, Conrad J. Gates and Kevin N. Rogers, *Resolving Grievances: A Practical Approach* (Reston, VA: Reston/Prentice-Hall, 1983); Michael E. Gordon and Sandra J. Miller, "Grievances: A Review of Research and Practice," *Personnel Psychology* (Spring 1984).

grievance arbitration, also called RIGHTS ARBITRATION, arbitration concerned with disputes that arise over the interpretation/application of an existing collective bargaining agreement. The grievance arbitrator interprets the contract for the parties. *See* Richard Mittenthal, "Making Arbitration Work: Alternatives in Designing the Machinery," *The Arbitration Journal* (September 1981).

grievance committee, those union and/or management representatives who are formally designated to review grievances left unresolved by lower elements of the grievance machinery.

See also ELGIN, JOLIET & EASTERN RAILWAY V. BURLEY.

grievance machinery, totality of the methods, usually enumerated in a collective bargaining agreement, used to resolve the problems of interpretation arising during the life of an agreement. Grievance machinery is usually designed so that those closest to the dispute have the first opportunity to reach a settlement. According to Walter E. Baer, *Grievance Handling* (N.Y.: American Management Associations, 1970),

the grievance machinery is the formal process, preliminary to any arbitration, that enables the parties to attempt to resolve their differences in a peaceful, orderly, and expeditious manner. It permits the company and the union to investigate and discuss their problems without interrupting the continued, orderly operation of the business. And, when the machinery works effectively, it can satisfactorily resolve the over-

whelming majority of disputes between the parties.

grievance procedure, specific means by which grievances are channeled for their adjustment through progressively higher levels of authority in both an organization and its union. Grievance procedures, while long considered the "heart" of a labor contract, are increasingly found in nonunionized organizations as managers realize the need for a process to appeal the decisions of supervisors that employees consider unjust. For a how-to-do-it book, *see* Maurice S. Trotta, *Handling Grievances: A Guide for Management and Labor* (Washington, D.C.: Bureau of National Affairs, 1976). *Also see* Steven Briggs, "The Grievance Procedure and Organizational Health," *Personnel Journal* (June 1981); David Lewin and Richard Peterson, "A Model for Measuring Effectiveness of the Grievance Process," *Monthly Labor Review* (April 1982).

For non-union grievance procedures, *see:* Donald A. Drost and Fabius P. O'Brien, "Are There Grievances Against Your Non-Union Grievance Procedure?" *Personnel Administrator* (January 1983); Alan Balfour, "Five Types of Non-Union Grievance Systems," *Personnel* (March–April 1984); Fabius P. O'Brien and Donald A. Drost, "Non-Union Grievance Procedures: Not Just an Anti-Union Strategy," *Personnel* (September–October 1984); James K. McCollum and Dwight R. Norris, "Nonunion Grievance Machinery In Southern Industry," *Personnel Administrator* (November 1984).

See also EMPORIUM CAPWELL CO. V. WESTERN ADDITION COMMUNITY ORGANIZATION, McDONALD V. CITY OF WEST BRANCH, MICHIGAN, and SMITH V. ARKANSAS STATE HIGHWAY EMPLOYEES, LOCAL 1315.

grievant, one who files a formal grievance; one who does so grieves. This person is not in a state of mourning, but one of complaining. A study of grievants and nongrievants in one company found that the grievants were more likely to be (1) better educated, (2) younger in terms of seniority, (3) more active in union matters, (4) lower paid, and (5) more likely to be absent or tardy. *See* Howard A. Sulkin and Robert W. Pranis, "Comparison of Grievants with Non-grievants in a Heavy Machinery Company," *Personnel Psychology* (Summer 1967).

Griffenhagen, Edwin O. (1886–   ), management engineer who became one of the pioneers in the development of position classification and job analysis. For his history of the origin of modern duties-classification systems, *see* "The Origin of Modern Occupation Classification in Personnel Administration," *Public Personnel Studies* (September 1924).

Griggs et al. v. Duke Power Company, 401 U.S. 424 (1971), is the most significant single Supreme Court decision concerning the validity of employment examinations. The court unanimously ruled that Title VII of the Civil Rights Act of 1964 "proscribes not only overt discrimination but also practices that are discriminatory in operation." Thus, if employment practices operating to exclude minorities "cannot be shown to be related to job performance, the practice is prohibited." The ruling dealt a blow to restrictive credentialism, stating that, while diplomas and tests are useful, the "Congress has mandated the commonsense proposition that they are not to become masters of reality." In essence, the court held that the law requires that tests used for employment purposes "must measure the person for the job and not the person in the abstract."

The *Griggs* decision applied only to the private sector until the Equal Employment Opportunity Act of 1972 extended the provisions of Title VII of the Civil Rights Act of 1964 to cover public as well as private employees. *See* Hugh Steven Wilson, "A Second Look at *Griggs* v. *Duke Power Company*: Ruminations on Job Testing, Discrimination and the Role of the Federal Courts," *Virginia Law Review* (May 1972); Alfred W. Blumrosen, "Strangers in Paradise: *Griggs* v. *Duke Power Co.* and the Concept of Employ-ment Discrimination," *Michigan Law Review* (November 1972).

Griner, John F. (1907–   ), president of the American Federation of Government Employees (AFGE) from 1962 to 1973.

grog privileges, practice of allowing laborers to stop work during the afternoon for a drink of grog or something similar. This custom has fallen into disuse, except among higher paid executives.

gross national product (GNP), monetary value of all of the goods and services produced in a nation in a given year.

group: *see* SMALL-GROUP RESEARCH.

group annuity, any of a variety of pension plans designed by insurance companies for a group of persons to cover all of those qualified under one contract.

group cohesiveness, measure of the degree of unity and solidarity that a group possesses.

group development, loose term concerned with the various processes and circumstances that occur when individuals organize themselves into goal orientated groups. For a survey of the theory and research, *see* John M. Ivancevich and J. Timothy McMahon, "Group Development, Trainer Style, and Carry-over Job Satisfaction and Performance," *Academy of Management Journal* (September 1976).

group dynamics, it is generally accepted that Kurt Lewin "invented" the field of group dynamics (that is, he was responsible, either directly or indirectly, for most of the pioneering research on group dynamics). Two of Lewin's close associates, Dorwin Cartwright and Alvin Zander, went on to produce what was for many years the standard text on the subject—*Group Dynamics: Research and Theory* (N.Y.: Harper & Row, 3rd ed., 1968). They defined "group dynamics" as the field of inquiry dedicated to advancing knowledge about the nature of groups, how they develop, and their relationships to individuals, other groups, and larger institutions. *See* Kurt Lewin, "Frontiers in Group Dynamics: Concept, Method and Reality in Social Science," *Human Relations* (June 1947).

group executive, manager responsible for the work of two or more organizational divisions.

group incentive plan: *see* INCENTIVE-WAGE PLAN.

group insurance, also GROUP HEALTH INSURANCE and GROUP LIFE INSURANCE, *group insurance* refers to any insurance plan that covers individuals (and usually their dependents) by means of a single policy issued to the employer or association with which the insured individuals are affiliated. The cost of group insurance is usually significantly lower than the costs for equivalent individual policies. Group insurance policies are written in the name of the employer so that individual employees are covered only as long as they remain with the insuring employer. Sometimes group insurance policies provide that an employee can continue his/her coverage upon resignation by buying an individual policy. The most common kinds of group insurance are *group health insurance* and *group life insurance.* Many employers pay a substantial portion of all of the cost of group insurance.

group of classes, two or more closely related job classes having a common basis of duties, responsibilities, and qualification requirements but differing in some particular (such as the nature of specialization) that is essential from the standpoint of recruitment and selection and requires that each class in the group be treated individually. Such classes have the same basic title but may be distinguished by a parenthetic. For example: Engineer (Chemical), Engineer (Electrical), etc.

group oral interview, also called GROUP ORAL EXAMINATION, measurement tool that involves a group of candidates (ideally 5-7) discussing a job-related problem. The evaluators do not actively participate in the group discussion; their role is to observe and evaluate the behavior of the participants. The value of this technique is heavily dependent on the ability of the evaluators.

group psychotherapy, any form of psychological treatment involving more than one subject. Organization development efforts can be considered a form of group psychotherapy. *See* Robert R. Dies, "Group Psychotherapy: Reflections on Three Decades of Research," *Journal of Applied Behavioral Science* (July-August-September 1979); George M. Gazda, *Basic Approaches to Group Psychotherapy and Group Counseling,* third edition (Springfield, Ill.: Charles C. Thomas, 1982).

See also ENCOUNTER GROUP and INTERNATONAL JOURNAL OF GROUP PSYCHOTHERAPY.

Group I Tenure/Group II Tenure/Group III Tenure, federal government terms for the tenure groupings of its employees. Employees who are serving in competitive positions are grouped as follows:

Group 1. Career employees who have completed their probationary period and who are not serving in obligated positions. (An obligated position is a position to which a former employee has mandatory reemployment or restoration rights.)

Group II. Career-conditional employees and career employees who have not completed probationary periods or who occupy obligated positions.

Group III. Employees serving under temporary appointments pending establishment of a register, employees serving under indefinite appointments, etc.

Employees serving under appointments to excepted positions, aliens, and attorneys are grouped according to their tenure of employment as follows:

Group I. Permanent employees whose appointments carry no restrictions or conditions.

Group II. Employees serving trial periods, those whose tenure is indefinite solely because they are occupying obligated positions and those serving under conditional appointments who have not completed the 3-year service requirement for appointment without condition or limitation.

Group III. This group includes all employees serving under appointments specifically identified as indefinite. It also includes employees serving under temporary excepted appointments limited to one year or less who have completed one year or more of current continuous employment in the excepted service.

groupthink, psychological drive for consensus, at any cost, which tends to suppress both dissent and the appraisal of alternatives in small decisionmaking groups. Groupthink, because it refers to a deterioration of mental efficiency and moral judgment due to ingroup pressures, has an invidious connotation. For the basic work on the subject, *see* Irving L. Janis, *Victims of Groupthink: A Psychological Study of Foreign-Policy Decisions and Fiascoes* (Boston: Houghton-Mifflin Co., 1972).

GS: *see* GENERAL SCHEDULE.

guaranteed annual wage (GAW), any of a variety of plans whereby an employer agrees to provide employees with a predetermined minimum (1) number of hours of work or (2) salary each year.

guaranteed base rate: *see* GUARANTEED RATE.

guaranteed earnings, provision in some union contracts that employees will be paid (guaranteed) a specified minimum wage, even when production must cease because of a machinery breakdown or some other cause beyond the control of the employee.

guaranteed income stream, an alternative to supplemental unemployment benefit plans (SUBs) in the auto industry which provides financial incentives for firms to avoid long-term layoffs and to find alternative employment for workers who are laid off. The guaranteed income stream can be thought of as negative income tax paid for by the firm, not the government. Eligible laid-off workers recieve a minimum benefit while outside earnings from alternative employment are "taxed" or offset by reductions in their benefits. Because the rate of offset is only 80 percent, workers have some incentive to find alternative employment. Benefits continue to be paid until workers reach a combined income level (benefits plus earnings) called the "break-even point" (1/tax rate), which in this case equals 125 percent of the minimum benefit. Beyond this point, additional earnings are completely offset by benefit reductions, and the plan ceases to function. *See* Peter Cappelli, "Auto Industry Experiments With the Guaranteed Income Stream," *Monthly Labor Review* (July 1983).

guaranteed rate, also called GUARANTEED BASE RATE, minimum wage guaranteed to an employee working under an incentive pay program.

guaranteed workweek, provision in some union contracts that an employee will be paid a full week's wages even when there is not enough actual work available to otherwise warrant a full week's pay.

Guest, Robert H. (1916-   ), known for his pioneering studies of life on the assembly line and of job design. Major works include: *The Man on the Assembly Line*, with Charles R. Walker (Cambridge, Mass.: Harvard University Press, 1952); *Organizational Change: The Effect of Successful Leadership* (Homewood, Ill.: Dorsey Press, 1962).

guest worker, European term for foreign workers allowed to enter and work in a country for a temporary period. *See* W. R. Bohning, "Estimating the Propensity of Guestworkers to Leave," *Monthly Labor Review* (May 1981).

guide chart, tool used by a factor-ranking system of job evaluation, which contains a narrative description and point value for each degree of each factor.

guideline method, job evaluation technique that determines the value of a position in an organization not by an analysis of the position's content, but by what the labor market says it is worth.

guidelines, also called GUIDEPOSTS, (1) general standards, usually expressed as a percentage, by which the federal government measures wage and price increases to determine if they are consistent with the national economic interest or (2) published outlines for action or suggested courses of conduct that many federal agencies issue for the guidance of their clients.

guideposts: see GUIDELINES.

guild, also called CRAFT GUILD, in medieval Western Europe, an association for mutual aid and/or for the furtherance of religious and business interests. Merchant guilds date from the 11th century. Although there was a craft-guild movement in ancient Rome, the modern union movement usually traces its lineage to the craft guilds of the Middle Ages, which paralleled the merchant guilds of the time. Craft guilds were associations of individual workers who sought to regulate production, establish standards, and fix prices. These craft guilds gave us the now familiar rankings for their classes of membership—apprentice, journeyman, and master.

Guild Socialism, political movement that advocated workers' control of industry by means of a system of national guilds. This movement had its greatest popularity in England just before and just after World War I.

Guilford-Zimmerman Temperament Survey (GZTS), personality inventory developed to provide a single comprehensive inventory of the following traits: general activity, restraint, ascendence, sociability, masculinity, emotional stability, objectivity, friendliness, thoughtfulness,

personal relations. TIME: Approximately 45 minutes. AUTHOR: J. P. Guilford and Wayne S. Zimmerman. PUBLISHER: Sheridan Psychological Services, Inc. (see TEST PUBLISHERS).

Gulick, Luther (1892-   ), highly honored reformer, researcher, and practitioner of public administration, best known to management generalists for having invented POSDCORB (see entry). Major works include: *Papers on the Science of Administration,* edited with Lyndall Urwick (N.Y.: Institute of Public Administration, 1937); *Administrative Reflections from World War II* (University of Alabama Press, 1948); *The Metropolitan Problem and American Ideas* (N.Y.: Knopf, 1962).

gypsy, slang term for an independent operator of a truck, taxi, etc., who owns his/her own vehicle.

GZTS: see   GUILFORD-ZIMMERMAN TEMPERAMENT SURVEY.

H

Hagglund, Joel Emmanuel: see HILL, JOE.

Hall v. *Cole,* 412 U.S. 1 (1973), U.S. Supreme Court case, which held that union members who successfully challenge a union action in court can be awarded attorney's fees if it could be shown that litigant's victory benefited the entire union.

Hall Occupational Orientation Inventory (HOOI), 345-item, free-choice test used to assess the attractiveness or relative importance to the individual of various occupational attributes or factors. The 23 scales measured include such items as: creativity/independence, risk, belongingness, security, aspiration, esteem, people-orientation, concerns about money, environment, co-workers, time, extremism, and defensiveness. TIME: 40/60 minutes. AUTHOR: L. G. Hall. PUBLISHER: Follett Educational Corporation (*see* TEST PUBLISHERS).

halo effect, bias in ratings arising from the tendency of a rater to be influenced in his/her rating of specific traits by his/her general impression of the person being rated. The concept was "discovered" by Edward L. Thorndike in "A Constant Error in Psychological Ratings," *Journal of Applied Psychology*, Vol. 4 (March 1920). *Also see* Larry M. King, John E. Hunter, and Frank L. Schmidt, "Halo in a Multi-dimensional Forced-Choice Performance Evaluation Scale," *Journal of Applied Psychology* (October 1980); Rich Jacobs and Steven W.J. Kozlowski, "A Closer Look at Halo Error in Performance Ratings," *Academy of Management Journal* (March 1985).

Halsey, Frederick Arthur (1856-1935), a pioneer in the development of wage payment systems.

Halsey Plan, Frederick A. Halsey's "premium plan" was first presented to the American Society of Mechanical Engineers in 1891. Halsey proposed that workers be allowed to use their individual past performance as a standard, with the value of any increased output divided between the employee and the employer.

Hammer v. Dagenhart, 247 U.S. 251 (1918), U.S. Supreme Court case, which held unconstitutional a federal statute barring goods made by child labor from interstate commerce. The court would not concede that the federal government could regulate child labor in interstate commerce until 1941, when it upheld the Fair Labor Standards Act of 1938 that put restrictions on the use of child labor. The landmark case was *United States v. Darby Lumber Company*, 312 U.S. 100 (1941).

Hampton v. Mow Sun Wong, 426 U.S. 88 (1976), U.S. Supreme Court case, which held that a U.S. Civil Service Commission regulation excluding resident aliens from the federal competitive service had been adopted in violation of the due process clause of the 5th Amendment. Because the court expressly decided only the validity of the regulations promulgated by the Civil Service Commission and reserved comment on the appropriateness of a citizenship requirement instituted by the president, on September 2, 1976, President Ford issued Executive Order 11935, which provides that only U.S. citizens and nationals may hold permanent positions in the federal competitive service except when necessary to promote the efficiency of the service. For a legal analysis, *see* Eric C. Scoones, "Procedural Due Process and the Exercise of Delegated Power: The Federal Civil Service Employment Restriction on Aliens," *The Georgetown Law Journal* (October 1977).

See also SUGARMAN V. DOUGALL.

handbilling, passing out leaflets urging consumers not to deal with an employer as part of a labor dispute. The employer who is the target of the handbill may be either a primary or secondary employer. In either case, the handbill must be truthful. Where it is aimed at a secondary employer, it must state that the dispute is with another employer. The status of handbilling is unusual because it can urge the consumer to engage in a total boycott of the secondary employer as long as that employer continues to do business with the primary employer. Unlike product picketing, handbilling does not have to be confined to urging boycotts of specific, individual products. The secondary boycott sought by handbilling is considered legal. Various other forms of notice, such as advertisements in the print and electronic media are treated as handbills in this context. The distinction between handbilling and picketing in terms of urging boycotts is derived from the more coercive nature of picketing.

handicapped employees, emotionally: *see* EMOTIONALLY HANDICAPPED EMPLOYEES.

handicapped individual, also QUALIFIED HANDICAPPED INDIVIDUAL, any person who (1) has a physical or mental impairment which substantially limits one or more of such person's major life activities, (2) has a record of such an impairment, or (3) is regarded as having such an impairment. A *qualified handicapped individual*, with respect to employment, is one who with reasonable accommodation can perform the essential functions of a job in question. Handicapped workers are protected from discrimination by Federal law if they are employed by companies that hold Federal contracts, are participants in programs or activites that receive Federal funds, or if they are employed by the Federal Government.

Under section 503 of the Rehabilitation Act of 1973, as amended, Federal contractors and subcontractors who have contracts in excess of $2,500 may not discriminate against persons otherwise qualified to do the job in hiring, firing, promotions, compensation, or other terms or conditions of employment because the person has a physical or mental handicap.

The Office of Federal Contract Compliance Programs (OFCCP), U.S. Department of Labor, enforces section 503 of the Rehabilitation Act. OFCCP regulations covering affirmative action obligations of Federal contractors and subcontractors require outreach and positive recruitment as well as individualized accommodation to the physical limitation of an applicant or employee, if necessary. The OFCCP enforcement process includes investigation and conciliation efforts as well as recourse to court action. Remedies include withholding of payments and debarment from Federal contracting. Some courts have held that an individual may sue privately under section 503, and others have held that only the Federal Government may pursue remedies under this section.

Section 504 of the Rehabilitation Act, as amended in 1978, forbids discrimination against handicapped individuals in programs or activities receiving Federal funds. Courts have held that section 504 permits individuals to take legal action against such programs for discriminatory

acts. Section 504 is enforced by the agency providing Federal assistance, under the general leadership of the Department of Justice. The EEOC provides leadership and guidance with respect to employment discrimination based on handicap.

Federal regulations prohibit Federal agencies from discriminating against qualified physically or mentally handicapped persons; require them to make reasonable accommodation to the known physical or mental limitations of qualified handicapped applicants or employees; and require them to issue regulations regarding the acceptance and processing of complaints of discrimination based on a physical or mental handicap. The Equal Employment Opportunity Commission enforces the regulations that apply to Federal employees.

A number of States prohibit unfair discrimination against handicapped individuals in State fair employment practices laws. For information about State protections, contact the State department of labor or human rights commission. *See* Robert B. Nathanson, "The Disabled Employee: Separating Myth from Fact," *Harvard Business Review* (May-June 1977); Sar A. Levitan and Robert Taggart, "Employment Problems of Disabled Persons" *Monthly Labor Review* (March 1977); Gopal C. Pati, "Countdown on Hiring the Handicapped," *Personnel Journal* (March 1978); Vigdor Grossman, *Employing Handicapped Persons: Meeting EEO Obligations* (Washington, D.C.: Bureau of National Affairs, Inc., 1980); Gopal C. Pati and John J. Adkins, "Hire the Handicapped—Compliance is Good Business," *Harvard Business Review* (January-February 1980); Ray B. Bressler and A. Wayne Lacy, "An Analysis of the Relative Job Progression of the Perceptibly Physically Handicapped," *Academy of Management Journal* (March 1980); Donald J. Peterson, "Paving the Way for Hiring the Handicapped," *Personnel* (March-April 1981); Sara M. Freedman and Robert T. Keller, "The Handicapped in the Workforce," *Academy of Management Review* (July 1981); Harriet McBryde Johnson, "Who is Handicapped? Defining the Protected Class Under the Employment Provisions of Title V of the Rehabilitation Act of 1973," *Review of Public Personnel Personnel Administration* (Fall 1981); Anne Waltz, "Integrating Disabled Workers into Your Workforce," *Public Personnel Management*, Vol. 10, No. 4 (Winter 1981); Sara M. Freedman and Robert T. Keller, "The Handicapped in the Workforce," *The Academy of Management Review* (July 1981).

See also the following entries:
ARCHITECTURAL BARRIERS
NATIONAL REHABILITATION ASSOCIATION
READING ASSISTANT
REASONABLE ACCOMMODATION
REHABILITATED OFFENDER PROGRAM
SHELTERED WORKSHOP
VOCATIONAL REHABILITATION ACT OF 1973
WAGNER-O'DAY ACT
WORK-ACTIVITIES CENTERS
WORK-READY

hands-on test, performance test that uses the actual tools of the job.

handwriting analysis, scientific name GRAPHOLOGY, psychological tool sometimes used to evaluate the personality and character of employment applicants. A handwriting analyst is a graphologist; the science is graphology. *See* Jitendra M. Sharma and Harsh Vardhan, "Graphology: What Handwriting Can Tell You About an Applicant," *Personnel* (March–April 1975).

Hanna Mining Co. v. District 2, Marine Engineers, 382 U.S. 181 (1965), U.S. Supreme Court case, which held that while supervisory personnel are not employees for purposes of the National Labor Relations Act, the act does not preempt state labor laws affecting supervisors.

hard cases, cases where fairness may require judges to be loose with legal principles; that's why "hard cases make bad law."

hard-core unemployed, those individuals who, because of racial discrimination, an impoverished background, or the lack of appropriate education, have never been able to hold a job for a substantial length of time. *See* Leonard Nadler, "Helping the Hard-Core Adjust to the World of Work," *Harvard Business Review* (March–April 1970); Keith C. Weir, "Hard Core Training and Employment," *Personnel Journal* (May 1971); Daniel M. Seifer, "Continuing Hard Problems: The 'Hard-Core' and Racial Discrimination," *Public Personnel Management* (May–June 1974); Albert A. Blum, "Hard-Core Unemployment: A Long-Term Problem," *Business and Society* (Spring 1983).

hardship allowance, additional money paid to an employee who accepts an assignment that offers difficult living conditions, physical hardships, unattractive climate, and/or a lack of the usual amenities found in the United States.

hardware, formally, the mechanical, magnetic, electrical, and electronic devices or components of a computer. Informally, any piece of computer or automatic-data-processing equipment. *See also* SOFTWARE.

Harvard Business Review (HBR), journal for professional managers, published bimonthly by the faculty of the Harvard University Graduate School of Business Administration. The editors modestly state that, in selecting articles for publication, they "try to pick those that are timeless rather than just timely." The *Harvard Business Review* is almost universally considered the foremost business journal in the United States.

Harvard Business Review
Editorial Address:
Harvard Business Review
Boston, MA 02163
Subscriptions:
Harvard Business Review
Subscription Service Department
P.O. Box 3000
Woburn, MA 01888

Harvard Business School (HBS), the

most prestigious of the prestigious "B" schools. Robert Townsend, in *Up the Organization* (N.Y.: Knopf, 1970), suggests that you "don't hire Harvard Business School graduates. This worthy enterprise confesses that it trains its students for only three posts—executive vice-president, president, and board chairman. The faculty does not blush when HBS is called the West Point of capitalism." For the "inside" story about the education of the managerial elite in the U.S., *see* Peter Cohn, *The Gospel According to the Harvard Business School* (Garden City, N.Y.: Doubleday & Co., 1973); Mark H. McCormak, *What They Don't Teach You At the Harvard Business School* (New York: Bantam, 1984).

Harvard Fatigue Laboratory (HFL), research organization that existed within the Harvard Business School from 1927 to 1947. According to Steven M. Horvath and Elizabeth C. Horvath, in *The Harvard Fatigue Laboratory: Its History and Contributions* (Englewood Cliffs, New Jersey: Prentice-Hall, Inc., 1973), its highly influential research efforts tended to focus on the notion that "group psychology, social problems and the physiology of fatigue of normal man must be studied, not only as individual factors in determining physical and mental health, but more especially to determine their interrelatedness and the effect upon work."

Hatch Act, collective popular name for two federal statutes. The Hatch Act of 1939, 53 Stat. 410 (1939), restricted the political activities of almost all federal employees, whether in the competitive service or not. The impetus for this legislation came primarily from a decrease in the proportion of federal employees who were in the competitive service. This was a direct result of the creation of several New Deal agencies that were placed outside the merit system. Senator Carl Hatch, a Democrat from New Mexico, had worked for several years to have legislation enacted that would prevent federal employees from being active in political conventions. He feared that their involvement and direction

by politicians could lead to the development of a giant national political machine.

A second Hatch Act in 1940, 54 Stat. 640 (1940), extended these restrictions to positions in state employment having federal financing. Penalties for violation of the Hatch Act by federal employees have been softened considerably over time. Originally, removal was mandatory, but, by 1962, the minimum punishment was suspension for 30 days.

It has never been possible to define completely the political activities prohibited by the Hatch Act. However, the following are among the major limitations:

1. serving as a delegate or alternate to a political party convention;
2. soliciting or handling political contributions;
3. being an officer or organizer of a political club;
4. engaging in electioneering;
5. with some exceptions, being a candidate for elective political office; and
6. leading or speaking to partisan political meetings or rallies.

The constitutionality of these regulations was first upheld by the Supreme Court in *United Public Workers* v. *Mitchell*, 330 U.S. 75 (1947) and reaffirmed in *Civil Service Commission* v. *National Association of Letter Carriers*, 413 U.S. 548 (1973). Repeal of the Hatch Act (or relaxation of some of its provisions) has been high on the legislative agenda of unions, especially since union legal challenges to the act have been unsuccessful. *See* Philip L. Martin, "The Hatch Act: The Current Movement for Reform," *Public Personnel Management* (May-June 1974); Henry Rose, "A Critical Look at the Hatch Act," *Harvard Law Review* (January 1962); Steven W. Hayes and Luther F. Carter, "The Myth of Hatch Act Reform," *Southern Review of Public Administration* (December 1980).

See also UNITED STATES CIVIL SERVICE COMMISSION V. NATIONAL ASSOCIATION OF LETTER CARRIERS.

hatchet man, according to Qass Aquarius, *The Corporate Prince: A Hand-*

book of Administrative Tactics (N.Y.: Van Nostrand Reinhold Co., 1971),

> when dirty work must be done, the wise administrator tries to keep his hands clean. Perhaps he may have a subordinate, a hatchet man, to do his dirty work for him, thereby avoiding the displeasure of those who do not approve of the actions. For this reason many administrators prefer to have their subordinates do their firing for them. Sometimes a board of directors deliberately brings in a president as a hatchet man to clean house, prune the corporate tree of its deadwood, thereby incurring great displeasure among people within the organization. After all the bloodletting has taken place, the board can find other work for the hatchet man and a new man can be brought in who immediately bestows benefits upon a grateful, relieved organization.

Hawkins v. Bleakly, 243 U.S. 210 (1917), U.S. Supreme Court case, which upheld the constitutionality of state workmen's compensation laws.

Hawthorne Effect, Elton Mayo and his associates, while conducting their now famous Hawthorne Studies, discovered that the researchers' concern for and attention to the workers led to increases in production. Any production increase due to known presence of benign observers can be attributed to a "Hawthorne Effect." For Mayo's account, *see* Elton Mayo, *The Human Problems of an Industrial Civilization* (N.Y.: Viking Press, 1933, 1960).

Hawthorne Studies, also called HAWTHORNE EXPERIMENTS, conducted at the Hawthorne Works of the Western Electric Company near Chicago are probably the most important single management study yet reported. Beginning in the late 1920s, a research team led by Elton Mayo of the Harvard Business School started a decade-long series of experiments aimed at determining the relationship between work environment and productivity. The experimenters, because they were initially unable to explain the results of their find-

ings, literally stumbled upon what today seems so obvious—that factories and other work situations are first of all social situations. The Hawthorne Studies are generally considered to be the genesis of the human relations school of management thought. The definitive account of the experiments is given in F. J. Roethlisberger and William J. Dickson's *Management and the Worker* (Cambridge, Mass.: Harvard University Press, 1939).

Work group behavior, output restriction, supervisory training, personnel research, interviewing methodology, employee counseling, socio-technical systems theory, small group incentive plans, and organizational theory became prime concerns of management, because, in one way or another, they were brought to the fore or elucidated by the Hawthorne Studies. For a re-examination of the studies a generation later, *see* Henry A. Landsberger, *Hawthorne Revisited* (Ithaca, N.Y.: Cornell University Press, 1958).

Hay, Edward N. (1891-1958), editor and publisher of the *Personnel Journal* from 1947 to 1958 who pioneered the development of modern testing and job evaluation techniques. Major works include: *Manual of Job Evaluation: Procedures of Job Analysis And Appraisal*, with Eugene J. Benge and Samuel L. H. Burk (N.Y.: Harper & Bros., 1941); *Psychological Aids in the Selection of Workers*, with G. W. Wadsworth, Jr., D. W. Cook and C. L. Shartle (N.Y.: American Management Association, 1941).

See also HAY SYSTEM.

Hay Guide Chart-Profile Method: *see* HAY SYSTEM.

Haymarket Riot, the 19th century's most famous confrontation between police and labor demonstrators. On May 3, 1886, police killed four strikers at the McCormick Harvesting Machine Company in Chicago. In response, labor leaders called a protest meeting for the night of May 4, 1886, in Chicago's Haymarket Square. Police arrived toward the end of the meeting and ordered the crowd to disperse. Suddenly, a bomb exploded among the approximately 180 police. Sixty-six were wounded; seven would die. The uninjured police opened fire on the crowd. Estimates of the killed vary from several to ten; of the wounded from 50 to 200. The identity of the bomb thrower was never determined. In the midst of an hysterical atmosphere, eight labor leaders were tried and convicted of murder on the grounds that they had conspired with or aided an unknown murderer. Four were hanged on November 11, 1887. One committed suicide, and the other three remained in prison until pardoned by Illinois Governor John P. Altgeld in 1893. For historics, *see* Frank Harris, *Bomb: The Haymarket Riot* (Chicago: University of Chicago Press, 1963). Wendy Snyder, *Haymarket* (Cambridge, Mass.: M.I.T. Press, 1970); Paul Avrich, *The Haymarket Tragedy* (Princeton University Press, 1984).

Hay System, Edward N. Hay developed one of the best known job evaluation methods. Essentially a modification of the factor-comparison technique, Hay's Guide Chart-Profile Method is based on three factors: know-how, problemsolving and accountability. Many organizations have adopted variations of the Hay System for job evaluation. For an analysis, *see* Charles W. G. Van Horn, "The Hay Guide Chart-Profile Method," *Handbook of Wage and Salary Administration*, Milton L. Rock (ed.), (N.Y.: McGraw-Hill, 1972),

Haywood, William Dudley (1869-1928), nicknamed BIG BILL HAYWOOD, a founder of the Industrial Workers of the World and one of the most violent and radical of the early labor leaders. For biographies, *see* Joseph R. Conlin, *Big Bill Haywood and the Radical Union Movement* (Syracuse: Syracuse University Press, 1969); Peter Carlson, *Roughneck: The Life and Times of Big Bill Haywood* (New York: W. W. Norton, 1983).

hazard pay, compensation paid to an employee above regular wages for work that is potentially dangerous to his/her health. *See* Craig A. Olson, "An Analysis of Wage Differentials Received by Workers on Dangerous Jobs," *The Journal of Human Resources* (Spring 1981).

Hazelwood School District* v. *United States, 433 U.S. 299 (1977), U.S. Supreme Court case, which held that a public employer did not violate Title VII of the Civil Rights Act of 1964 if, from March 24, 1972 (when Title VII became effective for public employers), all of its employment decisions were made in a "non-discriminatory way," even if it had "formerly maintained an all-white workforce by purposefully excluding Negroes."

HBR: *see* HARVARD BUSINESS REVIEW.

headhunter, also called CORPORATE HEADHUNTER and PEOPLE PLUCKER, slang terms for executive recruiter. For an account of the business, *see* Allan J. Cox, *Confessions of a Corporate Headhunter* (N.Y.: Trident Press, 1973). What should you do if a headhunter calls? According to Herbert E. Meyer, "The Headhunters Come Upon Golden Days," *Fortune* (October 1978),

> for those who have always wondered what is the proper response to this kind of telephone call, headhunters have a stock piece of advice: get up and close your office door. The purpose of the call is first, to verify that you are who the headhunter thinks you are, and second, to arrange a meeting if you are at all interested in considering a change of jobs. Not surprisingly, headhunters say that most people they call are willing, if not eager, to meet them.

> *Also see* A. Robert Taylor, *How to Select and Use an Executive Search Firm* (New York: McGraw-Hill Book Co., 1984); Robert H. Perry, *How to Answer a Headhunter's Call* (New York: AMACOM, 1984).

health benefits, total health service and health insurance programs that an organization provides for its employees.

health insurance, group: *see* GROUP INSURANCE.

Health Maintenance Organization (HMO), according to Robert Gumbiner, "Selection of a Health Maintenance Organization," *Personnel Journal* (August 1978), a HMO is

a nonprofit organization which maintains clinics and hospitals and supplies physicians, health care specialists and medication at little or no additional cost. It differs from indemnity insurance in that for a monthly fee, total health and medical care are provided. That is, indemnity insurance pays only in case of illness or accident, but an HMO allows a person to see a doctor for preventive care, and without extra charges. (Since an HMO commits itself to paying all medical expenses, it is in its own interest to keep people healthy.) Thus its subscribers are sometimes able to avoid serious illness.

Also see Jeffery Cohelan, "HMO's— How They Can Keep the Lid on Escalating Health Care Costs," *Pension World* (March 1978); Deborah H. Harrison and John R. Kimberly, "HMOs Don't Have to Fail," *Harvard Business Review* (July-August 1982); Allan Blostin and William Marclay, "HMOs and Other Health Plans: Coverage and Employee Premiums," *Monthly Labor Review* (June 1983).

Health Maintenance Organization Act of 1973, federal statute that sets standards of qualifications for an HMO and mandates that employers of 25 or more who currently offer a medical benefit plan offer the additional option of joining a qualified HMO, if one exists in the area.

hearing, legal or quasi-legal proceeding, in which arguments, witnesses, or evidence are heard by a judicial officer or administrative body.

hearing examiner/officer: *see* ADMINISTRATIVE LAW JUDGE.

HEARS: *see* HIGHER EDUCATION ADMINISTRATION REFERRAL SERVICE.

Heinz case: *see* H. J. HEINZ CO. V. NATIONAL LABOR RELATIONS BOARD.

helping interview, interview that consists of a genuine dialogue between the interviewer and the interviewee; the interviewer is an empathic listener rather than a mere technician recording information. *See* Alfred Benjamin, *The Helping Interview* (Boston: Houghton Mifflin, 2nd ed., 1974).

Helvering v. Davis, 301 U.S. 619 (1937), U.S. Supreme Court case, which held constitutional the Social Security Act of 1935.

Herzberg, Frederick (1923-   ), a major influence on the conceptualization of job design, especially job enrichment. His motivation-hygiene or two-factor theory of motivation is the point of departure and a common reference point for analyses of the subject. Major works include: *The Motivation To Work*, with Bernard Mausner and Barbara Snyderman (N.Y.: John Wiley & Sons, 1959); *Work And The Nature of Man* (Cleveland: World Publishers, 1966); and *The Managerial Choice* (Homewood, Ill.: Dow Jones-Irwin, 1976).

See also JOB ENRICHMENT and MOTIVATION-HYGIENE THEORY.

heuristic, short-cut process of reasoning that searches for a satisfactory, rather than an optimal, solution to a very large, complex and/or poorly defined problem. *See* Charles L. Hinkle and Alfred A. Kuehn, "Heuristic Models: Mapping the Maze for Management," *California Management Review* (Fall 1967).

Hicklin v. Orbeck, 57 L. Ed. 2d 397 (1978), U.S. Supreme Court case, which held unconstitutional an Alaska law granting employment preferences to Alaskan residents. The law violated the constitutional requirement that states grant all U.S. citizens the same "privileges and immunities" granted to its own citizens.

hidden agenda, unannounced or unconscious goals, personal needs, expectations, and strategies that each individual brings with his/her participation in a group.

Parallel to the group's open agenda are the private or hidden agendas of each of its members. *See* Priscilla Elfrey, *The Hidden Agenda: Recognizing What Really Matters at Work* (New York: Wiley, 1982).

hidden unemployed: *see* DISCOURAGED WORKERS.

hierarchy, any ordering of persons, things, or ideas by rank or level. *See* Arnold S. Tannenbaum, *Hierarchy in Organizations* (San Francisco: Jossey-Bass, 1974); Neely Gardner, "The Non-Hierarchical Organization of the Future: Theory v. Reality," *Public Administration Review* (September–October 1976); Thomas A. Mahoney, "Organizational Hierarchy and Position Worth," *Academy of Management Journal* (December 1979); John F. Padgett, "Managing Garbage Can Hierarchies," *Administrative Science Quarterly* (December 1980); Jon S. Ebeling and Michael King, "Hierarchical Position in the Work Organization and Job Satisfaction," *Human Relations* (July 1981); Patrica Yancey Martin, Dianne Harrison and Diana DiNitto, "Advancement for Women in Hierarchical Organizations: A Multilevel Analysis of Problems and Prospects," *The Journal of Applied Behavioral Science*, Vol. 19, No. 1 (1983).

Higher Education Administration Referral Service (HEARS), nonprofit organization that helps institutions locate qualified individuals for non-academic administrative vacancies. HEARS is co-sponsored by 19 major higher education associations.

HEARS
Suite 510
One Dupont Circle
Washington, D.C. 20036
(202) 857-0710

Hill, Joe (1879–1915), born JOEL EMMANUEL HAGGLUND, emigrated from Sweden to America in 1902 and became active as a union organizer. After joining the radical Industrial Workers of the World (IWW), he began writing "folk" songs dealing with union themes. In 1915, he was executed in Utah after being convicted on circumstantial evidence for the murder of a grocer and his son. His death made him a martyr to the union cause. One of his last requests was to be buried in another state, because "I don't want to be found dead in Utah." For accounts of his life and legend, *see* Vernon H. Jensen, "The Legend of Joe Hill," *Industrial and Labor Relations Review* (April 1951); Gibbs M. Smith, *Joe Hill* (Salt Lake City: University of Utah Press, 1969).

Hillman, Sidney (1887–1946), president of the Amalgamated Clothing Workers from its creation in 1913 to his death. A close political advisor of President Franklin D. Roosevelt, Hillman was the Sidney in FDR's famous order to "clear it with Sydney." For a biography, *see* Matthew Josephson, *Sidney Hillman: Statesman of American Labor* (Garden City, N.Y.: Doubleday, 1952). *See* CLEAR IT WITH SIDNEY.

Hines v. Anchor Motor Freight, 424 U.S. 554 (1976), U. S. Supreme Court case, which held that, if a union member can prove that he was erroneously discharged and that his union's representation tainted the decision of the arbitration committee which upheld the discharge, then he is entitled to take legal action against both the employer and the union.

hire: *see* EMPLOY.

hiring, preferential: *see* PREFERENTIAL HIRING.

hiring hall, also called UNION HIRING HALL and CENTRAL HIRING HALL, employment office usually run by the union to coordinate the referral of its members to jobs. Sometimes hiring halls are operated jointly with management and/or state government assistance. Hiring halls are especially important for casual or seasonal trades (such as construction and maritime work). For an analysis of the hiring-hall process, *see* Stuart B. Philpott, "The Union Hiring Hall as a Labor Market: A Sociological Analysis," *British Journal of Industrial*

Relations (March 1965). For a history, *see* Philip Ross, "Origin of the Hiring Hall in Construction," *Industrial Relations* (October 1972).

hiring rate: *see* ACCESSION RATE and ENTRANCE RATE.

Hishon* v. *King and Spalding, U.S. Supreme Court case, 81 L. Ed. 2d 59 (1984), which held that a law firm must comply with Federal anti-discrimination laws when deciding which members of the firm should be elevated to partners.

Hispanic Employment Program: *see* SPANISH SPEAKING PROGRAM.

histogram, bar graph of a frequency distribution.

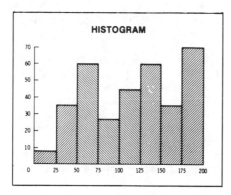

HISTOGRAM

hit the bricks, slang phrase for going out on strike.

H. J. Heinz Co.* v. *National Labor Relations Board, 311 U.S. 514 (1941), U.S. Supreme Court case, which held that a company had to sign a collective bargaining agreement, even when wages, hours and other terms and conditions of employment were not in dispute.

HMO: *see* HEALTH MAINTENANCE ORGANIZATION.

Hobbs Act: *see* ANTI-RACKETEERING ACT OF 1934.

Hodgson, James D. (1915-   ), Secretary of Labor from 1970 to 1973.

Hoffa, Jimmy, full name JAMES RIDDLE HOFFA (1913-1975), president of the International Brotherhood of Teamsters from 1957 to 1971 who was convicted of jury tampering and other charges in 1964. After exhausting appeals, he entered federal prison in 1967 to begin serving a 13-year term. His sentence was commuted by President Richard M. Nixon on condition that he not participate in union affairs until 1980. In 1975, Hoffa "disappeared" and is presumed dead. For an autobiography, *see The Trials of Jimmy Hoffa:* (Chicago: H. Regnery Co., 1970); for a biography, *see* Walter Sheridan, *The Fall and Rise of Jimmy Hoffa* (N.Y.: Saturday Review Press, 1972). *See also* Steven Brill, *The Teamsters* (N.Y.: Simon and Schuster, 1978).

Holden* v. *Hardy, 169 U.S. 336 (1898), U.S. Supreme Court case, which held that a state, in exercising its police power to protect the public health, had the right to legislate hours of work.

holiday, bank: *see* BANK HOLIDAY.

holiday pay, premium rate, usually provided for in union contracts, paid for work performed on holidays.

Hollerith cards, punched cards used by computers, which were first developed by Herman Hollerith of the U.S. Bureau of the Census in 1889.

Homans, George C. (1910-   ), industrial sociologist, best known for his early application of "systems" to organizational analysis. Major works include: *An Introduction to Pareto: His Sociology,* with C. P. Curtis, Jr., (N.Y.: Knopf, 1934); *The Fatigue of Workers: Its Relation to Industrial Production* (N.Y.: Reinhold Publishing Company, 1941); *The Human Group* (N.Y.: Harcourt Brace Jovanovich, 1950); *Sentiments and Activities* (N.Y.: The Free Press, 1962); *Nature of Social Science* (N.Y.: Harcourt Brace Jovanovich, 1967); *Social Behavior: Its Elementary Forms* (N.Y.: Harcourt Brace Jovanovich, rev. ed., 1974).

homeostasis, maintenance of equilibrium among bodily and systemic processes. The normal functioning of the body or system is dependent upon maintaining such internal stability. For an introduction to the concept, *see* L. L. Langley, *Homeostasis* (N.Y.: Reinhold Publishing, 1965).

Homestead Strike, in July 1892, the members of the Amalgamated Association of Iron, Steel and Tin Workers struck the Homestead (Pennsylvania) plant of the Carnegie Steel Company (forerunner of the United States Steel Corporation). The company thereupon hired 300 Pinkerton detectives to enable it to import strikebreakers. The strikers met the Pinkertons as they were arriving. After a 12-hour "battle," the Pinkertons, with three dead and dozens wounded, literally ran up a white flag, laid down their arms, and were allowed to go back to Pittsburgh. A week later, 8,000 state militia opened the plant to strikebreakers. By November 1892, the union was smashed—2,000 strikebreakers were at work and only 800 of the 4,000 who had gone out on strike were rehired. Unionism in the steel industry suffered a setback that would last for decades. For the history of the strike, *see* R. I. Finch, "Unionism in the Iron and Steel Industry," *Political Science Quarterly*, Vol. 24 (1909); Arthur G. Burgoyne, *Homestead* (N.Y.: Augustus M. Kelley, 1893; reprinted 1971); Leon Wolff, *Lockout: The Story of the Homestead Strike of 1892* (New York: Harper & Row, 1965).

hometown plan, voluntary affirmative action plan for the construction crafts and trades developed by a local construction industry, usually in cooperation with the U.S. Department of Labor.

homogeneity principle, principle of administration that advises the executive to group the major functions of an organization together according to their purpose, the process used, the persons served, or the places where it takes place, with each constituted as a single unit under the direction of a single administrator guided by a single plan of action.

honcho, slang word for a boss or any person in charge of a work detail. U.S. soldiers first adopted the term from the Japanese word *hancho* ("group leader").

honest graft, also DISHONEST GRAFT, the classic distinction between the two genre of graft was made by George Washington Plunkitt, a politico associated with New York's Tammany Hall early in this century. *Dishonest graft*, as the name implies, involves bribery, blackmailing, extortion and other obviously illegal activities. As for *honest graft*, let Plunkitt speak:

Just let me explain by examples. My party's in power in the city, and it's goin' to undertake a lot of public improvements. Well, I'm tipped off, say, that they're going to lay out a new park at a certain place.

I see my opportunity and I take it, I go to that place and I buy up all the land I can in the neighborhood. Then the board of this or that makes its plan public, and there is a rush to get my land, which nobody cared particular for before.

Ain't it perfectly honest to charge a good price and make a profit on my investment and foresight? Of course, it is. Well, that's honest graft.

For more of Plunkitt's wisdom, *see* William Riordon, *Plunkitt of Tammany Hall* (N.Y.: E. P. Dutton & Co., 1963).

honeymoon period, that period of time immediately following a major agreement between management and labor when both sides may seek to de-emphasize the normal difficulties inherent in their relationships.

HOOI: *see* HALL OCCUPATIONAL ORIENTATION INVENTORY.

hooking, also ROPING, slang term for convincing a worker to spy on fellow union members, usually by means of bribery or blackmail.

Hopf, Harry Arthur (1882-1949), management theorist who did pioneering work on executive compensation systems and the measurement of managerial performance. For the case that he originated many of the concepts of "management by objectives," *see:* Edmund R. Gray and Richard J. Vahl, "Harry Hopf: Management's Unheralded Giant," *Southern Journal of Business* (April 1971).

horizontal communication: *see* COMMUNICATION.

horizontal loading: *see* JOB LOADING.

horizontal occupational mobility: *see* OCCUPATIONAL MOBILITY.

horizontal promotion, advancement for an employee within his/her basic job category. For example, a promotion from Window Washer I to Window Washer II or from Junior Accountant to Intermediate Accountant.

horizontal union: *see* CRAFT UNION.

horizontal work group, work group that contains individuals whose positions are essentially the same in terms of rank, prestige, and level of skill.

hostile witness, a witness for one side in a trial or hearing who is seemingly so prejudiced or hostile to that side that he or she can also be cross-examined as if called by the opposition.

hospitalization, group insurance program that pays employees for all or part of their hospital, nursing, surgical, and other related medical expenses due to injury or illness to them or their dependents.

hot-cargo provisions, contract clauses that allow workers to refuse to work on or handle "unfair goods" or "hot cargo"—products coming from a factory where there is a labor dispute. The Labor-Management Reporting and Disclosure (Landrum-Griffin) Act of 1959 outlawed such provisions (except for those affecting suppliers or subcontractors in construction work and jobbers in the garment industry). For a legal analysis, *see* Paul A. Brinker, "Hot Cargo Cases Since 1958," *Labor Law Journal* (September 1971).

See also UNFAIR LABOR PRACTICES (UNIONS).

hot stove discipline, disciplinary practices that are immediate, painful, and impersonal.

hourly-rate workers, employees whose weekly pay is determined solely by the actual number of hours worked during a week.

house account, also called NO-COMMISSION ACCOUNT, account serviced by branch or home office executives. Usually no credit is given nor commissions paid when sales are made to such accounts.

housekeeping agency: *see* AUXILIARY AGENCY.

House of Labor, informal term for the AFL-CIO. *See* AMERICAN FEDERATION OF LABOR-CONGRESS OF INDUSTRIAL ORGANIZATIONS.

house organ, also INTERNAL HOUSE ORGAN and EXTERNAL HOUSE ORGAN, any publication—magazine, newspaper, newsletter, etc.—produced by an organization to keep its employees informed about the activities of the organization and its employees. *Internal house organs* are directed primarily to an organization's employees; *external house organs* find a wider distribution as part of the organization's public relations program. *See* Jim Mann, "Is Your House Organ A Vital Organ?" *Personnel Journal* (September 1977).

housework, domestic chores that one performs or has performed in one's domicile. *See* Ann Oakley, *The Sociology of Housework* (N.Y.: Pantheon, 1975).

housing allowance, special compensation, consisting of a flat rate or a salary percentage, for the purpose of subsidizing the living expenses of an employee, usually paid only to employees sent overseas.

Howard Johnson Co., Inc. v. Detroit Local Joint Executive Board, Hotel and Restaurant Employees, 417 U.S. 249 (1974), U.S. Supreme Court case, which held that one company, upon purchasing another, was not required to arbitrate the extent of its obligations to the purchased company's union under the so-called "successorship" doctrine announced in the case of *John Wiley & Sons* v. *Livingston,* 376 U.S. 543 (1964). In the *Wiley* case, the court held that a successor employer may be compelled, under certain circumstances, to arbitrate the question of his obligations toward the employees covered by his predecessor's labor contract. *See* Evan J. Spelfogel, "A Corporate Successor's Obligation to Honor His Predecessor's Labor Contract: The Howard Johnson Case," *Labor Law Journal* (May 1974); Gary A. Marsack and Phoebe M. Eaton, "Successorship Law: The Impact on Business Transfers and Collective Bargaining," *Marquette Law Review* (Winter 1981).

See also JOHN WILEY & SONS V. LIVINGSTON.

Hoxie, Robert Franklin (1868–1916), a professor of economics at the University of Chicago whose book, *Scientific Management and Labor* (New York: D. Appleton & Co., 1915), was the first to comprehensively deal with the relationship between scientific management and the labor movement.

HRM: *see* HUMAN RESOURCES MANAGEMENT.

H.R. 10 Plan: *see* KEOGH PLAN.

Hudgens v. National Labor Relations Board, 424 U.S. 507 (1976), U.S. Supreme Court case, which held that pickets did not have a 1st Amendment right to enter a shopping center (private property) for the purpose of advertising a strike against their employer.

human capital, a concept that views employees as assets in the same sense as financial capital. It presupposes that an investment in human potential will yield significant returns for the organization. *See* Theodore W. Schultz, *Investment in Human Capital* (N.Y.: The Free Press, 1971); Thomas K. Connellan, "Management as a Capital Investment," *Human Resource Management* (Summer 1972); Stanley A. Horowitz and Allan Sherman, "A Direct Measure of the Relationship Between Human Capital and Productivity," *Journal of Human Resources* (Winter 1980); William A. Darity, Jr., "The Human Capital Approach to Black-White Earnings Inequality: Some Unsettled Questions," *The Journal of Human Resources* (Winter 1982); R. U. Miller and M. A. Zaidi, "Human Capital and Multinationals: Evidence From Brazil and Mexico," *Monthly Labor Review* (June 1982).

human-factors engineering, also called ERGONOMICS, design for human use. The objective of human factors engineering, usually called ergonomics in Europe, is to increase the effective use of physical objects and facilities by people at work, while at the same time attending to concerns such as health, safety, job satisfaction, etc. These objectives are sought by the systematic application of relevant information about human behavior to the design of the things (usually machines) that people use and to the environments in which they work. The leading text is Ernest J. McCormick, *Human Factors Engineering* (N.Y.: McGraw-Hill, 3rd ed., 1970). *Also see* Roy J. Shepard, *Men at Work: Applications of Ergonomics to Performance and Design* (Springfield, Ill.: Charles C. Thomas, 1974); Vico Henriques and Charlotte LeGates, "Special Report: A Look at VDT's and Their Impact on the Workplace and an Overview of a New Science called Ergonomics, *"Personnel Administrator* (September 1984).

human relations, discipline concerned

with the application of the behavioral sciences to the analysis and understanding of human behavior in organizations.

Personnel operations still tend to live in the shadow of the old-style human-relations approach to management that emphasized sympathetic attitudes on the part of managers. Its critics contended that the human-relations approach (most popular during the late 1940s and 1950s) was little more than a gimmick—that there was sincere interest in the workers only to the extent that they could be manipulated for management's ends. The goal was to adjust the worker—the same old interchangeable part of the scientific management movement—so that he or she would be content in the industrial situation, not to change the situation so that the worker would find more contentment in his or her work.

Today, human relations is in a more mature period. Like the caterpillar that turned into the butterfly, it simply evolved into something much more desirable. By expropriating advances in the behavioral sciences as its own, it grew into its current definition. For texts, see Keith Davis, *Human Behavior at Work: Human Relations and Organizational Behavior* (N.Y.: McGraw-Hill, 1972); Aubrey C. Sanford, *Human Relations: Theory and Practice* (Columbus, Ohio: Charles E. Merrill, 1973); Robert M. Fulmer, *Practical Human Relations,* revised edition (Homewood, Ill.: Richard D. Irwin, 1983).

Human Relations, monthly journal founded on the belief that social scientists in all fields should work toward integration in their attempts to understand the complexities of human problems. Articles tend to be theoretical analyses of human interactions in the workplace, as well as society in general.

Editorial Address:
Editor
Human Relations
Tavistock Centre
120 Belsize Lane
London NW3 5BA
Subscriptions:
Plenum Publishing Corp.

233 Spring Street
New York, NY 10013

human resource accounting, concept that views the employees of an organization as capital assets similar to plant and equipment. While the concept is intuitively attractive, calculating the value, replacement cost, and depreciation of human assets poses significant problems. Consequently, it is viewed with considerable skepticism by managers and accountants. For the methodology, see Eric G. Flamholtz, "Human Resources Accounting: Measuring Positional Replacement Costs," *Human Resource Management* (Spring 1973); Robert Wright, "Managing Man as a Capital Asset," *Personnel Journal* (April 1970). For a text, see Edwin H. Caplan and Stephen Landekich, *Human Resource Accounting: Past, Present and Future* (N.Y.: National Association of Accountants, 1974). *Also see* Sue A. Ebersberger, "Human Resource Accounting: Can We Afford It?" *Training and Development Journal* (August 1981); Blair Y. Stephenson and Stephen G. Franklin, "Human Resource Accounting: Dollars and Sense for Management," *Business and Society* (Winter–Spring 1981-82); Bruce G. Meyers and Hugh M. Shane, "Human Resource Accounting for Managerial Decisions: A Capital Budgeting Approach," *Personnel Administrator* (February 1984).

Human Resource Management, previously titled MANAGEMENT OF PERSONNEL QUARTERLY, quarterly whose articles deal with a variety of topics related to personnel practices and human resource management. Most articles are written by academics and tend to be either theoretical analyses and/or reports of research.

Editorial Address:
Human Resource Management
Graduate School of Business Administration
University of Michigan
Ann Arbor, MI 48109
Subscriptions:
Subscription Department
John Wiley & Sons

605 Third Avenue
New York, NY 10157

Human Resource Planning, quarterly journal of the Human Resource Planning Society, which is devoted to the advancement of the practice, technology, and theory of planning for human resources.
Human Resource Planning
P.O. Box 2553
Grand Central Station
New York, NY 10163

Human Resource Planning Society, nonprofit organization devoted to the advancement of the practice, technology, and theory of planning for human resources. Its quarterly journal is Human Resource Planning.
Human Resource Planning Society
P.O. Box 2553
Grand Central Station
New York, NY 10163
(617) 837-0630

human resources, also called MANPOWER, general term for all of the employees in an organization or the workers in a society. It is gradually replacing the more sexist "manpower."

Human Resources Abstracts, formerly POVERTY AND HUMAN RESOURCES ABSTRACTS, quarterly publication that contains abstracts of current literature on human, social, and manpower problems and solutions ranging from slum rehabilitation and job development training to compensatory education, minority group problems, and rural poverty.
Human Resources Abstracts
Sage Publications, Inc.
275 South Beverly Drive
Beverly Hills, CA 90212

human resources administration, increasingly popular euphemism for the management of social welfare programs. Many jurisdictions that had Departments of Welfare have replaced them with Departments of Human Resources.

human resources development, a more impressive sounding phrase for the training and development function of personnel management. See Lue Rachelle Brim-Donohoe, "A Case for Human Resources Development," Public Personnel Management, Vol. 10, No. 4 (Winter 1981).

human resources management (HRM), although often used synonymously with personnel management, HRM transcends traditional personnel concerns, taking the most expansive view of the personnel department's mandate. Instead of viewing the personnel function as simply that collection of disparate duties necessary to recruit, pay, and discharge employees, a HRM approach assumes that personnel's appropriate mission is the maximum utilization of its organization's human resources. Recent textbooks are beginning to reflect this larger vision of the personnel function. See Andrew F. Sikula, Personnel Administration and Human Resources Management (N.Y.: John Wiley, 1976); William P. Anthony and Edward A. Nicholson, Management of Human Resources: A Systems Approach to Personnel Management (Columbus, Ohio: Grid, Inc., 1977); Lawrence A. Klatt, Robert G. Murdick and Fred E. Schuster, Human Resources Management: A Behavioral Systems Approach (Homewood, Ill.: Richard D. Irwin, 1978); Richard B. Peterson and Lane Tracy, Systematic Management of Human Resources (Reading, Mass.: Addison-Wesley, 1979); Andrew J. DuBrin, Personnel and Human Resources Management (N.Y.: D. Van Nostrand, 1981). Also see Joyce D. Ross, "A Definition of Human Resources Management," Personnel Journal (October 1981); Raymond E. Miles and Howard R. Rosenberg, "The Human Resources Approach to Management: Second-Generation Issues," Organizational Dynamics (Winter 1982); Donald Summers, "Human Resources Specialists: Working with Managers to Improve Productivity," Personnel (September-October 1984); John A. Hooper, "A Strategy for Increasing the Human Resource Department's Effectiveness," *Personnel Administrator* (June 1984).

human resources planning, also called MANPOWER PLANNING, there is no universally accepted definition of what human resources planning (or its more sexist equivalent, "manpower planning") is or consensus on what activities should be associated with it. Organizations claiming that they do such planning appear to use a wide variety of methods to approach their own unique problems.

Historically, manpower planning was most associated with the Johnson Administration's Great Society Programs of the 1960s. It was and remains an integral part of numerous government programs whose objective was to affect the labor market in order to improve the employment status and welfare of individuals. All such programs have a macro focus—they deal with the aggregate labor force of the country (all employed and unemployed individuals). At roughly the same time of the new manpower initiatives of the Johnson Administration, parallel thinking on human resources planning began to emerge at the firm and organizational level. Both situations involve projecting and managing the supply and demand of human resources,

only at different levels. Both are concerned with future demand aspects; that is, what will be the requirements for the future work force. At the macro level, this means projecting what skills will be in demand to service the economy. At the micro level, this entails projecting specific requirements for the work force of the organization, or what quantities and qualities of personnel will be needed to carry out organizational objectives. Both levels are concerned with future supply aspects. At the macro level this means that projections must be made on what the national work force will consist of in terms of future skills, both surpluses and deficits. For the micro level, the organization must forecast what its future work force will consist of as well as evaluate its competitive position in order to decide what quantities and qualities of personnel it can encourage to enter the organization as replacements.

Some of the better works on human resources planning include: D. J. Bell, *Planning Corporate Manpower* (London: Longman Group, 1974); Elmer H. Burack and James H. Walker, *Manpower Planning and Programming* (Boston: Allyn and Bacon, 1972); Edward B. Jakubauskas and Neil A. Palomba, *Manpower Economics* (Reading, Mass.: Addi-

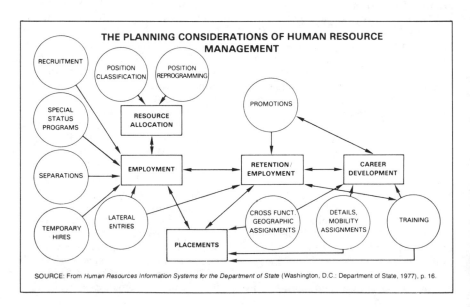

THE PLANNING CONSIDERATIONS OF HUMAN RESOURCE MANAGEMENT

SOURCE: From *Human Resources Information Systems for the Department of State* (Washington, D.C.: Department of State, 1977), p. 16.

son-Wesley, 1973); Ray A. Killian, *Human Resource Management* (N.Y.: American Management Association, 1976); James W. Walker, *Human Resources Planning* (New York: McGraw-Hill, 1980).

human resources planning models, also called MANPOWER PLANNING MODELS, according to Richard C. Grinold and Kneale T. Marshall, *Manpower Planning Models* (N.Y.: Elsevier North-Holland, 1977), personnel planning models use systems analysis to

(a) *Forecast* the future manpower requirements that will be satisfied by the current inventory of personnel; forecast the future manpower budget commitments represented by the current stock of personnel. (b) *Analyze* the impact of proposed changes in policy, such as changes in promotion or retirement rules, changes in salary and benefits, changes in transfers into and out of the organization, and changes in the organization's rate of growth. (c) *Test* the rationale of historical policy for consistency, and establish the relations among operating rules of thumb. (d) *Explore* regions of possible policy changes and allow a planner to experiment with and perhaps discover new policies. (e) *Understand* the basic flow process, and thus aid in assessing the relative operational problems. (f) *Design* systems that balance the flows of manpower, requirements, and costs. (g) *Structure* the manpower information system in a manner suitable for policy analysis and planning.

human resources requirements analysis, also called MANPOWER REQUIREMENTS ANALYSIS, analysis and projection of (a) the personnel movements and (b) the numbers and kinds of vacancies to be expected during each stage of management's workforce plan. According to the Office of Personnel Management, the essential steps in manpower requirements analysis are:

- *First,* to estimate what portion of the workforce present at the start of the planning period, or hired during the

period, will leave their positions during the period.
- *Second,* to estimate how many of these position leavers will move to other positions in the workforce during the period and how many will leave the service entirely.
- *Third,* to estimate the positions to be occupied by in-service movers at the end of the planning period.
- *Fourth,* by comparison of this retained workforce with the workforce specified in management's workforce plan, to identify the numbers and kinds of positions to be filled during the planning period.

Also see Richard B. Frantzreb, "Human Resource Planning: Forecasting Manpower Needs," *Personnel Journal* (November 1981); Norman Scarborough and Thomas W. Zimmerer, "Human Resources Forecasting: Why and Where to Begin," *Personnel Administrator* (May 1982).

human resources utilization, also called MANPOWER UTILIZATION, general terms for the selection, development and placement of human resources within an economic or organizational system in order to use these resources in the most efficient manner. *See* Edward B. Jakubauskas and Neil A. Palomba, *Manpower Economics* (Reading, Mass.: Addison-Wesley, 1973); Edward J. Giblin and Oscar A. Ornati, "Optimizing the Utilization of Human Resources," *Organizational Dynamics* (Autumn 1976).

human services, general term for organizations that seek to improve the quality of their client's lives by providing counseling, rehabilitative, nutritional, informational and related services.

Humphrey-Hawkins Act of 1977, formally the FULL EMPLOYMENT AND BALANCED GROWTH ACT OF 1977, federal statute that asserts it is the policy of the federal government to reduce overall unemployment to a rate of four percent by 1983, while reducing inflation to a rate of three percent. The act explicitly states that it is the "right of all Americans able, willing and seeking to work" to have "full opportunities for useful paid employment." However, the discussion of the act in the *Congressional Record* of December 6, 1977, states that "there is clearly no right to sue for legal protection of the right to a job." The popular name of the act comes from its co-sponsors, former Senator Hubert H. Humphrey (D-Minn.) and Representative Augustus F. Hawkins (D-Calif.)

Hutcheson case: *see* UNITED STATES V. HUTCHESON, ET AL.

Hutcheson, William L. (1874-1953), president of the Brotherhood of Carpenters from 1915 to 1953. For a biography, *see* Maxwell C. Raddock, *Portrait of An American Labor Leader: William L. Hutcheson* (N.Y.: American Institute of Social Science, Inc., 1955).

hypothesis, testable assertion, statement, or proposition about the relationship between two variables that are in some way related to each other. For example, a personnel manager might hypothesize that a specific kind of job performance can be predicted from a particular kind of knowledge about an applicant (such as scores on tests or grades in school). Hypotheses of this kind are proven—one way or another—by validation studies.

I

IAG: *see* INTERAGENCY ADVISORY GROUP.

IAPB: *see* INTERNATIONAL ASSOCIATION OF PROFESSIONAL BUREAUCRATS.

IAPES: *see* INTERNATIONAL ASSOCIATION OF PERSONNEL IN EMPLOYMENT SECURITY.

IAPW: *see* INTERNATIONAL ASSOCIATION OF PERSONNEL WOMEN.

ICMA: *see* INTERNATIONAL CITY MANAGEMENT ASSOCIATION.

ICMA Retirement Corporation, non-profit, tax-exempt organization providing a deferred compensation retirement plan for the mobile employees of state and local government. The Retirement Corporation was organized because of the inability of state and local governments to provide retirement security for those types of public servants whose careers require a periodic change in employment from one government or agency to another. State and local governments and agencies may also use the plan as a supplement to existing employee benefit programs.

The plan was developed by the International City Management Association, which underwrote the Retirement Corporation. In recognition of the plan's importance, most of the major public interest and professional associations related to state and local government have become sponsors of the plan.

ICSC: *see* INTERNATIONAL CIVIL SERVICE COMMISSION.

idle time, time for which employees are paid but not able to work because of mechanical malfunctions or other factors not within their control.

IDP: *see* INDIVIDUAL DEVELOPMENT PLAN.

illegal aliens, also called UNDOCUMENTED WORKERS, individuals from other countries who are living/working in the United States unlawfully. The U.S. Department of Labor prefers to refer to these individuals as "undocumented workers." See Jose A. Rivera, "Aliens Under the Law: A Legal Perspective," *Employee Relations Law Journal* (Summer 1977); Joanne G. Minarcini, "Illegal Aliens: Employment Restrictions and Responses," *Personnel Administrator* (March 1980); G. G. Gutierrez, "The Undocumented Immigrant: The Limits of Cost-Benefit Analysis," *Public Management* (October 1980); Ellen Sehgal and Joyce Violet, "Documenting the Undocumented,"

Monthly Labor Review (October 1980); Joan M. McCrea, "Illegal Labor Migration from Mexico to the United States," *Labour and Society* (October-December 1981); Jean Baldwin Grossman, "Illegal Immigrants and Domestic Employment," *Industrial and Labor Relations Review* (January 1984).

See also ALIENS and DE CANAS V. BICA and IMMIGRATION and NATURALIZATION SERVICE V. HERMAN DELGATO.

illegal bargaining items, any proposal made during the collective bargaining process that is expressly forbidden by law. For example, a union shop in a "right-to-work" state.

illegal strike, strike that violates existing law. While most public sector strikes are illegal, so are strikes that violate a contract, that are not properly authorized by the union membership, and that violate a court injunction.

ILO: *see* INTERNATIONAL LABOR ORGANIZATION.

immediate full vesting, pension plan that entitles an employee to all of the retirement income—both his/her contributions as well as those of his/her company—accrued during his/her time of participation in the plan.

Immigration and Naturalization Service v. Herman Delgato, U.S. Supreme Court case, 80 L. Ed. 247(1984), which held that it is constitutional for federal agents to conduct "factory surveys" to enforce immigration laws.

During each survey, which lasted from 1 to 2 hours, some agents were stationed near the exits, while other agents moved systematically through the factory approaching employees and, after identifying themselves, asking from one to three questions relating to their citizenship. If an employee gave a credible reply that he or she was a U.S. citizen or produced immigration papers, the agent moved to another employee. During the survey, employees continued with their work and

were free to walk around within the factory. The surveys resulted in the arrests of 164 of the 590 workers.

In the majority opinion, written by Justice Rehnquist, the Supreme Court held that the factory surveys did not result in the seizure of the entire work force and the individual questioning of the employees who initiated the case did not amount to a detention or seizure under the Fourth Amendment. Justice Rehnquist said that a "consensual encounter" between a police officer and a citizen could be transformed into a violation of the Fourth Amendment if, in view of all the circumstances surrounding the incident, a reasonable person would have believed that he was not free to leave. According to the Court, this did not occur during the surveys because employees were free to move about in the normal course of their duties, and the INS agents were stationed at the exits to insure that all employees were questioned, not to prevent them from leaving.

Finally, the Court said that because there was no seizure of the entire work force, the respondents could litigate only what happened to them, which, based on their own description of their encounters with the agents, were "classic consensual encounters," rather than violations of the Fourth Amendment.

immunity, an exemption from ordinary legal culpability while holding public office. Governmental officials generally need some protections against law suits, whether frivolous or not, which might be brought against them by individuals who are dissatisfied with their actions or adversely affected by them. Otherwise government could be brought to a standstill by such suits or crippled by the threat of them. In general, judges, executives, and legislators are well protected by judicial doctrines concerning immunities, whereas police officers, sheriffs, and similar officials are not. *See* David H. Rosenbloom, "Public Administrators' Official Immunity and the Supreme Court: Developments During the 1970's," *Public Administration Review* (March-April 1980); Walter S. Groszyk, Jr., and Thomas J. Madden,

"Managing Without Immunity: The Challenge for State and Local Government Officials in the 1980s," *Public Administration Review* (March–April 1981).

impact theory of discrimination, concept that asserts it is the consequences of employment practices that are relevant, not their intent. Even though an intent is benign, its consequences could foster systemic discrimination.

impact ratio, for employment decisions that offer people employment opportunities (such as hiring, training, promotion, etc.), the impact ratio for a group is the selection rate for that group divided by the selection rate for the group with the highest selection rate. For any adverse employment decision (such as disciplinary action, layoff, termination, etc.), the impact ratio is the rate for the group in question. Impact ratios are compared to the 80 percent rule of thumb to determine adverse impact.

impasse, a condition that exists during labor-management negotiations when either party feels that no further progress can be made toward reaching a settlement. Impasses are resolved either by strikes or the helpful intervention of neutral third parties. *See* Karl A. Van Asselt, "Impasse Resolution," *Public Administration Review* (March–April 1972); Jonathan Brock, *Bargaining Beyond Impasse: Joint Resolution of Public Sector Labor Disputes* (Boston, Mass.: Auburn House Publishing Co., 1982); Marian M. Extejt and James R. Chelius, "The Behavioral Impact of Impasse Resolution Procedures," *Review of Public Personnel Administration* (Spring 1985).

improvement factor, an annual wage increase provided for in a labor contract which anticipates that the rising productivity of workers will contribute to increased profits.

improper practice, an unfair labor practice.

implicit price deflator, a price index for the gross national product (GNP); the ratio of GNP in current prices to GNP in constant prices.

in-basket exercise, training technique and type of test frequently used in management assessment centers to simulate managerial problems by presenting the subject with an array of written materials (the kinds of items that might accumulate in an "in-basket") so that responses to the various items and problems can be evaluated. *See* F. M. Lopez, Jr., *Evaluating Executive Decision Making — The In-Basket Technique* (N.Y.: American Management Association, 1966); Cabot L. Jaffee, *Problems in Supervision: An In-Basket Training Exercise* (Reading, Mass.: Addison-Wesley Publishing Co., 1968); Betty Salem, Don Ellis and Douglas Johnson, "Development and Use of an In-Basket Promotional Exam for Police Sergeant," *Review of Public Personnel Administration* (Spring 1981).

incentive, reward, whether monetary or psychic, that motivates and/or compensates an employee for performance above standard.

incentive awards, also called INCENTIVE SCHEME, formal plan or program designed to motivate individual or group efforts to improve the economy and efficiency of organizational operations. There are essentially two kinds of awards—monetary and honorary.

incentive contract, that portion or clause of a collective bargaining agreement that establishes the terms and conditions of an incentive-wage system.

incentive pay, wage system that rewards a worker for productivity above an established standard.

incentive plan, individual/group: *see* INCENTIVE-WAGE PLAN.

incentive rate, special wage rate for production above a previously fixed standard of performance.

TYPES OF IMPASSE RESOLUTION

	Mediation	Fact-Finding	Arbitration
Process	Intervention by Federal Mediation and Conciliation Service or other appropriate third party at request of negotiating parties or on own proffering of services	A procedure for compelling settlement, frequently a final alternative to arbitration	A terminal procedure alternative to or following fact-finding
Subject Matter	Terms of new agreement being negotiated	Terms of agreement being negotiated	Terms of agreement being negotiated (also final step in grievance procedure)
Setting	*Mediator* tries to determine basis for agreement and persuade parties to reach agreement	*Parties* try to persuade fact-finder by arguments	*Parties* try to persuade arbitrator by arguments (same as fact-finding)
Third Party	*Mediator*—a Federal Commissioner of Mediation and Conciliation or other third party	*Fact-finder*—a public employee or a private citizen selected by parties or by an administrative agency	*Arbitrator*—a public employee or a private citizen selected by parties or by an administrative agency
Power Factor	*Mediator* limited to persuasion and ability to find compromise	*Fact-finder* may make recommendations for impasse resolution	*Arbitrator* makes binding decision
Publicity	Confidential process—no public record kept	Quasi-public process with recommendations recorded and reported	Quasi-public process with decisions recorded and reported

incentive scheme: *see* INCENTIVE AWARDS.

incentive-wage plan, also GROUP INCENTIVE PLAN, wage program that has wages rise with increases in productivity. Individual incentive plans are based on the performance of the individual employee while *group incentive plans* are based on the performance of the total work group. For a survey of the relevant research in both the U.S. and the U.K., *see* R. Marriott, *Incentive Payment Systems: A Review of Research and Opinion* (London: Staples, 4th ed., 1971). For a how-to-do-it approach, *see* H. K. Von Kaas, *Making Incentives Work* (N.Y.: American Management Association, 1971). For a critique of their faults, *see* Arch Patton, "Why Incentive Plans Fail," *Harvard Business Review* (May–June 1972). *Also see* Michael Schuster and Gary Florkowski, "Wage Incentive Plans and the Fair Labor Standards Act," *Compensation Review*, Vol. 14, No. 2 (1982); G. David Garson and D. S. Brenneman, "Incentive Systems and Goal Displacement in Personnel Resource Management," *Review of Public Personnel Administration* (Spring 1981); Bernard Dwortzan, "The ABCs of Incentive Programs," *Personnel Journal* (June 1982).

incidental learning, also called LATENT LEARNING, learning that takes place without formal instruction, intent to learn, or ascertainable motive. The information obtained tends to lie dormant until an occasion for its use arises.

income, the amount of money income received from each of the following sources: (1) money wages or salary; (2) net income from nonfarm self-employment; (3) net income from farm self-employment; (4) social security, veterans' payments, or other government or private

| Reported usage of incentive plans for production workers[1] | | |
| (in percent) | | |
Plans	Plants	Production workers
All plants..................................	100	100
Plants with any incentive plans	54	59
With personal incentive plans..............	31	38
Piecework................................	16	17
Bonuses for exceeding norms[2]............	16	23
Other[3]	2	1
With group incentive plans	32	33
Profit sharing or profit bonuses	21	12
Stock purchase	4	7
Bonuses based on aggregative indicators (production, sales, shipments)	9	14
Sharing cost savings, productivity increases .	3	3
With miscellaneous plans	1	0

[1]The data for each category are presented net of all duplications. Hence, the sums of the parts are larger than the reported total, with the differences reflecting the extent to which various plants have several types of plans.

[2]These include plans based on "standard hour" or "standard day" as well as "individual production bonuses."

[3]These include bonuses for good attendance and base-pay increases for "good work."

Source: Frederic L. Pryor, "Incentives in Manufacturing: The Carrot and the Stick," Monthly Labor Review *(July 1984).*

pensions; (5) interest (on bonds or savings), dividends, and income from annuities, estates, or trusts; (6) net income from boarders or lodgers, or from renting property to others; (7) all other sources such as unemployment benefits, public assistance, alimony, etc. The amounts received represent income before deductions for personal taxes, social security, bonds, etc.

incomes policy, general term for the totality of the federal government's influence upon wages, prices and profits. *See* Orley Ashenfelter and Richard Layard, "Incomes Policy and Wage Differentials," *Economica* (May 1983).

incompetence, demonstrated failure of an employee to meet minimum standards of job performance. For the classic analysis of why such people manage to hang in there despite their poor performance, *see* William J. Goode, "The Protection of the Inept," *American Sociological Review* (February 1967). *Also see* D. Keith Denton, "Survival Tactics: Coping With In-

competent Bosses," *Personnel Journal* (April 1985).

increment, also called STEP INCREASE, established salary increase between steps of a given salary grade, marking a steady progression from the minimum of the grade to the maximum.

incumbent, person presently serving in a position.

indemnify, act of compensating insured individuals for their losses.

indemnity, insurance contract to reimburse an individual or organization for possible losses of a particular type.

independent union, union that is not affiliated with the AFL-CIO. The United Mine Workers and the Teamsters are two of the largest independent unions.

indexing, system by which salaries, pensions, welfare payments and other kinds of income are automatically adjusted to account for inflation. *See* Geoffrey Brennan, "Inflation, Taxation, and Indexation," *Policy Studies Journal* (Spring 1977); Robert S. Kaplan, *Indexing Social Security: An Analysis of the Issues* (Washington, D.C.: American Enterprise Institute, 1977); Theodore Turnasella, "Market Indexed Compensation," *Personnel Administrator* (May 1984).

index of agreement, index, usually expressed as a percentage, showing the extent to which examiners agree on a candidate's scores.

index number, measure of relative value compared with a base figure for the same series. In a time series in index form, the base period usually is set equal to 100, and data for other periods are expressed as percentages of the value in the base period. Most indexes published by government agencies are presently expressed in terms of a 1967 = 100 base.

Index numbers possess a number of advantages over the raw data from which they are derived. First, they facilitate analysis by their simplicity. Second, they are a more useful basis for comparison of changes in data originally expressed in dissimilar units. Third, they permit comparisons over time with some common starting point—the index base period.

indirect compensation/income: *see* INDIRECT WAGES.

indirect labor: *see* DIRECT LABOR.

indirect labor costs, loose term for the wages of nonproduction employees.

indirect validity: *see* SYNTHETIC VALIDITY.

indirect wages, also called INDIRECT INCOME and INDIRECT COMPENSATION, nonfinancial benefits employees receive from their work situations—favorable organizational environment, nontaxable benefits, perquisites, and the authority, power, and/or status that may come with their jobs.

individual agreement, also called INDIVIDUAL CONTRACT, formal agreement between a single employee and his/her employer that determines the employee's conditions and terms of employment.

individual bargaining, negotiations between a single employee and his/her employer. Before the advent of modern collective bargaining, individual bargaining prevailed, and the employee was usually bargaining from a position of slight strength.

individual-contract pension trust, pension plan that creates a trust to buy and hold title to employees' individual insurance and/or annuity contracts. The employer makes payments to the trust, which then pays the insurance premiums on its various contracts.

individual development plan (IDP), periodically prepared schedule of developmental experiences, including both work assignments and formal training, designed to meet particular developmental objectives needed to improve current performance and/or to prepare the individual for positions of greater responsibility.

Individual Retirement Account (IRA), individual pensions that the Pension Reform Act of 1974, as amended, allows each person to create in order to put aside money that builds up tax free until retirement. Funds can be invested in savings accounts, mutual funds, annuities, government bonds, etc. Individuals *may* start withdrawing funds at age 59½ and *must* begin withdrawals by age 70½. Funds are taxed in the year they are withdrawn.

individual test, testing device designed to be administered (usually by a specially trained person) to only one subject at a time.

Industrial and Labor Relations Review, scholarly quarterly containing theoretical articles and research reports in the areas of labor-management relations; labor organizations; labor law; politics, government, and industrial relations; international and comparative industrial relations; labor market; income security, insurance, and benefits; labor conditions; manpower; personnel; management; organization; and work performance and satisfaction.

Industrial and Labor Relations Review
The New York State School of
    Industrial and Labor Relations
Cornell University
Ithaca, NY 14853

industrial and organizational psychology: *see* INDUSTRIAL PSYCHOLOGY.

industrial democracy, also PARTICIPATIVE MANAGEMENT, any of a variety of efforts designed to encourage employees to participate in an organization's decisionmaking processes by identifying problems and suggesting solutions to them in a formal manner. While the terms "industrial democracy" and "participative management" tend to be used almost interchangeably, there is a distinction. Industrial democracy was used as far back as 1897 by Beatrice and Sidney Webb to describe democratic practices within the trade union movement. The term's modern usage to cover innumerable types of joint or cooperative management programs dates from World War I. Then it connoted a scheme to avoid labor-management disputes which might adversely affect war production. Today industrial democracy connotes joint action by management and worker's representatives. *Participative management,* in contrast, connotes cooperative programs that are unilaterally implemented from on high. Nevertheless, both terms seem to be rapidly losing their distinctive connotations. The most comprehensive survey of the state of industrial democracy throughout the world is David Jenkins, *Job Power: Blue and White Collar Democracy* (Garden City, N.Y.: Doubleday, 1973). For a bibliography, *see* Ronald L. Weiher, "Sources on Industrial Democracy," *Harvard Business Review* (September-October 1975). For a review of practices in Sweden, Great Britain and the United States, *see* Nancy Foy and Herman

Gadon, "Worker Participation: Contrasts in Three Countries," *Harvard Business Review* (May-June 1976). For more on participative management, *see* William P. Anthony, *Participative Management* (Reading, Mass.: Addison-Wesley, 1978); Rosabeth Moss Kanter, "Dilemmas of Managing Participation," *Organizational Dynamics* (Summer 1982); Henry Mintzberg, "Why America Needs, But Cannot Have, Corporate Democracy," *Organizational Dynamics* (Spring 1983); William Foote Whyte, "Worker Participation: International and Historical Perspectives," *The Journal of Applied Behavioral Science,* Vol. 19, No. 3 (1963); Henry P. Guzda, "Industrial Democracy: Made in the U.S.A.," *Monthly Labor Review* (May 1984); Janice A. Klein, "Why Supervisors Resist Employee Involvement," *Harvard Business Review* (September-October 1984); S. A. Levitan and D. Werneke, "Work Participation and Productivity Change," *Monthly Labor Review* (September 1984).

See also SCANLON PLAN and WORKERS' COUNCILS.

industrial engineering, defined by the American Institute of Industrial Engineers as being

> concerned with the design, improvement, and installation of integrated systems of men, materials and equipment; drawing upon specialized knowledge and skill in the mathematical, physical, and social sciences together with the principles and methods of engineering analysis and design, to specify, predict, and evaluate the results to be obtained from such systems.

A basic reference is: H. B. Maynard (ed.), *Industrial Engineering Handbook* (N.Y.: McGraw-Hill, 3rd ed., 1971).

industrial gerontology: *see* GERIATRICS.

industrial health services, health services provided by physicians, dentists, nurses, or other health personnel in an industrial setting for the appraisal, protection, and promotion of the health of employees while on the job. Occupational health services is now the preferred term.

industrial hygiene, that branch of preventive medicine devoted to protecting the health of industrial workers. *See* Mary F. Davis, "Worksite Health Promotion," *Personnel Administrator* (December 1984).

industrial medicine, that branch of medicine that is concerned with protecting workers from hazards in the workplace and with dealing with health problems/emergencies that may occur during working hours. *See* Diana Chapman Walsh, "Is There a Doctor In-House?" *Harvard Business Review* (July–August 1984).

industrial paternalism: *see* PATERNALISM.

industrial policy, government regulation of industrial planning and production through law, tax incentives and subsidies. *See* Richard P. Nielsen, "Industrial Policy: Review and Historical Perspective," *Public Administration Review* (September–October 1983); Alan M. Kantrow, ed., "The Political Realities of Industrial Policy," *Harvard Business Review* (September–October 1983); J. L. Badaracco, Jr., and D. B. Yoffie, " 'Industrial Policy': It Can't Happen Here," *Harvard Business Review* (November–December 1983); Arthur Levitt, Jr., "Industrial Policy: Slogan or Solution," *Harvard Business Review* (March–April 1984).

industrial psychiatry: *see* OCCUPATIONAL PSYCHIATRY.

industrial psychology, also called OCCUPATIONAL PSYCHOLOGY, INDUSTRIAL AND ORGANIZATIONAL PSYCHOLOGY, and I/O PSYCHOLOGY, industrial or occupational psychology has traditionally been concerned with those aspects of human behavior related to work organizations; its focus has been on the basic relations in organizations between (1) employees and their co-workers, (2) employees and machines, and (3) employees and the organization. Because the term industrial psychology holds a restrictive connotation, the field is increasingly referred to as industrial and organizational psychology or I/O Psychology. For the most comprehensive summary of the state-of-the-art, *see* Marvin D. Dunnette (ed.), *Handbook of Industrial and Organizational Psychology* (Chicago: Rand McNally, 1976). *Also see* Earl C. Pence, Douglas Cederblom and Daniel L. Johnson, "The Image of Industrial/Organizational Psychologists," *Personnel Administrator* (April 1984).

industrial relations, generally used to refer to all matters of mutual concern to employers and employees and their representatives. In a more technical sense, its use should be limited to labor-management relationships in private sector manufacturing organizations. *See* Keith Bradley and Alan Gleb, *Worker Capitalism: The New Industrial Relations* (Cambridge: The MIT Press, 1983); Joseph W. Garbarino, "Unionism Without Unions: The New Industrial Relations?" *Industrial Relations* (Winter 1984); Thomas A. Kochan, Robert B. Mckersie and Peter Cappelli, "Strategic Choice and Industrial Relations Theory," *Industrial Relations* (Winter 1984); Sanford M. Jacoby, "The Future of Industrial Relations," *California Management Review* (Summer 1984); Jack Barbash, *The Elements of Industrial Relations* (Madison: University of Wisconsin Press, 1984).

Industrial Relations, this thrice-yearly journal publishes scholarly articles and symposia on all aspects of the employment relationship, with special attention given to pertinent developments in the fields of labor economics, sociology, psychology, political science and law.
Industrial Relations
Institute of Industrial Relations
University of California
Berkeley, CA 94720

industrial relations common law: *see* COMMON LAW OF THE SHOP.

Industrial Relations Law Journal, a quarterly dedicated to scholarly analysis and comments on issues and developments in the field of industrial relations.

Industrial Relations Research

Published by the students of the School of Law of the University of California, Berkeley, this is the only "law review" devoted exclusively to industrial relations.

> *Industrial Relations Law Journal*
> Boalt Hall, Room 1
> School of Law
> University of California
> Berkeley, CA 94720

industrial relations research: *see* PERSONNEL RESEARCH.

Industrial Relations Research Association (IRRA), private organization of 5000 members formed in 1947 to encourage and disseminate research on industrial relations.

> IRRA
> 7226 Social Science Building
> University of Wisconsin
> Madison, WI 53706
> (608) 262-2762

industrial revolution, a very general term that refers to a society's change from an agrarian to an industrial economy. The Industrial Revolution of the Western world is considered to have begun in England in the 18th century. For the case that it actually began much earlier, *see* Jean Gimpel, *The Industrial Revolution of the Middle Ages* (N.Y.: Holt, Rinehart and Winston, 1976). *Also see* Gene Bylinsky, "A New Industrial Revolution Is on the Way," *Fortune*, Oct. 5, 1981; Joseph Finkelstein and David A. H. Newman, "The Third Industrial Revolution: A Special Challenge to Managers," *Organizational Dynamics* (Summer 1984).

industrial sociology: *see* OCCUPATIONAL SOCIOLOGY.

Industrial Test, Flanagan: *see* FLANAGAN INDUSTRIAL TEST.

Industrial Training, International: see JOURNAL OF EUROPEAN INDUSTRIAL TRAINING.

industrial union, also called VERTICAL UNION, union whose members work in the same industry and encompass a whole range of skilled and unskilled occupations. *See* Harold W. Aurand, *From the Molly Maguires to the United Mine Workers: The Social Ecology of an Industrial Union 1869-1897* (Phila.: Temple University Press, 1971).

Industrial Workers of the World (IWW) nicknamed WOBBLIES, radical U. S. union whose main goal was to replace capitalism with a worker's democracy. It had its greatest strength before World War I, but most of its waning membership joined the American Communist Party after it was organized in 1919. For histories, *see* Melvyn Dubofsky, *We Shall Be All: A History of the Industrial Workers of the World* (Westminster, Md.: Quadrangle Books, 1969); Patrick Renshaw, *Wobblies: The Story of Syndicalism in the United States* (Garden City, N.Y.: Doubleday, 1967).

industry-wide bargaining, collective bargaining that results in a single master agreement negotiated by all of the major employers in an industry and one or more unions who represent workers throughout the industry.

inequity theory, also EQUITY THEORY, most fully developed by J. Stacy Adams (he premised his work upon Leon Festinger's theory of cognitive dissonance), who holds that inequity exists for Worker A whenever his/her perceived job inputs and outcomes are inconsistent with Worker B's job inputs and outcomes. Inequity would exist if a person perceived that he/she was working much harder than another person who received the same pay. Adams suggests that the presence of inequity creates tension within Person A to reduce the inequity by, for example, increasing (or decreasing) one's efforts if it is perceived to be low (or high) relative to others' work effort. *See* J. Stacy Adams, "Toward an Understanding of Inequity," *Journal of Abnormal and Social Psychology* (November 1963); Paul S. Goodman and Abraham Friedman, "An Examination of Adam's Theory of Inequity," *Administrative Science Quarterly*

(December 1971); Michael R. Carrell and John Dittrich "Equity Theory: The Recent Literature, Methodological Considerations, and New Directions," *Academy of Management Review,* (April 1978); John E. Dittrich and Michael R. Carrell, "Organizational Equity Perceptions, Employee Job Satisfaction, and Departmental Absence and Turnover Rates," *Organizational Behavior and Human Performance* (August 1979).

See also COGNITIVE DISSONANCE.

inflation, also DEFLATION. *Inflation* is a rise in the costs of goods and services which is equated to a fall in the value of a nation's currency. *Deflation* is the reverse, a fall in costs and a rise in the value of money. *Cost-push inflation* is inflation caused by increases in the costs of production which are independent of the state of demand. *Demand-pull inflation* is inflation caused by increased demand rather than by increases in the cost of production. *Hidden inflation* is a price increase achieved by selling smaller quantities (or a poorer quality) of a product for the same price as before. *Hyperinflation* is inflation so extreme that it practically destroys the value of paper money.

See Henry J. Aaron *(ed.), Inflation and the Income Tax* (Washington, D. C.: Brookings Institution, 1976); Arthur M. Okun, *Curing Chronic Inflation* (Washington, D.C.: Brookings Institution, 1978); John Case, *Understanding Inflation* (New York: William Morrow, 1981); T. Kristensen, *Inflation and Unemployment in Modern Society* (New York: Praeger, 1981); David P. Calleo, "Inflation and American Power," *Foreign Affairs* (Spring 1981); Thomas J. Dougherty, *Controlling the New Inflation* (Lexington, MA: Lexington Books, 1981); Wayne Vroman, *Wage Inflation: Prospects for Deceleration.* (Washington, D.C.: The Urban Institute Press, 1983).

informal organization, also FORMAL ORGANIZATION, within each formally structured organization there exists an informal organization consisting of spontaneously developed relationships and patterns of interaction between employees. According to Chester I. Barnard's classic statement on the subject, "Informal Organizations and Their Relation to Formal Organizations," Chapter IX from his *The Functions of the Executive* (Cambridge, Mass.: Harvard University Press, 1938),

> informal organization, although comprising the processes of society which are unconscious as contrasted with those of formal organization which are conscious, has two important classes of effects: (a) it establishes certain attitudes, understandings, customs, habits, institutions; and (b) it creates the condition under which formal organization may arise.

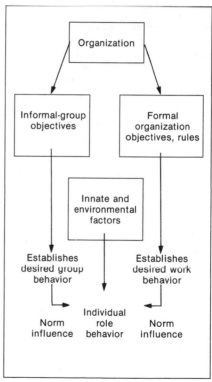

Formal and informal influences on individuals

Source: P. Bryans and T. P. Cronin, Organization Theory *(London: Mitchell Beazley, 1983), p. 84.*

initiation fees, payments required by unions of all new members and/or of employees who having once left the union wish to return. Initiation fees serve several purposes: (1) they are a source of revenue, (2) they force the new member to pay for the advantages secured by those who built the union, and (3) they (when the fees are high enough) can be used as a device to restrict membership.

injunction, also called LABOR INJUNCTION, court order forbidding specific individuals or groups from performing acts the court considers injurious to property or other rights of an employer or community. There are two basic types of injunctions: (1) *temporary restraining order*, which is issued for a limited time prior to a formal hearing and (2) *permanent injunction*, which is issued after a full formal hearing. Once an injunction is in effect, the court has contempt power to enforce its rulings through fines and/or imprisonment. For an analysis, *see* Richard D. Sibbernsen, "New Developments in the Labor Injunction," *Labor Law Journal* (October 1977).
     See also MUNIZ V. HOFFMAN.

injury, traumatic, under the Federal Employees' Compensation Act, for continuation of pay purposes, a wound or other condition of the body caused by external force, including stress or strain. The injury must be identifiable by time and place of occurrence and member or function of the body affected, and be caused by a specific event or incident or series of events or incidents within a single day or work shift.

injury, work related, for compensation under the Federal Employees' Compensation Act, a personal injury sustained while in the performance of duty. The term "injury" includes diseases proximately caused by the employment.

ink-blot test: *see* RORSCHACH TEST.

Inland Steel Co.* v. *National Labor Relations Board, decision by the U.S. Court of Appeals, 7th Circuit (1948), which held that a company was required to bargain with its union over retirement and pension matters. The decision was indirectly upheld by the U.S. Supreme Court when it denied certiorari in the case, 336 U.S. 960 (1949).

input, raw material of any process.

input-output table, a matrix table in which each of the producing (output) sectors of an economy is shown to be a consumer (input) of the output of one of the other producing sectors of the economy. The table consists of a vertical array (output sectors) mapped against a horizontal array (input sectors). Each one of the producers is listed also as a consumer. The table shows the high degree of interrelatedness and interdependence between the various sectors of an economy: a change in the figure in any one "box" of the table will precipitate an almost endless series of adjustments and readjustments in the other figures (boxes). The analysis of an input-output table reveals for each sector or industry what inputs it buys from every other industry in the table, and how much of its output it sells to every other industry.
     See also LEONTIEF, WASSILY.

in-service training, term used mainly in the public sector to refer to job-related instruction and educational experiences made available to employees. In-service training programs are usually offered during normal working hours. However, some programs, especially those offering college credit, are available to the employee only on his/her own time.

insolvent, the condition of some persons (or organizations) who either cannot pay debts as they come due or whose assets are less than liabilities.

Institute for Social Research (ISR), established at the University of Michigan in 1946, the ISR conducts research on a broad range of subjects within its four constituent research centers: (1) *Survey Research Center*—concerned primarily with the study of large populations, organizations, and special segments of society, and generally utilizes interview surveys; (2) *Research Center for Group Dynamics*—concerned with the development of the basic science of behavior in groups, seeking to explain the nature of the social forces which affect group behavior, the relations among members, and the activities of the group as a whole; (3) *Center for Research on Utilization of Scientific Knowledge*—studies the processes required for the full use of research findings and new knowledge; and (4) *Center for Political Studies*—investigates political behavior, focusing on national politics in many countries, and maintains a rich collection of election data.

Institute for Social Research
The University of Michigan
426 Thompson Street
Ann Arbor, MI 48104
(313) 764-8363

institutional discrimination, practices contrary to EEO policies that occur even though there was no intent to discriminate. Institutional discrimination exists whenever a practice or procedure has the effect of treating one group of employees differently from another.

instrumented laboratory, laboratory training experience that uses feedback from measurements taken during laboratory sessions of the behavior and feelings of the group and/or its component individuals. *See* Jay Hall, "The Use of Instruments in Laboratory Training," *Training and Development Journal* (May 1970).

insubordination, disobedience to higher authorities in an organization; refusing to take orders from those who are properly designated to give them.

insurable risk, a risk which has the following attributes: it is one of a large homogeneous group of similar risks; the loss produced by the risk is definable and quantifiable; the occurrence of loss in individual cases is accidental or fortuitous; the potential loss is large enough to cause

hardship; the cost of insuring is economically feasible; the chance of loss is calculable; and it is sufficiently unlikely that loss will occur in many individual cases at the same time.

insurance, also INSURANCE PREMIUM, contractual arrangement that has a customer pay a specified sum, the insurance premium, in return for which the insurer will pay compensation if specific events occur (*e.g.*, death for life insurance, fire for fire insurance, hospitalization for health insurance, etc.). The insurance premiums are calculated so that their total return to the insurance company is sufficient to cover all policyholder claims plus administrative costs and profit. For texts, *see* Mark S. Dorfman, *Introduction to Insurance* (Englewood Cliffs, N.J.: Prentice-Hall, 1978) and Robert I. Mehr and Emerson Cammack, *Principles of Insurance* (Homewood, Ill.: Richard D. Irwin, Inc., 7th ed., 1980).

See also the following entries:
DENTAL INSURANCE
DISABILITY INSURANCE
GROUP INSURANCE
LIFE INSURANCE
PLAN TERMINATION INSURANCE

Insurance Agents' decision: *see* NATIONAL LABOR RELATIONS BOARD V. INSURANCE AGENTS' INTERNATIONAL UNION.

insurance commissioner, the state official charged with the enforcement of laws pertaining to insurance in the respective states. The commissioner's title, status in government and responsibilities differ somewhat from state to state but all states have an official having such responsibilities regardless of his title. Sometimes called superintendent or director.

insurance pool, an organization of insurers or reinsurers through which particular types of risks are shared or pooled. The risk of high loss by any particular insurance company is transferred to the group as a whole (the insurance pool) with premiums, losses, and expenses shared in agreed amounts. The advantage of a pool is that the size of expected losses can be predicted for the pool with much more certainty than for any individual party to it. Pooling arrangements are often used for catastrophic coverage or for certain high risk populations like the disabled. Pooling may also be done within a single company by pooling the risks insured under various different policies so that high losses incurred by one policy are shared with others.

insurance premium: *see* INSURANCE.

insurance trust contributions, amounts derived from contributions, assessments, premiums, "taxes," etc., required of employers and employees for financing of compulsory or voluntary social insurance programs operated by a government.

insured, person who buys insurance on property or the person whose life is insured.

insurer, person, company, or governmental agency that provides insurance.

intangible rewards, satisfactions of no monetary value that an individual gains from a job.

intangibles, those benefits and costs which cannot be converted into dollar values.

integrated pension plan, a private pension plan that is explicitly coordinated with social security, either through the offset or excess approach. A common objective is to recognize employer costs for social security in setting private pension benefits. In addition, integrated private pension plans often provide greater benefits relative to preretirement earnings for the higher-paid workers.

integrative bargaining: *see* PRODUCTIVITY BARGAINING.

intelligence, there is no agreement on any single definition of intelligence, save that it is a hypothetical construct. Generally, it refers to an individual's ability to cope with his/her environment and deal with mental abstractions. The military, as well as some other organizations, use the word "intelligence" in its original Latin sense—as information.

intelligence quotient (IQ), measure of an individual's general intellectual capability. IQ tests have come under severe criticism because of their declining relevancy as a measurement tool for individuals past the age of adolescence and because of their inherent cultural bias, which has tended to discriminate against minorities. *See* Ashley Montagu, ed., *Race and IQ* (New York: Oxford University Press, 1975); Brigitte Berger, "A New Interpretation of the I.Q. Controversy," *The Public Interest* (Winter 1978).

intelligence test, any of a variety of standardized tests that seek to measure a range of mental abilities and social skills. *See* Charles Bahn, "Can Intelligence Tests Predict Executive Competence?" *Personnel* (July-August 1979).

IQ Classifications

The following table illustrates a traditional classification of IQ's and indicates the percentage of persons in a normal population who would fall into each classification.

Classification	IQ	Percentage of Population
Gifted	140 and above	1
Very Superior	130-139	2.5
Superior	120-129	8
Above Average	110-119	16
Average	90-109	45
Below Average	80-89	16
Dull or Borderline	70-79	8
Moron	60-69	2.5
Imbecile, idiot	59 and under	1

Intelligence Test, Cattell Culture Fair: *see* CATTELL CULTURE FAIR INTELLIGENCE TEST.

Interagency Advisory Group (IAG), the Office of Personnel Management's key link for the purposes of communication, consultation, and coordination with the rest of the federal personnel community. Its members are the top personnel officials from the departments and agencies of the federal government.

Interagency Committee on Handicapped Employees: see VOCATIONAL REHABILITATION ACT OF 1973.

intercity differential: see GEOGRAPHICAL DIFFERENTIAL.

interdisciplinary team: see TASK GROUP.

interest, community of: see COMMUNITY OF INTEREST.

interest arbitration, arbitration of a dispute arising during the course of contract negotiations where the arbitrator must decide what will or will not be contained in the agreement. See Ronald W. Haughton, "Some Successful Uses of 'Interest' Arbitration," *Monthly Labor Review* (September 1973); Betty Southard Murphy, "Interest Arbitration," *Public Personnel Management* (September-October 1977); Henry S. Farber, "Splitting-the-Difference in Interest Arbitration," *Industrial and Labor Relations Review* (October 1981); Clifford Scharman, "Interest Arbitration in the Private Sector," *The Arbitration Journal* (September 1981); Richard Johnson, "Interest Arbitration Examined," *Personnel Administrator* (January 1983); Patricia Compton-Forbes, "Interest Arbitration Hasn't Worked Well in the Public Sector," *Personnel Administrator* (February 1984); John Delaney and Peter Feuille, "Police Interest Arbitration: Awards and Issues," *Arbitration Journal* (June 1984); John Thomas Delaney and Peter Feuille, "Collective Bargaining, Interest Arbitration, and the Delivery of Police Services," *Review of Public Personnel Administration* (Spring 1985).

interest inventory, questionnaire designed to measure the intensity of interest that an individual has in various objects and activities. Interest inventories are widely used

in vocational guidance. See Donald G. Zytowski, *Contemporary Approaches to Interest Measurement* (Minneapolis: University of Minnesota Press, 1973).

See also SELF-DIRECTED SEARCH and STRONG-CAMPBELL INTEREST INVENTORY.

interest test, battery of questions designed to determine the interest patterns of an individual, particularly with regard to vocational choice.

interexaminer reliability: see INTERRATER RELIABILITY.

interface, point of contact, the boundary between organizations, people, jobs and/or systems. For analyses, see Frank T. Paine, "The Interface Problem," *The Personnel Administrator* (January-February 1965); Daniel A. Wren, "Interface and Interorganizational Coordination," *Academy of Management Journal* (March 1967); L. David Brown, *Managing Conflict at Organizational Interfaces* (Reading, Mass.: Addison Wesley, 1983).

interference, an unfair labor practice. Section 8 (a) (1) of the National Labor Relations Act makes it unlawful for an employer "to interfere with, restrain, or coerce employees" who are exercising their right to organize and bargain collectively.

Intergovernmental Personnel Act of 1970 (IPA), Public Law 91-648, federal statute designed to strengthen the personnel resources of state and local governments by making available to them a wide range of assistance. The act contains a declaration of policy that (1) the quality of public service at all levels can be improved through personnel systems that are consistent with merit principles, and (2) it is in the national interest for federal assistance to be directed toward strengthening state and local personnel systems in line with merit principles.

Specifically, IPA:
1. authorizes the U.S. Civil Service Commission (now the Office of Personnel Management) to make

grants to help meet the costs of strengthening personnel management capabilities of state and local governments in such areas as recruitment, selection, and pay administration, and for research and demonstration projects;

2. authorizes grants to help states and localities develop and carry out training programs for employees, particularly in such core management areas as financial management, automatic data processing and personnel management (the grant programs of the IPA Act were eliminated in 1981);

3. authorizes awards for Government Service Fellowship grants to support graduate-level study by employees selected by state and local governments;

4. authorizes a wide range of technical assistance in personnel management to be made available to state and local governments on a reimbursable, nonreimbursable, or partly reimbursable basis;

5. provides for the temporary assignment of personnel between federal agencies and state and local governments or institutions of higher education;

6. allows employees of state and local governments to benefit from training courses conducted for federal employees by federal agencies;

7. fosters cooperative recruitment and examining efforts; and

8. makes the Office of Personnel Management the sole federal agency responsible for prescribing and maintaining merit system standards required under federal grant programs.

interim agreement, collective bargaining agreement designed to avoid a strike and/or to maintain the current conditions of employment while the settlement of a dispute or the signing of a final comprehensive contract is pending.

intern: *see* INTERNSHIP.

internal alignment, relationship among positions in an organization in terms of rank and pay. In theory, the most desirable internal alignment calls for similar treatment of like positions, with the differences in treatment in direct proportion to differences in the difficulty, responsibilities, and qualifications needed for a position.

internal consistency reliability, measure of the reliability of a test based on the extent to which items in the test measure the same traits.

internal disputes plan, procedures established by the constitution of the AFL-CIO for resolving disputes among affiliated unions. *See* Joseph Krislov and John Mead, "Arbitrating Union Conflicts: An Analysis of the AFL-CIO Internal Disputes Plan," *Arbitration Journal* (June 1981).

internal equity: *see* EXTERNAL EQUITY.

internal house organ: *see* HOUSE ORGAN.

International Association of Personnel in Employment Security (IAPES), organization founded in 1913 for individuals working in job placement and unemployment compensation in the public sector. It now claims over 26,000 members.

IAPES
1101 Louisville Road
Frankfort, KY 40601
(502) 223-4459

International Association of Personnel Women (IAPW), a professional association of women personnel workers in business, government, and education established to expand and improve the professionalism of women working in personnel management.

IAPW
5820 Wilshire Blvd.
Suite 500
Los Angeles, CA 90036
(213) 937-9000

International Association of Professional Bureaucrats (IAPB), founded in 1968 and headed by James H. Boren (a former college professor, congressional staffer, and State Department official), IAPB is an organization dedicated to bureaucratic reform and maintaining the status quo. Its motto is: "When in charge, ponder. When in trouble, delegate. When in doubt, mumble." In addition to conducting seminars on fingertapping and eloquent mumbling, IAPB sponsors a number of annual awards banquets at which the organization's highest award, "The Order of the Bird," has been presented to leading bureaucrats in the governmental, corporate, and academic fields. The U.S. Postal Service was presented The Order of the Bird in recognition of its orderly postponement patterns in delivering special delivery mail. *See* James H. Boren, *When In Doubt, Mumble: A Bureaucrat's Handbook* (N.Y.: Van Nostrand Reinhold, 1972); James H. Boren, *Have Your Way With Bureaucrats* (Radnor, Pa.: Chilton Books Co., 1975).

IAPB
National Press Building
Washington, D.C. 20045
(202) 347-2490

International Brotherhood of Teamsters v. United States, 431 U.S. 324 (1977), U.S. Supreme Court case, which held that a seniority system is not unlawful merely because it perpetuates an employer's previous discriminatory policies. The majority found that Title VII protects "bonafide" seniority systems—those designed without discriminatory intent—even though they lock in the effects of illegal employment discrimination. The congressional judgment, the court said, was that Title VII should not "destroy or water down the vested seniority rights of employees simply because their employer had engaged in discrimination prior to the passage of the Act." For an analysis, *see* Stephen L. Swanson, "The Effect of the Supreme Court's Seniority Decisions," *Personnel Journal* (December 1977).

See also RETROACTIVE SENIORITY and SENIORITY.

International City Management Association (ICMA), professional organization founded in 1914 for appointed chief executives in cities, counties, towns, and other local governments. Its primary goals include strengthening the quality of urban government through professional management and developing and disseminating new concepts and approaches to management through a wide range of information services, training programs, and publications.

As an educational and professional association, ICMA is interested in the dissemination and application of knowledge for better urban management. To further these ends, ICMA utilizes a comprehensive research, data collection, and information dissemination program to facilitate reference and research by local government officials, university professors and students, researchers, and others concerned with urban affairs. Among ICMA publications are: Winston W. Crouch (ed.), *Local Government Personnel Administration* (1976), *The Municipal Year Book, The County Year Book*, and its monthly magazine, *Public Management*.

ICMA
1120 G Street
Washington, D.C. 20005
(202) 626-4600
See also ICMA RETIREMENT CORPORATION.

international civil service, term that does not refer to any particular government entity, but to any bureaucratic organization that is by legal mandate composed of differing citizenships and nationalities. Examples include the United Nations Secretariat, the International Labour Organization, and the Commission of the European Communities. Sometimes the term is used to collectively refer to the employees of all international bureaucracies. For a symposium, *see* Sidney Mailick (ed.), "Toward an International Civil Service," *Public Administration Review* (May–June 1970). For the standard work on the legal aspects of the subject, *see* M. B. Akehurst, *The Law Governing Employment in International Organizations* (Cambridge, England: Cambridge University Press, 1967). *See also* Robert S. Jordan,

"What Has Happened to Our International Civil Service: The Case of the United Nations," *Public Administration Review* (March–April 1981).

International Civil Service Commission (ICSC), 15-member commission created by the United Nations in 1974 to make recommendations concerning the personnel policies of the various United Nations secretariats. For a history and analysis, *see* John P. Renninger, "Staffing International Organizations: The Role of the International Civil Service Commission," *Public Administration Review* (July–August 1977).

International Journal of Group Psychotherapy, official quarterly of the American Group Psychotherapy Association. Devoted to reporting and interpreting research and practice in group psychotherapy in various settings in the United States and in other countries, it reflects the types of group psychotherapy now employed, and helps stimulate the study of validation of practice and results. It also serves as a forum of ideas and experiences, with a view toward clarifying and enlarging the scope of group psychotherapy techniques.

International Journal of Group Psychotherapy
American Group Psychotherapy Association, Inc.
1995 Broadway—14th Floor
New York, NY 10023

International Labor Organization (ILO), specialized agency associated with the United Nations, created by the Treaty of Versailles in 1919 as a part of the League of Nations. The United States joined this autonomous intergovernmental agency in 1934 and is currently one of 132 member countries that finance ILO operations. Governments, workers, and employers share in making the decisions and shaping its policies. This tripartite representation gives the ILO its balance and much of its strength and makes it distinct from all other international agencies.

The purpose of the ILO is to improve labor conditions, raise living standards, and promote economic and social stability as the foundation for lasting peace throughout the world. The standards developed by the annual ILO Conference are guides for countries to follow and form an international labor code that covers such questions as employment, freedom of association, hours of work, migration for employment, protection of women and young workers, prevention of industrial accidents, workmen's compensation, other labor problems, conditions of seamen, and social security. The only obligation on any country is to consider these standards; no country is obligated to adopt, accept, or ratify them. For a history, *see* Antony Alcock, *History of the International Labor Organization* (N.Y.: Octagon Books, 1972). *See also* Walter Galenson, *The International Labor Organization: An American View* (Madison: University of Wisconsin Press, 1981).

International Labor Organization
International Labor Office:
Geneva, Switzerland

Washington Branch:
1750 New York Ave., N.W.
Washington, D.C. 20006
(202) 376-2315

International Labour Documentation, see LABORDOC.

International Labour Office: *see* INTERNATIONAL LABOUR REVIEW and YEARBOOK OF LABOUR STATISTICS.

International Labour Review, this monthly has published original research, comparative studies, and articles of interest to the international labor community since 1897.

International Labour Review
International Labour Office
CH—1211 Geneva 22
Switzerland

International Personnel Management Association (IPMA), established in January 1973 through the consolidation of the Public Personnel Association (successor to the Civil Service Assembly of the United States and Canada) and the Society for Personnel Administration, IPMA is a nonprofit membership organization for agencies and persons in the public personnel field. Its members are located in federal, state, provincial and local governments throughout the United States, Canada, and elsewhere around the world. Among IPMA's continuing purposes are the improvement of personnel administration, promoting merit principles of employment, and assisting persons and agencies engaged in personnel work.

IPMA is divided into national sections (for example, the U.S. section is 'International Personnel Management Association-United States"), geographic regions, and local chapters.

IPMA
1850 K Street, N.W.
Washington, D.C. 20006
(202) 833-5860

internatonal representative, title sometimes used by agents of international unions.

International Trade Commission, United States, formerly the UNITED STATES TARIFF COMMISSION, commission that furnishes studies, reports, and recommendations involving international trade and tariffs to the president, the Congress, and other government agencies. It was created in 1916 as the *United States Tariff Commission* and changed to its present name in 1974.

U.S. I.T.C.
701 E Street, N.W.
Washington, D.C. 20436
(202) 523-0161

international union, also called NATIONAL UNION, parent union composed of affiliated unions known as "locals." Many international unions in the United States are "international" solely because of their affiliates in Canada. The international or national union is supported by a per capita tax on each of its locals' members.

internship, any of a variety of formal training programs for new employees or students that allows them to learn on-the-job by working closely with professionals in their field. Almost all professional educational programs at universities require or allow their students to undertake internships of one kind or another. *See* Daniel S. Golmmen and Francis B. Atkinson, "The Business Intern—New Source of Employees," *Management World* (January 1978); Thomas P. Murphy, *Government Management Internships and Executive Development* (Lexington, MA.: Lexington Books, 1973); Nicholas Henry, Symposium Editor, "Internships in Public Administration," *Public Administration Review* (May–June 1979); "NASPAA Guidelines for Public Service Internships," *Southern Review of Public Administration* (September 1979); Sigmund G. Ginsburg, "Try Before You Hire: Business Internship Programs," *Management Review* (January 1981); Edgar Mills, Richard J. Harris and Robert Brischetto, "Internships in an Instant Bureaucracy: Some Organizational Lessons," *The Journal of Applied Behavioral Science*, Vol. 19, No. 4 (1983); Daniel F. Griswold, "Student Internships," *Personnel Administrator* (July 1984).

interpersonal competence, measure of an individual's ability to work well in a variety of situations. To have interpersonal competence while occupying any given position, one would have to be proficient in meeting all of a position's role demands. *See* David Moment and Abraham Zaleznik, *Role Development and Interpersonal Competence* (Boston: Harvard University Graduate School of Business Administration, 1963); Chris Argyris and Roger Harrison, *Interpersonal Competence and Organizational Effectiveness* (Homewood, Ill.: Richard D. Irwin, 1962).

interpolation, process of estimating intermediate values between two known values.

interrater reliability, also called INTEREXAMINER RELIABILITY, extent to which examiners give the same score to like performing candidates. *See* J. M. Greenwood and W. J. McNamara, "Interrater Reliability in Situational Tests," *Journal of Applied Psychology* (April 1967).

interval, distance of time or space between two units.

intervention, one of the most basic techniques of organization development. According to Chris Argyris, *Intervention Theory and Method: A Behavioral Science View* (Reading, Mass.: Addison-Wesley, 1970),

> to intervene is to enter into an ongoing system of relationship, to come between or among persons, groups, or objects for the purpose of helping them. There is an important implicit assumption in the definition that should be made explicit: the system exists independently of the intervenor. There are many reasons one might wish to intervene. These reasons may range from helping the clients make their own decisions about the kind of help they need to coercing the clients to do what the intervenor wishes them to do. Examples of the latter are . . . executives who invite interventionists into their system to manipulate subordinates for them; trade union leaders who for years have resisted systematic research in their own bureaucratic functioning at the highest levels because they fear that valid information might lead to entrenched interests—especially at the top—being unfrozen.

Also see Iain Mangham, *Interactions and Interventions in Organizations* (New York: John Wiley, 1979); William G. Dyer, "Selecting an Intervention for Organizational Change," *Training and Development Journal* (April 1981); James Ledvinka and W. Bartley Hildreth, "Integrating Planned-Change Intervention and Computer Simulation Technology: The Case of Affirmative Action," *The Journal of Applied Behavioral Science*, Vol. 20, No. 2 (1984).

interview, also called EMPLOYMENT INTERVIEW and SELECTION INTERVIEW, conversation between two or more persons for a particular purpose. The purpose of an employment or selection interview is evaluation. According to Richard A. Fear, *The Evaluation Interview* (N.Y.: McGraw-Hill, rev. 2nd ed., 1978), "the interview is designed to perform three basic functions: (1) to determine the relevance of the applicant's experience and training to the demands of a specific job, (2) to appraise his personality, motivation, and character, and (3) to evaluate his intellectual functioning." For texts, *see* J. D. Drake, *Interviewing for Managers* (N.Y.: AMACOM, 1972); R. L. Gordon, *Interviewing* (Homewood, Ill.: Richard D. Irwin, rev. ed., 1975); Felix M. Lopez. *Personnel Interviewing* (N.Y.: McGraw-Hill, 2nd ed., 1975); Richard F. Olsen, *Managing the Interview* (New York: Wiley, 1980).

Interviewers who ask questions that are not job related could inadvertently violate EEO provisions. *See* Robert D. Gatewood and James Ledvinka, "Selection Interviewing and EEO: Mandate for Objectivity," *The Personnel Administrator* (May 1976); James G. Goodale, "Tailoring the Selection Interview to the Job," *Personnel Journal* (February 1976).

See also the following entries:
COMPLIMENTARY INTERVIEW
DIRECTED INTERVIEW
EXIT INTERVIEW
GROUP ORAL INTERVIEW
HELPING INTERVIEW
PATTERNED INTERVIEW
SCREENING INTERVIEW
STRESS INTERVIEW

interview schedule, formal list of questions that an interviewer puts to an interviewee.

intrinsic reward, also called PSYCHIC INCOME, reward contained in the job itself such as personal satisfaction, a sense of achievement, and the prestige of office. *See* William E. Reif, "Intrinsic Versus Extrinsic Rewards: Resolving The Controversy," *Human Resource Management* (Summer 1975); Lee Dyer and Donald F. Parker, "Classifying Outcomes in Work Motivation Research: An Examination of the Intrinsic-Extrinsic Dichotomy," *Jour-*

nal of Applied Psychology (August 1975). *See also* TITLES.

inventory, questionnaire designed to obtain non-intellectual information about a subject. Inventories are often used to gain information on an individual's personality traits, interests, attitude, etc. *See* Robert C. Droege and John Hawk, "Development of a U.S. Employment Service Interest Inventory," *Journal of Employment Counseling* (June 1977).

inventory, interest: *see* INTEREST INVENTORY.

inverse seniority, concept that allows workers with the greatest seniority to elect temporary layoff so the most recently hired (who would normally be subject to layoff) can continue working. The key to making the concept practical is the provision that senior workers who are laid off receive supplementary compensation in excess of state unemployment compensation and have the right to return to their previous jobs. *See* R. T. Lund, D. C. Bumstead, and S. Friedman, "Inverse Seniority: Timely Answer to the Layoff Dilemma?" *Harvard Business Review* (September–October 1975); S. Friedman, D. C. Bumstead, and R. T. Lund, "Inverse Seniority as an Aid to Disadvantaged Groups," *Monthly Labor Review* (May 1976).

involuntary demotion: *see* DEMOTION.

I/O psychology: *see* INDUSTRIAL PSYCHOLOGY.

IPA: *see* INTERGOVERNMENTAL PERSONNEL ACT OF 1970.

IPMA: *see* INTERNATIONAL PERSONNEL MANAGEMENT ASSOCIATION.

IQ: *see* INTELLIGENCE QUOTIENT.

IRA: *see* INDIVIDUAL RETIREMENT ACCOUNT.

iron-clad oath, also IRON-CLAD CON-

TRACT, a pre-World War I anti-union tactic that had employees take an oath and/or sign a contract agreeing not to join or encourage the formation of a union. Such practices were made illegal by the Norris-LaGuardia Act of 1932.

iron law of oligarchy, according to Robert Michels' "iron law of oligarchy," in *Political Parties* (Glencoe, Ill.: The Free Press, 1915, 1949), organizations are by their nature oligarchic because majorities within an organization are not capable of ruling themselves:

> Organization implies the tendency to oligarchy. In every organization, whether it be a political party, a professional union, or any other association of the kind, the aristocratic tendency manifests itself very clearly. The mechanism of the organization, while conferring a solidity of structure, induces serious changes in the organized mass, completely inverting the respective position of the leaders and the led. As a result of organization, every party or professional union becomes divided into a minority of directors and a majority of directed.

iron law of wages, also called SUBSISTENCE THEORY OF WAGES, concept, variously stated as a law or theory, which holds that in the long run workers will be paid merely the wages that they require for bare survival. It is premised upon the notion that as wages rise, workers have larger families. This increases the labor force and, in turn, drives down wages. The ensuing poverty causes family sizes to decline and, in turn, drives wages higher. Then the cycle begins again. While various writers popularized these notions in the last century, they are most fully stated in David Ricardo's *Principles of Political Economy and Taxation* (N.Y.: E. P. Dutton & Co., 1917, 1962).

IRRA: *see* INDUSTRIAL RELATIONS RESEARCH ASSOCIATION.

ISR: *see* INSTITUTE FOR SOCIAL RESEARCH.

item, smallest unit of an employment test; a test question.

See also RECALL ITEM and RECOGNITION ITEM.

item analysis, statistical description of how a particular question functioned when used in a particular test. An item analysis provides information about the difficulty of the question for the sample on which it is based, the relative attractiveness of the options, and how well the question discriminated among the examinees with respect to a chosen criterion. The criterion most frequently used is the total score on the test of which the item is a part. However, the criterion may be the score on a subtest, or some other test or, in general, on any appropriate measure that ranks the examinee from high to low.

item validity, extent to which a test item measures what it is supposed to measure.

itinerant worker, employee who finds work by traveling from one employer or community to another.

IWW: *see* INDUSTRIAL WORKERS OF THE WORLD.

J

Jackson, Andrew (1767-1845), president of the United States from 1829-1837 who has been blamed for inventing the spoils system. Prior to Jackson, the federal service was a stable, long-tenured corps of officials decidedly elitist in character and remarkably barren of corruption. Jackson, for the most part, continued with this tradition in practice, turning out of office about as many appointees as had Jefferson. In his most famous statement on the character of public office, Jackson asserted that the duties of public office are "so plain and simple that men of intelligence may readily qualify themselves for their performance; and I cannot but believe that more is lost by the long continuance of men in office than is generally to be gained by their experience." Jackson was claiming that all men, especially the newly enfranchised who did so much to elect him, should have an equal opportunity for public office. In playing to his plebian constituency, Jackson put the patrician civil service on notice that they had no natural monopoly on public office. His rhetoric on the nature of the public service was to be far more influential than his administrative example. While Jackson's personal indulgence in spoils were more limited than popularly thought, he did establish the intellectual and political rationale for the unmitigated spoils system that was to follow.

The classic work on Jackson's patronage policies is Erik M. Eriksson, "The Federal Civil Service Under President Jackson," *Mississippi Valley Historical Review* (March 1927). For later studies, *see* Sidney H. Aronson, *Status and Kinship in the Higher Civil Service* (Cambridge, Mass.: Harvard University Press, 1964); Leonard D. White, *The Jacksonians* (N.Y.: Macmillan, 1954); Matthew A. Crenson, *The Federal Machine: Beginnings of Bureaucracy in Jacksonian America.* (Baltimore: Johns Hopkins University Press, 1975).

jargon: *see* BUZZWORDS.

jargonaphasia, physiological disorder manifested by the intermingling of correct words with unintelligible speech. Many writers of organization memoranda and government regulations seem to suffer from this ailment.

jawboning, any presidential pressure on labor, management, or both to make their behavior more compatible with the national interest. The jawbone in jawboning refers to the biblical "jawbone of an ass" with which Samson "slew a thousand men." According to Theodore C. Sorenson, in *Kennedy* (N.Y.: Harper & Row, 1965), the term was first used by Walter Heller (then Chairman of the Council of

Economic Advisors) in reference to President Kennedy's efforts to impose his economic guidelines on price-setting and collective bargaining. While President Kennedy never used the term itself, his successor, President Johnson, admittedly used jawboning extensively because it neatly complimented both his policies and personality. Subsequent presidents have tried to avoid the term but stuck with the practice.

Jewish Labor Committee, seeks to combat totalitarianism and anti-semitism in cooperation with organized labor.
Jewish Labor Committee
25 E. 78th Street
New York, NY 10021
(212) 535-3700

J. I. Case Co.* v. *National Labor Relations Board, 321 U.S. 332 (1944), U.S. Supreme Court case, which held that individual contracts—no matter what the circumstances that justify their execution or what their terms—cannot be used to defeat or delay any procedures or rights under the National Labor Relations Act.

Jim Crow, a name given to any law requiring the segregation of the races. All such statutes are now unconstitutional. *See* Comer Vann Woodward, *The Strange Career of Jim Crow*, 3rd revised edition (New York: Oxford University Press, 1974).

Jimerson, Earl W. (1889-1957), president of the Amalgamated Meat Cutters and Butcher Workmen of North America who helped his union grow from 5,000 members in 1921 to 350,000 at the time of his death. For biographical information, *see* David Brody, *The Butcher Workmen: A Study of Unionization* (Cambridge, Mass.: Harvard University Press, 1964).

job, one of three common usages: (1) colloquial term for one's position or occupation, (2) group of positions that are identical with respect to their major duties and responsibilities, (3) discrete unit of work within an occupational specialty.

Historically, jobs were restricted to manual labor. Samuel Johnson's *English Dictionary* (1755) defines a job as "petty, piddling work; a piece of chance work." Anyone not dwelling in the lowest strata of employment had a position, a profession, a calling, or (at the very least) an occupation. However, our language strives ever toward egalitarianism and now even an executive at the highest level would quite properly refer to his position as a job.

job, bridge: *see* BRIDGE JOB.

job, covered: *see* COVERED JOB.

job action, a strike or work slowdown, usually by public employees. Russell K. Schutt, "Models of Militancy: Support for Strikes and Work Actions Among Public Employees," *Industrial and Labor Relations Review* (April 1982).

job analysis, determination of a position's specific tasks and of the knowledges, skills and abilities that an incumbent should possess. This information can then be used in making recruitment and selection decisions, creating selection devices, developing compensation systems, approving training needs, etc. *See* Clement J. Berwitz, *The Job Analysis Approach to Affirmative Action* (New York: John Wiley, 1975); Eugene Rouleau and Burton F. Krain, "Using Job Analysis to Design Selection Procedures," *Public Personnel Management* (September–October 1975); Edwin T. Cornelius III, Theodore J. Carron and Marianne N. Collins, "Job Analysis Models and Job Classification," *Personnel Psychology* (Winter 1979); Jai Ghropade and Thomas J. Atchison, "The Concept of Job Analysis: A Review and Some Suggestions," *Public Personnel Management* (Vol. 9, No. 3, 1980); Richard D. Arvey and others, "Potential Sources of Bias in Job Analytic Processes," *Academy of Management Journal* (September 1982); Stephen E. Bennis, Ann Holt Belenky and Dee Ann Soder, *Job Analysis: An Effective Management Tool* (Washington, D.C.: BNA Books, 1983); Sidney Gael, *Job Analysis* (San Francisco: Jossey-Bass, 1983).

job analysis, functional: *see* FUNCTIONAL JOB ANALYSIS.

job audit: *see* DESK AUDIT.

job bank, tool first developed in the late 1960s by the U.S. Employment Service so that its local offices could provide applicants with greater access to job openings and employers with a greater choice of workers from which to choose. The job bank itself is a computer. Each day the computer is fed information on new job openings and on jobs just filled. Its daily printout provides up-to-the-minute information for all jobseekers, greater exposure of employers' needs, and a faster referral of job applicants.

job categories, the nine designated categories of the EEO-1 report: officials and managers, professionals, technicians, sales workers, office and clerical, craft workers (skilled), operatives (semiskilled), laborers (unskilled), and service workers.

job ceiling, maximum number of employees authorized at a given time.

job classification evaluation method, method by which jobs are grouped into classes based on the job's level of difficulty. *See also* POSITION CLASSIFICATION.

job coding, numbering system used to categorize jobs according to their job families or other areas of similarity. For example, all positions in a clerical series might be given numbers from 200 to 299 or all management positions might be numbered from 500 to 599. Higher numbers usually indicate higher skill levels within a series.

job content, duties and responsibilities of a specific position.

Job Corps, federal program, presently authorized by the Comprehensive Employment and Training Act of 1973, which provides leadership and overall direction and guidance for the administration of a nationwide training program offering comprehensive development for disadvantaged youth through centers with the unique feature of residential facilities for all or most enrollees. Its purpose is to prepare these youth for the responsibilities of citizenship and to increase their employability by providing them with education, vocational training, and useful work experience in rural, urban, or inner-city centers.

Enrollees may spend a maximum of two years in the Job Corps. However, a period of enrollment, from six months to a year, is usually sufficient to provide adequate training and education to improve employability to a substantial degree.

Job Corps recruiting is accomplished primarily through state employment services. In certain areas, private organizations are the principal source of referrals. State employment services and private, nonprofit organizations provide assistance to enrollees in locating jobs after completion of training.

For the early history, *see* Christopher Weeks, *Job Corps: Dollars and Dropouts* (Boston: Little, Brown & Co., 1967); Sar A. Levitan, "Job Corps Experience with Manpower Training," *Monthly Labor Review* (October 1975); David A. Long, Charles D. Mallar and Craig V. D. Thornton, "Evaluating the Benefits and Costs of the Job Corps," *Journal of Policy Analysis and Management* (Fall 1981).

job cycle, amount of time required for an employee to perform a discrete unit of work.

job definition, formal statement of the task requirements of a job. The term is frequently used interchangeably with job description.

job depth, measure of the relative freedom that the incumbent of a position has in the performance of his assigned duties.

job description, also called POSITION GUIDE, summary of the duties and responsibilities of a job. According to Robert Townsend, in *Up the Organization* (N.Y.: Knopf, 1970),

at best, a job description freezes the job as the writer understood it at a particular instant in the past. At worst, they're prepared by personnel people who can't write and don't understand the jobs.

For how-to-do-it treatments, *see* W. J. Walsch, "Writing Job Descriptions: How and Why," *Supervisory Management* (February 1972); R. I. Henderson, "Job Descriptions—Critical Documents, Versatile Tools," *Supervisory Management* (December 1975). *Also see* John D. Ulery, *Job Descriptions in Manufacturing Industries* (New York: AMACOM, A division of American Management Associations, 1981); Mark A. Jones, "Job Descriptions Made Easy," *Personnel Journal* (May 1984).

See also SPECIFICATION.

job design, also called JOB REDESIGN, a general term for increasing job satisfaction or productivity by making jobs more interesting and efficient. It is one of the central concerns of industrial society. In addition to providing all of our goods and services, work provides our social identities and is the single most significant determinant of our physical and emotional health. Organizing work in a manner consistent with societal goals has been the basic task of management since prehistory. This task is made more difficult today by the ever-increasing educational levels and expectations of employees. During the first phase of industrialization, workers were content to be human interchangeable parts of machines (it was more desirable than the alternative of subsistence agriculture). But the modern day archetypical industrial citizens are highly educated individuals who exhibit little resemblance to their illiterate forebears. The scientific management movement, which grew up as an adjunct of industrial engineering, concerned itself solely with the physical considerations of work; it was human engineering. The research findings of medicine and the behavioral sciences of the last half century have thoroughly demonstrated that the social and psychological basis of work is as significant to long-term productivity and efficiency as are the traditional physiological factors. A modern job design purview seeks to address the

totality of these concerns. *See* Harold M. F. Rush, *Job Design for Motivation* (N.Y.: The Conference Board, 1971); Louis E. Davis and James C. Taylor (eds.), *The Design of Jobs* (Santa Monica, Calif.: Goodyear Publishing Co., 2nd ed., 1979); Sar A. Levitan and William B. Johnston, "Job Redesign, Reform, Enrichment—Exploring the Limitations," *Monthly Labor Review* (July 1973); Richard W. Woodman and John J. Sherwood, "A Comprehensive Look at Job Design," *Personnel Journal* (August 1977); Robert A. Karasek, Jr., "Job Demands, Job Decision Latitude, and Mental Strain: Implications for Job Redesign," *Administrative Science Quarterly* (June 1979); Russ Smith, "Job Redesign in the Public Sector: The Track Record," *Review of Public Personnel Personnel Administration* (Fall 1981); Allan R. Cohen, "Lucid Design for Work Redesign," *The Journal of Applied Behavioral Science*, Vol. 18, No. 1 (1982).

job diagnostic survey, research instrument developed by Hackman and Oldham to measure job characteristics and outcomes that might result from job redesign. The Hackman and Oldham approach is particularly concerned with the level of skill variety, task identity, task significance, autonomy, and feedback that characterize a job. *See* J. R. Hackman and G. R. Oldham, "Development of the Job Diagnostic Survey," *Journal of Applied Psychology* (April 1975).

job dilution, dividing a relatively sophisticated job into parts that can be performed by less skilled labor.

job element: *see* ELEMENT.

job enlargement: *see* JOB ENRICHMENT.

job enrichment, also JOB ENLARGEMENT, the term *job enrichment* is often confused or used interchangeably with *job enlargement*. However, enlarging a job—adding additional but similar duties—does not substantively change and by no means enriches it. For example, an assembly-line worker performing two menial tasks is not going to have his/her attitudes affected in any significant way if he/she is allowed to perform additional menial tasks. Job enrichment can only occur when motivational factors are designed into the work. Job enlargement is nothing more than horizontal loading—similar tasks laid along side one another. But job enrichment comes only with vertical loading—buiding into lower level jobs the very factors that make work at the higher levels of the organization more satisfying, more responsible, even more fun. Two such factors would be personal responsibility for discrete units of work and the ability to set one's own pace within an overall schedule.

The most influential individual in the movement toward more enriched jobs has been Frederick Herzberg. For summaries of his work, see "One More Time: How Do You Motivate Employees?" *Harvard Business Review* (January-February 1968); "The Wise Old Turk," *Harvard Business Review* (September-October 1974). *Also see* Robert N. Ford, "Job Enrichment Lessons from AT&T," *Harvard Business Review* (January-February 1973); J. Richard Hackman *et al.*, "A New Strategy for Job Enrichment," *California Management Review* (Summer 1975); Roy W. Walters and Associates, *Job Enrichment for Results* (Reading, Mass.: Addison-Wesley, 1975); Antone Alber and Melvin Blumberg, "Team vs. Individual Approaches to Job Enrichment Programs," *Personnel* (January-February 1981).

job evaluation, process that seeks to determine the relative worth of a position. It implies a formal comparison of the duties and responsibilities of various positions in order to ascertain the worth, rank, or classification of one position relative to all others in an organization. While job content is obviously the primary factor in evaluation, market conditions must also be considered. *See* Bryan Livy, *Job Evaluation: A Critical Review* (N.Y.: John Wiley, 1975); Philip M. Oliver, "Modernizing A State Job Evaluation and Pay Plan," *Public Personnel Management* (May-June 1976); Thomas H. Patten, Jr., "Job

Evaluation and Job Enlargement: A Collision Course?" *Human Resource Management* (Winter 1977); Committee on Occupational Classification and Analysis, National Research Council, *Job Evaluation: An Analytic Review* (Washington, D.C.: National Academy Press, 1979); Howard Risher, "Job Evaluation: Problems and Prospects," *Personnel* (January-February 1984); Edward C. Brett and Charles M. Cumming, "Job Evaluation and Your Organization: An Ideal Relationship?" *Personnel Administrator* (April 1984); Kenneth E. Foster and Sheryll Gimplin-Poris, "Job Evaluation: It's Time to Face the Facts," *Personnel Administrator* (October 1984).

See also WHOLE-JOB RANKING.

Job Evaluation and Pay Review Task Force, created by the Job Evaluation Policy Act of 1970 (Public Law 91-216), which asserted that it was the sense of the Congress that there be a coordinated position classification system for all civilian positions and authorized the Civil Service Commission to establish a temporary planning unit that would submit a report within two years. The unit became known as the Job Evaluation and Pay Review Task Force. Its final report, released in January 1972, is popularly known as the *Oliver Report* after the task force director, Philip M. Oliver. The report found the federal government's classification and ranking systems to be obsolete and recommended a new job evaluation system. The new system was field tested and revised and became the Civil Service Commission's factor evaluation system. For the report, *see Report of the Job Evaluation and Pay Review Task Force to the United States Civil Service Commission* (Committee on Post Office and Civil Service, Subcommittee on Employee Benefits, 92d Cong., 2d Sess., House Committee Print No. 16., January 12, 1972).

Job Evaluation Policy Act of 1970: *see* JOB EVALUATION AND PAY REVIEW TASK FORCE.

job factors, also called FACTORS, while

there are an infinite number of specific factors that pertain to differing jobs, the factors themselves can usually be categorized within the following groupings:

1. *Job Requirements* — the knowledges, skills, and abilities needed to perform the duties of a specific job.
2. *Difficulty of Work* — the complexity or intricacy of the work and the associated mental demands of the job.
3. *Responsibility* — the freedom of action required by a job and the impact of the work performed upon the organizational mission.
4. *Personal Relationships* — the importance of interpersonal relationships to the success of mission accomplishment.
5. *Other Factors* — Specific job-oriented elements which should be considered in the evaluation process. For example, physical demands, working conditions, accountability, number of workers directed.

job family, group or series of jobs in the same general occupational area, such as accounting or engineering. *See* L. R. Taylor, "The Construction of Job Families Based on the Component and Overall Dimensions of the PAQ," *Personnel Psychology* (Summer 1978).

See also POSITION ANALYSIS QUESTIONNAIRE.

job freeze, formal halt to an organization's discretionary hiring and promoting. Such an action is inherently temporary.

job grading; *see* POSITION RANKING.

job hopper, person who frequently changes jobs. *See* Larry Lang, "The Impact of Job-Hopping on Retirement Benefits," *Personnel Administrator* (May 1984).

job loading, also HORIZONTAL LOADING and VERTICAL LOADING, to load a job is to assign to it a greater variety of duties and responsibilities. It is *horizontal loading* when the newly assigned tasks are at the same level of interest and responsibility as the job's original tasks. It is *vertical loading* when the newly assigned tasks allow for increased responsibility, recognition, and personal achievement. The horizontal/vertical terminology comes from Frederick Herzberg, "One More Time: How Do You Motivate Employees?" *Harvard Business Review* (January–February 1968).

See also JOB ENRICHMENT.

job mobility, a measure of the degree to which an individual can move from job to job within one organization; or the degree to which an individual can market his or her skills to another organization. *See* John C. Anderson, George T. Milkovich and Ann Tsui, "A Model of Intra-Organizational Mobility," *Academy of Management Review* (October 1981).

job placement, assigning an individual to a job.

job posting, system that allows and encourages employees to apply for other jobs in their organization. According to Dave R. Dahl and Patrick R. Pinto, in "Job Posting: An Industry Survey," *Personnel Journal* (January 1977),

it is also a complicated system for employee self-development, which embraces internal recruitment, counseling regarding realistic job expectations, encouragement of training and development experiences, and support for the personal risk that any change incurs.

Also see Lawrence S. Kleiman and Kimberly J. Clark, "User's Satisfaction with Job Posting," *Personnel Administrator* (September 1984).

job preview: *see* WORK PREVIEW.

job pricing, determining the dollar value that a particular job is worth.

job range, a measure of the number of different tasks that a job has.

job ranking, also called RANKING, most rudimentary method of job evaluation, which simply ranks jobs in order of their importance to an organization.

job redesign: *see* JOB DESIGN.

job-relatedness, degree to which an applicant's knowledge, skills, abilities, and other qualification requirements have been determined to be necessary for successful job performance through a careful job analysis.

job restructuring, also called WORK RESTRUCTURING, element of job analysis that involves the identification of jobs within the context of the system of which they are a part and the analysis and rearrangement of their tasks to achieve a desired purpose. Although the term is relatively new, the concept is familiar. Employers frequently find it necessary to rearrange or adjust the contents (tasks performed) of jobs within a system because of economic conditions, technological changes, and the inability to fill vacant positions among other reasons. Because the interdependencies and relationships among jobs in a system cannot be ignored, job restructuring should be thought of not as changing one job but, rather, as rearranging the contents of jobs within a system. *See* Manpower Administration, U.S. Department of Labor, *A Handbook for Job Restructuring* (Washington, D.C.: U.S. Government Printing Office, 1970); Leonard A. Schlesinger and Richard E. Walton, "The Process of Work Restructuring, and Its Impact on Collective Bargaining," *Monthly Labor Review* (April 1977); Ernesto J. Poza and M. Lynn Markus, "Success Story: The Team Approach to Work Restructuring," *Organizational Dynamics* (Winter 1980); William A. Pasmore, "Overcoming the Roadblocks in Work-Restructuring Efforts," *Organizational Dynamics* (Spring 1982).

job rotation, transferring a worker from one assignment to another in order to minimize boredom and/or enhance skills. *See* Martin J. Gannon, Brian A. Poole, and Robert E. Prangley, "Involuntary Job Rotation and Worker Behavior," *Personnel Journal* (June 1972).

job sample: *see* WORK SAMPLE.

job sampling: *see* WORK SAMPLING.

job satisfaction, the totality of an employee's feelings about the various aspects of his or her work; an emotional appraisal of whether one's job lives up to one's values. *See* Edwin A. Locke, "The Nature and Causes of Job Satisfaction," in Marvin D. Dunnette (ed.), *Handbook of Industrial and Organizational Psychology* (Chicago: Rand McNally, 1976); Philip Janson and Jack K. Martin, "Job Satisfaction and Age: A Test of Two Views," *Social Forces* (June 1982); Jack F. McKenna and Paul L. Oritt, "Job Dissatisfaction: A Social Disease," *Business and Society* (Winter-Spring 1981-82); A. Chelte, J. Wright and C. Tausky, "Did Job Satisfaction Really Drop During the 1970's?" *Monthly Labor Review* (November 1982).

job scope, also CYCLE TIME, relative complexity of a particular task. This is usually reflected by the *cycle time*—the time it takes to complete the task.

job security, presence of safeguards that protect an employee from capricious assignments, demotion, or discharge. *See* Edward Yemin, "Job Security: Influence of ILO Standards and Recent Trends," *International Labour Review* (January-February 1976); Frederick V. Fox and Barry M. Staw, "The Trapped Administrator: Effects of Job Insecurity and Policy Resistance on Commitment to a Course of Action," *Administrative Science Quarterly* (September 1979); Kevin Williams and David Lewis, "Legislating for Job Security: The British Experience of Reinstatement and Reengagement," *Employee Relations Law Journal* (Winter 1982-83); James F. Bolt, "Job Security: Its Time Has Come," *Harvard Business Review* (November-December 1983); Marta Mooney, "Let's Use Job Security as a Productivity Builder," *Personnel Administrator* (February 1984).

See also EMPLOYMENT AT WILL and UNION SECURITY.

job sharing, concept that has two persons—each working part-time—sharing the same job. *See* Barney Olmsted, "Job-Sharing—A New Way to Work," *Personnel Journal* (February 1977); Gretl S. Meier, *Job Sharing: A New Pattern for Quality of Work and Life* (Kalamazoo, Mich.: W. E. Upjohn Institute for Employment Research, 1979); Michael Frease and Robert A. Zawacki, "Job-Sharing: An Answer to Productivity Problems," *The Personnel Administrator* (October 1979); Patricia Lee, *The Complete Guide to Job Sharing* (New York: Walker and Co., 1983).

See also WORKSHARING.

job specification: *see* SPECIFICATION.

job spoiler: *see* RATEBUSTER.

Job Tests Program, comprehensive battery of aptitude tests, personality/attitude questionnaires and biographical/experience questionnaires for use in selection for a wide variety of business and industry jobs (*i.e.,* clerical, mechanical, sales, technical, and supervisory/management areas). Tests in the battery include Factored Aptitude Series (J. E. King and H. B. Osborn, Jr.); Employee Attitude Series (R. B. Cattell, J. E. King and A. K. Schuettler); Application-Interview Series (J. E. King). TIME: Varies. PUBLISHER: Industrial Psychology Inc. (*see* TEST PUBLISHERS).

job ticket, a report of how much time was spent on a task; also known as a *time ticket.*

Job Training Partnership Act of 1983: *see* Comprehensive Employment and Training Act of 1973.

job upgrading, reclassifying a position from a lower to a higher classification.

job vacancy, also called JOB-VACANCY RATE, an available job for which an organization is actively seeking to recruit a worker. The *job-vacancy rate* is the ratio of the number of job vacancies to the sum of actual employment plus job vacancies. *See* Daniel Creamer, *Measuring Job Vacancies* (N.Y.: National Industrial Conference Board, 1967).

Johari Window, model, frequently used in laboratory training, for examining the mirror image of one's self. The window, developed by Joseph Luft and Harry Ingham (Joe + Harry = Johari), consists of the following four quadrants:
1. The first quadrant, the *public self,* contains knowledge that is known to both the subject and others.
2. The second quadrant, the *blind self,* contains knowledge that is known to others and unknown to the subject.
3. The third quadrant, the *private self,* contains all of those things that a subject keeps secret.
4. The fourth quadrant, the *unknown area,* contains information that neither the subject nor others know.

The Johari Window model is usually used as a visual aid for explaining the concepts of interpersonal feedback and disclosure. *See* Joseph Luft, *Group Processes: An Introduction to Group Dynamics* (Palo Alto, Calif.: National Press Books, 1963).

JOHARI WINDOW

	KNOWN TO SELF	NOT KNOWN TO SELF
KNOWN TO OTHERS	PUBLIC SELF (1)	BLIND SELF (2)
NOT KNOWN TO OTHERS	PRIVATE SELF (3)	UNKNOWN AREA (4)

John Wiley & Sons v. Livingston, 376 U.S. 543 (1964), U.S. Supreme Court case, which held that a successor employer may be compelled, under certain circumstances, to arbitrate the question of his obligations toward the employees covered by his predecessor's labor contract.

See also HOWARD JOHNSON CO., INC., V. DETROIT LOCAL JOINT EXECUTIVE BOARD, HOTEL AND RESTAURANT EMPLOYEES.

Johnson v. Railway Express, 421 U.S. 454 (1975), U.S. Supreme Court case, which held that the timely filing of an employment discrimination charge with the Equal Employment Opportunity Commission, pursuant to Title VII of the Civil Rights Act of 1964, does not toll the running of the limitation period applicable to an action.

joint bargaining, two or more unions united to negotiate with a single employer.

joint council, labor-management committee established to resolve disputes arising during the life of a contract.

joint training, training program that brings management and union officials together in a learning situation focusing on some aspect of labor relations.

Jones, Mother (1830–1930), formally MARY HARRIS JONES, first became an organizer for the United Mine Workers of America in her sixties and thereafter became famous as a colorful agitator for union causes. For her autobiography, *see* Mary Parton (ed.), *The Autobiography of Mother Jones* (Chicago: Charles H. Kerr & Co., 1925; reprint edition, ARNO Press, 1969). For a biography, *see* Dale Fetherling, *Mother Jones, the Miners' Angel: A Portrait* (Carbondale, Ill.: Southern Illinois University Press, 1974).

Jones and Laughlin decision: *see* NATIONAL LABOR RELATION BOARD V. JONES AND LAUGHLIN STEEL CORP.

Journal of Applied Behavioral Science, quarterly directed at those interested in in-

ducing social/organizational changes by means of the behavioral sciences.

> *Journal of Applied Behavioral Science*
> **Editorial Address**
> NTL Institute for Applied Behavioral Science
> P.O. Box 9155
> Rosslyn Station
> Arlington, VA 22209
> **Subscriptions**
> 36 Sherwood Place
> P.O. Box 1678
> Greenwich, CT 06836

Journal of Collective Negotiations in the Public Sector, quarterly that emphasizes practical strategies for resolving impasses and preventing strikes in the public sector.

> *Journal of Collective Negotiations in the Public Sector*
> Baywood Publishing Company
> 120-17 Marine Street
> P.O. Box D
> Farmingdale, NY 11735

Journal of Counseling and Development, monthly journal of the American Association for Counseling and Development which publishes articles of common interest to counselors and personnel workers in schools, colleges, community agencies, and government.

> *Journal of Counseling and Development*
> 5999 Stevenson Avenue
> Alexandria, VA 22304

Journal of European Industrial Training, bimonthly that emhasizes the practical application of training and development activities. While the *Journal* has contributors from both the business and academic worlds, it does not publish formal research papers. In 1977, *Industrial Training International* and the *Journal of European Training* merged to form the present *Journal of European Industrial Training.*

> *Journal of European Industrial Training*
> 200 Keighley Road
> Bradford, West Yorkshire
> England, BD9 4JQ

Journal of European Training: *see* JOURNAL OF EUROPEAN INDUSTRIAL TRAINING.

Journal of Human Resources, quarterly that provides a forum for analysis of the role of education and training in enhancing production skills, employment opportunities, and income, as well as of manpower, health, and welfare policies as they relate to the labor market and to economic and social development. It gives priority to studies having empirical content.

Journal of Human Resources
Editorial Office:
Social Science Building
1180 Observatory Drive
Madison, WI 53706
Subscriptions and Advertising Office:
Journals Department
114 North Murray Street
The University of Wisconsin Press
Madison, WI 53701

Journal of Labor Research, scholarly quarterly published by the Department of Economics of George Mason University.

Journal of Labor Research
Department of Economics
George Mason University
Fairfax, VA 22030

journeyman, also called JOURNEY WORKER, originally one of the three grades of workers recognized by the medieval guilds—masters, journeymen, and apprentices. The journeyman had completed apprenticeship training and was considered a fully skilled worker who was eligible to be hired by a master and receive specified wages. A master was a journeyman who was enterprising enough to "open his own store" and hire others as journeymen and apprentices.

Today, a *journey worker* (the de-sexed designation) is any worker who has completed a specified training program as an apprentice in learning a trade or craft or who can provide evidence of having spent a number of years qualifying for his/her trade or craft.

journeyman pay, also called JOURNEYMAN RATE and UNION SCALE, minimum wages paid to all journeymen/journey workers in a given community. Craft unions tend to refer to this minimum rate of pay as union scale.

Joy Silk Mills v. *National Labor Relations Board,* 185 F. 2d 732, decision of the U.S. Court of Appeals, which held that a company would have to bargain with a union that lost a representation election if it could be shown that the union's loss of strength was due to the employer's coercive activities. The decision was indirectly upheld by the U.S. Supreme Court when it denied certiorari in the case, 341 U.S. 914 (1951). For an analysis, *see* William A. Krupman, "The Joy Silk Rule—The Courts Weave a New Fabric," *Labor Law Journal* (October 1968).

judicial review, a court's power to review legislative acts or lower court (or quasi-judicial entities such as arbitration panels) decisions in order to either confirm or overturn them. It was first asserted by the Supreme Court in *Marbury* v. *Madison,* 1 Cranch 137 (1803). *See* Jesse H. Chopper, *Judicial Review and the National Political Process* (University of Chicago Press, 1980).

judiciary, the courts in general.

jurisdiction, the geographical area within which a court, public official, union, etc., has the right and power to operate.

jurisdictional dispute, disagreement between two unions over which should control a particular job or activity. *See* F. Bruce Simmons III, "Jurisdictional Disputes: Does the Board Really Snub the Supreme Court? *Labor Law Journal* (March 1985).

See also UNITED STATES V. HUTCHESON.

jurisdictional strike, strike that results when two unions have a dispute over whose members should perform a particular task and one or the other strikes in order to gain its way. For example, both electricians and carpenters may claim the right to do the same task at a construction site. Because the employer is caught in the middle, the Labor-Management Relations (Taft-Hartley) Act of 1947 makes jurisdictional strikes illegal.

See also STRIKE and UNFAIR LABOR PRACTICES (UNIONS).

jury-duty pay, the practice of giving employees leave with pay if they are called to jury duty. Many organizations reduce such pay by the amount the employee is paid by the court for his jury service. *See* T. J. Halatin and Jack D. Eure, Jr., "What to Do About Employee Absences for Jury Duty," *Supervisory Management* (May 1981).

See also DEAN V. GADSDEN TIMES PUBLISHING CORP.

K

Kafkaesque, bureaucratic to a ridiculous extreme. Franz Kafka's (1883-1924) novels and short stories often dealt with the theme of bureaucratic frustration.

Kahn, Robert L. (1918-), psychologist and a leading authority on organizational behavior. Major works include: *The Dynamics of Interviewing,* with Charles F. Cannell (N.Y.: John Wiley, 1957); *Organizational Stress: Studies in Role Conflict and Ambiguity,* with others (N.Y.: Wiley, 1964); *The Social Psychology of Organizations,* with Daniel Katz (N.Y.: John Wiley, 2nd ed., 1978).

Kaiser Aluminum & Chemical Corp. **v.** *Weber, et al.: see* UNITED STEELWORKERS OF AMERICA V. WEBER, ET AL.

Kaiser Permanente, a health maintenance organization. Kaiser is the surname of Henry J. Kaiser, the industrialist founder of Kaiser Industries, including Kaiser Aluminum, Kaiser Steel and Kaiser Cement. He also founded the non-profit organizations which became Kaiser Foundation Health Plans and Kaiser Foundation Hospitals. Today, there is no connection between any of the Kaiser Industries and the Kaiser Permanente Medical Care Program.

Permanente is the name of a stream in California's Santa Cruz Mountains where Henry J. Kaiser built his first plant in 1939. A Spanish word, "permanente" means permanent or everflowing. The name appealed to the Kaiser family, who used it in 1942 in naming their non-profit health and hospital foundations. Over the years, the foundations adopted the Kaiser name, while the physicians associated with the program chose to be known as Permanente Medical Groups.

Katz, Daniel (1903-), psychologist and a leading authority on organizational behavior. Major works include: *Bureaucratic Encounters: A Pilot Study in the Evaluation of Government Services* (Ann Arbor, Mich.: Institute for Social Research, University of Michigan, 1975); *The Social Psychology of Organizations,* with Robert L. Kahn (N.Y.: John Wiley, 2nd ed., 1978).

Kelley v. *Johnson,* 425 U.S. 238 (1976), U.S. Supreme Court case, which upheld a municipal regulation limiting the hair length of police.

Keogh Plan also called H.R. 10 PLAN, the Self-Employed Individuals Tax Retirement Act of 1962 encourages the establishment of voluntary pension plans by self-employed individuals. The act allows individuals to have tax advantages similar to those allowed for corporate pension plans. Congressman Eugene J. Keogh was the prime sponsor of the Act. H.R. 10 was the number assigned to the bill prior to its passage.

key classes, occupations or positions for which data are gathered from other employers (via a salary survey) in order to serve as a basis for establishing wage rates.

Keyishian v. *Board of Regents,* 385 U.S. 589 (1967), U.S. Supreme Court case, which held that laws "which make Communist Party membership, as such, prima facie evidence of disqualification for employment in the public school system are overbroad and therefore unconstitutional."

Keynes, John Maynard (1883-1946), English economist who wrote the most influential book on economics of this century, *The General Theory of Employment, Interest and Money* (London: Macmillan, 1936), founded a school of thought known as *Keynesian economics*, and developed the framework of modern macroeconomic theory. Keynes observed that "practical men, who believe themselves to be quite exempt from any intellectual influences, are usually the slaves of some defunct economist" and provided the definitive economic forecast when he asserted that "in the long run we are all dead." For biography, *see:* Robert Lekachman, *The Age of Keynes* (New York: Random House, 1975); John Fender, *Understanding Keynes: An Analysis of 'The General Theory,' "* (New York: Wiley, 1981); Charles H. Hession, *John Maynard Keynes: A Personal Biography of the Man Who Revolutionized Capitalism and the Way We Lived* (New York: Macmillan, 1984).

Also see: Amar Bhide, "Beyond Keynes: Demand-Side Economics," *Harvard Business Review* (July-August 1983); James Tobin, "A Keynesian View of the Budget Deficit," *California Management Review* (Winter 1984).

KGIS: *see* KUDER GENERAL INTEREST SURVEY.

Kheel, Theodore W. (1914-   ), New York lawyer and one of the nation's most visible labor mediators. For a profile, *see* Richard Karp, "The Many Worlds of Theodore Kheel," *New York* (January 8, 1979).

kickback, employers or third parties who extort money from employees or contractors by threatening to sever or have severed the employment relationship are soliciting kickbacks. Most kickbacks are obviously unethical if not illegal. The Anti-Kickback Act of 1934 (or the Copeland Act, as amended) prohibits kickbacks by federal contractors and subcontractors.

kicked upstairs, slang term for the removal of an individual from a position where his or her performance is not thought satisfactory by promoting him or her to a higher position in the organization.

kick-in-the-ass motivation: *see* KITA.

Kingsley, J. Donald (1908-   ), formerly Director-General of the United Nations' International Refugee Organization, co-author of the first full scale text on public personnel administration, and creator of the concept "representative bureaucracy." Major works include: *Public Personnel Administration,* with William E. Mosher (N.Y.: Harper & Bros., 1936); *Representative Bureaucracy: An Interpretation of the British Civil Service* (Yellow Springs, Ohio: Antioch Press, 1944).

Kirkland, Lane (1922-   ), became president of the AFL-CIO in 1979.

Kirkland v. New York State Department of Correctional Services, federal court of appeals case, 520 F. 2d 420 (2d Cir. 1975), cert. denied, 429 U.S. 974 (1976), dealt with the permissible range of remedies for illegal employment discrimination. While approving portions of a lower court ruling ordering New York State to develop an unbiased, job-related test for hiring correctional officials and instituting temporary hiring and promotion quotas until such a test could be developed, the appeals court overturned the portion of the order requiring a "permanent" quota to be followed until members of minority groups reached a specified proportion of correctional sergeants. See Roscoe W. Wisner, "The Kirkland Case—Its Implications for Personnel Selection," *Public Personnel Management* (July-August 1975).

KITA, mnemonic device used by Frederick Herzberg to refer to "kick-in-the-ass" attempts at worker motivation. Variants of KITA include "negative physical KITA" (literally using physical force); "negative psychological KITA" (hurting someone with a psychic blow); and "positive KITA" (offering rewards for performance). Herzberg states that KITA cannot create motivation; its only ability is to create movement. *See* Frederick Herzberg, "One More Time: How Do You Motivate Employees?" *Harvard Business Review* (January–February 1968).

Knights of Labor, first significant national labor organization in the United States, founded in 1869 as the Noble and Holy Order of the Knights of Labor. It was originally a secret society (to protect its members from employer reprisals), but its sundry rituals gained it the opposition of the Catholic Church. It lifted its veil of secrecy in 1881, removed the religious connotations from its rituals, saw the Catholic Church withdraw its condemnation, and grew to over 100,000 members within three years. It reached its peak of influence in 1886 when it claimed a national membership of 700,000. Then, a long series of strike failures caused membership to fall away as rapidly as it had grown. By the late 1880s, the Knights were increasingly overshadowed by the American Federation of Labor. Though weakened by loss of membership, the Knights of Labor persisted until 1917 when its formal organization was disbanded.

Because the Knights of Labor was a mass organization accepting all workers, it proved difficult for such a diverse group to agree upon particular courses of action, and so it tended to concentrate on broad political issues and social reform. Skilled workers found that they had little in common with the unskilled masses, nor with a leadership preaching social gospel instead of bread-and-butter issues. *See* Leon Fink, *Workingmen's Democracy: The Knights of Labor and American Politics* (University of Illinois Press, 1982).

Knights of St. Crispin, union of shoemakers formed in 1867, which grew to about 50,000 members and 600 chapters before it disappeared after the panic of 1873.

knocked off, slang term for being fired. But, be careful how you use it! It is also used as an underworld term for murder.

knock off work, it is thought that the phrase "knocking off" has its origins in the slave galleys of old. So that the oarsmen would row with the proper timing, an overseer would beat rhythmically on a block or drum. When it was time to stop, a special knock would indicate that the oarsmen could knock off or stop their work.

knowledge, understanding of facts or principles relating to a particular subject or subject area.

knowledge worker, Peter F. Drucker's term, in *The New Society: The Anatomy of Industrial Order* (N.Y.: Harper Torchbooks, 1949, 1962), for the largest and most rapidly growing group in the working population of the developed countries, especially the United States:

It is a group of "workers" though it will never identify itself with the "proletariat," and will always consider itself "middle-class" if not "part of management." And it is an independent group because it owns the one essential resource of production: knowledge. . . . It is this group whose emergence makes ours a "new" society. Never before has any society had the means to educate large numbers of its citizens, nor the opportunities for them to make their education productive. Our society, however, cannot get enough educated people, nor can it really effectively utilize any other resource but the educated man who works with his knowledge rather than with his animal strength or his manual skill.

Also see Donald B. Miller, "How to Improve the Performance and Productivity of the Knowledge Worker," *Organizational Dynamics* (Winter 1977); Edward Mandt, "Managing the Knowledge Worker of the Future," *Personnel Journal* (March 1978). *See also* DRUCKER, PETER.

KOIS: *see* KUDER OCCUPATIONAL INTEREST SURVEY.

Kreps, Juanita M. (1921–   ), Secretary of Commerce from 1977 to 1979.

Krislov, Samuel (1929-   ), constitutional law scholar who is best known outside of that field for his analyses of the link between broader political questions of representative bureaucracy and those emanating from equal employment opportunity concerns. Major works include: *The Supreme Court in the Political Process* (New York: Macmillan, 1965); *The Politics of Legal Advice* (New York: McGraw-Hill, 1965); *The Negro in Federal Employment: The Quest for Equal Opportunity* (University of Minnesota Press, 1967); *The Supreme Court and Political Freedom* (New York: The Free Press, 1968); *The Judicial Process and Constitutional Law* (Boston: Little, Brown, 1972); *Representative Bureaucracy* (Englewood Cliffs, N.J.: Prentice-Hall, 1974); *Representative Bureaucracy and the American Political System,* with David H. Rosenbloom (New York: Praeger, 1981).

Kuder General Interest Survey (KGIS), vocational interest inventory with 10 occupational scales (*i.e.,* outdoor, mechanical, scientific, artistic, musical, clerical, social services). Revision of Kuder Preference Record-Vocational. TIME: 45/60 minutes. AUTHOR: G. F. Kuder. PUBLISHER: Science Research Associates, Inc. (*see* TEST PUBLISHERS).

Kuder Occupational Interest Survey (KOIS), 100-triad interest inventory. Test subject picks most and least preferred occupational activity from three alternatives. This measures how an individual's preferences are like those typical of people in the various occupations and fields of study. TIME: 30/40 minutes. AUTHOR: G. F. Kuder. PUBLISHER: Science Research Associates, Inc. (*see* TEST PUBLISHERS).

Kuder Preference Record, self-report inventory designed to disclose relative interest in 38 broadly defined vocational interest areas (*i.e.,* outdoor, mechanical, clerical, artistic, musical, scientific, etc.). TIME: Untimed. AUTHOR: G. F. Kuder. PUBLISHER: Science Research Associates, Inc. (*see* TEST PUBLISHERS).

Kuder-Richardson Formulas, variety of formulas for estimating test reliability.

L

labor, collective term for an organization's workforce exclusive of management.
See also the following entries:
CASUAL LABOR
CHILD LABOR
CONTRACT LABOR
DIRECT LABOR
DIVISION OF LABOR
SKILLED LABOR

Labor, Department of (DOL), U.S. federal agency whose purpose is to foster, promote, and develop the welfare of the wage earners of the United States, to improve their working conditions, and to advance their opporunities for profitable employment. In carrying out this mission, DOL administers more than 130 federal labor laws guaranteeing workers' rights to safe and healthful working conditions, a minimum hourly wage and overtime pay, freedom from employment discrimination, unemployment insurance, and workers' compensation. DOL also protects workers' pension rights; sponsors job training programs; helps workers find jobs; works to strengthen free collective bargaining; and keeps track of changes in employment, prices, and other national economic measurements.
Department of Labor
200 Constitution Ave. N.W.
Washington, D.C. 20210
(202) 523-8165

Labor Affairs, Bureau of International: *see* BUREAU OF INTERNATIONAL LABOR AFFAIRS.

labor agreement, formal results achieved by collective bargaining. *See* Arnold M. Zack and Richard I. Block, *Labor Agree-*

ment in Negotiation and Arbitration (Washington, D.C.: BNA Books, 1983); James Suchan and Clyde Scott, "Readability Levels of Collective Bargaining Agreements," *Personnel Administrator* (November 1984).

Labor Arbitration Reports, published by the Bureau of National Affairs, Inc., this weekly report is the standard authority on awards and recommended settlements by arbitrators, emergency boards, factfinding bodies, permanent referees and umpires. Reports on company and union positions, dissenting opinions.

labor area, a central city or a city and the surrounding territory within commuting distance. It is an economically integrated geographical unit within which workers may readily change jobs without changing their place of residence.

laboratory education also called LABORATORY METHOD, method of learning about human behavior through experiencing group activities. According to Clayton P. Alderfer, in "Understanding Laboratory Education: An Overview," *Monthly Labor Review* (December 1970):

the various forms of laboratory education include a number of common elements such as acceptance of experience-based learning technology, recognition of the role of emotions in human relationships, and utilization of the small group (10 to 12 persons) as a central component in training designs.

The learning laboratory usually takes place on a "cultural island." Participants are taken away from their normal day-to-day activities to a setting where the learning experiences occur. Frequently this new setting is naturally beautiful, but at the very least it is different and thereby provides the participant with both safety from former distractions and a setting that does not necessarily reinforce his usual ways of behaving. A second component of the laboratory involves the use of unstructured or semistructured learning tools. The staff usually attempts to design a set of experiences

that serve to heighten certain aspects of human behavior and emotions. Participants learn by becoming actively involved in these activities and by developing skills which allow them to observe both themselves and others during these experiences. A person is asked to engage himself in the unfolding events and later to step back and try to see the patterns in his own and others' behavior. Much of the sense of excitement and high level of emotionality comes from the participant's becoming involved. Experiential learning is based on the assumption that experience precedes intellectual understanding.

laboratory training, also SENSITIVITY TRAINING and T-GROUP, generic term for those educational/training experiences that are designed (1) to increase an individual's sensitivity to his/her own motives and behavior, (2) to increase sensitivity to the behavior of others, and (3) to ascertain those elements of interpersonal interactions that either facilitate or impede a group's effectiveness. While laboratory training and *sensitivity training* tend to be used interchangeably, sensitivity training is the subordinate term (being the most common method of laboratory training) and the popular name given to almost all experience-based learning exercises. The basic vehicle for the sensitivity training experience is the *T-Group* (T for Training). According to Chris Argyris in "T-Groups for Organizational Effectiveness," *Harvard Business Review* (March–April 1964), the T-Group experience is designed to provide maximum possible opportunity for the individuals to expose their behavior, give and receive feedbacks, experiment with new behavior, and develop everlasting awareness and acceptance of self and others. The T-group, when effective, also provides individuals with the opportunity to learn the nature of effective group functioning. They are able to learn how to develop a group that achieves specific goals with minimum possible human cost.

See Robert T. Golembiewski and Arthur Blumberg (eds.), *Sensitivity Training and the Laboratory Approach* (Itasca, Ill.:

Peacock, 3rd ed., 1977); Henry Clay Smith, *Sensitivity Training: The Scientific Understanding of Individuals* (N.Y.: McGraw-Hill, 1973); C. L. Cooper and I. L. Mangham, *T-Groups: A Survey of Research* (N.Y.: Wiley, 1971); Dee G. Appley and Alvin E. Winder, *T-Groups and Therapy Groups in A Changing Society* (San Francisco: Jossey-Bass, 1973); Peter B. Smith, "The T-Group Trainer—Group Facilitator or Prisoner of Circumstance?" *Journal of Applied Behavioral Science* (January-February-March 1980).

See also the following entries:
INSTRUMENTED LABORATORY
NATIONAL TRAINING LABORATORIES
INSTITUTE FOR APPLIED
BEHAVIORAL SCIENCE
ROLE
TRAINERLESS LABORATORY

labor certification, certification by the U.S. Department of Labor which certain aliens (such as foreign medical graduates) seeking to immigrate to the United States in order to work must obtain before they may obtain a visa. People in occupations which the Department of Labor feels are in short supply throughout the country (such as physicians and nurses but not dentists) are given such certificates after review of the applicant's qualifications.

labor cost, that part of the cost of a product or service that is attributable to wages.

labor costs, also UNIT LABOR COST, total expenses an employer must meet in order to retain the services of employees. The *unit labor cost* is the expense for labor divided by the number of units of output produced.

labor costs audit, an audit made to determine whether the services received for the salaries paid are adequate and that salary expenditures are applied correctly in determining the costs of manufactured goods.

labor costs, indirect: *see* INDIRECT LABOR COSTS.

labor court, some European countries

have a permanent court of industrial arbitration available to settle labor disputes. *See* Joseph J. Shutkin, "One Nation Indivisible—A Plea for a U.S. Court of Labor Relations," *Labor Law Journal* (February 1969).

Labor Day, in 1894, the U.S. Congress mandated that the first Monday after the first Tuesday in September would be a federal holiday honoring the nation's workers.

labor demand, desire of employers to hire workers to fill job openings caused by growth or expansion of the firm or replacement of workers that have left the firm.

labor dispute, according to Section 2(9) of the National Labor Relations Act, as amended, the term "labor dispute" includes

any controversy concerning terms, tenure or conditions of employment, or concerning the association or representation of persons in negotiating, fixing, maintaining, changing, or seeking to arrange terms or conditions of employment.

See also LAUF V. E. G SHINNER AND COMPANY and LINN V. UNITED PLANT GUARD WORKERS.

Labordoc, the on-line version of *International Labour Documentation,* a bibliographic publication of the International Labour Organization. It is available through: System Development Corporation, 2500 Colorado Avenue, Santa Monica, CA 90406. (800) 421-7229.

labor economics, the subfield of economics concerned with wages and the supply/allocation of manpower. *See* F. Ray Marshall, Vernon M. Briggs, Jr., and Allan G. King, *Labor Economics: Wages, Employment, Trade Unionism, and Public Policy,* 5th ed. (Homewood, Ill.: Richard D. Irwin, 1984); Gordon F. Bloom and Herbert R. Northrup, *Economics of Labor Relations,* 9th ed. (Homewood, Ill.: Richard D. Irwin, 1981); Robert M. Fearn, *Labor Economics: The Emerging Syn-*

thesis (Cambridge, Mass.: Winthrop Publishers, 1981). For a how-to-do-it approach, *see* George S. Odiorne, "How to Become your Company's Labor Economist," *Management of Personnel Quarterly* (Spring 1968). For a history, see Paul J. McNulty, *The Origins and Development of Labor Economics* (Cambridge, MA: MIT Press, 1980).

labor efficiency variance, the difference between standard and actual direct labor hours expended in manufacturing under a standard cost system.

labor force, also CIVILIAN LABOR FORCE and TOTAL LABOR FORCE, according to the Bureau of Labor Statistics the *civilian labor force* consists of all employed or unemployed persons in the civilian non-institutional population; the *total labor force* includes military personnel. Persons not in the labor force are those not classified as employed or unemployed; this group includes persons retired, those engaged in their own housework, those not working while attending school, those unable to work because of long-term illness, those discouraged from seeking work because of personal or job market factors and those who are voluntarily idle. The noninstitutional population comprises all persons 16 years and older who are not inmates of penal or mental institutions, sanitariums, or homes for the aged, infirm, or needy. *See* Howard N. Fullerton, Jr., and Paul O. Flaim, "New Labor Force Projections to 1990," *Monthly Labor Review* (December 1976); Howard N. Fullerton, "How Accurate Were Projections of the 1980 Labor Force?" *Monthly Labor Review* (July 1982); H. N. Fullerton, Jr., and J. Tschetter, "The 1995 Labor Force: A Second Look," *Monthly Labor Review* (November 1983).

labor-force participation, rate at which a given group (women, blacks, handicapped, etc.) is represented (either nationally, regionally, or locally) in the labor force.

labor grade, one of a series of steps in a wage-rate structure established by a process of job evaluation or collective bargaining.

Labor History, quarterly, scholarly journal that publishes original research in U.S. labor history, studies of specific unions and of the impact labor problems have upon ethnic and minority groups, theory of labor history, biographical portraits of important trade union figures, comparative studies and analyses of foreign labor movements that shed light on U.S. labor developments, studies of radical groups or of radical history related to U.S. labor history.

> *Labor History*
> Bobst Library, Tamiment Institute
> New York University
> 70 Washington Square South
> New York, NY 10012

labor injunction: *see* INJUNCTION and BOYS MARKET V. RETAIL CLERKS' LOCAL 770.

labor intensive, any production process requiring a large proportion of human effort relative to capital investment.

labor law, body of law applied to concerns of employment, wages, conditions of work, unions, labor-management relations, etc. *See* Ronald A. Wykstra and Eleanour V. Stevens, *Labor Law and Public Policy* (N.Y.: Odyssey Press, 1970); Benjamin J. Taylor and Fred Witney, *Labor Relations Law*, 4th ed. (Englewood Cliffs, N.J.: Prentice-Hall, 1983); Bruce Feldacker, *Labor Guide to Labor Law*, 2nd ed., (Reston, VA: Reston/Prentice-Hall, 1983); James B. Atleson, *Values and Assumptions in American Labor Law* (Amherst: The University of Massachusetts Press, 1983); Benjamin Aaron, "Future Trends in Industrial Relations Law," *Industrial Relations* (Winter 1984).

Laborlaw, the on-line version of six BNA printed information services: *Labor Relations, Labor Arbitration Reports, Fair Employment Practice Cases, Wage and Hour Cases, Occupational Safety and Health Cases,* and *Mine Safety and Health*

Cases. Contains citations, summarized headnotes (abstracts), indexing, and other locator information to federal and state court decisions and administrative agency rulings. It is available through: Dialog Information Services, 3460 Hillview Avenue, Palo Alto, CA 94304. (800) 227-1927.

Labor Law Journal, monthly, devoted to legislative, administrative, and judicial developments pertaining to legal problems in the labor field.
Editorial Address:
Editor, *Labor Law Journal*
Suite 1100
1301 Pennsylvania Ave., N.W.
Washington, D.C. 20004
Subscriptions:
Commerce Clearing House, Inc.
4025 W. Peterson Ave.
Chicago, IL 60646

Labor Law Reform Bill of 1978, a series of reforms designed to make it more difficult and more costly for employers to fight union organizing efforts. It was never enacted into law.

labor lobby, those elements of organized labor that seek to influence legislation affecting labor's interests.

labor-management relations, general term referring to the formal and informal dealings and agreements between employees or employee organizations and managers.

Labor-Management Relations Act of 1947 (LMRA), also called TAFT-HARTLEY ACT, federal statute that modified what the Congress thought was pro-union bias of the National Labor Relations (Wagner) Act of 1935. Essentially a series of amendments to the National Labor Relations Act, Taft-Hartley provided:
1. that "National Emergency Strikes" could be put off for an 80 day cooling-off period during which the president might make recommendations to Congress for legislation that might cope with the dispute;

2. a list of unfair labor practices by unions, which balanced the list of unfair labor practices by employers delineated in the Wagner Act;
3. that the "closed shop" was illegal (this provision allowed states to pass "right-to-work" laws);
4. that supervisory employees be excluded from coverage under the act;
5. that suits against unions for contract violations were allowable (judgments enforceable only against union assets);
6. that a party seeking to cancel an existing collective bargaining agreement is required to give 60 days' notice;
7. that employers have the right to seek a representation election if a union claimed recognition as a bargaining agent;
8. that the National Labor Relations Board was reorganized and enlarged from 3 to 5 members; and
9. that the Federal Mediation and Conciliation Service be created to mediate labor disputes.

The Taft-Hartley Act was passed over the veto of President Truman.

See also NATIONAL LABOR RELATIONS BOARD V. WOOSTER DIVISION OF BORG-WARNER CORP. and UNFAIR LABOR PRACTICES (UNIONS).

Labor-Management Reporting and Disclosure Act of 1959, also called LANDRUM-GRIFFIN ACT, federal statute enacted in response to findings of corruption in the management of some unions. The purpose of the act is to provide for

the reporting and disclosure of certain financial transactions and administrative practices of labor organizations and employers, to prevent abuses in the administration of trusteeships by labor organizations, to provide standards with respect to the election of officers of labor organizations and for other purposes.

Congress determined that certain basic rights should be assured to members of labor unions, and these are listed in Title I of the act as a Bill of Rights. Existing rights and remedies of union members under other federal or state laws, before any court or tribunal, or under the constitution and bylaws of their unions are not limited by the provisions of Title I. Executive Order 11491 made these rights applicable to members of unions representing employees of the executive branch of the federal government.

Titles II through VI of the act deal primarily with the following: reporting by unions, by union officers and employees, by employers, by labor relations consultants, and by surety companies; union trusteeships; union safeguards. The Secretary of Labor has varying administrative and enforcement responsibilities under these titles. In addition, Titles II through VI contain a number of criminal provisions which involve enforcement responsibilities of the U.S. Department of Justice. Title VII contains amendments to

---

BILL OF RIGHTS OF MEMBERS OF LABOR ORGANIZATIONS

Sec. 101. (a)(1) Equal Rights.—Every member of a labor organization shall have equal rights and privileges within such organization to nominate candidates, to vote in elections or referendums of the labor organization, to attend membership meetings and to participate in the deliberations and voting upon the business of such meetings, subject to reasonable rules and regulations in such organization's constitution and bylaws.

(2) *Freedom of Speech and Assembly.*—Every member of any labor organization shall have the right to meet and assemble freely with other members; and to express any views, arguments, or opinions; and to express at meetings of the labor organization his views, upon candidates in an election of the labor organization or upon any business properly before the meeting, subject to the organization's established and reasonable rules pertaining to the conduct of meetings: *Provided,* That nothing herein shall be construed to impair the right of a labor organization to adopt and enforce reasonable rules as to the responsibility of every member toward the organization as an institution and to his refraining from conduct that would interfere with its performance of its legal or contractual obligations.

(3) *Dues, Initiation Fees, and Assessments.*—Except in the case of a federation of national or international labor organizations, the rates of dues and initiation fees payable by members of any labor organization in effect on the date of enactment of this Act shall not be increased, and no general or special assessment shall be levied upon such members, except—

(A) in the case of a local organization, (i) by majority vote by secret ballot of the members in good standing voting at a general or special membership meeting, after reasonable notice of the intention to vote upon such question, or (ii) by majority vote of the members in good standing voting in a membership referendum conducted by secret ballot; or

(B) in the case of a labor organization, other than a local labor organization or a federation of national or international labor organizations, (i) by majority vote of the delegates voting at a regular convention, or at a special convention of such labor organization held upon not less than thirty days' written notice to the principal office of each local or constituent labor organization entitled to such notice, or (ii) by majority vote of the members in good standing of such labor organization voting in a membership referendum conducted by secret ballot, or (iii) by majority vote of the members of the executive board of similar governing body of such labor organization, pursuant to express authority contained in the constitution and bylaws of such labor organization: *Provided,* That such action on the part of the executive board or similar governing body shall be effective only until the next regular convention of such labor organization.

(4) *Protection of the Right to Sue.*—No labor organization shall limit the right of any member thereof to institute an action in any court, or in a proceding before any administrative agency, irrespective of whether or not the labor organization or its officers are named as defendants or respondents in such action or proceeding, or the right of any member of a labor organization to appear as a witness in any judicial, administrative, or legislative proceeding, or to petition any legislature or to communicate with any legislator: *Provided,* That any such member may be required to exhaust reasonable hearing procedures (but not to exceed a four-month lapse of time) within such organization, before instituting legal or administrative proceedings against such organizations or any officer thereof: *And provided further,* That no interested employer or employer association shall directly or indirectly finance, encourage, or participate in, except as a party, any such action, proceeding, appearance, or petition.

(5) *Safeguards Against Improper Disciplinary Action.*—No member of any labor organization may be fined, suspended, expelled, or otherwise disciplined except for nonpayment of dues by such organization or by any officer thereof unless such member has been (A) served with written specific charges; (B) given a reasonable time to prepare his defense; (C) afforded a full and fair hearing.

(b) Any provision of the constitution and bylaws of any labor organization which is inconsistent with the provisions of this section shall be of no force or effect.

SOURCE: *The Labor-Management Reporting and Disclosure (Landrum-Griffin) Act of 1959.*

the Labor-Management Relations Act of 1947. *See* Doris B. McLaughlin and Anita L. W. Schoomaker, *The Landrum-Griffin Act and Union Democracy* (Ann Arbor: University of Michigan Press, 1978); Janice R. Bellace and Alan D. Berkowitz, *The Landrum-Griffin Act: Twenty Years of Federal Protection of Union Members' Rights* (Philadelphia: Wharton School, University of Pennsylvania, 1979); John Lawler, "Wage Spillover: The Impact of Landrum-Griffin," *Industrial Relations* (Winter 1981).

See also the following entries:
AMERICAN FEDERATION OF MUSICIANS
  V. WITTSTEIN
CLEANSING PERIOD
LABOR-MANAGEMENT RELATIONS
  ACT OF 1947
TRUSTEESHIP

Labor-Management Services Administration (LMSA), agency of the U.S. Department of Labor that provides a framework within which workers and employers can resolve their differences together. It helps both labor and management through special studies of collective bargaining problems and research on labor-management policy development. Unions are required to make annual reports to it and comply with standards for union elections under the Labor-Management Reporting and Disclosure Act of 1959. Under the Employee Retirement Income Security Act of 1974, the agency administers reporting and disclosure, fiduciary, and minimum standards that protect the benefits and rights of pension and welfare plan participants and beneficiaries. LMSA also administers the veterans' reemployment rights provisions of the Veterans' Readjustment Assistance Act of 1974 and similar earlier laws.

LMSA
Department of Labor
200 Constitution Ave., N.W.
Washington, D.C. 20210
(202) 523-6231

labor market, according to Everett Johnson Burtt, Jr., in *Labor Markets, Unions, and Government Policies* (N.Y.: St. Martin's Press, 1963), a labor market consists of those forces of demand and supply that establish a single price and the quantity sold of a particular labor service. Most labor markets can be defined spatially as local in character: the supply of machinists in Springfield, Vermont, for example, does not influence the price of machinists in Cleveland, Ohio. National markets can, however, be said to exist for some occupations, such as transistor engineers, airplane pilots, or certain types of government administrators. The factors determining the geographical size of a labor market depend upon the concentration demand in certain centers and upon the degree of mobility of labor supplies.

See Paul D. Montagna, *Occupations and Society: Toward A Sociology of the Labor Market* (N.Y.: John Wiley & Sons, 1977); Ivar Berg, ed., *Sociological Perspectives on Labor Markets* (New York: Academic Press, 1981); R. Bednarzik and R. Tiler, "Area Labor Market Response to National Unemployment Patterns," *Monthly Labor Review* (January 1982); Denis Maillat, "Mobility Channels: An Instrument for Analyzing and Regulating the Local Labour Market," *International Labour Review* (May–June 1984).

See also the following entries:
EFFECTIVE LABOR MARKET
EXTERNAL LABOR MARKET
SPLIT LABOR MARKET

labor mobility, degree of ease with which workers can change jobs and occupations.

labor monopoly, dominance over the supply of labor by a union or group of unions.

labor movement, inclusive term for the progressive history of U.S. unionism. Sometimes it is used in a broader sense to encompass the fate of the "workers." For histories, *see* Leon Litwack, *The American Labor Movement* (Englewood Cliffs, N.J.: Prentice-Hall, 1962); Joel Seidman, "The Labor Movement Today: A Diagnosis," *Monthly Labor Review* (February 1965); Jack Barbash, "Labor Movement Theory and the Institutional Setting," *Monthly Labor Review* (September 1981); Maurice F. Neufeld, "The Persistence of Ideas in the American Labor Movement: The Heritage of the 1930s," *Industrial and Labor Relations Review* (January 1982).

labor organization, as defined by Section 2(5) of the National Labor Relations act (as amended), a labor organization
means any organization of any kind, or any agency or employee representation committee or plan, in which employees participate and which exists for the purpose, in whole or part, of dealing with employers concerning grievances, labor disputes, wages, rates of pay, hours of employment, or conditions of work.
For the names, sizes, addresses, phone numbers, etc., of all U.S. labor organizations, *see* Courtney D. Gifford, *Directory of U.S. Labor Organizations: 1984-85* edition (Washington, D.C.: Bureau of National Affairs, Inc., 1984.

labor organizer: *see* ORGANIZER.

labor piracy, attracting employees away from one organization and into another by offering better wages and other benefits.

labor pool, set of trained workers from which prospective employees are recruited.

labor racketeer, broad term that applies to a union leader who uses his/her office

as a base for unethical and illegal activities. For a history, *see* John Hutchinson, *The Imperfect Union: A History of Corruption in American Trade Unions* (N.Y.: E. P. Dutton & Co., 1972).

See also ANTI-RACKETEERING ACT OF 1934 and UNFAIR LABOR PRACTICES (UNIONS).

labor rate variance, the difference between direct labor paid at the standard rate and at the actual rate in a standard cost system.

labor relations, totality of the interactions between an organization's management and organized labor. For texts, *see* Arthur A. Sloane and Fred Witney, *Labor Relations,* 4th ed. (Englewood Cliffs, N.J.: Prentice-Hall, 1981); Edward E. Herman and Alfred Kuhn, *Collective Bargaining and Labor Relations* (Englewood Cliffs, N.J.: Prentice-Hall, 1981); Gordon F. Bloom and Herbert R. Northrup, *Economics of Labor Relations,* 9th ed. (Homewood, Ill.: Richard D. Irwin, 1981); John A. Fossum, *Labor Relations: Development, Structure, Process* (Dallas: Business Publications, 1982); David H. Rosenbloom and Jay M. Shafritz, *Essentials of Labor Relations* (Reston, VA: Reston/Prentice-Hall, 1985).

Labor Research Association, conducts research and issues publications on economic and political issues of interest to unions.
Labor Research Association

THE LABOR RELATIONS LEGAL SYSTEM

Sector	Legal Base	Administrative Agency
Private industry	National Labor Relations Act, as amended	National Labor Relations Board
Railroads and airlines	Railway Labor Act, as amended	National Mediation Board
Postal Service	Postal Reorganization Act of 1970	National Labor Relations Board
Federal government	Civil Service Reform Act of 1978	Federal Labor Relations Authority
State and local government	Public employee relations acts	Public employment relations boards

80 E. 11th Street
New York, NY 10003
(212) 473-1042

labor reserve, general term that refers to potential members of the workforce. Historically the concept has been applied to the least skilled and the least able. For a modern definition, *see* Christopher G. Gellner, "Enlarging the Concept of a Labor Reserve," *Monthly Labor Review* (April 1975).

labor-saving equipment, any device that reduces an organization's need for human labor.

labor slowdown: *see* SLOWDOWN.

labor spy: *see* COMPANY SPY.

Labor Statistics, Bureau of: *see* BUREAU OF LABOR STATISTICS.

labor studies, formal academic degree concentrations or certificate programs concerned with the various aspects of labor relations. *See* Lois S. Gray, "Academic Degrees for Labor Studies—A New Goal for Unions," *Monthly Labor Review* (1977).

Labor Studies Journal, journal published three time a year by the University and College Labor Education Association, which offers articles and reviews on all aspects of labor studies.
Labor Studies Journal
Subscription Address:
Transaction Periodicals Consortium
Rutgers University
Box L
New Brunswick, NJ 08903
Editorial Address:
George Meany Center for Labor Studies
10,000 New Hampshire Ave.
Silver Springs, MD 20903

labor surplus area, an area of high unemployment for which the federal government sets aside procurement contracts for competition among firms that agree to perform a substantial portion of the production of the contract in the labor surplus area.

labor theory of value, notion that the value of a product is dependent or determined by the amount (or value) of the labor needed to produce it. Karl Marx used this concept (developed earlier by Adam Smith and David Ricardo) to denounce capitalists who exploited the working class by selling products at higher prices than the cost of the labor that went into them.

labor time ticket, a form or a computer record used to distribute the total hours worked to specific job orders or to types of production operations. In plants where workers are paid on a straight piece rate basis or salary plus production bonus, labor time tickets also include information on quantities produced for payroll purposes.

Laffer curve, a purported relationship between tax rates and government revenues stated by economist Arthur B. Laffer. According to Laffer, higher taxes reduce government revenue because high tax rates discourage taxable activity. Following this logic, beyond a certain tax rate a government can raise its total revenues by cutting taxes. This should stimulate new taxable activity, and the revenue from this should more than offset the loss from lower tax rates.

Laidlaw-Fleetwood doctrine, ruling of the Supreme Court in the case of *NLRB v. Fleetwood Trailer Company,* 389 U.S. 375 (1967) that if a striker has been replaced and no suitable employment is available, the status of the striker as an employee continues until he or she has obtained "other regular and substantially equivalent employment." Until then, the striker remains on a preferred hiring list, unless there is a "legitimate and substantial business justification" for not hiring him or her at all.

laissez-faire, "hands off" style of leadership that emphasizes loose supervision.

Lake, Mother: *see* BARRY, LEONORA.

Union officials' attitudes about the labor movement

Question	Survey date	Strongly agree	Agree	Neither agree nor disagree	Disagree	Strongly disagree	Mean[1]
Members do not understand what union does	1983	29.4	33.3	10.3	23.1	3.8	[2]2.38
	1963	10.7	42.9	9.5	26.2	10.7	[2]2.83
Need for formal opposition within unions	1983	5.1	22.8	32.9	20.3	19.0	3.25
	1963	8.3	21.4	16.7	39.3	14.3	3.30
Lack of vitality in labor movement..........	1983	29.1	44.3	8.9	12.7	5.1	2.20
	1963	27.4	36.9	6.0	23.8	6.0	2.40
Need for government involvement in internal union affairs	1983	7.6	32.9	10.1	27.8	21.6	3.23
	1963	10.7	37.6	3.6	24.7	23.5	3.13
Leader-held values of self-sacrifice, idealism, and dedication	1983	10.1	38.0	15.2	24.1	12.7	2.91
	1963	9.5	33.3	13.1	33.3	10.7	2.98
Less upward mobility in union hierarchy today.......	1983	3.8	19.2	16.7	47.4	12.8	[2]3.45
	1963	9.4	30.6	10.6	36.5	13.0	[2]3.16
More stress on organizing white-collar workers	1983	10.1	25.3	43.0	12.7	8.9	2.85
	1963	25.9	27.1	13.0	31.8	2.4	2.58
Future of labor movement is secure	1983	6.3	20.3	17.7	36.7	19.0	3.42
	1963	2.4	18.3	12.2	48.8	18.3	3.63
Internal problems are weakening the ability of labor union growth .	1983	7.6	20.3	12.7	34.2	25.3	3.49
	1963	9.8	17.1	8.5	42.7	22.0	3.50
Most important force behind social legislation......	1983	26.9	42.3	16.7	9.0	5.1	[2]2.23
	1963	38.6	45.8	6.0	9.6	0.0	[2]1.87

							Mean[1]
Federation should have more authority over organizing	1983	2.6	12.7	25.3	38.0	21.5	[2]3.63
	1963	8.6	25.9	13.6	34.6	17.3	[2]3.26
Labor's collective bargaining power is weaker today	1983	11.4	59.5	12.7	12.7	3.8	[2]2.38
	1963	12.2	39.0	11.0	32.9	4.9	[2]2.79
Too much political involvement, put more stress on collective bargaining	1983	8.9	7.6	10.1	34.2	39.2	3.87
	1963	6.0	7.2	3.6	37.3	45.8	4.10
Structure not adequate to meet challenge of robotics, automation	1983	15.2	26.6	12.7	36.7	8.9	[2]2.97
	1963	16.9	37.3	19.3	24.1	2.4	[2]2.58
Disregard economic situation of company in bargaining	1983	2.6	10.3	19.2	50.0	18.0	[2]3.71
	1963	3.7	25.6	13.4	47.6	9.8	[2]3.34
Not enough influence on foreign policy	1983	8.9	39.2	30.4	17.7	3.8	2.68
	1963	10.8	51.8	8.4	20.5	8.4	2.64
Should borrow more from European labor unions	1983	7.6	17.7	38.0	26.6	10.1	3.14
	1963	4.8	19.3	22.9	38.6	14.5	3.39
Closer ties with nonunion reform groups	1983	5.1	40.1	27.8	17.7	8.9	2.85
	1963	6.1	42.7	20.7	23.2	7.3	2.83
Unions doing all they can to bring blacks into the ranks	1983	13.9	32.9	27.8	17.7	7.6	2.72
	1963	12.9	34.1	11.8	28.2	13.0	2.94
Economic conditions weakening ability to get better wages and benefits	1983	32.9	60.8	0.0	5.1	1.3	[2]1.81
	1963	10.7	54.8	10.7	19.0	4.8	[2]2.52

[1]Attitudes were scaled from 1 to 5, with "strongly agree" equaling 1 and "strongly disagree," 5. The mean is the average value for responses to the question.

[2]Mean significantly different at .05 level or below.

Source: Brian Heshizer and Harry Graham, "Are Unions Facing a Crisis? Labor Officials are Divided," *Monthly Labor Review* (August 1984).

lame duck, in U.S. politics, any office-holder who is serving out the remainder of a fixed term after declining to run, or being defeated, for reelection. Since he/she will soon be leaving, his/her authority is considered impaired or "lame." The term is used in an organizational sense to refer to anyone whose leaving has been announced whether for retirement, promotion, transfer, etc.

Landrum-Griffin Act: see LABOR-MANAGEMENT REPORTING AND DISCLOSURE ACT OF 1959.

last offer arbitration: see FINAL OFFER ARBITRATION.

latent learning: see INCIDENTAL LEARNING.

lateral entry, appointment of an individual from outside of the organization to a position above the bottom level of a generally recognized career ladder.

lateral transfer: see TRANSFER.

Lauf v. E. G. Shinner and Company, 303 U.S. 323 (1938), U.S. Supreme Court case, which held that organizational picketing was a "labor dispute" within the meaning of the Norris-LaGuardia Act of 1932. This meant the employer could not seek an injunction in a federal court to stop the picketing.

law: see ACT, LABOR LAW.

Lawler, Edward E., III (1938-   ), psychologist who has written widely in the areas of organizational behavior and a leading authority on the relationship between pay and organizational effectiveness. Major works include: *Managerial Attitudes and Performance,* with L. W. Porter (Homewood, Illinois: Richard D. Irwin, 1968); *Managerial Behavior, Performance and Effectiveness,* with J. P. Campbell, M. D. Dunnette, and K. E. Weick, Jr. (N.Y.: McGraw-Hill, 1970); *Pay and Organizational Effectiveness: A Psychological View* (N.Y.: McGraw-Hill, 1971); *Motivation in Work Organizations* (Monterey, California: Brooks/Cole Publishing Company, 1973); *Behavior in Organizations,* with L. W. Porter and J. R. Hackman (N.Y.: McGraw-Hill, 1975).

Lawlor v. Loewe, also called DANBURY HATTERS' CASE, 235 U.S. 522 (1908), U.S. Supreme Court case, which held that the hatter's union which was seeking to organize a factory in Danbury, Connecticut, was in violation of the Sherman Anti-Trust Act of 1890 when it successfully organized a boycott against the company. The court ruled against the union because its boycott had the assistance of other affiliates of the American Federation of Labor and the Sherman Act prohibited "any combination whatever to secure action which essentially obstructs the free flow of commerce between the states, or restricts in that regard, the liberty of a trader to engage in business." The uproar over this decision led to the passage of the Clayton Act of 1914, which disallowed the application of the Sherman Act to combinations of labor.

law of demand, demand for an item falls as its price rises. There are many exceptions to the "law." The *first law of demand* holds that the rate of individual demand will not increase with a rise in prices. The *second law of demand* holds that the *substitution effect* (the purchase of less expensive products) is greater the longer that prices remain higher than they were before.

law of effect, fundamental concept in learning theory that holds that, other things being equal, an animal will learn those habits leading to satisfaction and will not learn (or learn only slowly) those habits causing annoyance. It was first formulated by Edward L. Thorndike, in *Education: A First Book* (N.Y.: MacMillan, 1920), as follows:

the greater the satisfyingness of the state of affairs which accompanies or follows a given response to a certain situation, the more likely that response is to be made to that situation in the future. Conversely, the greater the discomfort or annoyingness of the state of affairs which comes with or after a response to a situation, the more likely that response is not to be made to that situation in the future.

law of the situation, Mary Parker Follett's notion, in Henry C. Metcalf and Lyndall Urwick, eds., *Dynamic Administration, The Collected Papers of Mary Parker Follett* (N.Y.: Harper & Bros., 1940), that one person should not give orders to another person, but both should agree to take their orders from the situation. If orders are simply part of the situation, the question of someone giving and someone receiving does not come up.

law of triviality, C. Northcote Parkinson's discovery that "the time spent on any item of the agenda will be in inverse proportion to the sum invoked." Parkinson attempted to head off his critics by asserting

the statement that this law has never been investigated is not entirely accurate. Some work has actually been done in this field, but the investigators pursued a line of inquiry that led them nowhere. They assumed that the greatest significance should attach to the order in which items of the agenda are taken. They assumed, further, that most of the available time will be spent on items one to seven and that the latter items will be allowed automatically to pass. The result is well known. . . . We realize now that position on the agenda is a minor consideration.

For more, *see* C. Northcote Parkinson, *Parkinson's Law and other Studies in Administration* (Boston: Houghton Mifflin Co., 1957). For a methodological analysis, *see* Ross Curnow, "An Empirical Examination of the Parkinsonian Law of Triviality," *Public Personnel Review* (January 1971).

layoff, temporary or indefinite separation from employment, without prejudice or loss of seniority, resulting from slack work, a shortage of materials, decline in product demand, or other factors over which the worker has no control. The Bureau of Labor Statistics compiles monthly layoff rates

by industry. For an account of how a General Electric division sought to do it "nicely," *see* Ken Leinweber, "Showing Them the Door," *Personnel* (July–August 1976). *Also see* Robert W. Bednarzik, "Layoffs and Permanent Job Losses: Workers' Traits, Patterns," *Monthly Labor Review* (September 1983); R. Wayne Mondy and Shane R. Preameaux, "Management/Union Perceptions of Recent Layoffs," *Personnel Administrator* (November 1984).

The "last hired-first fired" policy of layoffs has come under increasing criticism because of the disparate impact that it has had upon minorities. For analyses of layoffs dealing with this problem, *see* William R. Walter and Anthony J. Obadal, "Layoffs: The Judicial View," *Personnel Administrator* (May 1975); James Ledvinka, "EEO, Seniority, and Layoffs," *Personnel* (January–February 1976); Robert N. Roberts, " 'Last-Hired, First-Fired' and Public Employee Layoffs: The Equal Employment Opportunity Dilemma," *Review of Public Personnel Administration* (Fall 1981).

See also the following entries:
DISCIPLINARY LAYOFF
RECALL
RE-EMPLOYMENT LIST
RETENTION STANDING

leading indicators, statistics that generally precede a change in a situation. For example, an increase in economic activity is typically preceded by a rise in the prices of stocks. Each month the Bureau of Economic Analysis of the Department of Commerce publishes data on hundreds of economic indicators in its *Business Conditions Digest*. Several dozen of these are classified as "leading." The Bureau's composite index of 12 leading indicators is a popular means of assessing the general state of the economy.

leadership, exercise of authority, whether formal or informal, in directing and coordinating the work of others. The literature on the concept of leadership is immense. The best one volume summary is Ralph M. Stogdill, *Handbook of Leadership: A*

Survey of Theory and Research (N.Y.: The Free Press, revised edition, 1981). The best quote on the problems of leadership comes from Harry S. Truman, who said while discoursing on his job as president of the United States: "I sit here all day trying to persuade people to do the things they ought to have sense enough to do without my persuading them." *Also see* Karen S. Koziara and others, "Becoming a Union Leader: The Path to Local Office," *Monthly Labor Review* (February 1982); John B. Miner, "The Uncertain Future of the Leadership Concept: Revisions and Clarifications," *The Journal of Applied Behavioral Science,* Vol. 18, No. 3 (1982).

See also the following entries:
CHARISMATIC LEADERSHIP
CONTINGENCY MODEL OF LEADERSHIP
   EFFECTIVENESS
FULL RESPONSIBILITY
FUNCTIONAL LEADERSHIP
LIFE CYCLE THEORY OF LEADERSHIP
PATH-GOAL THEORY OF LEADERSHIP

leadership effectiveness, contingency model of: *see* CONTINGENCY MODEL OF LEADERSHIP EFFECTIVENESS.

leadership style, patterns of a leader's interactions with his/her subordinates.

learning, generally, any behavior change occurring because of interaction with the environment, *See* Lee Hess and Len Sperry, "The Psychology of the Trainee as Learner," *Personnel Journal* (September 1973).

See also INCIDENTAL LEARNING and PROGRAMMED LEARNING.

learning curve, in industry the concept holds that when workers repeatedly perform a task, the amount of labor required per unit of output decreases according to a constant pattern. Generally speaking, with traditional, mass-production processes, each time output doubles, the new average of effort per unit should decline by a certain percentage, and so on for each successive doubling of output. Of course, as production processes become more dependent upon machines, the learning curve becomes less and less significant. *See* Raymond B. Jordan, *How To Use The Learning Curve* (Boston: Materials Management Institute, 1965). For a critique of its limitations, *see* William J. Abernathy and Kenneth Wayne, "Limits of the Learning Curve," *Harvard Business Review* (September-October 1974).

The learning curve as a concept in training describes a learning process in which increases of performance are large at the beginning but become smaller with continued practice. Learning of any new thing eventually levels off as mastery is attained, at which point the curve becomes horizontal. For further details, *see* Bernard M. Bass and James A. Vaughn, *Training in Industry: The Management of Learning* (Belmont, Calif.: Wadsworth Publishing Co., 1966). *See also* Winfred B. Hirschmann, "Profit from the Learning Curve," *Harvard Business Review* (January-February 1964).

learning plateau, that flat part of a learning curve that indicates there has been little or no additional learning.

leave, birth: *see* BIRTH LEAVE.

leave of absence: *see* FURLOUGH and LEAVE WITHOUT PAY.

leave without pay, a temporary nonpay status and short-term absence from duty, granted upon the employee's request. The permissive nature of leave without pay distinguishes it from absence without leave. A *leave of absence* is the same as leave without pay except for duration. A leave of absence implies a more substantial amount of time away from one's position.

L. Ed., abbreviation for *Lawyer's Edition* of the U.S. Supreme Court Reports.

Leffingwell, William Henry (1876-1934), the first person to apply the principles of scientific management to office management. His pioneering book, *Scientific Office Management* (Chicago: A. W. Shaw Co., 1917), is the forerunner of all subsequent studies of office work.

legitimacy, characteristic of a social institution such as a government or a family whereby it has both a legal and a perceived right to make binding decisions for its members. Legitimacy is granted to an institution by its public. *See* Seymour Martin Lipset, "Some Social Requisites of Democracy: Economic Development and Political Legitimacy," *American Political Science Review* (March 1959); Edgar H. Schein and J. Steven Ott, "The Legitimacy of Organizational Influence," *American Journal of Sociology* (May 1962); John Dowling and Jeffrey Pfeffer, "Organizational Legitimacy: Social Values and Organizational Behavior," *Pacific Sociological Review* (January 1975); Peter L. Berger, "New Attack on the Legitimacy of Business," *Harvard Business Review* (September–October 1981).

Leontief, Wassily (1906–), Nobel Prize winning developer of input-output analysis which has played an increasingly important role in econometric forecasting. *See:* Wassily Leontief, *Input-Output Economics* (New York: Oxford University Press, 1966).
Also see INPUT-OUTPUT TABLE.

leptokurtic, frequency distribution or curve that is more peaked, as opposed to flat-topped, than a normal curve.

lese majesty, in French LÈSE MAJESTÉ, literally injured majesty, originally an offense against one's sovereign or ruler. Now it quite properly refers to an insolent or slighting behavior towards one's bureaucratic superiors.

Letter Carriers decision: *see* UNITED STATES CIVIL SERVICE COMMISSION V. NATIONAL ASSOCIATION OF LETTER CARRIERS.

Letter Carriers v. Austin: *see* OLD DOMINION BRANCH NO. 496, NATIONAL ASSOCIATION OF LETTER CARRIERS V. AUSTIN.

level annual premium funding method, after the pension costs for a new employee are actuarially determined, pension contributions or premiums are paid into a fund (or to an insurance company) in equal installments during the employee's remaining working life so that upon retirement the pension benefit is fully funded.

Levinson, Harry (1922–), psychologist and a leading authority on organizational mental health and work motivation. Major works include: *Men, Management and Mental Health,* with C. R. Price, H. J. Munden & C. M. Solley (Cambridge, Mass.: Harvard University Press, 1962); *Emotional Health in the World of Work* (N.Y.: Harper & Row, 1964); *Organizational Diagnosis* (Cambridge, Mass.: Harvard University Press, 1972); *The Exceptional Executive: A Psychological Conception* (Cambridge, Mass.: Harvard University Press, 1968); *Executive Stress* (N.Y.: Harper & Row, 1970); *The Great Jackass Fallacy* (Boston: Harvard Graduate School of Business Administration, 1973).

Lewin, Kurt (1890–1947), popularly noted for his assertion that "there is nothing so practical as a good theory," was the most influential experimental psychologist of the twentieth century. His research originated the modern concepts of group dynamics, action research, field theory, and sensitivity training. Major works include: *Principles of Topological Psychology* (N.Y.: McGraw-Hill, 1936); *Resolving Social Conflicts: Selected Papers on Group Dynamics* (N.Y.: Harper & Row, 1948); *Field Theory In Social Science. Selected Theoretical Papers,* edited by Dorwin Cartwright (London: Tavistock, 1963). For a biography, *see* Alfred J. Marrow, *The Practical Theorist: The Life and Work of Kurt Lewin* (N.Y.: Basic Books, 1969).

Lewis, John L. (1880–1969), president of the United Mine Workers of America from 1920 to 1960, a founder and first president of the Congress of Industrial Organizations (CIO), and probably the most controversial, most hated, and most revered labor leader of his time. For biographies, *see* Saul Alinsky, *John L. Lewis: An Unauthorized Biography* (N.Y.: G. P.

Putnam's Sons, 1949); Melvyn Dubofsky and Warren Van Tine, *John L. Lewis: A Biography* (N.Y.: Quadrangle, 1977).

Lewis, Joseph Slater (1852-1901), British industrialist whose book, *The Commercial Organization of Factories* (London and New York: Spon Books, 1896) was one of the first comprehensive analyses of industrial administration.

license, a permission granted to an individual or organization by competent authority, usually public, to engage in a practice, occupation or activity otherwise unlawful. Licensure is the process by which the license is granted. Since a license is needed to begin lawful practice, it is usually granted on the basis of examination and/or proof of education rather than measures of performance. License when given is usually permanent but may be conditioned on annual payment of a fee, proof of continuing education, or proof of competence. Common grounds for revocation of a license include incompetence, commission of a crime (whether or not related to the licensed practice) or moral turpitude.

See also OCCUPATIONAL LICENSING.

lie detector, also called POLYGRAPH, also VOICE STRESS ANALYZER, and PSYCHOLOGICAL STRESS ANALYZER, an instrument for recording physiological phenomena such as blood pressure, pulse rate, and the respiration rate of individuals as they answer questions put to them by an operator. The technique is based on the assumption that when an individual experiences apprehension, fear, or emotional excitement, his/her respiration rate, blood pressure, etc., will sharply increase. These physiological data are then interpreted by an operator who makes judgments on whether or not a subject is lying. Only one thing is certain about polygraph tests; they are not 100 percent accurate. Lie detectors have been used in police investigations since the 1920s, and have been increasingly used for employee screening since World War II. However the authority of employers to use polygraph tests in per-

sonnel investigations has been challenged. Many state and local legislative actions have placed legal limitations on the public and private employers' use of lie detectors. Thirteen states prohibit the use of polygraphs as a condition of employment or continued employment. In addition, labor arbitrators often refuse to admit test results as evidence of "just cause" for discharge and have upheld a worker's right to refuse to take such a test. According to David T. Lykken, in "Psychology and The Lie Detector Industry," *American Psychologist* (October 1974), "the general use of lie detectors in employee screening cannot be justified, however, and psychologists have a professional responsibility to oppose this growing practice." For other analyses, *see* Burke M. Smith, "The Polygraph," *Scientific American* (January 1967); Mary Ann Coghill, *The Lie Detector In Employment* (Ithaca, N.Y.: New York State School of Industrial and Labor Relations, Cornell University, rev. ed., 1973); John A. Beit and Peter B. Holden, "Polygraph Usage Among Major U.S. Corporations," *Personnel Journal* (February 1978); David J. Carr, "Employer Use of the 'Lie Detector:' The Arbitration Experience," *Labor Law Journal* (November 1984).

The *voice stress analyzer* or *psychological stress analyzer* is a lie detector that can be used without the subject knowing that he/she is being tested. By simply analyzing the stress in the subject's voice it purports to tell whether or not the truth is being told. As such devices have only been available since the mid 1970s, their use should still be considered experimental.

life cycle theory of leadership, theory put forth by Paul Hersey and Kenneth R. Blanchard, which suggests that the appropriate leadership style for a particular situation should be primarily dependent upon the task maturity level of the follower(s). Maturity is defined as a function of task relevant education and experience, achievement motivation, and willingness and ability to accept responsibility. Leadership is seen as a combination of two types of behavior: "Task Behavior" (Directive), ranging from low to high, and "Relationships Behavior" (Supportive), ranging from low to high. If a follower is assessed to be extremely "immature," the theory suggests that high task-low relationships is the appropriate leadership style. As the follower matures the theory suggests that the leader's behavior should move from high task-low relationships (Quadrant I), to high task-high relationships (Quadrant II), to high relationship-low task (Quadrant III), to low task-low relationships (Quadrant IV).

Also see Ichak Adizes, "Organizational Passages: Diagnosing and Treating Lifecycle Problems of Organizations," *Organizational Dynamics* (Summer 1979).

life insurance, insurance that provides for the payment of a specific amount to a designated beneficiary in the event of the death of the insured. *See* Viviana A. Rotman Zelizer, *Morals and Markets: The Development of Life Insurance in the United States* (New York: Columbia University Press, 1979); Allan P. Blostin, "Is Employer-Paid Life Insurance Declining Relative to Other Benefits?" *Monthly Labor Review* (September 1981).

See also the following entries:
ACCIDENTAL DEATH BENEFIT
GROUP LIFE INSURANCE
INSURANCE
SPLIT-DOLLAR LIFE INSURANCE
TERM LIFE INSURANCE
VARIABLE LIFE INSURANCE

Likert, Rensis (1903-1981), one of the pioneers of organizational survey research and director of the Institute of Social Research at the University of Michigan from 1948 to 1970. He is perhaps best known for his linking-pin theory and his concepts of Systems 1, 2, 3, and 4. Major works include: *New Patterns of Management* (N.Y.: McGraw-Hill, 1961); *The Human Organization: Its Management and Value* (N.Y.: McGraw-Hill, 1967); *New Ways of Managing Conflict,* with Jane Gibson Likert (N.Y.: McGraw-Hill, 1976).

Likert Scale, also called LIKERT-TYPE SCALE, one of the most widely used scales in social research. Named after Rensis Likert, who first presented it in "A Technique for the Measurement of Attitudes," *Archives of Psychology* (No. 140, 1932), the scale presents a subject with a statement to which the subject expresses his/her reaction or opinion by selecting one of five (or more) possible responses arranged at equidistant intervals.

Typical Questions on a Likert Scale
1. The sick-leave policies of this company are not liberal enough.
   (a) strongly agree
   (b) agree
   (c) no opinion
   (d) disagree
   (e) strongly disagree
2. My supervisor is a good leader.
   (a) strongly agree
   (b) agree
   (c) uncertain
   (d) disagree
   (e) strongly disagree

Lincoln Incentive Plan, combination profit sharing and piecework incentive system developed in 1934 by J. F. Lincoln of the Lincoln Electric Company of Cleveland. The plan incorporates many aspects of industrial democracy and is famous for the fact that employees have received bonuses of up to 150 percent of their base pay.

Lincoln Mills **case:** *see* TEXTILE WORKERS V. LINCOLN MILLS.

Lindblom, Charles E. (1917-   ), leading proponent of the incremental approach to policy/decisionmaking. In his most famous work, "The Science of Muddling Through," *Public Administration Review* (Spring 1959), Lindblom took a hard look at the rational models of decisional processes. He rejected the notion that most decisions are made by rational—total information—processes. Instead he saw such decisions—indeed, the whole policymaking process—dependent upon small incremental decisions that tended to be made in response to short-term considerations. Lindblom's thesis essentially held that decisionmaking was controlled infinitely more by events and circumstances than by the will of those in policymaking positions.

line of authority: *see* SCALAR CHAIN.

line organization, those segments of a larger organization that perform the major functions of the organization and have the most direct responsibilities for achieving organizational goals.

line personnel, those who directly carry out the essential tasks of an organization. Production, sales, and finance departments are usually considered line or operating units. *See* John T. Thompson, "Helping Line Managers to be Change Agents," *Training and Development Journal* (April 1981).

line-staff conflict, according to Charles Coleman and Joseph Rich, "Line, Staff and the Systems Perspective," *Human Resources Management* (Fall 1973),

one of the pillars of traditional organization theory is the concept that line officers possess command authority in core areas of the organization and that staff officers provide them with specialized assistance. However, empirical studies have shown time and again that the traditional line-staff idea leads to large amounts of conflict.

See Melville Dalton, "Conflict Between Staff and Line Managerial Officers," *American Sociological Review* (June 1950); Robert T. Golembiewski, *Organizing Men and Power: Patterns of Behavior and Line-Staff Models* (Chicago: Rand McNally, 1967); Philip J. Browne and Robert T. Golembiewski, "The Line-Staff Concept Revisited: An Empirical Study of Organizational Images," *Academy of Management Journal* (September 1974); Vivian Nossiter, "A New Approach Toward Resolving the Line and Staff Dilemma," *Academy of Management Review* (January 1979).

linking pin, concept developed by Rensis Likert in his *New Patterns of Management* (New York: McGraw-Hill, 1961). A "linking pin" is anyone who belongs to two groups within the same organization, usually as a superior in one and as a subordinate in the other. *See* George Graen *et al.,* "Effects of Linking-Pin Quality on the Quality of Working Life of Lower Partici-

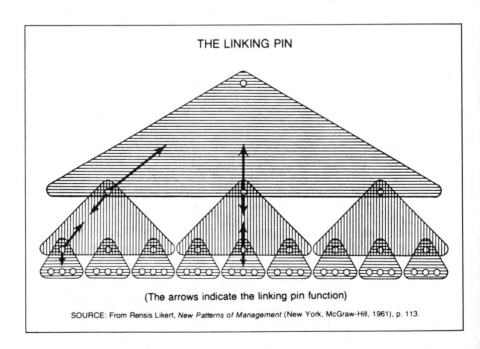

THE LINKING PIN

(The arrows indicate the linking pin function)

SOURCE: From Rensis Likert, *New Patterns of Management* (New York, McGraw-Hill, 1961), p. 113.

pants," *Administrative Science Quarterly* (September 1977).

Linn v. United Plant Guard Workers, 383 U.S. 53 (1966), U.S. Supreme Court case, which held that the National Labor Relations Act does not bar libel actions brought by either party to a labor dispute who alleges the circulation of false and defamatory statements during a union organizing campaign as long as the complainant pleads and proves that the statements were made with malice and injured him/her.

listening, one of the oldest and most useful of personnel management techniques. According to John A. Wilson, *The Culture of Ancient Egypt* (Chicago: University of Chicago Press, 1951), the ancient Egyptians advised their leaders to

be calm as thou listenest to what the petitioner has to say. Do not rebuff him before he has swept out his body or before he has said that for which he came. . . . It is not [necessary] that everything about which he has petitioned should come to pass, [for] a good hearing is soothing to the heart.

Some things haven't changed much in 4000 years! For modern pep talks on how to be a good listener, *see* Thomas G. Banville, *How to Listen—How to be Heard* (Chicago: Nelson-Hall, 1978); A. W. Clausen, "Listening and Responding to Employees' Concerns," *Harvard Business Review* (January-February 1980); Robert L. Montgomery, *Listening Made Easy: How to Improve Listening on the Job, at Home and in the Community* (New York, AMACOM, 1981).

list of eligibles: *see* ELIGIBLE LIST.

Little, Frank H. (1879-1917), one of the most radical leaders of the Industrial Workers of the World (IWW). He became a major IWW martyr when, after agitating against U.S. involvement in World War I and being branded a traitor by the press, he was murdered in Montana by six men who were never identified. *See* Arnon Gutfeld, "The Murder of Frank Little," *Labor History* (Spring 1969).

Little Steel: *see* BIG STEEL.

living wage, also STARVATION WAGES, although one might suspect that *starvation wages* would be necessarily of limited duration, many a union leader will assert that the workers have been putting up with them far too long. A *living wage,* in contrast, wards off starvation and even provides for some of the comforts of life. However, the ultimate goal of the union must be a "decent living wage," which affords a standard of luxury that can hardly be imagined by those on starvation wages.

Lloyd-LaFollette Act of 1912, federal statute that guarantees civilian employees of the federal government the right to petition Congress, either individually or through their organizations. The act was the only statutory basis for the organization of federal employees until the Civil Service Reform Act of 1978. In addition, it provided the first statutory procedural safeguards for federal employees facing removal. It provides that "no person in the classified civil service of the United States shall be removed or suspended without pay therefrom except for such cause as will promote the efficiency of such service and for reasons given in writing."

LMRA: *see* LABOR-MANAGEMENT RELATIONS ACT OF 1947.

LMSA: *see* LABOR-MANAGEMENT SERVICES ADMINISTRATION.

loading, job/horizontal/vertical: *see* JOB LOADING.

lobster shift: *see* GRAVEYARD SHIFT.

local: *see* COSMOPOLITAN-LOCAL CONSTRUCT.

local independent union, local union not affiliated with a national or international union.

local industrial union, local union consisting of workers in a variety of occupations in an industry.

Local 174, Teamsters* v. *Lucas Flour Co., 369 U.S. 95 (1962), U.S. Supreme Court case, which held that a strike to settle a dispute which a collective bargaining agreement provides shall be settled by compulsory arbitration is a violation of the agreement.

local union, regional organization of union members who are part of a national or international union. A local union is chartered by the national or international union with which it is affiliated.

The local union remains the basic organizational unit for the governance of labor unions. The local performs so many functions that it is in some ways an organizational microcosm of the labor movement as a whole. Locals in industrial unions are generally organized on a plant basis, while craft locals tend to draw their members from a specific geographical area. In either case, the local is a highly political organization because it is the level of the union with which the members identify most. It is most salient to them, and their voices carry more weight within it than at any other level of the union structure. The election of officers at the local level is often hotly contested, and the turn-

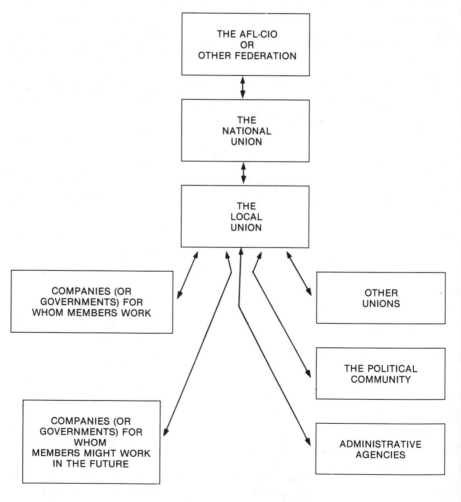

THE LOCAL UNION'S RELATIONSHIPS

over of leaders at this level is generally greater than at the regional or international levels.

The local is critically important to the member because it is the unit that engages in contract enforcement. It also engages in collective bargaining, though much of this function now rests with the national or international union. Locals also enforce the international union's rules and regulations pertaining to the conduct of members and their obligations. The locals also administer and implement the general policies and programs of the international unions. They also provide a variety of services to their members including opportunities for further education, and channels for involvement in politics and community affairs.

The typical local has a number of officers and some have paid staff. The officers are often designated as president, secretary-treasurer, and members of an executive board. Locals are also likely to have a number of committees to carry out specific functions. Some locals, especially the larger ones, employ a business agent. This functionary is responsible for the administration of union affairs, including such activities as record keeping, maintaining files, membership lists, overseeing the operation of hiring halls in the construction industry, arranging for meetings and participating in the setting of their agendas, and engaging in many facets of the collective bargaining process itself. The influence of business agents varies widely. Much depends on the size of the local, the personality of the business agent and the desires of the elected leaders and members. Some locals have come to rely very heavily on their business agents, who more or less "run" the local on a day to day basis. Business agents in larger locals may also have a considerable number of staff at their disposal. Many elected union officials at the local level continue to hold their regular jobs, depending again, largely on the size of the local.

See Robert W. Miller, Frederick A. Zeller and Glenn W. Miller, *The Practice of Local Union Leadership* (Columbus, Ohio: Ohio State University Press, 1965); Leonard R. Sayles and George Strauss, *The Local Union* (New York: Harcourt, Brace & World, 1967).

Lochner v. New York, 198 U.S. 45 (1905), U.S. Supreme Court case, which declared unconstitutional a New York law which sought to regulate the hours of employment.

lockout, employer's version of a strike—the closing of a business in order to pressure the employees and/or the union to accept the employer's offered terms of employment. This early weapon against the union movement lost much of its effect when locked-out employees became eligible for unemployment compensation. Almost all union contracts with a no-strike clause contain a similar ban against lockouts. For an analysis, *see* Willard A. Lewis, "The 'Lockout as Corollary of Strike' Controversy Reexamined," *Labor Law Journal* (November 1972).

See also AMERICAN SHIPBUILDING CO. V. NATIONAL LABOR RELATIONS BOARD and TEXTILE WORKERS V. DARLINGTON MANUFACTURING COMPANY.

lodge, organizational unit of some labor unions, equivalent to a local union.

Lodge 76, International Association of Machinists v. Wisconsin Employment Relations Commission, 427 U.S. 132 (1976), U.S. Supreme Court case, which held that a state cannot interfere with a union's power to collectively refuse overtime during contract negotiations or to engage in other partial strike activities unregulated by federal labor laws.

longevity pay, also called LONGEVITY RATE, salary additions based on length of service. Contracts or pay plans frequently state specific time periods to qualify for such upward wage adjustments.

longitudinal survey, study of a group of subjects that follows them through time. *See* Herbert S. Parnes, "Longitudinal Surveys: Prospects and Problems," *Monthly Labor Review* (February 1972); Wesley

Mellow, "Unionism and Wages: A Longitudinal Analysis," *The Review of Economics and Statistics* (February 1981); Mary Corcoran, Greg J. Duncan and Michael Ponza, "A Longitudinal Analysis of White Women's Wages," *The Journal of Human Resources* (Fall 1983).

Lordstown strike, three-week wildcat strike at the General Motors automobile assembly plant at Lordstown, Ohio, in April 1972. One of the most technically sophisticated plants of its kind in the world, the plant could produce about 100 Chevrolet Vega cars per hour. In 1971, assembly-line workers began to purposely disrupt production, while claiming that management was seeking to "speedup" the assembly line. This problem festered and led to the strike. While the strike gained no economic benefits for the workers, it did focus national attention on the problems of job monotony and worker alienation. For accounts, *see* Barbara Garson, "Luddites in Lordstown," *Harpers* (June 1972); Stanley Aronwitz, *False Promise: The Shaping of American Working Class Consciousness* (N.Y.: McGraw-Hill, 1973); James O'Toole, "Lordstown: Three Years Later," *Business and Society Review* (Spring 1975).

Lordstown syndrome, workers perception that they are required to perform dehumanized and monotonous work. Among the dysfunctional aspects of this syndrome are high absenteeism, low productivity, sabotage, and wildcat strikes. While the term has its origins in the 1972 strike at the General Motors plant in Lordstown, Ohio, the phenomenon itself is more widespread. For a discussion, *see* "The Spreading Lordstown Syndrome," *Business Week* (March 4, 1972).

Lorenz curve, most commonly used in macroeconomics to show the unequal distribution of national income, the Lorenz curve can be applied to wage and salary structures to demonstrate the spread of wages from the lowest paid employee to the highest paid. A curve is constructed by plotting the cumulative percentage of employees against the cumulative percentage of wages and salaries. This curve is compared to a 45° line and the area between the two computed as a value L. The greater the L value, the greater the inequality of wages. *See* T. M. Husband and A. P. Schofield, "The Use of the Lorenz Curve and the Pareto Distribution in Internal Pay Structuring: A Research Note," *The Journal of Management Studies* (October 1976).

Los Angeles Department of Water and Power* v. *Manhart: *see* CITY OF LOS ANGELES, DEPARTMENT OF WATER & POWER V. MANHART.

love, also called OFFICE ROMANCE, when individuals working in the same organization discover that they have an emotional and/or physical attraction for each other, that may be very nice for them but a potential problem for their organization's management. For general advice on handling this kind of situation, *see* Auren Uris, *The Blue Book of Broadminded Business Behavior* (N.Y.: Thomas Y. Crowell, Co., 1977). For scholarly analyses, *see* Robert E. Quinn, "Coping with Cupid: The Formation, Impact, and Management of Romantic Relationships in Organizations," *Administrative Science Quarterly* (March 1977); Eliza G. C. Collins, "Managers and Lovers," *Harvard Business Review* (September–October 1983).
See also SEXUAL HARASSMENT.

Lowell system, the practices associated with Lowell, Massachusetts, during the early 1800s whereby workers, mainly young women, lived in boarding houses owned and run by the company.

low man on the totem pole, refers to the lowest person in any organizational hierarchy. The phrase is credited to Fred Allen, who, while writing an introduction to a book by H. Allen Smith, said, "If Smith were an Indian, he would be low man on any totem pole." Smith then used the phrase as the title of his next book, *Low Man on A Totem Pole* (Garden City, N.Y.: Doubleday Doran and Co., 1941).

loyalty, *also* LOYALTY OATH, loyalty is allegiance. A *loyalty oath* is an affirmation of allegiance. Many public employers may legitimately require their employees to swear of affirm their allegiance to the Constitution of the United States and of a particular state. *See* Paul E. Donnelly, "The Pervasive Effect of McCarthyism on Recent Loyalty Oath Cases," *St. Louis University Law Journal* (Spring 1972); T. W. Fletcher, "The Nature of Administrative Loyalty," *Public Administration Review* (Winter 1958); O. Glenn Stahl, "Loyalty, Dissent, and Organizational Health," *Bureaucrat* (July 1974); Paul M. Sniderman, *A Question of Loyalty* (Berkeley, Calif.: University of California Press, 1981).

Luddite, the original "Luddities,"—they first appeared in Nottingham, England, in 1811—were organized bands of handicraftsmen who, masked and operating at night, sought to destroy the new textile machinery that was displacing them. Their name is thought to have come from Ned Ludd, a village idiot who gained local notoriety in 1779 by destroying some stocking frames belonging to his employer. While Ned Ludd has the same historical stature as Robin Hood (that is, more likely to be mythical than real), his namesakes today would include anyone who seeks to destroy machinery in order to protect a job. For a history, *see* Malcolm I. Thomis, *The Luddites: Machine-Breaking in Regency England* (N.Y.: Schocken Books, 1972).

Ludlow Massacre, because of a strike called by the United Mine Workers (UMW) against various Colorado coal companies in 1913, "guards" employed by the companies attacked a tent city where strikers were living and otherwise harrassed the UMW. Martial law was thereupon imposed by the governor. Then, in April 1914, the state militia sought to clear out the strikers from their tent city in Ludlow. The soldiers killed three people while clearing the camp and then burned it. The next day, the bodies of two women and eleven children were discovered in the remains. The miners called the incident "The Ludlow Massacre." Thoughts of revenge became reality when the miners armed themselves and literally attacked both the state militia and the company guards. After a week of the most ferocious warfare in U.S. labor history, federal troops were sent in to restore order. In the end the UMW lost, it formally called off the strike in December 1914. The most comprehensive account of the whole affair is George S. McGovern and Leonard F. Guttridge, *The Great Coalfield War* (Boston: Houghton Mifflin Co., 1972). This is a "re-write" of Senator McGovern's 1953 Northwestern University Ph. D. dissertation. But, be assured, it has been thoroughly rewritten and reads like a "real" book.

M

Machiavelli, Niccolò (1469-1527), most famous management analyst of the Italian Renaissance, is often credited with having established the moral foundations of modern personnel management. In *Discorsi sopra la prima deca di Tito Livio* ("Discourses on the First Decade of Tito Livy") he offers his advice to all staff specialists:

> If you tender your advice with modesty, and the opposition prevents its adoption, and, owing to someone else's advice being adopted, disaster follows, you will acquire very great glory. And, though you cannot rejoice in the glory that comes from disasters which befall your country or your prince, it at any rate counts for something.

For a modern appreciation, *see* Anthony Jay, *Management and Machiavelli: An Inquiry into the Politics of Corporate Life* (N.Y.: Holt, Rinehart, and Winston, 1967).

machinery, the totality of the methods, usually enumerated in a collective bargaining agreement, used to resolve the problems of interpretation arising during the life of the agreement.

MacKay Rule: *see* NATIONAL LABOR RELATIONS BOARD V. MACKAY RADIO & TELEGRAPH COMPANY.

macroeconomics, study of the relationships between broad economic aggregates such as national income, consumer savings and expenditures, capital investment, employment, money supply, prices, and balance of payments. Macroeconomics is especially concerned with government's role in affecting these aggregates. For texts, *see* Robert L. Heilbroner and Lester C. Thurow, *Understanding Macroeconomics* (Englewood Cliffs, N.J.: Prentice-Hall, 6th ed., 1978); Paul Wonnacott, *Macroeconomics* (Homewood, Ill.: Richard D. Irwin, Inc., 3rd ed., 1984); Michael R. Edgmand, *Macroeconomics: Theory and Policy* (Englewood Cliffs, N.J.: Prentice-Hall, 1979); Jan Walter Elliott, *Macroeconomic Analysis* (Englewood Cliffs, N.J.: Prentice-Hall, 2nd ed., 1979).

Magnavox **decision:** *see* NATIONAL LABOR RELATIONS BOARD V. MAGNAVOX.

Mahon, William D. (1861-1949), president of the Amalgamated Association of Street, Electric Railway and Motor Coach Employees of America from 1893 to 1946. For biographical information, *see* Emerson P. Schmidt, *Industrial Relations in Urban Transportation* (Minneapolis: University of Minnesota Press, 1937).

Maier, Norman R. F. (1900-1977), psychologist best known for his research in industrial psychology, human relations, and executive development. Major works include: *Principles of Human Relations* (N.Y.: John Wiley, 1952); *The Appraisal Interview* (N.Y.: John Wiley, 1958); *Psychology in Industrial Organizations* (Boston: Houghton Mifflin, 4th ed., 1973).

maintenance-of-membership shop, union security provision found in some collective bargaining agreements, holds that employees who are members of the union at the time the agreement is negotiated, or who voluntarily join the union subsequently, must maintain their membership for the duration of the agreement as a condition of employment.

maintenance-of-standards clause, a contract provision that prevents an employer from changing the conditions of employment unless such changes are negotiated with the union.

Magna Carta, this was the charter of liberties that English nobles forced from King John in 1215; now the term is also used to refer to any document offering fundamental guarantees of rights.

major dispute, a *major dispute* in transportation labor law concerns the creation or change of a labor contract, while a *minor dispute* concerns the meaning of an existing contract as it applies to specific situations.

major duty, any duty or responsibility, or group of closely related tasks, of a position that (1) determines qualification requirements for the position, (2) occupies a significant amount of the employee's time, and (3) is a regular or recurring duty.

major-medical insurance, insurance designed to offset the heavy medical expenses resulting from catastrophic or prolonged illness or injuries. Generally, such policies do not provide first dollar coverage, but do provide benefit payments of 75 to 80 percent of all types of medical expenses above a certain base amount paid by the insured. Most major medical policies sold as private insurance contain maximums on the total amount that will be paid (such as $50,000); thus, they do not provide last dollar coverage or complete protection against catastrophic costs. However, there is a trend toward $250,000 limits or even unlimited plans. In addition, benefit payments are often 100 percent of expenses after the individual has incurred some large amount ($500 to $2,000) of out-of-pocket expenses. *See* D. Hedger and D. Schmitt, "Major Medical Coverage During a Period of Rising Costs," *Monthly Labor Review* (July 1983).

make-up pay, allowances paid to piece workers to make-up the difference between actual piece work earnings and guaranteed rates (or statutory minimum wages).

make whole, legal remedy that provides for an injured party to be placed, as near as may be possible, in the situation he or she would have occupied if the wrong had not been committed. The concept was first put forth by the U.S. Supreme Court in the 1867 case of *Wicker* v. *Hoppick*. In 1975, the Court held, in the case of *Albermarle Paper Company* v. *Moody* (422

U.S. 405), that Title VII of the Civil Rights Act of 1964 (as amended) intended a "make whole" remedy for unlawful discrimination.

See also RETROACTIVE SENIORITY and RIGHTFUL PLACE.

make-work, any effort to reduce or limit labor output so that more labor must be employed.

Malek Manual, guidebook concerning the operations of the federal personnel system that was prepared for Fred Malek, the manager of the White House Personnel Office during the early part of the Nixon Administration. Its Machiavellian character (it asserted that "There is no merit in the merit system") gave it tremendous notoriety. For a dispassionate analysis, *see* Frank

---

MALEK MANUAL EXCERPT

The best way to appreciate the usefulness of the Malek Manual is to read its own "example of the rape of the merit system."

Let us assume that you have a career opening in your Department's personnel office for a Staff Recruitment Officer. Sitting in front of you is your college roommate from Stanford University in California who was born and raised in San Francisco. He received his law degree from Boalt Hall at the University of California. While studying for the bar he worked at an advertising agency handling newspaper accounts. He also worked as a reporter on the college newspaper. Your personnel experts judge that he could receive an eligibility rating for a GS-11.

The first thing you do is tear up the old job description that goes with that job. You then have a new one written, to be classified at GS-11, describing the duties of that specific Staff Recruitment Officer as directed toward the recruitment of recent law graduates for entry level attorney positions, entry level public information officers for the creative arts and college news liaison sections of your public information shop, and to be responsible for general recruiting for entry level candidates on the West Coast. You follow that by listing your selective criteria as follows: Education. BA and LLD, stating that the candidate should have extensive experience and knowledge by reason of employment or residence on the West Coast. Candidate should have attended or be familiar with law schools, and institutions of higher education, preferably on the West Coast. The candidate should also possess some knowledge by reasons of education or experence of the fields of college journalism, advertising, and law.

You then trot this candidate's Application for Federal Employment over to the Civil Service Commission, and shortly thereafter he receives an eligibility rating for a GS-11. Your personnel office then sends over the job descriptions (GS-11) along with the selective criteria which was based on the duties of the job description. When the moment arrives for the panel to "spin the register" you insure that your personnel office sends over two "friendly" bureaucrats. The register is then spun and your candidate will certainly be among the only three who even meet the selective criteria, much less be rated by your two "friendly" panel members as among the "highest qualified" that meet the selection criteria. In short, you write the job description and selective criteria around your candidate's Form 171.

There is no merit in the merit system!

SOURCE: *Executive Session Hearings Before the Select Committee on Presidential Campaign Activities of the United States Senate, Watergate and Related Activities,* BOOK 19 (Washington, D.C.: U.S. Government Printing Office, 1974).

J. Thompson and Raymond G. Davis, "The Malek Manual Revisited," *The Bureaucrat* (Summer 1977). For Malek Manual excerpts, *see* Frank J. Thompson (ed.), *Classics of Public Personnel Policy* (Oak Park, Ill.: Moore Publishing Company, 1979).

Maloney, William E. (1884-1964), president of the International Union of Operating Engineers from 1940 to 1958, when the union grew from 58,000 to 294,000. For biographical information, *see* Garth L. Mangum, *The Operating Engineers: The Economic History of a Trade Union* (Cambridge, Mass.: Harvard University Press, 1964).

management, can refer to both (1) the people responsible for running an organization and (2) the running process itself—the utilizing of numerous resources to accomplish an organizational goal. For general histories, *see* Claude S. George, Jr., *The History of Management Thought* (Englewood Cliffs, N.Y.: Prentice-Hall, 1972); Daniel A. Wren, *The Evolution of Management Thought* (N.Y.: John Wiley & Sons, 2nd ed., 1979).

    See also the following entries:
    CAREER MANAGEMENT
    CONTINGENCY MANAGEMENT
    EUPSYCHIAN MANAGEMENT
    FIRST-LINE MANAGEMENT
    GRAND CANYON MANAGEMENT
    INDUSTRIAL DEMOCRACY
    MUSHROOM MANAGEMENT
    PRINCIPLES OF MANAGEMENT
    PROJECT MANAGEMENT
    REACTION MANAGEMENT
    SANDWICH MANAGEMENT
    SCIENTIFIC MANAGEMENT
    SYSTEMS MANAGEMENT

management audit, any comprehensive examination of the administrative operations and organizational arrangements of a company or government agency which uses generally accepted standards of practice for the purposes of evaluation. The pioneering work on this is Jackson Martindell, *The Scientific Appraisal of Management* (N.Y.: Harper and Row, 1950). *Also*

see William P. Leonard, *The Management Audit* (Englewood Cliffs, N.J.: Prentice-Hall, 1962).

management by exception, management control process that has a subordinate report to an organizational superior only exceptional or unusual events that might call for decision-making on the part of the superior. In this way, a manager may avoid unnecessary detail that only confirms that all is going according to plan. This concept originated with Frederick Taylor. For an update, *see* Lester R. Bittel, *Management by Exception* (N.Y.: McGraw-Hill, 1964).

management by objectives (MBO), approach to managing whose hallmark is a mutual—by both organizational subordinate and superior—setting of measurable goals to be accomplished by an individual or team over a set period of time. According to George S. Odiorne, in *Management by Objectives* (New York: Pitman Publishing Company, 1965), "The superior and subordinate managers of an organization jointly define its common goals, define each individual's major areas of responsibility in terms of the results expected of him and use these measures as guides for operating the unit and assessing the contribution of each of the members." The phrase and concept of MBO was first popularized by Peter F. Drucker, in his *The Practice of Management* (N.Y.: Harper & Row, 1954).

    One of the major uses of MBO is for formal performance appraisals. For an assertion that this use is dysfunctional, *see* Harry Levinson, "Management by Whose Objectives?" *Harvard Business Review* (July-August 1970). *Also see* Charles H. Ford, "MBO: An Idea Whose Time Has Gone?" *Business Horizons* (December 1979); Jack N. Kondrasuk, "Studies in MBO Effectiveness," *Academy of Management Review* (July 1981); Richard Gruner, "Employment Discrimination in Management by Objectives Systems," *Labor Law Journal* (June 1983).

    For analysis of MBO in the public sector, *see* Dale D. McConkey, *MBO for*

Nonprofit Organizations (N.Y.: AMACOM, 1975); George L. Morrisey, *Management by Objectives and Results in the Public Sector* (Reading, Mass.: Addison-Wesley Publishing Co., 1976); Perry D. Moore and Ted Staton, "Management by Objectives in American Cities," *Public Personnel Management,* Vol. 10, No. 2 (Summer 1981). In addition, there is a symposium on MBO in *Public Administration Review* (January-February 1976).

management clause: *see* MANAGEMENT RIGHTS CLAUSE.

management development, also called EXECUTIVE DEVELOPMENT, any conscious effort on the part of an organization to provide a manager with skills that he might need for future duties, such as rotational assignments or formal educational experiences, constitutes management development. The semantic difference between training workers and developing managers is significant. A manager is trained so that he can be of greater organizational value not only in his present but in his future assignments as well. In such a context the development investment made by the organization in a junior manager may only pay off when and if that individual grows into a bureau or division chief. For an analysis, *see* Edgar H. Schein, "Management Development: Full Spectrum Training," *Training and Development Journal* (March 1975); Raymond Pomerleau, "The State of Management Development in the Federal Service," *Public Personnel Management* (January-February 1974); John Sauter, "Purchasing Public Sector Executive Development," *Training and Development Journal* (April 1980); Robert E. Boynton, "Executive Development Programs: What Should They Teach?" *Personnel* (March-April 1981); David Bresnick, "University/Agency Collaboration in Management Development Efforts," *Public Administration Review* (November-December 1981); Stanley D. Truskie, "Guidelines for Conducting in-House Management Development," *Personnel Administrator* (July 1981); Stanley D. Truskie, "Getting the Most From Management Development Programs," *Personnel Journal* (January 1982); H. Wayne Smith and Clay E. George, "Evaluating Internal Advanced Management Programs," *Personnel Administrator* (August 1984).

management games, also called BUSINESS GAMES, any of a variety of simulation exercises used in management development and education. *See* Joel M. Kibbee, Clifford J. Craft, and Burt Nanus, *Management Games: A New Technique for Executive Development* (N.Y.: Van Nostrand Reinhold, 1961); Robert G. Graham and Clifford F. Gray, *Business Games Handbook* (N.Y.: American Management Association, 1969); David W. Zukerman and Robert E. Horn, *The Guide to Simulations/Games for Education and Training* (Lexington, Mass.: Information Resources, 1973). For a view of all of modern business as a game, *see* John McDonald, *The Games of Business* (Garden City, N.Y.: Doubleday, 1975). For an analysis of the players, *see* Michael Maccoby, *The Gamesman: The New Corporate Leaders* (N.Y.: Simon & Schuster, 1976).

management information system (MIS), any formal process in an organization that provides managers with facts that they need for decisionmaking. Modern management information systems are almost invariably dependent upon computers. For the theory behind a modern MIS, *see* Jagjit Singh, *Great Ideas in Information Theory, Language and Cybernetics* (N.Y.: Dover Publications, 1966). For what can go wrong, *see* Russell L. Ackoff, "Management Misinformation Systems," *Management Science* (December 1967). Also *see* Richard L. Nolan, "Managing Information Systems By Committee," *Harvard Business Review* (July-August 1982); Alfred J. Walker, "The Newest Job in Personnel: Human Resources Data Administrator," *Personnel Journal* (December 1982); Albert L. Lederer, "Planning and Developing a

Human Resource Information System," *Personnel Administrator* (August 1984).

Management of Personnel Quarterly: *see* HUMAN RESOURCE MANAGEMENT.

management movement, the totality of events, starting in the last century, that led to the recognition of *management* as a professional discipline. The movement is usually dated from 1886 when Henry R. Towne told the American Society of Mechanical Engineers that "The matter of shop management is of equal importance with that of engineering."

management prerogatives: *see* MANAGEMENT RIGHTS.

management prerogatives: *see* MANAGEMENT RIGHTS.

management rights, also called MANAGEMENT PREROGATIVES and RESERVED RIGHTS, those rights reserved to management that management feels are intrinsic to its ability to manage and, consequently, not subject to collective bargaining. According to Paul Prasow and Edward Peters, "New Perspectives on Management's Reserved Rights," *Labor Law Journal* (January 1967),

management's authority is supreme in all matters except those it has expressly conceded in the collective agreement, or in those areas where its authority is restricted by law. Put another way, management does not look to the collective agreement to ascertain its rights; it looks to the agreement to find out which and how much of its rights and powers it has conceded outright or agreed to share with the union.

For further analyses of management rights, *see* George Bennett, "Management Rights in the Public Sector," *Labor Law Journal* (Sept. 1977); Bruno Stein, "Management Rights and Productivity," *The Arbitration Journal* (December 1977).

management rights clause, also called MANAGEMENT CLAUSE, that portion of a collective bargaining agreement that defines the scope of management rights, functions, and responsibilities—essentially all those activities which management can undertake without the consent of the union. A typical management rights clause might read: "It is the intention hereof that all of the rights, powers, prerogatives, authorities that the company had prior to the signing of this agreement are retained by the company except those that are specifically abridged, delegated, granted, or modified by the agreement." *See* Richard F. Groner and Leon E. Lunden, "Management Rights Provisions in Major Agreements," *Monthly Labor Review* (February 1966); Frank P. Zeidler, *Management's Rights Under Public Sector Collective Bargaining Agreements* (Washington, D.C.: International Personnel Management Association, 1980); Ronald L. Blevins, "Maximizing Company Rights Under the Contract," *Personnel Administrator* (June 1984).

management science, also called OPERATIONS RESEARCH, approach to management dating from World War II that seeks to apply the scientific method to managerial problems. Because of its emphasis on mathematical techniques, management science as a term is frequently used interchangeably with operations research. Management science should not be confused with Frederick W. Taylor's Scientific Management Movement. For an elementary introduction, *see* Stafford Beer, *Management Science: The Business Use of Operations Research* (N.Y.: Doubleday and Co., 1968). For a governmental perspective, *see* Michael J. White, *Management Science in Federal Agencies: The Adoption and Diffusion of a Socio-Technical Innovation* (Lexington, Mass.: Lexington Books, 1975); *also see* Jack Byrd, *Operations Research Models for Public Administration* (Lexington, Mass.: Lexington Books, 1975); Charles E. Pinkus and Anne Dixson, *Solving Local Government Problems: Practical Applications of Operations Research in Cities and Regions* (London: Allen & Unwin, 1981).

"Management Theory Jungle," title of an

article by Harold Koontz that appeared in the *Journal of the Academy of Management* (December 1961), wherein Koontz sought to classify the major schools of management theory into six groupings: (1) the management process school, (2) the empirical school, (3) the human behavior school, (4) the social system school, (5) the decision theory school and (6) the mathematical school. Koontz noted that the terminology and principles of the various schools of management thought have resulted in a "semantics jungle." For an update, Harold Koontz, "The Management Theory Jungle Revisited," *Academy of Management Review* (April 1980).

management trainee, administrative job title loosely assigned to a wide variety of entry-level positions that are usually reserved for new college graduates. *See* Hal Anderson, "Selecting Management Trainees," *Personnel Journal* (November 1976).

manager, generally speaking, any organization member whose job includes supervising others. A *top manager* is one of those who makes policy for, and is responsible for, the overall success of the organization. A *middle manager* is responsible for the execution and interpretation of top management policies and for the operation of the various departments. A *supervisory manager* is responsible for the final implementation of policies by rank and file employees.

manager, project: *see* PROJECT MANAGER.

managerial grid, the basis of Robert R. Blake and Jane S. Mouton's widely implemented organization development program. By using a graphic gridiron format, which has an X axis locating various degrees of orientation toward production and a Y axis locating various degrees of orientation toward people, individuals scoring this "managerial grid" can place themselves at one of 81 available positions that register their relative orientations toward people or production. Grid scores

can then be used as the point of departure for a discussion of individual and organizational growth needs. *See* Robert R. Blake and Jane S. Mouton, *The Managerial Grid* (Houston: Gulf Publishing, 1964).

managerial obsolescence: *see* OCCUPATIONAL OBSOLESCENCE.

managerial philosophy, all organizations are guided by a philosophy of management. It need not be formally expressed. Indeed, many managers would deny that they have one. But it's always there, somewhere—whether stated or unstated, conscious or unconscious, intentional or unintentional. It is this philosophy that facilitates management's decisionmaking process. Of course, different managerial philosophies have evolved in reflection of differing organizational environments and work situations. For example, a managerial philosophy appropriate for a military combat unit would hardly be suitable for a medical research team seeking to find a cure for cancer. The sincerity and rigor of an employee's motivation toward his or her duties is a direct reflection of the host organization's managerial philosophy. *See* Michael Albert and Murray Silverman, "Making Management Philosophy A Cultural Reality, Part I: Get Started," *Personnel* (January–February 1984); Michael Albert and Murray Silverman, "Making Management Philosophy A Cultural Reality, Part 2: Design Human Resources Programs Accordingly," *Personnel* (March–April 1984).

managerial psychology, generally, all those concepts of human behavior in organizations that are relevant to managerial problems. A standard text is Harold J. Leavitt, *Managerial Psychology: An Introduction to Individuals, Pairs, and Groups in Organizations* (Chicago: University of Chicago Press, 3rd ed., 1972).

managerial revolution, refers to James Burnham's concept that as the control of the large corporations passes from the hands of the owners into the hands of professional administrators, the society's new governing class will not be the possessors of wealth but of technical administrative expertise. *See* James Burnham, *The Managerial Revolution* (N.Y.: The John Day Co., 1941). For a history of this managerial class, *see* Alfred D. Chandler, Jr., *The Visible Hand: The Managerial Revolution in American Business* (Cambridge, Mass.: Harvard University Press, 1977).

mandamus, also called WRIT OF MANDAMUS, court order that compels the performance of an act.

mandatory bargaining items, those collective bargaining items that each party must bargain over if introduced by the other party. *See* Peter A. Susser, "NLRB Restricts Mandatory Bargaining Over Managerial Changes," *Labor Law Journal* (July 1984).

man-day, amount of work that can be accomplished in a single normal day of work.

man Friday or GIRL FRIDAY, in Daniel Defoe's 1719 novel, *Robinson Crusoe*, the hero, a castaway on a desolate island, was fortunate to find a black man who developed into a hardworking helper. He was named Friday because that was the day of the week when Crusoe rescued him from acquaintances who thought he was good enough to eat. Over time, a man Friday or girl Friday became synonymous with a general and cheerful helper.

Manhart **decision:** *see* CITY OF LOS ANGELES, DEPARTMENT OF WATER & POWER V. MANHART.

manit, contraction for man-minute.

man-machine systems, according to W. T. Singleton, in his *Man-Machine Systems* (Baltimore: Penguin Books, 1974), man-machine systems have

to do with the design of work, on the assumption that work nowadays is never done by men, nor is it done by machine, it is always done by man-machine

systems. The man-machine system has proved enormously successful because men and machines are so different, each compensates for the weaknesses of the other. There are therefore, problems of deciding what men should do and what machines should do in the pursuit of any objective. That is what the man-machine allocation function is about.

Also see: Henry M. Parsons, *Man-Machine System Experiments* (Baltimore: The Johns Hopkins University Press, 1972).

manning table, also called PERSONNEL INVENTORY, listing of all of the employees in an organization by job and personal characteristics, which serves as a basic reference for planning and other purposes.

manpower: *see* HUMAN RESOURCES.

Manpower Development and Training Act of 1962 (MDTA), federal statute that authorized the U.S. Department of Labor to identify the skills and capability needs of the economy and to initiate and find appropriate training programs. It was superseded by the Comprehensive Employment and Training Act of 1973. *See* Garth L. Mangum, *MDTA: Foundation of Federal Manpower Policy* (Baltimore: Johns Hopkins Press, 1968).

manpower planning: *see* HUMAN RESOURCES PLANNING.

manpower planning models: *see* HUMAN RESOURCES PLANNING MODELS.

manpower requirements analysis: *see* HUMAN RESOURCES REQUIREMENTS ANALYSIS.

manpower utilization: *see* HUMAN RESOURCES UTILIZATION.

manufacturing sector, the segment of the national economy that produces things such as furniture and machines, as opposed to those segments that sell or repair them.

March, James G. (1928-   ), social psychologist best known for his application of behavioral science concepts to organizational concerns. He wrote (with Herbert A. Simon) a landmark book in organizational behavior, *Organizations* (New York: John Wiley & Sons, 1958). Other major works include: *A Behavioral Theory of the Firm*, with R. M. Cyert (Englewood Cliffs, N.J.: Prentice-Hall, 1963); *Handbook of Organizations*, editor (Chicago: Rand McNally, 1965).

marginal analysis, any technique that seeks to determine the point at which the cost of something (for example, an additional employee or machine) will be worth while or pay for itself.

marginal cost, the cost of adding one more identical item to a bulk purchase, of manufacturing one more item in a production run, of borrowing one more dollar in a loan, etc.

marginal employees, those members of an organization who contribute least to the organization's mission because of their personal sloth or the inherent nature of their duties. *See* Charles A. O'Reilly, III, and Barton A. Weitz, "Managing Marginal Employees: The Use of Warnings and Dismissals," *Administrative Science Quarterly* (September 1980).

marginal productivity theory of wages, theory holding the wages of workers will be determined by the value of the productivity of the marginal worker; additional workers will not be hired if the value of the added production is less than the wages that must be paid them. Consequently, wages will tend to equal the value of the product contributed by the last (the marginal) worker hired. The theory, first formulated by John Bates Clark in 1899, has been severely criticized for being premised upon business circumstances that tend to be uncommon in real life. For the original source, *see* John Bates Clark, *The Distribution of Wealth* (N.Y.: Macmillan, 1899). For analysis, *see* J. R. Hicks, *The Theory of Wages* (London: Macmillan, 2nd ed., 1963).

marginal propensity, the ratio of a change in economic activity to an underlying change in income. The *marginal propensity to consume* is the rate of change in consumption which follows an increase in income. The *marginal propensity to save* is the rate of change in saving with respect to a change in income.

Marshall, F. Ray (1928-   ), labor economist, Secretary of Labor from 1977 to 1981. Major works include: *The Negro Worker* (N.Y.: Random House, 1967); *Cooperatives and Rural Poverty in the South*, with Lamond Godwin (Baltimore: Johns Hopkins Press, 1971); *Labor Economics: Wages, Employment and Trade Unionism*, with Allan Murray Cartter (Homewood, Ill.: R. D. Irwin, rev. ed., 1972); *Human Resources and Labor Markets*, with Sar A. Levitan and Garth L. Mangum (N.Y.: Harper & Row, 1972).

Marshall v. Barlow's, Inc., 56 L. Ed. 2d 305 (1978), U.S. Supreme Court case, which interpreted the 4th Amendment's prohibition on unreasonable searches to impose a warrant requirement on Occupational Safety and Health Administration Inspections. The court ruled that such warrants do not require evidence establishing probable cause that a violation has occurred on the premises. Rather, a judge can issue an OSHA warrant upon a showing that the inspection follows a reasonable administrative or legislative plan for enforcing the Occupational Safety and Health Act.

martinet, strict disciplinarian. The word comes from an inspector general in the army of France's Louis XIV, Jean Martinet, who was so despised for his spit-and-polish discipline that he was "accidentally" killed by his own soldiers while leading an assault in 1672.

Maryland v. Wirtz: see NATIONAL LEAGUE OF CITIES V. USERY.

Marxism, the doctrine of revolution based on the writings of Karl Marx (1818-1883) and Friedrich Engels (1820-1895) which maintains that human history is a history of struggle between the exploiting and exploited classes. They wrote the *Communist Manifesto* (1848) "to do for history what Darwin's theory has done for biology." The basic theme of Marxism holds that the proletariat will suffer so from alienation that they will rise up against the bourgeoisie who own the means of production and overthrow the system of capitalism which has so neglected the labor theory of value. After a brief period of rule by "the dictatorship of the proletariat" the classless society of communism would be forthcoming. While Marxism currently has a strong influence on the economics of the second, third, and fourth worlds, its intent has never been fully achieved. Indeed, because Marx's writings are so vast and often contradictory, serious Marxists spend considerable time arguing about just what Marx "really" meant. Marx's magnum opus, *Das Capital (1867),* is frequently referred to as the "bible of socialism."

Maslow, Abraham H. (1908-1970), psychologist best known for his theory of human motivation, which was premised upon a "needs hierarchy" within which an individual moved up or down as the needs of each level were satisfied or threatened. Major works include: *Motivation and Personality* (N.Y.: Harper & Row, 1954; 2nd ed., 1970); *Eupsychian Management* (Homewood, Ill.: Richard D. Irwin, 1965). For a biography, *see* Frank G. Goble, *The Third Force: The Psychology of Abraham Maslow* (N.Y.: Grossman Publishers, 1970).

See also SELF-ACTUALIZATION.

Massachusetts Board of Retirement* v. *Murgia, 427 U.S. 307 (1976), U.S. Supreme Court case, which held that a state statute requiring uniformed state police to retire at age 50 was not a violation of equal protection. The court ruled that the state had met its burden of showing some rational relationship between the statute and the purpose of maintaining the physical condition of its police.

mass picketing, when a union wants to indicate broad support for a strike it sometimes assembles a "mass" of strikers to picket a place of business in order to discourage nonstrikers from entering the premises.

mass production, generally, a high volume of output; but more specifically, mass production also assumes product simplification, standardization of parts, continuous production lines, and the maximum possible use of automatic equipment. *See:* Ray Wild, *Mass Production Management: The Design and Operation of Production Flow-Line Systems* (New York: Wiley, 1972); David A. Hounshell, *From the American System to Mass Production, 1800-1932: The Development of Manufacturing Technology in the United States* (Baltimore: The Johns Hopkins University Press, 1984).

master, skilled worker in a trade who is qualified to train apprentices.
See also JOURNEYMAN.

master agreement, also called MASTER CONTRACT, collective bargaining contract that serves as a model for an entire industry or segment of that industry. While the master agreement serves to standardize the economic benefits of all of the employees covered by it, it is often supplemented by a local contract which deals with the varying circumstances of the various local unions.

mastery, perfect performance on a test.

***Mastro Plastics Corp.* v. National Labor Relations Board,** 350 U.S. 270 (1956), U.S. Supreme Court case, which held that in the absence of contractual or statutory provision to the contrary, an employer's unfair labor practices provide adequate ground for an orderly strike. In such circumstances, the striking employees "do not lose their status and are entitled to reinstatement with back pay, even if replacements for them have been made."

MAT: *see* (1) MILLER ANALOGIES TEST and (2) MULTIPLE APTITUDE TESTS.

matching item, test item that asks which one of a group of words, pictures, etc., matches up with those of another group.

maternity leave, formally approved absence from work for childbirth and its aftermath.

See also the following entries:
BIRTH LEAVE
CLEVELAND BOARD OF EDUCATION V. LAFLEUR
MONELL V. DEPT. OF SOCIAL SERVICES, NEW YORK CITY
NASHVILLE GAS CO. V. SATTY
PREGNANCY DISCRIMINATION ACT OF 1978

Mathews v. Eldridge, 424 U.S. 319 (1976), U.S. Supreme Court case, which held that while due process requires pretermination hearings for recipients of welfare benefits, it does not require such hearings for those who receive disability benefits.

matrix diamond, basic structural form of matrix organizations; this is in contrast to the pyramid—the basic structural form of traditional organizations.

matrix manager, any manager who shares formal authority over a subordinate with another manager.

matrix organization, any organization using a multiple command system whereby an employee might be accountable to one superior for overall performance as well as to one or more leaders of particular projects. "Matrix" is a generic term that is used to refer to various organizational structures. For an exhaustive analysis, see Stanley M. Davis and Paul R. Lawrence, *Matrix* (Reading, Mass.: Addison-Wesley Publishing Co., 1977). For critiques, see Kenneth Knight, "Matrix Organization: A Review," *Journal of Management Studies* (May 1976); Harvey F. Kolodny, "Evolution to a Matrix Organization," *Academy of Management Review* (October 1979); Mary Ellen Simon, "Matrix Management at the U.S. Consumer Product Safety Commission," *Public Administration Review* (July–August 1983).

See also PROJECT MANAGEMENT and TASK FORCE.

maturity curve also called CAREER CURVE and SALARY CURVE, technique for determining the salaries of professional and technical employees that relates the employee's education and experience to on-the-job performance. For example, after it is determined what the average compensation for a professional employee is for each of various categories of experience, the individual employee is assigned a salary based upon whether he or she is considered average, below average, or above average in performance. See H. C. Rickard, "Maturity Curve Surveys," *Handbook of Wage and Salary Administration,* M. L. Rock, ed. (N.Y.: McGraw-Hill, 1972); Robert L. McCornack, "A New Method for Fitting Salary Curves," *Personnel Journal* (October 1967).

May Day, in 1889, the International Socialist Congress fixed May 1 as the day to publicize the eight-hour day because the American Federation of Labor planned a major demonstration on May 1, 1890. Since then May Day has become a major holiday in socialist countries. In 1955, President Eisenhower proclaimed May 1 as "Loyalty Day."

Mayo, Elton (1880-1949), principle organizer and researcher of the famous Hawthorne experiments and considered the founder of the human-relations approach in industry. Major works include: *The Human Problems of An Industrial Civilization* (N.Y.: The Viking Press, 1933); *The Social Problems of An Industrial Civilization* (N.Y.: The Viking Press, 1945). For a biography, see Lyndall F. Urwick, *The Life and Work of Elton Mayo* (London: Urwick, Orr & Partners, Ltd., 1960).

MBA also MPA, Master of Business Administration and Master of Public Administration, respectively. These are the leading managerial degrees for practitioners in both the private and public sectors. While such

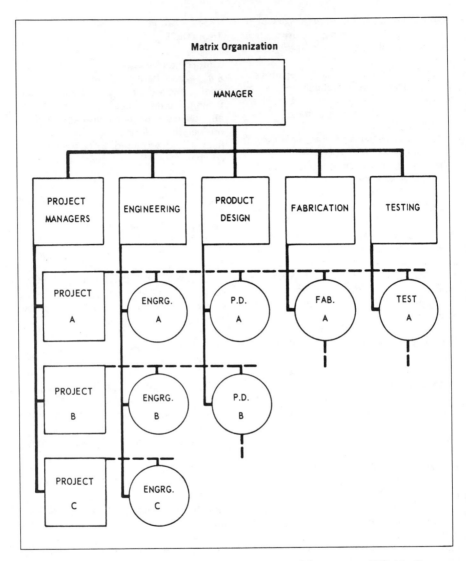

Matrix Organization

SOURCE: T. Roger Manley, "Have You Tried Project Management?" Public Personnel Management (May-June 1975).

degrees are obviously helpful, it has long been established that there is no direct relationship between scholastic performance and success in management. For an analysis of this seeming contradiction, *see* J. Sterling Livingston, "Myth of the Well-Educated Manager," *Harvard Business Review* (January-February 1971). *See also* Philip T. Crotty, "The Value of MBA

and Executive Development Programs," *Training and Development Journal* (May 1972); George Grode and Marc Holzer, "The Perceived Utility of MPA Degrees," *Public Administration Review* (July-August 1975); J. N. Behrman and R. I. Levin, "Are Business Schools Doing Their Job?" *Harvard Business Review* (January-February 1984); R. L. Jenkins,

R. C. Reizenstein and F. G. Rodgers, "Report Cards on the MBA," *Harvard Business Review* (September-October 1984).

MBO: *see* MANAGEMENT BY OBJECTIVES.

McAuliffe v. *Mayor of New Bedford,* 155 Mass. 216 (1892), Massachusetts Supreme Court case concerning the constitutionaltiy of a city rule prohibiting policemen from joining labor unions. Justice Oliver Wendell Holmes' immortal words were iterated here:

> The petitioner may have a constitutional right to talk politics, but he has no constitutional right to be a policeman. There are few employments for hire in which the servant does not agree to suspend his constitutional right of free speech, as well as of idleness, by the implied terms of his contract. The servant cannot complain, as he takes the employment on the terms which are offered him.

The logic of this decision has been rejected by the Supreme Court in more recent years. *See* David H. Rosenbloom, *Federal Service and the Constitution* (Ithaca: Cornell University Press, 1971).

McCarthy v. *Philadelphia Civil Service Commission,* 424 U.S. 645 (1976), U.S. Supreme Court case, which upheld an ordinance requiring that city employees live within city limits.

McClellan Committee, in the late 1950s, Senator John L. McClellan (1896-1977) of Arkansas chaired the Senate Committee on Improper Activities in Labor-Management Relations. The committee's findings of violence and corruption spurred the passage of the Labor-Management Reporting and Disclosure (Landrum-Griffin) Act of 1959. For accounts of the committee's work by its chairman and legal counsel, *see* John L. McClellan, *Crime Without Punishment* (N.Y.: Duell, Sloan and Pearce, 1962); Robert F. Kennedy, *The Enemy Within* (N.Y.: Harper & Row, 1960).

McClelland, David C. (1917-   ), psychologist widely considered the foremost authority on achievement motivation. The body of McClelland's work asserts that achievement motivation can be developed within individuals, provided that the environment in which they live and work is supportive. Major works include: *The Achievement Motive,* with J. W. Atkinson, R. A. Clark, and E. A. Lowell (N.Y.: Appleton-Century-Crofts, 1953); *The Achieving Society* (Princeton, N.J.: Van Nostrand, 1961); *Motivating Economic Achievement,* with D. G. Winter (N.Y.: The Free Press, 1969).

McDonald, David John (1902-1979), president of the United Steelworkers of America from 1953 to 1965 when he was defeated for reelection by I. W. Abel. For an account of his last election contest, *see* John A. Orr, "The Steelworker Election of 1965," *Labor Law Journal* (February 1969). For McDonald's autobiography, *see Union Man* (N.Y.: E. P. Dutton, 1969).

McDonald v. *City of West Branch, Michigan,* U.S. Supreme Court case, 80 L.Ed. 2d 302 (1984), which held that a discharged police officer could seek redress in court, even though he had fully utilized the grievance procedure in his union's contract, culminating in an arbitrator's ruling that the discharge was warranted.

McDonald v. *Sante Fe Trail Transportation Co.,* 424 U.S. 952 (1976), U.S. Supreme Court case, which held an employer could not impose racially discriminatory discipline on employees guilty of the same offense.

McDonnell Douglas Corporation v. *Green,* 411 U.S. 792 (1973), U.S. Supreme Court case, which held that an employee could establish a prima facie case of discrimination by initially showing (1) that he or she was a member of a racial minority; (2) that he or she applied and was qualified in an opening for which the employer sought applicants; (3) that despite qualifications he or she was rejected; (4) that after rejection the position remained open and the employer continued to seek applicants.

McGregor, Douglas M. (1906-1964), organizational humanist and managerial philosopher who is best known for his conceptualization of Theory X and Theory Y. Major works include: *The Human Side of Enterprise* (N.Y.: McGraw-Hill, 1960); *The Professional Manager* (N.Y.: McGraw-Hill, 1967). For an evaluation of McGregor's impact and contribution, *see* Warren G. Bennis, "Chairman Mac in Perspective," *Harvard Business Review* (September-October 1972).

MCT: *see* MINNESOTA CLERICAL TEST.

MDTA: *see* MANPOWER DEVELOPMENT AND TRAINING ACT OF 1962.

mean, simple average of a set of measurements, obtained by summing the measurements and dividing by the number of them.

mean deviation: *see* AVERAGE DEVIATION.

Meany, George (1894-1979), labor leader who started out as a plumber in a Bronx local and was president of the AFL-CIO from its creation in 1955 to 1979. For biographies, *see* Joseph C. Goulden, *Meany* (N.Y.: Atheneum, 1972); Archie Robinson, *George Meany and His Times: A Biography* (New York: Simon and Schuster, 1981).

measure of dispersion, aslo called MEASURE OF VARIABLITY, any statistical measure showing the extent to which individual test scores are concentrated about or spread out from a measure of central tendency.

measured day work, also called MEASURED DAY RATE, an incentive wage plan that is premised upon a guaranteed base wage rate that is based upon previous job performance. *See* Andrew J. Waring, "The Case for the Measured Day Rate Plan," *Personnel Journal* (October 1961).

mechanical aptitude tests, tests designed to measure how well an individual can learn to perform tasks that involve the understanding and manipulation of mechanical devices. Classified in two subgroups—mechanical reasoning and spatial relations.

Mechanical Comprehension Test, Bennett: *see* BENNETT MECHANICAL COMPREHENSION TEST.

mechanistic system, organization form, proven to be most appropriate under stable conditions, which is characterized by: (1) a high-degree of task differentiation and specialization with a precise delineation of rights and responsibilities; (2) a high degree of reliance on the traditional hierarchical structure; (3) a tendency for the top of the hierarchy to control all incoming and outgoing communications; (4) an emphasis on vertical interactions between superiors and subordinates; (5) a demand for loyalty to the organization and to superiors; and (6) a greater importance placed on internal (local) knowledge, skill, and experience, in contrast to more general (cosmopolitan) knowledge, experience, and skill. The classic analysis of mechanistic systems is to be found in Tom Burns and G. M. Stalker, *The Management of Innovation* (Chicago: Quadrangle Books, 1961).

See also ORGANIC SYSTEM.

mechanization: *see* AUTOMATION.

med-arb, a combination of mediation and arbitration which engages a third party neutral in both mediation and arbitration. The main idea is to mediate in an effort to resolve the impasse or at least reduce the number of issues going to arbitration. Then, where mediation is unsuccessful, some form of binding arbitration is used. *See* James L. Stern, "The Mediation of Interest Disputes by Arbitrators Under the Wisconsin Med-Arb Law for Local Government Employees," *Arbitration Journal* (June 1984).

median, middle score in a distribution, the

MECHANISTIC AND ORGANIC ORGANIZATIONS COMPARED

Mechanistic		Organic
High: many and sharp differentiation	Specialization	Low: no hard boundaries relative few different jobs
High: methods spelled out	Standardization	Low: individuals decide own methods
Means	Orientation of Members	Goals
By superiority	Conflict Resolution	Interaction
Hierarchy based on contractual relations	Authority, Control and Communication	Wide net based on common commitment
At top of organization	Locus of Superior Competence	Wherever there is skill and competence
Direction, orders	Communication Content	Advice, information
To organization position	Loyalty Prestige	To project and groups personal contribution

SOURCE: Reprinted from Jerome B. McKinney and Lawrence C. Howard, *Instructor's Manual* for *Public Administration: Balancing Power and Accountability* (Oak Park, Ill.: Moore Publishing, 1979), p. 19. Copyright © 1979 Moore Publishing Company, Inc.

50th percentile, the point that divides the group into two equal parts. Half of a group of scores fall below the median and half above it.

mediation, also CONCILIATION, any attempt by an impartial third party to help settle disputes between labor and management. A mediator has no power but that of persuasion. The mediator's suggestions are advisory in nature and may be rejected by both parties. Mediation and conciliation tend to be used interchangeably to denote the entrance of an impartial third party into a labor dispute. However, there is a distinction. *Conciliation* is the less active term. It technically refers simply to efforts to bring the parties together so that they may resolve their problems themselves. *Mediation,* in contrast, is a more active term. It implies that an active effort will be made to help the parties reach agreement by clarifying issues, asking questions, and making specific proposals. However, the usage of the two terms has been so blurred that the only place where it is absolutely necessary to distinguish between them is in a dictionary. For a text, *see* William E. Simkin, *Mediation and the Dynamics of Collective Bargaining* (Washington, D.C.: Bureau of National Affairs, 1971). For a legal analyses, *see* Lon L. Fuller, "Mediation—Its Forms and Functions," *Southern California Law Review* (Winter 1971). For a public sector perspective, *see* Paul D. Staudohar, "Some Implications of

Mediation for Resolution of Bargaining Impasses in Public Employment," *Public Personnel Management* (July–August 1973); Ronald Hoh, "The Effectiveness of Mediation in Public Sector Arbitration Systems: The Iowa Experience," *Arbitration Journal* (June 1984); Arnold M. Zak, *Public Sector Mediation* (Washington D.C.: Bureau of National Affairs, Inc., 1985). For a bibliography, *see* Edward Levin and Daniel V. DeSantis, *Mediation: An Annotated Bibliography* (Ithaca, N.Y.: New York State School of Industrial and Labor Relations, Cornell University, 1978). *Also see* Ahmad Karim and Richard Pegnetter, "Mediator Strategies and Qualities and Mediation Effectiveness," *Industrial Relations* (Winter 1982); John R. Stepp and others, "Helping Labor and Mangement See and Solve Problems," *Monthly Labor Review* (September 1982).

See also PREVENTIVE MEDIATION.

Mediation Service, abbreviated way of referring to the Federal Mediation and Conciliation Service or state agencies performing a similar function.

mediator, individual who acts as an impartial third party in order to help resolve labor-management disputes. Appointed by an administrative agency or by the parties involved, the mediator's role is to help the parties reach an agreement short of a strike. *See* Arthur S. Meyer, "Function of the Mediator in Collective Bargaining," *In-*

dustrial and Labor Relations Review (January 1960); Deborah M. Kolb, "Roles Mediators Play: State and Federal Practice," *Industrial Relations* (Winter 1981); Perry A. Zirkel and J. Gary Lutz, "Characteristics and Functions of Mediators: a Pilot Study," *The Arbitration Journal* (June 1981); Deborah M. Kolb, *The Mediators* (Cambridge, Mass.: MIT Press, 1983).

medical insurance, supplemental: *see* SUPPLEMENTAL MEDICAL INSURANCE.

Medicare, the National Health Insurance Program for the elderly and the disabled. The two parts of Medicare—hospital insurance and medical insurance—help protect people 65 and over from the high costs of health care. Also eligible for Medicare are disabled people under 65 who have been entitled to social security disability benefits for 24 or more consecutive months (including adults who are receiving benefits because they have been disabled since childhood). Insured workers and their dependents who need dialysis treatment or a kidney transplant because of permanent kidney failure also have Medicare protection. For a history of how the medicare bill passed, *see* Max J. Skidmore, *Medicare and the American Rhetoric of Reconciliation* (University: University of Alabama Press, 1970). *Also see* Theodore Marmor, *The Politics of Medicare* (Chicago: Aldine, 1973).

Mee, John F. (1908-   ), industrial psychologist known for his advocacy that motivation be considered a management function. He edited the first practical handbook on the modern personnel function, *Personnel Handbook*, (N.Y.: Ronald Press Company, 1951).

meet-and-confer discussions, technique, used mostly in the public sector, of determining conditions of employment whereby the representatives of the employer and the employee organization hold periodic discussions to seek agreement on matters within the scope of representation. Any written agreement is in the form of a non-binding memorandum of understanding. This technique is often used where formal collective bargaining is not authorized.

Memorial Day Massacre, strike violence at Republic Steel's South Chicago mill where police killed ten and wounded over eighty steelworkers on May 30, 1937.

menial, originally a household servant. For centuries, it has been used as a term of disparagement and contempt to describe work of degrading drudgery. According to Albert L. Porter, "Repugnance for 'Menial Jobs,' " *Management of Personnel Quarterly* (Winter 1971),

a man's sense of well-being and meaningfulness in work is not so much a matter of external circumstances—the kind of job he has—as it is of his deep-down belief that he is a worthy human being. If he lacks that, any job can seem dissatisfying and "menial." Executives may suffer from this (or related behaviors) as much as assembly-line workers.

mentally handicapped employees, also called MENTALLY RETARDED EMPLOYEES, individuals with less than normal intellectual abilities. On standard tests, an intelligence quotient of 70 is usually thought to be the upper borderline for those who are classified as retarded. Until comparatively recently, the retarded had only the most limited opportunities in the open job market. But more enlightened attitudes toward dealing with retarded individuals and an employment climate influenced by the concept of equal employment opportunity for all are rapidly improving the employment prospects for the mentally handicapped/retarded. Mental deficiency and vocational deficiency are not synonymous. According to Donn E. Prolin, *Vocational Preparation of Retarded Citizens* (Columbus, Ohio: Charles E. Merrill, 1976), "one of the greatest problems that persons with mental retardation encounter is the continual underestimation of their potentials by the general public and professional workers." *Also see* Howard F. Rudd, "Supervising the Mentally Handicapped: The Procedures, the Rewards," *Supervisory Management* (December 1976); The National Association for Retarded Citizens, "Mentally Retarded Persons in the Open Job Market," *Personnel Journal* (May 1977).

mentally ill employees: *see* EMOTIONALLY HANDICAPPED EMPLOYEES.

mentally retarded employees: *see* MENTALLY HANDICAPPED EMPLOYEES.

mentor, wise counselor. The word comes from Homer's *The Odyssey*. When Odysseus set off for the war at Troy, he left his house and wife in the care of a friend named Mentor. When things got rough at home for Odysseus' family, Athene, the goddess of wisdom, assumed the shape of Mentor and provided Telemachus, the son of Odysseus, with some very helpful advice about how to deal with the problems of his most unusual adolescence. For an analysis of the importance of mentoring in organizational careers, *see* Eileen C. Shapiro, Florence P. Haseltine, and Mary P. Rowe, "Moving Up: Role Models, Mentors and the 'Patron System,'" *Sloan Management Review* (Spring 1978). For a case study, *see* Barbara Kellerman, "Mentoring in Political Life: The Case of Willy Brandt," *American Political Science Review* (June 1978).

Also see Mary C. Johnson, "Speaking From Experience: 'Mentors—The Key to Development and Growth,'" *Training and Development Journal* (July 1980); Gerard R. Roche, "Much Ado About Mentors," *Harvard Business Review* (January–February 1979); T. J. Halatin, "Why Be a Mentor," *Supervisory Management* (February 1981); Michael G. Zey, "Mentor Programs: Making the Right Moves," *Personnel Journal* (February 1985).

merchant guild: *see* GUILD.

merit increase, raise in pay based upon a favorable review of an employee's performance. This is the way most organizations seek to relate quality of performance to financial rewards. *See* A. Mikalachki,

"There Is No Merit in Merit Pay!" *The Business Quarterly* (Spring 1976); Ernest C. Miller, "Top- and Middle-Management Compensation—Part 2: Incentive Bonus and Merit Increase Plans," *Compensation Review* (Fourth Quarter 1976); Douglas L. Fleuter, "A Different Approach to Merit Increases," *Personnel Journal* (April 1979); James T. Brinks, "Is There Merit in Merit Increases?" *The Personnel Administrator* (May 1980); Jeffrey D. Schwartz, "Maintaining Merit Compensation in a High Inflation Economy," *Personnel Journal* (February 1982).

merit pay system, also called MERIT PAY PROGRAM, set of procedures designed to reward employees with salary increases reflective of their on-the-job performance. According to Myles H. Goldberg, "Another Look at Merit Pay Programs," *Compensation Review* (Third Quarter 1977),

Many merit pay programs are built around the concept of a fixed pool of merit increase dollars. This pool is derived usually by applying a percentage merit increase factor to the salaries of currently employed staff. Administrative guidelines define the average merit increase (usually as a percentage of salary) and restrict the increase to an amount within a set range. Typically, satisfactory or acceptable performance merits an average pay increase, better-than-acceptable performance merits a larger increase, and less-than-acceptable performance merits a lower increase.

Also see Don R. Marshall, "Merit Pay Without Headaches: How to Design a Plan for Nonexempts," *Compensation Review* (Second Quarter 1975); Edward E. Lawler, "Merit Pay: Fact or Fiction?" *Management Review* (April 1981); James G. Goodale and Michael W. Mouser, "Developing and Auditing a Merit Pay System," *Personnel Journal* (May 1981); Richard E. Kopelman and Leon Reinharth, "Research Results: The Effect of Merit Pay Practices on White Collar Performance," *Compensation Review* (Fourth Quarter 1982); Jone L. Pearce and James L. Perry, "Federal Merit Pay: A Longitudinal Analysis," *Public Administration Review* (July–August 1983), Robert A. Printz and David A. Waldman, "The Merit of Merit Pay," *Personnel Administrator* (January 1985).

merit principle, the concept that members of an organization are selected and promoted based on achievements measured in a standard way through open competition.

merit promotion, selection to a higher grade made solely on the basis of job-related qualifications without regard to factors such as race, color, religion, national origin, sex, age, political belief, marital status, or physical handicap.

merit raise: *see* MERIT INCREASE.

merit system, a public sector concept of staffing, which implies that no test of party membership is involved in the selection, promotion, or retention of government employees and that a constant effort is made to select the best qualified individuals available for appointment and advancement. For a classic analysis of why it ain't necessarily so, *see* E. S. Savas and Sigmund G. Ginsburg, "The Civil Service: A Meritless System?" *The Public Interest* (Summer 1973). *Also see* Nicholas P. Lovrich, Jr., *et al.,* "Do Public Servants Welcome or Fear Merit Evaluation of Their Performance?" *Public Administration Review* (May-June 1980); Lawrence D. Greene, "Federal Merit Requirements: A Retrospective Look," *Public Personnel Management* (Spring 1982).

merit system principles, the Civil Service Reform Act of 1978 put into law the nine basic merit principles that should govern all personnel practices in the federal government and defined prohibited practices. The principles and prohibitions are:

Personnel Practices
and Actions in the
Federal Government Require:
- Recruitment from all segments of society, and selection and advancement on the basis of ability, knowledge, and skills, under fair and open competition.
- Fair and equitable treatment in all personnel management matters, without regard to politics, race, color, religion, national origin, sex, marital status, age, or handicapping condition, and with proper regard for individual privacy and constitutional rights.
- Equal pay for work of equal value, considering both national and local rates paid by private employers, with incentives and recognition for excellent performance.
- High standards of integrity, conduct, and concern for the public interest.
- Efficient and effective use of the Federal work force.
- Retention of employees who perform well, correcting the performance of those whose work is inadequate, and separation of those who cannot or will not meet required standards.
- Improved performance through effective education and training.
- Protection of employees from arbitrary action, personal favoritism, or political coercion.
- Protection of employees against reprisal for lawful disclosures of information.

Officials and Employees Who Are Authorized to Take Personnel Actions Are Prohibited From:
- Discriminating against any employee or applicant.
- Soliciting or considering any recommendation on a person who requests or is being considered for a personnel action unless the material is an evaluation of the person's work performance, ability, aptitude, or general qualifications, or character, loyalty, and suitability.
- Using official authority to coerce political actions, to require political contributions, or to retaliate for refusal to do these things.
- Willfully deceiving or obstructing an individual as to his or her right to compete for Federal employment.
- Influencing anyone to withdraw from competition, whether to improve or worsen the prospects of any applicant.
- Granting any special preferential treat-

ment or advantage not authorized by law to a job applicant or employee.

- Appointing, employing, promoting, or advancing relatives in their agencies.
- Taking or failing to take a personnel action as a reprisal against employees who exercise their appeal rights; refuse to engage in political activity; or lawfully disclose violations of law, rule, or regulation, or mismanagement, gross waste of funds, abuse of authority, or a substantial and specific danger to public health or safety.
- Taking or failing to take any other personnel action violating a law, rule, or regulation directly related to merit system principles.

Merit Systems Protection Board (MSPB), independent federal government agency created by the Civil Service Reform Act of 1978 and designed to safeguard both the merit system and individual employees against abuses and unfair personnel actions. The MSPB is headed by three board members, appointed on a bipartisan basis to 7-year nonrenewable terms. The MSPB hears and decides employee appeals and orders corrective and disciplinary actions against an employee or agency when appropriate. It also oversees the merit system and reports annually to Congress on how the system is functioning.

Within the MSPB is an independent special counsel, appointed by the president for a 5-year term. The special counsel has the power to investigate charges of prohibited personnel practices (including reprisals against whistleblowers), to ask MSPB to stop personnel actions in cases involving prohibited personnel practices, and to bring disciplinary charges before the MSPB against those who violate merit system law.

Merit Systems Protection Board
1120 Vermont Ave., N.W.
Washington, DC 20419
(202) 653-7124

meritocracy, word coined by Michael Young, in his *The Rise of the Meritocracy, 1870-2033* (London: Thames & Hudson,

1958; Penguin Books, 1961). Referred to a governing class that was both intelligent and energetic, yet sowed the seeds of its own destruction because of its obsession with test scores and paper qualifications that eventually forced those deemed to have lesser IQs to revolt. A favorite slogan of the revolutionaries was "Beauty is achievable by all." Today meritocracy is often used to refer to any elitist system of government or education. The grisly connotation of the word's original use has been effectively forgotten.

Merrick differential piece rate, also called MERRICK MULTIPLE PIECE RATE, incentive wage plan that establishes three different piece rates on the basis of performance— one for beginners, one for average workers, and one for superior workers.

Merton, Robert K. (1910-   ), sociologist who did pioneering work on the concepts of bureaucratic goal displacement and bureaucratic dysfunctions. Major works include: "Bureaucratic Structure and Personality," *Social Forces* 18 (1940); *Social Theory and Social Structure* (New York: The Free Press, 1949; revised edition enlarged, 1957); *Reader in Bureaucracy,* edited with others (New York: The Free Press, 1952); *The Focused Interview,* with others (New York: The Free Press, 1956); *The Sociology of Science: Theoretical and Empirical Investigations* (Chicago: University of Chicago Press, 1973); *Sociological Ambivalence and Other Essays* (New York: The Free Press, 1976).

Metcalf, Henry C. (1867-1942), a leading advocate of a "humanized industrialism" and co-author of one of the earliest and most influential texts on personnel administration. Major works include: *Personnel Administration: Its Principles and Practices,* with Ordway Tead (N.Y.: McGraw-Hill, 1920); *Scientific Foundations of Business Administration* (Baltimore: The Williams & Wilkins Co., 1926); *Dynamic Administration: The Collected Papers of Mary Parker Follett,* edited with Lyndall Urwick (N.Y.: Harper & Bros., 1942).

Metcalfe, Henry (1847-1917), a Captain in the U.S. Army who developed pioneering concepts of shop management at the Frankford Arsenal. See his *The Cost of Manufactures and the Administration of Workshops, Public and Private* (New York: Wiley & Sons, 1885).

MGD data: *see* MINORITY GROUPS DESIGNATOR DATA.

Mickey Mouse, pejorative term for many aspects of personnel administration. When Walt Disney's famous mouse made it "big" in the 1930s, he appeared in a variety of cartoon shorts that had him building something that would later fall apart (such as a house or boat) or generally going to a great deal of trouble for little result. So Mickey Mouse gradually gave his name to anything requiring considerable effort for slight result, including many of the Mickey Mouse requirements of personnel. The term is also applied to policies or regulations felt to be needless, silly, or mildly offensive.

microeconomics, the study of how small economic units (*i.e.*, the consumer, the household, etc.) interrelate with the market in determining the relative price of goods and the factors of production. For texts, *see* Robert L. Heilbroner and Lester C. Thurow, *Understanding Microeconomics* (Englewood Cliffs, N.J.: Prentice-Hall, 4th ed., 1978); R. Stephen Polkinghorn, *Micro-Theory and Economic Choices* (Homewood, Ill.: Richard D. Irwin, Inc., 1979); William P. Albrecht, Jr., *Microeconomic Principles* (Englewood Cliffs, N.J.: Prentice-Hall, 1979); J. P. Gould, *Microeconomic Theory* (Homewood, Ill.: Richard D. Irwin, Inc., 5th ed., 1980).

mid-career change: *see* CAREER CHANGE.

mid-career crisis, also MID-LIFE CRISIS, terms used to refer to a period in a person's life, usually during his/her 30s, which is marked by feelings of (1) personal frustration and (2) professional failure. Such feelings may or may not have a basis in fact. For general accounts of mid-life crisis, *see* Gail Sheehy, *Passages: Predictable Crises of Adult Life* (N.Y.: E. P. Dutton, 1976); Roger Gould, *Transformations* (N.Y.: Simon and Schuster, 1978). For analyses of the problem of mid-career crises, *see* Harry Levinson, "On Being a Middle-Aged Manager," *Harvard Business Review* (July-August, 1969); Robert T. Golembiewski, "Mid-Life Transition and Mid-Career Crisis: A Special Case For Individual Development," *Public Administration Review* (May-June, 1978); Daniel J. Levinson *et al.*, *The Seasons of a Man's Life* (New York: Knopf, 1978); Barbara S. Lawrence, "The Myth of the Midlife Crisis," *Sloan Management Review* (Summer 1980); Raymond E. Hill and Edwin L. Miller, "Job Change and the Middle Seasons of a Man's Life," *Academy of Management Journal* (March 1981); Richard A. Payne, "Mid-Career Block," *Personnel Journal* (April 1984).
See also STRESS.

middle management, vague delineation of organizational authority and leadership that lies below top management and above first-level supervisors. *See* Emmanuel Kay, *The Crises in Middle-Management* (N.Y.: American Management Association, 1974); Steven H. Appelbaum, "The Middle Manager: An Examination of Aspirations and Pessimism," *The Personnel Administrator* (January 1977); Rosabeth Moss Kanter, "The Middle Manager as Innovator," *Harvard Business Review* (July-August 1982); Bernard Keys and Robert Bell, "Four Faces of the Fully Functioning Middle Manager," *California Management Review* (Summer 1982).

mid-level managers: *see* MIDDLE MANAGEMENT.

mid-life crisis: *see* MID-CAREER CRISIS.

midnight shift, tour of duty that usually runs from midnight to 8 A.M.

migratory worker, individual whose principal income is earned from temporary employment (typically in agriculture) and who, in order to find work, moves several times a year through as many states. For accounts of the life of migrant workers, *see* Robert Coles, *Uprooted Children: The Early Life of Migrant Farm Workers* (N.Y.: Harper & Row, 1971); Carey McWilliams, *Ill Fares the Land: Migrants and Migratory Labor in the United States* (N.Y.: Barnes & Noble, 1967); Ronald L. Goldfarb, *Migrant Farm Workers: A Caste of Despair* (Ames: Iowa State University Press, 1981).

mileage allowance, specific amount an employee is reimbursed for each mile that his personal automobile is used on company business. For how to determine a mileage allowance rate, *see* Joseph A. Capolarello, "Employee Mileage Allowances: Too High or Too Low?" *Personnel Journal* (February 1975).

military-industrial complex, a nation's armed forces and their industrial suppliers. President Dwight D. Eisenhower warned during his farewell address in 1961 that "In the councils of government we must guard against the acquisition of unwarranted influence, whether sought or unsought, by the military-industrial complex. The potential for the disastrous rise of misplaced power exists and will persist."

military leave, lengthy leave of absence for service in the armed forces of the United States or a short-term leave of absence for service in the military reserves.

military service, as a general rule, military service for civil service retirement purposes is creditable provided it was active service, was terminated under honorable conditions, and was performed before separation from a civilian position under the retirement system. The federal government defines military service for retirement purposes as "service in the Army, Navy, Air Force, Marine Corps, and Coast Guard, including the service academies, and, after June 30, 1960, in the Regular Corps or Reserve Corps of the Public Health Service, and, after June 30, 1961, as a commissioned officer of the Coast and Geodetic Survey."

Miller Analogies Test (MAT), 100 verbal analogies designed to measure scholastic aptitude at the graduate school level and to aid in the selection of individuals for personnel positions. Primarily a measure of verbal ability that covers a broad range of knowledge. TIME 50/55 minutes. AUTHOR: W. S. Miller. PUBLISHER: Psychological Corporation (*see* TEST PUBLISHERS).

Miller, Arnold (1922-1985), president of the United Mine Workers of America from 1972 to 1979. *See* Paul F. Clark, *The Miners' Fight for Democracy: Arnold Miller and the Reform of the United Mine Workers* (Ithaca, N.Y.: Cornell University, New York State School of Industrial and Labor Relations, 1981).

Miller v. Wilson, 236 U.S. 373 (1915), U.S. Supreme Court case, which held that a state law limiting the employment of women to eight hours a day was constitutional.

Mine Safety and Health Administration (MSHA), agency of the Department of Labor created by the Federal Mine Safety and Health Amendments Act of 1977 to bring all mines in the United States under a single safety and health program.
Mine Safety and Health Administration
4015 Wilson Blvd.
Arlington, VA 22203
(703) 235-1452

minimum wage, smallest hourly rate that may be paid to a worker. While many "minimum wages" are established by union contracts and organizational pay policies, "the" minimum wage usually refers to the federal minimum wage law — the Fair Labor Standards Act (FLSA). The minimum wage at any given time is established by Congress via FLSA amendments. The Secretary of Labor regulates some exceptions to the minimum wage. Persons with impaired earning or production capacity because of age, physical or mental deficiencies, or injury may be paid as low as 50 percent of the wage paid to a nonhandicapped worker for the same type, quality and quantity of work.

Mini-Shift

FLSA Minimum Wage Standards

Legislation	Hourly Rate	Effective Date
Act of 1938	$ .25	Oct. 24, 1938
	.30	Oct. 24, 1939
	.40	Oct. 24, 1945
Amendments of:		
1949	.75	Jan. 25, 1950
1955	1.00	Mar. 1, 1956
1961	1.15	Sept. 3, 1961
	1.25	Sept. 3, 1963
1966	1.40	Feb. 1, 1967
	1.60	Feb. 1, 1968
1974	2.00	May 1, 1974
	2.10	Jan. 1, 1975
	2.30	Jan. 1, 1976
1977	2.65	Jan. 1, 1978
	2.90	Jan. 1, 1979
	3.10	Jan. 1, 1980
	3.35	Jan. 1, 1981

Forty-one States, the District of Columbia, and Puerto Rico have minimum wage laws for adults with minimum rates currently in effect. State minimum wage laws are of two basic types: those that contain a minimum in the law itself (a statutory rate) and those that authorize an administrator or wage board to set minimum rates by occupation or industry. Several States combine the two types and have both a statutory minimum for most employment and provisions for wage orders to establish rates and/or working conditions for certain occupations or industries. Only the legislature can change statutory rates, but wage orders can be modified by the administrator or wage board. Under both types of minimum wage law, lower rates are generally payable to learners and apprentices, handicapped persons, and minors.

Statutory State minimum wage rates for experienced adults varied widely in mid-1982—from a low of $1.25 an hour in Georgia to a high of $3.85 in Alaska. Some States provide for automatic upward adjustment if the Federal minimum wage rate is increased. When workers are covered by both the Federal minimum wage law (the Fair Labor Standards Act, or FLSA) and a State law, they are entitled to the higher rate.

Full-time students may be employed at 85 percent of the minimum wage under certain conditions. For an analysis of how youth unemployment, particularly black youth, would be reduced if a lower minimum wage was available for teenagers, see "Would the 'Teenwage' Cut Unemployment?" *Business Week* (September 19, 1977). *Also see* Peyton Elder, "The 1977 Amendments to the Federal Minimum Wage Law," *Monthly Labor Review* (January 1978); Sar A. Levitan and R. S. Belous, "The Minimum Wage Today: How Well Does It Work?" *Monthly Labor Review* (July 1979); D. Quinn Mills and Shirley Frobes, "Impact of Increases in the Federal Minimum Wage on Target Groups in Urban Areas," *Public Policy* (Summer 1981); Robert Swidinsky and David A. Wilton, "Minimum Wages, Wage Inflation, and the Relative Wage Structure," *The Journal of Human Resources* (Spring 1982); John Z. Drabicki and Akira Takayama, "Minimum Wage Regulation and Economic Growth," *Journal of Economics and Business,* Vol. 34, No. 3 (1982); Curtis L. Gilroy, "The Effects of the Minimum Wage on Farm Employment: A New Model," *Monthly Labor Review* (June 1982); Brigitte H. Sellekaerts and Stephen W. Welch, "An Econometric Analysis of Minimum Wage Noncompliance," *Industrial Relations* (Spring 1984).

See also NATIONAL LEAGUE OF CITIES V. USERY and WEST COAST HOTEL V. PARRISH.

mini-shift, tour of duty for a permanent part-time employee. For an analysis of its utility, *see* William B. Werther, Jr., "Mini-Shifts: An Alternative to Overtime," *Personnel Journal* (March 1976).

Minnesota Clerical Test (MCT), test of clerical ability that measures perception of detail and perceptual speed. The two test parts (numbers and names) list identical and nonidentical pairs for the subject to detect unlike pairs. TIME: 15/20 minutes. AUTHORS: D. C. Andrew, D. G. Paterson, and H. P. Longstaff. PUBLISHER: Psychological Corporation (*see* TEST PUBLISHERS).

Minnesota Multiphasic Personality Inventory (MMPI), 566-item, paper-and-pencil inventory that measures degrees of hypochondriasis, depression, hysteria, psychopathic deviation, masculinity-femininity, paranoia, psychasthenia, schizophrenia, hypomania, and social introversion. Originally designed to reveal pathological tendencies, this test is now widely used by business and industry in personnel selection and counseling procedures. However, proper interpretation of test results requires considerable psychological sophistication. TIME: Untimed. AUTHORS: S. R. Hathaway, J. C. McKinley. PUBLISHERS: Psychological Corporation (see TEST PUBLISHERS).

Minnesota Rate of Manipulation Test, two-part test that measures arm-hand dexterity. The test requires an individual to place 58 round blocks into a board with matching slots, turn the blocks out, and again place them in the holes. Person is scored on total time required to complete the task. TIME: 30/40 minutes. AUTHOR: Minnesota Employment Stabilization Research Institute. PUBLISHER: American Guidance Services, Inc. (see TEST PUBLISHERS).

Minnesota Spatial Relations Test, test that measures both manual dexterity and spatial perceptions. It consists of four form boards with 58 cut-out geometric shapes to be placed in appropriate cut-out slots. TIME: 20 minutes. AUTHOR: Minnesota Employment Stabilization Research Institute. PUBLISHER: American Guidance Services, Inc. (see TEST PUBLISHERS).

Minnesota Vocational Interest Inventory (MVII), consists of 158 forced-choice items that provide 21 occupational and 9 area scales of interest patterns. Designed for those (age 15 and over) contemplating occupations at the semiskilled and skilled levels (i.e., baker, printer, carpenter/painter, truck driver, sales and office clerk, electronics, etc.). TIME: 45/50 minutes. AUTHORS: K. E. Clark and David P. Campbell. PUBLISHER: Psychological Corporation (see TEST PUBLISHERS).

minority groups designator data, also called MGD DATA, data base or system which provides statistical employment information by race or national origin. In theory, such data should only be used in studies and analyses that evaluate an organization's equal employment opportunity programs.

MIS: see MANAGEMENT INFORMATION SYSTEM.

misery index, the total of the rates of inflation and unemployment.

mission agency, any government department or agency whose legislation gives it responsibility for promotion of some cause or operation of some system as its primary reason for existence (mission) and which is appropriated funds for the conduct of this mission.

Mitbestimmungsrecht: see CO-DETERMINATION.

Mitchell, James P. (1900-1964), Secretary of Labor from 1953 to 1961.

Mitchell, John (1870-1919), president of the United Mine Workers from 1898 to 1907 when membership grew from 33,000 to 260,000. For a biography, see Elsie Gluck, *John Mitchell, Miner* (N.Y.: John Day Co., 1929; reprinted AMS Press, 1971).

mixed economy, if at one end of a continuum were laissez-faire capitalism and at the other end were socialism, then an economic system that lies somewhere in the middle would be a *mixed economy*. All of the industrialized countries of the free world have mixed economies; some are just more mixed up than others.

MLR: see MONTHLY LABOR REVIEW.

MMPI: see MINNESOTA MULTIPHASIC PERSONALITY INVENTORY.

mobility: see OCCUPATIONAL MOBILITY.

mobility assignment, term generally used

for the sharing of talent between the federal government and states, local governments, and institutions of higher education, as authorized by Title IV of the Intergovernmental Personnel Act of 1970, Public Law 91-648. Title IV is designed to: (1) improve the delivery of government services at all levels of government by bringing the specialized knowledge and experience of skilled people to bear on problems that are of mutual concern to state or local jurisdictions and the federal government; (2) strengthen intergovernmental understanding, broaden perspective and increase capacity of personnel resources; and (3) help preserve the rights and benefits of employees so they will be better able to accept temporary assignments.

mode, score or value that occurs most frequently in a distribution.

model, a simplification of reality, a reduction in time and space that allows for a better understanding of reality. The representation may be expressed in words, numbers, or diagrams. A *deterministic model* is one in which the variables take definite values; that is, a model that does not permit any risk as to the magnitude of the variables; for example, a set of simultaneous equations for which there is a unique solution. A *probabilistic model* is one in which each variable may take on more than one value. Such models are sometimes called *stochastic,* and values are assigned according to probability distributions. An *econometric model* is a mathematical formulation of economic relationships. An *economic model* is a construct which reflects the assumptions of a particular economic theory.

model agreement, collective bargaining agreement developed by a national or international union to serve as a standard for its locals.

modeling, the identification of the fixed and variable components in a system, assigning them numerical or economic values, and relating them to each other in a logical fashion to derive optimal solutions to operational problems by manipulating the components of the model.

modified union shop, variation of the union shop that exempts certain classes of employees from joining the union. Such exemptions might include employees who were employed before a certain date, seasonal workers, work study students, etc.

mole: *see* SANDHOG.

Molly Maguires, originally members of an Irish secret society—the Ancient Order of Hibernians (founded in 1843), to prevent the eviction of tenant farmers by process-servers of the English landlords—the Molly Maguires got their name because of their tendency to disguise themselves as women while engaging in their terrorist activities. After the U.S. Civil War, they established themselves as secret worker societies in the coal fields of Pennsylvania and West Virginia. Their terror tactics ceased and their organization disappeared in 1876 when 10 of their leaders were executed and 14 others jailed. For a history, *see* Wayne G. Broehl, Jr., *The Molly Maguires* (Cambridge, Mass.: Harvard University Press, 1964). *See also* Sidney Lens, *The Labor Wars: From the Molly Maguires to the Sitdowns* (Garden City, N.Y.: Doubleday, 1973).

Monell v. Dept. of Social Services, New York City, 56 L. Ed. 2d 611 (1978), U.S. Supreme Court case, which held that cities and municipalities may be held liable when their official policies (in this case a mandatory maternity leave policy) or customs violate a person's constitutional rights.

monetary policy, a government's formal efforts to manage the money in its economy in order to realize specific economic goals. Three basic kinds of monetary policy decisions can be made: (1) decisions about the amount of money in circulation; (2) decisions about the level of interest rates; and (3) decisions about the functioning of credit markets and the banking system.

money purchase benefit, pension that is entirely dependent on contributions made to an individual's account.

monotony curve: *see* FATIGUE CURVE.

Monte Carlo techniques, operations research processes premised upon the laws of probability.

Monthly Labor Review (MLR), major publication of the U.S. Bureau of Labor Statistics. Articles deal with labor relations, trends in the labor force, new laws and court decisions effecting workers, etc. Lists the major labor agreements expiring each month and gives monthly current labor statistics on employment, unemployment, wages and prices, and productivity.

> *Monthly Labor Review*
> **Editorial Address:**
> Bureau of Labor Statistics
> U.S. Department of Labor
> Washington, D.C. 20210
> **Subscriptions:**
> Superintendent of Documents
> Government Printing Office
> Washington, D.C. 20402

Mooney, Tom (1882-1942), full name THOMAS JOSEPH MOONEY, socialist and radical unionist sentenced to hang because of a bombing that killed ten people in a San Francisco parade in 1916. Because it later became obvious that he was convicted on false testimony, his case became a *cause celèbre* of the union movement. The governor of California commuted his death sentence to life imprisonment in 1918; a later governor pardoned him in 1939. For accounts of his troubles, *see* Richard H. Frost, *The Mooney Case* (Stanford, Calif.: Stanford University Press, 1968); Curt Gentry, *Frame-Up: The Incredible Case of Tom Mooney and Warren Billings* (N.Y.: Norton, 1967).

moonlighting, in the 19th century, moonlighting referred to any illicit nighttime activity. In the mid 1950s, it gained currency as a slang term for a second job. Employee moonlighting may impede primary job productivity and otherwise cause problems when there are questions about sick leave claims, absenteeism, tardiness, overtime scheduling, and potential conflict of interest. Many employers—because of union contracts, civil service regulations, or company policy—formally restrict moonlighting by their employees. Typically, such restrictions require advance approval and stipulate that moonlighting be done outside of regularly scheduled work periods. According to the Bureau of Labor Statistics of the U.S. Department of Labor, 4.7 percent of all employed persons hold two or more jobs. Men employed in the protective services (primarily police and fire) and as teachers (except college) had the highest rates of moonlighting—10.4 percent and 16.3 percent respectively. For a complete analysis, *see* Kopp Michelotti, "Multiple Jobholding in May 1975," *Monthly Labor Review* (November 1975). *Also see* Lawrence Stessin, "Moonlighting: The Employer's Dilemma," *Personnel* (January-February 1981).

Moore, Ely (1798-1861), first president of the New York General Trades' Union in 1833 who later served in the U.S. Congress. For a biography, *see* Walter E. Hugins, "Ely Moore: The Case History of a Jacksonian Labor Leader," *Political Science Quarterly* (March 1950).

morale, collective attitude of the workforce toward their work environment and a crude measure of the organizational climate. Peter F. Drucker insists that the only true test of morale is performance. As such, morale is one of the most significant indicators of organizational health. "What physical health is to a physical organization, morale is to a cooperative system," said Fritz J. Roethlisberger, in *Management and Morale* (Cambridge, Mass.: Harvard University Press, 1941).

Also see Louis C. Schroeter, *Organizational Elan* (N.Y.: American Management Association, 1970); Robert G. Pajer, "The Relationship of Morale to Productivity," *Public Personnel Review* (October 1970); Christian F. Paul and Albert C. Gross, "Increasing Productivity and Morale in Municipality: Effects of Organization Development," *Journal of Applied Behavioral Science* (January–February–March 1981); Robert H. Garin and John F. Cooper, "The Morale-Productivity Relationship: How Close?" *Personnel* (January–February 1981).

Mosher, Frederick C. (1913–   ), a major voice in public administration who wrote the standard historical analysis of the civil service in the United States, *Democracy and the Public Service* (N.Y.: Oxford University Press, 1968). Other works include: *Governmental Reorganizations: Cases and Commentary* (Indianapolis, Indiana: Bobbs-Merrill, 1967); *Programming Systems and Foreign Affairs Leadership* (N.Y.: Oxford University Press, 1970); *American Public Administration: Past, Present, and Future* (University, Alabama: University of Alabama Press, 1975).

Mosher, William E. (1877–1945), founder and first president (1940–1941) of the American Society for Public Administration. Co-author, with J. Donald Kingsley, of the first public personnel text, *Public Personnel Administration* (N.Y.: Harper Bros., 1936).

most-favored nation, trade policy whereby countries agree to give each other the most favorable trade concessions that they might separately give to any other country.

most-favored-nation clause, also called MORE-FAVORABLE-TERMS CLAUSE, that portion of a collective bargaining agreement where a union agrees not to sign contracts with any other employers under more favorable terms.

Mother Lake: *see* BARRY, LEONORA.

motion study, according to Benjamin W. Niebel, *Motion and Time Study* (Homewood, Ill.: Richard D. Irwin, 6th ed., 1976), motion study

> may be defined as the study of the body motions used in performing an operation, with the thought of improving the operation by eliminating unnecessary

motions and simplifying necessary motions, and then establishing the most favorable motion sequence for maximum efficiency.

See also TIME STUDY.

motivation, also WORK MOTIVATION, an emotional stimulus that causes a person to act. *Work motivation* is an amalgam of all of the factors in one's working environment that foster (positively or negatively) productive efforts. Classic analyses of worker motivation include: A. H. Maslow, *Motivation and Personality* (N.Y.: Harper & Row, 1954); F. Herzberg, B. Mausner, and B. Snyderman, *The Motivation to Work* (N.Y.: John Wiley, 1959); V. H. Vroom, *Work and Motivation* (N.Y.: John Wiley, 1964).

See also Kae H. Chung, *Motivational Theories and Practices* (Columbus, Ohio: Grid, Inc., 1977); Bernard L. Rosenbaum, *How to Motivate Today's Workers: Motivational Models for Managers and Supervisors,* (New York: McGraw-Hill Book Co., 1982); Gene Milbourn, Jr., "The Relationship of Money and Motivation," *Compensation Review* (Second Quarter 1980); Philip C. Grant, "Why Employee Motivation Has Declined in America," *Personnel Journal* (December 1982); William Rabinowitz, Kenneth Falkenbach, Jeffrey R. Travers, C. Glenn Valentine and Paul Weener, "Worker Motivation: Unsolved Problem or Untapped Resource?" *California Management Review* (January 1983); Larry L. Cummings, "Compensation, Culture and Motivation: A Systems Perspective," *Organizational Dynamics* (Winter 1984); Michael E. Cavanagh, "In Search of Motivation," *Personnel Journal* (March 1984); Leonard Ackerman and Joseph P. Grunenwald, "Help Employees Motivate Themselves," *Personnel Journal* (July 1984).

See also the following entries:
EXTRINSIC MOTIVATION
REINFORCEMENT
SELF-ACTUALIZATION
STROKING

Motivation-Hygiene Theory, also called TWO-FACTOR THEORY, put forth in a land-

Theorist	Assumptions of man	Contribution
Scientific management (Taylor)	Economic man	Man primarily motivated by financial reward
Human Relations School (Mayo)	Social man	Importance of informal organizations on human behavior
Maslow	Self-actualizing man	Hierarchy of needs
Herzberg	Self-actualizing man	Motivation-hygiene theory
McGregor	Self-actualizing man	Theory X, Theory Y views of man
Vroom	Complex man (Contingency view)	Expectancy theory

Major contributors to theories of motivation.

Source: P. Bryans and T. P. Cronin, Organization Theory (London: Mitchell Beazley, 1983), p. 54.

mark study by Frederick Herzberg, Bernard Mausner, and Barbara Snyderman, in *The Motivation to Work* (N.Y.: John Wiley & Sons, 1959). It was one of the first extensive empirical demonstrations of the primacy of internal worker motivation. Five factors were isolated as determiners of job satisfaction: achievement, recognition, work itself, responsibility and advancement. Similarly, the factors associated with job dissatisfaction were realized: company policy and administration, supervision, salary, interpersonal relations, and working conditions. The satisfying factors were all related to job content, the dissatisfying factors to the environmental context of the job. The factors that were associated with job satisfaction were quite separate from those factors associated with job dissatisfaction. According to Herzberg, in "The Motivation-Hygiene Concept and the Problems of Manpower," *Personnel Administration* (January–February 1964):

Since separate factors needed to be considered depending on whether job satisfaction or job dissatisfaction was involved, it followed that these two feelings were not the obverse of each other. The opposite of job satisfaction would not be job dissatisfaction but rather NO job satisfaction; and similarly the opposite of job dissatisfaction is NO job dissatisfaction—not job satisfaction.

Because the environmental context of jobs, such as working conditions, interpersonal relations, and salary, served primarily as preventatives, they were termed hygiene factors; as an analogy to the medical use of hygiene meaning preventative and environmental. The job-content factors such as achievement, advancement, and responsibility were termed motivators because these are the things that motivate people to superior performance. Again according to Herzberg, in *Work and the Nature of Man* (Cleveland: World Publishers, 1966):

The principal result of the analysis of this data was to suggest that the hygiene or maintenance events led to job dissatisfaction because of a need to avoid unpleasantness; the motivator events led to job satisfaction because of a need for growth or self-actualization. At the psychological level, the two dimensions of job attitudes reflected a two-dimensional need structure: one need system for the avoidance of unpleasantness and a parallel need system for personal growth.

Since its original presentation, a considerable number of empirical investigations by a wide variety of researchers has tended to confirm the Motivation-Hygiene Theory. Its chief fault seems to be its rejection of the view that pay is a unique incentive capable, in differing circumstances, of being a hygiene as well as a motivator factor. But the theory's main holding—that worker motivation is essentially internal—remains largely unchallenged.

See also HERZBERG, FREDERICK.

Motor Coach Employees v. Lockridge:
see AMALGAMATED ASSOCIATION OF

STREET, ELECTRIC RAILWAY, AND MOTOR COACH EMPLOYEES OF AMERICA V. LOCKRIDGE.

Mountain Timber Company v. Washington, 343 U.S. 238 (1917), U.S. Supreme Court case, which held constitutional state workmen's compensation laws.

Mouton, Jane S.: see BLAKE, ROBERT R. AND JANE S. MOUTON.

MPA: see MBA.

Ms., title of courtesy for a woman, which is used without regard to her marital status. On January 26, 1977, the U.S. Civil Service Commission announced that it would revise all of its personnel forms—including job application forms—to make "Ms." available for those who prefer it. As present stocks are depleted and the forms are reprinted, the change will be incorporated in all forms that require a title. The commission also instructed all federal agencies under its jurisdiction to incorporate "Ms." in addition to "Miss," "Mrs.," and "Mr." on their internal personnel forms.

MSHA: see MINE SAFETY AND HEALTH ADMINISTRATION.

MSPB: see MERIT SYSTEMS PROTECTION BOARD.

Mt. Clemens case: see ANDERSON V. MT. CLEMENS POTTERY.

Mt. Healthy Board of Education v. Doyle, 429 U.S. 274 (1977), U.S. Supreme Court case, which held that the first amendment does not demand that a discharged employee be placed "in a better position as a result of the exercise of constitutionally protected activity than he would have occupied had he done nothing." An employer should not be inhibited from evaluating an employee's performance and "reaching a decision not to rehire on the basis of that record, simply because the protected conduct makes the employer more certain of the correctness of its decision." See William H. DuRoss, III,

"Toward Rationality in Discriminatory Cases: The Impact of *Mt. Healthy Board of Education v. Doyle* Upon the NLRA," *The Georgetown Law Journal* (April 1978).

Muller v. Oregon, 208 U.S. 412 (1908), U.S. Supreme Court case, which held constitutional an Oregon law that limited the employment of women to ten hours a day as a health measure.

multicraft union, craft union that encompasses several different skilled occupations.

multiemployer bargaining, collective bargaining involving more than one company, usually in the same industry. *See* Richard Pegnetter, *Multiemployer Bargaining in the Public Sector: Purposes and Experiences* (Chicago: International Personnel Management Association, 1975); Robert B. Hoffman, "The Trend Away from Multiemployer Bargaining," *Labor Law Journal* (February 1983).

Multiple Aptitude Tests (MAP), battery of nine tests used for vocational guidance. Measures word meaning, paragraph meaning, language usage, routine clerical facility, arithmetic reasoning, arithmetic computation, applied science and mechanical and spatial relations. TIME: 175/220 minutes (3 sessions). AUTHORS: David Segel and Evelyn Raskin. PUBLISHER: California Test Bureau/McGraw-Hill (*see* TEST PUBLISHERS).

multiple-choice test, test consisting entirely of multiple-choice items, which require the examinee to choose the best or correct answer from several that are given as options. *See* J. Marshall Trieber, "The Use of Multiple-Choice for Testing," *Training and Development Journal* (October 1980).

multiple cutting score, assignment of a cutting score to each of several tests (or other standards) and the requirement that an applicant achieve a passing score on each of them to be hired or eligible for hire.

multiple regression analysis: *see* REGRESSION ANALYSIS.

multiple time plan, wage incentive plan that provides for higher base rates as progressively higher levels of production are reached.

Muniz v. Hoffman, 422 U.S. 454 (1975), U.S. Supreme Court case, which held that a union did not have a statutory or constitutional right to a jury trial on charges of criminal contempt stemming from its violation of an injunction issued under the authority of the National Labor Relations Act.

Munsterberg, Hugo (1863–1916), German psychologist who spent his later years at Harvard and earned the title of "father" of industrial or applied psychology by proposing the use of psychology for practical purposes. His major book is *Psychology and Industrial Efficiency* (Boston: Houghton Mifflin, 1913). For a sympathetic biography, *see* Margaret Munsterberg, *Hugo Munsterberg: His Life and Work* (N.Y.: Appleton-Century-Crofts, 1922).

Also see Merle J. Moskowitz, "Hugo Munsterberg: A Study in the History of Applied Psychology," *American Psychologist* (October 1977); Matthew Hale, Jr., *Human Science and Social Order: Hugo Munsterberg and the Origins of Applied Psychology* (Philadelphia: Temple University Press, 1980).

Murgia **decision:** *see* MASSACHUSETTS BOARD OF RETIREMENT V. MURGIA.

Murphy's Law, *Public Administration Review* (July 1976) published the following Murphy's Laws:
1. Anything that can go wrong will go wrong.
2. Anything that can go wrong will—at the worst possible time.
3. Nothing is as easy as it seems.
4. If there is a possibility of several things going wrong, the one that will go wrong is the one that will do the most damage.
5. Everything takes longer than it should.
6. Left to themselves, things will go from bad to worse.
7. Nature always sides with the hidden flaw.
8. If everything seems to be going well, you have obviously overlooked something.

Murphy seems related to that famous literary wit, Anonymous. Only one thing seems certain—Murphy's laws were not written by Murphy, but by another person with the same name. *Also see* William C. Waddell, *Overcoming Murphy's Law* (New York: AMACOM, 1981).

Murray, Philip (1886–1952), first president of the United Steelworkers of America and president of the Congress of Industrial Organizations (CIO) from 1940 until his death.

mushroom management, all that mushrooms need in order to grow is to be left undisturbed in the dark and fed fertilizer frequently. Mushroom managers keep subordinates in the dark and feed them lots of manure. Unfortunately, this technique works better on real mushrooms than it does on subordinates—they cease to grow at all. *Source:* William Thomas, "Humor for Hurdling the Mystique in Management," *Management of Personnel Quarterly* (Winter 1970).

Muste, A. J. (1885–1967), in full ABRAHAM JOHANNES MUSTE, labor leader until the late 1930s when he turned his major efforts toward Christian pacifism. For biographies, *see* Nat Hentoff, *Peace Agitator: The Story of A. J. Muste* (N.Y.: MacMillan, 1963); Jo Ann Robinson, *Abraham Went Out: A Biography of A. J. Muste* (Philadelphia: Temple University Press, 1981).

mutuality: *see* DOCTRINE OF MUTUALITY.

mutual rating: *see* PEER RATING.

mutual strike aid, also called EMPLOYER STRIKE INSURANCE, formal strike insurance program that has employees in a particular industry share the financial burden of a strike. Companies operating normally return a portion of their additional earnings to the company whose employees are on strike. Some mutual strike aid programs operate by assessing their member companies on an annual basis. *See* John S. Hirsch, Jr., "Strike Insurance and Collective Bargaining," *Industrial and Labor Relations Review* (April 1969). For a legal analysis, *see* Frank M. Tuerkheimer, "Strike Insurance: An Analysis of the Legality of Inter-Employer Economic Aid Under Present Federal Legislation," *New York University Law Review* (January 1963).

MVII: *see* MINNESOTA VOCATIONAL INTEREST INVENTORY.

Myers-Briggs Type Indicator (MBTI), 166 item paper-and-pencil test of four bipolar aspects of personality: Introversion-Extroversion, Sensing-Intuition, Thinking-Feeling, and Judging-Perceptive. The subjects are classified as one of two "types" on each scale. The test is heavily influenced by Jungian theories of personality types and the ways in which these types express their personality traits through perceptions, judgments, interests, values and motivations. A theoretical background in dynamic psychology is helpful in maximizing the benefits of research compiled for this test. TIME: Untimed. AUTHORS: Isabel Briggs Myers and Katharine C. Briggs. PUBLISHER: Consulting Psychologists Press (*see* TEST PUBLISHERS).

Myers, M. Scott (1922-   ), industrial psychologist and leading authority on job design and motivation. Major works include: *Every Employee a Manager: More Meaningful Work Through Job Enrichment,* 2nd ed. (N.Y.: McGraw-Hill, 1981); "Overcoming Union Opposition to Job Enrichment," *Harvard Business Review* (May-June 1971); *Managing with Unions* (Reading, Mass.: Addison-Wesley, 1978).

N

N, mathematical symbol commonly used to represent the number of cases in a distribution, study, etc. The symbol of the number of cases in a subgroup of *N* is *n*.

NAACP v. Federal Power Commission: *see* NATIONAL ASSOCIATION FOR THE ADVANCEMENT OF COLORED PEOPLE V. FEDERAL POWER COMMISSION.

NAB: *see* NATIONAL ALLIANCE OF BUSINESS.

Nagler, Isidore (1895-1959), one of the pioneering labor organizers and leaders of the garment industry.

NALC decision: *see* UNITED STATES CIVIL SERVICE COMMISSION V. NATIONAL ASSOCIATION OF LETTER CARRIERS.

NAM: *see* NATIONAL ASSOCIATION OF MANUFACTURERS.

NAPA: *see* NATIONAL ACADEMY OF PUBLIC ADMINISTRATION.

Nashville Gas Co. v. Satty, 434 U.S. 136 (1977), U.S. Supreme Court case, which held that pregnant women, forced to take maternity leave, cannot be denied their previously accumulated seniority rights when they return to work.

NASS: *see* NATIONAL ASSOCIATION OF SUGGESTION SYSTEMS.

NATB: *see* NONREADING APTITUDE TEST BATTERY.

national, a union composed of a variety of widely dispersed affiliated local unions. The Bureau of Labor Statistics defines a national union as one with agreements with different employers in more than one state. The terms "national union" and "international union" tend to be used interchangeably; the only difference being (in the American context) that "international" unions have locals in Canada.

National Academy of Arbitrators, founded in 1947 "to establish and foster high standards and competence among those engaged in the arbitration of labor-management disputes on a professional basis; to adopt canons of ethics to govern the conduct of arbitrators; to promote the study and understanding of the arbitration of labor-management disputes." The Academy is not an agency for the selection or appointment of arbitrators. It does invite and sponsor activities designed to improve general understanding of the nature of arbitration and its use as a means of settling labor disputes.

Membership in the National Academy of Arbitrators is conferred by vote of the Board of Governors upon recommendation of the Membership Committee.

In considering applications for membership, the Academy applies the following standards: (1) the applicant should be of good moral character, as demonstrated by adherence to sound ethical standards in professional activities; (2) the applicant should have substantial and current experience as an impartial arbitrator of labor-management disputes, so as to reflect general acceptability by the parties; and (3) as an alternative to (2), the applicant with limited but current experience in arbitration should have attained general recognition through scholarly publication or other activities as an impartial authority on labor-management relations. Membership will not be conferred upon applicants who serve partisan interests as advocates or consultants for Labor or Management in labor-management relations or who are associated with or are members of a firm which performs such advocate or consultant work. The Academy had about 600 members in 1984. See J. Timothy Sprehe and Jeffrey Small, "Members and Nonmembers of the National Academy of Arbitrators: Do They

Differ?" *Arbitration Journal* (September 1984).
> *National Academy of Arbitrators*
> Office of the Secretary
> Graduate School of Business
>   Administration
> University of Michigan
> Ann Arbor, MI 48109
> (313) 763-9714

National Academy of Conciliators, an organization of about 1,000 members founded in 1979 to foster alternatives to litigation through dispute settlement consultation and training.
> *National Academy of Conciliators*
> 5530 Wisconsin Ave.
> Suite 1130
> Chevy Chase, MD 20815
> (301) 654-6515

National Academy of Public Administration (NAPA), organization of more than 300 distinguished practitioners and scholars in public administration, supported by a small staff and dedicated to improving the role of public management in a democratic society. The Academy was founded in 1967 to serve as a source of advice and counsel to government and public officials on problems of public administration; to help improve the policies, processes, and institutions of public administration through early identification of important problems and significant trends; to evaluate program performance and assess administrative progress; and to increase public understanding of public administration and its critical role in a democratic society.
> *National Academy of Public*
>   *Administration*
> 1120 G Street, N.W.
> Washington, D.C. 20004
> (202) 347-3190
See also AMERICAN SOCIETY FOR PUBLIC ADMINISTRATION.

National Alliance of Business (NAB), business group formed in 1968 to work in partnership with the federal government in order to find permanent jobs for the hard core unemployed.

National Alliance of Business
1015 15th Street, N.W.
Washington, D.C. 20005
(202) 457-0040

National Association for the Advancement of Colored People (NAACP), founded in 1909, the largest and historically most influential of the Black interest groups.
NAACP
270 W. 96th Street
New York, New York 10014
(212) 749-2323

National Association for the Advancement of Colored People v. Federal Power Commission, 425 U.S. 663 (1976), U.S. Supreme Court case, which held that the Federal Power Commission is authorized to consider the consequences of discriminatory employment practices on the part of its regulatees only insofar as such consequences are directly related to its establishment of just and reasonable rates in the public interest. To the extent that illegal, duplicative, or unnecessary labor costs are demonstrably the product of a regulatee's discriminatory employment practices and can be or have been demonstrably quantified by judicial decree or the final action of an administrative agency the Federal Power Commission should disallow them.

National Association of Manufacturers (NAM), largest (13,000 members) nontrade employer's association in the United States. NAM's purpose is to unite the manufacturers of the country in order to promote public progress and general prosperity. While NAM supports the abstract rights of labor, its specific policies tend to be thought of (by organized labor at least) as being anti-labor.
National Association of Manufacturers
1776 F Street
Washington, DC 20006
(202) 626-3700

National Association of Suggestion Systems (NASS), non-profit organization founded in 1942 to promote and develop suggestion systems in industry and government. NASS seeks to develop new technology and disseminate information about suggestion systems to its more than 800 members and to all others interested in suggestion systems.
National Association of Suggestion Systems
230 North Michigan Ave.
Chicago, IL 60601
(312) 372-1770

National Center for Productivity and Quality of Working Life, federal agency that existed from 1975 to 1978. In 1970, the National Commission on Productivity was formed to focus public attention on the importance of productivity and to enlist the cooperation of labor, management, government, and the public in a sustained effort to improve the economy's performance. In 1975, Public Law 94-136 created the National Center for Productivity and Quality of Working Life as an independent agency with no regulatory authority to work with Congress and federal agencies to develop a national policy for greater productivity, improved worker morale and work quality. The new National Center thereupon assumed much of the work and the staff of the expired National Commission. After publishing a variety of reports, the National Center expired on September 30, 1978.

National Center for the Study of Collective Bargaining in Higher Education and the Professions, a clearinghouse and research center for information on all aspects of labor relations in higher education and other areas of professional employment.
National Center for the Study of Collective Bargaining in Higher Education and the Professions
Baruch College, CUNY
17 Lexington Ave.
New York, N.Y. 10010
(212) 725-3390

National Civil Service League (NCSL), a good-government lobby formed in 1881 by patrician reformers concerned with the debilitating and corrupting effects of patronage and the "spoils system" on the efficiency and moral stature of government. The Pendleton Act, drawn up by the League and sponsored by a League member, Senator George Pendleton of Ohio, introduced merit principles into federal employment.

The League continues its reform efforts. Its Model Public Personnel Administration Law of 1970, which advocates replacing civil service commissions with personnel directors appointed by the chief executive, has been adopted in whole or in part by hundreds of governmental jurisdictions.

National Civil Service League
3600 Gunston Road
Alexandria, VA 22302
See also COUTURIER, JEAN J. and PENDLETON ACT OF 1883.

National Commission for Industrial Peace, presidential advisory commission established in 1961 as the President's Advisory Committee on Labor-Management Policy. It became the National Commission for Industrial Peace in 1973 and was abolished by Executive Order 11823 of December 12, 1974.

National Commission on Productivity: *see* NATIONAL CENTER FOR PRODUCTIVITY AND QUALITY OF WORKING LIFE.

National Commission on State Workmen's Compensation Laws: *see* WORKER'S COMPENSATION.

National Committee for Labor Israel, American unionists organized to support the labor movement in Israel.

National Committee for Labor Israel
33 E. 67th Street
New York, N.Y. 10021
(212) 628-1000

national consultation rights, generally a union of federal government employees may be accorded national consultation rights if it holds exclusive recognition for either 10 percent or more, or 5,000 or more, of the employees of an agency. According to Section 7113 of the Civil Service Reform Act of 1978:

When a labor organization holds national consultation rights, the agency must give the labor organization notice of proposed new substantive personnel policies and proposed changes in established personnel policies and an opportunity to comment on such proposals. The labor organization has a right to suggest changes in personnel policies and to have those suggestions carefully considered. The labor organization also has a right to consult, in person at reasonable times, upon request, with appropriate officials on personnel policy matters and a right to submit its views in writing on personnel policy matters at any time. National consultation rights do not include the right to negotiate. Further, the agency is not required to consult with a labor organization on any matter which would be outside the scope of negotiations if the labor organization held national exclusive recognition in that agency.

National consultation rights were first granted to federal employees under Executive Order 11491 of October 29, 1969.

national convention, the governmental body having the greatest formal authority in most unions. It is elected directly or indirectly by the membership, although apportionment schemes vary. Election may be on a per capita basis within locals, which serve as electoral districts in this sense. Representation may also be apportioned according to the size of the locals. For instance, the American Federation of State, County, and Municipal Employees (AFSCME), which is the largest union restricted to public employees, has apportioned delegates to its international convention in the following fashion: 1 delegate per 100 members in a local up to 400 members, 1 delegate for each additional 1,000 members or fraction of that number, with the proviso that every local has to have at least one delegate.

The convention is usually a union's highest legislative body. It passes rules, declares policies, and gives direction to union officials. In some cases, the convention can also adopt amendments to the

279

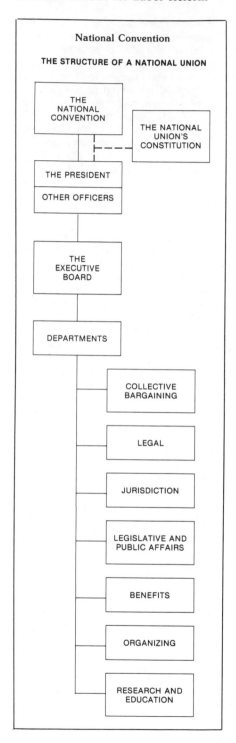

National Convention

THE STRUCTURE OF A NATIONAL UNION

- THE NATIONAL CONVENTION
- THE NATIONAL UNION'S CONSTITUTION
- THE PRESIDENT
- OTHER OFFICERS
- THE EXECUTIVE BOARD
- DEPARTMENTS
  - COLLECTIVE BARGAINING
  - LEGAL
  - JURISDICTION
  - LEGISLATIVE AND PUBLIC AFFAIRS
  - BENEFITS
  - ORGANIZING
  - RESEARCH AND EDUCATION

union's constitution. When the convention is in session, the union's leaders preside over its meetings, serving in the capacity of moderators. There are two major differences between conventions and governmental legislative bodies in general. First, the convention may meet infrequently. In about 35 percent of all national unions in the United States conventions are held every four or five years. During the interim, legislative authority is typically vested in the union's officers, who are supposed to act in accordance with the guidance passed on from the convention. Second, conventions are large relative to the membership and consequently take on the air of a "town meeting" more than a professionalized legislature such as the U.S. Congress. They are not in session very long. They are as much a governmental as a social event, since they also serve to bring delegates elected from the various locals into contact with one another.

National Council for Labor Reform, an anti-union group whose goal is to help employees and employers maintain "their constitutional rights against monopoly labor practices."
National Council for Labor Reform
406 S. Plymouth Court
Chicago, Ill. 60605
(312) 427-0206

national emergency, a condition determined by the president under provisions of the Taft-Hartley Act.

National Employ the Handicapped Week, also called NETH WEEK, the first full week in October, which has been set aside by the U.S. Congress to emphasize the employment of the handicapped.

national income, the total earnings of labor and property from the production of goods and services; the income earned, but not necessarily received, by all people and companies in a given country during a stated period. This is an important measure of economic growth which can be derived from the gross national product if certain taxes, depreciation, subsidies, and other items are subtracted.

National Industrial Recovery Act of 1933 (NIRA), federal statute that guaranteed employees "the right to organize and bargain collectively through representatives of their own choosing . . . free from the interference, restraint or coercion of employers." The act, which created the National Recovery Administration (NRA) to administer its provisions, was designed to establish self-government of industry through codes of fair competition which tended to eliminate competitive practices. Companies adopting their industries' codes of fair practice were entitled to display the "Blue Eagle," a flag or poster indicating compliance. The Supreme Court declared the act to be unconstitutional in 1935, but the Wagner Act of that year provided employees with even stronger collective bargaining guarantees.

National Institute for Occupational Safety and Health (NIOSH), established within the Department of Health, Education, and Welfare under the provisions of the Occupational Safety and Health Act of 1970 (P.L. 91-596). As the federal agency responsible for formulating new or improved occupational safety and health standards, NIOSH not only carries out responsibilities under the Occupational Safety and Health Act, but also the health program of the Federal Coal Mine Health and Safety Act of 1969 (P.L. 91-173). NIOSH is the principal federal agency engaged in research, education and training in a national effort to eliminate on-the-job hazards to the health and safety of U.S. working men and women.

Under the Occupational Safety and Health Act, NIOSH has the responsibility for conducting research designed to produce recommendations for new occupational safety and health standards. These recommendations are transmitted to the Department of Labor which has the responsibility for the final setting, promulgation and enforcement of the standards.

In the case of the Federal Coal Mine Health and Safety Act, NIOSH transmits recommended health standards to the Department of the Interior, which has the enforcement responsibilities under that law.

> *National Institute for Occupational Safety and Health*
> 1600 Clifton Road, N.E.
> Atlanta, GA 30333
> (404) 329-3644

National Labor-Management Foundation, business group hoping to correct abuses committed by both labor and management through remedial legislation and training.

> *National Labor-Management Foundation*
> 1901 L Street, N.W.
> Washington, D.C. 20036
> (202) 296-8577

National Labor Relations Act of 1935 (NLRA), also called WAGNER-CONNERY ACT and WAGNER ACT, the nation's principal labor relations law applying to all interstate commerce except railroad and airline operations (which are governed by the Railway Labor Act). The NLRA seeks to protect the rights of employees and employers, to encourage collective bargaining, and to eliminate certain practices on the part of labor and management that are harmful to the general welfare. It states and defines the rights of employees to organize and to bargain collectively with their employers through representatives of their own choosing. To ensure that employees can freely choose their own representatives for the purpose of collective bargaining, the act establishes a procedure by which they can exercise their choice at a secret ballot election conducted by the National Labor Relations Board. Further, to protect the rights of employees and employers, and to prevent labor disputes that would adversely affect the rights of the public, Congress has defined certain practices of employers and unions as unfair labor practices. The NLRA is administered and enforced principally by the National Labor Relations Board, which was created by the act.

In common usage, the National Labor

Relations Act refers not to the act of 1935, but to the act as amended by the Labor-Management Relations (Taft-Hartley) Act of 1947 and the Labor-Management Reporting and Disclosure (Landrum-Griffin) Act of 1959.
See also the following entries:

National Labor Relations Board

(NLRB), federal agency that administers the nation's laws relating to labor relations. The NLRB is vested with the power to safeguard employees' rights to organize, to determine through elections whether workers want unions as their bargaining representatives, and to prevent and remedy unfair labor practices (see also AMERICAN FEDERATION OF LABOR V. NATIONAL LABOR RELATIONS BOARD).

The NLRB is an independent agency created by the National Labor Relations Act of 1935 (Wagner Act), as amended in 1947 (Taft-Hartley Act) and 1959 (Landrum-Griffin Act). The act affirms the right of employees to self-organization and to bargain collectively through representatives of their own choosing or to refrain from such activities. The act prohibits certain unfair labor practices by employers and labor organizations or their agents and authorizes the NLRB to designate appropriate units for collective bargaining and to conduct secret ballot elections to determine whether employees desire representation by a labor organization. The Postal Reorganization Act of 1971 conferred jurisdiction upon the NLRB over unfair labor practice charges and representation elections affecting U.S. Postal Service employees. Jurisdiction over all privately operated health care institutions was conferred on the NLRB by an amendment to the act in 1974.

The NLRB has two principal functions—preventing and remedying unfair labor practices by employers and labor organizations or their agents, and conducting secret ballot elections among employees in appropriate collective bargaining units to determine whether or not they desire to be represented by a labor organization. The NLRB also conducts secret ballot elections among employees who have been covered by a union-shop agreement to determine whether or not they wish to revoke their union's authority to make such agreements; in jurisdictional disputes, decides and determines which competing group of workers is entitled to perform the work involved; and conducts secret ballot elections among employees concerning employers' final settlement offers in national emergency labor disputes.

The NLRB's general counsel has final authority in unfair labor practice cases to investigate charges, issue complaints, and prosecute such complaints before the board. The general counsel, on behalf of the board, prosecutes injunction proceedings; handles courts of appeals proceedings to enforce or review NLRB orders; participates in miscellaneous court litigation; and obtains compliance with NLRB ordrs and court judgments. The general counsel is responsible for the processing by field personnel of the several types of employee elections referred to above.

Under general supervision of the general counsel, 33 regional directors and their staffs process representation, unfair labor practice, and jurisdictional dispute cases. (Some regions have subregional or resident offices.) They issue complaints in unfair labor practice cases; seek settlement of unfair labor practice charges; obtain compliance with Board orders and court judgments; and petition district courts for injunctions to prevent or remedy unfair labor practices. The regional directors also direct hearings in representation cases; conduct elections pursuant to agreement or the decisionmaking authority delegated to them by the NLRB, or pursuant to NLRB directions; and issue certifications of representatives when unions win or certify the results when unions lose employee elections. They process petitions for bar-

NATIONAL LABOR RELATIONS BOARD

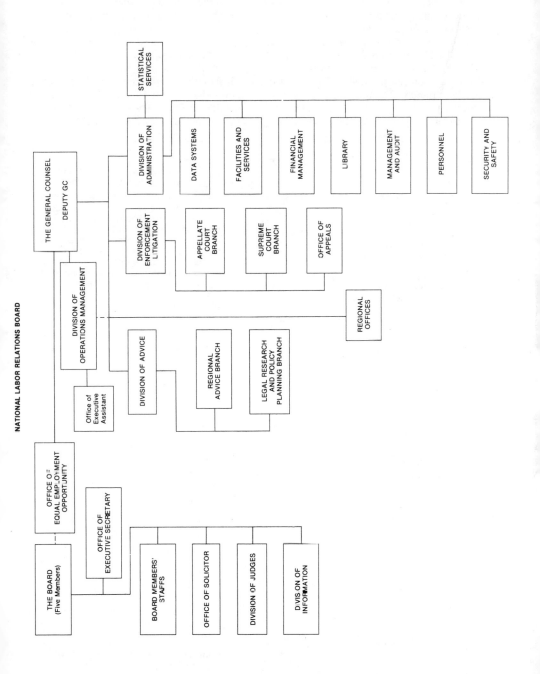

THE BOARD (Five Members)

OFFICE OF EQUAL EMPLOYMENT OPPORTUNITY

OFFICE OF EXECUTIVE SECRETARY

BOARD MEMBERS' STAFFS

OFFICE OF SOLICITOR

DIVISION OF JUDGES

DIVISION OF INFORMATION

THE GENERAL COUNSEL DEPUTY GC

DIVISION OF OPERATIONS MANAGEMENT

Office of Executive Assistant

DIVISION OF ADVICE

REGIONAL ADVICE BRANCH

LEGAL RESEARCH AND POLICY PLANNING BRANCH

DIVISION OF ENFORCEMENT LITIGATION

APPELLATE COURT BRANCH

SUPREME COURT BRANCH

OFFICE OF APPEALS

REGIONAL OFFICES

STATISTICAL SERVICES

DIVISION OF ADMINISTRATION

DATA SYSTEMS

FACILITIES AND SERVICES

FINANCIAL MANAGEMENT

LIBRARY

MANAGEMENT AND AUDIT

PERSONNEL

SECURITY AND SAFETY

283

gaining unit clarification, for amendment of certification, and for rescission of a labor organization's authority to make a union-shop agreement. They also conduct national emergency employee referendums.

The NLRB can act only when it is formally requested to do so. Individuals, employers, or unions may initiate cases by filing charges of unfair labor practices or petitions for employee representation elections with the NLRB field offices serving the area where the case arises.

In the event a regional director declines to proceed on a representation petition, the party filing the petition may appeal to the NLRB. Where a regional director declines to proceed on an unfair labor practice charge, the filing party may appeal to the general counsel. Administrative law judges conduct hearings in unfair labor practice cases, make findings, and recommend remedies for violations found. Their

---

NLRB ELECTION PETITIONS

The National Labor Relations Board will conduct secret ballot elections when any of the kinds of petitions listed below are properly filed with the appropriate NLRB Regional Office:

1) Certification of Representative

This petition, which is normally filed by a union, seeks an election to determine whether employees wish to be represented by a union or not. It must be supported by the signatures of 30 percent or more of the employees in the bargaining unit being sought. These signatures may be on separate cards or on a single piece of paper. Generally, this designation or "showing of interest" contains a statement that the employees want to be represented for purposes of collective bargaining by a specific labor organization. The showing of interest must be signed by each employee, and each employee signature must be dated.

2) Decertification

This petition, which can be filed by an individual, seeks an election to determine whether the authority of a union to act as a bargaining representative of employees should continue. It must be supported by the signatures of 30 percent or more of the employees in the bargaining unit represented by the union. These signatures may be on separate cards or on a single piece of paper. Generally, this "showing of interest" contains a statement that the employees do not wish to be represented for purposes of collective bargaining by the existing labor organization. The showing of interest must be signed by each employee and each employee signature must be dated.

3) Withdrawal of Union-Shop Authority

This petition, which can also be filed by an individual, seeks an election to determine whether the union's contractual authority to require the payment of union dues and initiation fees as a condition of employment should be continued. It must be supported by the signatures of 30 percent or more of the employees in the bargaining unit covered by the union-shop agreement. These signatures may be on separate cards or on a single piece of paper. Generally, this "showing of interest" states that the employees no longer want their collective bargaining agreement to contain a union-shop provision. The showing of interest must be signed by each employee and each employee signature must be dated.

4) Employer Petition

This petition is filed by an employer for an election where one or more unions claim to represent the employer's employees or when the employer has reasonable grounds for believing that the union, which is the current bargaining representative, no longer represents a majority of employees.

5) Unit Clarification

This petition seeks to clarify the scope of an existing bargaining unit by, for example, determining whether a new classification is properly a part of that unit. The petition may be filed by either the employer or the union.

6) Amendment of Certification

This petition seeks the amendment of an outstanding certification of a union to reflect changed circumstances such as changes in the name or affiliation of the union. This petition may be filed by a union or an employer.

SOURCE: NLRB

Field Offices—National Labor Relations Board

Office	Address	Telephone
Albany, N.Y. 12207	Clinton Ave. at N. Pearl St	518-472-2215
Albuquerque, N. Mex. 87110	5000 Marble Ave. NE	505-766-2508
Anchorage, Alaska 99513	701 C St	907-271-5015
Atlanta, Ga. 30323	101 Marietta St. NW	404-221-2896
Baltimore, Md. 21202	109 Market Pl	301-962-2822
Birmingham, Ala. 35203	2026 2d Ave. N.................	205-254-1492
Boston, Mass. 02116............	120 Boylston St	617-223-3300
Brooklyn, N.Y. 11241............	16 Court St....................	212-330-7713
Buffalo, N.Y. 14202	111 W. Huron St	716-846-4931
Chicago, Ill. 60604..............	219 S. Dearborn St	312-353-7570
Cincinnati, Ohio 45202	550 Main St	513-684-3686
Cleveland, Ohio 44199	1240 E. 9th St	216-522-3715
Denver, Colo. 80202	721 19th St	303-837-3555
Des Moines, Iowa 50309	907 Walnut St	515-284-4391
Detroit, Mich. 48226	477 Michigan Ave	313-226-3200
El Paso, Tex. 79901.............	109 N. Oregon St..............	915-541-7737
Fort Worth, Tex. 76102.........	819 Taylor St	817-334-2921
Grand Rapids, Mich. 49503	82 Ionia NW	616-456-2679
Hartford,Conn. 06103	750 Main St	203-722-2540
Hato Rey, P.R. 00918	Carlos E. Chardon Ave	809-753-4347
Honolulu, Hawaii 96850	300 Ala Moana Blvd	808-546-5100
Houston, Tex. 77002...........	515 Rusk St	713-229-3748
Indianapolis, Ind. 46204	575 N. Pennsylvania Ave	317-269-7430
Jacksonville, Fla. 32202	400 W. Bay St	904-791-3768
Kansas City, Kans. 66101.......	4th at State	913-236-3846
Las Vegas, Nev. 89101	720 S. 7th St	702-385-6416
Little Rock, Ark. 72201	1 Union National Plaza.........	501-378-6311
Los Angeles, Calif. 90024 ...... Region 31.	11000 Wilshire Blvd	213-209-7352
Los Angeles, Calif. 90014 ...... Region 21.	606 S. Olive St.	213-688-5200
Memphis, Tenn. 38174	1407 Union Ave	901-521-2725
Miami, Fla. 33130	51 SW. 1st Ave	305-350-5391
Milwaukee, Wis. 53203	310 W. Wisconsin Ave	414-291-3861
Minneapolis, Minn. 55401	110 S. 4th St	612-725-2611
Nashville, Tenn. 37203	801 Broadway..................	615-251-5921
Newark, N.J. 07102	970 Broad St	201-645-2100
New Orleans, La. 70130	600 South St	504-589-6361
New York, N.Y. 10278	26 Federal Plaza	212-264-0300
Oakland, Calif. 94604	2201 Broadway.................	415-273-7200
Peoria, Ill. 61602	411 Hamilton Blvd.............	309-671-7080
Philadelphia, Pa. 19106.........	615 Chestnut St...............	215-597-7601
Phoenix, Ariz. 85012	3030 N. Central Ave	602-241-2350
Pittsburgh, Pa. 15222	1000 Liberty Ave	412-644-2977
Portland, Oreg. 97205	921 SW. Washington St	503-221-3085
St. Louis, Mo. 63101	210 Tucker Blvd. N	314-425-4167
San Antonio, Tex. 78206	727 E. Durango Blvd	512-229-6140
San Diego, Calif. 92189	940 Front St	619-293-6184
San Francisco, Calif. 94102	450 Golden Gate Ave	415-556-3107
Seattle, Wash. 98174	915 2d Ave	206-442-4532
Tampa, Fla. 33601	700 Twiggs St	813-228-2641
Tulsa, Okla. 74127	440 S. Houston Ave	918-581-7951
Washington, D.C. 20037	2120 L St. NW	202-254-7612
Winston-Salem, N.C. 27101	251 N. Main St	919-761-3201

decisions are reviewable by the NLRB if exceptions to the decision are filed.

National Labor Relations Board
1717 Pennsylvania Ave., N.W.
Washington, DC 20570
(202) 655-4000

See James A. Gross, *The Making of the National Labor Relations Board: A Study in Economics, Politics, and the Law* (Albany: State University of New York Press, 1974); James A. Gross, *The Reshaping of the National Labor Relations Board: National Labor Policy in Transition, 1937-1947* (Albany: State University of New York Press, 1981); John R. Van de Water, "New Trends in NLRB Law," *Labor Law Journal* (October 1982). See also the following entries:

MASTRO PLASTICS CORP. V. NATIONAL
   LABOR RELATIONS BOARD
NEWPORT NEWS SHIPBUILDING AND DRY
   DOCK CO. V. SCHAUFFLER
PORTER CO. V. NATIONAL LABOR
   RELATIONS BOARD
SEARS, ROEBUCK, & CO. V. SAN DIEGO
   COUNTY DISTRICT COUNCIL OF
   CARPENTERS

National Labor Relation Board v. Allis-Chalmers, 388 U.S. 175 (1967), U.S. Supreme Court case, which held that a union could fine its members for breaking a lawful strike and could obtain a judgment in court in order to enforce payment of the fine.

National Labor Relations Board v. Babcock and Wilcox, 351 U.S. 105 (1956), U.S. Supreme Court case, which held that non-employee union organizers may have access to an employer's grounds for organizational purposes only if there is no other practical means of access to the employees.

National Labor Relations Board v. Bildisco & Bildisco, U.S. Supreme Court case, 79 L. Ed. 2d 89 (1984), which held that employers filing for reorganization in Federal bankruptcy court may temporarily terminate or alter collective bargaining agreements even before the judge has heard their case. The Court also held that

the termination or alteration could be made permanent if the employer can demonstrate to the judge that the agreement "burdens" chances of recovery. In arriving at a decision, the bankruptcy judge should determine if the company has made a "reasonable" effort to negotiate a less burdensome contract, the Court said. If the negotiators are not able to arrive at a "satisfactory" solution, the judge still may cancel the contract.

See also CHAPTER 11.

National Labor Relations Board v. Boeing, 412 U.S. 67 (1973), U.S. Supreme Court case, which held that the validity of a fine imposed by a union upon a member does not depend upon the fine being reasonable in amount.

National Labor Relations Board v. Burns International Security Services, 406 U.S. 272 (1972), U.S. Supreme Court case, which ruled that a successor employer who does not change the nature of the acquired business and hires most of its employees represented by a certified union is duty-bound to recognize and bargain with the union, but is not obligated to honor his predecessor's labor contract unless he has agreed to do so. See Robert E. Wachs, "Successorship: The Consequences of Burns," *Labor Law Journal* (April 1973).

National Labor Relations Board v. Exchange Parts, 375 U.S. 405 (1964), U.S. Supreme Court case, which held that the conferral of employee benefits while a representation election is pending, for the purpose of inducing employees to vote against the union, interferes with the right to organize guaranteed by the National Labor Relations Act.

National Labor Relations Board v. Fansteel Metallurgical Corp.: see SIT-DOWN STRIKE.

National Labor Relations Board v. Fruit Packers, 377 U.S. 58 (1964), U.S. Supreme Court case that upheld picketing at independent retail stores by workers urging consumers not to buy items produced by their employer. *See* Robert C. Castle and Richard Pegnetter, "Secondary Picketing: The Supreme Court Limits the *Tree Fruit* Exception," *Labor Law Journal* (January 1982).

National Labor Relations Board v. General Motors, 373 U.S. 734 (1963), U.S. Supreme Court case, which held that the agency shop is not an unfair labor practice.

National Labor Relations Board v. Gissel Packing Co.: *see* AUTHORIZATION CARD.

National Labor Relations Board v. Granite State Joint Board, Textile Workers, 409 U.S. 213 (1972), U.S. Supreme Court case, which held that a union could not collect fines imposed upon employees who had returned to work after resigning their membership during a strike. Since at the time there were no valid restraints on their freedom of resignation, the employees' action was an exercise of their statutory rights. "When a member lawfully resigns from the union, its power over him ends," said Justice Douglas in delivering the court's opinion.

National Labor Relations Board v. Insurance Agents' International Union, 361 U.S. 477 (1960), U.S. Supreme Court case, which held that a union does not fail to bargain in good faith by sponsoring on-the-job conduct designed to interfere with the employer's business and place economic pressure on him at the same time that it is negotiating a contract.

National Labor Relations Board v. Iron Workers: *see* PRE-HIRE AGREEMENT.

National Labor Relations Board v. Jones and Laughlin Steel Corp., 301 U.S. 1 (1937), U.S. Supreme Court case, that upheld the National Labor Relations Act (Wagner Act) of 1935, which gave labor the right to organize and bargain collectively. The NLRB, created by the act to enforce its provisions, ordered the Jones and Laughlin Steel Corporation to reinstate some employees it had discharged because of their union activities. The corporation responded by challenging both the authority of the NLRB to issue such an order and the legality of the act itself. The court ruled that

> Employees have as clear a right to organize and select their representatives for lawful purposes as the respondent to organize its business and select its own officers and agents. Discrimination and coercion to prevent the free exercise of the right of employees to self-organization and representation is a proper subject for condemnation by competent legislative authority.

National Labor Relations Board v. J. Weingarten, Inc., 420 U.S. 251 (1975), U.S. Supreme Court case, which held that an employee under company investigation for misconduct has a right to the presence of a union representative while being interrogated by a company investigator. *See* Lewis H. Silverman and Michael J. Soltis, "*Weingarten:* An Old Trumpet Plays the Labor Circuit," *Labor Law Journal* (November 1981).

National Labor Relations Board v. Local 103, International Association of Bridge, Structural, and Ornamental Iron Workers: *see* PRE-HIRE AGREEMENT.

National Labor Relations Board v. MacKay Radio & Telegraph Company, 304 U.S. 33 (1938), U.S. Supreme Court case, which held that an employer could hire permanent replacements for workers on strike for economic reasons. The court expanded the *MacKay* rule in the *Fleetwood Trailer Co.* decision, 389 U.S. 375, (1967), when it held that if a striker has been replaced and no suitable employment is available, the status of a striker as an employee continues until he has obtained "other regular and substantially equivalent employment." Until then, the striker remains on a preferred hiring list, unless there is a "legitimate and substantial business justification" for not hiring him at all.

National Labor Relations Board v. Magnavox, 415 U.S. 322 (1974), U.S. Supreme Court case, which held that a union cannot waive the distribution rights of employees who seek to distribute literature in support of the bargaining unit.

National Labor Relations Board v. Robbins Tire and Rubber Co., 57 L. Ed. 2d 159 (1978), U.S. Supreme Court case, which held that witness' statements in pending unfair labor practice cases are exempt from disclosure under the Freedom of Information Act.

National Labor Relations Board v. Truitt Manufacturing, 351 U.S. 149 (1956), U.S. Supreme Court case, which held that a refusal by an employer to attempt to substantiate a claim of inability to pay increased wages may support a finding of a failure to bargain in good faith.

National Labor Relations Board v. Wooster Division of Borg-Warner Corp., 356 U.S. 342 (1958), U.S. Supreme Court case, which held there were three categories of bargaining proposals under the Labor-Management Relations (Taft-Hartley) Act of 1947—illegal subjects, mandatory subjects, and voluntary subjects.

National Labor Relations Board v. Wyman-Gordon Co.: see EXCELSIOR RULE.

National Labor Relations Board v. Yeshiva University, U.S. Supreme Court case, 444 U.S. 672 (1980), which held that university faculty members who were involved in the governance (management) of their institutions were excluded from the protections and rights offered nonmanagerial employees by the National Labor Relations Act. See Joel M. Douglas, "Distinguishing *Yeshiva:* A Troubling Task for the NLRB," *Labor Law Journal* (February 1983); Clarence R. Deitsch and David A. Dilts, "*NLRB v. Yeshiva University:* A Positive Perspective," *Monthly Labor Review* (July 1983).

National Labor Union, union of local unions and reform grups that fostered an active political program. Born in 1866, it collapsed in 1872.

National League of Cities (NLC), formerly AMERICAN MUNICIPAL ASSOCIATION, known until 1964 as the American Municipal Association, NLC was founded in 1924 by and for reform-minded state municipal leagues. Membership in NLC was opened to individual cities in 1947, and NLC now has more than 1100 direct member cities. The 27 U.S. cities with populations greater than 500,000 are all NLC direct members, as are 87 percent of all cities with more than 100,000 residents. NLC is an advocate for municipal interests before Congress, the executive branch, and the federal agencies and in state capitals across the nation where other matters of importance to cities are decided.

National League of Cities
1301 Pennsylvania Ave., N.W.
Washington, D.C. 20004
(202) 626-3000

National League of Cities v. Usery, 426 U.S. 833 (1976), U.S. Supreme Court case, which held that the doctrine of federalism as expressed in the Tenth Amendment invalidates the 1974 amendments to the Fair Labor Standards Act (FLSA) extending minimum-wage and overtime provisions to state and local employees performing traditional governmental functions. This decision reversed the Court's decision in *Maryland v. Wirtz,* 392 U.S. 183 (1968), which approved the extension of the FLSA to certain state-operated hospitals, institutions, and schools. *NCL v. Usery* was, in turn, reversed by the Supreme Court in *Garcia v. San Antonio Metropolitan Transit Authority,* 83 L. Ed. 2nd 1016 (1985).

National Mediation Board, federal agency that provides the railroad and airline industries with specific mechanisms for the adjustment of labor-management disputes; that is, the facilitation of agreements through collective bargaining, investigation of questions of representation, and the arbitration and establishment of procedures for emergency disputes. First created by the Railway Labor Act of 1934, today the board's major responsibilities are: (1) the mediation of disputes over wages, hours, and working conditions which arise between rail and air carriers and organizations representing their employees, and (2) the investigation of representation disputes and certification of employee organizations as representatives of crafts or classes of carrier employees.

Disputes growing out of grievances or out of interpretation or application of agreements concerning rates of pay, rules, or working conditions in the railroad industry are referable to the National Railroad Adjustment Board. In the airline industry no national airline adjustment board has been established for settlement of grievances. Over the years the employee organizations and air carriers with established bargaining relationships have agreed to grievance procedures with final jurisdiction resting with a system board of adjustment. The National Mediation Board is frequently called upon to name a neutral referee to serve on a system board when the parties are deadlocked and cannot agree on such an appointment themselves.

The board is charged with mediating disputes between carriers and labor organizations relating to initial contract negotiations or subsequent changes in rates of pay, rules, and working conditions. When the parties fail to reach accord in direct bargaining either party may request the board's services or the board may on its own motion invoke its services. Thereafter, negotiations continue until the board determines that its efforts to mediate have been unsuccessful, at which time it seeks to induce the parties to submit the dispute to arbitration. If either party refuses to arbitrate, the board issues a notice stating that the parties have failed to resolve their dispute through mediation. This notice commences a 30-day cooling off period after which resort to self-help is normally available to either or both parties.

If a dispute arises among a carrier's employees as to who is to be the representative of such employees, it is the board's duty to investigate such disputes and to determine by secret ballot election or other appropriate means whether or not and to whom a representation certification should be issued. In the course of making this determination, the board must determine the craft or class in which the employees seeking representation properly belong.

Additional duties of the board are: the interpretation of agreements made under its mediatory auspices; the appointment of neutral referees when requested by the National Railroad Adjustment Board, the appointment of neutrals to sit on System Boards and Special Boards of Adjustments; and finally, the duty of notifying the president when the parties have failed to reach agreement through the board's mediation efforts and the labor dispute, in the judgment of the board, threatens substantially to interrupt interstate commerce to a degree such as to deprive any section of the country of essential transportation service. In these cases, the president may, at his discretion, appoint an emergency board to investigate and report to him on the dispute.

National Mediation Board
1425 K Street, N.W.
Washington, DC 20572
(202) 523-5920

national origin discrimination, Title VII of the Civil Rights Act of 1964 prohibits disparate treatment whether overt or covert, of any individual or group of individuals because of their national origin except when such treatment is necessary because of a bona fide occupational qualification; for example it might be lawful to require native fluency in Spanish for a position as a translator. The Equal Employment Opportunity Commission (EEOC) gives as examples of national origin discrimination,

the use of tests in the English language where the individual tested came from circumstances where English was not that person's first language or mother tongue, and where English language skill is not a requirement of the work to be performed; denial of equal opportunity to persons married to or associated with persons of a specific national origin; denial of equal opportunity because of membership in lawful organizations identified with or seeking to promote the interests of national groups; denial of equal opportunity because of attendance at schools or churches commonly utilized by persons of a given national origin; denial of equal opportunity because their name or that of their spouse reflects a certain national origin, and denial of equal opportunity to persons who as a class of persons tend to fall outside national norms for height and weight where such height and weight specifications are not necessary for the performance of the work involved.

Some states have laws prohibiting the employment of noncitizens in varying circumstances. According to the EEOC, "where such laws have the purpose or effect of discriminating on the basis of national origin, they are in direct conflict with and are, therefore, superseded by Title VII of the Civil Rights Act of 1964, as amended." *See* Charles J. Hollon and Thomas L. Bright, "National Origin Harassment in the Work Place: Recent Guideline Development from the EEOC," *Employee Relations Law Journal* (Autumn 1982).

National Panel of Arbitrators: *see* AMERICAN ARBITRATION ASSOCIATION.

National Public Employer Labor Relations Association (NPELRA), professional association of state and local government labor relations specialists who solely represent management.
> *NPELRA*
> 55 E. Monroe Street
> Chicago, IL 60603
> (312) 782-1752

National Railroad Adjustment Board, federal agency created by the Railway Labor Act of 1934. The National Railroad Adjustment Board has the responsibility of deciding disputes growing out of grievances or out of interpretation or application of agreements concerning rates of pay, rules, or working conditions in the railroad industry.
> *National Railroad Adjustment Board*
> 10 West Jackson Blvd.
> Chicago, IL 60604
> (312) 886-7300

National Recovery Administration: *see* NATIONAL INDUSTRIAL RECOVERY ACT OF 1933.

National Rehabilitation Association (NRA), founded in 1925, a private, nonprofit organization of 18,000 people whose purpose is to advance the rehabilitation of all handicapped persons.
> *National Rehabilitation Association*
> 633 S. Washington Street
> Alexandria, VA 22314
> (703) 836-0850

National Right to Work Committee, also NATIONAL RIGHT TO WORK LEGAL DEFENSE FOUNDATION, INC., the *National Right to Work Committee* advocates legislation to prohibit all forms of forced union membership. The *National Right to Work Legal Defense Foundation, Inc.* seeks to establish legal precedents protecting workers against compulsory unionism.
> *National Right to Work Committee*
> 8001 Braddock Road
> Springfield, VA 22160
> (703) 321-9820

National Safety Council, nongovernmental, nonprofit, public service organization dedicated to reducing the number and severity of all kinds of accidents by gathering and distributing information about the causes of accidents and ways to prevent them.
> *National Safety Council*
> 444 North Michigan Avenue
> Chicago, IL 60611
> (312) 527-4800

National Technical Information Service (NTIS), established in 1970 to simplify and improve public access to Department of

Commerce publications and to data files and scientific and technical reports sponsored by federal agencies. It is the central point in the United States for the public sale of government-funded research and development reports and other analyses prepared by federal agencies, their contractors, or grantees.

National Technical Information Service
5285 Port Royal Road
Springfield, VA 22161
(703) 487-4660

National Training Laboratories Institute for Applied Behavioral Science (NTL), also called NTL INSTITUTE, founded as the National Training Laboratories in 1947 in Bethel, Maine. The early years at Bethel were devoted to the development of human relations laboratories. It was during this period that NTL proved the effectiveness of the new concept of the T Group ("T" for training). NTL's concept of the T Group—in which individuals, working in small groups, develop new insights into self and others—is still an important element in NTL programs and has been widely imitated. During the 1950s and 1960s, major areas for experimentation and development were expanded to include group dynamics, organization development and community development. During the 1960s and early 1970s, the development of individual potential in personal growth programs became an added thrust, as did innovation in working with large systems. In the late 1970s, NTL helped men and women recognize and develop their potential in response to the array of alternatives in life-styles, careers and patterns of interaction available to them. It worked toward keeping change from becoming chaos by promoting flexibility and innovation and by providing help in planning for individuals, organizations and large systems.

Today, NTL Institute is internationally recognized as a focal agency for experience-based learning programs. It is also known as the institution which has had most to do with developing the new profession of laboratory education, with exploring new means of relating, with new approaches to social change, and with new methods of managing organizations. Interest in laboratory education has grown rapidly, and NTL defines as one of its roles helping to maintain professional standards in a field now popularized and often misunderstood.

National Training Laboratories Institute
Mailing Address:
P.O. Box 9155
Rosslyn Station
Arlington, VA 22209
Address:
1501 Wilson Blvd.
Arlington, VA 22209
(703) 527-1500

National Woodwork Manufacturers Association v. National Labor Relations Board, 386 U.S. 612 (1967), U.S. Supreme Court case, which held that when a boycott is used as a shield to preserve customary jobs, rather than as a sword to gather new ones, it does not violate the National Labor Relations Act's proscription against secondary boycotts, Section 8(6)(4)(B).

native ability, actual ability. A test score is usually interpreted to mean that an individual's native ability lies somewhere in a range (plus or minus 50 points, for example) surrounding the score.

NCSL: *see* NATIONAL CIVIL SERVICE LEAGUE.

needs analysis, any of a variety of approaches that seek to establish the requirements of a particular situation in order to determine what, if any, program activity should be initiated.

needs hierarchy, in the July 1943 issue of *Psychological Review,* Abraham H. Maslow published his now classic, "A Theory of Human Motivation," in which he put forth his hierarchical conception of human needs. Maslow asserted that humans had five sets of goals or basic needs arranged in a hierarchy of prepotency: physiological needs, safety needs, love or affiliation needs, esteem needs and the need for self-actualization—the desire "to become everything that one is capable of becoming." Once lower needs are satisfied, they cease to be motivators of behavior. Conversely, higher needs cannot motivate until lower needs are satisfied. It is commonly recognized that there are some inescapable incongruities in Maslow's needs hierarchy. Some lower needs in some people, such as security, love and status, never seem to be satiated. However, this does not take away from the importance of the desire for higher level needs as a motivational force in others. *See* Abraham Maslow, *Motivation and Personality* (N.Y.: Harper & Row, 1954, 2nd ed., 1970); Edwin C. Nevis, "Using An American Perspective in Understanding Another Culture: Toward a Hierarchy of Needs for the People's Republic of China," *The Journal of Applied Behavioral Science,* Vol. 19, No. 3 (1983).

See also SELF-ACTUALIZATION.

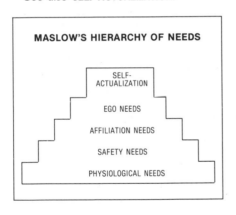

MASLOW'S HIERARCHY OF NEEDS

SELF-ACTUALIZATION

EGO NEEDS

AFFILIATION NEEDS

SAFETY NEEDS

PHYSIOLOGICAL NEEDS

negative entropy: *see* ENTROPY.

negatively skewed: *see* SKEWNESS.

negative reinforcement: *see* REINFORCEMENT.

negative strike: *see* POSITIVE STRIKE.

negative stroking: *see* STROKING.

negative transfer: *see* TRANSFER OF LEARNING.

negotiating committee, continuous: *see* CONTINUOUS NEGOTIATING COMMITTEE.

negotiation, process by which representatives of labor and management bargain, directly discuss proposals and counterproposals, in order to establish the conditions of work—wages, hours, benefits, the machinery for handling grievances, etc. For general theories on the negotiating process, *see* Gerald I. Nierenberg, *The Art of Negotiating: Psychological Strategies for Gaining Advantageous Bargains* (N.Y.: Hawthorn Books, 1968); Otomar J. Bartos, *Process and Outcome of Negotiations* (N.Y.: Columbia University Press, 1974); Jeffrey Z. Rubin and Bert R. Brown, *The Social Psychology of Bargaining and Negotiation* (N.Y.: Academic Press, 1975). For a specific application to labor relations, *see* Richard E. Walton and Robert B. McKersie, *A Behavioral Theory of Labor Negotiations* (N.Y.: McGraw-Hill, 1965).

Also see William E. Klay, "Combating Inflation Through Wage Negotiations: A Strategy for Public Administration," *Public Administration Review* (September/October 1981); John J. Hoover, "Negotiating the Initial Union Contract," *Personnel Journal* (September 1982); David W. Ewing, "How To Negotiate With Employee Objectors," *Harvard Business Review* (January-February 1983); Michael E. Gordon, Neal Schmitt and Walter G. Schneider, "Laboratory Research on Bargaining and Negotiations: An Evaluation," *Industrial Relations* (Spring 1984); Colette A. Frayne and Phillip L. Hunsaker, "Strategies for Successful Interpersonal Negotiating," *Personnel* (May-June 1984).

negotiation, career: *see* CAREER NEGOTIATION.

negotiations, collective: *see* COLLECTIVE NEGOTIATIONS.

Negotiations & Contracts, Collective Bargaining: *see* COLLECTIVE BARGAINING NEGOTIATIONS & CONTRACTS.

neoclassical organization theory: *see* ORGANIZATION THEORY.

nepotism, any practice by which office-holders award positions to members of their immediate family. It is derived from the Latin *nepos,* meaning nephew or grandson. The rulers of the medieval church were often thought to give special preference to their nephews in distributing churchly offices. At that time, "nephew" became a euphemism for their illegitimate sons. *See* Leonard Bierman and Cynthia D. Fisher, "Antinepotism Rules Applied to Spouses: Business and Legal Viewpoints," *Labor Law Journal* (October 1984).

nervous breakdown, catch-all expression for mental illness that does not refer to any particular disorder. Individuals in high pressure jobs who can no longer cope with the associated mental strains are frequently said to have had nervous breakdowns, but the actual clinical reason for their incapacity could be any of a large variety of mental and/or physical maladies.

See also OCCUPATIONAL NEUROSIS and STRESS.

Nestor, Agnes (1880-1948), a leader of the International Glove Workers Union and Women's Trade Union League. For an autobiography, *see Women's Labor Leader: Autobiography of Agnes Nestor* (Rockford, Ill.: Bellevue Books Pub. Co., 1954).

NETH Week: *see* NATIONAL EMPLOY THE HANDICAPPED WEEK.

net pay: *see* TAKE-HOME PAY.

network, pattern of "interrelated and interconnected individuals, groups and/or organizations that form a system of communication." *See* Jeffalyn Johnson, "Networking: A Management Tool," *The Bureaucrat* (Winter 1977); Philomena, D. Warihay, "The Climb to the Top: Is the Network the Route for Women?" *Personnel Administrator* (April 1980).

neutral, any third party who is actively engaged in labor-management negotiations in order to facilitate a settlement.

New Deal, the domestic programs and policies of the administration of President Franklin D. Roosevelt (1933-1945).

new girls' network: *see* OLD BOYS' NETWORK.

new hire, individual who has just joined an organization as an employee.
See also PROBATIONARY EMPLOYEE.

new industrial state, John Kenneth Galbraith's concept (from his 1967 book of the same name) which holds that modern organizations have become so complex that traditional leaders are no longer able to "make" major decisions: they can only ratify the decisions made for them by a technostructure of specialists who may be more interested in maintaining themselves than generating profits.

Newport News Shipbuilding and Dry Dock Co. v. Schauffler, 303 U.S. 54 (1938), U.S. Supreme Court case, which held that a company was subject to the authority of the National Labor Relations Board even if its participation in interstate commerce was limited to receiving goods from other states.

Newport News Shipbuilding and Dry Dock Co. v. EEOC, U.S. Supreme Court case, 77 L.Ed. 2d 18 (1983), which ruled that the company had discriminated against a male employee by providing limited health insurance coverage of his wife's pregnancy costs, while providing full coverage of health costs for the spouses of female employees. Writing for the majority, Justice John Stevens said that the Newport News plan violated the Pregnancy Discrimination Act of 1978. Continuing, Justice Stevens said that in enacting the law, the Congress had "unambiguously expressed its disapproval" of the Court's 1976 ruling in *General Electric Co. v. Gilbert* that the exclusion of disabilities caused by pregnancy from an employer's disability plan did not constitute discrimination based on sex.

293

New York Telephone Co. v. New York State Department of Labor, 59 L. Ed. 2d 553 (1979), U.S. Supreme Court case, which held that the payment of unemployment compensation to strikers was not in conflict with the policy of free collective bargaining established by the National Labor Relations Act.

New York Times v. Sullivan, 376 U.S. 254 (1964), U.S. Supreme Court case, which held that a state cannot, under the 1st and 14th Amendments, award damages to a public official for defamatory falsehood relating to his official conduct unless he proves "actual malice"—that the statement was made with knowledge of its falsity or with reckless disregard of whether it was true or false.

nibbling, also called PIECE RATE NIBBLING, practice of cutting the piece rates paid to employees upon an increase in their output.

night premium, also called NIGHT DIFFERENTIAL, addition to regular wage rates that is paid to employees who work on shifts other than the regular day shift.

NIOSH: see NATIONAL INSTITUTE FOR OCCUPATIONAL SAFETY AND HEALTH.

NIRA: see NATIONAL INDUSTRIAL RECOVERY ACT OF 1933.

NLC: see NATIONAL LEAGUE OF CITIES.

NLC v. USERY: see NATIONAL LEAGUE OF CITIES V. USERY.

NLRA: see NATIONAL LABOR RELATIONS ACT OF 1935.

NLRB: see NATIONAL LABOR RELATIONS BOARD.

noble, slang term for an armed guard hired by industry to escort strikebreakers or otherwise harass the budding union movement.

no-commission account: see HOUSE ACCOUNT.

Noise Regulation Reporter, bi-weekly notification and reference service published by the Bureau of National Affairs, Inc., which covers all significant legislative and administrative efforts to control noise. Includes information on regulations and programs under the Noise Control Act of 1972, the Occupational Safety and Health Act, the Noise Pollution Abatement Act, the Federal Aviation Act, and state statutes.

Nolde Brothers, Inc., v. Local No. 358, Bakery Workers, 430 U.S. 243 (1977), U.S. Supreme Court case, which held that a "party to a collective-bargaining contract may be required to arbitrate a contractual dispute over severance pay pursuant to the arbitration clause of that agreement even though the dispute, although governed by the contract, arises after its termination." See Irving M. Geslewitz, "Case Law Development Since Nolde Brothers: When Must Post-Contract Disputes Be Arbitrated?" Labor Law Journal (April 1984).

noncompetitive appointment, government employment obtained without competing with others, in the sense that it is done without regard to civil service registers. Includes reinstatements, transfers, reassignments, demotions, and some promotions.

noncontributory pension plan, pension program that has the employer paying the entire cost.

nondirective interview: see DIRECTED INTERVIEW.

nonproduction bonus, also called CHRISTMAS BONUS and YEAR-END BONUS, payments to workers that are, in effect, gratuities upon which employees cannot regularly depend. Richard P. Helwig, in "The Christmas Bonus: A Gift or a Give-Away?" Personnel Journal (November 1973), warns that
it is an unfair labor practice if an

employer refuses to bargain as to wages, hours of employment, or other conditions of employment. The factual question to be determined is whether a Christmas gift constitutes a condition of employment such as compensation for service, as distinguished from a mere discretionary gift? If so, the discontinuance of such a program is a bargainable matter and must be discussed with the union prior to taking such action.

nonprofit sector, all those businesses and organizations set up for religious, charitable, educational or other purposes that would entitle them to a special tax exempt status. *See* P. H. Mirvis and E. J. Hackett, "Work and the Work Force in the Nonprofit Sector," *Monthly Labor Review* (April 1983).

Nonreading Aptitude Test Battery (NATB), form of the General Aptitude Test Battery designed by the United States Employment Service for individuals so disadvantaged that testing premised upon literacy would be inappropriate. *See* Patricia Marshall, "Tests Without Reading," *Manpower* (May 1971).

nonsuability clause, that portion of a labor contract where a company agrees that it will not sue a labor union because of a wildcat strike, provided that the union lives up to its obligation to stop the strike.

nonverbal communication, any means of projecting opinion, attitudes and desires through the use of body postures, movements, expressions, gestures, eye contact, use of space and time, or other means of expressing such ideas short of written and/or verbal communications. For the classic work, *see* Edward T. Hall, *The Silent Language* (Garden City, N.Y.: Doubleday, 1959). For a text, *see* Mark L. Knapp, *Nonverbal Communication In Human Interaction* (N.Y.: Holt, Rinehart and Winston, Inc., 1972).

Also see Fernando Poyatos, *New Perspectives in Nonverbal Communication* (New York: Pergamon Press, 1983); Peter Bull, *Body Movement and Interpersonal Communication* (New York: Wiley, 1983); Walburga Von Raffler-Engle, *The Perception of Nonverbal Behavior in the Career Interview* (Amsterdam: John Benjamins Publishing, 1983).

norm, standard or criteria against which an individual's test score or production rate can be compared and evaluated.

normal distribution, frequency distribution that follows the pattern of the normal "bell shaped" curve, characterized by symmetry about the mean and a standard relationship between width and height of the curve.

normal time: *see* ALLOWED TIME.

normative, those findings or conclusions that are premised upon morally established norms of right or wrong.

normative standard, standard of performance obtained by examining the relative performance of a group or sample of candidates.

norm-referenced test, any test that describes a candidate's performance in terms of its relation to the performance of other candidates.

norms, in psychological testing, norms are tables of scores from a large number of people who have taken a particular test. For an analysis of norm referenced test scores, *see* H. B. Lyman, *Test Scores and What They Mean* (Englewood Cliffs, N.J.: Prentice-Hall, 2nd ed., 1971).

Norris-LaGuardia Act of 1932, federal statute that generally removed the power of the federal courts to prevent coercive activities by unions if such actions did not involve fraud or violence. The act was significant because it finally allowed unions to exert effective economic pressures against employers. It also declared yellow-dog contracts to be unenforceable. Many states have "Little Norris-LaGuardia" acts that cover industries not engaged in interstate commerce.

See also YELLOW-DOG CONTRACT.

Northwest Airlines v. Air Line Pilots & Transport Workers, U.S. Supreme Court case, 447 U.S. 920 (1981), which held that an employer found guilty of job bias does not have the right to force a union to pay part of the damages, even though the discrimination results from provisions of a collective bargaining agreement.

no-show jobs, government positions for which the incumbent collects a salary but is not required to report to work. While no-show jobs are by their nature illegal, they are not uncommon. In 1975, when a New York State assemblyman was tried in Albany County Court for authorizing no-show jobs on his legislative payroll, he claimed discriminatory prosecution and asked that his case be dismissed because the practice was so commonplace. The judge concurred and the case was dismissed. *See* Albany, N.Y., *Times-Union,* September 23-28, 1975.

no-solicitation rule, employer's rule that prohibits solicitation of employees for any purpose during working hours.

notary public, semi-public official who can administer oaths, certify the validity of documents, and perform a variety of formal witnessing duties.

nothing job, a job that offers nothing (no satisfaction, prestige, etc.) to a worker except wages; or an easy task that can be quickly done.

NRA: *see* (1) NATIONAL INDUSTRIAL RECOVERY ACT OF 1933 or (2) NATIONAL REHABILITATION ASSOCIATION.

NTIS: *see* NATIONAL TECHNICAL INFORMATION SERVICE.

NTL: *see* NATIONAL TRAINING LABORATORIES FOR APPLIED BEHAVIORAL SCIENCE.

null hypothesis, hypothesis used in statistics that asserts there is no difference between two populations that cannot be explained by chance.

O

OASDI: *see* OLD AGE, SURVIVORS, AND DISABILITY INSURANCE.

objective, also ABSTRACT OBJECTIVE, INTANGIBLE OBJECTIVE, CONCRETE OBJECTIVE, and TANGIBLE OBJECTIVE. An *objective* is a point to be reached, the end result of an action or the broad overall purposes of an agency.

Abstract or *intangible objectives* are the qualities one seeks to attain in people and the environment that exemplify the application of the highest management principles. They are the broad, general goals cited by management as theoretical considerations, ideals or qualities to be attained. These abstractions or ideals are found in such objectives as: improve employee morale, increase individual employee productivity, be cost conscious, provide better on-the-job training, etc.

Concrete or *tangible objectives* are the translation of broad, strategic goals into the specific, realistic goals containing identifiable and/or measurable performance from the application of resources.

objective test, any examining device whose scoring is not dependent upon the discretion of the examiners.

objectivity, an applicant appraisal procedure is objective (that is, it has objectivity) if it elicits observable responses that can be recorded and reported in a precise, specified way. Objectivity seeks to remove personal opinion by reducing the impact of individual judgment.

obligatory arbitration, arbitration requested by one party in a situation where the other party is obligated (for example, by a contract provision) to accept it.

obsolescence: *see* OCCUPATIONAL OBSO-LESCENCE.

occupation, relatively continuous pattern of activity that (1) provides a livelihood for an individual and (2) serves to define an individual's general social status.

occupational career, according to Walter L. Slocum, in "Occupational Careers in Organizations: A Sociological Perspective," *Personnel and Guidance Journal* (May 1965), "an occupational career, ideally, consists of entry into a position at the lowest rung of a career ladder, followed by an orderly sequence of promotions to positions at successively higher status levels and finally to retirement."

occupational certification, also called CERTIFICATION, practice that permits prac-

Twenty most rapidly declining occupations, 1982–95	
Occupation	**Percent decline in employment**
Railroad conductors	− 32.0
Shoemaking machine operatives.	− 30.2
Aircraft structure assemblers	− 21.0
Central telephone office operators	− 20.0
Taxi drivers	− 18.9
Postal clerks	− 17.9
Private household workers	− 16.9
Farm laborers	− 15.9
College and university faculty	− 15.0
Roustabouts	− 14.4
Postmasters and mail superintendents	− 13.8
Rotary drill operator helpers	− 11.6
Graduate assistants	− 11.2
Data entry operators	− 10.6
Railroad brake operators	− 9.8
Fallers and buckers.	− 8.7
Stenographers	− 7.4
Farm owners and tenants	− 7.3
Typesetters and compositors.	− 7.3
Butchers and meatcutters	− 6.3

Note: Includes only detailed occupations with 1982 employment of 25,000 or more. Data for 1995 are based on moderate-trend projections.

Source: George T. Silvestri, John M. Lukasiewicz and Marcus E. Einstein, "Occupational Employment Projections Through 1995," Monthly Labor Review *(November 1983).*

Twenty fastest growing occupations, 1982–95	
Occupation	**Percent growth in employment**
Computer service technicians	96.8
Legal assistants	94.3
Computer systems analysts	85.3
Computer programmers	76.9
Computer operators	75.8
Office machine repairers	71.7
Physical therapy assistants	67.8
Electrical engineers	65.3
Civil engineering technicians	63.9
Peripheral EDP equipment operators	63.5
Insurance clerks, medical	62.2
Electrical and electronic technicians	60.7
Occupational therapists	59.8
Surveyor helpers	58.6
Credit clerks, banking and insurance	54.1
Physical therapists.	53.6
Employment interviewers	52.5
Mechanical engineers	52.1
Mechanical engineering technicians.	51.6
Compression and injection mold machine operators, plastics . . .	50.3

Note: Includes only detailed occupations with 1982 employment of 25,000 or more. Data for 1995 are based on moderate-trend projections.

titioners in a particular occupation to claim minimum levels of competence. While certification enables some practitioners to claim a competency which others cannot, this type of regulation does not prevent uncertified people from supplying the same services as certified people. *See* Kenneth K. Henning, "Certification as a Recognition of Professional Development," *State and Local Government Review* (May 1981).

See also OCCUPATIONAL LICENSING.

Occupational Check List, Gordon: *see* GORDON OCCUPATIONAL CHECK LIST.

occupational decisionmaking: *see* CAREER DECISIONMAKING.

occupational disease: *see* OCCUPATIONAL ILLNESS.

occupational grouping, grouping of classes within the same broad occupational category, such as engineering, nursing, accounting, etc.

occupational hazard, any danger directly associated with one's work. *See* Nicholas A. Ashford, *Crisis in the Workplace: Occupational Disease and Injury – A Report to the Ford Foundation* (Cambridge, Mass.: The MIT Press, 1976); N. Root and D. Sebastian, "BLS Develops Measure of Job Risk by Occupation," *Monthly Labor Review* (October 1981).

occupational health, all the activities related to protecting and maintaining the health and safety of employees. *See* Joseph A. Page and Mary-Win O'Brien, *Bitter Wages: Ralph Nader's Study Group Report on Disease and Injury on the Job* (N.Y.: Grossman, 1973); John Mendeloff, *Regulating Safety: An Economic and Political Analysis of Occupational Safety and Health Policy* (Cambridge, Mass.: The MIT Press, 1979); Steven Deutsch, ed., "Theme Issue: Occupational Safety and Health," *Labor Studies Journal* (Spring 1981); W. B. Creighton and E. J. Micallef, "Occupational Health and Safety as an Industrial Relations Issue: The Rank-General Electric Dispute, 1981," *The Journal of Industrial Relations* (September 1983).

occupational illness, also called OCCUPATIONAL DISEASE, any abnormal condition or disorder, other than one resulting from an occupational injury, caused by exposure to environmental factors associated with employment. It includes acute and chronic illnesses or diseases which may be caused by inhalation, absorption, ingestion, or direct contact. *See* H. J. Hilaski and C. L. Wang, "How Valid are Estimates of Occupational Illness?" *Monthly Labor Review* (August 1982).

occupational injury, any injury (such as a cut, fracture, sprain, amputation, etc.), that results from a work accident or from exposure involving a single incident in the work environment. *See* Fred Siskind, "Another Look at the Link Between Work Injuries and Job Experience," *Monthly Labor Review* (February 1982).

occupational licensing, also called LICENSING, according to Clifford Elliott and Vincent H. Smith, "occupational Licensing: An Empirical Approach," *University of Michigan Business Review* (July 1978), occupational licensing

> requires that all non-licensed persons cease to practice and be excluded from future participation in the licensed occupation. The additional benefit provided to the community from licensing occupations is to protect the community from the spillover costs that might result if individual consumers choose low quality services. A classic example of this possibility is to be found in medicine. A man with a contagious disease who hires the services of a low-cost quack and consequently fails to be cured, may impose the disease on people who might not have caught it if he had been forced to utilize the services of a more competent person.

Also see Alex Maurizi, "Occupational Licensing and the Public Interest," *Journal of Political Economy* (March–April 1974); Barbara F. Esser, Daniel H. Kruger, and Benjamin Shimberg, *Occupational Licensing: Practices and Politics* (Washington, D.C.: Public Affairs Press, 1973); Stuart Dorsey, "The Occupational Licensing Queue," *Journal of Human Resources* (Summer 1980).
See also OCCUPATIONAL CERTIFICATION.

occupational mobility, also HORIZONTAL and VERTICAL OCCUPATIONAL MOBILITY, *occupational mobility* refers to the movement of individuals from one occupation to another. A change from one occupation to another of similiar occupational status is an example of *horizontal occupational mobility*. A change of occupational status levels within the same occupation

Distribution of occupational fatalities in establishments in the private sector with 11 employees or more, by cause, 1981–82 average

(In percent)

Cause[1]	Total, all industries[2]	Agriculture, forestry, and fishing	Mining, oil and gas extraction only	Construction	Manufacturing	Transportation and public utilities[3]	Wholesale and retail trade	Finance, insurance, and real estate	Services
Total, all causes	100	100	100	100	100	100	100	100	100
Over-the-road motor vehicles	27	18	26	15	20	52	20	35	29
Falls	12	12	9	31	10	6	5	9	10
Heart attacks	10	6	8	8	10	6	12	23	16
Industrial vehicles or equipment	10	27	21	17	9	3	4	0	9
Nonaccidental injuries	7	3	(*)	(*)	2	2	30	8	15
Struck by objects other than vehicles or equipment	6	1	9	5	8	3	12	0	2
Electrocutions	6	16	4	11	5	6	1	0	5
Caught in, under, or between objects other than vehicles or equipment	6	1	3	4	5	9	8	17	2
Aircraft crashes	4	2	5	1	3	6	1	7	7
Fires	3	8	7	1	6	2	(*)	1	(*)
Plant machinery operations	3	1	1	2	10	(*)	1	0	(*)
Explosions	2	0	2	2	4	2	1	0	1
Gas inhalations	2	1	3	1	4	1	1	0	1
All other	3	2	3	3	4	2	3	(*)	3

[1] Cause is defined as the object or event associated with the fatality.

[2] Excludes coal, metal and nonmetal mining, and railroads for which data are not available.

[3] Excludes railroads.

(*) Less than 1 percent.

NOTE: It is impossible to estimate year-to-year changes precisely because at the industry division level sampling errors are large. Therefore, the results are for both years rather than a comparison between them. Because of rounding, percentages may not add to 100.

Source: Janet Macon: "BLS' 1982 Survey of Work-Related Deaths," Monthly Labor Review *(March 1984)*.

is an example of *vertical occupational mobility.* See Dixie Sommers and Alan Eck, "Occupational Mobility in the American Labor Force," *Monthly Labor Review* (January 1977); Harrison C. White, *Chains of Opportunity: System Models of Mobility in Organizations* (Cambridge, Mass.: Harvard University Press, 1970); Marshall I. Pomer, *Intergenerational Occupational Mobility in the United States: A Segmentation Perspective* (Gainesville: University Presses of Florida, 1981); Ellen Sehgal, "Occupational Mobility and Job Tenure in 1983," *Monthly Labor Review* (October 1984).

occupational neurosis, development of incapacitating physical symptoms that make it impossible to continue one's work.

occupational obsolescence, concept usually associated with professional employees who lack currency with their discipline. For example, an engineer who has served as an administrator for a significant number of years may, in consequence, be unable to function in his/her engineering speciality because the "state of the art" has moved too far. For thorough analyses of the concept and the problem, *see* H. G. Kaufman, *Obsolescence and Professional Career Development* (New York: AMACOM, 1974); Samuel S. Dubin, "Obsolesence or Lifelong Education: A Choice for the Professional," *American Psychologist* (May 1972); Clayton Reeser, "Managerial Obsolescence—An Organization Dilemma," *Personnel Journal* (January 1977); Benson Rosen and Thomas H. Jerdee, "A Model Program for Combatting Employee Obsolescence," *Personnel Administrator* (March 1985).

Occupational Orientation Inventory, Hall: *see* HALL OCCUPATIONAL ORIENTATION INVENTORY.

Occupational Outlook Handbook, the Bureau of Labor Statistics' biennial survey of employment trends that contains descriptive information and employment prospects for hundreds of occupational categories.

Occupational Outlook Quarterly, the U.S. Bureau of Labor Statistics' magazine designed to help high school students and guidance counselors assess career opportunities.

Occupational Outlook Quarterly
Superintendent of Documents
Government Printing Office
Washington, DC 20402

occupational parity: *see* PARITY.

Occupational Preference Survey, California: *see* CALIFORNIA OCCUPATIONAL PREFERENCE SURVEY.

occupational prestige, also called OCCUPATIONAL STATUS, ascribed status associated with an individual's employment. Opinion surveys typically find physicians, college professors, psychologists, bankers, and architects at the top of a hierarchy of occupational prestige, while unskilled farm workers and garbage collectors compete for the lowest rankings. According to Donald J. Treiman, in *Occupational Prestige in Comparative Perspective* (N.Y.: Academic Press, 1977),

> people in all walks of life share understandings about occupations—how much skill they require, how physically demanding they are, whether they are considered men's work or women's work, and so on—but particularly about their prestige. Every adult member of society ordinarily is able to locate occupations on a hierarchy of prestige. These perceptions form part of the *conscience collective.* This permits one to rank oneself and others with respect to the social honor derived from occupational status.

See also Andre L. Delebec and James Vigen, "Prestige Ratings of Business and Other Occupations," *Personnel Journal* (February 1970); Anthony P. M. Coxon and Charles L. Jones, *Class and Hierarchy: The Social Meaning of Occupations* (New York: St. Martin's Press, 1979).

occupational psychiatry, also called INDUSTRIAL PSYCHIATRY, any of the professional activities of psychiatry conducted at the workplace of the clients. *See* W. E. Powles and W. D. Ross, "Industrial and Occupational Psychiatry," in S. Arieti (ed.), *American Handbook of Psychiatry,* 2nd ed. (N.Y.: Basic Books, 1975).

occupational psychology: *see* IN-DUSTRIAL PSYCHOLOGY.

occupational registration, simple require-ment that persons active in a particular oc-cupation file their names with an appro-priate authority. As such regulations place no restrictions upon the persons engaged in the particular occupation, registration is no indication of competence.

Occupational Safety and Health Act of 1970, also called WILLIAMS-STEIGER ACT, federal government's basic legislation for providing for the health and safety of employees on the job. The act created the Occupational Safety and Health Review Commission, the Occupational and Health Administration, and the National Institute for Occupational Safety and Health. It covers every employer in a business affect-ing commerce, except where the work-place is covered under a special Federal law such as those for the mining and atomic energy industries. Federal employees are covered by an Executive order, and State and local government employees may be covered by the State, operating under a plan approved by the Federal Government. The law encourages States to operate occupational safety and health programs by providing grants for those whose plans demonstrate that the program can be "at least as effective as" the Federal program.

Under the general duty clause of the law, each employer must provide a workplace free from recognized hazards that are causing or are likely to cause death or serious physical harm. The Occupa-tional Safety and Health Administration (OSHA) of the U.S. Department of Labor establishes standards which require condi-tions or the use of practices or methods necessary to protect workers on the job. OSHA has issued standards on the follow-ing substances: acrylonitrile, inorganic arsenic, asbestos, benzene, 14 car-cinogens, coke oven emissions, cotton dust, dibromochloropropane (DBCP), lead, and vinyl chloride. It is the employer's responsibility to become familiar and comply with the standards, to put them into effect, and to assure that employees have and use personal protec-tive equipment required for safety and health.

Employees have a right:
- to request that OSHA conduct an in-spection if they believe hazardous conditions or violations of standards exist in their workplace;
- to file a written request for an im-mediate inspection whenever they fear that an imminent danger is present in the workplace. If OSHA decides an in-spection is unnecessary, they must notify the employee in writing;
- to refuse in good faith to expose themselves to a hazardous condition if there is no reasonable alternative. The condition must be of such a nature that, to a reasonable person, there is a real danger of death or serious in-jury and there is not enough time to do away with the danger through the complaint process;
- to have an authorized employee representative accompany the OSHA representative during an inspection tour;
- to respond to questions from an OSHA inspector;
- to review employer information about job-related accidents and injuries at the workplace;
- to participate in establishing standards;
- to be advised by their employer of hazards, prohibited by the law, that ex-ist at the workplace and of possible ex-posure to toxic or dangerous materials;
- to be notified of any citations issued against their employer.

Several cities and states have enacted laws requiring employers to inform their employees about toxic substances they are exposed to at the workplace. The National Labor Relations Board has also ruled that unions who request them must be given the names of chemicals and other substances the workers they represent are exposed to in the workplace. *See* George C. Guenther, "The Significance of the Occupational Safety and Health Act to the Worker in the United States," *International Labor Review* (January 1972); Judson MacLaury, "The Job Safety Law of 1970: Its Passage was Perilous," *Monthly Labor Review* (March 1981).

Occupational Safety and Health Administration (OSHA), established by the Occupational Safety and Health Act of 1970, OSHA develops and promulgates occupational safety and health standards, develops and issues regulations, conducts investigations and inspections to determine the status of compliance with safety and health standards and regulations, and issues citations and proposes penalties for noncompliance with safety and health standards and regulations. The Assistant Secretary for Occupational Safety and Health has responsibility for occupational safety and health activities. OSHA has ten regional offices. *See* Albert L. Nichols and Richard Zeckhauser, "Government Comes to the Workplace: An Assessment of OSHA," *The Public Interest* (Fall 1977); Benjamin W. Mintz, OSHA: History, Law, and Policy (Washington, DC: Bureau of National Affairs, Inc., 1985).

OSHA
U.S. Department of Labor
Washington, DC 20210
(202) 523-8017
See also MARSHAL V. BARLOW'S, INC. and MINE SAFETY AND HEALTH ADMINISTRATION.

Occupational Safety & Health Reporter, weekly notification and reference service published by the Bureau of National Affairs, Inc. Covers significant legislative, administrative, judicial, and industrial developments under the Occupational Safety and Health Act. Includes information on standards, legislation, regulations, enforcement, research, advisory committee recommendations, union activities, and state programs.
See also BUREAU OF NATIONAL AFFAIRS, INC.

Occupational Safety and Health Review Commission (OSHRC), independent adjudicatory agency established by the Occupational Safety and Health Act of 1970 to adjudicate enforcement actions initiated under the act when they are contested by employers, employees, or representatives of employees.

Within OSHRC there are two levels of adjudication. All cases which require a hearing are assigned to a OSHRC judge who will decide the case. Each such decision is subject to discretionary review by the three OSHRC members upon the motion of any one of the three. However, approximately 90 percent of the decisions of the judges become final orders without any change whatsoever.

The Occupational Safety and Health Act covers virtually every employer in the country. It requires employers to furnish their employees with employment and a place of employment free from recognized hazards that are causing or are likely to cause death or serious physical harm to employees and to comply with occupational safety and health standards promulgated under the act.

The Secretary of Labor has promulgated a substantial number of occupational safety and health standards, which, pursuant to the act, have the force and effect of law. He has also initiated a regular program of inspections in order to check upon compliance. A case for adjudication by OSHRC arises when a citation is issued against an employer as the result of such an inspection and it is contested within 15 working days thereafter.

When a case is docketed, it is assigned for hearing to a OSHRC judge. The hearing will ordinarily be held in or near the community where the alleged violation occurred. At the hearing, the Secretary of Labor will have the burden of proving his case.

After the hearing, the judge must issue a report, based on findings of fact, affirming, modifying, or vacating the secretary's citation or proposed penalty, or directing other appropriate relief. His report will become a final order of OSHRC 30 days thereafter unless, within such period, any

OSHRC member directs that such report shall be reviewed by OSHRC itself. When that occurs, the OSHRC members will thereafter issue their own decision on the case.

Once a case is decided, any person adversely affected or aggrieved thereby, may obtain a review of such a decision in a United States court of appeals.

OSHRC
1825 K Street N.W.
Washington, DC 20006
(202) 634-7943

occupational socialization, process by which an individual absorbs and adopts the values, norms, and behavior of the occupational role model with whom he/she interacts. Occupational socialization is complete when an individual internalizes the values and norms of the occupational group. *See* Wilbert E. Moore, "Occupational Socialization," in David A. Goslin (ed.), *Handbook of Socialization Theory and Research* (Chicago: Rand McNally & Co., 1969).

occupational sociology, also called INDUSTRIAL SOCIOLOGY and SOCIOLOGY OF WORK, subspecialty of sociology concerned with examining the social structures and institutions which a society develops to facilitate its work. For texts, *see* Walter S. Neff, *Work and Human Behavior* (Chicago: Aldine Publishing Company, 1968); Lee Taylor, *Occupational Sociology* (N.Y.: Oxford University Press, 1968); Elliott A. Krause, *The Sociology of Occupations* (Boston: Little, Brown, 1971).

occupational status: *see* OCCUPATIONAL PRESTIGE.

occupational survey, an organization's study of all positions in a given class, series of classes, or occupational group in whatever departments or divisions they may be located.

occupational therapy, health profession providing services to people whose lives have been disrupted by physical injury or illness, developmental problems, the aging process and social or psychological difficulties.

OD: *see* OGRANIZATION DEVELOPMENT.

Odiorne, George S. (1920-   ), one of the foremost authorities on MBO. Major works include: *Management by Objectives—A System of Managerial Leadership* (N.Y.: Pitman, 1965); *Management Decisions by Objectives* (Englewood Cliffs, N.Y.: Prentice-Hall 1969); *Personnel Policy: Issues and Practices* (Columbus, Ohio: Charles E. Merrill, 1963); *Training by Objectives* (N.Y.: Macmillan, 1970); *Personnel Administration by Objectives* (Homewood, Ill.: Richard D. Irwin, 1971).

OFCCP: *see* OFFICE OF FEDERAL CONTRACT COMPLIANCE PROGRAMS.

office: *see* OPEN OFFICE and TURKEY FARM.

office automation, a loose term for any significant use of machines in offices. In the 1960s, it referred to any use of computers to process paperwork. Today it refers to word processing and other information retrieval equipment; but, it has also taken on a larger connotation—the "office of the future"—in which electronic office devices are linked by telecommunications to other offices throughout a company, a region, or the world.

Office of Federal Contract Compliance Programs (OFCCP), agency within the Department of Labor delegated the responsibility for ensuring that there is no employment discrimination by government contractors because of race, religion, color, sex, or national origin, and to ensure affirmative action efforts in employing Vietnam Era veterans and handicapped workers. *See* Frank Erwin, "The New OFCCP Guidelines: What Happened?" *The Personnel Administrator* (February 1977).

OFCCP
200 Constitution Ave., N.W.
Washington, D.C. 20210
(202) 523-9475

Office of Personnel Management (OPM), the central personnel agency of the federal government, created by the Civil Service Reform Act of 1978. OPM took over many of the responsibilities of the U.S. Civil Service Commission, including central examining and employment operations, personnel investigations, personnel program evaluation, executive development, and training. OPM administers the retirement and insurance programs for federal employees and exercises management leadership in labor relations and affirmative action. As the central personnel agency, OPM develops policies governing civilian employment in executive branch agencies and in certain agencies of the legislative and judicial branches. Subject to its standards and review, OPM delegates certain personnel powers to agency heads.
Office of Personnel Management
1900 E. Street, N.W.
Washington, D.C. 20415
(202) 632-5491

office romance: *see* LOVE.

office title, job title that differs from the classified title assigned to a job and is used to describe a particular position for other than payroll, budget, or official purposes. For example, a Head Clerk position might have an "office" title of Office Supervisor.

off-line, computer system whose operations are not under the control of a central processing unit, or a computer system that does not process information as it is received, but stores and processes it at a later time.

offset plan, an integrated pension plan that reduces private benefits by a portion of an employee's social security benefit.

ogive, a cumulative frequency graph.

Ohio Bureau of Employment Services v. Hodory, 431 U.S. 471 (1977), U.S. Supreme Court case, which ruled that a "State can withhold jobless benefits from workers laid off as a result of a strike against their employer even when they are not involved in the strike because it occurs at another location."

Ohio Vocational Interest Survey (OVIS), interest inventory used in vocational guidance and counseling. Consists of 280 items that yield a profile of interests in 24 occupational scales (*i.e.,* teaching, art, management, sales, medical, manual labor, nursing, clerical work, etc.). TIME: 60/90 minutes. AUTHORS: A. G. D'Costa, J. G. Odgers, D. W. Wineford-ner, P. B. Koons, Jr. PUBLISHER: Harcourt, Brace, Jovanovich, Inc. (*see* TEST PUBLISHERS).

Oil Workers **v.** ***Mobile Oil Co.,*** 426 U.S. 407 (1976), U.S. Supreme Court case, which considered the express authorization in the National Labor Relations Act for states to enact "right-to-work" laws forbidding union shops. Texas, a right-to-work state, tried to apply its statute to oil-tanker workers who were hired and often based in Texas. Because the workers spent the bulk of their working time on the high seas, however, the court decided that Texas law should not govern these workers and upheld a union-shop clause in their contract.

Old Age, Survivors, and Disability Insurance (OASDI), federal program, created by the Social Security Act, which taxes both workers and employers to pay benefits to retired and disabled people, their dependents, widows, widowers, and children of deceased workers.
See also SOCIAL SECURITY.

old boys' network also NEW GIRLS' NETWORK, colloquial way of referring to the fact that men who went to school together or belong to the same clubs tend to help each other in the business world as the occasion arises. Many a career was advanced because a college roommate was in a critical position 20 years later. In an effort to develop similar ties for similar advantages, some women have been purposely trying to create a "new girls' network" by sponsoring appropriate social events. As Sarah Weddington, President Carter's "women's advisor," told one such group, "where you are tomorrow may well depend upon whom you meet tonight." *See* Stephen L. Slavin, "The Old Boy Network at Six Big Banks," *Business and Society Review* (Fall 1977).

Old Dominion Branch No. 496, National Association of Letter Carriers v. Austin, 418 U.S. 264 (1974), U.S. Supreme Court case, which held use of the epithet "scab," which was literally and factually true and in common parlance in labor disputes, was protected under federal law.

oligarchy: *see* IRON LAW OF OLIGARCHY.

Oliver Report: *see* JOB EVALUATION AND PAY REVIEW TASK FORCE.

OLMAT: *see* OTIS-LENNON MENTAL ABILITY TEST.

ombudsman, also ORGANIZATION OMBUDSMAN, official whose job is to investigate the complaints of the citizenry concerning public services. Originally a Swedish word meaning "representative of the King," ombudsmen are now found in many countries at a variety of jurisdictional levels. For a comprehensive discussion, *see* Stanely V. Anderson (ed.), *Ombudsmen for American Government?* (Englewood Cliffs, N.J.: Prentice-Hall, 1968).

An *organization ombudsman* is a high-level staff officer who receives complaints and grievances about his organization directly from the employees. Such an officer mainly serves as an open channel of communication between employees and top management. *See* Isidore Silver, "The Corporate Ombudsman," *Harvard Business Review* (May–June 1967); Marshall Dimock, "The Ombudsman and

Public Administration," *Public Administration Review* (September/October 1983).

one big union, the slogan of the IWW which stressed the inclusion of everyone, regardless of trade, in one all-encompassing union.

on-line, computer system whose operations are under the control of a central processing unit or a computer system in which information is processed as received. *See* Raymond E. Casper, "On-Line Recruitment," *Personnel Journal* (April 1985).

on-the-job training, any training that takes place during regular working hours and for which normal wages are paid. *See* Earl R. Gomersall and M. Scott Myers, "Breakthrough in On-the-Job Training," *Harvard Business Review* (July–August 1966); Martin M. Broadwell, "It Pays to Increase Your Support of On-the-Job Training," *Training* (October 1977); Delbert W. Fisher, "Educational Psychology Involved in On-the-Job Training," *Personnel Journal* (October 1977).
See also UNDERSTUDY.

open-book test, test that allows candidates to consult textbooks or other relevant material while the examination is in progress.

open-end agreement, collective bargaining agreement providing for a contract that will remain in effect until one of the parties wants to reopen negotiations.

open enrollment, a period when new subscribers may elect to enroll in a health insurance plan or prepaid group practice. Open enrollment periods may be used in the sale of either group or individual insurance and be the only period of a year when insurance is available.

open office, completely open room without walls, doors, or dividers; room with partitions and potted plants where walls once were; room with partitioned cubicles that curve and connect; and/or an office laid out according to how information flows from one person to the next.

open shop, any work organization that is not unionized. The term also applies to organizations that have unions but do not have union membership as a condition of employment. Historically, an "open shop" was one that tended to discriminate against unions.

open system, any organism or organization that interacts with its environment.

open union, union willing to admit any qualified person to its membership upon payment of initiation fees.

operational validity, the three basic elements of operational validity are test administration, interpretation, and application. According to William C. Byham and Stephen Temlock, in "Operational Validity—A New Concept in Personnel Testing," *Personnel Journal* (September 1972), "operational validity includes everything that happens with and to a test after test research has been completed. Operational validity can never make invalid tests predictive; it can only assure maximum prediction within the limits of the tests used." According to Dennis M. Groner, in "A Note on 'Operational'

Validity," *Personnel Journal* (March 1977), "in the strictest sense of the word, operational validity is not validity at all, but a source of error which reduces the correlation between a predictor and a criterion."

operations research, a group of mathematical methods for the efficient allocation of scarce resources such as capital, labor and materials. *See also* MANAGEMENT SCIENCE for partially overlapping definitions. For history, *see:* Russell L. Ackoff, "The Development of Operations Research as a Science," *Operations Research* (June 1956).

opportunity cost, also called ALTERNATIVE COST, true cost of choosing one alternative rather than another; represents the implicit cost of the highest foregone alternative.

OPM: *see* OFFICE OF PERSONNEL MANAGEMENT.

oral board, committee formed for the purpose of interviewing candidates for employment, promotion, or evaluation.

oral examination, group: *see* GROUP ORAL INTERVIEW.

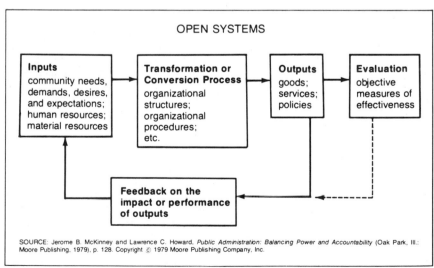

OPEN SYSTEMS

Inputs	Transformation or Conversion Process	Outputs	Evaluation
community needs, demands, desires, and expectations; human resources; material resources	organizational structures; organizational procedures; etc.	goods; services; policies	objective measures of effectiveness

Feedback on the impact or performance of outputs

SOURCE: Jerome B. McKinney and Lawrence C. Howard, *Public Administration: Balancing Power and Accountability* (Oak Park, Ill.: Moore Publishing, 1979), p. 128. Copyright © 1979 Moore Publishing Company, Inc.

oral interview, group: *see* GROUP ORAL INTERVIEW.

oral test, any test that has an examiner ask a candidate a set of questions, as opposed to a paper-and-pencil test.

organic system, that organization form that has proved to be most appropriate under changing conditions. It is characterized by: (1) constant reassessment of tasks, assignments, and the use of organizational expertise; (2) authority, control, and communication are frequently *ad hoc* depending upon specific commitments and tasks; (3) communications and interactions between members are both very open and extensive; (4) leadership stressing consultation and group decisional processes; and (5) greater commitment to the organization's tasks and goals than to traditional hierarchical loyalty. The classic analysis of organic systems is to be found in Tom Burns and G. M. Stalker, *The Management of Innovation* (Chicago: Quadrangle Books, 1961). For the contrast, *see* MECHANISTIC SYSTEM.

organization, any structure and process of allocating jobs so that common objectives may be achieved. *See* James G. March and Herbert A. Simon, *Organizations* (N.Y.: John Wiley, 1958); James G. March (ed.), *Handbook of Organizations* (Chicago: Rand McNally, 1965); Harold J. Leavitt, William R. Dill, and Henry B. Eyring, *The Organizational World* (N.Y.: Harcourt Brace Jovanovich, 1973).

organization, flat/tall: *see* FLAT ORGANIZATION.

organization, formal/informal: *see* INFORMAL ORGANIZATION.

organizational behavior, academic discipline consisting of those aspects of the behavioral sciences that focus on the understanding of human behavior in organizations. *See* Walter E. Natemeyer (ed.), *Classics of Organizational Behavior* (Oak Park, Ill.: Moore Publishing Co., 1979); William B. Eddy, *Public Organiza-*

tion Behavior and Development (Cambridge, Mass.: Winthrop Publishers, 1981).

organizational conflict: *see* CONFLICT RESOLUTION.

Organizational Dynamics, quarterly publication of the American Management Associations that is a review of organizational behavior for professional managers.
Organizational Dynamics
Editorial Address:
American Management Associations
135 West 50th Street
New York, NY 10020
Subscriptions:
Box 319
Saranac Lake, NY 12983

organizational humanism, movement to create more humane work environments.

organizational iceberg, concept that the formal or overt aspects of an organization are just the proverbial tip of the iceberg. The greater part of the organization—the feelings, attitudes, and values of its members, for example—remain covert or hidden from obvious view. In short, the formal organization is visible, while the informal is hidden and waiting to sink any ship that ignores it.

organizational identification, according to Douglas T. Hall, Benjamin Schneider, and Harold T. Nygren, in "Personal Factors in Organizational Identification," *Administrative Science Quarterly* (June 1970), organization identification "is the process by which the goals of the organization and those of the individual become increasingly integrated or congruent."

organizational mirror, according to Jack K. Fordyce and Raymond Weil, in *Managing with People* (Reading, Mass.: Addison-Wesley, 1971),

> an organization mirror is a particular kind of meeting that allows an organizational unit to collect feedback from a number of key organizations to which it relates (*e.g.,* customers, suppliers,

users of services within the larger organization). The meeting closes with a list of specific tasks for improvement of operations, products, or services.

organizational picketing, picketing an employer in order to encourage union membership.

organizational pyramids: see PYRAMIDS.

Organization Behavior & Human Performance, published bimonthly (beginning each year in February), this journal of fundamental research and theory in applied psychology seeks papers describing original empirical research and theoretical developments in all areas of human performance theory and organizational psychology. Preference is given to those articles contributing to the development of theories relevant to human performance or organizational behavior.

> *Organizational Behavior & Human*
> *Performance*
> Academic Press, Inc.
> 111 Fifth Avenue
> New York, NY 10003

organization chart, graphic description of the structure of an organization, usually in the form of a diagram.

organization climate, as a concept that can both explain and describe, organization climate studies seek (1) to show why things are as good or as bad as they are in a particular organization and/or (2) to characterize an organization's overall ambience. For comprehensive introductions to the concept, see Fritz Steele and Stephen Jenks, *The Feel of the Work Place: Understanding and Improving Organization Climate* (Reading, Mass.: Addison-Wesley Publishing Co., 1977); Terrence E. Deal and Allan A. Kennedy, *Corporate Cultures: The Rituals of Corporate Life* (Reading, Mass.: Addison-Wesley, 1982). For how to evaluate the climate in your organization, see William R. LaFollette, "How Is the Climate in Your Organization," *Personnel Journal* (July 1975); Alan L. Wilkins, "The Culture

Audit: A Tool for Understanding Organizations," *Organizational Dynamics* (Autumn 1983); Daniel R. Denison, "Bringing Corporate Culture to the Bottom Line," *Organizational Dynamics* (Autumn 1984). *Also see* Allan P. Jones and Lawrence R. James, "Psychological Climate: Dimensions and Relationships of Individual and Aggregated Work Environment Perceptions," *Organizational Behavior and Human Performance* (April 1979); Andrew M. Pettigrew, "On Studying Organizational Cultures," *Administrative Science Quarterly* (December 1979); Benjamin Schneider, "The Service Organization: Climate Is Crucial," *Organizational Dynamics* (Autumn 1980); Edgar H. Schein, "The Role of the Founder in Creating Organizational Culture," *Organizational Dynamics* (Summer 1983); Vijay Sathe, "Some Action Implications of Corporate Culture: A Manager's Guide to Action," *Organizational Dynamics* (Autumn 1983).

organization design, formal structure of the organization. Organization design is a relatively new term that implies that the structure is a consciously manipulatable variable. The term emerges from a resurgence of concern about the question "what is the most appropriate structure in a given situation?" See J. Galbraith, *Organization Design* (Reading, Mass.: Addison-Wesley, 1977); Henry Mintzberg, "Organization Design: Fashion or Fit?" *Harvard Business Review* (January–February 1981).

organization development (OD), premised upon the notion that any organization wishing to survive must periodically divest itself of those parts or characteristics that contribute to its malaise, OD is a process for increasing an organization's effectiveness. As a process it has no value bias, yet it is usually associated with the idea that maximum effectiveness is to be found by integrating an individual's desire for personal growth with organizational goals. Wendell L. French and Cecil H. Bell, Jr., in *Organization Development: Behavioral Science Interventions for Organization Im-*

provement (Englewood Cliffs, N.J.: Prentice-Hall, 1973), provide a formal definition:

> organization development is a long-range effort to improve an organization's problem-solving and renewal processes, particularly through a more effective and collaborative management of organization culture—with special emphasis on the culture of formal work teams—with the assistance of a change agent, or catalyst, and the use of the theory and technology of applied behavioral science, including action research.

Other major texts include: Warren Bennis, *Organization Development: Its Nature, Origin, and Prospects* (Reading, Mass.: Addison-Wesley, 1969); Chris Argyris, *Management and Organizational Development: The Path From XA to YB* (N.Y.: McGraw-Hill, 1971); Edgar F. Huse, *Organization Development and Change* (St. Paul, Minn.: West Publishing, 1975); Stanley P. Powers, F. Gerald Brown, and David S. Arnold, *Developing the Municipal Organization* (Washington, D.C.: International City Management Association, 1974). *Also see* Robert T. Golembiewski and William B. Eddy, editors, *Organization Development in Public Administration*, 2 Volumes (New York: Marcel Dekker, 1978); Wendell L. French, Cecil H. Bell, Jr., and Robert A. Zawacki (eds.), *Organization Development: Theory, Practice, and Research* (Dallas, Texas: Business Publications, Inc., 1978); Glen H. Varney, *Organization Development for Managers* (Reading, Mass.: Addison-Wesley, 1977); Warner Woodworth and Reed Nelson, "Witch Doctors, Messianics, Sorcerers, and OD Consultants: Parallels and Paradigms," *Organizational Dynamics* (Autumn 1979); Dennis D. Umstot, "Organization Development Technology and the Military: A Surprising Merger?" *Academy of Management Review* (April 1980); W. Warner Burke, "Organization Development and Bureaucracies in the 1980s," *Journal of Applied Behavioral Science* (July-August-September 1980); Anthony T. Cobb and Newton Margulies, "Organization Development: A Political Perspective," *Academy of Management Review* (January 1981); David A. Nadler, "Managing Organization Change: An Integrative Perspective," *Journal of Applied Behavioral Science* (April-May-June 1981); Robert T. Golembiewski, Carl W. Proehl, Jr., and David Sink, "Success of OD Applications in the Public Sector: Toting Up the Score for a Decade, More or Less," *Public Administration Review* (November/December 1981); W. Warner Burke, *Organization Development: Principles and Practices* (Boston: Little, Brown and Co., 1982); Fred E. Fiedler and Joseph E. Garcia, "Comparing Organization Development and Management Training," *Personnel Administrator* (March 1985).

See also the following entries:

ARGYRIS, CHRIS
BENNIS, WARREN
BLAKE, ROBERT R. AND JANE S. MOUTON
CONFRONTATION MEETING
NATIONAL TRAINING LABORATORIES INSTITUTE FOR APPLIED BEHAVIORAL SCIENCE
PROCESS CONSULTATION
SMALL-GROUP RESEARCH
TEAM BUILDING

organization man, now generic term to describe any individual within an organization who accepts the values of the organization and finds harmony in conforming to its policies. The term was popularized by William H. Whyte, Jr., in his best selling book, *The Organization Man* (New York: Simon & Schuster, 1956). Whyte wrote that these individuals were "the ones of our middle class who have left home, spiritually as well as physically, to take the vows of organization life, and it is they who are the mind and soul of our great self-perpetuating institutions." For the organization man's replacement, *see* Robert Stephen Silverman and D. A. Heming, "Exit The Organization Man: Enter the Professional Person," *Personnel Journal* (March 1975).

organization ombudsman: *see* OMBUDSMAN.

organization theory, also CLASSICAL

ORGANIZATION THEORY and NEOCLASSICAL ORGANIZATION THEORY, theory that seeks to explain how groups and individuals behave in varying organizational structures and circumstances.

Classical organization theory, as its name implies, was the first theory of its kind, is considered traditional, and will continue to be the base upon which subsequent theories are built. The development of any theory must be viewed in the context of its time. The beliefs of early management theorists about how organizations worked or should work was a direct reflection of the social values of their times. And the times were harsh. Individual workers were not viewed as individuals, but as the interchangeable parts in an industrial machine whose parts were made of flesh when it was impractical to make them of steel. Consequently, the first theories of organizations were concerned with the anatomy, with the structure, of formal organizations. This is the hallmark of classical organization theory—a concern for organizational structure that is premised upon the assumed rational behavior of its human parts.

There is no firm definition as to just what "neoclassical" means in *neoclassical organization theory*, but the general connotation is that of a theoretical perspective that revises and/or is critical of traditional (classical) organization theory because it does not pay enough attention to the needs and interactions of organizational members. The watershed between classical and neoclassical organization theory is World War II. The major writers of the classical school (Taylor, Fayol, Weber, Gulick, etc.) did their most significant work before World War II. The major neoclassical writers (Simon, March, Selznick, Parsons, etc.) gained their reputations as organization theorists by attacking the classical writers after the war.

For the historical evolution of organization theory, *see* William G. Scott, "Organization Theory: An Overview And An Appraisal," *Academy of Management Journal* (April 1961); Charles Perrow, "The Short and Glorious History of Organizational Theory," *Organizational Dynamics* (Summer 1973); Jay M. Shafritz and Philip H. Whitbeck, *Classics of Organization Theory* (Oak Park, Illinois: Moore Publishing Company, 1978).
See also REALPOLITIK.

organized labor, collective term for members of labor unions. *See* Sanford Cohen, *Labor in the United States* (Columbus, Ohio: Charles E. Merrill, 5th ed., 1979).

organizer, also called LABOR ORGANIZER and UNION ORGANIZER, individual, employed by a union, who acts to encourage employees of a particular plant or organization to join the union that the organizer represents. *See* Stephen L. Schlossberg and Judith A. Scott, *Organizing and the Law: A Handbook for Union Organizers* (Washington, D.C.: Bureau of National Affairs, Inc., 3rd ed., 1983); James H. Hopkins and Robert D. Binderup, "Employee Relations and Union Organizing Campaigns," *The Personnel Administrator* (March 1980); William E. Fulmer, *Union Organizing: Management and Labor Conflict* (New York: Praeger Publishers, 1982); John J. Hoover, "Union Organization Attempts: Management's Response," *Personnel Journal* (March 1982); Kenneth Gagala, *Union Organizing and Staying Organized* (Reston, VA: Reston/Prentice-Hall, 1983); Paula B. Voos, "Does It Pay to Organize? Estimating the Cost to Unions," *Monthly Labor Review* (June 1984).
See also the following entries:
> BETH ISRAEL HOSPITAL V. NATIONAL LABOR RELATIONS BOARD
> NATIONAL LABOR RELATIONS BOARD V. BABCOCK AND WILCOX
> PANDOL & SONS V. AGRICULTURAL LABOR RELATIONS BOARD

organizing: *see* CENTRAL HARDWARE CO. V. NATIONAL LABOR RELATIONS BOARD and PANDOL & SONS V. AGRICULTURAL LABOR RELATIONS BOARD.

orientation, formal introduction and guided adjustment of new employees to their new job, new co-workers, and new working environment. *See* Murray Lubliner, "Employee Orientation," *Personnel Journal* (April 1978); Daniel N. Kanouse and Philomena Warihay, "A New Look at Employee Orientation," *Training and Development Journal* (July 1980); Mark S. Tauber, "New Employee Orientation: A Comprehensive Systems Approach," *Personnel Administrator* (January 1981); Edmund J. McGarrell, Jr., "An Orientation System that Builds Productivity," *Personnel Administrator* (October 1984); Ronald E. Smith, "Employee Orientation: 10 Steps to Success," *Personnel Journal* (December 1984).

orientation checklist, a listing in an orderly and logical sequence of all of the items about which a new employee should be informed or must do as part of the orientation process.

Oscar Mayer & Co. v. Evans, 60 L. Ed. 2d 609 (1979), U.S. Supreme Court case, which held an employee must exhaust state remedies for age discrimination before bringing federal action under the Age Discrimination in Employment Act.

OSHA: *see* OCCUPATIONAL SAFETY AND HEALTH ADMINISTRATION.

OSHRC: *see* OCCUPATIONAL SAFETY AND HEALTH REVIEW COMMISSION.

Otis-Lennon Mental Ability Test (OLMAT), test battery widely used for industrial personnel screening to measure general reasoning ability or scholastic aptitude by sampling a broad range of cognitive abilities. Most commonly used in the placement of individuals in lower level jobs—clerks, office machine operators, and assembly-line workers, etc. TIME: 30/45 minutes. AUTHORS: Arthur S. Otis and Roger T. Lennon. PUBLISHER: Psychological Corporation (*see* TEST PUBLISHERS).

outlaw strike: *see* WILDCAT STRIKE.

out-of-title work, also called OUT-OF-CLASS EXPERIENCE, duties performed by an incumbent of a position that are not appropriate to the class to which the position has been assigned.

outplacement, according to John Scherba, in "Outplacement: An Established Personnel Function," *The Personnel Administrator* (July 1978),

outplacement is the extension of services to a terminated employee to: 1) minimize the impact of termination, 2) reduce the time necessary to secure a new position, 3) improve the person's job search skills and 4) ultimately bring about the best possible match between the person and available jobs.

Also useful is J. D. Erdlen, "Guidelines for Retaining an Outplacement Consultant," *The Personnel Administrator* (January 1978); Dick Schaaf, "Training for Outplacement and Retirement," *Training* (May 1981); Dane Henriksen, "Outplacement: Guidelines That Ensure Success," *Personnel Journal* (August 1982); Lawrence M. Brammer and Frank E. Humberger, *Outplacement and Inplacement Counseling* (Englewood Cliffs, N.J.: Prentice-Hall, 1984).

See also DEHIRING.

output, end result of any process.

output curve: *see* WORK CURVE.

outstationing, placement of direct service personnel of one organization into another organization's physical facility. However, the service personnel remain accountable to and are paid by their own organization.

overachievement, also UNDERACHIEVEMENT, psychological concepts that describe a discrepancy between predicted and actual achievement/performance. Individuals whose performance exceeds or goes below expectations are described as overachievers or underachievers. *See* Robert L. Thorndike, *The Concepts of Over and Underachievements* (N.Y.: Columbia University Press, 1963).

overhead, the general and administrative expenses of a business that cannot be directly allocated to a particular product or department; includes such things as power, water, supervision, maintenance, rent, real estate tax, etc.

overhead agency: *see* AUXILIARY AGENCY.

overrate: *see* FLAGGED RATE.

overseas premium, payment that serves to induce an employee to accept a foreign assignment. It is usually paid each year that the employee is overseas and can either be a fixed dollar amount or a percentage of salary. Overseas premiums are designed to reimburse an employee for the cost of living in a foreign country in excess of what it would normally cost to live in the United States. *See* Cecil G. Howard, "Overseas Compensation Policies of U.S. Multinationals," *The Personnel Administrator* (November 1975).

overtime, work performed in excess of the basic workday/workweek as defined by law, collective bargaining, or company policy. For economic analyses, *see* Ronald G. Ehrenberg, *Fringe Benefits and Overtime Behavior: Theoretical and Econometric Analysis* (Lexington, Mass.: D.C. Heath, 1971); Ronald G. Ehrenberg and Paul L. Schumann, "Compliance With the Overtime Provisions of the Fair Labor Standards Act," *Journal of Law and Economics* (April 1982).

   See also BAY RIDGE COMPANY V. AARON and LODGE 76, INTERNATIONAL ASSOCIATION OF MACHINISTS V. WISCONSIN EMPLOYMENT RELATIONS COMMISSION.

overtime computations, for employees covered by the Fair Labor Standards Act, overtime must be paid at a rate of at least 1½ times the employee's regular pay rate for each hour worked in a workweek in excess of the maximum allowable in a given type of employment. Generally, the regular rate includes all payments made by the employer to or on behalf of the employee (excluding certain statutory exceptions). The following examples are based on a maximum 40-hour workweek:

1. **Hourly rate** (regular pay rate for an employee paid by the hour). If more than 40 hours are worked, at least 1½ times the regular rate for each hour over 40 is due. *Example:* An employee paid $3.80 an hour works 44 hours in a workweek. The employee is entitled to at least 1½ times $3.80, or $5.70, for each hour over 40. Pay for the week would be $152 for the first 40 hours, plus $22.80 for the four hours of overtime—a total of $174.80.

2. **Piece rate.** The regular rate of pay for an employee paid on a piecework basis is obtained by dividing the total weekly earnings by the total number of hours worked in the same week. The employee is entitled to an additional ½ of this regular rate for each hour over 40, besides the full piecework earnings. *Example:* An employee paid on a piecework basis works 45 hours in a week and earns $162. The regular pay rate for that week is $162 divided by 45, or $3.60 an hour. In addition to the straight time pay, the employee is entitled to $1.80 (half the regular rate) for each hour over 40. Another way to compensate pieceworkers for overtime, if agreed to before the work is performed, is to pay 1½ times the piece rate for each piece produced during overtime hours. The piece rate must be the one actually paid during nonovertime hours and must be enough to yield at least the minimum wage per hour.

3. **Salaries.** The regular rate for an employee paid a salary for a regular or specified number of hours a week is obtained by dividing the salary by the number of hours. If, under the employment agreement, a salary sufficient to meet the minimum wage requirement in every workweek is paid as straight time for whatever number of hours are worked in a workweek, the regular rate is obtained by dividing the salary by the number of hours

worked each week. To illustrate, suppose an employee's hours of work vary each week and the agreement with the employer is that the employee will be paid $200 a week for whatever number of hours of work are required. Under this pay agreement, the regular rate will vary in overtime weeks. If the employee works 50 hours, the regular rate is $4 ($200 divided by 50 hours). In addition to the salary, ½ the regular rate, or $2 is due for each of the 10 overtime hours, for a total of $220 for the week. If the employee works 54 hours, the regular rate will be $3.70 ($200 divided by 54). In that case, an additional $1.85 is due for each of the 14 overtime hours, for a total of $225.90 for the week.

In no case may the regular rate be less than the minimum wage required by the Act. If a salary is paid on other than a weekly basis, the weekly pay must be determined in order to compute the regular rate and overtime. If the salary is for a half month, it must be multiplied by 24 and the product divided by 52 weeks to get the weekly equivalent. A monthly salary should be multiplied by 12 and the product divided by 52.

OVIS: see OHIO VOCATIONAL INTEREST SURVEY.

Owen, Robert (1771–1858), Welsh industrialist, social reformer and utopian socialist who was one of the first writers to consider the importance of the human factor in industry. His model factory communities, New Lanark in Scotland and New Harmony in Indiana, were among the first to take a modern approach to personnel management. For biographies, see: J. F. C. Harrison, *Quest for the New Moral World: Robert Owen and the Owenites in Britain and America* (New York: Scribner, 1969); Arthur L. Morton, *The Life and Ideas of Robert Owen* (New York: International Publishers, 1969); and Sidney Pollard, editor, *Robert Owen, Prophet of the Poor* (Lewisburg, PA: Bucknell University Press, 1971).

P

PACE: see PROFESSIONAL AND ADMINISTRATIVE CAREERS EXAMINATION.

package settlement, term that describes the total money value (usually quoted as cents per hour) of an increase in wages and benefits achieved through collective bargaining. For example, a new contract might give employees an increase of 50¢ an hour. However, when the value of increased medical and pension benefits are included, the "package settlement" might come to 74¢ an hour. *See* John G. Kilgour, " 'Wrapping the Package' of Labor Agreement Costs," *Personnel Journal* (June 1977).

pact, an agreement.

PAIR, acronym for "personnel and industrial relations"; or for "personnel administration/industrial relations."

Pandol & Sons v. Agricultural Labor Relations Board, 429 U.S. 802 (1976), U.S. Supreme Court case, which upheld state regulations permitting union organizers access to private property for the purpose of organizing California's farmworkers.

paper locals, local unions created as vehicles for unethical or illegal actions.

PAQ: see POSITION ANALYSIS QUESTIONNAIRE.

PAR: see PUBLIC ADMINISTRATION REVIEW.

paradox of thrift, while individual increases in savings may be good for the individual, the totality of such increases can lead to an overall reduction in income and employment if not offset by an increase in investment.

paradox of value, the fact that so many of the absolute necessities of life (such as water) are cheap or relatively inexpensive compared to the price of luxury items (such as diamonds); in effect, great utility does not necessarily yield economic value and economic value does not mean that an item is useful.

paralegal: *see* PARAPROFESSIONAL.

parallel forms, two or more forms of a test that are assembled as closely as possible to the same statistical and content specifications so that they will provide the same kind of measurement at different administrations.

parallel ladder: *see* DUAL LADDER.

paramedic: *see* PARAPROFESSIONAL.

paraprofessional, any individual with less than standard professional credentials who assists a fully credentilized professional with the more routine aspects of his/her professional work. For example, paralegals assist lawyers and paramedics assist medical doctors. *See* Robert Cohen, *"New Careers" Grows Older: A Perspective on the Paraprofessional Experience, 1965-1975* (Baltimore: The Johns Hopkins University Press, 1976); Charlotte Mugnier, *The Paraprofessional and the Professional Job Structure* (Chicago: American Library Association, 1980); Greg H. Firth, *The Role of the Special Education Paraprofessional* (Springfield, Ill.: Charles C. Thomas, 1982).

Pareto, Vilfredo (1848-1923), Italian sociologist and economist who is considered the "father" of the idea of social systems. The *Pareto optimality* is an equilibrium point reached in a society when resource allocation is most efficient; that is, no further changes in resource allocation can be made that will increase the welfare of one person without decreasing the welfare of other persons. *Pareto's law*

holds that the pattern of income tends to become distributed in the same proportion in every country no matter what political or taxation conditions exist. Thus, the only way to increase the income of the poor is to increase overall production. Another of Pareto's laws is the *law of the trivial many and the critical few* (also called the *80-20 rule*) which holds that 80 percent of the traffic in a group of items is accounted for by only 20 percent of the items themselves. *See* Warren J. Samuels, *Pareto on Policy* (New York: Elsevier Scientific, 1974); Renato Cirillo, *The Economics of Vilfredo Pareto* (Totowa, N.J.: Cass, 1979).

parity, also EMPLOYMENT PARITY, OCCUPATIONAL PARITY, and WAGE PARITY, long term goal of all affirmative action efforts, which will exist after all categories of an organization's employees are proportionately representative of the population in the organization's geographic region. *Employment parity* exists when the proportion of protected groups in the external labor market is equivalent to their proportion in an organization's total work force without regard to job classifications. *Occupational parity* exists when the proportion of an organization's protected group employees in all job classifications is equivalent to their respective availability in the external labor market.

Wage parity requires that the salary level of one occupational classification be the same as for another. The most common example of wage parity is the linkage between the salaries of police and firefighters. Over two thirds of all cities in the United States have parity policies for their police and firefighters. But according to David Lewin, in "Wage Parity and the Supply of Police and Firemen," *Industrial Relations* (February 1973),

parity contributes to the problem of attracting and retaining qualified personnel in police ranks; it also inflates wages in the fire services beyond the level necessary to secure adequate staffing, thus imposing a heavy burden on local taxpayers. Furthermore, parity implies that police and fire occupations are similar

314

in nonpay characteristics when, in fact, policemen and firemen not only perform substantially different functions, but also have different promotional opportunities. Thus, from the perspective of the external labor market and from considerations of internal equity, wage parity is a deficient policy and should no longer guide the wage setting process for the protective services.

For legal analysis of the police/fire parity issue, see Hoyt N. Wheeler, Richard Berger, and Stephen McGarry, "Parity: An Evaluation of Recent Court and Board Decisions," *Labor Law Journal* (March 1978); Paul A. Lafranchise, Sr., and Michael T. Leibig, "Collective Bargaining for Parity in the Public Sector," *Labor Law Journal* (September 1981).

Parkinson's Law, C. Northcote Parkinson's famous law that "work expands so as to fill the time available for its completion" first appeared in his *Parkinson's Law and Other Studies in Administration* (Boston: Houghton Mifflin Co., 1957). With mathematical precision, he "discovered" that any public administrative department will invariably increase its staff an average of 5.75 percent per year. In anticipation of suggestions that he advise what might be done about this problem, he asserted that "it is not the business of the botanist to eradicate the weeds. Enough for him if he can tell us just how fast they grow."

See also LAW OF TRIVIALITY.

Parsons, Albert R(oss) (1848-1887), anarchist and radical labor leader who was convicted (with seven others) of the murder of seven policemen during the Haymarket "riot" of 1886. For a biography, see Alan Calmer, *Labor Agitator: The Story of Albert R. Parsons* (N.Y.: International Publishers, 1937).

Parsons, Talcott (1902-1979), preeminent sociologist whose theories of social action and structural-functionalism furthered the development of organization theory. Major works include: *The Structure of Social Action* (New York: McGraw-

Hill, 1937); *The Social System* (New York: The Free Press, 1951); *Structure and Process in Modern Societies* (New York: The Free Press, 1960); *Social Structure and Personality* (New York: The Free Press, 1964); *Politics and Social Structure* (New York: The Free Press, 1969); *Social Systems and the Evolution of Action Theory* (New York: The Free Press, 1977).

participative management: *see* INDUSTRIAL DEMOCRACY.

part-time workers: *see* FULL-TIME WORKERS.

passing point: *see* CUTTING SCORE.

passing score: *see* CUTTING SCORE.

passing the buck: *see* BUCKOLOGY.

passionate leave: *see* COMPASSIONATE LEAVE.

pass rate, proportion of candidates who pass an examination.

past practice, manner in which a similar issue was resolved before the occasion of a present grievance.

PATCO: *see* AIR TRAFFIC CONTROLLERS' STRIKE.

paternalism, also called INDUSTRIAL PATERNALISM and EMPLOYER PATERNALISM, in the United States, the word is a derogatory reference to an organization's "fatherly" efforts to better the lot of its employees. Historically, the U.S. labor movement has considered paternalistic efforts to be a false and demeaning charity which inhibited the growth of union membership. In other societies where there are well established paternalistic traditions, the derogatory connotations of the word may be absent. Japan is undoubtedly the most paternalistic of all the major industrial societies. For a history and analysis of the concept, *see* John W. Bennett, "Paternalism," David L. Sills (ed.), *International Encyclopedia of* *the Social Sciences* (N.Y.: Macmillan Co. & The Free Press, 1968).

paternity leave, *see* BIRTH LEAVE.

path-goal theory of leadership, a leadership style that has the leader indicate to his or her followers the "path" by which to accomplish their individual and organizational goals, then help to make that "path" as easy to follow as possible. According to Robert J. House, in "A Path-Goal Theory of Leader Effectiveness," *Administrative Science Quarterly* (September 1971),

> The motivational function of the leader consists of increasing personal pay-offs to subordinates for work-goal attainment, and making the path to these pay-offs easier to travel by clarifying it, reducing roadblocks and pitfalls, and increasing the opportunities for personal satisfaction in route.

Also see Robert J. House and T. R. Mitchell, "Path-Goal Theory of Leadership," *Journal of Contemporary Business* (Autumn 1974); Charles N. Greene, "Questions of Causation in the Path-Goal Theory of Leadership," *Academy of Management Journal* (March 1979).

patronage, the power of elected officials to make partisan appointments to office or to confer contracts, honors, or other benefits to their political supporters. For the most comprehensive survey of U.S. patronage practices, *see* Martin and Susan Tolchin, *To the Victor: Political Patronage from the Clubhouse to the White House* (N.Y.: Random House, 1971).

Also see Frank Sorauf, "The Silent Revolution in Patronage," *Public Administration Review* (Winter 1960); James Q. Wilson, "The Economy of Patronage," *Journal of Political Economy* (August 1961); Kenneth J. Meier, "Ode to Patronage: A Critical Analysis of Two Recent Supreme Court Decisions," *Public Administration Review* (September/October 1981); William M. Timmins, "Relations Between Political Appointees and Careerists," *Review of Public Personnel Administration* (Spring 1984).

See also the following entries:
APPOINTMENT CLAUSE
BRANTI V. FINKEL
CIVIL SERVICE REFORM
ELROD V. BURNS
MALEK MANUAL
MYERS V. UNITED STATES
NO-SHOW JOBS
PLUM BOOK
PUBLIC PERSONNEL POLITICS
SINECURE

patronage jokes, the definitive statement on the disillusioning aspects of political patronage is credited to President William Howard Taft, who was moved to conclude that whenever he made a patronage appointment, he created "nine enemies and one ingrate." Actually, this quip is generally attributed to all sophisticated dispensers of patronage from Thomas Jefferson to Louis XIV. U.S. presidents have produced only two memorable patronage jokes (other than many of the appointees themselves). In addition to President Taft's remark, there is the story that Abraham Lincoln, while lying prostrate in the White House with an attack of smallpox, said to his attendants: "Tell all the office-seekers to come in at once, for now I have something I can give to all of them."

pattern bargaining, collective bargaining in which key contract terms agreed to by one bargaining unit are copied by other companies in the same industry during subsequent negotiations. *See* Audrey Freedman and William E. Fulmer, "Last Rites For Pattern Bargaining, *Harvard Business Review* (March–April 1982).

See also UNITED MINE WORKERS V. PENNINGTON.

patterned interview, also UNPATTERNED INTERVIEW, interview that seeks to ask the same questions of all applicants. An *unpatterned interview* does not seek such uniformity. *See* Barbara Felton and Sue Ries Lamb, "A Model for Systematic Selection Interviewing," *Personnel* (January–February 1982).

pay: *see* the following entries:
  BASIC RATE OF PAY
  CALL-BACK PAY
  CALL-IN PAY
  COMPENSATION
  DOWN-TIME PAY
  HAZARD PAY
  HOLIDAY PAY
  INCENTIVE PAY
  JOURNEYMAN PAY
  JURY-DUTY PAY
  LONGEVITY PAY
  MAKE-UP PAY
  RETROACTIVE PAY
  SEVERANCE PAY
  STRIKE PAY
  TAKE-HOME PAY
  VACATION PAY
  WELL PAY
  WORK PREMIUM

pay-as-you-go plan, pension plan that has employers paying pension benefits to retired employees out of current income.

Pay Board, 15-member tripartite board consisting of business, labor, and public representatives whose function was to set and administer wage and salary policies. The Pay Board, authorized by the Economic Stabilization Act of 1970 and established by Executive Order 11627 on October 28, 1971, officially functioned under the Economic Stabilization Program of the Executive Office of the President. It was abolished by Executive Order 11695 on January 11, 1973.

pay compression, a situation where the salaries of all classes of employees are forced so close together that there ceases to be meaningful differences in the various pay grades. *See* James W. Steele, *Paying for Performance and Position: Dilemmas in Salary Compression and Merit Pay* (New York: American Management Associations, 1982); Thomas J. Bergmann, Frederick S. Hills and Laurel Priefert, "Pay Compresssion: Causes, Results, and Possible Solutions," *Compensation Review* (Second Quarter 1983).

pay criteria: *see* WAGE CRITERIA.

pay for performance, concept of paying an employee on the basis of job performance—all bonuses, raises, promotions, etc., would be directly related to the measurable results of the employee's efforts. *See* Thomas H. Patten, Jr., "Pay for Performance or Placation?" *The Personnel Administrator* (September 1977); Paula Cowan, "How Blue Cross Put Pay-for-Performance to Work," *Personnel Journal* (May 1978); James W. Steele, *Paying for Performance and Position: Dilemmas in Salary Compression and Merit Pay* (New York: American Management Associations, 1982); Robert H. Rock, "Pay for Performance: Measures and Standards," *Compensation Review* (Third Quarter 1984).

pay grade, also called PAY LEVEL, an increment that makes up a pay structure. Each represents a range of pay or a standard rate of pay for a specific class of jobs.

pay increase, any permanent raise in an employee's basic salary or wage level. *See* Linda A. Krefting and Thomas A. Mahoney, "Determining the Size of a Meaningful Pay Increase," *Industrial Relations* (February 1977); Poondi Varadarajan and Charles Futrell, "Factors Affecting Perceptions of Smallest Meaningful Pay Increases," *Industrial Relations* (Spring 1984).

paying your dues, the experiences that one must have before being ready for advancement. In effect, "you have to pay your dues" before you can be perceived as a legitimate occupant of a higher position.

pay level: *see* PAY GRADE.

payments in kind, noncash payments for services rendered.

pay plan, a listing of rates of pay for each job category in an organization. A *pay range,* also known as *salary* or *wage range,* indicates the minimum through maximum rates of pay for a job. The various increments that make up the pay range are known as the *pay steps*. The *pay grade* or *pay level* is the range of pay or a standard rate of pay for a specific job. The totality of the pay grades make up the *pay structure.*

While a position classification plan essentially arranges positions in classes on the basis of their similarities, a pay plan establishes rates of pay for each class of positions. Consequently, if a position is improperly classified, the corresponding salary can not be in accord with the principle of "equal pay for equal work." *See* Donald E. Hoag and Robert J. Trudel, *How to Prepare a Sound Pay Plan* (Chicago: International Personnel Management Association, 1976).

payroll, listing of all the wages and/or salaries earned by employees within an organization for a specific time period (usually weekly, bimonthly, or monthly).

payroll taxes: *see* EMPLOYMENT TAXES.

pay satisfaction, according to Edward E. Lawler, III, in *Pay and Organizational Effectiveness: A Psychological View* (N.Y.: McGraw-Hill, 1971), pay satisfaction "is basically determined by the difference between pay and the person's belief about what his pay should be." If employees find themselves assuming substantially similar duties and responsibilities as co-workers, who, because of seniority or education, have higher paying classifications, they are going to be dissatisfied with their pay. It is very difficult to convince employees that their pay is determined fairly if they have before them on a daily basis other more highly paid employees, who serve not as role models that one should strive to emulate, but rather as glaring examples of the inequities of the pay program.

pay secrecy, policy of keeping confidential the compensation levels of various categories of employees, most usually those in managerial positions. For analyses, *see* Mary G. Miner, "Pay Policies: Secret or Open? And Why?" *Personnel Journal* (February 1974); Jay R. Schuster and Jerome A. Colletti, "Pay Secrecy: Who Is For and Against It?" *Academy of Management Journal* (March 1973); Thomas A. Mahoney and William Weitzer, "Secrecy and Managerial Compensation," *Industrial Relations* (May 1978).

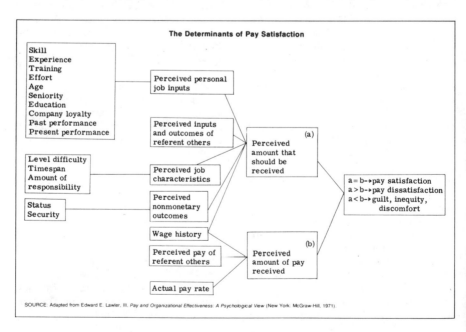

The Determinants of Pay Satisfaction

SOURCE: Adapted from Edward E. Lawler, III, *Pay and Organizational Effectiveness: A Psychological View* (New York: McGraw-Hill, 1971).

pay step, each of the various increments that make up a pay range.

pay survey: *see* WAGE SURVEY.

pay system, dual: *see* DUAL PAY SYSTEM.

pay system, Foreign Service: *see* FOREIGN SERVICE PAY SYSTEM.

PBGC: *see* PENSION BENEFIT GUARANTY CORPORATION.

P-C: *see* PROCESS CONSULTATION.

peaked out, negative way of referring to an employee who has reached the maximum step in his salary range or has already made his or her maximum contributions to the organization.

pecking order, ever since social psychologists discovered that chickens have a pecking order—the strongest or most aggressive fowl get to eat, or to peck, first—the term has been used to describe the comparative ranks that humans hold in their social organizations. No aspect of our society is immune from the pecking order's fowl antics. According to Lyndon Johnson's former press secretary, George E. Reedy, in *The Twilight of the Presidency* (Cleveland: World Publishing, 1970),

the inner life of the White House is essentially the life of the barnyard, as set forth so graphically in the study of the pecking order among chickens which every freshman sociology student must read. It is a question of who has the right to peck whom and who must submit to being pecked. There are only two important differences. The first is that the pecking order is determined by the individual strength and forcefulness of each chicken, whereas in the White House it depends upon the relationship to the barnyard keeper. The second is that no one outside the barnyard glorifies the chickens and expects them to order the affairs of mankind. They are destined for the frying pan and that is that.

peer rating, also called MUTUAL RATING,

performance evaluation technique that calls for each employee to evaluate all of the other employees in his/her work unit. *See* Allen I. Kraut, "Prediction of Managerial Success by Peer and Training-Staff Ratings," *Journal of Applied Psychology* (February 1975); R. G. Downey, F. F. Medland, and L. G. Yates, "Evaluation of a Peer Rating System for Predicting Subsequent Promotion of Senior Military Officers," *Journal of Applied Psychology* (April 1976); Kevin G. Love, "Empirical Recommendations for the Use of Peer Rankings in the Evaluation of Police Officer Performance," *Public Personnel Management* (Spring 1983); Fred C. Olson, "How Peer Review Works at Control Data," *Harvard Business Review* (November–December 1984).

Pendleton Act of 1883, this "Act to Regulate and Improve the Civil Service of the United States" introduced the merit concept into federal employment and created the U.S. Civil Service Commission. *See* David H. Rosenbloom, editor, *Centenary Issues of the Pendleton Act of 1883: The Problematic Legacy of Civil Service Reform* (New York: Marcel Dekker, 1982).

See also the following entries:
   CIVIL SERVICE REFORM ACT OF 1978
   GRANT'S CIVIL SERVICE COMMISSION
   NATIONAL CIVIL SERVICE LEAGUE

penetration rate, also PENETRATION RATIO, in the context of equal employment opportunity, the *penetration rate* for an organization is the proportion of its workforce belonging to a particular minority group. The *penetration ratio* is the ratio of an organization's penetration rate to the penetration rate for its geographic region (usually the standard metropolitan statistical area or SMSA). The rate and ratio are derived as follows:

$$\text{Penetration Rate} = \frac{\text{Total Minority Employment}}{\text{Total Employment}}$$

$$\text{Penetration Ratio} = \frac{\text{Penetration Rate for an Organization}}{\text{Penetration Rate for the SMSA}}$$

See also REPRESENTATIVE BUREAUCRACY.

Pennington decision: see UNITED MINE WORKERS V. PENNINGTON.

pension, periodic payments to an individual who retires from employment (or simply from a particular organization) because of age, disability, or the completion of a specific period of service. Such payments usually continue for the rest of the recipient's life and sometime extend to legal survivors.

While pensions have a long history as royal beneficences, the populace did not always view such royal largess as deserving. Samuel Johnson, in his 1755 *English Dictionary,* defined pension by stating, "in England it is generally understood to mean pay given to a state hireling for treason to his country." While early industrial pension plans were informal and based upon oral agreements, the first formal pension plan in the United States was the 1875 program of the American Express Company. In the public sector, the first civilian pension plans appeared just before World War I for some of the larger municipal police and fire departments. Federal civilian employees had to wait for the Retirement Act of 1920 before they were eligible for any retirement benefits.

Pension plans generally have either defined benefits or defined contributions. In *defined benefit plans* the amount of the benefit is fixed, but not the amount of contribution. These plans usually gear benefits to years of service and earnings or a stated dollar amount. About 60 percent of all pension plan participants are covered by defined benefit plans. In *defined contribution plans,* the amount of contributions is fixed, but the amount of benefit is not. These plans usually involve profit sharing, stock bonus or money purchase arrangements where the employer contributes an agreed percentage of profits or wages to the worker's individual account. The eventual benefit is determined by the amount of total contributions and investment earnings in the years during which the employee is covered.

The Employee Retirement Income Security Act of 1974 protects the interest of workers and their beneficiaries who de-

pend on benefits from employee pension and welfare plans. The law requires disclosure of plan provisions and financial information; establishes standards of conduct for trustees and administrators of welfare and pension plans; and sets up funding, participation, and vesting requirements for pension plans and an insurance system for certain defined benefit plans that terminate without enough money to pay benefits. *The law prohibits discharging a worker in order to avoid paying a pension benefit.* As a result of changes made by the Economic Recovery Tax Act of 1981, it also provides that any employed person may put aside a certain amount of income each year in a tax-free individual retirement account. ERISA does *not* require that employers establish pension plans, nor does it set benefit levels.

The Department of Labor and the Internal Revenue Service share the responsibility for administration of the law. The pension plan termination insurance program is administered by the Pension Benefit Guaranty Corporation.

For a history and analysis of pension programs, *see* William C. Greenough and Francis P. King, *Pension Plans and Public Policy* (N.Y.: Columbia University Press, 1976). *See also* William D. Hall and David L. Landsittel, *A New Look at Accounting for Pension Costs* (Homewood, Ill.: Richard D. Irwin, 1977); Everett T. Allen, Jr., Joseph J. Melone, and Jerry S. Rosenbloom, *Pension Planning* (Homewood, Ill.: Richard D. Irwin, 3rd ed., 1976); Wesley S. Mellow, "Health and Pension Coverage by Worker Characteristics," *Monthly Labor Review* (May 1982); Robert J. Lynn, *The Pension Crisis* (Lexington, Mass.: Lexington Books, 1983); Robert W. Hartman, *Pay and Pensions for Federal Workers* (Washington DC: The Brookings Institution, 1983); Dennis E. Logue and Richard J. Rogalski, *Managing Corporate Pension Plans: The Impacts of Inflation* (Washington, D.C.: American Enterprise Institute for Public Policy Research, 1984).

See also the following entries:

Pension Benefit Guaranty Corporation (PBGC), federal agency that guarantees basic pension benefits in covered private plans if they terminate with insufficient assets. Title IV of the Employee Retirement Income Security Act of 1974 (ERISA) established the corporation to guarantee payment of insured benefits if covered plans terminate without sufficient assets to pay such benefits. The PBGC, a self-financing, wholly-owned government corporation is governed by a Board of Directors consisting of the Secretaries of Labor, Commerce and the Treasury. The Secretary of Labor is chairman of the board and is responsible for administering the PBGC in accordance with policies established by the board. A seven-member Advisory Committee, composed of two labor, two business, and three public members appointed by the President, advises the PBGC on various matters.

Title IV of ERISA provides for mandatory coverage of most private defined benefit plans. These are those plans that provide a benefit, the amount of which can be determined from a formula in the plan, for example, based on factors such as age, years of service, average or highest salary, etc. *See* David M. Walker, "The PBGC's Role in Protecting Lump-Sum Benefit Values," *Labor Law Journal* (November 1984).

Pension Benefit Guaranty Corporation
2020 K Street N.W.
Washington, DC 20006
(202) 254-4817

pension fund socialism, Peter F. Drucker's term for the phenomenon that is turning traditional thinking about the "inherent" and historical separation of capital and labor upside down—namely, that the "workers" of the United States are rapidly and literally becoming the owners of the nation's industry through their pension fund investments in diverse common stocks. According to Drucker, by 1985 pension funds "will own at least 50—if not 60—percent of equity capital." For Drucker's complete analysis, *see* his *The Unseen Revolution: How Pension Fund Socialism Came to America* (N.Y.: Harper & Row, 1976).

pension plan, contributory, *see* CONTRIBUTORY PENSION PLAN.

pension plan, fully funded: *see* FULLY FUNDED PENSION PLAN.

pension plan, funded: *see* FUNDED PENSION PLAN.

Pension Reform Act of 1974: *see* EMPLOYEES RETIREMENT INCOME SECURITY ACT OF 1974.

Pension Reporter: see BNA PENSION REPORTER.

pension trust, individual-contract: *see* INDIVIDUAL-CONTRACT PENSION TRUST.

peonage, forced labor. The 13th Amendment prohibits such involuntary servitude.

people plucker: *see* HEADHUNTER.

per capita, Latin meaning: "by heads." In a per capita election each member would have one vote.

per capita income, the mean income computed for every man, woman and child in a particular group. It is derived by dividing the total income of a particular group by the total population (including patients or inmates in institutional quarters) in that group.

per capita tax, tax on each head and the regular payment made on the basis of membership by a local union to its national organization.

percentile, that point or score in a distribution below which falls the percent of cases indicated by the given percentile.

PENSION BENEFIT GUARANTY CORPORATION

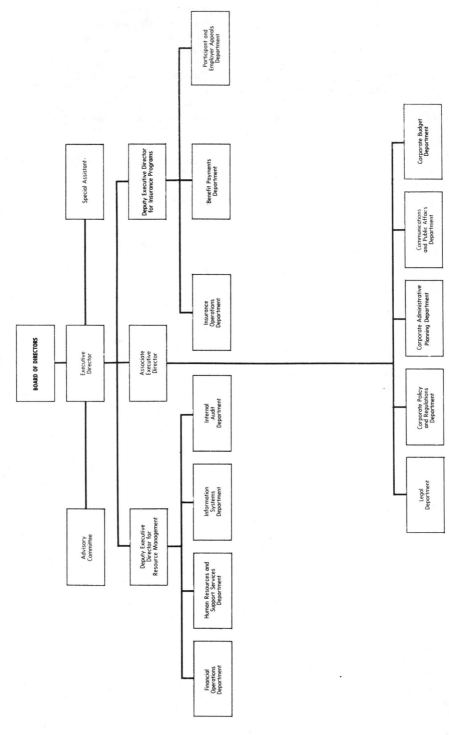

Source: U.S. Government Manual, p. 853.

Thus the 15th percentile denotes the score or point below which 15 percent of the scores fall.

percentile band, interval between percentiles, corresponding to score limits one standard error of measurement above and below an obtained score. The chances are approximately 2 out of 3 that the true score of an examinee with a particular obtained score is within these score limits.

percentile rank, percent of scores in a distribution equal to or lower than a particular obtained score.

per diem, Latin for "by the day." Temporary employees may be paid a "per-diem" rate or a travel expense program may reimburse employees using a flat "per-diem" amount.

performance, demonstration of a skill or competence.

performance appraisal, also called PER-FORMANCE EVALUATION and PERFORMANCE REPORTING, title usually given to the formal method by which an organization documents the work performance of its employees. Performance appraisals are designed to serve a variety of functions, such as:
1. changing or modifying dysfunctional work behavior;
2. communicating to employees managerial perceptions of the quality and quantity of their work;
3. assessing future potential of an employee in order to recommend appropriate training or developmental assignments;
4. assessing whether the present duties of an employee's position have an appropriate compensation level; and
5. providing a documented record for disciplinary and separation actions.

For a classic analysis of the problems of performance appraisal, *see* Douglas McGregor, "An Uneasy Look at Performance Appraisal," *Harvard Business Review* (May-June 1957; reprinted May-June 1975). For legal analyses, *see* William H. Holley and Hubert S. Field, "Performance Appraisal and the Law," *Labor Law Journal* (July 1975); Dena B. Schneier, "The Impact of EEO Legislation on Performance Appraisals," *Personnel* (July-August 1978); Gary L. Lubben *et al.,* "Performance Appraisal: The Legal Implications of Title VII," *Personnel* (May-June 1980); Patricia Linenberger and Timothy J. Keaveny, "Performance Appraisal Standards Used by the Courts," *Personnel Administrator* (May 1981); William Holley and Hubert S. Field, "Will Your Performance Appraisal System Hold Up in Court?" *Personnel* (January-February, 1982); David H. Rosenbloom, "Public Sector Performance Appraisal in the Contemporary Legal Environment," *Public Personnel Management* (Winter 1982). For an overview, *see* Alan H. Locher and Kenneth S. Teel, "Performance Appraisal—A Survey of Current Practices," *Personnel Journal* (May 1977); Albert C. Hyde and Wayne F. Cascio, eds., "Special Issue: Performance Appraisal," *Public Personnel Management* (Winter 1982); Richard I. Henderson, *Performance Appraisal,* second edition (Reston, VA: Reston/Prentice-Hall, 1983). *Also see* Peter Allan and Stephen Rosenberg, "Getting a Managerial Performance Appraisal System Under Way: New York City's Experience," *Public Administration Review* (July/August 1980); Ann M. Morrison and Mary Ellen Kranz, "The Shape of Performance Appraisal in the Coming Decade," *Personnel* (July-August 1981); Fred C. Thayer, "Civil Service Reform and Performance Appraisal: A Policy Disaster," *Public Personnel Management,* Vol. 10, No. 1 (1981); Stephen J. Carrol and Craig E. Schneier, *Performance Appraisal and Review Systems: The Identification, Measurement, and Development of Performance in Organizations* (Glenview, IL: Scott, Foresman and Co., 1982); Robert L. Taylor and Robert A. Zawacki, "Trends in Performance Appraisal: Guideline for Managers," *Personnel Administrator* (March 1984); Robert G. Pajer, "Performance Appraisal: A New Era for Federal Government Managers," *Personnel Administrator* (March 1984); Ed-

---

The Ultimate Performance Appraisal Scale

Check One

1. Individual is inept *within* tolerable organizational standards. ___

2. Individual is inept *beyond* tolerable organizational standards. ___

3. Individual is *hopelessly* inept. ___

4. Individual is a *classic case* of *dysfunctional ineptness*. ___

5. Individual is so *totally* and *completely inept* that even the *ineptitude* is marred by *ineptness*. ___

---

ward E. Lawler III, Allan M. Mohrman, Jr., and Susan M. Resnick, "Performance Appraisal Revisited," *Organizational Dynamics* (Summer 1984).

See also the following entries:
BEHAVIORALLY ANCHORED RATING SCALES
EFFICIENCY RATING
SCHLESINGER V. BALLARD
SELF-APPRAISAL

performance evaluation: *see* PERFORMANCE APPRAISAL.

performance incentive: *see* INCENTIVE.

performance objective, also called CRITERION OBJECTIVE, statement specifying exactly what behavior is to be exhibited, the conditions under which behavior will be accomplished, and the minimum standard of acceptable performance.

performance reporting: *see* PERFORMANCE APPRAISAL.

performance standards: *see* STANDARDS OF PERFORMANCE.

performance test, examination that has candidates perform a sample of the actual work that would be found on the job. *See* Roscoe W. Wisner, "Construction and Use of Performance Tests," J. J. Donovan (ed.), *Recruitment and Selection in the Public Service* (Chicago: Public Personnel Association, 1968); Wayne F. Cascio and

Neil F. Phillips, "Performance Testing: A Rose Among Thorns?" *Personnel Psychology* (Winter 1979).

PEG: *see* PERSONNEL EFFECTIVENESS GRID.

peripheral employees, according to Martin J. Gannon, "The Management of Peripheral Employees," *Personnel Journal* (September 1975), peripheral employees are those that
are not totally committed to the organization and, in fact, view their work, not as a career, but as a job which can be easily discarded. Included in this segment of the labor force would be part-time employees, temporary employees, working students, moonlighters and women who decide to take a job only for a short period of time.

See also Dean Morse, *The Peripheral Worker* (N.Y.: Columbia University Press, 1969).

Perkins, Frances (1882-1965), Secretary of Labor from 1933 to 1945 and the first woman to hold a cabinet post in the U.S. government. For a biography, *see* George Martin, *Madam Secretary: Frances Perkins* (Boston: Houghton Mifflin, 1976).

perks: *see* PERQUISITES.

permanent arbitrator, arbitrator who hears all disputes during the life of a contract or other stipulated term.

permanent injunction: *see* INJUNCTION.

perquisites, also called PERKS, the special benefits, frequently tax exempt, made available only to the top executives of an organization. There are two basic kinds of executive perquisites: (1) those with "take-home" value (such as company cars, club memberships, etc.) and (2) those that have no "take-home" value, but serve mainly to confer status (such as the proverbial executive washroom, office size and decor, etc.). Historically, the U.S. Internal Revenue Service has striven to restrict the tax exempt status of executives perquisites. According to Robert C. Coffin, in "Developing A Program of Executives Benefits and Perquisites," *The Personnel Admini-strator* (February 1977),

the possibilities of executive benefits are numerous. Some are clearly tax advan-taged. Some are tax advantaged under certain circumstances—conceivably they could be tax advantaged for some ex-ecutives and not for others. Some ex-ecutive benefits, though valuable, have no tax advantage—their value is the same as the equivalent in direct pay. Re-member, however, that the legal niceties are not always observed by small com-panies not heavily subject to public, stockholder or IRS scrutiny, that certain perquisites are easily hidden even by large, exposed corporations and that in some cases (expense accounts, for ex-ample), the tax aspect is a private mat-ter between the beneficiary of the perquisite and IRS.

Also see Michael F. Klein, "Executive Perquisites," *Compensation Review* (Fourth Quarter 1979); Karen M. Evans, "The Power of Perquisites," *Personnel Ad-ministrator* (May 1984).

Perry v. **Sinderman,** 408 U.S. 593 (1972), U.S. Supreme Court case, which held that while a teacher's subjective "ex-pectancy" of tenure is not protected by procedural due process, an allegation that a school had a *de facto* tenure policy en-titles one to an opportunity of proving the legitimacy of a claim to job tenure. Such proof would obligate a school to hold a re-quested hearing when the teacher could both be informed of the grounds for nonretention and challenge the sufficien-cy of those grounds.

persona, term developed by Carl Jung that refers to the personality or facade that each individual shows to the world. The persona is distinguished from our inner be-ing, because it is adopted and put on like a mask to meet the demands of social life. Persona is the word for the masks that ac-tors wore in ancient Greece.

personal, having to do with a human be-ing's thoughts, possessions, feelings and things.

personality inventory, also called SELF-REPORT INVENTORY, questionnaire con-cerned with personal characteristics and behavior that an individual answers about himself/herself. Then, the individual's self-report is compared to norms based upon the responses given to the same question-naire by a large representative group.

See also the following entries:
BERNREUTER PERSONALITY INVENTORY
EYSENCK PERSONALITY INVENTORY
MINNESOTA MULTIPHASIC PERSONALITY INVENTORY
PERSONALITY RESEARCH FORM.

personal-rank system: *see* RANK-IN-MAN SYSTEM.

Personality Research Form (PRF), self-report personality inventory. Available in Standard Edition (300 items, 15 scores) and Long Edition (440 items, 22 scores). TIME: varies. AUTHOR: D. N. Jackson. PUBLISHER: Research Psychologists Press, Inc. (*see* TEST PUBLISHERS).

personality test, test designed to measure any of the non-intellectual aspects of an individual's psychological disposition. It seeks information on a person's motiva-tions and attitudes as opposed to his or her abilities.

personal pension plans, personal re-tirement plans that federal income tax laws encourage individuals to set up according to IRS regulations. Contributions to these plans, which are subject to specific legal requirements, may be deducted from in-come for tax purposes, and the plans and the income from them will be exempt from taxes until the money is drawn from the account. There are two types of personal plans—individual retirement accounts (IRA's) which any employed person may establish, and Keogh, or HR-10 plans, which are designed for self-employed per-sons and their employees.

personal space, the area that individuals actively maintain around themselves, in-to which others cannot intrude without a-rousing discomfort. *See* Leslie Alec Hayduk, "Personal Space: An Evaluative and Orienting Overview," *Psychological Bulletin* (January 1978).

personal time, that time an employee uses to tend to personal needs. This time is usually separate from lunch and rest breaks and is sometimes written into union contracts.

personnel, collective term for all of the employees of an organization. The word is of military origin—the two basic components of a traditional army being materiel and personnel. Personnel is also commonly used to refer to the personnel management function or the organizational unit responsible for administering personnel programs. *See* Cyril Curtis Ling, *The Management of Personnel Relations: History and Origins* (Homewood, Ill.: Richard D. Irwin, 1965).

Personnel, bimonthly magazine of the American Management Associations, which contains articles by scholars and practitioners on every phase of human resource management and personnel administration.

Personnel
Editorial Address:
American Management Associations
135 West 50th Street
New York, NY 10020
Subscriptions:
Subscription Services
Box 319
Saranac Lake, NY 12983

Personnel Accreditation Institute, a personnel accreditation program sponsored by the American Society for Personnel Administration, which is designed to raise and maintain professional standards in the field. Through testing and peer reviews, the program identifies persons who have mastered the various functions and levels of personnel and industrial relations.

Personnel Accreditation Institute
606 N. Washington Street
Alexandria, VA 22314
(703) 684-8327

personnel administration, also PERSON-NEL MANAGEMENT, that aspect of management concerned with the recruitment, selection, development, utilization, and compensation of the members of an organization. While the terms *personnel administration* and *personnel management* tend to be used interchangeably, there is a distinction. The former is mainly concerned with the technical aspects of maintaining a full complement of employees within an organization, while the latter concerns itself as well with the larger problems of the viability of an organization's human resources. For analyses of how personnel administration has been evolving into personnel management, *see* Henry Eilbirt, "The Development of Personnel Management in the United States," *Business History Review* (Autumn 1959); Edward J. Giblin, "The Evolution of Personnel," *Human Resource Management* (Fall 1978); Lawrence A. Wangler, "The Intensification of the Personnel Role," *Personnel Journal* (February 1979).
See also STAFFING.

Personnel Administrator, this is the official monthly publication of the American Society for Personnel Administration. Its major purpose is to further the professional aims of the ASPA and the human resources management profession. Articles cover all aspects of personnel management, human resources development, and industrial relations.

The Personnel Administrator
American Society for Personnel Administration
606 N. Washington Street
Alexandria, VA 22314

Personnel Administrator of Massachusetts v. Feeney, 60 L.Ed. 2d 870 (1979), U.S. Supreme Court case, which held that a state law operating to the advantage of males by giving veterans lifetime preference for state employment was not in violation of the equal protection clause of the 14th Amendment. The court found that a veterans preference law's disproportionate impact on women did not prove intentional bias.
See also VETERANS PREFERENCE.

Major Activities of the Corporate Personnel Unit

(668 companies)

Activity	All Corporate Staffs	Corporate Unit Is Only Unit	Personnel Units also at Intermediate Level	Personnel Units also at Intermediate and Plant Levels	Personnel Units also at Group Intermediate and Plant Levels
	100%	100%	100%	100%	100%
Compensation	67	61	74	78	78
Equal employment opportunity	66	58	71	80	74
Benefits	64	49	72	77	74
Recruitment, selection, employment	64	69	64	64	52
Contract negotiations	59	25	46	61	57
Training and development	58	54	66	63	48
Compensation of managers	57	42	67	73	74
Labor relations	54	35	66	75	65
Recruitment of managers	53	42	59	66	70
Compensation of senior management	49	30	59	71	78
Managerial training	48	38	57	57	56
Occupational safety and health	47	38	52	56	48
General administration	45	58	43	35	30
Communication	44	36	48	52	52
Planning and research	44	35	48	56	56
Monitoring compliance re OSHA	42	31	43	53	44
Organization development	41	27	51	56	74
Manpower forecasting and planning	40	31	46	53	44
Compensation, hourly and nonsupervisory	39	40	41	37	35
Medical programs	36	28	38	44	44
Employee publications	36	26	45	44	48
Organization structure	36	23	44	54	44
Recruitment, selection, employment-hourly	32	28	31	27	35
Safety	31	26	32	36	30
Employee services	30	28	36	35	9
Grievance handling	28	29	33	20	22
Sales compensation	28	21	34	22	26
Employee attitude surveys	26	18	30	35	35
Training, hourly	25	32	29	15	22
Industrial hygiene	24	18	22	32	22
Sales recruitment	23	20	29	23	26
Human resource accounting	23	18	25	33	26
Training of the disadvantaged	19	20	25	17	9
Recreation	19	21	19	20	0
Sales training	19	17	22	16	17
Human productivity analysis	18	14	22	21	26
Food service	16	15	18	16	9

SOURCE: Allen R. Janger, *The Personnel Function: Changing Objectives and Organization* (N.Y.: The Conference Board, Inc., 1977), p. 63.

Personnel and Guidance Journal, The, see JOURNAL OF COUNSELING AND DEVELOPMENT.

personnel audit, evaluation of one or more aspects of the personnel function. See Eugene Schmuckler, "The Personnel Audit: Management's Forgotten Tool," *Personnel Journal* (November 1973); Paul Sheibar, "Personnel Practices Review: A Personnel Audit Activity," *Personnel Journal* (March 1974).

personnel director, manager responsible for all of an organization's personnel programs. In larger corporations, the personnel director is frequently a vice-president for personnel. *See* Herbert E. Myers, "Personnel Directors Are the New Corporate Heroes," *Fortune* (February 1976).

personnel effectiveness grid, a device used to assess the effectiveness of an organization's human resources management system from three dimensions: (1) top management support, (2) lower, management cooperation, and (3) the perceived quality of the personnelists and their programs. *See* D. J. Petersen and R. L. Malone, "The Personnel Effectiveness Grid (PEG): A New Tool for Estimating Personnel Department Effectiveness," *Human Resource Management* (Winter 1975).

personnel examiner, job title for an individual who is a professional staff member of that unit of a personnel department which is concerned with selection.

personnel files: *see* PERSONNEL RECORDS.

personnel function, service to line management. Fred K. Foulkes and Henry M. Morgan, in "Organizing and Staffing the Personnel Function," *Harvard Business Review* (May–June 1977), warn that "personnel must, however, guard against becoming a servant to, as opposed to a service to, the line organization." *Also see* Harold C. White and Michael N. Wolfe, "The Role Desired for Personnel Administration," *The Personnel Administrator* (June 1980); William H. Smits, Jr., "Personnel Administration—A Viable Function in Government?" *Public Personnel Management Journal* (Summer 1982); Roy Foltz, Karn Rosenberg and Julie Foehrenbach, "Senior Management Views the Human Resource Function," *Personnel Administrator* (September 1982); Harish C. Jain and V. V. Murray, "Why the Human Resources Management Function Fails," *California Management Review* (Summer 1984).
    See also TRASHCAN HYPOTHESIS.

personnel game, the way some personnel directors, personnel officers, personnel technicians, personnel examiners, and vice presidents for personnel refer to their occupation.

personnel generalist, personnelist who, instead of concentrating in one subspecialty, is minimally competent in a variety of personnel management subspecialties.

personnel inventory, a listing of all employees in an organization by job and personal characteristics which serves as a basic reference for planning and other purposes.

personnelist, also called PERSONNEL MANAGER, one who is professionally engaged in the practice of personnel management. *See* George Ritzer and Harrison M. Trice, *An Occupation in Conflict: A Study of the Personnel Manager* (Ithaca, N.Y.: New York State School of Industrial and Labor Relations, Cornell University, 1969); Tony J. Watson, *The Personnel Managers: A Study in the Sociology of Work and Employment* (London: Routledge and Kegan Paul, 1977).

personnel jacket, file folder containing all personnel data on, and personnel actions pertaining to, an employee.

Personnel Journal, monthly that publishes articles on all aspects of industrial relations, human relations, and personnel management.
    Personnel Journal
    A. C. Croft, Inc.
    Box 2440
    Costa Mesa, CA 92628

personnel journals, see separate entries for the following:
    Academy of Management Journal
    Academy of Management Review
    Administrative Science Quarterly
    Arbitration Journal
    California Management Review
    Civil Service Journal
    Compensation Review
    Employee Assistance Quarterly
    Fortune

Harvard Business Review
Human Relations
Human Resources Abstracts
Human Resource Management
Human Resources Planning
Industrial and Labor Relations Review
Industrial Relations
Industrial Relations Law Journal
International Journal of Group
Psychotherapy
Journal of Applied Behavioral Science
Journal of Collective Negotiations in
the Public Sector
Journal of Counseling and
Development
Journal of European Industrial
Training
Journal of Human Resources
Journal of Labor Research
Labor History
Labor Law Journal
Labor Studies Journal
Monthly Labor Review
Organizational Behavior and Human
Performance
Organizational Dynamics
Personnel
Personnel Administrator
Personnel and Guidance Journal
Personnel Journal
Personnel Literature
Personnel Management Abstracts
Personnel Psychology
Psychological Review
Public Administration Review
Public Personnel Management
Public Productivity Review
Review of Public Personnel
Administration
Sloan Management Review
Supervisory Management
Training
Training and Development Journal

Personnel Literature, monthly bibliography compiled by the library of the U.S. Office of Personnel Management.
Personnel Literature
Superintendent of Documents
Government Printing Office
Washington, DC 20402

personnel management: *see* PERSONNEL ADMINISTRATION.

Personnel Management Abstracts (PMA), this quarterly abstracts major articles in personnel management magazines, journals, and books that relate to the management of people and organizational behavior.
Personnel Management Abstracts
704 Island Lake Road
Chelsa, MI 48118

personnel management evaluation, formal effort to determine the effectiveness of any or all of an organization's personnel management programs. *See* Michael E. Gordon, "Three Ways to Effectively Evaluate Personnel Programs," *Personnel Journal* (July 1972); Donald J. Peterson and Robert L. Malone, "The Personnel Effectiveness Grid (PEG): A New Tool for Estimating Personnel Department Effectiveness," *Human Resource Management* (Winter 1975); Albert S. King, "A Programmatic Procedure for Evaluating Personnel Policies," *Personnel Administrator* (September 1982); Anne S. Tsui, "Personnel Department Effectiveness: A Tripartite Approach," *Industrial Relations* (Spring 1984).

personnel manager: *see* PERSONNELIST.

personnel manual, written record of an organization's personnel policies and procedures. *See* William B. Cobaugh, "When It's Time to Rewrite Your Personnel Manual," *Personnel Journal* (December 1978).
See also FEDERAL PERSONNEL MANUAL.

personnel officer, common job title for the individual responsible for administering the personnel program of an organizational unit.

personnel planning, process that (1) forecasts future supply and demand for various categories of personnel, (2) determines net shortages or excesses, and (3) develops plans for remedying or balancing these forecasted situations.
See also HUMAN RESOURCES PLANNING.

personnel practices, prohibited: *see* MERIT SYSTEM PRINCIPLES.

personnel psychology, that branch of psychology "concerned with individual differences in behavior and job performance and with measuring and predicting such differences," according to Wayne F. Cascio, in *Applied Psychology in Personnel Management* (Reston, VA: Reston Publishing Company, 1978). *Also see* Thelma Hunt, "Contemporary Personnel Psychology: An Overview," *Public Personnel Management* (Spring 1982); Kenneth N. Wexley and Gary A. Yukl, *Organizational Behavior and Personnel Psychology* (Homewood, Ill.: Richard D. Irwin, 1983).

See also INDUSTRIAL PSYCHOLOGY.

Personnel Psychology, quarterly aimed at operating personnel officials, personnel technicians and industrial psychologists. The articles in each issue are confined to reports on personnel management research and reviews of books relating to industrial psychology, human resource management, personnel practices, and organizational behavior.

Personnel Psychology
P.O. Box 6965
College Station
Durham, NC 27708

personnel ratio, number of full-time employees of a personnel department (usually exclusive of clerical support) per 100 employees of the total organization. *See* Thomas L. Wood, "The Personnel Staff: What Is a Reasonable Size?" *Personnel Journal* (March 1967).

personnel records, also called PERSONNEL FILES, all recorded information about employees kept by an employer, usually in the form of, and under the name, "personnel files." *See* Mordechai Mironi, "The Confidentiality of Personnel Records: A Legal and Ethical View," *Labor Law Journal* (May 1974); Joan Johnson Schliebner and Joy Sandberg, "Record Retention and Posting Requirements of the Federal Government," *Personnel Administrator* (April 1979); John G. Fox and Paul J. Ostling, "Employee and Government Access to Personnel Files: Rights and Requirements," *Employee Relations Law Journal* (Summer 1979).

personnel research, also called INDUSTRIAL RELATIONS RESEARCH, systematic inquiry into any or all of those problems, policies, programs, and procedures growing out of the employee-employer relationship. For a summary of the origins and importance of personnel management research, *see* Thomas H. Patten, Jr., "Personnel Research: Status Key," *Management of Personnel Quarterly* (Fall 1965). *See also* John R. Hinrichs, "Characteristics of the Personnel Research Function," *Personnel Journal* (August 1969); Allen P. O. Williams, editor, *Using Personnel Research* (Aldershot, Hants, England: Gower Publishing, 1983).

personnel runaround, what happens to job applicants who apply for positions for which individuals have been preselected. *See also* REALPOLITIK.

personnel selection, also called SELECTION and EMPLOYEE SELECTION, the object of a personnel/employee selection program is to choose for employment those applicants who best meet an organization's needs in particular jobs. *See* Mary Green Miner and John B. Miner, *Employee Selection Within the Law* (Washington, D.C.: The Bureau of National Affairs, Inc., 1979); Alfred J. Walker, "Management Selection Systems that Meet the Challenges of the '80s," *Personnel Journal* (October 1981); James P. Springer, "The Importance of Selection in Public Sector Administration," *Public Personnel Management* (Spring 1982); Paul R. Sackett and Michael M. Harris, "Honesty Testing for Personnel Selection: A Review and Critique," *Personnel Psychology* (Summer 1984).

personnel technician, job title for an individual who is a professional staff member of a specialized unit (recruitment, classification and pay, examinations, etc.) of a personnel department.

Personnel Tests for Industry (PTI), short, low-level intelligence battery used for screening of industrial personnel applicants (*i.e.*, laborer, maintenance and service worker, messenger). Battery includes a 5-minute Verbal Test, a 20-minute Numerical Test, and a 15-minute Oral Direction Test. Tests may be used together or separately. TIME: 5-40 minutes. AUTHOR: Charles R. Langmuir. PUBLISHER: Psychological Corporation (see TEST PUBLISHERS).

personnel textbooks, personnel textbooks abound. Listed below is a representative sample:

Dale J. Beach, *Personnel: The Management of People at Work* (N.Y.: Macmillan, 5th ed., 1985); Richard W. Beatty and Craig Eric Schneier, *Personnel Administration: An Experiential/Skill-Building Approach* (Reading, Mass.: Addison-Wesley, 1977); Elmer H. Burack and Robert D. Smith, *Personnel Management: A Human Resource Systems Approach* (St. Paul, Minn.: West Publishing, 1977); Lloyd L. Byars and Leslie W. Roe, *Personnel Management: Concepts and Applications* (Philadelphia: W. B. Saunders Co., 1979); Herbert J. Chruden and Arthur W. Sherman, Jr., *Personnel Management* (Cincinnati: South-Western Publishing, 7th ed., 1984); Gary Dessler, *Personnel Management: Modern Concepts and Techniques*, 3rd ed. (Reston, VA: Reston Publishing Co., 1984); Wendell L. French, *The Personnel Management Process* (Boston: Houghton Mifflin, 5th ed., 1982); William F. Glueck, *Personnel: A Diagnostic Approach* (Dallas, Texas: Business Publications, rev. ed., 1978); Michael J. Jucius, *Personnel Management* (Homewood, Ill.: Richard D. Irwin, 9th ed., 1979); Robert L. Mathis and John H. Jackson, *Personnel: Human Resource Management* (St. Paul, Minn.: West Publishing, 4th ed., 1985); Leon C. Megginson, *Personnel Management: A Human Resources Approach* (Homewood, Ill.: Richard D. Irwin, 4th ed., 1981); John B. Miner and Mary Green Miner, *Personnel and Industrial Relations: A Managerial Approach* (N.Y.: Macmillan, 4th ed., 1985); Mitchel S. Novit, *Essentials of Personnel Management* (Englewood Cliffs, N.J.: Prentice-Hall, 1979); George S. Odiorne, *Personnel Administration by Objectives* (Homewood, Ill.: Richard D. Irwin, 1971); Thomas H. Patten, Jr. (ed.), *Classics of Personnel Management* (Oak Park, Ill.: Moore Publishing Co., 1979); Paul Pigors and Charles A. Myers, *Personnel Administration: A Point of View and a Method* (N.Y.: McGraw-Hill, 1973); Stephen P. Robbins, *Personnel: The Management of Human Resources* (Englewood Cliffs, N.J.: Prentice-Hall, 1978); George Strauss and Leonard R. Sayles, *Personnel: The Human Problems of Management* (Englewood Cliffs, N.J.: Prentice-Hall, 3rd ed., 1972); Joseph P. Yaney, *Personnel Management: Reaching Organizational and Human Goals* (Columbus, Ohio: Charles E. Merrill, 1975); Dale Yoder, *Personnel Management and Industrial Relations* (Englewood Cliffs, N.J.: Prentice-Hall, 6th ed., 1970).

See also PUBLIC PERSONNEL MANAGEMENT.

PERT, acronym for "program evaluation and review technique," a planning and control process that requires identifying the accomplishments of programs and the time and resources needed to go from one accomplishment to the next. A PERT diagram would show the sequence and interrelationships of activities from the beginning of a project to the end. See J. D. Wiest and F. K. Levy, *A Management Guide to PERT/CPM* (Englewood Cliffs, N.J.: Prentice-Hall, 2nd ed., 1977).

Peter Principle, promulgated by Laurence J. Peter, in his worldwide best seller, *The Peter Principle: Why Things Always Go Wrong*, with Raymond Hull (N.Y.: William Morrow, 1969), the "principle" held that "in a hierarchy every employee tends to rise to his level of incompetence." Corollaries of the Peter Principle hold that "in time, every post tends to be occupied by an employee who is incompetent to carry out its duties." In answer to the logical question of who then does the work

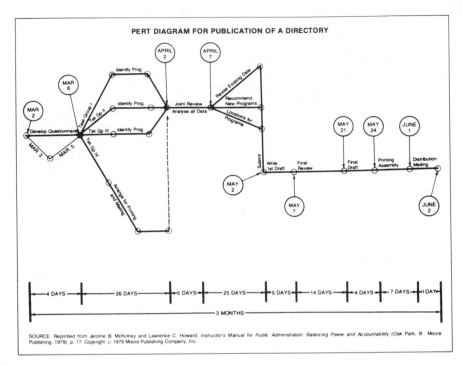

PERT DIAGRAM FOR PUBLICATION OF A DIRECTORY

SOURCE: Reprinted from Jerome B. McKinney and Lawrence C. Howard, *Instructor's Manual for Public Administration: Balancing Power and Accountability* (Oak Park, Ill.: Moore Publishing, 1979), p. 17. Copyright © 1979 Moore Publishing Company, Inc.

that has to be done, Peter asserts that "work is accomplished by those employees who have not yet reached their level of incompetence."

See also REALPOLITIK.

Petrillo, James Caesar (1892–1984), president of the American Federation of Musicians from 1940 to 1958. For a biography, *see* Robert D. Leiter, *The Musicians and Petrillo* (N.Y.: Bookman Associates, 1953).

phantom-stock plan, incentive plan that grants an executive a theoretical number of shares of stock—phantom stock. Since the executive is told that he or she will be paid a cash bonus at some later date that is equal to the then value of the theoretical or phantom shares, there should exist within the executive a great desire to see the value of the company's stock appreciate.

phantom unemployment, jobless citizens who, for a variety of reasons, fall between the statistical cracks and are never official-

ly counted among the unemployed. They have the double misfortune of being both unemployed and "invisible" to their government. For an analysis, *see* Alan Mark Mendelson, "Phanton Unemployment: What Government Figures Don't Tell," *Washington Journalism Review* (April–May 1978).

phased testing, also called PROGRESS TESTING, testing of those in a training program after specific phases of the program.

phatic language, any language used to create an atmosphere of sociability rather than to convey information. For example, a manager might observe that "It's nice weather today" or ask an employee "How are you?" before being critical of some aspect of the employee's work. The initial phatic language is an attempt to make the employee more receptive to the ensuing criticism.

Phelps Dodge Corp. v. National Labor Relations Board, 313 U.S. 177 (1946), U.S. Supreme Court case, which held that an employer subject to the National Labor Relations Act cannot refuse to hire individuals solely because of their affiliation with a union.

phenomenology, frame of reference with which to view organizational phenomena. To a phenomenologist, an organization exists on two planes—in reality and in the mind of the person perceiving its actions. Phenomenology is the integrated study of reality as well as its perceptions. According to Howard E. McCurdy, in "Fiction, Phenomenology, and Public Administration," *Public Administration Review* (January-February 1973), "Under phenomenology, concepts as 'hierarchy' and 'patterned behavior' are not seen as objects; rather they are concepts created intuitively and supported by fictions in order to help us conceptualize and eventually manipulate reality." For a broad introduction to the concept, *see* Pierre Thevenaz, *What Is Phenomenology?* (Chicago: Quadrangle Books, 1962).

Philadelphia Plan, equal opportunity compliance program that requires bidders on all federal and federally-assisted construction projects exceeding $500,000 to submit affirmative action plans setting specific goals for the utilization of minority employees. The plan went into effect on July 18, 1969, in the Philadelphia area and affected six of the higher-paying trades in construction—iron work, plumbing and pipefitting, steamfitting, sheetmetal work, electrical work, and elevator construction work.

The plan was issued under Executive Order 11246 of 1965, which charges the Secretary of Labor with responsibility for administering the government's policy requiring equal employment opportunity in federal contracts and federally-assisted construction work.

Phillips Curve, graphic presentation of the theory put forth in 1958 by the British economist, A. W. Phillips, holding that there is a measurable, direct relationship between unemployment and inflation. In short, as unemployment declines, wages

and prices can be expected to rise. For analyses, *see* N. J. Simler and A. Tella, "Labor Reserve and The Phillips Curve," *Review of Economics and Statistics* (February 1968); Maurice D. Levi and John H. Makin, "Inflation Uncertainty and the Phillips Curve: Some Empirical Evidence," *The American Economic Review* (December 1980).

Phillips v. Martin Marietta: *see* SEX PLUS.

philosophy: *see* MANAGERIAL PHILOSOPHY.

physical examination, medical review to determine if an applicant is able to perform the duties of a position. *See* Mitchell S. Novit, "Physical Examinations and Company Liability: A Legal Update," *Personnel Journal* (January 1982).

Pickering v. Board of Education 391 U.S. 563 (1968), U.S. Supreme Court case, which held that when public employee's rights to freedom of speech are in question, the special duties and obligations of public employees cannot be ignored; the proper test is whether the government's interest in limiting public employees' "opportunities to contribute to public debate is . . . significantly greater than its interest in limiting a similar contribution by any member of the general public." The court identified six elements which would generally enable the state to legitimately abridge a public employee's freedom of expression:

1. The need for maintaining discipline and harmony in the workforce.
2. The need for confidentiality.
3. The possibility that an employee's position is such that his or her statements might be hard to counter due to his or her presumed greater access to factual information.
4. The situation in which an employee's statements impede the proper performance of work.
5. The instance where the statements are so without foundation that the individual's basic capability to per-

form his or her duties comes into question.

6. The jeopardizing of a close and personal loyalty and confidence.

In addition to the above factors, it has been held that the nature of the remarks or expression, degree of disruption, and likelihood that the public will be prone to accepting the statements of an employee because of his or her position must be weighed. In general, however, only expressions on matters of public concern, as opposed to those primarily of interest to co-workers, are subject to constitutional protection.

picketing, occurs when one or more persons are present at an employer's business in order (1) to publicize a labor dispute, (2) to influence others (both employees and customers) to withhold their services or business, and/or (3) to demonstrate a union's desire to represent the employees of the business being picketed.

The U.S. Supreme Court held, in the case of *Thornhill* v. *Alabama*, 310 U.S. 88 (1940), that the dissemination of information concerning the facts of a labor dispute was within the rights guaranteed by the 1st Amendment. However, picketing may be lawfully enjoined if it is not peaceful, for an unlawful purpose, or in violation of some specific state or federal law.

See also the following entries:

AMERICAN STEEL FOUNDRIES V. TRI-CITY CENTRAL TRADES COUNCIL
ANTI-STRIKEBREAKER ACT OF 1936
CHAIN PICKETING
COMMON SITUS PICKETING
CROSS PICKETING
HUDGENS V. NATIONAL LABOR RELATIONS BOARD
LAUF V. E.G. SHINNER AND COMPANY
MASS PICKETING
NATIONAL LABOR RELATIONS BOARD V. FRUIT PACKERS
ORGANIZATIONAL PICKETING
RECOGNITION PICKETING
SEARS ROEBUCK & CO. V. SAN DIEGO COUNTY DISTRICT COUNCIL OF CARPENTERS
SENN V. TILE LAYERS' PROTECTIVE UNION

TEAMSTERS, LOCAL 695 V. VOGT
UNFAIR LABOR PRACTICES (UNIONS)
UNITED STATES V. HUTCHESON

picket line, dues: *see* DUES PICKET LINE.

piece rate, also called PIECE-WORK RATE, incentive wage program in which a predetermined amount is paid to an employee for each unit of output. *See* Ian Wood and Edward E. Lawler III, "Effects of Piece-Rate Overpayment on Productivity," *Journal of Applied Psychology* (June 1970).

See also DIFFERENTIAL PIECE RATE.

piece rate nibbling: *see* NIBBLING.

piece work, differential: *see* DIFFERENTIAL PIECE WORK.

piece-work rate: *see* PIECE RATE.

pilot study, method of testing and validating a survey research instrument by administering it to a small sample of the subject population. According to Sigmund Nosow, in "The Use of the Pilot Study in Behavioral Research," *Personnel Journal* (September 1974), "there is a significant latent use for the pilot study, in a sense somewhat related to feasibility, and that is the creation of a climate of acceptance for such research. For organizations which have not used such research, it is very possible that the acceptance function may be the most important one for a pilot study."

pilot testing, experimental testing of a newly devised test in order to discover any problems before it is put into operational use.

pink-collar jobs, those jobs in which non-college women form the bulk of the labor force, in which the pay is usually low in comparison to men of the same or lower educational levels, in which unionization is nil or weak, and where "equal-pay-for-equal-work" provisions are of little effect because women tend to compete only with other women. *Pink-color workers* include nurses, elementary school teachers, typists, telephone operators, secretaries, hairdressers, waiters and waitresses, private household workers, etc. *See* Louise Kapp Howe, *Pink Collar Workers* (New York: G. P. Putnam's Sons, 1977); Martin F. Payson, "Wooing the Pink Collar Work Force," *Personnel Journal* (January 1984).

Pittsburgh Press Co.* v. *The Pittsburgh Commission on Human Relations, 413 U.S. 376 (1973), U.S. Supreme Court case, which held that a municipal order forbidding newspapers to segregate job announcements according to sex when gender is not a required qualification did not violate the constitutional freedom of the press.

placement, acceptance by an employer or hiring authority of a candidate for a position as a direct result of the efforts of an employment agency or central personnel office. *See* Ronald C. Pilenzo, "Placement by Objectives," *Personnel Journal* (September 1973).

planning, the formal process of making decisions for the future of individuals and organizations. There are two basic kinds of business planning: *strategic* and *operational. Strategic planning,* also known as long-range, comprehensive, corporate, integrated, overall, and managerial planning, has three dimensions: the identification and examination of future opportunities, threats and consequences; the process of analyzing an organization's environment and developing compatible objectives along with the appropriate strategies and policies capable of achieving those objectives; and the integration of the various elements of corporate planning into an overall structure of plans so tha each unit of the organization knows in advance what must be done, when and by whom. *Operational planning,* also known as divisional planning, is concerned with: the implementation of the larger goals and strategies that have been determined by strategic planning; improving current operations; and the allocation of resources through the operating budget.

planning, career: *see* CAREER PLANNING.

planning horizon, the time limit of organizational planning beyond which the future is considered too uncertain or unimportant to waste time on.

plan termination insurance, pension insurance available through the Pension Benefit Guarantee Corporation, which provides that in the event of the financial collapse of a private pension fund wherein the pension fund assests are not sufficient to meet its obligations, the interests of vested employees will be protected. *See* Powell Niland, "Reforming Private Pension Plan Administration," *Business Horizons* (February 1976).

platykurtic, frequency distribution or curve that is more flat-topped, as opposed to peaked, than a normal curve.

Plum Book, also known as the POLICY AND SUPPORTING POSITIONS BOOK. First published in 1960, the Plum Book lists the jobs that are the current leading positions in the U.S. government.

The Plum Book is often viewed as a list of "political jobs" available to a new administration to which it can make appointments. The available jobs include a large variety of positions exempt from competitive civil service rules as well as vacancies in the judiciary and jobs in the legislative branch filled by presidential appointment. Among these are:

1. Appointments made by the president.
2. Noncareer executive assignment positions.
3. Positions under Schedule C of the Office of Personnel Management rules.
4. Other excepted positions at GS-14 or equivalent, and above.
5. Selected positions under Schedules A and B of the Office of Personnel Management rules.

The Plum Book is prepared by the Committee on Post Office and Office of Personnel Management of the House of Representatives after every presidential election and is printed quadrennially by the U.S. Government Printing Office.

See also PATRONAGE.

plural executive, concept that has a committee assuming the normal responsibilities of an executive. For an account of this in action, *see* William H. Mylander, "Management by Executive Committee," *Harvard Business Review* (May–June 1955).

PMA: *see* PERSONNEL MANAGEMENT ABSTRACTS.

pneumoconiosis: *see* BLACK LUNG DISEASE.

point system, also called POINT METHOD, most widely used method of job evaluation, in which the relative worth of the jobs being evaluated is determined by totaling the number of points assigned to the various factors applicable to each of the jobs.

See also BEDAUX POINT SYSTEM.

Policy and Practice Series: *see* BNA POLICY AND PRACTICE SERIES.

political action, any attempt to influence the political process from lobbying legislators to seeking the election (or defeat) of particular candidates.

political machine, an informal system of governance in which power is concentrated into the hands of a central figure, the "boss," who may or may not have a formal position of power. The "boss" manages a hierarchy that is usually created and maintained by the use of patronage and largess.

political neutrality, the concept that public employees should not actively participate in partisan politics. The Hatch Acts of 1939 and 1940 restrict the political activities of almost all federal employees and those in state employment having federal financing. Many states have "little" Hatch Acts which further limit the possible political activities of public employees.

polygraph: *see* LIE DETECTOR.

population, also called SET and UNIVERSE, a population, set or universe is composed of all of the cases in a class of things under statistical examination.

See also CANDIDATE POPULATION.

pork chopper, disrespectful term for a union official, who in the opinion of the workers he represents, is mainly concerned with his own pay and perquisites.

pork chops, slang term for the benefits that union workers expect from a strike.

portability, characteristic of a pension plan that allows participating employees to have the monetary value of accrued pension benefits transfered to a succeeding pension plan should they leave their present organization. According to Susan Meredith Phillips and Linda Pickthorne Fletcher, "The Future of the Portable Pension Concept," *Industrial and Labor Relations Review* (January 1977), "the portable pension concept has been offered as a solution to the problem of providing a secure retirement income to a mobile labor force."

portal-to-portal pay, wages paid while traveling from a plant, factory, or mine's entrance to the employee's specific work station and vice versa.

Portal-to-Portal Pay Act of 1947, federal statute that established a cutoff date for back claims of portal-to-portal pay (May 14, 1947) except where a written contract or established custom was already in effect.

Porter Co. v. National Labor Relations Board, 397 U.S. 99 (1970), U.S. Supreme Court case, which held that the National Labor Relations Board did not have the power to compel a company or union to agree to a substantive provision of a collective bargaining agreement.

POSDCORB, mnemonic device invented by Luther Gulick in 1937 to call attention to the various functional elements of the work of a chief executive. POSDCORB stands for the following activities:

Planning, that is working out in broad outline the things that need to be done and the methods for doing them to accomplish the purpose set for the enterprise;

Organizing, that is the establishment of the formal structure of authority through which work subdivisions are arranged, defined and co-ordinated for the defined objective;

Staffing, that is the whole personnel function of bringing in and training the staff and maintaining favorable conditions of work;

Directing, that is the continuous task of making decisions and embodying them in specific and general orders and instructions and serving as the leader of the enterprise;

Co-ordinating, that is the all important duty of interrelating the various parts of the work;

Reporting, that is keeping those to whom the executive is responsible informed as to what is going on, which thus includes keeping himself and his subordinates informed through records, research and inspection;

Budgeting, with all that goes with budgeting in the form of fiscal planning, accounting and control.

Source: Luther Gulick, "Notes on the Theory of Organization," in Luther Gulick and L. Urwick (eds.), Papers on the Science of Administration (N.Y.: Institute of Public Administration, 1937). For a re-examination, see David S. Brown, "POSDCORB Revisited and Revised," *Personnel Administration* (May-June 1966).

position, group of duties and responsibilities requiring the full or part-time employment of one individual. A position may, at any given time, be occupied or vacant.

position analysis, a systematic method of identifying, summarizing and documenting the most important elements of an individual position; including (1) the results expected from the incumbent's work activity, (2) a summary of that work activity

in terms of the tasks performed, and (3) a description of the qualifications needed to perform the necessary tasks. Position analysis is distinguished from job analysis in that the latter focuses on an analysis of a representative sample of positions included in a job classification. *See* Robert D. White, "Position Analysis and Characterization," *Review of Public Personnel Administration* (Spring 1984).

position, benchmark: *see* BENCHMARK POSITION.

Position Analysis Questionnaire (PAQ), job analysis questionnaire that is a tool for quantitatively describing the various aspects of a job. It was developed and copyrighted by the Purdue University Research Foundation and is available from the Purdue University Book Store, 360 West State Street, West Lafayette, IN 47906. *See* Ernest J. McCormick, Angelo S. DeNisi and James B. Shaw, "Uses of Position Analysis Questionnaires in Personnel Administration," *The Personnel Administrator* (July 1978); P. R. Jenneret, "Equitable Job Evaluation and Classification with the Position Analysis Questionnaire," *Compensation Review* (First Quarter 1980).

position ceiling: *see* JOB CEILING.

position classification, process of using formal job descriptions to organize all jobs in a given organization into classes on the basis of duties and responsibilities for the purpose of delineating authority, establishing chains of command, and providing equitable salary scales. The principles and practices of position classification that are generally used in the public service are throwbacks to the heyday of the scientific management movement. They were conceived at a point in time the second two decades of this century—when this school of management thought held sway, and they have never really adapted to modern currents of management thought. While position classifications tend to be required of public personnel programs, their allegiance to notions of the past occasions

WORK PLAN FOR UPDATE OF A TRADITIONAL POSITION CLASSIFICATION AND COMPENSATION PLAN

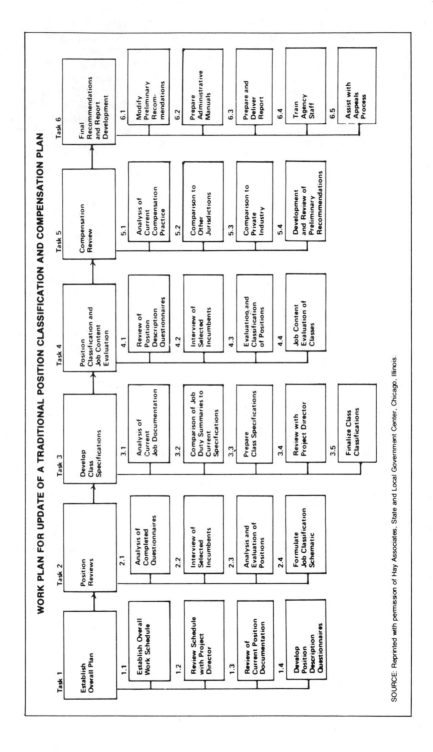

Task 1 — Establish Overall Plan

- 1.1 Establish Overall Work Schedule
- 1.2 Review Schedule with Project Director
- 1.3 Review of Current Position Documentation
- 1.4 Develop Position Description Questionnaires

Task 2 — Position Reviews

- 2.1 Analysis of Completed Questionnaires
- 2.2 Interview of Selected Incumbents
- 2.3 Analysis and Evaluation of Positions
- 2.4 Formulate Job Classification Schematic

Task 3 — Develop Class Specifications

- 3.1 Analysis of Current Job Documentation
- 3.2 Comparison of Job Duty Summaries to Current Specifications
- 3.3 Prepare Class Specifications
- 3.4 Review with Project Director
- 3.5 Finalize Class Classifications

Task 4 — Position Classification and Job Content Evaluation

- 4.1 Review of Position Description Questionnaires
- 4.2 Interview of Selected Incumbents
- 4.3 Evaluation, and Classification of Positions
- 4.4 Job Content Evaluation of Classes

Task 5 — Compensation Review

- 5.1 Analysis of Current Compensation Practice
- 5.2 Comparison to Other Jurisdictions
- 5.3 Comparison to Private Industry
- 5.4 Development and Review of Preliminary Recommendations

Task 6 — Final Recommendations and Report Development

- 6.1 Modify Preliminary Recommendations
- 6.2 Prepare Administrative Manuals
- 6.3 Prepare and Deliver Report
- 6.4 Train Agency Staff
- 6.5 Assist with Appeals Process

SOURCE: Reprinted with permission of Hay Associates, State and Local Government Center, Chicago, Illinois.

their frequent denunciation as unreasonable constraints on top management, sappers of employee morale, and for being little more than polite fictions in substance. For a "how-to-do-it" text, *see* Harold Suskin (ed.), *Job Evaluation and Pay Administration in the Public Sector* (Chicago: International Personnel Management Association, 1977). For a critical analysis, *see* Jay M. Shafritz, *Position Classification: A Behavorial Analysis for the Public Service* (N.Y.: Praeger, 1973).

See also SERIES OF CLASSES and SPECIFICATION.

position classification principles, basic principles of position classification that constitute the foundation of most position classification systems in government were promulgated by the 1919 Congressional Joint Commission on Reclassification of Salaries. The commission's 1920 Report recommended that:

1. positions and not individuals should be classified;
2. the duties and responsibilities pertaining to a position constitute the outstanding characteristics that distinguish it from, or mark its similarity to, other positions;
3. qualifications in respect to education, experience, knowledge, and skill necessary for the performance of certain duties are determined by the nature of those duties (Therefore, the qualifications for a position are an important factor in the determination of the classification of a position.);
4. the individual characteristics of an employee occupying a position should have no bearing on the classification of the position; and
5. persons holding positions in the same class should be considered equally qualified for any other position in that class.

For the total report, *see Report of the Congressional Joint Commission on Reclassification of Salaries* (H. Doc. 686, 66th Cong.2nd Sess., March 12, 1920).

position classifier, a specialist in job analysis who determines the titles, occupational groups, series, and grades of positions.

position description, formal statement of the duties and responsibilities assigned to a position.

position excepted by law/executive order/civil service rule: *see* EXCEPTED POSITION.

position guide: *see* JOB DESCRIPTION.

position management, term used to describe the key management actions involved in the process of organizing work to accomplish the missions of federal departments and agencies. It involves, essentially, the determination of the needs for positions, the determination of required skills and knowledges, and the organization, grouping, and assignment of duties and responsibilities among positions. There are no absolute rules for managers to follow in the complex and evolving art of position management; however, there are basic *system* requirements for position management in government agencies, which are designed to assure that work structures and organizational designs are systematically being assessed for improvement, that positions are correctly classified, and that the allocation of positions and deployment of people reflect the best that is known about managing human resources. *See* Tim E. Winchell, Sr., "Federal Position Control Programs in an Era of Cutback Management," *Public Personnel Management Journal* (Fall 1982).

position ranking, also called JOB GRADING, method of comparing jobs on a "whole job" basis in order to rank such jobs in a hierarchy from highest to lowest.

positive economics, economic analysis which limits itself to what *is* rather than to normative concerns of what *ought to be*. *See* James R. Wible, "Friedman's Positive Economics and Philosophy of Science," *Southern Economic Journal* (October 1982).

positively skewed: see SKEWNESS.

positive recruitment, aggressive action designed to encourage qualified individuals to apply for positions, as opposed to just waiting for the right person to "knock on the door."

positive reinforcement: see REINFORCEMENT.

positive strike, also NEGATIVE STRIKE, a *positive strike* is one whose purpose is to gain new benefits. A *negative strike* is one whose purpose is to prevent the loss of present benefits.

positive stroking: see STROKING.

positive transfer: see TRANSFER OF LEARNING.

Postal Reorganization Act of 1970, federal statute that converted the Post Office Department into an independent establishment—within the executive branch of the government, but free from direct political pressures—to own and operate the nation's postal system known as the United States Postal Service. The act also provided for collective bargaining by postal workers—the first instance of true collective bargaining in the federal service. *See* John J. Morrison, *Postal Reorganization: Managing the Public's Business* (Boston, MA: Auburn House Publishing, 1981).

postbureaucratic organizations, in 1952, Dwight Waldo, in the *American Political Science Review*, prophesied a future society in which "bureaucracy in the Weberian sense would have been replaced by more democratic, more flexible, though more complex, forms of large-scale organization." Waldo called such a society "postbureaucratic." However, it remained for Warren G. Bennis, in the 1960s, to make the term particularly his own with a series of articles and books predicting the "end of bureaucracy." In its place, "there will be adaptive, rapidly changing *temporary systems*. These will be task forces composed of groups of relative strangers with diverse professional backgrounds and skills organized around problems to be solved. The groups will be arranged in an organic, rather than mechanical, model, meaning that they will evolve in response to a problem rather than to preset, programmed expectations. People will be evaluated not vertically according to rank and status, but flexibly according to competence. Organizational charts will consist of project groups rather than stratified functional groups." Warren G. Bennis and Philip E. Slater, *The Temporary Society* (N.Y.: Harper & Row, 1968). *Also see* Warren G. Bennis, *Changing Organizations* (N.Y.: McGraw-Hill, 1966). For a reader in organizational futures, *see* Jong S. Jun and William B. Storm, eds., *Tomorrow's Organizations: Challenges and Strategies* (Glenview, Ill.: Scott, Foresman and Co., 1973).

post-entry training, activities designed to upgrade the capabilities of an employee once he has joined an organization. Everything from executive development seminars constructed to improve the decision making skills of top management to an orientation program which has as its objective acquainting new employees with the purposes and structure of the organization may be identified as post-entry training.

post-industrial society, term coined by Daniel Bell to describe the new social structures evolving in modern societies in the second half of the twentieth century. Bell holds that the "axial principle" of post-industrial society is the centrality of theoretical knowledge as the source of innovation and of policy formation for the society. Hallmarks of post-industrial society include a change from a goods-producing to a service economy, the pre-eminence of a professional and technical class, and the creation of a new "intellectual" technology. For the definitive work to date, *see* Daniel Bell, *The Coming of Post-Industrial Society: A Venture in Social Forecasting* (N.Y.: Basic Books, 1973). *Also see* John Schmidman, *Unions in Postindustrial Society* (University Park, Penn.: The

Pennsylvania State University Press, 1979); Hank E. Koehn, "The Post-Industrial Worker," *Public Personnel Management* (Fall 1983).

post-test, test given at the end of a training program to determine if the training objectives have been met.

Potofsky, Jacob S. (1895-1979), president of the Amalgamated Clothing Workers of America from 1946 to 1972.

Poverty and Human Resources Abstracts: see HUMAN RESOURCES ABSTRACTS.

Powderly, Terence Vincent (1849-1924), grand worthy foreman of the Knights of Labor (1879-1893), three-term mayor of Scranton, Pennsylvania, U.S. Commissioner General of Immigration (1897-1902), and chief of the Division of Information in the Bureau of Immigration (1907-1921). For an autobiography, *see* Harry J. Carman, Henry David, and Paul N. Guthrie (eds.), *The Path I Trod: The Autobiography of Terence V. Powderly* (N.Y.: Columbia University Press, 1940).

power, the ability or the right (or both) to do something. Power enables leaders to exercise influence over other people. John R. P. French and Bertram Raven, in "The Bases of Social Power," suggest that there are five major bases of power: (1) *expert power*, which is based on the perception that the leader possesses some special knowledge or expertise; (2) *referent power*, which is based on the follower's liking, admiring, or identifying with the leader; (3) *reward power*, which is based on the leader's ability to mediate rewards for the follower; (4) *legitimate power*, which is based on the follower's perception that the leader has the legitimate right or authority to exercise influence over him or her; and (5) *coercive power*, which is based on the follower's fear that non-compliance with the leader's wishes will lead to punishment. Subsequent research on these power bases has indicated that emphasis on expert and referent power are more positively related to subordinate performance and satisfaction than utilization of reward, legitimate, or coercive power. For the French and Raven study, *see* Dorwin Cartwright (ed.), *Studies in Social Power* (Ann Arbor, Michigan: Institute for Social Research, University of Michigan, 1959). *Also see* Norton E. Long, "Power and Administration," *Public Administration Review* (Autumn 1949); R. G. H. Siu, *The Craft of Power* (New York: John Wiley & Sons, 1979); Karen Van Wagner and Cheryl Swanson, "From Machiavelli to Ms.: Differences in Male-Female Power Styles," *Public Administration Review* (January-February 1979); R. G. H. Siu, *Transcending the Power Game: The Way to Executive Serenity* (New York: John Wiley, 1980); Samuel B. Bacharach and Edward J. Lawler, "Power and Tactics in Bargaining," *Industrial and Labor Relations Review* (January 1981); Anthony T. Cobb, "Informal Influence in the Formal Organization: Perceived Sources of Power Among Work Unit Peers," *Academy of Management Journal* (March 1981); Jeffrey Pfiffer, *Power in Organizations* (Marshfield, MA: Pitman Publishing, Inc., 1981); Donald C. Hambrick, "Environment, Strategy, and Power Within Top Management Teams," *Administrative Science Quarterly* (June 1981); Carleton S. Bartlem and Edwin A. Locke, "The Coch and French Study: A Critique and Reinterpretation," *Human Relations* (July 1981); Andrew Kakabadse and Christopher Parker, *Power, Politics and Organizations: A Behavioral Science View,* (New York: Wiley, 1984).

See also LEADERSHIP.

power of attorney, document authorizing one person to act as attorney for, or in the place of, the person signing the document.

power test, test intended to measure level of performance unaffected by speed of response—there is either no time limit or a very generous one.

practice effect, the influence of previous experience with a test on a later administration of the same test or a similar test—usually an increase in score on the second testing that can be attributed to increased familiarity with the directions, kinds of questions, or content of particular questions. Practice effect is greatest when the interval between testings is small, when the materials in the two tests are very similar, and when the initial test taking represents a relatively novel experience for the subjects.

precedent, a legal decision on a question of law that gives authority and direction on how similar cases should be decided in the future.

prediction, differential: *see* DIFFERENTIAL VALIDATION.

predictive efficiency, measure of accuracy of a test or other predictive device in terms of the proportion of its predictions that have been shown to be correct.

predictive validity, obtained by giving a test to a group of subjects and then comparing the test results with the job performance of those tested. Predictive validity is the type of validity most strongly advocated by the EEOC, because predictively valid tests are excellent indicators of future performance.

predictor, any test or other employment procedure used to assess applicant characteristics and from which predictions of future performance may be made.

preferential hiring, union security agreement under which an employer, in hiring new workers, will give preference to union members.

preferential shop, work unit where the employer must give union members preference in hiring.

pregnancy, according to Equal Employment Opportunity Commission guidelines, a written or unwritten employment policy or practice which excludes from employment applicants or employees because of pregnancy is in prima facie violation of Title VII (of the Civil Rights Act of 1964).

Disabilities caused or contributed to by pregnancy, miscarriage, abortion, childbirth, and recovery therefrom are, for all job-related purposes, temporary disabilities and should be treated as such under any health or temporary disability insurance or sick leave plan available in connection with employment. Written and unwritten employment policies and practices involving matters such as the commencement and duration of leave, the availability of extensions, and the accrual of seniority and other benefits and privileges, reinstatement and payment under any health or temporary disability insurance or sick leave plan, formal or informal, shall be applied to disability due to pregnancy or childbirth on the same terms and conditions as they are applied to other temporary disabilities. Where the termination of an employee who is temporarily disabled is caused by an employment policy under which insufficient or no leave is available, such a termination violates the Act if it has a disparate impact on employees of one sex and is not justified by business necessity.

See also the following entries:
  GEDULDIG V. AIELLO
  GENERAL ELECTRIC CO. V. GILBERT
  MATERNITY LEAVE
  NASHVILLE GAS CO. V. SATTY
  NEWPORT NEWS SHIPBUILDING AND DRY
      DOCK CO. V. EEOC
  SEX DISCRIMINATION
  TITLE VII

Pregnancy Discrimination Act of 1978, an amendment to Title VII of the Civil Rights Act of 1964, which holds that discrimination on the basis of pregnancy, childbirth or related medical conditions constitutes unlawful sex discrimination. The amendment was enacted in response to the Supreme Court's ruling in *General Electric Co. v. Gilbert*, 429 U.S. 125 (1976) that an employer's exclusion of pregnancy related disabilities from its comprehensive disability plan did not violate Title VII. The amendment asserts that:

1. A written or unwritten employment policy or practice which excludes from employment opportunities applicants or employees because of pregnancy, childbirth or related medical conditions is in prima facie violation of Title VII.

2. Disabilities caused or contributed to by pregnancy, childbirth, or related medical conditions, for all job-related purposes, shall be treated the same as disabilities caused or contributed to by other medical conditions, under any health or disability insurance or sick leave plan available in connection with employment. Written or unwritten employment policies and practices involving matters such as the commencement and duration of leave, the availability of extensions, the accrual of seniority and other benefits and privileges, reinstatement, and payment under any health or disability insurance or sick leave plan, formal or informal, shall be applied to disability due to pregnancy, childbirth, or related medical conditions on the same terms and conditions as they are applied to other disabilities. Health insurance benefits for abortion, except where the life of the mother would be endangered if the fetus were carried to term or where medical complications have arisen from an abortion, are not required to be paid by an employer; nothing herein, however, precludes an employer from providing abortion benefits or otherwise affects bargaining agreements in regard to abortion.

3. Where the termination of an employee who is temporarily disabled is caused by an employment policy under which insufficient or no leave is available, such a termination violates the Act if it has a disparate impact on employees of one sex and is not justified by business necessity.

The law does not require an employer to provide a specific number of weeks for maternity leave, or to treat pregnant employees in any manner different from other employees with respect to hiring or promotions, or to establish new medical, leave, or other benefit programs where none currently exist.

The law requires that women affected by pregnancy, childbirth or related medical conditions be treated the same for all employment-related purposes, including receipt of benefits under fringe benefit programs, as persons not so affected but similar in their ability or inability to work. The amendment does not require employers to pay health insurance benefits for abortions, except where the life of the mother would be endangered or where medical complications have arisen from an abortion. On the other hand, it does not preclude employers from providing abortion benefits or otherwise affect bargaining agreements in regard to abortion. Employers may not fire or refuse to hire a woman simply because she has exercised her right to have an abortion.

Pregnant workers in a number of States are entitled to benefits under statewide temporary disability insurance laws, special sections of fair employment or labor codes, and regulations or court decisions interpreting statutory bans on sex discrimination in employment.

pre-hire agreement, in the U.S. Supreme Court case of *National Labor Relations Board* v. *Iron Workers*, 54 L. Ed. 2d 586 (1978), the court accepted the NLRB's claim that, although the Taft-Hartley amendments to the National Labor Relations Act authorizes "pre-hire" agreements in construction (under which a union is not required to establish its majority status before bargaining with an employer), employers are nevertheless free to renounce the agreements at any time. Under the NLRB's ruling as affirmed by the Supreme Court, a pre-hire agreement is valid until an employer chooses to renounce it, at which time a union is limited to 30 days of recognitional picketing before it must either stop picketing or face an election to determine whether it represents a majority of the employees. *See* Warren C. Ogden and Judd H. Lees, "Challenging the Prehire Agreement," *Labor Law Journal* (February 1985).

premium pay: *see* WORK PREMIUM.

prepaid legal services, employee benefit that has the employee and/or employer contribute to a fund that pays for legal services in the same way that medical insurance pays for hospitalization. *See* Guvenc G. Alpander and Jordon I. Kobritz, "Prepaid Legal Services: An Emerging Fringe Benefit," *Industrial and Labor Relations Review* (January 1978).

pre-retirement counseling, efforts on the part of an organization to give to those of its employees who will be eligible to retire information about all of the options that retirement entails. *See* Don F. Pellicano, "Overview of Corporate Pre-Retirement Counseling," *Personnel Journal* (May 1977); William Arnone, "Preretirement Planning: An Employee Benefit That Has Come of Age," *Personnel Journal* (October 1982); Judith Raffel, "How to Select a Preretirement Consultant," *Personnel Journal* (November 1982).

See also RETIREMENT COUNSELING.

preselection, process by which a person is informally selected for a position prior to the normal competitive selection procedures. The ensuing selection process is necessarily a sham. *See* Shelby McIntyre, Dennis J. Moberg, and Barry Z. Posner, "Preferential Treatment in Preselection Decisions According to Sex and Race," *Academy of Management Journal* (December 1980).

President's Advisory Commission on Labor-Management Policy: see NATIONAL COMMISSION FOR INDUSTRIAL PEACE.

President's Commission on Executive Interchange, federal government program, established in 1969 by Executive Order 11451, which arranges for managers from the public and private sector to work in a different sector for a year or more. *See* Herman L. Weiss, "Why Business and Government Exchange Executives," *Harvard Business Review* (July–August 1974).

President's Commission on Executive
    Interchange
144 Jackson Place, N.W.

Washington, D.C.: 20503
(202) 395-4616

Presidential Management Intern Program, established August 25, 1977, by Executive Order 12008, the Presidential Management Intern Program provides a special means of entry into the federal service for recipients of graduate degrees in general management with a public sector focus. Each year, up to 250 interns receive two-year appointments to developmental positions throughout the executive branch of the federal government. These internships differ from most entry-level positions in their emphasis on career development. Through rotational assignments, on-the-job training, seminars, discussion groups, career counseling, and other activities, interns are exposed to a variety of management areas and issues. At the successful completion of the two-year term, the interns are eligible for conversion to regular civil service appointments without further competition.

Presidential Management Intern
    Program
Office of Presidential Management
    Internships
1900 E Street, N.W.
Washington, D.C. 20415

Presser, Jackie (1926–   ), became president of the Teamsters in 1983.

pressure bargaining: *see* PRODUCTIVITY BARGAINING.

pre-test, test given before training in order to measure existing levels of proficiency. Such levels should later be compared to end-test scores in order to evaluate the quality of the training program as well as the attainments of the individuals being trained. Also a test designed for the purpose of validating new items and obtaining statistics for them before they are used in a final form.

prevailing hours of labor, prevailing hours of labor for a given trade or craft means the hours of labor per day and per week worked within the area by a larger number of workers in the same trade or craft than are employed within the area (in the same trade or craft) for any other number of hours per day or per week.

prevailing wage, average pay for a specific job in a given geographical region. Because wages in the private sector are determined to a large extent by market forces, the prevailing wage concept is used more extensively in the public sector where wage "comparability" is frequently mandated by law. For an analysis, *see* David Lewin, "The Prevailing-Wage Principle and Public Wage Decisions," *Public Personnel Management* (November–December 1974).

Prevailing Wage Law: *see* DAVIS-BACON ACT OF 1931.

preventive discipline, premised on the notion that knowledge of disciplinary policies tends to inhibit infractions, preventive discipline seeks to heighten employees' awareness of organizational rules and policies. *See* Alan W. Bryant, "Replacing Punitive Discipline with a Positive Approach," *Personnel Administrator* (February 1984).

preventive mediation, in order to avoid last minute crisis bargaining, the negotiating parties sometimes seek preventive mediation—the use of a mediator before an impasse has been reached.

PRF: *see* PERSONALITY RESEARCH FORM.

primary boycott, concerted effort by a union to withdraw and to induce others to withdraw from economic relationships with an offending employer. While the mere withholding of patronage is not unlawful, all contracts, combinations and conspiracies to do so are.

principled negotiations, an approach to collective bargaining advocated by Roger Fisher and William Ury in *Getting to Yes: Negotiating Agreement Without Giving In* (Boston: Houghton Mifflin, 1981) which seeks to avoid the pitfalls of conventional bargaining. One should:

a) "Separate the people from the problem." Recognize that the problem is arriving at a workable and desirable agreement. Don't let personalities get in the way.

b) "Focus on interests, not positions." Each side will have different, but often overlapping interests. By focusing on the areas where the interests are compatible, or can be redefined to make them compatible, negotiators can avoid getting locked into initial positions. This is the antithesis of boulwareism.

c) "Invent options for mutual gain." Explore the possibilities for harmony and compatibility. Although labor and management are adversarial in important respects, it is also important to avoid concluding that they are adversaries in all respects.

d) "Insist on using objective criteria" as a means of determining what is acceptable. Since one cannot expect to dominate in every bargaining situation, it is important that the acceptability of an agreement turn on objective factors, fairly applied. For example, if management and labor have agreed to cost of living increases in principle, it is important to adopt an objective measure of what the increase has actually been.

principles of classification: *see* POSITION CLASSIFICATION PRINCIPLES.

principles of management, fundamental truths or working hypotheses that serve as guidelines to management thinking and action. The first complete statement of the prnciples of management was produced by Henri Fayol in 1916. *See* his *General and Industrial Management*, trans. by Constance Storrs (London: Pitman, 1949). For a modern treatment, *see* George R. Terry and Stephen G. Franklin, *Principles of Management* (Homewood, Ill.: Richard D. Irwin, 8th ed., 1982).

See also the following entries:
POSDCORB
PROVERBS OF ADMINISTRATION
SPAN OF CONTROL

Prisoner Rehabilitation Act of 1965, federal statute that permits selected federal prisoners to work in the community while still in an inmate status.

Privacy Act of 1974, (Public Law 93-579), federal statute that reasserts the fundamental right to privacy as derived from the Constitution of the United States and provides a series of basic safeguards for the individual to prevent the misuse of personal information by the federal government.

The act provides for making known to the public the existence and characteristics of all personal information systems kept by every federal agency. It permits an individual to have access to records containing personal information on that individual and allows the individual to control the transfer of that information to other federal agencies for nonroutine uses. The act also requires all federal agencies to keep accurate accountings of transfers of personal records to other agencies and outsiders, and to make the accountings available to the individual. It further provides for civil remedies for the individual whose records are kept or used in contravention of the requirements of the act.

Virtually all agencies of the federal government have issued regulations implementing the Privacy Act. These regulations generally inform the public how to determine if a system of records contains information on themselves, how to gain access to such records, how to request amendment of such records, and the method of internal appeal of an adverse agency determination on such a request. The Office of the Federal Register publishes an annual compilation, which includes descriptions of all the systems of records maintained by each agency of the federal government, the categories of individuals about whom each record system is maintained, and the agency rules and procedures whereby an individual may obtain further information. The most recent compilation, entitled Privacy Act Issuances, 1976 Compilation, is divided into five volumes, and is available at many public libraries or from the Superintendent of Documents. For an ex-amination of the adequacy of privacy legislation, *see* John Raliya, "Privacy Protection and Personnel Administration: Are New Laws Needed?" *The Personnel Administrator* (April 1979); *Freedom of Information Guide: Citizen's Guide to the Use of the Freedom of Information and Privacy Acts* (Washington, D.C.: Want Publishing Co., 1982).

See also FREEDOM OF INFORMATION ACT.

private law, statute passed to affect only one person or group in contrast to a public law.

private sector organization, all of those industries or activities considered to be within the domain of free enterprise. *See* Michael A. Murray, "Comparing Public and Private Management: An Exploratory Essay," *Public Administration Review* (July/August 1975); Kenneth A. Gold, "Managing for Success: A Comparison of the Private and Public Sectors," *Public Administration Review* (November/December 1982).

See also THIRD SECTOR.

probability, chance of an occurrence—the likelihood that an event will occur, expressed as a number from 0 to 1.

probationary employee, also PROBATIONARY PERIOD, new employees are frequently considered probationary until they satisfactorily complete a period of on-the-job trial—the *probationary period*. During this time they have no seniority rights and may be discharged without cause, so long as such a discharge does not violate laws concerning union membership and equal employment opportunity.

See also SAMPSON V. MURRAY.

probationary rate: *see* ENTRANCE RATE.

pro bono publico, Latin phrase meaning "for the public good." When abbreviated to *pro bono*, it usually stands for work done by lawyers without pay for some charitable or public purpose.

procedural rights, various protections that

DISTINCTIONS BETWEEN THE PUBLIC AND PRIVATE SECTORS

Public	Private

1. MAJOR PURPOSE

Public	Private
A. Provides nonprofit goods and services	**A.** Sells goods and services for a profit.
B. Individual agencies survive based upon continuing legislative authorization.	**B.** Survival depends upon both profits and growth.
C. Decisions reflect client or constituent preferences.	**C.** Decisions are governed partly, at least by market factors (consumer demands).

2. CONSTRAINTS

Public	Private
A. Legal constraints permeate the entire administrative process.	**A.** Laws provide the outside limits of business activity. There is a large body of regulation, but compliance is secondary to profit-making.
B. Administrators are sensitive to the political climate in which their agencies must operate. Solutions reached through compromise are standard.	**B.** The market is the major constraining force and format. As long as customers are willing to buy, producers will endeavor to provide the quantity yielding the maximum profit.

3. FINANCIAL BASE

Public	Private
A. Resources obtained through the ability to borrow and to tax.	**A.** Resources obtained from return on investments
B. The budget process is fragmented and politicized.	**B.** Financial planning is integrated and related to income.

4. MANAGING PERSONNEL

Public	Private
A. The public service comprises persons selected through merit systems or by political appointment. The effort is to build a career service. Much of recruitment and the monitoring of promotions is handled by an independent regulatory commission.	**A.** The private workforce is generally selected on the basis of qualifications for a needed task, although nepotism is also common. There is usually little assurance of tenure. The promotion or separation of personnel is free of external rules and procedures.
B. The idea prevails that government is staffed by less efficient personnel, although supporting evidence for this view is limited.	**B.** The idea prevails that business operates with efficiency and free from the influence of politics. What might be called waste in government is often hidden under labels of research and development.

5. MEASURES OF EFFECTIVENESS

Public	Private
A. The legitimacy of the acts performed is a primary measure of effectiveness. Also concerns with building consensus and reducing conflict rank ahead of assessment of the costs of providing a public good. The criteria for effectiveness are likely to be subjective.	**A.** Effectiveness is gauged by such measures as the ratio of net sales to working capital, profit per dollar of sales, and net return on capital. The social costs associated with making a profit are seldom assessed.

SOURCE: Reprinted from Jerome B. McKinney and Lawrence C. Howard, *Public Administration: Balancing Power and Accountability* (Oak Park, Ill.: Moore Publishing, 1979), p. 43. Copyright © 1979 Moore Publishing Company, Inc.

all citizens have against arbitrary actions by public officials.

process consultation (P-C), the standard work on process consultation, Edgar H. Schein's *Process Consultation: Its Role in Organization Development* (Reading, Mass.: Addison-Wesley Publishing Co., 1969), defines it as "a set of activities on the part of the consultant which help the client to perceive, understand, and act upon process events which occur in the client's environment."

According to Schein, P-C makes the following seven assumptions:

1. Managers often do not know what is wrong and need special help in diagnosing what their problems actually are.
2. Managers often do not know what kinds of help consultants can give to them; they need to be helped to know what kind of help to seek.
3. Most managers have a constructive intent to improve things but need help in identifying what to improve and how to improve it.
4. Most organizations can be more effective if they learn to diagnose their own strengths and weaknesses. No organizational form is perfect; hence every form of organization will have some weaknesses for which compensatory mechanisms need to be found.
5. A consultant could probably not, without exhaustive and time-consuming study, learn enough about the culture of the organization to suggest reliable new courses of action. Therefore, he must work jointly with members of the organization who do know the culture intimately from having lived within it.
6. The client must learn to see the problem for himself, to share in the diagnosis, and to be actively involved in generating a remedy. One of the process consultant's roles is to provide new and challenging alternatives for the client to consider. Decision-making about these

alternatives must, however, remain in the hands of the client.
7. It is of prime importance that the process consultant be expert in how to diagnose and how to establish effective helping relationships with clients. Effective P-C involves the passing on of both these skills.

Also see Robert E. Kaplan, "The Conspicuous Absence of Evidence that Process Consultation Enhances Task Performance," *Journal of Applied Behavioral Science* (July-August-September 1979).

prodigy, any individual who demonstrates phenomenal ability in an activity at an unusually early age. The 30-year-old president of a major corporation would either be a management prodigy or the inheritor of a controlling interest in the corporation.

Producer Prices and Price Indexes, U.S. Bureau of Labor Statistics' comprehensive monthly report on price movements of both farm and industrial commodities, by industry and stage of processing.
Producer Prices and Price Indexes
Superintendent of Documents
Government Printing Office
Washington, D.C. 20402

production bonus, regularly scheduled additional payments to workers for exceeding production quotas.

production workers, those employees directly concerned with the manufacturing or operational processes of an organization, as opposed to supervisory and clerical employees.

productivity, measured relationship between the quantity (and quality) of results produced and the quantity of resources required for production. Productivity is, in essence, a measure of the work efficiency of an individual, a work unit, or a whole organization. Productivity can be measured in two ways. One way relates the output of an enterprise, industry, or economic sector to a single input such as labor or capital. The other relates output to a composite of inputs, combined so as to account for their relative importance. The choice of a particular productivity measure depends on the purpose for which it is to be used.

The most generally useful measure of productivity relates output to the input of labor time—output per hour, or its reciprocal, unit labor requirements. This kind of measure is used widely because labor productivity is relevant to most economic analyses, and because labor is the most easily measured input. Relating output to labor input provides a tool not only for analyzing productivity, but also for examining labor costs, real income, and employment trends.

Labor productivity can be measured readily at several levels of aggregation: the business economy, its component sectors, industries, or plants. Depending on the components of the measure used and the context, labor productivity will be called output per hour of all persons engaged in the productive process, output per employee hour, or just output per hour.

The use of labor productivity indexes does not imply that labor is solely or primarily responsible for productivity growth. In a technologically advanced society, labor effort is only one of many sources of productivity improvement. Trends in output per hour also reflect technological innovation, changes in capital stock and capacity utilization, scale of production, materials flow, management skills, and other factors whose contribution often cannot be measured.

The output side of the output per hour ratio refers to the finished product or the amount of real value added in various enterprises, industries, sectors, or the economy as a whole. Few plants or industries produce a single homogeneous commodity that can be measured by simply counting the number of units produced. Consequently, for the purpose of measurement, the various units of a plant's or an industry's output are combined on some common basis—either their unit labor requirements in a base period or their dollar value. When information on the amount of units produced is not available, as is often the case, output must be ex-

pressed in terms of the dollar value of production, adjusted for price changes. *See* Solomon Fabricant, *A Primer on Productivity* (N.Y.: Random House, 1969); Marc Holzer (ed.), *Productivity in Public Organizations* (Port Washington, N.Y.: Kennikat Press, 1976); Allan S. Udler, "Productivity Measurement of Administrative Services," *Personnel Journal* (December 1978); Jerome A Mark, "Measuring Productivity in Service Industries," *Monthly Labor Review* (June 1982); Arnold S. Judson, "The Awkward Truth About Productivity," *Harvard Business Review* (September-October 1982); Donald M. Fisk, "Measuring Productivity in State and Local Government," *Monthly Labor Review* (June 1984).

productivity bargaining, collective bargaining that seeks increases in productivity in exchange for increases in wages and benefits. There are two basic approaches to productivity bargaining—integrative bargaining and pressure bargaining. The latter is the stuff of confrontation and is best illustrated by the adversary model of labor relations—the most commonly adopted model in the United States. Its dysfunctional consequences—strikes and hostility—are well known. The other approach—integrative bargaining—is, in essence, participative management. It is premised upon the notions that a decrease in hostility is mutually advantageous and that management does not have a natural monopoly on brains. The crucial aspect of integrative bargaining is its joint procedures in defining problems, searching for alternatives, and selecting solutions.

The two productivity bargaining strategies are not mutually exclusive. Each side develops what it believes to be the best mix of both approaches for any given situation. While the end of labor-management conflict is far from at hand, mixed strategies are a step in the right direction. Since financial resources are finite and imagination is frequently infinite, a mixed approach to productivity bargaining holds out more hope for radical changes in job design and organization environment than for radical changes in salaries.

The best survey of productivity bargaining tactics in the private sector is R. B. McKersie and L. C. Hunter, *Pay, Productivity and Collective Bargaining* (London: The Macmillan Press, Ltd., 1973). For a public sector analysis, *see* Raymond D. Horton, "Productivity and Productivity Bargaining in Government: A Critical Analysis," *Public Administration Review* (July–August 1976).

product picketing, picketing a store to urge consumers to boycott a particular item for sale. It occurs at a secondary location and is legal as long as the picketing does not urge a total boycott of the store, but rather only a boycott of a specific product.

The Little Red Hen:
A Productivity Fable

Once upon a time there was a little red hen who scratched about the barnyard until she uncovered some grains of wheat. She turned to other workers on the farm and said: "If we plant this wheat, we'll have bread to eat. Who will help me plant it?"

"We never did that before," said the horse, who was the supervisor.

"I'm too busy," said the duck.

"I'd need complete training," said the pig.

"It's not in my job description," said the goose.

"Well, I'll do it myself," said the little red hen. And she did. The wheat grew tall and ripened into grain. "Who will help me reap the wheat?" asked the little red hen.

"Let's check the regulations first," said the horse.

"I'd lose my seniority," said the duck.

"I'm on my lunch break," said the goose.

"Out of my classification," said the pig.

"Then I will," said the little red hen, and she did.

At last it came time to bake the bread. "Who will help me bake the bread?" asked the little red hen.

"That would be overtime for me," said the horse.

"I've got to run some errands," said the duck.

"I've never learned how," said the pig.

"If I'm to be the only helper, that's unfair," said the goose.

"Then I will," said the little red hen.

She baked five loaves and was ready to turn them in to the farmer when the other workers stepped up. They wanted to be sure the farmer knew it was a group project.

"It needs to be cleared by someone else," said the horse.

"I'm calling the shop steward," said the duck.

"I demand equal rights," yelled the goose.

"We'd better file a copy," said the pig.

But the little red hen turned in the loaves by herself. When it came time for the farmer to reward the effort, he gave one loaf to each worker.

"But I earned all the bread myself!" said the little red hen.

"I know," said the farmer, "but it takes too much paperwork to justify giving you all the bread. It's much easier to distribute it equally, and that way the others won't complain."

So the little red hen shared the bread, but her co-workers and the farmer wondered why she never baked any more.

SOURCE: *Federal News Clip Sheet* (June 1979).

---

profession, occupation requiring specialized knowledge that can only be gained after intensive preparation. Professional occupations tend to possess three features: (1) a body of erudite knowledge which is applied to the service of society; (2) a standard of success measured by accomplishments in serving the needs of society rather than purely serving personal gain; and (3) a system of control over the professional practice which regulates the education of its new members and maintains both a code of ethics and appropriate sanctions. The primary characteristic that differentiates it from a vocation is its theoretical commitment to rendering a public service. *See* Kenneth S. Lynn (ed.), *The Professions in America* (Boston: Houghton Mifflin, 1965); Edgar H. Schein, *Professional Education* (N.Y.: McGraw-Hill, 1972); Judith V. May, *Professionals and Clients: A Constitutional Struggle* (Beverly Hills, Calif.: Sage Publications, 1976); Marina Angel, "White-

Collar and Professional Unionization," *Labor Law Journal* (February 1982).

Professional and Administrative Careers Examination (PACE), this was the principal means of entry into the federal government for liberal arts graduates, although it was open to all majors and applicants with equivalent experience. Each year, thousands of hires were made through this route for more than 100 different positions and career fields. PACE replaced the Federal Service Entrance Examination (FSEE) in 1975; but suffered a similar fate in 1982. It was discontinued in response to a legal challenge to its validity as a selection tool by the NAACP.

See also FEDERAL SERVICE ENTRANCE EXAMINATION.

professionalism, conducting one's self in a manner that characterizes a particular occupation. For example, a professional fireman is a full-time fireman who is thoroughly skilled in his trade. Nevertheless, a fireman is not a "professional" in the traditional sense. *See* Cheryl Haigley, "Professionalism in Personnel," *Personnel Administrator* (June 1984); William I. Sauser, Jr., and Elton C. Smith, "Toward An Empirical Definition of Public Sector Professionalism," *Review of Public Personnel Administration* (Spring 1984).

professionalization, process by which occupations acquire professional status. For example, U.S. police departments are becoming more professional as increasing numbers of their members gain advanced degrees and take their ethical responsibilities more seriously. This process of professionalization will be complete only when the overwhelming majority of police officers meet the same high standards of the present minority. *See* M. S. Larson, *The Rise of Professionalism: A Sociological Analysis* (Berkeley, Calif.: University of California Press, 1977).

proficiency test, device to measure the skill or knowledge that a person has acquired in an occupation.

profit sharing, in 1889, profit sharing was defined at the International Congress on Profit Sharing as "an agreement freely entered into, by which the employees receive a share fixed in advance, of the profits." The Council of Profit-Sharing Industries of America has defined a profit sharing plan as "any procedure under which an employer pays to all employees in addition to good rates of regular pay, special current or deferred sums based not only upon individual or group performances but on the business as a whole."

Profit sharing plans fall into three basic categories
1. *immediate*—profits paid as soon as they are determined;
2. *deferred*—profits are credited to individual employee accounts and paid out according to specific withdrawal provisions; and
3. *combined*—any combination of the above.

For the history of profit sharing, *see* Lyle W. Cooper, "Profit Sharing," *Encyclopedia of the Social Sciences* (N.Y.: MacMillan, 1934). For a survey on current thinking, *see Guide to Modern Profit Sharing* (Chicago: Profit Sharing Council of America, 1973). *Also see* Carla S. O'Dell, *Gainsharing: Incentive, Involvement, and Productivity* (New York: AMACOM, 1981); Brian E. Graham-Moore and Timothy L. Ross, *Productivity Gainsharing: How Employee Incentive Programs Can Improve Business Performance* (Englewood Cliffs, NJ: Prentice-Hall, 1983); Raymond E. Majerus, "Workers Have a Right to a Share of Profits," *Harvard Business Review* (September-October 1984).

program, major organizational endeavor, mission oriented, that fulfills statutory or executive requirements and is defined in terms of the principal actions required to achieve a significant end objective.

program, also PROGRAMMER and PROGRAMMING, in computer terminology, a set of instructions telling the computer what to do. A *programmer* is a person who writes a computer program. As the programmer does his or her job, he or she can be said to be *programming* the computer.

program evaluation, systematic examination of any activity or group of activities undertaken by an organization to make a determination about their impact or effects, both short and long range. A program evaluation should be distinguished from a management evaluation or an organization evaluation because these are limited to concentrating on a program's internal administrative procedures. While program evaluations will use information such as workload measures, staffing levels, or operational procedural data, the main thrust is necessarily on overall program objectives and impact. *See* Jerome T. Murphy, *Getting the Facts: A Fieldwork Guide for Evaluators & Policy Analysts* (Santa Monica, Calif.: Goodyear Publishing Co., 1980); A. C. Hyde and J. M. Shafritz (eds.), *Program Evaluation in the Public Sector* (New York: Praeger Publishers, 1979).

Program Evaluation and Review Technique: *see* PERT.

program management: *see* PROJECT MANAGEMENT.

programmed instruction: *see* PROGRAMMED LEARNING.

programmed learning, also called PROGRAMMED INSTRUCTION, technique that has learning materials presented in a predetermined order, with provisions that permit the learner to proceed at his/her own pace and gain immediate feedback on his/her answers. Programmed learning usually requires the use of a teaching machine or programmed text. The rationale for and methodology of programmed learning is generally credited to B. F. Skinner. *See* J. G. Holland and B. F. Skinner, *The Analysis of Behavior: A Program for Self-Instruction* (N.Y.: McGraw-Hill, 1961). For a report of the efficacy of programmed instruction, *see* J. W. Buckley, "Programmed Instruction in Industry," *California Management Review* (Winter

1967). *Also see* Angus Reynolds, "An Introduction to Computer-Based Learning," *Training and Development Journal* (May 1983).

programmer: *see* PROGRAM.

programming: *see* PROGRAM.

progression line charts, lists of job titles in a broad job family, generally starting with the less difficult, lower paying jobs, and progressing to the more difficult, higher paying jobs.

progression sequences, a hierarchy of job titles through which an employee may progress in following a career path or ladder. Such sequences generally begin with lower paying job titles and ascend, through intermediate job titles, to higher paying job titles.

progressive discipline, concept predicated on the notion that employees are both aware of the behavior expected of them and subject to disciplinary action to the extent that they violate the norms of the organization. A policy of progressive discipline would then invoke penalties appropriate to the specific infraction and its circumstances.

progress testing: *see* PHASED TESTING.

prohibited personnel practices: *see* MERIT SYSTEM PRINCIPLES.

projective test, also called PROJECTIVE TECHNIQUE, any method which seeks to discover an individual's attitudes, motivations, and characteristic traits through responses to unstructured stimuli such as ambiguous pictures or inkblots. *See* D. L. Grant, W. Katkovsky, and D. W. Bray, "Contributions of Projective Techniques to Assessment of Management Potential," *Journal of Applied Psychology* (June 1967).
  See also RORSCHACH TEST and THEMATIC APPERCEPTION TEST.

project manager, manager whose task is to achieve a temporary organizational goal using as his/her primary tool the talents of diverse specialists from the larger organization. The authority and responsibility of a project manager varies enormously with differing projects and organizations. See Paul O. Gaddis, "The Project Manager," *Harvard Business Review* (June 1959).

project management, also called PRO-GRAM MANAGEMENT, a project is an organizational unit created to achieve a specific goal. While a project may last from a few months to a few years, it has no further future. Indeed, a primary measure of its success is its dissolution. The project staff necessarily consists of a mix of skills from the larger organization. The success of project management is most dependent upon the unambiguous nature of the project's goal and the larger organization's willingness to delegate sufficient authority and resources to the project manager. Project or program management is an integral part of matrix organizations. See Charles C. Martin, *Project Management: How to Make it Work* (N.Y.: AMACOM, 1976); Arthur G. Butler, "Project Management: A Study in Organizational Conflict," *Academy of Management Journal* (March 1973); Clifford F. Gray, *Essentials of Project Management* (Princeton, N.J.: Petrocelli, 1981); Harold Kerzner, *Project Management for Executives* (New York: Van Nostrand Reinhold, 1982); David I. Cleland, *Systems Analysis and Project Management,* 3rd ed. (New York: McGraw-Hill, 1983). For a comparative focus, see Per Jonason, "Project Management, Swedish Style," *Harvard Business Review* (November–December 1971).

See also MATRIX ORGANIZATION and TASK FORCE.

proletariat, in ancient Rome, the word referred to those members of society who were so poor that they could contribute nothing to the state but their offspring. In the 19th century, Karl Marx used it to refer to the working class in general. Because of the word's political taint, it should not be used to refer simply to workers, but only to the "oppressed" workers.

promotion, process of advancing employees to positions that usually carry more responsibilities and greater salaries. For analyses of what it takes to get promoted, see Sexton Adams and Don Fyffe, *The Corporate Promotables* (Houston: Gulf Publishing Co., 1969); Vinay Kothari, "Promotional Criteria—Three Views," *Personnel Journal* (August 1976). For what to do when you can't get promoted, see Edward Roseman, *Confronting Unpromotability: How To Manage A Stalled Career* (New York, AMACOM, 1977). Also see Alfred W. Swinyard and Floyd A. Bond, "Who Gets Promoted?" *Harvard Business Review* (September–October 1980).

See also the following entries:
CAREER PROMOTION
COMPETITIVE PROMOTION
HORIZONTAL PROMOTION
MERIT PROMOTION

promotion plan, a federal government promotion plan covers a group of positions, such as all regional positions below GS-12, or all regional supervisory positions, or all central office positions at GS-5 and below. The plan describes the methods to be followed in locating, evaluating, and selecting employees for promotion. It also explains what records will be kept, how information will be given to employees about the promotion program, etc.

protected classes/groups: see AFFIRMATIVE ACTION GROUPS.

protest, not agreeing with legality of an action taken against you; but complying with it while reserving all legal rights to challenge it.

Protestant ethic, also called WORK ETHIC, Max Weber's term from his 1904-05 book, *The Protestant Ethic and the Spirit of Capitalism,* which refers to his theory that modern capitalism has its origins in the Calvinistic concern for moral obligation and economic success. While some dispute Weber's historical analysis, any society whose members have a strong drive for work and the accumulation of wealth is colloquially said to have a "Protestant" or work ethic. For histories of the U.S. work ethic, see Daniel T. Rodgers, *The Work Ethic in Industrial America: 1850-1920* (Chicago: University of Chicago Press, 1978); Richard Stott, "British Immigrants and the American 'Work Ethic' in the Mid-Nineteenth Century," *Labor History* (Winter 1985). For present day analyses, see M. Scott Meyers and Susan S. Myers, "Toward Understanding the Changing Work Ethic," *California Management Review* (Spring 1974); Roger E. Calhoun, "The New Work Ethic," *Training and Development Journal* (May 1980); Ann Howard and James A. Wilson, "Leadership in a Declining Work Ethic," *California Management Review* (Summer 1982); Perry Pascarella, *The New Achievers: Creating a Modern Work Ethic* (New York: The Free Press, A Division of Macmillan, Inc., 1984).

proverbs of administration, a significant landmark in the history of administrative theory was Herbert A. Simon's refutation of the principles approach that dominated administrative thinking until after World War II. Simon asserted, in "The Proverbs of Administration," *Public Administration Review* (Winter 1946), that the principles of administration, like proverbs, almost always occur in mutually contradictory pairs:

> Most of the propositions that make up the body of administrative theory today share, unfortunately, this defect of proverbs. For almost every principle one can find an equally plausible and acceptable contradictory principle. Although the two principles of the pair will lead to exactly opposite organizational recommendations, there is nothing in the theory to indicate which is the proper one to apply.

provisional appointment, usually government employment without competitive examination because there is no appropriate eligible list available. Most jurisdictions have a 3, 6, or 12 month limitation on provisional appointments.

pseudo-effectiveness, according to Chris Argyris, in *Integrating the Individual and the Organization* (N.Y.: John Wiley & Sons, 1964), organizational pseudo-effectiveness is "a state in which no discomfort is reported but in which, upon diagnosis, ineffectiveness is found." Since the underlying ineffectiveness is not evident, the true costs of continuing in such a state remain hidden by compensatory mechanisms. Eventually, such compensatory mechanisms will require so much energy that they will influence the organization negatively and call attention to the underlying problem.

psychiatry, industrial/occupational: *see* OCCUPATIONAL PSYCHIATRY.

psychic income: *see* INTRINSIC REWARD.

psychobabble, indiscriminate use of psychological concepts and terms as an affected style of speech. R. D. Rosen, in *Psychobabble* (N.Y.: Atheneum, 1977), says that psychobabblers

> free-float in an all-purpose linguistic atmosphere, a set of repetitive verbal formalities that kills off the very spontaneity, candor, and understanding it pretends to promote. It's an idiom that reduces psychological insight to a collection of standardized observations, that provides a frozen lexicon to deal with an infinite variety of problems. *Uptight,* for instance, is a word used to describe an individual experiencing anything from mild uneasiness to a clinical depression. . . . One is no longer fearful; one is *paranoid.* . . . Increasingly, people describe their moody acquaintances as *manic-depressives,* and almost anyone you don't like is *psychotic* or at the very least *schizzed-out.*

psychological contract, Edgar H. Schein, in his *Organizational Psychology* (Englewood Cliffs, N.J.: Prentice-Hall, 2nd ed., 1970), asserts that the

> notion of a psychological contract implies that the individual has a variety of expectations of the organization and that the organization has a variety of expec-

tations of him. These expectations not only cover how much work is to be performed for how much pay, but also involve the whole pattern of rights, privileges, and obligations between worker and organization. For example, the worker may expect the company not to fire him after he has worked there for a certain number of years and the company may expect that the worker will not run down the company's public image or give away company secrets to competitors. Expectations such as these are not written into any formal agreement between employee and organization, yet they operate powerfully as determinants of behavior.

For a discussion of this concept in the context of employment, *see* Emanuel C. Salemi and John B. Monohan, "The Psychological Contract of Employment: Do Recruiters and Students Agree?" *Personnel Journal* (December 1970); Michael H. Dunahee and Lawrence A. Wangler, "The Psychological Contract: A Conceptual Structure for Management/Employee Relations," *Personnel Journal* (July 1974).
  See also EXPECTANCY THEORY.

Psychological Inventory, California: *see* CALIFORNIA PSYCHOLOGICAL INVENTORY.

Psychological Review, bimonthly that publishes articles making theoretical contributions to any area of scientific psychology. Preference is given to papers that advance theory rather than review it.
  Psychological Review
  American Psychological Association, Inc.
  1200 Seventeenth Street, N.W.
  Washington, D.C. 20036

psychological stress analyzer: *see* LIE DETECTOR.

psychological test, a general term for any effort (usually a standardized test) that is designed to measure the abilities or personality traits of individuals or groups. *See* A. Anastasi, *Psychological Testing* (N.Y.: Macmillan, 4th ed., 1976); J. Lee Cronback, *Essentials of Psychological Testing,*

4th ed. (New York: Harper & Row, 1983).

psychology, generally, the scientific study of human and animal behavior. According to Bergen Evans and Cornelia Evans, *A Dictionary of Contemporary American Usage* (N.Y.: Random House, 1957),
  in an age which James Joyce has described as "jung and easily freudened," *psychology* is a word thrown about knowingly by about everyone capable of articulating a four-syllabled word, though not necessarily of spelling it. Basically it means the science of mind, of mental states or processes, the science of human nature.
  See also the following entries:
    BEHAVIORISM
    DYNAMIC PSYCHOLOGY
    INDUSTRIAL PSYCHOLOGY
    PERSONNEL PSYCHOLOGY
    VOCATIONAL PSYCHOLOGY

psychometrician, psychologist who deals with mental tests and their associated statistical procedures.

psychometrics, that branch of psychology that deals with mental tests and their associated statistical procedures. *See* Judson Gooding, "Psychometrics: The Use and Misuse of Psychological Tests in Executive Employment," *Across The Board* (November 1976).

psychometry, mental measurements and/or testing.

psychomotor test: *see* DEXTERITY TEST.

PTI: *see* PERSONNEL TESTS FOR INDUSTRY.

Public Administration Review (PAR), leading professional journal on all apsects of managing public and nonprofit institutions.
  Public Administration Review
  American Society for Public Administration
  1120 G Street, N.W.
  Washington, D.C. 20005

public employee, any person who works for a governmental agency. Civilian public employment in the United States totaled 16 million in 1984.

public employee relations, labor-management relations in the public sector. For texts, see Winston W. Crouch, *Organized Civil Servants: Public Employer-Employee Relations in California* (Berkeley: University of California Press, 1978); Hugh D. Jascourt (ed.), *Government Labor Relations* (Oak Park, Ill.: Moore Publishing Co., 1979); Marvin J. Levine and Eugene C. Hagburg, *Public Sector Labor Relations* (St. Paul, Minn.: West Publishing, 1979); Richard C. Kearney, *Labor Relations in the Public Sector* (New York: Marcel Dekker, 1984).

Public Employees' Fair Employment Act: see TAYLOR LAW.

public enterprise, a company that trades its debt or equity securities in a stock exchange or over-the-counter market; and is required to file financial statements with the Securities and Exchange Commission.

public goods, commodities typically produced by government that cannot be separately parceled out to individuals since no one can be excluded from their benefits. Examples include national defense, clean air, public safety, etc. *See* Mancur Olson, Jr., *The Logic of Collective Action: Public Goods and the Theory of Groups* (Cambridge, Mass.: Harvard University Press, 1965); Dwight R. Lee, "On the Pricing of Public Goods," *Southern Economic Journal* (July 1982).

public personnel management, personnel management in government. The essential difference between personnel management in the private sector and personnel management in the public sector can be summed up in one word—politics. The public personnel process is a political process; except in the most sophisticated jurisdictions, management processes are decidedly subordinate to political considerations. For texts, see N. Joseph

Cayer, *Public Personnel Administration in the United States* (N.Y.: St. Martin's Press, 1975); N. Joseph Cayer, *Managing Human Resources: An Introduction to Public Personnel Administration* (New York: St. Martin's Press, 1980); Winston W. Crouch, ed., *Local Government Personnel Administration* (Washington, D.C.: International City Management Association, 1976); Donald E. Klingner, ed., *Public Personnel Management: Readings in Contexts and Strategies* (Palto Alto, CA: Mayfield Publishing Co., 1981); Marvin J. Levine, ed., *Public Personnel Management: Readings, Cases and Contingency Plans* (Salt Lake City: Brighton Publishing Co., 1980); O. Glenn Stahl, *Public Personnel Administration* (N.Y.: Harper & Row, 7th ed., 1976); Jay M. Shafritz, ed., *The Public Personnel World: Readings on the Professional Practice* (Chicago: International Personnel Management Association, 1977); Jay M. Shafritz, Albert C. Hyde, and David H. Rosenbloom, *Personnel Management in Government: Politics and Process*, 2nd edition (N.Y.: Marcel Dekker, 1981); Frank J. Thompson (ed.), *Classics of Public Personnel Policy* (Oak Park, Ill.: Moore Publishing Company, 1979).

See also:
CIVIL SERVICE REFORM
CIVIL SERVICE REFORM ACT OF 1978
PATRONAGE
PENDLETON ACT
PERSONNEL TEXTBOOKS
POSITION CLASSIFICATION
PUBLIC PERSONNEL POLITICS

Public Personnel Management (PPM), bimonthly journal of the International Personnel Management Association, which offers articles dealing with all aspects of personnel management in government.
Public Personnel Management
Suite 870
1850 K Street, N.W.
Washington, D.C. 20006

public personnel politics, the perversion of most civil service merit systems for private, administrative, and especially partisan ends. This is one of the worst-kept, yet least-written-about, secrets in government. While the general textbooks on state and local government frequently take cognizance of this situation, traditional texts on public personnel administration have tended to deal with this subject as if it were an abnormal malignancy instead of an inherent and frequently beneficial part of governmental personnel management. This is faulty perspective. Senator Daniel P. Moynihan (N.Y.) long ago noted that corruption must be recognized as "a normal condition of American local government." Similarly, it must be recognized that the perversion of merit system principles is a normal condition of the public personnel process. This latter situation is not necessarily as unhealthy and undesirable as the former. Frequently such "perversions" are essential if actual merit is to be rewarded within the "merit" system. Unfortunately, other considerations seem just as likely to apply.

Throughout the United States, public personnel merit systems tend to operate on two different planes within the same jurisdiction. The great majority of civil service employees within merit systems are able to enter and advance on the basis of their own talents and the design of the system. However, at the same time and within the same system there are two groups of individuals that enter and advance according to criteria other than that provided for in the merit system regulations.

This first group of employees consists of all those who were appointed for considerations other than personal fitness. Here are hidden the political appointees in excess of those policymaking and confidential positions that are usually the executive's legal prerogative. The extent of such placements depends upon such factors as the strength and longevity of the merit system, the political culture of the community, and the integrity of the executive who, having taken an oath to uphold all the laws of his jurisdiction, can only make such appointments in violation of the spirit, if not the letter, of his oath.

While the merit system is frequently perverted for traditional political ends, it is similarly abused for more scrupulous purposes. The excessively rigid procedures for entering and advancing in most merit systems have long been recognized as being a decided hindrance to effective management practices. In order to compensate for the lack of managerial discretion occasioned by such rigidities, career civil servants as well as other highly qualified individuals have either been advanced or initially installed through a fudging of the civil service regulations—this is the same process by which politicos are foisted upon the merit system. The procedural morass designed to keep out the bad is frequently as effective in keeping out the good. In consequence, what exists in fact, although it is nowhere de jure, is a first-class and second-class civil service. This classification is not a reflection on the quality of any individual or of the productive value of each class, but merely a reference as to how they are treated by those who work the merit system. While the members of the civil service proletariat must be content with careers bounded by the full force of the frequently unreasonable and always constraining regulations, others—those fortunate enough to be recognized for their talents as well as those recognized in spite of their talents—benefit markedly by having these same regulations waived, fraudulently complied with, or simply ignored when it is to their advantage. See Jay M. Shafritz, *Public Personnel Management: The Heritage of Civil Service Reform* (New York: Praeger, 1975); Frank J. Thompson, *Personnel Policy in the City: The Politics of Jobs in Oakland* (Berkeley, CA: University of California Press, 1975); Wilbur G. Rich, *The Politics of Urban Personnel Policy: Reformers, Politicians, and Bureaucrats* (Port Washington, N.Y.: Kennikat Press, 1981).

See also the following entries:
CIVIL SERVICE REFORM
CIVIL SERVICE REFORM ACT OF 1978
GRANT'S CIVIL SERVICE COMMISSION
JACKSON, ANDREW
PATRONAGE

Public Productivity Review, quarterly

devoted to all of the concerns of productivity enhancement in the public sector.

Public Productivity Review
National Center for Public Productivity
John Jay College of Criminal Justice
City University of New York
445 West 59th Street
New York, NY 10019

public sector organization, any agency or institution funded, directly or indirectly, by public taxation.
See also THIRD SECTOR.

Purdue Pegboard Test, two-part, timed test designed to measure two types of activity, one requiring gross movements of hands, fingers, and arms, and the other involving tip-of-the finger dexterity needed in small assembly work. TIME: 10/20 minutes. AUTHOR: Purdue Research Foundation. PUBLISHER: Science Research Association, Inc. (*see* TEST PUBLISHERS).

public works, generic term for government sponsored construction projects. *See* Ellis Armstrong (ed.), *History of Public Works in the United States: 1776-1976* (Chicago: American Public Works Association, 1976).

Pullman Strike, a strike in 1894 by workers at the Pullman Palace Car Company in response to an arbitrary wage cut by the company. The strike was so effective—no member of the American Railway Union would handle trains with Pullman (sleeper) cars—that it spread to twenty-seven states. The federal government used federal troops to break the strike. *See:* Colston Estey Warne, *The Pullman Boycott of 1894: The Problem of Federal Intervention* (Boston: D. C. Heath, 1955); Almont Lindsey, *The Pullman Strike: The Story of a Unique Experiment and of a Great Labor Upheaval* (Chicago: University of Chicago Press, 1964); Leon Stein, *The Pullman Strike* (New York: Arno, 1969).

putting-out system, as the next step in the evolution of production methods from the domestic system, the *putting-out system* has entrepreneurs act as brokers to contract for a family's entire domestic production of goods at a fixed price.

pyramid, also called ORGANIZATIONAL PYRAMID, colloquial term for an organization's hierarchy. According to Vance Packard, *The Pyramid Climbers* (N.Y.: McGraw-Hill, 1962),

> The number of ledges—or steps—in a company's hierarchy varies of course with the company's size and philosophy of organization. Some like tall, slender pyramids, with only a few people under each leader; others prefer short, squat pyramids. Occasionally, one literally sees these modern pyramids in brick and mortar, where the home office occupies a skyscraper with the suites of the highest officers at the pinnacle.

This is equally true for government. For example, in the U.S. State Department, the highest officials occupy the seventh and highest floor of their building. Policy is frequently said to come—not from any particular official—but simply from the "seventh floor."
See also FLAT ORGANIZATION.

Q

qualification requirements, education, experience, and other prerequisites to employment or placement in a position.

Qualifications Review Board, panel attached to the federal government's Office of Personnel Management (OPM) that determines whether a candidate for career appointment in the Senior Executive Service meets the managerial criteria established by law.

Quality B School, when recruiting notices say that they are looking for someone who has an MBA from a "Quality B School," they are usually referring to the graduate programs in business from any of the following universities: Harvard, Stanford, Chicago, Penn (Wharton), Michigan, MIT (Sloan), Carnegie-Mellon, Northwestern, Dartmouth (Tuck), Columbia, UCLA, and New York University. However, quality, which is ignorant of ascribed status, is also to be found in hundreds of other schools of management, if only in smaller concentrations.

quality circles, small groups of employees working in the same organizational unit who, with the approval of management, voluntarily meet on a regular basis to identify and solve problems that directly affect their work. *See* Elaine Rendall, "Quality Circles—A 'Third Wave' Intervention," *Training and Development Journal* (March 1981); Edwin G. Yager, "The Quality Control Circle Explosion," *Training and Development Journal* (April 1981); Kenneth M. Jenkins and Justin Shimada, "Quality Circles in the Service Sector," *Supervisory Management* (August 1981); Philip C. Thompson, *Quality Circles: How to Make Them Work in America* (New York: AMACOM, 1982); George Munchus, III, "Employer-Employee Based Quality Circles in Japan: Human Resource Policy Implications for American Firms," *The Academy of Management Review* (April 1983).

quality control, the totality of concern for, including the inspection of, the goods and services that are produced by an organization.

quality increase, additional within-grade increase granted to federal General Schedule employees for high quality performance above that ordinarily found in the type of position concerned.

quality of working life, area of concern that addresses the problem of creating more humane working environments. For a summary of the "state of the art," *see* Louis E. Davis & Albert B. Cherns (eds.), *The Quality of Working Life* (N.Y.: The Free Press, 1975), volumes I and II. For

analyses of cooperative union-management projects, *see* Edward E. Lawer III and John A. Drexler, Jr., "Dynamics of Establishing Cooperative Quality-of-Worklife Projects," *Monthly Labor Review* (March 1978); William H. Holley, Hubert S. Field and James C. Crowley, "Negotiating Quality of Worklife, Productivity and Traditional Issues: Union Members' Preferred Roles of Their Union," *Personnel Psychology* (Summer 1981); David Lewin, "Collective Bargaining and the Quality of Worklife," *Organizational Dynamics* (Autumn 1981); Michael Maccoby, "Helping Labor and a Firm Set Up a Quality-of-Worklife Plan," *Monthly Labor Review* (March 1984). *Also see* Robert H. Guest, "Quality of Work Life—Learning From Tarrytown," *Harvard Business Review* (July-August 1975); Jerome M. Rosow, "Quality of Work Life Issues for the 1980s," *Training and Development Journal* (March 1981); David A. Nadler and Edward E. Lawler III, "Quality of Work Life: Perspectives and Directions," *Organizational Dynamics* (Winter 1983); David A. Whitsett and Lyle Yorks, "Looking Back at Topeka: General Foods and the Quality-of-Worklife Experiment," *California Management Review* (Summer 1983); Leonard A. Schlesinger and Barry Oshry, "Quality of Work Life and the Manager: Muddle in the Middle," *Organizational Dynamics* (Summer 1984).

See also NATIONAL CENTER FOR PRODUCTIVITY AND QUALITY OF WORKING LIFE.

quartile, one of three points that divide the test scores in a distribution into four equal groups.

quasi-judicial agency, quasi is Latin for "sort of" or "analogous to." A quasi-judicial agency, such as a regulatory commission, may perform many courtlike functions in the course of enforcing its rules. For example, it may bring charges, hold hearings and render judgments.

quasi-legislative, the rulemaking functions of administrative agencies.

questionnaire, set of questions to be answered by a subject. *See* J. L. Stone, "The Use of an Applicant Service Questionnaire," *Public Personnel Management* (March–April 1974); Donald P. Warwick and Charles A. Lininger, *The Sample Survey* (N.Y.: McGraw-Hill, 1975).

questionnaire, exit: *see* EXIT INTERVIEW.

quickie strike, spontaneous or unannounced strike of short duration.

quid pro quo, Latin meaning "something for something"; the giving of one valuable thing for another.

Quill, Mike (1905–1966), full name MICHAEL JOSEPH QUILL, one of the founders of the Transport Workers Union of America and president of that union from 1936 until his death. For a biography, *see* L. H. Whittemore, *The Man Who Ran the Subways: The Story of Mike Quill* (N.Y.: Holt, Rinehart, and Winston, 1968).

quit, volunteered resignation. According to Ken Jennings, in "When A Quit Is Not a Quit," *Personnel Journal* (December 1971), a quit can be considered a discharge for the purposes of arbitral review if "intent to resign is not evidenced." Arbitrators have reasoned "that if this treatment of quit as discharge were not applied, management could escape from the 'just cause' provisions of the labor contract by insisting that an undesirable employee's quit (voluntary or coerced) was not subject to the grievance procedure." *Also see* Francine D. Blau and Lawrence M. Kahn, "Race and Sex Differences in Quits by Young Workers," *Industrial and Labor Relations Review* (July 1981); Gary Solon, "The Effects of Unemployment Insurance Eligibility Rules on Job Quitting Behavior," *Journal of Human Resources* (Winter 1984).

quota: *see* GOAL.

R

r: see CORRELATION COEFFICIENT.

race, a United Nations publication, *Race and Science* (N.Y.: UNESCO, 1961), has found that

the term 'race' designates a group or population characterized by some concentrations, relative as to frequency and distribution, of hereditary particles (genes) or physical characters, which appear, fluctuate, and often disappear in the course of time by reason of geographic and/or cultural isolation. The varying manifestations of these traits in different populations are perceived in different ways by each group. What is perceived is largely preconceived, so that each group arbitrarily tends to misinterpret the variability which occurs as a fundamental difference which separates that group from all others.

A more expansive definition is provided by G. E. Simpson and J. M. Yinger in *Racial and Cultural Minorities* (N.Y.: Harper & Row, 3rd ed., 1965). They find that there are really three basic approaches to race: (1) the "mystical" or "political" approach "has been the stock in trade in the chicanery of rabble rousers, fanatics, demagogues, adventurers, and charlatans (rational or psychopathic)"; (2) the "administrative conception of race" has government actions based on certain "racial" categories established by legislative act or bureaucratic practice; (3) and the biological approach based on crude observations of obvious physical differences. *Also see* Anne Wortham, *The Other Side of Racism: A Philosophical Study of Black Race Consciousness* (Ohio State University Press, 1981).

race categories, also ETHNIC CATEGORIES, the race/ethnic categories that the Equal Employment Opportunity Commission insists be used for EEO reporting purposes follow:

White, not of Hispanic Origin. Persons having origins in any of the original peoples of Europe, North Africa, or the Middle East.

Black, not of Hispanic Origin. Persons having origins in any of the black racial groups of Africa.

Hispanic. Persons of Mexican, Puerto Rican, Cuban, Central or South American or other Spanish culture or origin, regardless of race.

American Indian or Alaskan Native. Persons having origins in any of the original peoples of North America and who maintain cultural identification through tribal affiliation or community recognition.

Asian or Pacific Islander. Persons having origins in any of the original peoples of the Far East, Southeast Asia, the Indian subcontinent, or the Pacific Islands. This area includes, for example, China, Japan, Korea, the Philippine Islands, and Samoa.

race differential: *see* SEX DIFFERENTIAL.

racist, any person or organization that consciously or unconsciously practices racial discrimination. *See* Benjamin P. Bowser and Raymond G. Hunt, eds., *Impacts of Racism on White Americans* (Beverly Hills, Calif.: Sage Publications, Inc., 1981); John P. Fernandez, *Racism and Sexism in Corporate Life: Changing Values in American Business* (Lexington, Mass.: D.C. Heath and Co., Lexington Books, 1981); Terry L. Leap and Larry R. Smeltzer, "Racial Remarks in the Workplace: Humor or Harassment?" *Harvard Business Review* (November–December 1984).

racketeering, a broad term for using a union leadership position as a base for illegal or unethical activities.

radius clause, provision used in some training program agreements that requires an employee not to seek other employment for a specified time over a specified geographic area, so that the investment made in the employee's training cannot be used to benefit a competitor.

raiding, generally, efforts by one organization to gain members of a competing organization for their own. As a tactic, raiding is used by both management and labor.

Railroad Retirement Act, the Railroad Retirement Act of 1934 was declared unconstitutional by the U.S. Supreme Court in *Railroad Retirement Board v. Alton Railroad Company,* 295 U.S. 330 (1935). The Railroad Retirement Act of 1935, as amended, provides for a federal retirement program for employees in the railroad industry and their families.

Railroad Retirement Board (RRB), federal agency that administers retirement-survivor and unemployment-sickness benefit programs provided by federal laws for the nation's railroad workers and their families. Under the Railroad Retirement Act, annuities are paid by the RRB to rail employees with at least 10 years of service who retire because of age or disability and to their eligible wives. When other requirements are met, annuities are also provided to the surviving widows and children or parents of deceased employees. These retirement-survivor benefit programs are closely coordinated with social security benefit programs and include Medicare health insurance coverage. Under the Railroad Unemployment Insurance Act, biweekly benefits are payable by the RRB to workers with qualifying railroad earnings who become unemployed or sick. About 100 field offices are maintained across the country.

The RRB is composed of three members appointed by the president by and with the advice of the Senate—one upon recommendations of representatives of employees, one upon recommendations of carriers, and one, the chairman, as a public member.

Railroad Retirement Board
844 Rush Street

Chicago, IL 60611
(312) 751-4776
Washington Liaison Office
Room 630
425 Thirteenth Street, N.W.
Washington, DC 20004
(202) 724-0787

Railroad Retirement Board v. Alton Railroad Co.: *see* RAILROAD RETIREMENT ACT.

Railroad Unemployment Insurance Act of 1938, federal statute that created a national system to provide railroad employees with unemployment and sickness benefits.

Railway Labor Act of 1926, federal statute, amended in 1934 to include airlines, that protects the collective bargaining rights of employees and established the National Railroad Adjustment Board to arbitrate grievances that arise from labor-management contracts. *See* Leonard A. Lecht, *Experience Under Railway Labor Legislation* (New York: AMS Press, 1955, 1968); George S. Roukis, "Should the Railway Labor Act Be Amended?" *The Arbitration Journal* (March 1983).

R & D: *see* RESEARCH AND DEVELOPMENT.

Randolph, A(sa) Philip (1889-1979), one of the founders and first president of the Brotherhood of Sleeping Car Porters; one of the most significant voices in the labor and civil rights movements. For biographies, *see:* Jervis Anderson, *A. Philip Randolph: A Biographical Portrait* (New York: Harcourt Brace Jovanovich, 1973); William Hamilton Harris, *Keeping the Faith: A. Philip Randolph, Milton P. Webster, and the Brotherhood of Sleeping Car Porters, 1925-37* (Urbana: University of Illinois Press, 1977).

Randolph, Woodruff (1892-1966), president of the International Typographical Union from 1944 to 1958. For biographical information, *see* Seymour M. Lipset, et al., *Union Democracy: The Internal Politics of the International Typographical*

Union (Glencoe, Ill.: The Free Press, 1956).

random sample, sample of members of a population drawn in such a way that every member of the population has an equal chance of being included in the sample.

range, difference between the lowest and highest scores obtained on a test by some group.

rank, place in a hierarchical ordering of positions.

rank and file, colloquial expression referring to the masses. When used in an organizational context, it refers to those members of the organization who are not part of management. The term is frequently used to describe those members of a union having no status as officers or shop stewards. Rank and file was originally a military term referring to the enlisted men who had to line up in ranks, side by side, and files, one behind the other. Officers, being gentlemen, were spared such indignities. *See* George W. Bohlander, "How the Rank and File Views Local Union Administration—A Survey," *Employee Relations Law Journal* (Autumn 1982); Samuel R. Friedman, *Teamster Rank and File: Power, Bureaucracy, and Rebellion at Work and in a Union* (New York: Columbia University Press, 1982); Philip W. Nyden, *Steelworkers Rank-and-File: The Political Economy of a Union Reform Movement* (New York: Praeger Publishers, 1984).

ranking: *see* JOB RANKING.

ranking test, examination used to rank individuals according to their scores so that those with the higher scores have an advantage in gaining employment or promotion.

rank-in-man system, also called PERSONAL-RANK SYSTEM, method of establishing pay primarily on the basis of an employee's qualifications without consideration given to the specific duties and responsibilities that would be performed by the employee. Such personal rank systems tend to be restricted to the military, the U.S. Foreign Service, and other similar officer corps systems. *See* Harold H. Leich, "Rank in Man or Job? Both!" *Public Administration Review* (Spring 1960).

rank performance rating, method of performance appraisal that requires superiors to rank order employees according to their merit.

rapport, generally, a spirit of harmony, accord, and mutual confidence between individuals.

rate, beginner's: *see* BEGINNER'S RATE.

rate, incentive: *see* INCENTIVE RATE.

rate, trainee: *see* BEGINNER'S RATE.

ratebuster, also called JOB SPOILER, general term for any employee whose production level far exceeds the norms established by the majority of the work force. Ratebusters usually face considerable peer pressure to conform to average production levels, and sometimes this pressure can be physical. A *job spoiler* is a British ratebuster. For a study of the personality traits of ratebusters, *see* Melville Dalton, "The Industrial 'Ratebuster': A Characterization," *Applied Anthropology* (Winter 1948).

rate fixing, the power of some administrative agencies, public utility commissions, for example, to set the prices a company may charge for its services. This differs from price fixing, which is done by sellers of goods or services and may be illegal.

ratification, formal confirmation by the union membership of a contract that has been signed on their behalf by union representives.

rating, efficiency: *see* EFFICIENCY RATING.

rating, rank-performance: *see* RANK-PERFORMANCE RATING.

rating chart, graphic: *see* GRAPHIC RATING CHART.

rating system, deferred: *see* DEFERRED RATING SYSTEM.

ratio, efficiency: *see* EFFICIENCY.

ratio delay, work sampling technique that uses a large number of observations taken at random intervals in order to determine the parts of the work day (expressed in minutes or hours) during which an employee is working productively or is engaged in activities other than productive work. *See* L.H.C. Tippett, "The Ratio-Delay Technique," *Time and Motion Study* (May 1953).

rational validity, involves the use of a detailed job analysis to determine the knowledges, skills, and abilities that are necessary for effective performance in a particular job. Measurement instruments are then designed to measure such factors. For example, if a job requirement is the ability to type errorless copy at 50 words a minute, a test can be designed to measure that ability.

rat race, slang phrase for the relentless pursuit of success. The "race" is usually engaged in and won by workaholics who can't think of anything better to do anyway. Vermin lovers consider the phrase a gross libel of a species that would be innocent save for the bubonic plague. *See* Millard C. Faught, *Split-Week Living: A Way Out of the American Rat Race Toward More Timewealth for All* (Houston, Texas: DaVinci Press, 1969).
See also WORKAHOLIC.

raw score, also called CRUDE SCORE, number of items correct, when there is no correction for guessing, or the formula score, when a correction for guessing has been applied.

R cases, representation election cases before the NLRB.

reaction management, management

posture that is limited to responding to immediate problems and pressures.

reading assistant, reader for a blind employee. Public Law 87-614 of 1962 authorizes the employment of readers for blind federal employees. These reading assistants serve without compensation from the government, but they can be paid by the blind employees, nonprofit organizations, or state offices of vocational rehabilitation. They may also serve on a volunteer basis.

Reading Test, Davis: *see* DAVIS READING TEST.

Reagan, Ronald (1911-   ), the only American president who was previously an elected union official; he was President of the Screen Actors Guild from 1947 to 1952 and again from 1959 to 1960.

Reaganomics: *see* SUPPLY-SIDE ECONOMICS.

reallocate: *see* ALLOCATE.

reallocation, also called RECLASSIFICATION, change in the position classification of an existing position resulting from significant changes in assigned duties and responsibilities.

Realpolitik, originally a German word meaning "realist politics." Applied to politics—whether of the organizational or societal variety—that are premised upon material or practical factors rather than theoretical or ethical considerations. According to John E. Fisher, in "Playing Favorites in Large Organizations," *Business Horizons* (June 1977),

the realpolitiks of business offices may be overlooked by students of business administration who are surfeited in the literature of management techniques. Yet the literature actually reveals far less about how organizations operate internally than can be learned from studying office patronage and politics. Pre-occupation with management techniques may be misleading to callow

youth just coming from the halls of academe into the occupational armies of business. Unsophisticated tyros are led to believe that their technical qualifications will be highly regarded and will play a significant role in their advancement. And so it may, in some instances. In organizations dominated by authoritarians, however, office patronage and politics hold the key to what is to be accomplished and what is forbidden. Office patronage provides a means for people of indifferent ability who have acquired power to be secure in its exercise.

Also see Albert Somit, "Bureaucratic Realpolitik and Teaching of Administration," *Public Administration Review* (Autumn 1956); Nestor Cruz, " 'Realpolitik' and Affirmative Action," *Public Personnel Management* (Vol. 9, No. 3, 1980); Gerald F. Cavanagh, Dennis J. Moberg and Manuel Velasquez, "The Ethics of Organizational Politics," *Academy of Management Review* (July 1981); Frank M. Machovec and Howard R. Smith, "Fear Makes the World Go Round: The 'Dark' Side of Management," *Management Review* (January 1982); Manuel Velasquez, Dennis J. Moberg and Gerald F. Cavanagh, "Organizational Statesmanship and Dirty Politics: Ethical Guidelines for the Organizational Politician," *Organizational Dynamics* (Autumn 1983).

real time, computer term that describes an information processing speed sufficient to control an ongoing process.

real wages, wages after they have been adjusted for changes in the level of prices. The buying power of wages, the "real" wages, are computed by dividing the dollar amount by an index measuring changes in prices (such as the Consumer Price Index).

reasonable accommodation, once a handicapped employee is hired, an employer is required to take reasonable steps to accommodate the individual's disability unless such steps would cause the employer undue hardship. Examples of "reasonable accommodations" include providing a reader for a blind employee, an interpreter for a deaf person requiring telephone contacts, or adequate workspace for an employee confined to a wheelchair. *See* Janet Asher and Jules Asher, "How To Accommodate Workers in Wheelchairs," *Job Safety and Health* (October 1976); Leslie Milk, "What is Reasonable Accommodation?" *Civil Service Journal* (October-December 1978); Dorothy J. Steffanic, *Reasonable Accommodation for Deaf Employees in White Collar Jobs* (Washington, D.C.: U.S. Office of Personnel Management, 1982).

reassignment, transfer of an employee while serving continuously within the same organization, from one position to another without promotion or demotion.

Rebnick v. *McBride,* 277 U.S. 350 (1928), U.S. Supreme Court case, which held that the activities of employment offices were subject to state regulation.

recall, rehiring employees from a layoff. In a recall, union contracts usually require that the union be given both notice of the recall and the names of the employees to be recalled. This enables the union to determine if employees are being called back in the order required by the agreement. *See* Bureau of Labor Statistics, U.S. Department of Labor, *Major Collective Bargaining Agreements: Layoff, Recall, and Worksharing Procedures* (Washington, D.C.: U.S. Government Printing Office, Bulletin 1425-13, 1972).

recall item, test question that requires the examinee to supply the correct answer from memory, in contrast to a recognition item where the examinee need only identify the correct answer.

receiver, person appointed by a court to manage the affairs of an organization facing litigation and/or reorganization.

recess appointment, an appointment to federal office of a person, by the president, to fill a vacancy while the Senate is not in session.

A person appointed to office while the Senate is in recess may begin his or her duties before his or her name has been submitted to the Senate. However, the president must submit the nomination when the Senate reconvenes and the recess appointment expires at the end of the next session unless the Senate has confirmed the appointment by a majority vote. Moreover, the recess appointment expires and the office is declared vacant even earlier than the end of the next session if the Senate acts before that time to reject a nominee.

recession, a decline in overall business activity that is pervasive, substantial and of at least several months' duration. Historically, a decline in real gross national product for at least two consecutive quarters has been considered a recession.

reclassification: *see* REALLOCATION.

reclassify: *see* CLASSIFY.

recognition, employer's acceptance of a union as the bargaining agent for all of the employees in a particular bargaining unit. *See also* EXCLUSIVE RECOGNITION.

recognition item, test question that calls for the examinee to recognize or select the correct answer from among two or more alternatives.

recognition picketing, picketing to encourage an employer to recognize a particular union as the bargaining agent for his or her employees. Recognition picketing is usually an unfair labor practice. *See also* PRE-HIRE AGREEMENT.

recognition strike, work stoppage that seeks to force an employer to formally recognize and deal with a union.

record copy, copy of a document that is regarded by an organization as the most important or the key official copy.

recruitment, total process by which an organization gathers individuals to occupy its various positions. *See* Rober M. Guion, "Recruiting, Selection, and Job Placement," in Marvin D. Dunnette (ed.), *Handbook of Industrial and Organization Psychology* (Chicago: Rand McNally, 1976); Erwin S. Stanton, *Successful Personnel Recruiting and Selection within EEO/Affirmative Action Guidelines* (N.Y.: AMACON, 1977); John P. Wanous, *Organizational Entry: Recruitment, Selection, and Socialization of Newcomers* (Reading, Mass.: Addison-Wesley, 1980); Christine White and Abbie Willard Thorner, *Managing the Recruitment Process* (New York: Law & Business, Inc., 1982); Bernard S. Hodes, *The Principles and Practices of Recruitment Advertising: A Guide for Personnel Professionals* (New York: F. Fell Publishers, 1982); Donn L. Dennis, "Evaluating Corporate Recruitment Efforts," *Personnel Administrator* (January 1985).

See also POSITIVE RECRUITMENT.

red circle (position classification): *see* EARMARK.

red-circle rate, also called RINGED RATE, rate of pay that is higher than the established rate for a particular job.

red rash, job action by firefighters who, because they cannot legally strike, call in sick. When police suffer from this affliction, it is called the "blue flu."

See also BLUE FLU and STRIKE.

red tape, this despised symbol of excessive formality and attention to routine has its origins in the red ribbon with which clerks bound up official documents in the last century. The ribbon has disappeared, but the practices it represents linger on.

Herbert Kaufman's *Red Tape: Its Origins, Uses, and Abuses* (Washington, D.C.: The Brookings Institution, 1977), finds that the term "is applied to a bewildering variety of organizational practices and features." After all, "one person's 'red tape' may be another's treasured procedural safeguard." Kaufman concludes that "red tape turns out to be at the core of our institutions rather than an excrescence on them."

reduction in force: *see* RIF.

redundat, no longer needed; to be laid off. *See* Peter F. Drucker, "Planning for 'Redundant' Workers," *Personnel Administrator* (January 1980); Edward Yemin, editor, *Workforce Reductions in Undertakings: Policies and Measures for the Protection of Redundant Workers in Seven Industrialized Market Economy Countries* (Geneva: International Labour Office, 1982).

re-employed annuitant, employee who, having retired with a pension from an organization, is again employed by the same organization. Most of the re-employed annuitants working for the federal government are subject to a law that has their salary reduced by the amount of the annuity.

re-employment list, also called RE-EMPLOYMENT ELIGIBILITY LIST, most merit systems and union contracts require that, in the event of lay-offs, employees will be ranked on a re-employment list in order of their seniority. Usually, re-employment lists must be exhausted before new hires can be considered.

reference checking, verifying information provided by a job applicant. *See* Edward L. Levine, "Legal Aspects of Reference Checking for Personnel Selection," *The Personnel Administrator* (November 1977); John D. Rice, "Privacy Legislation: Its Effect on Pre-employment Reference Checking," *The Personnel Administrator* (February 1978); Edward L. Levine and Stephone M. Rudolph, *Reference Checking for Personnel Selection: The State of the Art* (Berea, Ohio: American Society for Personnel Administration, 1978); Paula Lippin, "The Delicate Art of Checking References," *Administrative Management* (August 1979); James D. Bell, James Castagnera and Jane Patterson Young, "Employment References, Do You Know the Law?" *Personnel Journal* (February 1984); Bruce D. Wonder and Kenneth S. Keleman, "Increasing the Value of Reference Information," *Personnel Administrator* (March 1984).

reference group, also called SOCIAL REFERENCE GROUP, social group with which an individual identifies to the extent that his/her personal values are derived from the group's norms and attitudes. See Herbert H. Hyman and Eleanor Singer (eds.), *Readings in Reference Group Theory and Research* (N.Y.: The Free Press, 1968).

referendum, a procedure for submitting a proposed law to the voters for ratification and enactment. See Darold T. Barnum and I. B. Helburn, "Influencing the Electorate: Experience with Referenda on Public Employee Bargaining," *Industrial and Labor Relations Review* (April 1982).

Regents of the University of California v. Allan Bakke, 438 U.S. 265 (1978), U.S. Supreme Court case, which upheld a white applicant's claim of reverse discrimination because he was denied admission to the University of California Medical School at Davis when 16 out of the school's 100 class spaces were set aside for minority applicants. The court ruled that Bakke must be admitted to the Davis Medical School as soon as possible, but that the university had the right to take race into account in its admissions criteria. The imprecise nature of taking race into account as one factor among many has created considerable speculation about the potential impact this case may have on voluntary affirmative action programs concerning employment. See Allen P. Sindler, *Bakke, Defunis, and Minority Admissions: The Quest for Equal Opportunity* (N.Y.: Longman, 1978); Joel Dreyfuss and Charles Lawrence III, *The Bakke Case: The Politics of Inequality* (New York: Harcourt, Brace, Jovanovich, 1979); J. Harvie Wilkinson III, *From Brown to Bakke: The Supreme Court and School Integration 1954-1978* (New York: Oxford University Press, 1979); C. G. Bakaly and G. E. Krischer, "Bakke: Its Impact on Public Employment Discrimination," *Employee Relations Law Journal* (Spring 1979); William Kelso, "From Bakke to Fillilove: Has the Supreme Court Finally Settled the Affirmative Action Contro-

versy?" *Review of Public Personnel Administration* (Fall 1980).
 See also the following entries:
  DEFUNIS V. ODEGAARD
  REVERSE DISCRIMINATION
  UNITED STEEL WORKERS OF AMERICA V.
   WEBER, ET AL.

regional bargaining, collective bargaining between a union and the representatives of an industry in a given region.

register of eligibles: see ELIGIBLE LIST.

registration: see OCCUPATIONAL REGISTRATION.

regression analysis, also MULTIPLE REGRESSION ANALYSIS, method for describing the nature of the relationship between two variables, so that the value of one can be predicted if the value of the other is known. *Multiple regression analysis* involves more than two variables. See James L. Danielson and Russ Smith, "The Application of Regression Analysis to Equality and Merit in Personnel Decisions," *Public Personnel Management,* Vol. 10, No. 1 (1981); Walter W. Hudson, "Simplified Multiple Regression for Applied Behavioral Science," *The Journal of Applied Behavioral Science,* Vol. 18, No. 4 (1982).

regulation, a government control on the behavior of people or organizations that is decided upon by administrative agencies such as the National Labor Relations Board. See Thomas K. McCraw, "Regulation in America: A Historical Overview," *California Management Review* (Fall 1984).

rehabilitants, emotional: see EMOTIONALLY HANDICAPPED EMPLOYEES.

Rehabilitated Offender Program, federal government's program to assure fair federal employment opportunity for qualified applicants convicted of a crime who are subsequently declared rehabilitated offenders. The federal government seeks to carefully and selectively hire rehabilitated offenders for jobs where they are needed and for which they are qualified by experience, education, and training, as determined by normal competitive examining procedures. Rehabilitated offenders who are mentally retarded or otherwise severely handicapped are appointed under the same procedures used for other such handicapped persons, with appointing officials taking into account their record, conduct, and rehabilitative efforts. In both competitive and excepted appointments, the hiring agency makes the final decision on whether an applicant would be the right person for a particular opening.

reindustrialization, a loose term for public and private efforts to make American industry more competitive in world markets by rejuvenating its physical plant. *See* Milton D. Lower, "The Reindustrialization of America," *Journal of Economic Issues* (June 1982).

reinforcement, also POSITIVE REINFORCE-MENT and NEGATIVE REINFORCEMENT, inducement to perform in a particular manner. *Positive reinforcement* occurs when an individual receives a desired reward that is contingent upon some prescribed behavior. *Negative reinforcement* occurs when an individual works to avoid an undesirable reward. *See* B. F. Skinner, *Contingencies of Reinforcement: A Theoretical Analysis* (N.Y.: Appleton-Century-Crofts, 1969); Harry Wiard, "Why Manage Behavior? A Case for Positive Reinforcement," *Human Resource Management* (Summer 1972); Jerry A. Wallinand and Ronald D. Johnson, "The Positive Reinforcement Approach to Controlling Employee Absenteeism," *Personnel Journal* (August 1976); Norman C. Hill, "The Need For Positive Reinforcement in Corrective Counseling," *Supervisory Management* (December 1984).

reinstatement, restoration of an employee to his/her previous position without any loss of seniority or other benefits. In a governmental context, reinstatement is the noncompetitive reentrance into the competitive service of a person who acquired eligibility for such action as a result of previous service. Reinstatement is a privilege accorded in recognition of and on the basis of former service and is not a "right" to which one is entitled.

relevance: *see* CRITERION RELEVANCE.

relevant labor market, in the context of equal employment opportunity this is the geographic area from which an organization should recruit in order to satisfy affirmative action requirements. *See* Howard R. Bloch and Robert L. Pennington, "Measuring Discrimination: What is a Relevant Labor Market," *Personnel* (July-August 1980).

reliability, dependability of a testing device, as reflected in the consistency of its scores when repeated measurements are made of the same group. When a test is said to have a high degree of reliability, it means that an individual tested today and tested again at a later time with the same test and under the same conditions will get approximately the same score. In short, a test is reliable if it gives a dependable measure of whatever it seeks to measure.

See also INTERNAL CONSISTENCY RELIABILITY and INTERRATER RELIABILITY.

reliability coefficient, numerical index of reliability that is obtained by correlating scores on two forms of a test, from statistical data on individual test items, or by correlating scores on different administrations of the same test. A reliability coefficient can be a perfect 1.00 or a perfectly unreliable -1.00. A reliability of .90 or greater is generally considered adequate for a test used as a personnel selection device.

relief, also WORK RELIEF, terms usually refer to the public assistance program available during the depression of the 1930s. *Relief* or *direct relief* referred to straight welfare payments. *Work relief* referred to any of the numerous public works projects initiated specifically to provide jobs for the unemployed. *See* Bruno Stein, *On Relief:*

The Economics of Poverty and Public Welfare (New York: Basic Books, 1971).

religious discrimination, any act that manifests unfavorable or inequitable treatment toward employees or prospective employees because of their religious convictions. Because of section 703(a) (1) of the Civil Rights Act of 1964, an individual's religious beliefs or practices cannot be given any consideration in making employment decisions. The argument that a religious practice may place an undue hardship upon an employer—for example, where such practices require special religious holidays and hence absence from work—has been upheld by the courts. However, because of the sensitive nature of discharging or refusing to hire an individual on religious grounds, the burden of proof to show that such a hardship exists is placed upon the employer. *See* Charles J. Hollon and Thomas L. Bright, "Avoiding Religious Discrimination in the Workplace," *Personnel Journal* (August 1982); I. B. Helburn and John R. Hill, "The Arbitration of Religious Practice Grievances," *Arbitration Journal* (June 1984).

relocation allowance, payment by an employer of all or part of the cost of moving one's self and one's household to a distant place of employment. *See* Peter J. DiDomenico, Jr., "Relocation Benefits for New Hires," *The Personnel Administrator* (February 1978).

remuneration: *see* COMPENSATION.

reopener clause, also WAGE REOPENER CLAUSE, provision in a collective bargaining agreement stating the circumstances under which portions of the agreement, usually concerning wages, can be renegotiated before the agreement's normal expiration date. Typically such clauses provide for renegotiation at the end of a specified time period (such as one year) or when the Consumer Price Index increases by an established amount.

reorganization, any restructuring of a large organization. A reorganization under federal bankruptcy laws allows an insolvent corporation to continue functioning while financial reforms are implemented.

replacement demand, the demand for workers existing because employers need to replace workers who die, retire, or leave their jobs to migrate to different areas or transfer to different occupations.

reporting pay: *see* CALL-IN PAY.

Report of the Job Evaluation and Pay Review Task Force to the United States Civil Service Commission: *see* JOB EVALUATION AND PAY REVIEW TASK FORCE.

representation, any system of governance which has all of its citizens (or members) elect agents to represent their interests in another (possibly legislative) forum.

representation election: *see* AUTHORIZATION ELECTION.

representative bureaucracy, concept originated by J. Donald Kingsley, in *Representative Bureaucracy* (Yellow Springs, Ohio: Antioch Press, 1944), which asserts that all social groups have a right to participation in their governing institutions. In recent years, the concept has developed a normative overlay—that all social groups should occupy bureaucratic positions in direct proportion to their numbers in the general population. For defenses of this normative position, *see* Samuel Krislov, *Representative Bureaucracy* (Englewood Cliffs, N.J.: Prentice-Hall, 1974); Harry Kranz, *The Participatory Bureaucracy: Women and Minorities in a More Representative Public Service* (Lexington, Mass.: Lexington-Books, 1976); Samuel Krislov and David H. Rosenbloom, *Representative Bureaucracy and the American Political System* (New York: Praeger, 1981).

representative sample, sample that corresponds to or matches the population of which it is a sample with respect to characteristics important for the purposes under investigation. For example, a representative national sample of secondary school students should probably contain students from each state, from large and small schools, and from public and independent schools in approximately the same proportions as these exist in the nation as a whole.

reprimand, formal censure for some job related behavior. A reprimand is less severe than an adverse action; more forceful than an admonition.

reprivatization, assignment of functions to the private sector that were previously performed by the government *(i.e., trash collection, fire protection, etc.). See* E. S. Sayas, *Privatizing the Public Sector* (Chatham, N.J.: Chatham House, 1982).

requisite skills, those skills that make a person eligible for consideration for employment in a particular job.

research and development, the systematic and intensive study of a subject in order to direct that knowledge toward the production of new materials, systems, methods, or processes. Corporate research uncovers facts and principles in order to benefit development. *Pure* or *basic* research attempts to uncover new scientific knowledge and understanding with little regard to when, or specifically how, the new facts will be used; and *applied* research is conducted with a special purpose in mind. It is usually directed toward a specific problem, or toward a series of problems that stand in the way of progress in a particular area. *See* David B. Balkin and Luis R. Gomez-Mejia, "Determinants of R and D Compensation Strategies in the High Tech Industry," *Personnel Psychology* (Winter 1984).

reserved rights: *see* MANAGEMENT RIGHTS.

residency requirement: *see* the following entries:
DOMICILE
HICKLIN V. ORBECK
MCCARTHY V. PHILADELPHIA CIVIL
   SERVICE COMMISSION

residual unemployment, no matter how many jobs are available, there will always be some people out of work because of illness, indolence, movement from one job or community to another, etc. The total number of these individuals is a measure of residual unemployment.

resignation, employee's formal notice that his or her relationship with the employing organization is being terminated.

resignation, volunteered: *see* QUIT.

response rate, in survey research, the percentage of those given questionnaires who complete and return them.

rest period, recuperative pause during working hours. The federal wage and hour law does *not* require rest periods or "breaks." Guidelines issued under Title VII of the Federal Civil Rights Act state that where rest periods are required for women they also shall be provided for men, unless precluded by business necessity. In this case, the employer may not provide rest periods for members of only one sex. *See* Stephen E. Bechtold, Ralph E. Janaro and DeWitt L. Sumners, "Maximization of Labor Productivity Through Optimal Rest-Break Schedules," *Management Science* (December 1984).

restraining order, temporary: *see* INJUNCTION.

restriction of output, reduced productivity on the part of a worker or workforce because of informal group norms, personal grievances, or sloth. For the classic study of this phenomenon, *see* Stanley B. Mathewson, *Restriction of Output Among Unorganized Workers* (Carbondale: Southern Illinois University Press, 1931, 1969). *Also see* Harry Cohen, "Dimensions of Restriction of Output," *Personnel Journal* (December 1971).

restrictive credentialism, general term for any selection policy adversely affecting disadvantaged groups because they lack the formal qualifications for positions that, in the opinion of those adversely affected, do not truly need such formal qualifications.

resume, also CURRICULUM VITA, brief account of one's education and experience that job applicants typically prepare for prospective employers to review. In the academic world, a resume is more pompously called a *curriculum vita. See* Robert P. Vecchio, "The Problem of Phony Resumes: How to Spot a Ringer Among the Applicants," *Personnel* (March–April 1984).

Retail/Services Labor Report, weekly report published by the Bureau of National Affairs, Inc., for management and unions in the retail/services field. Covers personnel administration, legislative developments, equal employment opportunity, union organizing, collective bargaining, contract settlements, equal pay, job safety, and hours and earnings. Provides full texts of important court and labor board rulings.
See also BUREAU OF NATIONAL AFFAIRS, INC.

retention period, stated period of time during which personnel records are to be retained.

retention register, federal government's record of employees occupying positions in a competitive level. Employees on the register are arranged by tenure groups and subgroups and according to their relative retention standing within the subgroups.

retention standing, precise rank among employees competing for a position in the event of a reduction-in-force or layoff. It is determined by tenure groups and subgroups and by length of creditable service.

retirement, voluntary or involuntary termination of employment because of age, disability, illness or personal choice. *See* James W. Walker and Harriet L. Lazer, *The End of Mandatory Retirement: Implications for Management* (N.Y.: John Wiley, 1978); Thomas S. Litras, "The Battle over Retirement Policies and Practices,"

Personnel Journal (February 1979); William Graebner, *A History of Retirement: The Meaning and Function of an American Institution, 1885–1978* (New Haven: Yale University Press, 1980); James B. Shaw and Lisa L. Grubbs, "The Process of Retiring: Organizational Entry in Reverse," *Academy of Management Review* (January 1981); Malcolm H. Morrison, "Retirement and Human Resource Planning for the Aging Work Force," *Personnel Administrator* (June 1984).
See also the following entries:
    ALLIED CHEMICAL WORKERS V. PITTS-
        BURGH PLATE GLASS CO.
    CANNON V. GUSTE
    CIVIL SERVICE RETIREMENT AND
        DISABILITY FUND
    DISABILITY RETIREMENT
    INLAND STEEL COMPANY V. NATIONAL
        LABOR RELATIONS BOARD
    MASSACHUSETTS BOARD OF RETIRE-
        MENT V. MURGIA
    PRE-RETIREMENT COUNSELING
    RE-EMPLOYED ANNUITANT
    SURVIVORS BENEFITS
    VANCE V. BRADLEY

Retirement Account, Individual: *see* IN-DIVIDUAL RETIREMENT ACCOUNT.

retirement age, a 1978 amendment to the Age Discrimination in Employment Act raised the minimum mandatory retirement age to 70 years for workers in private companies and state and local governments. It banned forced retirement at any age for federal workers.

retirement counseling, systematic efforts by an organization to help its employees who are retiring to adjust to their new situation. For how to establish a retirement counseling program, *see* Douglas M. Bartlett, "Retirement Counseling: Make Sure Employees Aren't Dropouts," *Personnel* (November–December 1974); Don Pellicano, "Retirement Counseling," *Personnel Journal* (July 1973); Don Underwood, "Toward Self-Reliance in Retirement Planning," *Harvard Business Review* (May–June 1984).
See also PRE-RETIREMENT COUNSELING.

Retirement Equity Act of 1984, broadens the conditions under which spouses receive retirement benefits. Under the act, spouses of employees who die after attaining eligibility for pensions are guaranteed a benefit beginning at age 55; a prospective survivor must agree in a signed, notarized statement before a pension plan member can waive the option of providing a survivorship benefit (previously, the plan member had the sole right to decide); and the divorced spouse of a plan member is entitled to part of a pension, if stipulated in the separation papers or ordered by a judge.

Also, the new act:

- Requires employers to count all service from age 18 in calculating when an employee becomes vested (legally entitled to a pension, which usually requires 10 years of service). In computing the amount of benefits, all employee earnings from age 21 must be considered. (Previously, service accrual toward vesting began at age 22 and benefits were based on earnings from age 25.)
- Permits pension plan members to leave the work force for up to 5 consecutive years without losing pension credits.
- Allows plan members to take maternity or paternity leave of up to 1 year without loss of service credit for the period.
- Permits employees of companies that have thrift (savings) plans to join as early as age 21. These plans generally provide for employers to match some of the money the employee invests.
- Requires employers to explain to employees the tax consequences of taking lump-sum amounts from pension or profit-sharing plans.

The new provisions, which amend the Employee Retirement Income Security Act of 1974, are effective December 31, 1984. For pension plans established through collective bargaining, provisions take effect when the contract pertaining to the pension plan expires, or January 1, 1987, whichever comes first.

retirement plan, fixed-benefit: *see* FIXED-BENEFIT RETIREMENT PLAN.

retreating, assigning an employee to a position from or through which the employee was promoted, when the position is occupied by someone with lower retention standing.

retroactive pay, wages for work performed during an earlier time at a lower rate. Retroactive pay would make up the difference between the new and old rates of pay.

retroactive seniority, seniority status that is retroactively awarded back to the date that a woman or minority group member was proven to have been discriminatorily refused employment. The U.S. Supreme Court has interpreted the "make whole" provision of Title VII of the Civil Rights Act of 1964 to include the award of retroactive seniority to proven discriminatees; however, retroactive seniority cannot be awarded further back than 1964—the date of the act. *See* Hindy Lauer Schachter, "Retroactive Seniority and Agency Retrenchment," *Public Administration Review* (January–February 1983).

See FRANKS V. BOWMAN TRANSPORTATION CO. and INTERNATIONAL BROTHERHOOD OF TEAMSTERS V. UNITED STATES.

Reuther, Walter P. (1907–1970), president of the United Automobile Workers from 1946 until his death. For biographies, *see* Frank Cormier and William J. Eaton, *Reuther* (Englewood Cliffs, N.J.: Prentice-Hall, 1970; Jean Gould and Lorena Hickok, *Walter Reuther: Labor's Rugged Individualist* (N.Y.: Dodd, Mead, 1972); John Barnard, *Walter Reuther and the Rise of the United Auto Workers* (Boston: Little, Brown, 1983).

reverse collective bargaining, occurs when economic conditions force collective bargaining agreements to be renegotiated so that employees end up with a less favorable wage package. *See* Peter Henle, "Reverse Collective Bargaining? A Look at Some Union Concession Situations," *In-*

dustrial and Labor Relations Review (April 1973).

reverse discrimination, although generally understood to mean preferential treatment for women and minorities, as opposed to white males, the practice has no legal standing. Indeed, Section 703 (j) of Title VII of the Civil Rights Act of 1964 holds that nothing in the title shall be interpreted to require any employer to "grant preferential treatment to any individual or group on the basis of race, color, religion, sex or national origin." Yet, affirmative action programs necessarily put some otherwise innocent white males at a disadvantage that they would not have otherwise had. The whole matter may have been summed up by George Orwell in his 1945 novella, *Animal Farm,* when he observed that "All animals are equal, but some animals are more equal than others." For analyses of the problem, *see* Gopal C. Pati, "Reverse Discrimination: What Can Managers Do?" *Personnel Journal* (July 1977); Alan H. Goldman, *Justice and Reverse Discrimination* (Princeton University Press, 1979); Robert K. Fullinwider, *The Reverse Discrimination Controversy: A Moral And Legal Analysis* (Totowa, N.J.: Rowman and Littlefield, 1980); Ralph A. Rossum, *Reverse Discrimination: The Constitutional Debate* (New York: Marcel Dekker, 1980). For a political analysis, *see* Nathan Glazer, *Affirmative Discrimination* (N.Y.: Basic Books, 1975). For a defense, *see* Boris Bittker, *The Case for Black Reparations* (N.Y.: Random House, 1973). For a philosophic approach, *see* Barry R. Gross, *Discrimination in Reverse: Is Turnabout Fair Play?* (N.Y.: New York University Press, 1978). *Also see* Marianne A. Ferber and Carole A. Green, "Traditional or Reverse Sex Discrimination? A Case Study of a Large Public University," *Industrial and Labor Relations Review* (July 1982); R. Kent Greenawalt, *Discrimination and Reverse Discrimination* (New York: Knopf, 1983).

See also the following entries:
DEFUNIS V. ODEGAARD
REGENTS OF THE UNIVERSITY OF CALIFOR-
NIA V. ALLAN BAKKE
UNITED STEELWORKERS OF AMERICA V. WEBER, ET AL.

Review of Public Personnel Administration, a journal of public personnel management and labor relations.
> *Review of Public Personnel Administration*
> Bureau of Governmental Research and Service
> University of South Carolina
> Columbia, SC 29208

Revised Minnesota Paper Form Board Test, paper-and-pencil instrument consisting of 64 multiple-choice items that measure mechanical aptitude. Each item consists of a figure cut into two or more parts. The individual must determine how the pieces would fit together into a complete figure, then choose the drawing that correctly shows the arrangement. Valid instrument for measuring the ability to visualize and manipulate objects in space. TIME: 20/25 minutes. AUTHORS: Rensis Likert and W. H. Quasha. PUBLISHER: Psychological Corporation (*see* TEST PUBLISHERS).

Ricardo, David (1772-1823), the English economist who developed the first comprehensive economic model, formulated the concept of comparative advantage in international trade, and promulgated the iron law of wages.

RIF, acronym for "reduction in force"— the phrase the federal government uses when it eliminates specific job categories in specific organizations. While an employee who has been "riffed" has not been fired, he or she is nevertheless still without a job. This acronym has become so common that it is often used as a verb and seems to be spreading well beyond the federal bureaucracy. *See* Robert Rudary and J. Garrett Ralls, Jr., "Manpower Planning for Reduction-in-Force," *University of Michigan Business Review* (November 1978); George H. Cauble, Jr., "Alternative to a Reduction in Force," *Public Personnel Management* (Spring 1982);

Richard I. Lehr and David J. Middle-brooks, "Work Force Reduction: Strategies and Options," *Personnel Journal* (October 1984).

See also the following entries:
LAYOFF
RECALL
RE-EMPLOYMENT LIST
REINSTATEMENT
RETENTION REGISTER
RETENTION STANDING

rightful place, judicial doctrine that an individual who has been discriminated against should be restored to the job—to his or her "rightful place"—as if there had been no discrimination and given appropriate seniority, merit increases, and promotions.

rights arbitration: *see* GRIEVANCE ARBITRATION.

right-to-work laws, state laws that make it illegal for collective bargaining agreements to contain maintenance of membership, preferential hiring, union shop, or any other clauses calling for compulsory union membership. A typical "right-to-work" law might read: "No person may be denied employment and employers may not be denied the right to employ any person because of that person's membership or nonmembership in any labor organization."

It was the Labor-Management Relations (Taft-Hartley) Act of 1947 that authorized right-to-work laws, when it provided in section 14(b) that "nothing in this Act shall be construed as authorizing the execution or application of agreements requiring membership in a labor organization as a condition of employment in any State or Territory in which such execution or application is prohibited by State or Territorial law."

The law does not prohibit the union or closed shop; it simply gives each state the option of doing so. Twenty states have done so: Alabama, Arizona, Arkansas, Florida, Georgia, Iowa, Kansas, Louisiana, Mississippi, Nebraska, Nevada, North Carolina, North Dakota, South Carolina, South Dakota, Tennessee, Texas, Utah, Virginia, and Wyoming. *See* David T. Ellwood and Glenn A. Fine, *"The Impact of Right-to-Work Laws on Union Organizing"* (Cambridge, Mass.: National Bureau of Economic Research, Inc., 1983); Henry S. Farber, *Right-to-Work Laws and the Extent of Unionization* (Cambridge, Mass.: National Bureau of Economic Research, Inc., 1983).

See also NATIONAL RIGHT TO WORK COMMITTEE and OIL WORKERS V. MOBIL OIL COMPANY.

ringed rate: *see* RED-CIRCLE RATE.

rival unionism, competition between two or more unions for the same prospective members.

robber barons, label applied to the big business titans of the United States toward the end of the 19th century. Now it is an insidious term for corporate leadership in general. For the historical account, *see* Matthew Josephson, *The Robber Barons: The Great American Capitalists, 1861-1901* (N.Y.: Harcourt, Brace & Co., 1934).

Robbins **decision:** *see* NATIONAL LABOR RELATIONS BOARD V. ROBBINS TIRE AND RUBBER CO.

Robertson, David Brown (1876-1961), president of the Brotherhood of Locomotive Firemen and Enginemen from 1922 to 1953.

Robins, Margaret Dreier (1868-1945), a leader of the Women's Trade Union League and president of the International Federation of Working Women from 1921 to 1923. For a biography, *see* Mary Dreier, *Margaret Dreier Robins: Her Life, Letters and Work* (N.Y.: Island Press Cooperative, 1950).

Robinson **v.** *Lorrilard Corp.:* *see* BUSINESS NECESSITY.

robot, general term for any machine that does the work that a person would otherwise have to do. The word comes from *robotnik*, the Czech word for slave. *See* S. A. Levitan and C. M. Johnson, "The Future of Work: Does it Belong to Us or to the Robots?" *Monthly Labor Review* (September 1982); James Lambrinos and W. G. Johnson, "Robots to Reduce the High Cost of Illness and Injury," *Harvard Business Review* (May-June 1984); F. K. Foulkes and J. L. Hirsch, "People Make Robots Work," *Harvard Business Review* (January-February 1984).

robotics, the use of the robots. *See* H. Allan Hunt and Timothy L. Hunt, *Human Resource Implications of Robotics* (Kalamazoo, Mich.: The W. E. Upjohn Institute for Employment Research, 1983); Linda Argot, Paul S. Goodman and David Schkade, "The Human Side of Robotics: How Workers React to a Robot," *Sloan Management Review* (Spring 1983).

Roethlisberger, Fritz J. (1898-1974), with Elton Mayo, one of the founders of the human relations movement in industry. As one of the prime researchers of the Hawthorne experiments, he co-authored the definitive report on them—*Management and the Worker*, with William J. Dickson (Cambridge, Mass.: Harvard University Press, 1939). Other major works include: *Management and Morale* (Cambridge, Mass: Harvard University Press, 1941); *Man-in-Organization* (Cambridge, Mass.: Harvard University Press, 1968); *The Elusive Phenomena: An Autobiographical Account of My Work in the Field of Organizational Behavior at the Harvard Business School*, edited by George F. F. Lombard (Cambridge: Harvard University Press, 1977). *Also see* George F. F. Lombard (ed.), *The Contributions of F. J. Roethlisberger to Management Theory and Practice* (Cambridge, Mass: Harvard University Graduate School of Business, 1976).

Rogers Act of 1924, federal statute that created a merit-based career system for the Foreign Service of the U.S. Department of State.

role, also ROLE PLAYING, in social psychology, the term "role" is used to describe the behavior expected of an individual occupying a particular position. Just as an actor acts out his role on the stage, a personnel manager, for example, performs his role in real life. Role playing is a very common training technique and is based on the assumption that the process of acting out a role will enable an individual to gain insights concerning the behavior of others that cannot be realized by reading a book or listening to a lecture. *See* R. J. Corsini, M. Shaw, and R. Blake, *Roleplaying in Business and Industry* (N.Y.: Free Press, 1961); Norman R. F. Maier, Allen Solem, and Ayesha A. Maier, *The Role-Play Technique: A Handbook for Management and Leadership Practice* (La Jolla, Calif.: University Associates, 1975); Frank Sherwood, "The Role Concept in Administration," *Public Personnel Review* (January 1964); George Graen, "Role-Making Processes within Complex Organizations," in Marvin D. Dunnette, ed., *Handbook of Industrial and Organizational Psychology* (Chicago: Rand McNally, 1976).

See also STRUCTURED ROLE PLAYING.

role conception: *see* ROLE PERCEPTION.

role conflict, when an individual is called upon to perform mutually exclusive acts by parties having legitimate "holds" on him/her, role conflict may be said to exist. For example, a rising young manager may not make it to the "big" meeting if he must at that moment rush his child to the hospital for an emergency appendectomy. When such conflicts arise, most individuals invoke a hierarchy of role obligation that gives some roles precedence over others. To most fathers, their child's life would be more important than a business meeting—no matter how "big." Real life is not always so unambiguous, however, and role conflict is a common dilemma in the world of work. *See* J. R. Rizzo, R. J. House, and S. I. Lirtzman, "Role Conflict and Ambiguity in Complex Organizations," *Administrative Science Quarterly* (June 1970); R. H. Miles and W. D. Perreault, Jr., "Organizational Role Conflict: Its Antecedents and Consequences," *Organizational Behavior and Human Performance* (October 1976); James H. Morris, Richard M. Steers, and James L. Koch, "Influence of Organizational Structure on Role Conflict and Ambiguity for Three Occupational Groupings," *Academy of Management Journal* (March 1979); Mary Van Sell, Arthur P. Brief and Randall S. Schuler, "Role Conflict and Role Ambiguity: Integration of the Literature and Directions for Future Research," *Human Relations* (January 1981).

role perception, also called ROLE CONCEPTION, an individual's role perception or role conception delineates the position that the individual occupies in his/her organization and establishes for the individual the minimum and maximum ranges of permissible behavior in "acting" out his/her organizational role. For empirical studies, *see* Andrew D. Szilagyi, "An Empirical Test of Causal Inference between Role Perceptions, Satisfaction with Work, Performance and Organizational Level," *Personnel Psychology* (Autumn 1977); Randell S. Schuler, "The Effects of Role Perceptions on Employee Satisfaction and Performance Moderated by Employee Ability," *Organizational Behavior and Human Performance* (February 1977); Barbara Ley Toffler, "Occupational Role Development: The Changing Determinants of Outcomes for the Individual," *Administrative Science Quarterly* (September 1981); Kevin W. Mossholder, Arthus G. Bedeian and Achilles A. Armenakis, "Role Perceptions, Satisfaction, and Performance: Moderating Effects of Self-Esteem and Organizational Level," *Organizational Behavior and Human Performance* (October 1981).

role playing: *see* ROLE and STRUCTURED ROLE PLAYING.

romance: *see* LOVE.

Roney, Frank (1841-1925), West Coast labor organizer in the late 1800s. For an autobiography, *see* Ira B. Cross, editor, *Frank Roney: Irish Rebel and Labor Leader* (Berkeley, Calif.: University of California Press, 1931).

roping: *see* HOOKING.

Rorschach test, also called INK-BLOT TEST, projective test in which the responses to standard ink blots are interpreted to gain clues to the subject's personality. Developed by the Swiss psychiatrist, Hermann Rorschach (1884-1922), the Rorschach test is no longer considered to be a valid tool for predicting vocational success.

See also PROJECTIVE TEST and THEMATIC APPERCEPTION TEST.

Rosenbloom, David H. (1943-   ), the leading authority on the constitutional aspects of public employment. Major works include: *Federal Service and the Constitution* (Ithaca: Cornell University Press, 1971); *Federal Equal Employment Opportunity* (New York: Praeger, 1977). He is coauthor of: *Bureaucratic Culture: Citizens and Administrators in Israel* (New York: St. Martin's Press, 1978); *Bureaucratic Government, USA* (New York: St. Martin's Press, 1980); *Representative Bureaucracy and the American Political System* (New York: Praeger, 1981); *Personnel Management in Government: Politics and Process,* second edition (New York: Marcel Dekker, Inc., 1981).

roster of eligibles: *see* ELIGIBLE LIST.

rotating shift, work schedule designed to give employees an equal share of both day and night work.

Roth decision: *see* BOARD OF REGENTS V. ROTH.

Rowan, James (1851-1906), British industrialist who in 1898 created a premium bonus system for rewarding labor.

Rowan Plan, incentive wage plan that gives a worker a standard rate for completing a job within an established time, plus a premium determined on the basis of the percentage of time saved.

Rowntree, Benjamin Seebohm (1871-1954), British industrialist and scientific management advocate who during the early part of this century introduced innovative and influential employee welfare and profit sharing plans.

RRB: see RAILROAD RETIREMENT BOARD.

Rucker Plan, employee incentive plan developed in the 1950s by Allen W. Rucker of the Eddy-Rucker-Nickels consulting firm. According to R. C. Scott, in "Rucker Plan of Group Incentives," Carl Heyel (ed.), *The Encyclopedia of Management* (N.Y.: Van Nostrand Reinhold Co., 2nd ed., 1973), the plan

uses day-to-day employee participants and broad coverage to develop cost reductions and improve profits. It is backed by a precise measurement of productivity gains in money terms (not physical units). It recognizes and reinforces those gains with an equitable, automatic method of sharing them between the participants (added pay) and the company (added margin).

rule, a regulation made by an administrative agency. *See* William F. Kent, "The Politics of Administrative Rulemaking," *Public Administrative Review* (September/October 1982).

rule-making authority, powers exercised by administrative agencies that have the force of law.

Agencies begin with some form of legislative mandate and translate their interpretation of that mandate into policy decisions, specifications of regulations, and statements of penalties and enforcement provisions. The exact process to be followed in formulating regulations is only briefly described in the federal Administration Procedure Act (APA). There are no more constitutional procedural requirements for enacting rules than for legislatures enacting statutes. Agencies are required only to provide advance notice of their intent to formulate new rules or changes in existing rules.

The APA does distinguish between rule-making requiring a hearing and rule-making requiring only notice and opportunity for public comment. Bernard Schwartz sees these categories as two different procedural requirements; formal rule-making which must be preceded by a trial-type hearing and informal rule-making which is termed "notice and comment rule-making." But the test of whether the formal or informal procedure will be used is the specification in the enabling statute. This was affirmed in the Supreme Court's decision in *United States* v. *Florida East Coast Railway,* 410 U.S. 224 (1973), that formal rule-making need only be followed when the enabling statute expressly requires an agency hearing prior to rule formulation.

What remains in the APA provisions for rule-making is the requirement that rules be published thirty days before their effective date and that agencies afford any interested party the right to petition for issuance, amendment, or repeal of a rule. In effect, while APA establishes a process of notice and time for comment, it accords administrative rule-making the same prerogatives as legislatures have in enacting statutes. There is, of course, the additional requirement that the rule enacted be consistent with the enabling statute directing the rule-making. *See* J. Skelly Wright, "Court of Appeals Review of Federal Agency Rulemaking," *Administrative Law Review* (Winter 1974); Bernard Schwartz, "Administrative Law in the Next Century," *Ohio State Law Journal,* No. 4 (1978).

rule of three, also RULE OF ONE and RULE OF THE LIST, practice of certifying to an appointing authority the top three names on an eligible list. The rule of three is intended to give the appointing official an opportunity to weigh intangible factors, such as personality, before making a formal offer of appointment. The *rule of one* has only the single highest ranking person on the eligible list certified. The *rule of the list* gives the appointing authority the opportunity to choose from the entire list of eligibles.

runaway shop, term used by unionists to describe a company or company subdivision that moves to another state or area to avoid a union or state labor laws. *See* Martin J. Klaper, "The Right to Relocate Work During the Term of an Existing Collective Bargaining Agreement," *Labor Law Journal* (February 1983); Peter A. Susser, "National Labor Relations Board Reverses Its Position on Midterm Relocations," *Personnel Administrator* (June 1984).

run-off election, when no single union receives a majority in a representation election, a second election—the run-off election—is held and participants choose between the two unions that got the most votes in the first election.

S

sabbath: *see* TRANS WORLD AIRLINES V. HARDISON.

sabbatical, lengthy paid leave for professional, intellectual or emotional refurbishment. It was an ancient Hebrew tradition to allow fields to lie fallow every seventh year. The words sabbath and sabbatical both come from the Hebrew word *shabath,* meaning to rest. In modern times, a sabbatical has been a period of paid leave and rejuvenation for teachers at colleges and universities, but it has recently gained a broader meaning. *See* Angelos A. Tsaklanganos, "Sabbaticals for Executives," *Personnel Journal* (May 1973).

sabotage, deliberate destruction of property or the slowing down of work in order to damage a business. During a 1910 railway strike in France, strikers destroyed some of the wooden shoes or *sabots* that held the rails in place. Sabotage soon came

into English, but it wasn't until World War II that the word gained widespread popularity as a description of the efforts of secret agents to hinder an enemy's industrial/military capabilities.

There is also the story of the French wool finishers who, in the 1820s rioted to protest the use of machinery that might supplant them. They were said to have used their wooden shoes or *sabots* to kick the machines to pieces. While this may have been the first instance of sabotage, the use of the word in English dates from the 1910 railway strike.

safety, *also* SAFETY DEPARTMENT, an organization's total effort to prevent and eliminate the causes of accidents. Some organizations have a safety department responsible for administering the various aspects of the safety program. For a text, *see* John V. Grimaldi and Rollin H. Simonds, *Safety Management,* 4th ed. (Homewood, Ill.: Richard D. Irwin, Inc., 1985). For how to staff a safety department, *see* Robert E. McClay, "Professionalizing the Safety Function," *Personnel Journal* (February 1977). *Also see* Robert W. Crandall and Lester B. Lave (eds.), *The Scientific Basis of Health and Safety Regulations* (Washington, D.C.: Brookings Institution, 1981); Alan J. Harrison, "Managing Safety and Health," *Labor Law Journal* (September 1981); L. Parmeggiani, "State of the Art: Recent Legislation on Workers' Health and Safety," *International Labour Review* (May–June 1982); Kathryn A. Gellens, "Resolving Industrial Safety Disputes: To Arbitrate or Not to Arbitrate," *Labor Law Journal* (March 1983).
    See also the following entries:
    GATEWAY COAL CO. V. UNITED MINE
        WORKERS
    MINE SAFETY AND HEALTH ADMINIS-
        TRATION
    NATIONAL SAFETY COUNCIL
    OCCUPATIONAL SAFETY AND HEALTH
        ADMINISTRATION
    TRIANGLE SHIRTWAIST FACTORY FIRE

Safety, an on-line database covering the worldwide literature on the broad interdisciplinary science of safety. It is available

job safety and health protection

The Occupational Safety and Health Act of 1970 provides job safety and health protection for workers through the promotion of safe and healthful working conditions throughout the Nation. Requirements of the Act include the following:

Employers: Each employer shall furnish to each of his employees employment and a place of employment free from recognized hazards that are causing or are likely to cause death or serious harm to his employees; and shall comply with occupational safety and health standards issued under the Act.

Employees: Each employee shall comply with all occupational safety and health standards, rules, regulations and orders issued under the Act that apply to his own actions and conduct on the job.

The Occupational Safety and Health Administration (OSHA) of the Department of Labor has the primary responsibility for administering the Act. OSHA issues occupational safety and health standards, and its Compliance Safety and Health Officers conduct jobsite inspections to ensure compliance with the Act.

Inspection: The Act requires that a representative of the employer and a representative authorized by the employees be given an opportunity to accompany the OSHA inspector for the purpose of aiding the inspection.

Where there is no authorized employee representative, the OSHA Compliance Officer must consult with a reasonable number of employees concerning safety and health conditions in the workplace.

Complaint: Employees or their representatives have the right to file a complaint with the nearest OSHA office requesting an inspection if they believe unsafe or unhealthful conditions exist in their workplace. OSHA will withhold, on request, names of employees complaining.

The Act provides that employees may not be discharged or discriminated against in any way for filing safety and health complaints or otherwise exercising their rights under the Act.

An employee who believes he has been discriminated against may file a complaint with the nearest OSHA office within 30 days of the alleged discrimination.

Citation: If upon inspection OSHA believes an employer has violated the Act, a citation alleging such violations will be issued to the employer. Each citation will specify a time period within which the alleged violation must be corrected.

The OSHA citation must be prominently displayed at or near the place of alleged violation for three days, or until it is corrected, whichever is later, to warn employees of dangers that may exist there.

Proposed Penalty: The Act provides for mandatory penalties against employers of up to $1,000 for each serious violation and for optional penalties of up to $1,000 for each nonserious violation. Penalties of up to $1,000 per day may be proposed for failure to correct violations within the proposed time period. Also, any employer who willfully or repeatedly violates the Act may be assessed penalties of up to $10,000 for each such violation.

Criminal penalties are also provided for in the Act. Any willful violation resulting in death of an employee, upon conviction, is punishable by a fine of not more than $10,000 or by imprisonment for not more than six months, or by both. Conviction of an employer after a first conviction doubles these maximum penalties.

Voluntary Activity: While providing penalties for violations, the Act also encourages efforts by labor and management, before an OSHA inspection, to reduce injuries and illnesses arising out of employment.

The Department of Labor encourages employers and employees to reduce workplace hazards voluntarily and to develop and improve safety and health programs in all workplaces and industries.

Such cooperative action would initially focus on the identification and elimination of hazards that could cause death, injury, or illness to employees and supervisors. There are many public and private organizations that can provide information and assistance in this effort, if requested.

More Information: Additional information and copies of the Act, specific OSHA safety and health standards, and other applicable regulations may be obtained from your employer or from the nearest OSHA Regional Office in the following locations:

Atlanta, Georgia
Boston, Massachusetts
Chicago, Illinois
Dallas, Texas
Denver, Colorado
Kansas City, Missouri
New York, New York
Philadelphia, Pennsylvania
San Francisco, California
Seattle, Washington

Telephone numbers for these offices, and additional Area Office locations, are listed in the telephone directory under the United States Department of Labor in the United States Government listing.

Washington, D.C.
1981
OSHA 2203

Raymond J. Donovan
Secretary of Labor

U. S. Department of Labor

Occupational Safety and Health Administration

☆U.S. Government Printing Office: 1984—421-271/11157

through: System Development Corporation, 2500 Colorado Avenue, Santa Monica, CA 90406. (800) 421-7229.

safety net, President Ronald Reagan's term for the totality of social welfare programs which, in his opinion, assure at least a subsistence standard of living for all Americans.

salary: *see* WAGES.

salary, straight: *see* STRAIGHT SALARY.

salary compression, also called WAGE COMPRESSION, according to M. Sami Kassem, in "The Salary Compression Problem," *Personnel Journal* (April 1971), salary/wage compression is "the shrinking difference of pay being given newcomers as opposed to the amount paid to the experienced regulars."

salary curve: *see* MATURITY CURVE.

salary range: *see* PAY RANGE.

Salary Reform Act of 1962, (Public Law 87-793) federal statute that provided "federal salary rates shall be comparable with private enterprise salary rates for the same levels of work."

salary review, formal examination of an employee's rate of pay in terms of his or her recent performance, changes in the cost of living and other factors.

salary structures, according to Robert E. Sibson, in "New Practices and Ideas in Compensation Administration," *Compensation Review* (Third Quarter 1974), salary structures were originally

largely conceived as boxes within which salaries must be paid. Increasingly, though, companies are viewing their salary structures essentially as a uniform accounting system, intended primarily as an information source, rather than a control mechanism. Furthermore, the use of salary structures is changing in very fundamental ways. For instance,

the use of the bottom part of the salary range in management positions is seldom used in many companies today, because paying managers at the bottom part of the range suggests that they are trainees or not qualified to do the work.

salary survey: *see* WAGE SURVEY.

salary survey, community: *see* COMMUNITY WAGE SURVEY.

sales commission: *see* COMMISSION EARNINGS.

SAM: *see* SOCIETY FOR THE ADVANCEMENT OF MANAGEMENT.

sample, any deliberately chosen portion of a larger population that is representative of that population as a whole. *See* Donald P. Warwick and Charles A. Lininger, *The Sample Survey: Theory and Practice* (New York: McGraw-Hill, 1975).
   See also BIASED SAMPLE, RANDOM SAMPLE, and REPRESENTATIVE SAMPLE.

sampling error, error caused by generalizing the behavior of a population from a sample of that population that is not representative of the population as a whole.

sampling population, entire set or universe from which a sample is drawn.

Sampson v. Murray, 415 U.S. 61 (1974), U.S. Supreme Court case, which held that the federal courts did not have the authority to issue a temporary restraining order (pending an administrative appeal to the U.S. Civil Service Commission) on behalf of a probationary federal government employee who had been discharged. A federal court's authority to review agency action does not come into play until it may be authoritatively said that the administrative decision to discharge an employee does, in fact, fail to conform to the applicable regulations. Until administrative action has become final, no court is in a position to say that such action did or did not conform to the regulations.

sandhogs, slang term for a worker who works underground digging subways, tunnels, *etc.*

sandwich management. This technique is one that is adopted most innocently. In fact, it has been perpetrated for years as managers have been encouraged to manipulate people rather than level with them. A typical statement by a sandwich manager goes something like this. "Fred, you've been doing a splendid job in many respects since you came aboard. On the other hand, there have been times when your work was so late, it caused problems for the whole department. You will have to get on the ball, son, or else we might have to transfer you to a job you can handle for sure. But I am sure we can count on you to do the right thing. Your past history indicates you have great potential." Upon analyzing that statement closely you can see a loss of "bread," neatly sandwiched between two slices of baloney. *Source:* William Thomas, "Humor for Hurdling the Mystique in Management," *Management of Personnel Quarterly* (Winter 1970).

satisfactory-performance increase, annual incremental salary step increase awarded for satisfactory performance within a single salary grade.

satisficing, also called BOUNDED RATIONALITY, term coined by Herbert A. Simon, in *Administrative Behavior* (N.Y.: Macmillan, 1947), while explaining his concept of *bounded rationality.* Simon asserts that it is impossible to ever know "all" of the facts that bear upon any given decision. Because truly rational research on any problem can never be completed, humans put "bounds" on their rationality and make decisions, not on the basis of optimal information, but on the basis of satisfactory information. Humans tend to make their decisions by satisficing— choosing a course of action that meets one's minimum standards for satisfaction. *See* John Forester, "Bounded Rationality and the Politics of Muddling Through,"

Public Administration Review (January– February 1984).

Say's law, the assertion of French economist Jean-Baptiste Say (1767– 1832) which held that general overproduction is not possible because supply creates its own demand.

scab, also called BLACKLEG, generally, an employee who continues to work for an organization while it is being struck by coworkers. Since the 1500s, scab has been used as a term for a rascal or scoundrel. Early in the 1800s, Americans started using it to refer to workers who refused to support organized efforts on behalf of their trade. A scab should be distinguished from a fink or strikebreaker who is brought into an organization only after a strike begins. Samuel Gompers, the first president of the American Federation of Labor, said that "a 'scab' is to his trade what a traitor is to his country. He is the first to take advantage of any benefit secured by united action, and never contributes anything toward its achievement." *Blackleg* is the British word for scab.

See also OLD DOMINION BRANCH NO. 496, NATIONAL ASSOCIATION OF LETTER CARRIERS V. AUSTIN and STRIKEBREAKER.

What is a Scab?

*by Jack London**

After God had finished the rattlesnake, the toad and the vampire, He had some awful substance left with which He made a SCAB. A SCAB is a two-legged animal with a corkscrew soul, a waterlogged brain, and a combination backbone made of jelly and glue. Where others have hearts he carries a tumor of rotten principles.

When a SCAB comes down the street men turn their backs and angels weep in heaven, and the devil shuts the gates of hell to keep him out. No man has a right to SCAB as long as there is a pool of water deep enough to drown his body in, or a rope long enough to hang his carcass with. Judas Iscariot was a gentleman compared with a SCAB. For betraying his Master, he had character enough to hang himself. A SCAB HASN'T!

Esau sold his birthright for a mess of pottage. Judas Iscariot sold his Savior for thirty pieces of silver. Benedict Arnold sold his country for a promise of a commission in the British Army. The modern strikebreaker sells his birthright, his country, his wife, his children, and his fellowmen for an unfulfilled promise from his employer, trust or corporation.

Esau was a traitor to himself. Judas Iscariot was a traitor to his God. Benedict Arnold was a traitor to his country.

A STRIKEBREAKER IS A TRAITOR TO HIS GOD, HIS COUNTRY, HIS FAMILY AND HIS CLASS!

---

*Jack London (1876–1916) was the author of novels such as *The Call of the Wild* (1903), *The Sea-Wolf* (1904), and *Martin Eden* (1909). He was also an avid socialist and enthusiastic union supporter.

scalar chain, also LINE OF AUTHORITY, according to Henri Fayol, *General and Industrial Management*, trans. by Constance Storrs (London: Pitman Publishing, Ltd., 1949),

the scalar chain is the chain of superiors ranging from the ultimate authority to the lowest ranks. The *line of authority* is the route followed—via every link in the chain—by all communications which start from or go to the ultimate authority. This path is dictated both by the need for some transmission and by the principle of unity of command, but it is not always the swiftest. It is even at times disastrously lengthy in large concerns, notably in governmental ones.

scaled score, score on a test when the raw score obtained has been converted to a number or position on a standard reference scale. Test scores reported to examinees and users of tests are usually scaled scores. The purpose of converting scores to a scale is to make reported scores as independent as possible of the particular form of a test an examinee has taken and of the composition of the candidate group at a particular administration. For example, the College Board Achievement tests are all reported on a scale of 200 to 800.

A score of 600 on a College Board Achievement test is intended to indicate the same level of ability from year to year.

Scanlon Plan, employee incentive plan developed in the 1930s by Joseph N. Scanlon (then an officer of the United Steelworkers of America), which seeks to enhance productivity and organizational harmony through bonus and suggestion systems. The suggestion system demanded by a "true" Scanlon Plan is so sophisticated that it is more properly considered a form of participatory management. For details, *see* Frederick G. Lesieur, *The Scanlon Plan: A Frontier in Labor-Management Cooperation* (N.Y. and Cambridge: John Wiley and the Technology Press of MIT, 1958); Frederick G. Lesieur and Elbridge Pluckett, "The Scanlon Plan Has Proved Itself," *Harvard Business Review* (October 1969); Brian E. Moore and Timothy L. Ross, *The Scanlon Way to Improved Productivity: A Practical Guide* (N.Y.: John Wiley & Sons, 1978); Michael Schuster, "The Scanlon Plan: A Longitudinal Analysis," *The Journal of Applied Behavioral Science*, Vol. 20, No. 1 (1984).

SCAT: *see* COOPERATION SCHOOL AND COLLEGE ABILITY TEST.

scapegoating, shifting the blame for a problem or failure to another person, group or organization—a common bureaucratic and political tactic. *See* Jeffrey Eagle and Peter M. Newton, "Scapegoating in Small Groups: An Organizational Approach," *Human Relations* (April 1981).

scatter diagram, display of the relationship between variables using dots on a graph.

Schecter Poultry Corp v. United States, 295 U.S. 495 (1935), Supreme Court case concerning the constitutionality of congressional delegations of authority. The court held that the separation of powers provided for in the Constitution means that

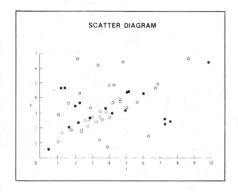

SCATTER DIAGRAM

"Congress is not permitted to abdicate or to transfer to others the essential legislative functions with which it is . . . vested." Consequently, legislative delegations would be constitutional only if Congress ". . . has itself established the standards of legal obligation. . ." Based upon these premises the court held that the promulgation of a "Live Poultry Code" under the National Industrial Recovery Act was constitutionally defective. Although *Schecter* has never been directly overruled, the courts have subsequently taken a more flexible view of legislative delegations. Had the *Schecter* rule been forcefully applied since 1935, the discretion exercised by the federal bureaucracy would have been severely constricted.

Schedule A, category used by the Office of Personnel Management (OPM) for those excepted federal positions for which it is not practicable to hold any examinations and which are not of a confidential or policy determining nature. Included here are teachers in dependent school systems overseas, faculty members of the service academies, narcotics agents for undercover work, certain part-time positions at isolated localities, positions on vessels operated by the Military Sealift Command, and many purely seasonal positions not of a continuing nature. In addition, because the OPM is forbidden by law to examine for attorneys, they have also been placed in Schedule A. There are about 75,000 positions in this schedule (This number increases during the summer months to include temporary seasonal personnel).

Schedule B, category used by the Office of Personnel Management for those excepted federal positions for which competitive examinations are impracticable, but for which the person must pass a *noncompetitive* examination. Included here are positions assigned to Navy or Air Force Communications Intelligence activities and national bank examiners in the Treasury Department. Only about 3,000 positions are covered by Schedule B.

Schedule C, category used by the Office of Personnel Management (OPM) for the excepted positions which are policy-determining or which involve a close personal relationship between the incumbent and the agency head or his/her key officials. It contains key positions that should be filled by the administration in power with persons who will fully support its political aims and policies as well as the positions of secretaries, special assistants, and other members of the immediate staffs of key officials. There are about 1,200 positions in Schedule C.

No examination is required for appointment to Schedule C jobs. Departments and agencies may recommend to OPM that a position be placed in Schedule C if they feel the duties assigned are either policy-determining or require the incumbent to serve in a confidential relationship to a key official. If OPM considers the duties of the position are actually policy-determining in nature or if they establish a confidential relationship to a key official, it places the position in Schedule C. If not, OPM rejects the recommendation. Each job is considered on an individual basis.

Schein, Edgar H. (1928–), psychologist who has written some of the most influential work on organizational psychology, organization development, and career management. Major works include: *Personnel and Organizational Change Through Group Methods: The Laboratory Approach,* with Warren Bennis (N.Y.: John Wiley, 1965); *Process*

Consultation: Its Role in Organization Development (Reading, Mass.: Addison-Wesley, 1969); *Organizational Psychology* (Englewood Cliffs, N.J.: 3rd ed., Prentice-Hall, 1980); *Professional Education: Some New Directions* (N.Y.: McGraw-Hill, 1972); *Career Dynamics: Matching Individual and Organizational Needs* (Reading, Mass.: Addison-Wesley, 1978).

Scheuer v. Rhodes, 416 U.S. 232 (1974), Supreme Court case holding that officers of the executive branch of state governments had a qualified immunity from civil suits for damages.

Schlesinger v. Ballard, 419 U.S. 498 (1975), U.S. Supreme Court case, which held that women could be judged by a more lenient standard than men in measuring their performance in the military services because their promotional opportunities were fewer.

schmoozing, collective term for all of the social interactions engaged in by employees that are seemingly unrelated to their organization's productivity.

scholarship plan, company: *see* COMPANY FELLOWSHIP PLAN.

Schwellenbach, Lewis B. (1894–1948), Secretary of Labor from 1945 to 1948.

scientific management, systematic approach to managing that seeks the "one best way" of accomplishing any given task by discovering the fastest, most efficient, and least fatiguing production methods. The job of the scientific manager, once the "one best way" was found, was to impose this procedure upon the workforce. Frederick W. Taylor is considered to be the "father" of scientific management. *See* his *Principles of Scientific Management* (N.Y.: Harper & Bros., 1911). *Also see* Samuel Haber, *Efficiency and Uplife: Scientific Management in the Progressive Era 1890-1920* (Chicago: University of Chicago Press, 1964).

See also the following entries:

GILBRETH, FRANK BUNKER AND LILLIAN MOLLER
MOTION STUDY
TAYLOR, FREDERICK W.
TIME STUDY

scientific method, an approach to research which starts with the observation of a phenomenon, then develops an hypothesis about it, and finally tests the hypothesis through experimentation. Then the process or cycle of observation-hypothesis-experimentation begins all over again.

SCII: *see* STRONG-CAMPBELL INTEREST INVENTORY.

scope of bargaining, those issues over which management and labor negotiate during the collective bargaining process. *See* Joan Weitzman, *The Scope of Bargaining in Public Employment* (N.Y.: Praeger, 1975); Robert M. Tobias, "The Scope of Bargaining in the Federal Sector: Collective Bargaining or Collective Consultation," *The George Washington Law Review* (May 1976); Stephen A. Woodbury, "The Scope of Bargaining and Bargaining Outcomes in the Public Schools," *Industrial & Labor Relations Review* (January 1985).

score, crude/raw: *see* RAW SCORE.

score, formula: *see* FORMULA SCORE.

score, scaled: *see* SCALED SCORE.

score, standard: *see* STANDARD SCORE.

Scott, Walter Dill (1869–1955), psychologist who was one of the pioneers of modern personnel management and industrial psychology. He is generally credited with having convinced the U.S. Army to use psychological techniques for the classification and assignment of men during World War I. For biography, *see* Edmund C. Lynch, *Walter Dill Scott: Pioneer in Personnel Management* (Austin, Texas: Bureau of Business Research, The University of Texas at

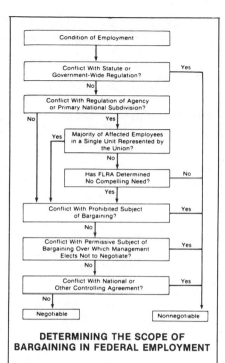

| Condition of Employment |
| Conflict With Statute or Government-Wide Regulation? | Yes |
| No |
| Conflict With Regulation of Agency or Primary National Subdivision? |
| No | Yes |
| Yes | Majority of Affected Employees in a Single Unit Represented by the Union? |
| No |
| Has FLRA Determined No Compelling Need? | No |
| Yes |
| Conflict With Prohibited Subject of Bargaining? | Yes |
| No |
| Conflict With Permissive Subject of Bargaining Over Which Management Elects Not to Negotiate? | Yes |
| No |
| Conflict With National or Other Controlling Agreement? | Yes |
| No |
| Negotiable | Nonnegotiable |

DETERMINING THE SCOPE OF BARGAINING IN FEDERAL EMPLOYMENT

Austin, 1968); Edmund C. Lynch, "Walter Dill Scott: Pioneer Industrial Psychologist," *Business History Review* (Summer 1968).

Scott, William G. (1926-), a leading authority on organizational theory and behavior. Major works include: *Human Relations in Management* (Homewood, Ill.: Richard D. Irwin, 1962); *The Management of Conflict: Appeal Systems in Organizations* (Homewood, Ill.: Richard D. Irwin, 1965); *Organizational Concepts and Analysis* (Belmont, Calif.: Dickenson, 1969); *Organization Theory: A Structural and Behavioral Analysis* (Homewood, Ill.: Richard D. Irwin, 4th ed., 1981).

screening interview, initial interview for a job that serves to determine which applicants are to be given further consideration. *See* Jack Bucalo, "The Balanced Approach to Successful Screening Interviews," *Personnel Journal* (August 1978); Larry F. Moore and J. Cameron Craik,

"Video Tape and the Screening Interview," *Personnel Journal* (March 1972).

SCSA: *see* STANDARD CONSOLIDATED STATISTICAL AREA.

scrip, temporary document entitling the bearer to something of value. This token money was once commonly used to pay workers in lieu of cash. As the scrip could only be redeemed at a company store with inflated prices, some states passed laws making it illegal to pay employees with anything but legal tender.

SDS: *see* SELF-DIRECTED SEARCH.

Sears, Roebuck, & Co. v. San Diego County District Council of Carpenters, 56 L. Ed. 2d 209 (1978), U.S. Supreme Court case, which ruled that courts may apply state trespass law to cases involving picketing that might either be protected or prohibited by the National Labor Relations Act. This holding carved out an exception for the traditional rule of federal preemption by permitting the application of state law in situations where an employer has no right to seek relief from the National Labor Relations Board if the union does not present the case to the NLRB.

seasonal adjustments, statistical modifications made to compensate for fluctuations in a time series which recur more or less regularly each year. The cause of these movements may be climatic (farm income, for example, is highest in the fall) or institutional (retail sales reach a peak just before Christmas). These seasonal movements are often so strong that they distort the underlying changes in economic data and tend to obscure trends that might be developing.

seasonal employment, also SEASONAL UNEMPLOYMENT, work that is available only during certain times of the year, such as (1) jobs picking or canning fruit in the fall, (2) jobs playing Santa Claus in a shopping mall, and (3) jobs as lifeguards at summer resorts. *Seasonal unemployment* is unemployment occasioned by the seasonal variations of particular industries. Jobs affected by the weather as in construction and agriculture are particularly susceptible to seasonal unemployment.

secondary boycott, concerted effort by a union engaged in a dispute with an employer to seek another union to boycott a fourth party (usually their employers) who, in response to such pressure, might put like pressure on the original offending employer. Secondary boycotts are forbidden by the Labor-Management Relations (Taft-Hartley) Act of 1947. For a legal analysis, *see* Ralph M. Dereshinsky, *The NLRB and Secondary Boycotts* (Philadelphia: University of Pennsylvania Press, 1972).
　　See also the following entries:
　　　BOYCOTT
　　　NATIONAL WOODWORK MANUFAC-
　　　　TURERS ASSOCIATION V. NATIONAL
　　　　LABOR RELATIONS BOARD
　　　UNFAIR LABOR PRACTICES (UNIONS)

secondary strike, strike against an employer because it is doing business with another employer whose workers are on strike.

second career: *see* CAREER CHANGE.

selection: *see* PERSONNEL SELECTION.

selection guidelines: *see* UNIFORM GUIDELINES ON EMPLOYEE SELECTION.

selection interview: *see* INTERVIEW.

selection out, euphemism for terminating an employee from a training program or employment.

selection procedure, according to the "Uniform Guidelines on Employee Selection," a selection procedure is
　　any measure, combination of measures, or procedures used as a basis for an employment decision. Selection procedures include the full range of assessment techniques from traditional paper and pencil tests, performance tests, training programs, or probationary periods and physical, educational, and work experience requirements through informal or casual interviews and unscored application forms.
　　See also UNIFORM GUIDELINES ON EMPLOYEE SELECTION.

selection ratio, number of job applicants selected compared to the number of job applicants who were available.

self-actualization, apex of Abraham Maslow's needs hierarchy, where an individual theroretically reaches self-fulfillment and becomes all that he or she is capable of becoming. The importance of the concept of self-actualization was established long before Maslow gave it voice. The 19th century poet, Robert Browning, described its essence when he said "a man's reach should exceed his grasp, or what's a heaven for?" Maslow's needs hierarchy was originally presented in "A Theory of Human Motivation," *Psychological Review* (July 1943). For a technique to measure self-actualization, *see* Charles Bonjean and Gary Vance, "A Short Form Measure of Self-Actualization," *Journal of Applied Behavioral Science* (July-August-September 1968). Also see Harold R. McAlindon, "Education for Self-Actualization," *Training and Development Journal* (October 1981).

self-appraisal, performance evaluation technique in which the employee takes the initiative in appraising his/her own performance. *See* Kenneth S. Teel, "Self-Appraisal Revisited," *Personnel Journal* (July 1978); Robert P. Steel and Nestor K. Ovalle 2nd, "Self-Appraisal Based Upon Supervisory Feedback," *Personnel Psychology* (Winter 1984).

Self-Directed Search (SDS), vocational interest inventory commonly used in vocational guidance and counseling. Administration, scoring and interpretation is performed by the individual. Consists of two booklets, the Assessment Booklet (for evaluation of individual's abilities and interests) and an Occupation Finder (a listing of 95 percent of all job types). TIME: Un-

timed. AUTHOR: John L. Holland, PUB-
LISHER: Consulting Psychologists Press,
Inc. (see TEST PUBLISHERS).

self-employed, members of the workforce
who work for themselves—in their own
trade or business—as opposed to wage
earners who are in the employ of others.
See Eugene H. Becker, "Self-Employed
Workers: An Update to 1983," *Monthly
Labor Review* (July 1983).

**Self-Employed Individuals Tax Retire-
ment Act of 1962:** see KEOGH PLAN.

self-employment tax, means by which
persons who work for themselves are provided social security coverage. Each
self-employed person must pay self-employment tax on part or all of his or her
income to help finance social security benefits, which are payable to self-employed
persons as well as wage earners.

self-fulfilling prophecy, causing something to happen by believing it will. If a
manager or teacher believes that his or her
employees or students are not capable,
they will eventually live up or down to the
manager's or teacher's expectations. For
a case study of how a manager's expectations about employee performance become a self fulfilling prophecy, see J.
Sterling Livingston, "Pygmalion in Management," *Harvard Business Review*
(July-August 1969).

self-report inventory: see PERSONALITY
INVENTORY.

semiskilled workers, employees whose
jobs are confined to well established work
routines, usually requiring a considerable
degree of manipulative ability and a limited
exercise of independent judgment.

senior civil service, as recommended by
the Hoover Commission of the 1950s, the
federal government should establish a
senior civil service "consisting of career administrators selected from all agencies of
the Government solely on the basis of
demonstrated competence to fill positions

requiring a high degree of managerial
competence." The senior civil service concept was only realized when the Civil Service Reform Act of 1978 created the
Senior Executive Service. See Leonard D.
White, "The Senior Civil Service," *Public
Administration Review* (Autumn 1955);
Paul P. Van Riper, "The Senior Civil Service and the Career System," *Public Administration Review* (Summer 1958);
William Pincus, "The Opposition to the
Senior Civil Service," *Public Administration Review* (Autumn 1958).

Senior Executive Service (SES), federal
government's top management corps, established by the Civil Service Reform Act
of 1978.

The SES includes managers at GS 16
through Executive Level IV or their equiv-
alents in the executive branch. The large
majority of SES executives are career
managers; there is a 10 percent, gov-
ernment-wide ceiling on the number who
may be noncareer. In addition, about 45
percent of SES positions are career-
reserved; that is, they can be filled only by
career executives. See "All You Ever
Wanted to Know About SES," *Civil Service Journal* (April-June 1979); Bruce
Buchanan, "The Senior Executive Service:
How Can We Tell If It Works," *Public Administration Review* (May-June 1981);
Norton E. Long, "The S.E.S. and the Public Interest," *Public Administration Review*
(May-June 1981); Bernard Rosen, "Uncertainty in the Senior Executive Service,"
Public Administration Review (March-
April 1981); William J. Lanouette, "SES
in Flames," *National Journal* (July 18,
1981); Patricia W. Ingraham and Peter W.
Colby, "Individual Motivation and Institutional Changes Under the Senior Executive Service," *Review of Public Personnel
Administration* (Spring 1982); Michael A.
Pagano, "The SES Performance Management System and Bonus Awards," *Review
of Public Personnel Administration* (Spring
1984).

See also CIVIL SERVICE REFORM ACT OF
1978.

seniority, social mechanism that gives priority to the individuals who are the most senior—have the longest service—in an organization. Seniority is often used to determine which employees will be promoted, subjected to layoff, or given/denied other employment advantages. For a legal analysis, *see* Barry A. Friedman, "Seniority Systems and the Law," *Personnel Journal* (July 1976). For contractual provisions, *see* Winston L. Tillery, "Seniority Administration in Major Agreements, *"Monthly Labor Review"* (December 1972). *Also see* Maryellen R. Kelley, "Discrimination in Seniority Systems: A Case Study," *Industrial and Labor Relations Review* (October 1982); Gene M. Grossman, "Union Wages, Temporary Layoffs, and Seniority," *The American Economic Review* (June 1983); Elaine Gale Wrong, "Arbitrator's Decisions in Seniority-Discrimination Cases," *Arbitration Journal* (December 1984).

See also the following entries:

BENEFIT SENIORITY
COMPETITIVE SENIORITY
DEPARTMENTAL SENIORITY
DOVETAIL SENIORITY
FIRE FIGHTERS LOCAL UNION NO. 1784 V. STOTTS
INTERNATIONAL BROTHERHOOD OF TEAMSTERS V. UNITED STATES
INVERSE SENIORITY
RETROACTIVE SENIORITY
SUPERSENIORITY
TRANS WORLD AIRLINES V. HARDISON

Senn v. *Tile Layer's Protective Union,* 301 U.S. 468 (1937), U.S. Supreme Court case, which held that a state anti-injunction law supporting peaceful picketing was constitutional.

sensitivity training: *see* LABORATORY TRAINING and BRADFORD, LELAND P.

separation, termination of an individual's employment for whatever reason.

separation interview: *see* EXIT INTERVIEW.

separation pay: *see* SEVERANCE PAY.

separation rate, ratio of the number of separations per hundred employees over a specified time span.

series of classes, all classes of positions involving the same kind of work, but which may vary as to the level of difficulty and responsibility and have differing grade and salary ranges. The classes in a series either have differing titles (*e.g.,* assistant accountant, associate accountant, senior accountant) or numerical designations (*e.g.,* Accountant I, Accountant II, Accountant III). Be wary of numerical designations, however. There is no uniformity in their use; an Accountant I could be either the most junior or most senior level.

See also POSITION CLASSIFICATION.

service fee, money (usually the equivalent of union dues) that non-union members of an agency shop bargaining unit pay the union for negotiating and administering the collective bargaining agreement.

See also ABOOD V. DETROIT BOARD OF EDUCATION.

service occupations, the category of jobs performed in and around private households; serving individuals in institutions and in commercial and other establishments; and protecting the public against crime, fire, accidents and acts of war. All industries employ workers in service classifications. Some of the larger groups of service workers include culinary and related food workers, cosmetologists, attendants in hospitals, barbers, janitors and porters. *See* R. E. Kutscher, J. A. Mark, "The Service-Producing Sector: Some Common Perceptions," *Monthly Labor Review* (April 1983); Michael Urquhart, "The Employment Shift to Services: Where Did It Come From?" *Monthly Labor Review* (April 1984); Irving D. Canton, "Learning to Love the Service Economy," *Harvard Business Review* (May–June 1984).

SET: *see* SHORT EMPLOYMENT TEST.

set: *see* POPULATION.

set-up time, time during the normal work

day when a worker's machine is being set up (usually by the machine's operator) prior to commencing production. Union contracts frequently provide time standards for set-up operations.

70-percent syndrome: *see* CUTTING SCORE.

706 agency, state and local fair employment practices agency named for Section 706(c) of Title VII of the Civil Rights Act of 1964, which requires aggrieved individuals to submit claims to state or local fair employment practices agencies before they are eligible to present their cases to the federal government's Equal Employment Opportunity Commission. State and local agencies that have the ability to provide the same protections provided by Title VII as would the EEOC are termed 706 agencies. The EEOC maintains a list of the 706 agencies that it formally recognizes.

sever: *see* FIRE.

severance pay, also called DISMISSAL PAY, SEPARATION PAY, and TERMINATION PAY, lump-sum payment by an employer to an employee who has been permanently separated from the organization because of a work force reduction, the introduction of labor-saving machinery, or for any reason other than "cause." The amount of a severance payment is usually determined by a schedule based on years of service and earnings. About 40 percent of all union contracts contain provisions for severance pay. *See* Edward P. Lazear, *Severance Pay, Pensions and Efficient Mobility* (Cambridge, Mass.: National Bureau of Economic Research, Inc., 1982).

Eligible federal government employees have severance pay computed on the basis of one week's salary for each year of the first 10 years of service and 2 week's salary for each year of service after 10 years. For employees over age 40, an age adjustment allowance is added to the basic allowance by computing 10 percent of the basic allowance of each year over age 40. The total severance pay that a federal employee may receive is limited to one year's pay at the rate of pay received immediately prior to separation.

See also NOLDE BROTHERS, INC. V. LOCAL NO. 358, BAKERY WORKERS.

sex differential, also RACE DIFFERENTIAL, lower than "regular" wage rate paid by an employer to female and/or black employees. Such differentials were paid before the advent of current equal employment opportunity laws and are now illegal.

sex discrimination, any disparate or unfavorable treatment of an individual in an employment situation because of his or her sex. The Civil Rights Act of 1964 makes sex discrimination illegal except where a bona fide occupational qualification is involved. For a legal analysis, *see* Jerri D. Gilbreath, "Sex Discrimination and Title VII of the Civil Rights Act," *Personnel Journal* (January 1977). *See also* Paul Osterman, "Sex Discrimination in Professional Employment: A Case Study," *Industrial and Labor Relations Review* (July 1979); Joan Acker and Donald R. Van Houten, "Differential Recruitment and Control: The Sex Structuring of Organizations," *Administrative Science Quarterly* (June 1974); Sandra Sawyer and Arthur A. Whatley, "Sexual Harassment: A Form of Sex Discrimination," *The Personnel Administrator* (January 1980); Nancy F. Rytina, "Earnings of Men and Women: A Look at Specific Occupations," *Monthly Labor Review* (April 1982); Harish C. Jain, "Canadian Legal Approaches to Sex Equality in the Workplace," *Monthly Labor Review* (October 1982).

See also the following entries:
CITY OF LOS ANGELES, DEPARTMENT OF WATER & POWER V. MANHART
DAVIS V. PASSMAN
DISCRIMINATION
GOESAERT V. CLEARY
PITTSBURGH PRESS CO. V. THE PITTSBURGH COMMISSION ON HUMAN RELATIONS
PREGNANCY DISCRIMINATION ACT OF 1978
SCHLESINGER V. BALLARD

sexist, person or organization that consciously or unconsciously practices sex discrimination. *See* Betty J. Collier and Louis N. Williams, "Towards a Bilateral Model of Sexism," *Human Relations* (February 1981).

sex plus, situation where an employer does not discriminate against all males or all females, but discriminates against a subset of either sex. *Phillips* v. *Martin Marietta,* 400 U.S. 542 (1971), is the U.S. Supreme Court case that dealt with the "sex plus" criterion for evaluating applicants for employment. Martin Marietta had a policy of hiring both sexes for a particular job but refused to hire any women with pre-school-aged children. The court found this "sex plus" policy to be in violation of Title VII of the Civil Rights Act of 1964.

sexual harassment, exists whenever an individual in a position to control or influence another's job, career, or grade uses such power to gain sexual favors or punish the refusal of such favors. Sexual harassment on the job varies from inappropriate sexual innuendo to coerced sexual relations.

Sexual harassment is an unlawful employment practice under Title VII of the Civil Rights Act of 1964, as amended. The EEOC "Guidelines on Discrimination Because of Sex" provide that unwelcome sexual advances, requests for sexual favors, and other verbal or physical conduct of a sexual nature constitute sexual harassment when:

- Submission to such conduct is made either explicitly or implicitly a term or condition of an individual's employment.
- Submission to or rejection of such conduct by an individual is used as the basis for employment decisions affecting that person
- Such conduct has the purpose or effect of unreasonably interfering with an individual's work performance or creating an intimidating, hostile, or offensive working environment.

Under the Guidelines, an employer, employment agency, joint apprenticeship

Median usual weekly earnings of men and women, full-time wage and salary workers, May 1967–78, and quarterly and annual averages, 1979–83

Date	Median weekly earnings			
	Total	Men	Women	Female-to-male ratio
May:[1]				
1967	$109	$125	$78	62.4
1969	121	142	86	60.6
1970	130	151	94	62.3
1971	138	162	100	61.7
1972	144	168	106	63.1
1973	159	188	116	61.7
1974	169	204	124	60.8
1975	185	221	137	62.0
1976	196	233	145	62.2
1977	211	252	156	61.9
1978	226	271	166	61.3
1979:				
I	238	290	182	62.8
II	242	295	183	62.0
III	243	298	187	62.8
IV	252	309	192	62.1
Annual average	244	298	186	62.4
1980:				
I	260	315	200	63.5
II	261	317	200	63.1
III	266	321	205	63.9
IV	277	334	211	63.2
Annual average	266	322	204	63.4
1981:				
I	283	342	220	64.3
II	284	343	221	64.4
III	287	345	224	64.9
IV	300	360	232	64.4
Annual average	289	347	224	64.6
1982:				
I	304	363	238	65.6
II	308	370	240	64.9
III	307	371	240	64.7
IV	316	379	248	65.4
Annual average	309	371	241	65.0
1983:				
I	319	385	252	65.5
II	320	383	253	66.1
III	320	388	251	64.7
IV	327	393	260	66.2
Annual average	322	387	254	65.6

[1]Data for 1967–78 are not strictly comparable to those for later years.
NOTE: Data are not seasonally adjusted. Earnings data were not collected in 1968.

Source: Earl F. Mellor, "Investigating the Differences in Weekly Earnings of Women and Men," Monthly Labor Review *(June 1984).*

committee, or labor organization is responsible for the acts of its agents and supervisory employees, regardless of whether the specific acts complained of were forbidden and regardless of whether the employer knew of their occurrence. An employer is also responsible for sexual harassment by co-workers where the employer knew or should have known of the conduct, unless immediate and appropriate corrective action was taken. An employer may also be responsible for sexual harassment by clients or customers. *See* Kerri Weisel, "Title VII: Legal Protection Against Sexual Harassment," *Washington Law Review* (December 1977); Lin Farley, *The Sexual Harassment of Women on the Job* (N.Y.: McGraw-Hill, 1979); Patricia A. Somers and Judith Clementson-Mohr, "Sexual Extortion in the Workplace," *The Personnel Administrator* (April 1979); Catharine A. MacKinnon, *Sexual Harassment of Working Women* (New Haven, Conn.: Yale University Press, 1979); Dail Ann Neugarten and Jay M. Shafritz, editors, *Sexuality in Organizations* (Oak Park, Ill.: Moore Publishing Co., 1980); Mary Coeli Meyer and others, *Sexual Harassment* (New York: Petrocelli, 1981); U.S. Merit Systems Protection Board, *Sexual Harassment in the Federal Workplace: Is It a Problem?* (Washington, D.C.: U.S. Government Printing Office, 1981); Patrice D. Horn and Jack C. Horn, *Sex in the Office: Power and Passion in the Workplace* (Reading, Mass.: Addison-Wesley, 1982); Robert E. Quinn and Patricia L. Lees, "Attraction and Harassment: Dynamics of Sexual Politics in the Workplace," *Organizational Dynamics* (Autumn 1984).

Shakespeare, William (1564–1616), English writer who created now classic studies in personnel management and organizational behavior. His more famous works include:

MacBeth—the story of a ruthless workaholic who allows his too ambitious wife to egg him on to the top, only to find that he can't hack it when up against a "C" section rival.

Romeo and Juliet—illustrates the dys-

functional aspects of a breakdown in communications between two competing paternalistic organizations. This situation is only temporarily rectified when informal inter-organizational communications are established at the employee level—unfortunately with poisonous results.

Hamlet—poignant case study of a sensitive young executive who fails to move up in the organizational hierarchy because of his inability to make decisions.

Othello—minority employee makes it to the top, only to find that jealousy at the office leads to murder.

King Lear—chief executive of a family business learns the perils of early retirement.

Shanker, Albert (1928–   ), became president of the United Federation of Teachers in New York City in 1964 and president of the American Federation of Teachers in 1974.

shape-up, a declining method of hiring—long common in the maritime industry—which had men line up at the beginning of each day so that they could be selected (or rejected) for work.

Shaw, Lemuel (1781–1861), chief justice of the Supreme Judicial Court of Massachusetts from 1830 to 1860 who wrote a landmark decision, in the case of *Commonwealth v. Hunt,* 4 Metcalf, 45 Mass., III (1842), which held that it was not a criminal act of conspiracy for a combination of employees or a union to refuse to work for an employer who hires non-union labor. This decision established the legality of the right to strike for higher wages. For a biography, *see* Leonard W. Levy, *Law of the Commonwealth and Chief Justice Shaw* (Cambridge, Mass.: Harvard University Press, 1957).

sheepskin psychosis: *see* CREDENTIALISM.

Sheldon, Oliver (1894–1951), English businessman who was the first to provide a philosophical basis for the identification of management as a profession. In *The Philosophy of Management* (London: Pitman, 1923), he asserted that management was separate from both capital and labor; and that, as a profession, its primary responsibility was "social and communal."

sheltered workshops, places of employment that offer a controlled, noncompetitive environment for persons unable to compete in the regular world of work because of physical or mental disabilities. For a history, *see* Nathan Nelson, *Workshops for the Handicapped in the United States: An Historical and Developmental Perspective* (Springfield, Ill.: Charles C. Thomas, 1971).
　　See also WAGNER-O'DAY ACT.

Shelton v. Tucker, 364 U.S. 479 (1960), U.S. Supreme Court case, which dealt with the questions of whether public employees could have membership in subversive organizations, organizations with illegal objectives, and unions. Their right to join the latter was upheld. With regard to the former, it was held that there could be no general answer. Rather, each case has to be judged on the basis of whether a public employee actually supports an organization's illegal aims, because, as the Supreme Court expressed it, "Those who join an organization but do not share its unlawful purposes and who do not participate in its unlawful activities surely pose no threat, either as citizens or as public employees." Consequently, it is incumbent upon public employers seeking to dismiss employees for membership in subversive organizations or those with illegal purposes to prove that the employees actually shared in the subversive organization's objectionable aims and activities.

Sherbert v. Verner, 374 U.S. 398 (1963), U.S. Supreme Court case, which held it was unconstitutional to disqualify a person for unemployment compensation benefits solely because that person refused to accept employment that would require working on Saturday contrary to his or her religious belief.

Sherman Antitrust Act of 1890, also called SHERMAN ACT, federal statute that held "every contract, combination in the form of trust or otherwise, or conspiracy, in restraint of trade or commerce . . . , is hereby declared to be illegal." While the statute was directed at industrial monopolies, the courts used the act punitively against the budding union movement. Subsequent legislation (the Clayton Act of 1914) exempted unions from the Sherman Act prohibitions on the restraint of trade.
　　See also the following entries:
　　　ANTITRUST LAWS
　　　BEDFORD CUT STONE COMPANY V. JOURNEYMEN STONE CUTTERS' ASSOCIATION
　　　LAWLOR V. LOEWE
　　　UNITED MINE WORKERS V. PENNINGTON
　　　UNITED STATES V. HUTCHESON

shift, fixed: *see* FIXED SHIFT.

shift, split: *see* BROKEN TIME.

shift premium, also called SHIFT DIFFERENTIAL, extra compensation paid as an inducement to accept shift work.

shift work, formal tour of duty that is mostly outside of "normal" daytime business hours. According to Richard A. Edwards, in "Shift Work: Performance and Satisfaction," *Personnel Journal* (November 1975), an examination of the research on the efficiency of night or shift workers seems to indicate that it is "a physiological fact of life that night shift workers will never perform with the same efficiency as the other two shifts."
　　Also see Peter Finn, "The Effects of Shift Work on the Lives of Employees," *Monthly Labor Review* (October 1981); Jane C. Hood and Nancy Milazzo, "Shiftwork, Stress and Well-being," *Personnel Administrator* (December 1984); Gerald A. Benjamin, "Shift Workers," *Personnel Journal* (June 1984).

shop committee, group of union members in the same organizational unit who have been selected to speak for the union membership on any of a variety of issues.

shop steward: *see* STEWARD.

Short Employment Test (SET), three tests that measure verbal, numerical and clerical abilities of applicants for clerical positions. Developed to supplement tests being used by member banks of the American Bankers Association in their selection of clerical workers.. TIME: 15/20 minutes. AUTHORS: G. K. Bennett and Marjorie Gelink. PUBLISHER: Psychological Corporation (*see* TEST PUBLISHERS).

Short Tests of Clerical Ability, series of tests for job applicants in various clerical areas used for employment selection and placement in business and industry settings. Test series includes: Short Occupational Knowledge Test for Bookkeepers, Short Occupational Knowledge Test for Office Machine Operators, and Short Occupational Knowledge Test for Secretaries. TIME: 10/15 minutes each test. AUTHORS: Bruce A. Campbell and Suellen O. Johnson. PUBLISHER: Science Research Associates, Inc. (*see* TEST PUBLISHERS).

showing of interest, evidence of membership—the requirement that a union must show that it has adequate support from employees in a proposed bargaining unit before a representation election can be held. A "showing of interest" is usually demonstrated by signed authorization cards.

Shultz, George P. (1920-   ), Secretary of Labor from 1969 to 1970, director of the Office of Management and Budget from 1970 to 1972, Secretary of the Treasury from 1972 to 1974, and Secretary of State from 1982 to present.

sick leave, leave of absence, usually with pay, granted to employees who cannot attend work because of illness. *See* Charles N. Weaver, "Influence of Sex, Salary and Age on Seasonal Use of Sick Leave," *Personnel Journal* (August 1970); Maureen

Heneghan and Sigmund G. Ginsberg, "Use of Sick Leave," *Personnel Administration* (September–October 1970).

sick-leave bank, arrangement that allows employees to pool some of their paid sick-leave days in a common fund so that they may draw upon that fund if extensive illness uses up their remaining paid time off. Sick-leave banks have tended to discourage absenteeism; because, with everyone jointly owning days in the bank, there is some psychological pressure on workers not to use their sick-leave unless they are really sick.

Sidney: *see* CLEAR IT WITH SIDNEY.

significance, also called STATISTICAL SIGNIFICANCE, degree to which one can be confident in the reliability of a statistical measure. For example, a confidence level of .05 means that the statistical finding would occur by chance in only one sample out of every twenty.

Silicon Valley, that part of the San Francisco Bay Area where there is a concentration of manufacturers who produce semiconductors, microelectronic chips out of silicon, and computers. The phrase is gradually coming to mean any concentration of computer related industries. *See* Everett M. Rogers and Judith K. Larsen, "Silicon Valley Confronts Japan," *Society* (July–August 1982); Dirk Hanson, *The New Alchemists: Silicon Valley and the Microelectronics Revolution* (Boston: Little, Brown, 1982); Everett M. Rogers and Judith K. Larson, *Silicon Valley Fever: Growth of High-Technology Culture* (New York: Basic Books, 1984).

silver-circle rate, higher than standard pay rate based upon length of service.

Simon, Herbert A. (1916-   ), awarded the Nobel Prize for Economics in 1978 for his pioneering work in management decision making, Simon is best known to the personnel world for his equally impressive contributions to our understanding of organizational behavior. Major works include: *Administrative Behavior* (N.Y.: Macmillan, 1947); *Public Administration,* with D. Smithburg and V. Thompson (N.Y.: Knopf, 1950); *Models of Man: Social and Rational* (N.Y.: John Wiley, 1958); *The New Science of Management Decision* (N.Y.: Harper & Row, 1960); *The Shape of Automation for Men and Management* (N.Y.: Harper & Row, 1965); *Human Problem Solving,* with Allen Newell (Englewood Cliffs, N.J.: Prentice-Hall, 1972).

See also PROVERBS OF ADMINISTRATION and SATISFICING.

simulation: *see* GAMING SIMULATION.

Sinclair Refining* v. *Atkinson: *see* BOYS MARKET V. RETAIL CLERKS' LOCAL 770.

sinecure, any position for which a salary is extracted but little or no work is expected. This was originally an eccelesiastical term, which meant a church office that did not require the care of souls. Sinecure is Latin for "without care."

Siney, John (1831-1880), president of the first national miner's union, the Miners' National Association. For a biography, *see* Edward Pinkowski, *John Siney: The Miners Martyr* (Philadelphia: Sunshine Press, 1963).

single rate: *see* FLAT RATE.

SIT: *see* SLOSSON INTELLIGENCE TEST.

sit-down strike, also STAY-IN STRIKE, any work stoppage during which the strikers remain at their work stations and refuse to leave the employer's premises in order to forestall the employment of strikebreakers. This kind of strike gained widespread publicity in the 1930s as a tactic of the unions in the rubber and automobile industries. A sit-down strike that lasts for a substantial period of time is then called a *stay-in strike.* For a history, *see* Daniel Nelson (ed.), "The Beginning of the Sit-Down Era: The Reminiscences of Rex Murray," *Labor History* (Winter 1974); Sidney Fine, *Sit-Down: The General Motors Strike of*

1936-1937 (Ann Arbor: University of Michigan Press, 1969).

In 1939, the U.S. Supreme Court in *National Labor Relations Board* v. *Fansteel Metallurgical Corp.,* 306 U.S. 240 (1939), ruled that the right to strike did not extend to the use of sit-down strikes and that employees discharged under such circumstances had no reinstatement rights under the National Labor Relations (Wagner) Act of 1935. The Court held that a sit-down strike

> was an illegal seizure of the buildings in order to prevent their use by the employer in a lawful manner and thus by acts of force and violence to compel the employer to submit. When the employees resorted to that sort of compulsion they took a position outside the protection of the statute and accepted the risk of the termination of their employment upon grounds aside from the exercise of the legal rights which the statute was designed to conserve . . . .

situational management: *see* CONTINGENCY MANAGEMENT.

Sixteen Personality Factor Questionnaire (16PF), assesses sixteen basic personality dimensions (*i.e.,* practical vs. imaginative, relaxed vs. tense, introversion vs. extraversion, trusting vs. suspicious, humble vs. assertive, emotionally stable vs. affected by feelings, etc. Designed for use with individuals age 16 and over. TIME: Varies. AUTHORS: R. B. Cattell, H. W. Eber, and M. M. Tatsuoka. PUBLISHER: Institute for Personality and Ability Testing (*see* TEST PUBLISHERS).

skewness, tendency of a distribution to depart from symmetry or balance around the mean. If the scores tend to cluster at the lower end of the distribution, the distribution is said to be positively skewed; if they tend to cluster at the upper end of the distribution, the distribution is said to be negatively skewed.

skill differential, differences in wage rates paid to workers employed in occupational categories requiring varying levels of skill.

skilled labor, workers who, having trained for a relatively long time, have mastered jobs of considerable skill requiring the exercise of substantial independent judgment. *See* W. Franke and D. Sokel, *The Shortage of Skilled and Technical Workers* (Lexington, Mass.: Lexington Books, 1970); Russell W. Rumberger, "The Changing Skill Requirements of Jobs in the U. S. Economy," *Industrial and Labor Relations Review* (July 1981).

skills, physical or manipulative activities requiring knowledge for their execution.

skills survey, also called SKILLS INVENTORY, comprehensive collection and examination of data on the workforce to determine the composition and level of employees' skills, knowledges, and abilities so that they can be more fully utilized and/or developed to fill the staffing needs of an organization. A skills survey or inventory may at times be the process of collecting data and at other times the product as represented by a collection of data in a variety of forms. To be effective, skills data must also be arranged in such a manner that the information gathered can be readily accessible for management use. *See* John A. R. Jons, "A Skills Audit," *Training and Development Journal* (September 1980).

Skinner, B. F. (1904–), full name FREDERIC BURRHUS SKINNER, one of the most influential of behavioral psychologists, inventor of the teaching machine, and generally considered to be the "father" of programmed instruction. Major works include: *Waldon Two* (N.Y.: Macmillan 1948, 1966); *Science and Human Behavior* (N.Y.: Free Press, 1953, 1965); *The Technology of Teaching* (N.Y.: Appleton-Century-Crofts, 1968); *Beyond Freedom and Dignity* (N.Y.: Knopf, 1971).

slide-rule discipline, approach to discipline that eliminates supervisory discretion and sets very specific quantitative standards as the consequences of specific violations. For example, a discipline policy based on this concept might hold that any

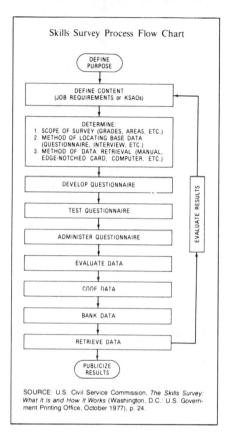

Skills Survey Process Flow Chart

DEFINE PURPOSE

DEFINE CONTENT (JOB REQUIREMENTS or KSAOs)

DETERMINE:
1. SCOPE OF SURVEY (GRADES, AREAS, ETC.)
2. METHOD OF LOCATING BASE DATA (QUESTIONNAIRE, INTERVIEW, ETC.)
3. METHOD OF DATA RETRIEVAL (MANUAL, EDGE-NOTCHED CARD, COMPUTER, ETC.)

DEVELOP QUESTIONNAIRE

TEST QUESTIONNAIRE

ADMINISTER QUESTIONNAIRE

EVALUATE DATA

CODE DATA

BANK DATA

RETRIEVE DATA

PUBLICIZE RESULTS

EVALUATE RESULTS

SOURCE: U.S. Civil Service Commission, *The Skills Survey: What It Is and How It Works* (Washington, D.C.: U.S. Government Printing Office, October 1977), p. 24.

employee who is late for work more than four times in a 30-day period would be "automatically" suspended for three days.

Sloan Management Review, professional management journal of the Alfred P. Sloan School of Management at the Massachusetts Institute of Technology. It is published three times each academic year (Fall, Winter, and Spring) and has as its principal goal the exchange of information between academic and business communities.

Sloan Management Review
Alfred P. Sloan School of Management
Massachusetts Institute of Technology
Cambridge, MA 02139

Slosson Intelligence Test (SIT), brief intelligence test that is individually and verbally administered. Scores correlate highly with tests that normally take one hour or more. Items are based in part upon the Stanford-Binet Intelligence Scale, Third Revision and the Gesell Developmental Schedules. TIME: 10/30 minutes. AUTHOR: Richard L. Slosson. PUBLISHER: Slosson Educational Publications (*see* TEST PUBLISHERS).

slot, position in an organization.

slowdown, deliberate reduction of output by employees. Such efforts are usually designed to bring economic pressure upon an employer without incurring the costs of a strike. *See* Richard S. Hammett, Joel Seidman, and Jack London, "The Slowdown as a Union Tactic," *Journal of Political Economy* (April 1957).

small-group research, also GROUP, study of small groups. A *group* consists of a number of individuals who interact with each other in a particular social setting. Generally, groups are classified as "small" when each member can at least take personal cognizance of all other members. This distinguishes small groups from social units that are so large that it is impossible for each member to be aware of all others. For the pioneering concepts of small-group research, *see* George C. Homans, *The Human Group* (N.Y.: Harcourt, Brace, Jovanovich, 1950); Robert T. Golembiewski, *The Small Group: An Analysis of Research Concepts and Operations* (Chicago: University of Chicago Press, 1962); A. Paul Hare, *Handbook of Small Group Research* (N.Y.: The Free Press, 2nd ed., 1976).
　　See also GROUP DYNAMICS and ORGANIZATION DEVELOPMENT.

Small Parts Dexterity Test, Crawford: *see* CRAWFORD SMALL PARTS DEXTERITY TEST.

Smith Act: *see* ALIEN REGISTRATION ACT OF 1940.

Smith, Adam (1723-1790), the Scottish economist who provided the first systematic analysis of economic phenomena and the intellectual foundation for laissez-faire capitalism. In *The Wealth of Nations* (1776) Smith discovered an "invisible hand" that automatically promotes the general welfare so long as individuals are allowed to pursue their self-interest. It has become customary for organization theorists to trace the lineage of present day theories to Smith's concept of the division of labor. Greater specialization of labor was one of the pillars of the "invisible hand" market mechanism with which the greatest rewards would go to those who were the most efficient in the competitive marketplace. As Smith's work marks the beginning of economics as an identifiable discipline, he is often referred to as the "father" of economics. *See* N. R. Goodwin and Bruce Mazlish, "The Wealth of Adam Smith," *Harvard Business Review* (July-August 1983).

Smith-Hughes Act of 1917, federal vocational educational act that established the principles of federal financial aid and cooperation with the states in promoting public vocational education.

Smith, Oberlin (1840-1926), a precursor of Frederick W. Taylor who is credited with creating the first system of mnemonic symbols for machine parts.

Smith v. Arkansas State Highway Employees, Local 1315, 60 L. Ed. 2d 360 (1979), U.S. Supreme Court case, which held that the Arkansas State Highway Commission's refusal to consider a Highway Department employee's grievance, when submitted by a union rather than by the employee, did not violate 1st Amendment rights.

smoking, a form of worksite air pollution. For the controversy, *see* Robert L. Jauvtis, "The Rights of Nonsmokers in the Workplace: Recent Developments," *Labor Law Journal* (March 1983); William L. Weis, Horace R. Kornegay and Lewis Solomon, "The Fiery Debate Over Smoking At Work," *Business and Society Review* (Fall 1984).

smorgasbord benefits plan: see CAFE-TERIA BENEFITS PLAN.

social audit, defined by Raymond A. Bauer and Dan H. Fenn, Jr., in "What *is* a Corporate Social Audit?" *Harvard Business Review* (January-February 1973), as "a commitment to systematic assessment of and reporting on some meaningful, definable domain of a company's activities that have social impact." *Also see:* John William Humble, *Social Responsibility Audit: A Management Tool for Survival* (New York: AMACOM, 1973); Clark C. Abt, *The Social Audit for Management* (New York: AMACOM, 1977).

social darwinism, Charles Darwin's concept of the "survival of the fittest" applied to human society.

social equity, normative standard holding that equity, rather than efficiency, is the major criterion for evaluating the desirability of a policy or program. *See* H. George Frederickson, Symposium Editor, "Social Equity and Public Administration," *Public Administration Review* (January-February 1974); Arthur M. Oken, *Equity and Efficiency: The Big Tradeoff* (Washington, D.C.: Brookings Institution, 1975).

social indicators, statistical measures that aid in the description of conditions in the social environment (*i.e.,* measures of income distribution, poverty, health, physical environment). *See* Raymond Bauer, *Social Indicators* (Cambridge, Mass.: M.I.T. Press, 1967); Raymond D. Gastil, "Social Indicators and Quality of Life," *Public Administration Review* (November-December 1970); Bureau of the Census, U.S. Department of Commerce, *Social Indicators 1976; Selected Data on Social Conditions and Trends in the United States* (Washington, D.C.: Government Printing Office, 1977); W. A. McIntosh, G. E. Klonglan and L. D. Wilcox, "Theoretical Issues and Social Indicators: A Societal Process Approach," *Policy Sciences* (September 1977); Fremont Kast, "Scanning the Future Environment: Social Indicators," *California Management Review* (Fall 1980).

social insurance, any benefit program that a state makes available to the members of its society in time of need and as a matter of right.

socialism, a system of government in which many of the means of production and trade are owned or run by the government and in which many human welfare needs are provided directly by the government. *Socialism* may or may not be democratic.

social reference group: see REFERENCE GROUP.

social responsibility of business, a vague term which implies that a business has an obligation to its society other than seeking a profit in a legal manner. The *social audit,* a systematic assessment of a company's actions that have social impact, is a major way of measuring just how socially responsible a company is—at least in the eyes of the "social auditor." *See* Phillip L. Cochran and Robert A. Wood, "Corporate Social Responsibility and Financial Performance," *Academy of Management Journal* (March 1984); Melanie Lawrence, "Social Responsibility: How Companies Become Involved in Their Communities," *Personnel Journal* (July 1982).

social security, once defined by Britain's Lord Beveridge as "a job when you can work and an income when you can't." In the United States, social security is the popular name for the Old Age, Survivors, and Disability Insurance (OASDI) system established by the Social Security Act of 1935. At first, social security only covered private sector employees upon retirement. In 1939, the law was changed to pay survivors when the worker died, as well as certain dependents when the worker retired. In the 1950s, coverage was extended to include most self-employed persons, most state and local employees, household and farm employees, members of the armed forces, and members of the clergy. Today, almost all U.S. jobs are covered by social security.

Disability insurance was added in 1954 to give workers protection against loss of earnings due to total disability. The social security program was expanded again in 1965 with the enactment of Medicare, which assured hospital and medical insurance protection to people 65 and over. Since 1973, Medicare coverage has been available to people under 65 who have been entitled to disability checks for 2 or more consecutive years and to people with permanent kidney failure who need dialysis or kidney transplants. Amendments enacted in 1972 provide that social security benefits will increase automatically with the cost of living. *See* Alicia H. Munnell, *The Future of Social Security* (Washington D.C.: The Brookings Institution, 1977); Robert M. Ball, *Social Security: Today and Tomorrow* (N.Y.: Columbia University Press, 1978); Martha Derthick, *Policymaking for Social Security* (Washington, D.C.: The Brookings Institution, 1979); Edward Wynne, *Social Security: A Reciprocity System Under Pressure* (Boulder, Colo.: Westview Press, 1980); Henry J. Aaron, *Economic Effects of Social Security* (Washington, D.C., The Brookings Institution, 1982).

See also the following entires:
HELVERING V. DAVIS
MEDICARE
OLD AGE, SURVIVORS, AND DISABILITY
INSURANCE

Social Security Act of 1935, federal statute that, as amended, is the foundation of the nation's social insurance program. For histories, *see* Edwin E. White, *The Development of the Social Security Act* (Madison: University of Wisconsin Press, 1963); Roy Lubove, *The Struggle for Social Security: 1900-1935* (Cambridge, Mass.: Harvard University Press, 1968); J. Douglas Brown, *An American Philosophy of Social Security: Evolution and Issues* (Princeton: Princeton University Press, 1972).

See also OLD AGE, SURVIVORS, AND DIS-

ABILITY INSURANCE and UNEMPLOYMENT INSURANCE.

Society for Personnel Administration: *see* INTERNATIONAL PERSONNEL MANAGEMENT ASSOCIATION.

Society for the Advancement of Management (SAM), formed in 1912 by colleagues of Frederick W. Taylor as a professional society dedicated to the discussion and promotion of scientific management, SAM is now a peer training organization "devoted to helping managers develop professionally through communication and interaction with other managers."

> *Society for the Advancement of Management*
> 135 West 50th Street
> New York, NY 10020
> (212) 586-8100

sociogram, diagram showing the interactions between members of a group. Typically, it has circles representing people and arrows extending from those circles pointing out the other people (circles) that are liked, disliked, etc.

sociology, occupational: *see* OCCUPATIONAL SOCIOLOGY.

sociology of work: *see* OCCUPATIONAL SOCIOLOGY.

sociometry, technique for discovering the patterns of interpersonal relationships that exist within a group. A sociometric analysis typically has each member of the group express his or her choices for or against other members of the group. A common question on such surveys is "who should be the leader of the group?" The ensuing preference and rejection patterns can be used to construct sociograms or social maps. For the pioneering work in sociometric methodologies, *see* J. L. Moreno, "Contributions of Sociometry to Research Methodology in Sociology," *American Sociological Review* (June 1947); J. L. Moreno (ed.), *The Sociometry Reader* (Glencoe, Ill.: The Free Press, 1960). For an evaluation of its usefulness, *see* B. J. Speroff, "Sociometry: A Key to the Informal Organization," *Personnel Journal* (February 1968).

socio-technical systems, concept that a work group is neither a technical nor a social system, but an interdependent socio-technical system. Research on this concept was pioneered in the early 1950s by the Tavistock Institute of Human Relations in London. For accounts by the original researchers, *see* F. E. Emery and E. L. Trist, "Socio-Technical Systems," C. W. Churchman and M. Verhulst (eds.), *Management Science, Models, and Techniques* (London: Pergamon, 1960), Vol II; Fred E. Emery, "Characteristics of Socio-Technical Systems," Louis E. Davis and James C. Taylor (eds.), *Design of Jobs* (Baltimore: Penguin Books, 1972). *See also* Thomas G. Cummings and Suresh Srivastva, *Management of Work: A Socio-Technical Systems Approach* (Kent State University Press, 1977); William A. Pasmore and John J. Sherwood, *Socio-technical Systems: A Sourcebook* (La-Jolla, Calif.: University Associates, 1978).

Socrates (470-399 B.C.), ancient Greek philosopher who established the intellectual foundations of modern employment testing when he asserted that "The unexamined life is not worth living."

soldier, in the industrial world, to mal-inger, to shrink one's duty, to feign illness, or to make a pretense of working. The usage comes from naval history. In earlier centuries, soldiers aboard ship did not have duties as arduous as those of the regular ship's company. So the sailors made soldiering synonymous with loafing and other nonproductive activities.

solidarity, union unity; a sense of common purpose. Solidarity is also the name of the Polish workers' free union movement led by Lech Walesa. *See* Robert Eringer, *Strike for Freedom: The Story of Lech Walesa and the Polish Solidarity* (New York: Dodd, Mead, 1982); Horst Brand, "Solidarity's Proposals for Reforming Poland's Economy," *Monthly Labor Review* (May 1982); Alain Touraine and others, *Solidarity — The Analysis of a Social Movement: Poland 1980-1981* (New York: Cambridge University Press, 1983).

Solidarity Forever, perhaps the most famous of all union songs. Like many union songs it was a parody of a well-known hymn and should be sung to the tune of *The Battle Hymn of the Republic.*

> It is we who plowed the prairies, built the cities where they trade,
> Dug the mines and built the workshops, endless miles of railroad laid;
> Now we stand outcast and starving mid the wonders we have made
> But the union makes us strong!

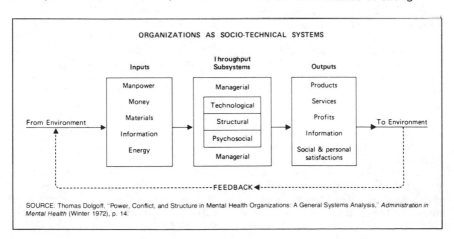

ORGANIZATIONS AS SOCIO-TECHNICAL SYSTEMS

SOURCE: Thomas Dolgoff, "Power, Conflict, and Structure in Mental Health Organizations: A General Systems Analysis," *Administration in Mental Health* (Winter 1972), p. 14.

Solidarity forever!
Solidarity forever!
Solidarity forever!
For the union makes us strong!

sovereign immunity, a government's freedom from being sued for damages in all but special situations where it consents to suit by passing statutes allowing it.

See also IMMUNITY.

sovereignty, the concept that there must be a single repository of supreme political authority and power in a society; for example, a king is a sovereign. In the United States the people are sovereign and government is considered their agent. But sovereignty presents serious problems to public sector collective bargaining—at least in theory.

First of all, it makes it impossible to consider the collective bargaining process as negotiations between co-equal partners. What does it mean to say that a public sector union is the equal of the government? Would anyone consider the National Association of Letter Carriers to be the equal of the United States government?

Second, a strike against the agent of the sovereign can be viewed as an extremely antisocial act, aimed at harming the society itself. This is all the more so when the governmental function that is struck directly deals with the exercise of sovereignty, such as policing.

Third, there are many matters in public employment that involve considerations of working conditions *and* public policy. For example, should there be a civilian review board to examine police activities? Should teachers be able to bargain over school calendars and the number of pupils per classroom? Generally speaking, any society prefers to make these and other public policies through its political institutions, rather than through collective bargaining between its government and a private association.

The courts and state statutes have gradually eroded the importance of sovereignty as a barrier to collective bargaining by public employees. But even as recently as 1968 it was used by the state of Nevada to prohibit collective bargaining with its public employees. More importantly, though, contemporary restrictions on the scope of bargaining in the public sector can be traced to concerns that stem directly from the matter of sovereignty. In essence, collective bargaining demands that the sovereign sacrifice some of its authority; but this has not been done quietly, cheerfully or even completely. *See* Sar Levitan and Alexandra B. Noden, *Working for the Sovereign: Employee Relations in the Federal Government* (Baltimore, Md.: The Johns Hopkins University Press, 1983).

Spalding* v. *Vilas, 161 U.S. 483 (1896), Supreme Court case granting absolute immunity from civil suit for damages to the Postmaster General of the United States and, by implication, to the heads of other federal departments.

See also the following entries:
  BARR V. MATTEO
  BUTZ V. ECONOMOU
  WOOD V. STRICKLAND

Spanish Speaking Program, also HISPANIC EMPLOYMENT PROGRAM, federal government program established on November 5, 1970 to call attention to the needs of the Spanish-speaking in federal employment. It is an integral part of the government's total EEO effort and is designed to assure equal employment opportunity for the Spanish-speaking in all aspects of federal employment. In March 1978, the name of the Spanish Speaking Program was changed to the Hispanic Employment Program. *See* Office of the Spanish Speaking Program, U.S. Civil Service Commission, *Spanish Speaking Program: A Guidebook for Coordinators* (Washington, D.C.: U.S. Government Printing Office, 1975). *See also* Harry P. Pachon, "Hispanics in Local Government: A Growing Force," *Public Management* (October 1980).

span of control, extent of a manager's responsibility. The span of control has usually been expressed as the number of subordinates that a manager should supervise. Sir Ian Hamilton, *The Soul and Body* of an Army (London: Edward Arnold & Co., 1921), is generally credited with having first asserted that the "average human brain finds its effective scope in handling from three to six other brains." A. V. Graicunas took a mathematical approach to the concept and demonstrated, in "Relationship in Organization," Luther Gulick and Lyndall Urwick (eds.), *Papers on the Science of Administration* (N.Y.: Institute of Public Administration, 1937), that as the number of subordinates reporting to a manager increases arithmetically, the number of possible interpersonal interactions increased geometrically. Building upon Graicunas' work, Lyndall F. Urwick boldly asserts, in "The Manager's Span of Control," *Harvard Business Review* (May-June 1956), that "no superior can supervise directly the work of more than five or, at the most, six subordinates whose work interlocks." Studies on the concept of span of control abound but there is no consensus on an "ideal" span. *Also see* John Udell, "An Empirical Test of Hypotheses Relating to Span of Control," *Administrative Science Quarterly* (December 1967); Michael Keren and David Levhari, "The Optimum Span of Control in a Pure Hierarchy," *Management Science* (November 1979); Robert D. Dewar and Donald P. Simet, "A Level Specific Prediction of Spans of Control Examining the Effects of Size, Technology, and Specialization," *Academy of Management Journal* (March 1981).

spatial relations, measure of an individual's ability for rapid and dexterous manipulation of pieces and parts relative to one another (*i.e.*, perceiving geometric relationships).

Spearman-Brown Formula, formula for determining the relationship between the reliability of a test and its length.

specification, also called JOB SPECIFICATION and CLASS SPECIFICATION, written description of the duties and responsibilities of a class of positions. Specifications usually include: the title of the position; a general statement of the nature of the work; examples of typical tasks; the minimum requirements and qualifications for the position; the knowledges, skills, and abilities essential for satisfactory performance; and the assigned salary range.

Specifications are designed to highlight those aspects of a position that are significant for classification purposes. They are descriptive, not restrictive. They are not expected to include all of the possible duties that might make up an individual position.

See also POSITION CLASSIFICATION.

speededness, appropriateness of a test in terms of the length of time allotted. For most purposes, a good test will make full use of the examination period but not be so speeded that an examinee's rate of work will have an undue influence on the score received.

speed rating, performance rating that compares the speed with which an employee performs specific tasks against an observer's standard or norm.

speed test, term loosely applied to any test that few can complete within the allotted time or, more technically, a test consisting of a large number of relatively easy items so that a high score depends on how fast an examinee can work within a time limit.

speed-up, also STRETCH-OUT, terms referring to any effort by employers to obtain an increase in productivity without a corresponding increase in wages.

speed-up boy, derogatory term for an "efficiency expert."

spillover effect, also EXTERNALITIES, benefits or costs that accrue to parties other than the buyer of a good or service. For the most part, the benefits of private goods and services enure to the exclusive benefit of the buyer (*i.e.*, new clothes, a television set, etc.). In the case of public goods, however, the benefit or cost usually spills over onto third parties. A new airport, for example, not only benefits its users but spills over onto the population at large in both positive and negative ways. Benefits might include improved air service for a community, increased tourism and attraction of new businesses while costs might include noise, pollution and traffic congestion. *See* E. J. Mishan, "The Postwar Literature on Externalities: An Interpretive Essay," *Journal of Economic Literature* (March 1971); Guy Black, "Externalities and Structure in PPB," *Public Administration Review* (November-December 1971).

spiral-omnibus test, test in which the various kinds of tasks are distributed throughout the test (instead of being grouped together) and are in cycles of increasing difficulty. There is only one timing and one score for such a test.

split commission, awarding of partial credit and compensation to each of several sales persons when each is directly involved in completing a sale. The normal commission is divided among the recipients.

split-dollar life insurance, also called SUPPLEMENTAL LIFE INSURANCE, life insurance for employees paid for by an employer. In the event of the covered employee's death, the employer totally recovers the paid premiums from the benefit sum with the remainder distributed to the employee's beneficiaries. *See* Robert B. Morley, "New Uses of Supplemental Life Insurance," *The Personnel Administrator* (May 1975).

split-half reliability, measure of the reliability of a test obtained by correlating scores on one half of a test with scores on the other half and correcting for the reduced size.

split labor market, according to Edna Bonacich, in "A Theory of Ethnic Antagonism: The Split Labor Market," *American Sociological Review* (October 1972), "to be split, a labor market must contain at least two groups of workers whose price

of labor differs for the same work, or would differ if they did the same work."

split shift: *see* BROKEN TIME.

split-the-difference, collective bargaining tactic in which both sides agree to a settlement half way between their bargaining positions. For a lesson on strategy, *see* Roger L. Bowlby and William R. Schriver, "Bluffing and the 'Split-the-Difference' Theory of Wage Bargaining," *Industrial and Labor Relations Review* (January 1978).

Sprading, Abe L. (1885-1970), president of the Amalgamated Association of Street, Electric Railway and Motor Coach Employees of America from 1946 to 1959.

SSI: *see* SUPPLEMENTAL SECURITY INCOME.

staff, specialists who assist line managers in carrying out their duties. Generally, staff units do not have the power of decision, command, or control of operations. Rather, they make recommendations (which may or may not be adopted) to the line personnel.

staffing, one of the most basic functions of management and usually considered synonymous with employment—that is, the process of hiring people to perform work for the organization. Staffing defines the organization by translating its objectives and goals into a specific work plan. It structures the responsibilities of the organization's human resources into a work system by establishing who will perform what function, and have what authority. Staffing must also make the employment, advancement, and compensation processes satisfy the criteria of equity and due process while at the same time relating their processes to the overall organizational structure in order to ensure their relevance. Staffing is the essence of the personnel management process. *See* Ruth G. Shaeffer, *Staffing Systems: Managerial and Professional Jobs* (New York: Conference Board, 1972); Benjamin Schneider, *Staffing Organizations* (Pacific

Palisades, CA: Goodyear Publishing Co., 1976); Oscar A. Ornati, Edward J. Giblin and Richard R. Floersch, *The Personnel Department: Its Staffing and Budgeting* (New York: American Management Associations, 1982); Judy D. Olian and Sara L. Rynes, "Organizational Staffing: Integrating Practice with Strategy," *Industrial Relations* (Spring 1984).

staffing dynamics, phrase used by those who are not content with calling turnover turnover.

staffing plan, planning document that minimally (1) lists an organization's projected personnel needs by occupation and grade level and (2) identifies how these needs will be met.

staffing program planning, determination by organization personnel management of the numbers and kinds of personnel management actions necessary during each stage of the planning period to staff the workforce required in management's program plan.

staff organization, those segments of a larger organization that provide support services and have no direct responsibilities for line operations or production. Personnel administration has traditionally been a staff function. See Ernest Dale and Lyndall F. Urwick, *Staff in Organization* (N.Y.: McGraw-Hill, 1960).

staff out, process that involves soliciting a variety of views or recommendations on an issue so that a decisionmaker will be aware of all reasonable options.

staff principle, the principle of administration which states that the executive should be assisted by officers who are not in the line of operations but are essentially extensions of the personality of the executive and whose duties consist primarily of assisting the executive in controlling and coordinating the organization and, secondly, of offering advice.

stagflation, high levels of unemployment

and inflation at the same time. *See* Martin L. Weitzman, *The Share Economy: Conquering Stagflation* (Cambridge, MA, Harvard University Press, 1984).

See also PHILLIPS CURVE.

Stahl, O. Glenn (1910-   ), until his retirement in 1969, the director of the Bureau of Policies and Standards, U.S. Civil Service Commission, and the author of one of the leading texts on public personnel administration. Major works include: *The Personnel Job of Government Managers* (Chicago: International Personnel Management Association, 1971); *Public Personnel Administration* (N.Y.: Harper & Row, 8th ed., 1983).

Stakhanovite, decidedly dated term for a ratebuster. Alexei Stakhanov was a Russian miner who regularly exceeded his production quota. During Stalin's regime, he was a well published example of the "ideal" Russian worker. Rumor has it that Stakhanov increased his production output on secret orders from the Communist Party. For his efforts, he was promoted from worker to commissar and even awarded the Order of Lenin.

standard, employment: *see* EMPLOYMENT STANDARD.

standard allowance, established amount of time by which the normal time for employees to complete their tasks is increased in order to compensate for the expected amount of personal and/or unavoidable delays.

Standard Consolidated Statistical Area (SCSA), creation of the U.S. Census Bureau combining continguous standard metropolitan statistical areas in order to more accurately portray urban population patterns.

standard deviation, measure of the variability of a distribution about its mean or average. In distributions of test scores, for example, a low standard deviation would indicate a tendency of scores to cluster about the mean; a high standard deviation would indicate a wide variation in scores. In a normal distribution, approximately 68 percent of the cases lie between + 1 S.D. and − 1 S.D. from the mean and approximately 96 percent of the cases between + 2 S.D. and − 2 S.D. from the mean.

standard error of measurement, number expressed in score units that serves as another index of test reliability. It can be interpreted as indicating the probability that if an error of measurement of a test is 20 points, there are approximately 2 chances out of 3 that an individual's "true score" will be within ± 20 points of his/her "obtained score" on the test. Similarly, the chances are approximately 96 out of 100 that his/her "true score" will be within ± 40 points of his/her "obtained score."

standard federal regions, geographic subdivisions of the U.S. established to achieve more uniformity in the location and geographic jurisdiction of federal field offices as a basis for promoting some systematic coordination among agencies and among federal-state-local governments and for securing management improvements and economies through greater interagency and intergovernmental cooperation. Boundaries were drawn and regional office locations designed for 10 regions, and agencies are required to adopt the uniform system when changes are made or new offices established.

Standard Form 171, the federal government's "Personal Qualifications Statement" and its universal employment application.

standard hour, the normally expected amount of work to be done in an hour. It is a unit of measurement for use in nearly all production activities. Standard hours do not correspond to clock times; the standard hour notation on an incoming job order may indicate that the job will require 40 standard hours, but this does not mean that the job can be completed by one person in a regular 40-hour work week. The available clock time of a facility does not take into account, for example, personal

time, absenteeism, stoppages, and reduced efficiency. The only way to correlate standard hours and maximum gross hours is to reduce the maximum gross hours available by total lost time.

standard-hour plan, incentive plan that rewards an employee by a percent premium that equals the percent by which performance beats the standard.

Standard Industrial Classification System, the federal government's numbering system for the classification of industries and enterprises which develops comparable statistics on the composition and structure of the economy. This system is an important resource for marketing research because census reports based upon this data allow companies to easily determine the location and size of potential customer groups.

standardization, specification of consistent procedures to be followed in administering, scoring, and interpreting tests.

standardized test, any objective test given under constant conditions and/or any test for which a set of norms is available.

Standard Metropolitan Statistical Area (SMSA), creation of the U.S. Census Bureau so as to more accurately portray urban population. It includes the population in all counties contiguous to an urban county (that is one with a city over 50,000, in a common total) if the population of those counties is involved in the urban county work force. Being designated a SMSA is important to cities and counties because only SMSAs are eligible for certain federal government grants.

standard of living, measure of the material affluence enjoyed by a nation or by an individual. The "standard of living" refers to the *way* people live. The "cost of living" refers to *how much* it costs them to live that way. Thus, the cost-of-living is a reflection of the prices people have to pay in order to enjoy their life style, or living standard. The cost of living is constantly changing because price movements are often a daily occurrence. On the other hand, changes in one's standard of living occur less frequently, and for workers usually result from increases in pay or compensation.

standard rate: *see* FLAT RATE.

standards: *see* CLASSIFICATION STANDARDS.

standard score, any transformed test

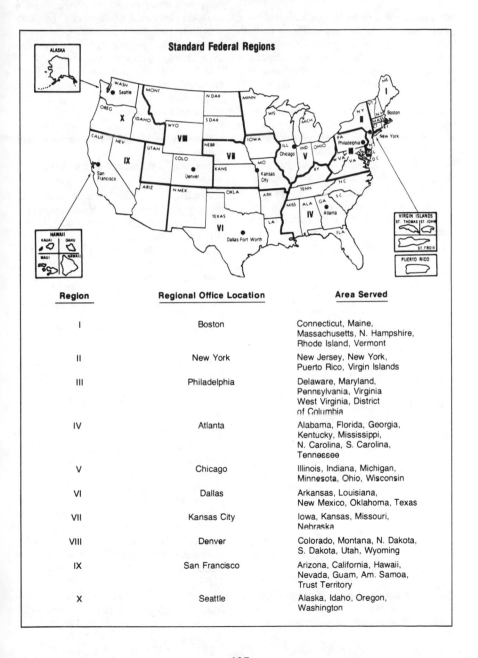

Standard Federal Regions

Region	Regional Office Location	Area Served
I	Boston	Connecticut, Maine, Massachusetts, N. Hampshire, Rhode Island, Vermont
II	New York	New Jersey, New York, Puerto Rico, Virgin Islands
III	Philadelphia	Delaware, Maryland, Pennsylvania, Virginia West Virginia, District of Columbia
IV	Atlanta	Alabama, Florida, Georgia, Kentucky, Mississippi, N. Carolina, S. Carolina, Tennessee
V	Chicago	Illinois, Indiana, Michigan, Minnesota, Ohio, Wisconsin
VI	Dallas	Arkansas, Louisiana, New Mexico, Oklahoma, Texas
VII	Kansas City	Iowa, Kansas, Missouri, Nebraska
VIII	Denver	Colorado, Montana, N. Dakota, S. Dakota, Utah, Wyoming
IX	San Francisco	Arizona, California, Hawaii, Nevada, Guam, Am. Samoa, Trust Territory
X	Seattle	Alaska, Idaho, Oregon, Washington

score, in terms of which raw scores are expressed for convenience and ease of interpretation.

standards of conduct, an organization's formal guidelines for ethical behavior.

Standards of Conduct For Labor Organization. In the federal sector, a code governing internal democratic practices and fiscal responsibility, and procedures to which a labor organization must adhere to be eligible to receive any recognition.

standards of performance, statements that tell an employee how well he or she must perform a task to be considered a satisfactory employee. Standards cover how much, how accurately, in what time period, or in what manner, the various job tasks are to be performed. The performance standards, whether written or unwritten, will specify the minimum level of performance at which an employee must work in order to attain a satisfactory performance rating.

standing, a person's right to initiate legal action because he or she is directly affected by the issues raised. *See* Karen Orren, "Standing to Sue: Interest Group Conflict in the Federal Courts," *American Political Science Review* (September 1976).

starvation wages: *see* LIVING WAGE.

state of the art, level of development in a given scientific or technological field at a given time, usually the present. *See* Edward M. Glaser, "Using Behavioral Science Strategies for Defining the State-of-the-Art," *Journal of Applied Behavioral Science* (January-February-March 1980).

static system: *see* DYNAMIC SYSTEM.

statistical inference, use of information observed in a sample to make predictions about a larger population.

statistical significance: *see* SIGNIFICANCE.

statistical validation, also called CRI-TERION RELATED VALIDATION, validation that involves definition of what is to be measured (*i.e.*, criterion) by some systematic method based upon observations of the job behavior of individuals. Possible measures of the knowledges, skills, abilities, and other employee characteristics are then obtained for individuals. Through statistical means, the strength of the relationship between the criterion and the measures is evaluated (validity).

If the criterion has been defined rationally through a careful empirical analysis of job duties, job-relatedness of the appraisal procedure is considered to be present. If the criterion has not been defined in this way, job-relatedness is inferred but not assured.

See also VALIDATION and VALIDITY.

statistics, any gathered numerical data and any of the processes of analyzing and of making inferences from the data. While there are innumerable works on the collection and interpretation of statistics, the classic work on statistical presentation is: Darrell Huff, *How to Lie with Statistics* (N.Y.: W. W. Norton & Co., 1954). This work is valuable for those who would lie, those who would not, and those who would like not to be lied to.

status, abstraction of one's relative position or ranking within an organization or society.

status symbols, visible signs of an individual's social status or importance in an organization. Status symbols are a significant element of the psychic compensation of every job. Under varying circumstances almost anything can be a status symbol—a private secretary, a key to the executive washroom, an assigned parking space, wood as opposed to metal office furniture, etc. For an account of the relentless search for greater status, *see* Vance Packard, *The Status Seekers* (N.Y.: David McKay Co., 1959).

statutory, referring to laws passed by legislatures. A statute is such a law.

stay-in strike: *see* SIT-DOWN STRIKE.

Steelworkers' Trilogy, three decisions of the U.S. Supreme Court, which held that: (1) a labor-management dispute could not be judged to be nonarbitrable unless the parties specifically excluded the subject from the arbitration process; (2) the role of the federal courts is limited when the parties have agreed to submit all questions of contract interpretation to an arbitrator; and (3) the interpretation of a collective bargaining agreement is a question for the arbitrator and the courts do not have the right to overrule the arbitrator because of his interpretation.

The trilogy cases are, respectively: *United Steelworkers of America* v. *Warrior and Gulf Navigation Co.,* 363 U.S. 574 (1960); *United Steelworkers of America* v. *American Manufacturing Co.,* 363 U.S. 564 (1960); and *United Steelworkers of America* v. *Enterprise Wheel and Car Corp.,* 363 U.S. 593 (1960).

step bonus, feature of wage incentive plans that call for a substantial increase in incentive payments when the quantity and/or quality of output reaches a specified level.

Stephens, Uriah Smith (1821-1882), Grand Master Workman of the Knights of Labor from its founding in 1869 to 1879.

step increases: *see* INCREMENT.

steward, also called SHOP STEWARD and UNION STEWARD, local union's most immediate representative in a plant or department. Usually elected by fellow employees (but sometimes appointed by the union leadership), the shop steward handles grievances, collects dues, solicits new members, etc. A shop steward usually continues to work at his or her regular job and handles union matters on a part-time basis, frequently on the employer's time. According to the *AFL-CIO Manual for Shop Stewards* (July 1978),

it is important that the steward understands his relationship with management. Although the foreman, forelady or supervisor exercises certain authority over him in his role as a worker in the department, when they meet to discuss grievances the steward acts as an official representative of the union and, therefore, has equal status. He has every right to be expected to be treated as an equal as well as the right to express himself fully on the problem under discussion.

See Allan N. Nash, *The Union Steward: Duties, Rights, and Status,* 2nd ed. (Ithaca, N.Y.: New York State School of Industrial and Labor Relations, Cornell University, 1983).

steward chief, union representative who supervises the activities of a group of shop stewards.

stint-plan wage system, system that assigns a definite output as an employee's day's work; and, if the work is completed in less than normal time, the employee is credited with a full day's work and allowed to go home.

Stock Acquisition Plan, Executive: *see* EXECUTIVE STOCK ACQUISITION PLAN.

stock-option plan, any of a variety of plans that allow employees to purchase shares of the company's stock at a future date at a price that is significantly lower than the stock's market value. If the price of the stock rises, the employee would find it profitable to exercise the option and buy the stock at a discount unavailable on the open market. Stock options tend to be limited to those key managers who can significantly influence the success of the company. As such they have a certain status value. For the studies of various plans, *see* Donald R. Simpson, "Stock Options," Milton L. Rock (ed.), *Handbook of Wage and Salary Administration* (N.Y.: McGraw-Hill, 1972); V. Henry Rothschild II and Jack B. Salwen, "Stock Option Plans in Transition," *Conference Board Record* (June 1973); Fred O. Nwokobia, "Profit-Related Stock Options: Immunizing Grants Against the Market," *Compensation Review* (Third Quarter 1975);

Harland Fox, *Incentive Stock Option Plans* (New York: The Conference Board, 1983).

stoop labor, farm work involving the picking of crops that grow close to or into the ground.

Stotts decision: *see* FIRE FIGHTERS LOCAL UNION NO. 1784 V. STOTTS.

straight commission, method of compensating sales employees by solely paying them a percentage of the value of the goods they sell.

straight salary, method of compensating sales employees by solely paying them a fixed salary without regard to the dollar value of the sales that they generate within a specified time period.

stranger laboratory, laboratory experience for individuals from differing organizations.

stranger pickets, workers who picket an employee who has never employed them.
    See also AMERICAN FEDERATION OF LABOR V. SWING.

Strasser, Adolph, *see* BUSINESS UNION.

strategic management, a decisional process that combines an organization's capabilities with the opportunities and threats found in both the internal and external organizational environment. *See* Jeffrey Bracker, "The Historical Development of the Strategic Management Concept," *Academy of Management Review* (April 1980); Edward H. Bowman, "A Risk/Return Paradox for Strategic Management," *Sloan Management Review* (Spring 1980); J. Krieken, "Formulating and Implementing a More Systematic Approach to Strategic Management," *Management Review* (July 1980); Alan J. Rowe, Richard O. Mason and Karl Dickel, *Strategic Management & Business Policy: A Methodological Approach* (Reading, Mass.: Addison-Wesley, 1982); Noel M. Tichy, "Managing Change

Strategically: The Technical, Political, and Cultural Keys," *Organizational Dynamics* (Autumn 1982); Max S. Wortman, Jr., "Strategic Management and Changing Leader-Follower Roles," *The Journal of Applied Behavioral Science,* Vol. 18, No. 3 (1982); Lee Dyer, "Studying Human Resources Strategy: An Approach and an Agenda," *Industrial Relations* (Spring 1984).

strategic planning. According to William R. King and David I. Cleland, *Strategic Planning and Policy* (New York: Van Nostrand Reinhold Co., 1978), strategic planning "provides procedures, processes, information support, and a facilitative organizational structure to permit managers to 'break out' of an emphasis on day-to-day operating problems and give appropriate attention to the development of *controlled organizational change." Also see* Peter Lorange and Richard F. Vancil, *Strategic Planning Systems* (Englewood Clfifs, N.J.: Prentice-Hall, 1977); Michael H. Moskow, *Strategic Planning in Business and Government* (New York: Committee for Economic Development, 1978); Lewis F. McLain, Jr., "How Strategic Planning Can Help Put Budgeting in Perspective," *Governmental Finance* (June 1981); Eddie C. Smith, "Strategic Business Planning and Human Resources: Part 1," *Personnel Journal* (August 1982); Laurence J. Styble, "Linking Strategic Planning and Management Manpower Planning," *California Management Review* (Fall 1982).

straw boss, colloquial term for a supervisor who has no real authority, power or status with which to back up his orders.

stress, engineering term applied to humans in reference to any condition or situation that forces the body to respond to it. Prolonged stress can overtax an individual's emotional and/or physical ability to cope with it. The pioneering work on "stress on the whole person" was done by Hans Seyle, *The Stress of Life* (N.Y.: McGraw-Hill, rev. ed., 1976). *Also see* David E. Morrison, "Stress and the Public Administrator," *Public Administration*

Review (July–August 1977); John E. Newman and Terry A. Beehr, "Personal and Organizational Strategies for Handling Job Stress: A Review of Research and Opinion," *Personnel Psychology* (Spring 1979); Michael T. Matteson and John M. Ivancevich, "Organizational Stressors and Heart Disease: A Research Model," *Academy of Management Review* (July 1979); Manfred F. R. Kets de Vries, "Organizational Stress: A Call for Management Action," *Sloan Management Review* (Fall 1979); Randell S. Schuler, "Definition and Conceptualization of Stress in Organizations," *Organizational Behavior and Human Performance* (April 1980); Herbert Benson and Robert L. Allen, "How Much Stress Is Too Much?" *Harvard Business Review* (September–October 1980); John M. Ivancevich and Michael T. Matteson, "Optimizing Human Resources: A Case for Preventive Health and Stress Management," *Organizational Dynamics* (Autumn 1980); Kim R. Kanaga and Mark Flynn, "The Relationship Between Invasion of Personal Space and Stress," *Human Relations* (March 1981); Robert L. Kahn, "Work, Stress, and Individual Well-Being," *Monthly Labor Review* (May 1981); Cary L. Cooper and Marilyn J. Davidson, "The High Cost of Stress on Women Managers," *Organizational Dynamics* (Spring 1982); Srinika Jayaratne and Wayne A. Chess, "The Effects of Emotional Support on Perceived Job Stress and Strain," *The Journal of Applied Behavioral Science*, Vol. 20, No. 2 (1984); James C. Quick and Jonathan D. Quick, "Preventive Stress Management at the Organizational Level," *Personnel* (September–October 1984).

The definitive compendium on occupational stress is the 1980 Addison-Wesley series of 6 books on the subject. Titles include: *Work Stress* by Alan McLean, *Managing Stress* by Leon Warshaw, *Blue-Collar Stress* by Arthur B. Shostak, *Work Stress and Social Support* by James S. House, *Management and Stress* by Leonard Moss, and *Preventing Work Stress* by Lennart Levi.

See also the following entries:
MID-CAREER CRISIS

NERVOUS BREAKDOWN
OCCUPATIONAL NEUROSIS

stress carriers, fellow workers who are crisis oriented and tend to induce stress in others in addition to suffering from it themselves.

stress interview, interview in which the interviewer deliberately creates a stressful situation for the interviewee in order to see how the interviewee might behave under such pressure. Common tactics used to induce stress include: critically questioning the opinions of the interviewee, frequent interruptions of interviewee's answers to possibly hostile questions, silence on the part of the interviewer for an extended period, etc.

stretch-out: see SPEED-UP.

strike, also called WALKOUT, mutual agreement among workers (whether members of a union or not) to a temporary work stoppage in order to obtain or resist a change in their working conditions. The term is thought to have nautical origins, because sailors would stop work by striking or taking down their sails. A strike or potential strike is considered an essential element of the collective bargaining process. Many labor leaders would claim that collective bargaining can never be more than a charade without the right to strike. For histories, see P. K. Edwards, *Strikes in the United States, 1881–1974* (New York: St. Martin's Press, 1981); Bruce E. Kaufman, "The Determinants of Strikes in the United States, 1900–1977," *Industrial and Labor Relations Review* (July 1982). For a defense of the right to strike, see T. Kennedy, "Freedom to Strike Is in the Public Interest," *Harvard Business Review* (July–August 1970); Grace Sterrett and Antone Aboud, *The Right to Strike in Public Employment* (Ithaca, N.Y., Cornell University, New York State School of Industrial and Labor Relations, 1982). To prepare for a strike, see Lee T. Paterson and John Liebert, *Management Strike Handbook* (Chicago: International Personnel Management Associations, 1974).

WORK STOPPAGE DATA

WORK STOPPAGES include all known strikes or lockouts involving 1,000 workers or more and lasting a full shift or longer. Data are based largely on newspaper accounts and cover all workers idle one shift or more in establishments directly involved in a stoppage. They do not measure the indirect or secondary effect on other establishments whose employees are idle owing to material or service shortages.

Estimates of days idle as a percent of estimated working time measure only the impact of larger strikes (1,000 workers or more). Formerly, these estimates measured the impact of strikes involving 6 workers or more; that is, the impact of virtually *all* strikes. Due to budget stringencies, collection of data on strikes involving fewer than 1,000 workers was discontinued with the December 1981 data.

Work stoppages involving 1,000 workers or more, 1947 to date

Month and year	Number of stoppages		Workers involved		Days idle	
	Beginning in month or year	In effect during month	Beginning in month or year (in thousands)	In effect during month (in thousands)	Number (in thousands)	Percent of estimated working time
1947	270	....	1,629	....	25,720	—
1948	245	....	1,435	....	26,127	.22
1949	262	....	2,537	....	43,420	.38
1950	424	....	1,698	....	30,390	.26
1951	415	....	1,462	....	15,070	.12
1952	470	....	2,746	....	48,820	.38
1953	437	....	1,623	....	18,130	.14
1954	265	....	1,075	....	16,630	.13
1955	363	....	2,055	....	21,180	.16
1956	287	....	1,370	....	26,840	.20
1957	279	....	887	....	10,340	.07
1958	332	....	1,587	....	17,900	.13
1959	245	....	1,381	....	60,850	.43
1960	222	....	896	....	13,260	.09
1961	195	....	1,031	....	10,140	.07
1962	211	....	793	....	11,760	.08
1963	181	....	512	....	10,020	.07
1964	246	....	1,183	....	16,220	.11
1965	268	....	999	....	15,140	.10
1966	321	....	1,300	....	16,000	.10
1967	381	....	2,192	....	31,320	.18
1968	392	....	1,855	....	35,567	.20
1969	412	....	1,576	....	29,397	.16
1970	381	....	2,468	....	52,761	.29
1971	298	....	2,516	....	35,538	.19
1972	250	....	975	....	16,764	.09
1973	317	....	1,400	....	16,260	.08
1974	424	....	1,796	....	31,809	.16
1975	235	....	965	....	17,563	.09
1976	231	....	1,519	....	23,962	.12
1977	298	....	1,212	....	21,258	.10
1978	219	....	1,006	....	23,774	.11
1979	235	....	1,021	....	20,409	.09
1980	187	....	795	....	20,844	.09
1981	145	....	729	....	16,908	.07
1982	96	....	656	....	9,061	.04
1983	81	....	909	....	17,461	.08
1983						
January	1	3	1.6	38.0	794.8	.04
February	5	7	14.0	50.4	844.4	.05
March	5	10	10.5	54.9	1,131.5	.05
April	2	9	2.8	52.4	789.5	.04
May	12	17	24.9	34.2	488.5	.03
June	16	25	63.3	81.2	689.1	.03
July	10	23	64.5	99.8	1,270.1	.07
August	7	19	615.8	669.7	8,673.2	.41
September	7	19	20.8	49.5	567.1	.03
1984[p]						
January	6	12	28.9	43.0	507.3	.03
February	2	12	8.7	37.2	365.5	.02
March	2	9	3.0	14.6	284.2	.01
April	7	13	28.5	38.1	651.0	.03
May	5	15	8.1	39.2	581.2	.03
June	5	14	23.7	45.7	754.8	.04
July	[r]8	[r]20	[r]68.4	[r]104.1	[r]1,221.7	.06
August	5	19	24.0	103.4	1,633.3	.07
September	8	17	102.9	119.7	736.4	.04

p = preliminary   r = revised

Source: Monthly Labor Review *(November 1984).*

For alternatives, see Theodore E. Kheel et al., "Exploring Alternatives to the Strike," *Monthly Labor Review* (September 1973); Thomas P. Gies, "Employer Remedies for Work Stoppages that Violate No-Strike Provisions," *Employee Relations Law Journal* (Autumn 1982). *Also see* Robert B. Fouler, "Normative Aspects of Public Employee Strikes," *Public Personnel Management* (March–April 1974); Eugene H. Becker, "Analysis of Work Stoppages in the Federal Sector, 1962-81," *Monthly Labor Review* (August 1982); Woodruff Imberman, "Who Strikes—and Why," *Harvard Business Review* (November–December 1983); Peter A. Veglahn, "Public Sector Strike Penalties and Their Appeal," *Public Personnel Management* (Summer 1983); Gary L. Tidwell, "The Meaning of the No-Strike Clause," *Personnel Administrator* (November 1984); Ben Burdetsky and Marvin S. Katzman, "Is the Strike Iron Still Hot?" *Personnel Journal* (July 1984); Edward Levin and Candace Reid, "Arbitration of Strike Misconduct Cases Arising out of Legal Strikes," *Arbitration Journal* (September 1984).

See also the following entries:

strike authorization, also called STRIKE VOTE, formal vote by union members that (if passed) invests the union leadership with the right to call a strike without additional consultation with the union membership.

strike benefits, payments by a union to its striking members or to non-members who are out on strike in support of the union. The U.S. Supreme Court has held, in *United States* v. *Allen Kaiser,* 363 U.S. 299 (1960), that, for tax purposes, strike benefits are to be considered as gifts and thus not taxable as part of a worker's gross income. See Sheldon M. Kline, "Strike Benefits of National Unions," *Monthly Labor Review* (March 1975); John Gennard, *Financing Strikers* (N.Y.: John Wiley, 1977).

strike-bound, any organization that is being struck by its employees and/or attemping to function in spite of the strike.

strikebreaker, person who accepts a position vacated by a worker on strike or a worker who continues to work while others are on strike. The Labor-Management Relations (Taft-Hartley) Act of 1947 guarantees a strikebreaker's right to work and makes it illegal for unions to attempt to prohibit strikebreakers from crossing picket lines.

See also the following entries:

ANTI-STRIKEBREAKER ACT OF 1936
NOBLE
SCAB

strike counselors: *see* COUNSELORS.

strike duty, tasks assigned to union members by the union leadership during the course of a strike (for example, picketing, distributing food, preventing violence, creating violence, etc.).

strike fund, monies reserved by a union to be used during a strike to cover costs such as strike benefits or legal fees. Strike funds are not necessarily separate from a union's general fund. The amount of strike funds available may mean the success or failure of a strike.

strike notice, formal notice of an impending work stoppage that is presented by a union to an employer or to an appropriate government agency. *See* John G. Kruchko and Jay R. Fries, "Hospital Strikes: Complying with NLRA Notice Requirements," *Employee Relations Law Journal* (Spring 1984).

strike pay, union payments to union members as partial compensation for income loss during a strike.

strike vote: *see* STRIKE AUTHORIZATION.

stroking, also POSITIVE STROKING and NEGATIVE STROKING. Eric Berne, in *Games People Play: The Psychology of Human Relationships* (N.Y.: Grove Press, 1964), took the intimate physical act of stroking and developed its psychological analogy in conversation. All of human intercourse can be viewed from the narrow perspective of the giving and receiving of physical and psychological strokes. In an organizational context, *positive stroking* consists of the laying of kind words on employees. *Negative stroking* involves using less than kind words—being critical. *See* Thomas C. Clary, "Motivation Through Positive Stroking," *Public Personnel Management* (March–April 1973).
See also MOTIVATION.

Strong-Campbell Interest Inventory (SCII), vocational interest inventory that allows individuals to compare their preferences with reference groups in a large range of occupations; helps the test taker identify a general section of the occupational world for more intensive study. This inventory is a 1974 revision of the Strong-Vocational Interest Blank (SVIB) that combined the men's and women's scales to reduce or remove sex bias and is widely used in vocational and/or career counseling. TIME: Untimed-approximately 30/40 minutes. AUTHORS: Edward K. Strong and David P. Campbell. PUBLISHER: Stanford University Press (*see* TEST PUBLISHERS).

Strong Vocational Interest Blank (SVIB), paper-and-pencil vocational inventory used primarily for vocational counseling at the high school and college student level for career choice and in personnel counseling. There are separate scales for men and women. Usage has been replaced by the SCII which integrated the two scales (non-discriminatory). TIME: 30/60 minutes. AUTHORS: E. K. Strong, Jr., D. P. Campbell, R. F. Berdie, K. E. Clark. PUBLISHER: Stanford University Press (*see* TEST PUBLISHERS).

struck work, products produced by strikebreakers.

structural change, alterations in the relative significance of the productive components of a national or international economy that take place over time. Expansion in the economy as a whole or temporary shifts in the relationship of its components as a result of cyclical developments would *not* be considered structural changes. Since the industrial revolution, structural change in most countries has resulted principally from changes in comparative advantage associated with technological advance, but also to a lesser degree from changes in consumer preference. It has involved shifts from subsistence agriculture to commercial agriculture, an increase in the relative significance of manufacturing and, at a later stage, a further shift toward service industries. Other major structural changes involve shifts in the economic importance between various industries, shifts between regions of large national economies, and changes in the composition of exports and imports.

structural-functional theory, also called STRUCTURAL-FUNCTIONALISM, an approach in sociology in which societies, communities or organizations are viewed as systems; then their particular features are explained in terms of their contributions—their functions—in maintaining the system. This approach is generally credited to Talcott Parsons. *See* his *The Social System* (New York: The Free Press, 1951).

structural unemployment, unemployment resulting from changes in technology, consumption patterns or government policies—a mismatch between available labor and demand for skills. Structural unemployment can be said to be an inherent part of a dynamic economic system. The "cure" for structural unemployment is worker retraining. *See* Eleanor G. Gilpatrick, *Structural Unemployment And Aggregate Demand* (Baltimore: The Johns Hopkins University Press, 1966); Paul G. Schervish, *The Structural Determinants of Unemployment: Vulnerability and Power in Market Relations* (New York: Academic Press, 1983).

structured role playing, role-play exercise or simulation in which the players receive oral or written instruction giving them cues as to their roles.

Stump* v. *Sparkman, 435 U.S. 349 (1978), Supreme Court case reaffirming the principle of *Bradley* v. *Fisher*, 13 Wall 335 (1872), that judges have absolute immunity from liability in civil suits based upon their official acts.

SUB: *see* SUPPLEMENTAL UNEMPLOYMENT BENEFIT.

subemployment, concept that tries to capture two major dimensions of labor market functioning that produce, and reproduce poverty—the lack of opportunity for work and substandard wage employment. *See* T. Vietorisz, R. Mier, and J. Giblin, "Subemployment: Exclusion and Inadequacy Indexes," *Monthly Labor Review* (May 1975).

subemployment index, includes persons who are: unemployed; working part-time, but seeking full-time work; discouraged workers (those who have dropped out because they sought but could not find work); and full-time workers paid less than the official poverty level. This is a measure developed by the Bureau of the Census because the conventional unemployment rate did not adequately describe the employment situation of disadvantaged persons.

subsistence allowance, payments for an employee's reasonable expenses (meals, lodging, transportation, etc.) while traveling on behalf of his or her employer.

subsistence theory of wages: *see* IRON LAW OF WAGES.

subordinate rating, evaluation of an organizational superior by someone of lesser rank.

substandard rate, wage rate below established occupational, prevailing, or legal levels.

substantive law, the basic law of rights and duties (contract law, criminal law, accident law, law of wills, etc.) as opposed to procedural law (law of pleading, law of evidence, law of jurisdiction, etc.).

Sugarman* v. *Dougall, 413 U.S. 634 (1973), U.S. Supreme Court case, which held that a ban on the employment of resident aliens by a state was unconstitutional, because it encompassed positions that had little, if any, relation to a legitimate state interest in treating aliens differently from citizens. However, the court also stated that alienage might be reasonably taken into account with regard to specific positions.

See also the following entries:

suggestion system, formal effort to encourage employees to make recommendations that would improve the operations of their organizations. *See* Charles Foos, "How to Administer A Suggestion System," *Management Review* (August 1968); Edward H. Downey and Walter L. Balk, *Employee Innovation and Government Productivity: A Study of Suggestion Systems in the Public Sector* (Chicago: International Personnel Management Association, 1976). For a history, *see* Stanley J. Seimer, *Suggestion Plans in American Industry* (Syracuse, N.Y.: Syracuse University Press, 1959).
     See also SCANLON PLAN.

summons, written order issued by a judicial officer requiring a person accused of a criminal offense to appear in a designated court at a specified time to answer the charge(s).

sunk costs, resources committed to the achievement of an organizational objective that cannot be regained if the objective is abandoned.

sunshine bargaining, also called GOLDFISH-BOWL BARGAINING, collective bargaining sessions open to the press and public. This process is more likely to be used in public sector negotiations (in response to the assertion that since the spending of public funds are the essence of the negotiations, the negotiating process should be open to public scrutiny).

superannuated rate, pay rate below the

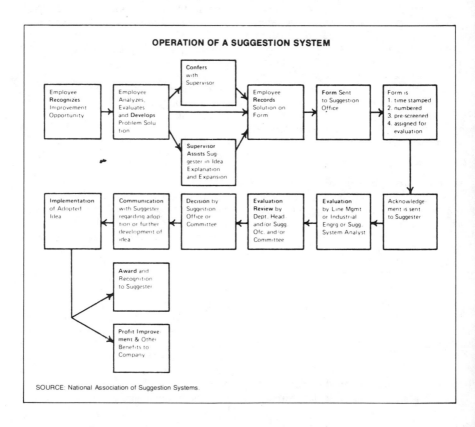

OPERATION OF A SUGGESTION SYSTEM

SOURCE: National Association of Suggestion Systems.

prevailing rate that is paid to older employees who are in need or are needed because of a labor shortage. A ratio for superannuated workers is sometimes provided for in union agreements. The lower rate is justified on the theory that these older, otherwise retired, workers are not as productive as younger employees. Some superannuated rate policies may be in violation of age discrimination laws.

supergrades, federal government executives in grades GS-16, 17, and 18.

supernumerary income, that portion of a worker's income which is not needed for the essentials of everyday life and consequently available for luxuries and other optional spending. See Fabian Linden, "Supernumerary Income: A Statistical Measure of Consumer Affluence," *Conference Board Record* (April 1968).

superseniority, also called SYNTHETIC SENIORITY, seniority that supercedes ordinary seniority, which is dependent on an individual's length of service. Because a union may be detrimentally affected if its key union officials are subject to layoffs, union contracts often grant them superseniority. This synthetic seniority is designed to ensure continued representation for workers remaining following a reduction in force. Superseniority also provides an advantage to management since established lines of communication with the union and its members continues without interruption. Sometimes union contracts provide for superseniority for special categories of employees (such as the aged or physically handicapped and key personnel essential if production is to be maintained). See Max S. Wortman, "Superseniority—Myth or Reality?" *Labor Law Journal* (April 1967); George K. Leonard, "Practical Applications of Superseniority," *Labor Law Journal* (January 1975).

supervision, directing the performance of one or more workers towards the accomplishment of organizational goals. See Robert M. Fulmer, *Supervision: Principles*

of Professional Management (Beverly Hills, Calif.: Glencoe Press, 1976). Fred Luthans and Mark J. Martinko *The Practice of Supervision and Management* (New York: McGraw-Hill, 1979; Andrew J. DuBrin, *The Practice of Supervision: Achieving Results Through People* (Dallas, Texas: Business Publications, 1980); Michael J. Austin, *Supervisory Management for Human Services* (Englewood Cliffs, N.J.: Prentice-Hall, 1981); Jack Halloran, *Supervision: The Art of Management* (Englewood Cliffs, N.J.: Prentice-Hall, 1981). Leonard A. Schlesinger, *The Quality of Work Life and the Supervisor* (New York: Praeger, 1982); Edward E. Scannell, *Supervisory Communications* (Dubuque, Iowa: Kendall/Hunt Pub. Co., 1982); Ann Majchrzak, *The Manipulation of Supervisory Behaviors: Results of a Field Experiment* (West Lafayette, Indiana: Krannert Graduate School of Management, Purdue University, 1984).

supervisor, according to Section 2(11) of the National Labor Relations Act, as amended, the term "supervisor" means

any individual having authority, in the interest of the employer, to hire, transfer, suspend, lay off, recall, promote, discharge, assign, reward, or discipline other employees, or responsibly to direct them, or to adjust their grievances, or effectively to recommend such action, if in connection with the foregoing the exercise of such authority is not of a merely routine or clerical nature, but requires the use of independent judgment.

See also HANNA MINING CO. V. DISTRICT 2, MARINE ENGINEERS.

Supervisory Management, monthly magazine that deals with all aspects of supervisory management.

Supervisory Management
Editorial Address
American Management Associations
135 West 50th St
New York, NY 10020
Subscriptions:
P.O. Box 319
Saranac Lake, NY 12983

supplemental compensation, executive: see EXECUTIVE SUPPLEMENTAL COMPENSATION.

supplemental compensation: see BONUS and FEDERAL SUPPLEMENTAL COMPENSATION.

supplemental dental insurance: see SUPPLEMENTAL MEDICAL INSURANCE.

supplemental life insurance: see SPLIT-DOLLAR LIFE INSURANCE.

supplemental medical insurance: also SUPPLEMENTAL DENTAL INSURANCE, fringe benefit usually offered only to top management, whereby all expenses from medical and/or dental care not covered by the general medical/dental policy offered by the company are reimbursable.

Supplemental Security Income (SSI), federal program that assures a minimum monthly income to needy people with limited income and resources who are 65 or older, blind, or disabled. Eligibility is based on income and assets. Although the program is administered by the Social Security Administration, it is financed from general revenues, not from social security contributions. See Marilyn Moon, "Supplemental Security Income, Asset Tests, and Equity," *Policy Analysis* (Winter 1980).

supplemental unemployment benefit (SUB), payments to laid off workers from private unemployment insurance plans that are supplements to state unemployment insurance compensation. The first SUB plan was negotiated by the Ford Motor Company and the United Auto Workers in 1955. By 1973, about 29 percent of the members of major unions worked under contracts containing SUB plans. There are two basic SUB plans— the individual account and the pooled fund. With the former, contributions are credited to each employee's account and a terminated employee may take his benefits with him. With the latter, benefits are paid from a common fund and individual

employees have no vested rights should they leave the company. For the history of SUB, see Joseph M. Becker, *Guaranteed Income for the Unemployed: The Story of SUB* (Baltimore: Johns Hopkins Press, 1968). For a financial analysis, see Emerson H. Beier, "Financing Supplemental Unemployment Benefits," *Monthly Labor Review* (November 1969). *Also see* Audrey Freedman, "Reexamining Income Security: SUB vs. Guaranteed Work," *The Conference Board Record* (May 1976); Audrey Freedman, *Security Bargains Reconsidered: SUB, Severance Pay, Guaranteed Work* (New York: The Conference Board, 1978).

supply, in economics, this is the quantity of goods and services available for purchase if income and other factors are held constant. Increases in price either induce increases in supply or serve to ration the supply.

supply-side economics/Reaganomics, the essence of supply side economics is a belief that lower tax rates, especially on marginal income, will encourage fresh capital to flow into the economy; which will, in turn, generate jobs and growth and new tax revenue. Because this concept was widely adopted by President Reagan and his advisors, it has been popularly called "Reaganomics."

Economist Arthur Laffer is generally credited with having "discovered" supply-side economics. See Bruce R. Bartlett, *Reaganomics: Supply-Side Economics in Action* (Westport, Conn.: Arlington House, 1981); R. T. McNamar, "President Reagan's Economic Program," *Presidential Studies Quarterly* (Summer 1981); Paul Craig Roberts, "Will Reaganomics Unravel?" *Fortune*, November 16, 1981; John Kenneth Galbraith, "Why Reaganomics Can't Work," *The New Republic*, September 23, 1981; Robert B. Reich, "Beyond Reaganomics," *The New Republic*, November 18, 1981; Robert Lekachman, *Greed is not Enough: Reaganomics* (N.Y.: Pantheon, 1982).

See also LAFFER CURVE and TRICKLE DOWN ECONOMICS.

surface bargaining, not taking the bargaining process seriously; just going through the motions.

Survey Research Center: *see* INSTITUTE FOR SOCIAL RESEARCH.

survivors benefits, totality of the benefits that are paid upon the death of an employee to his/her legal survivors. Employees are frequently required to make a decision at the time of retirement whether or not to take a reduced pension that allows for survivors benefits.

suspension, removing an individual from employment for a specified period. Suspensions, by their nature temporary, are disciplinary acts—more severe than a reprimand yet less severe than a discharge.

SVIB: *see* STRONG VOCATIONAL INTEREST BLANK.

swap maternity, a provision in group health insurance plans providing immediate maternity benefits to a newly covered woman, but terminating coverage on pregnancies in progress upon termination of a woman's coverage.

sweat shop, work sites where employees worked long hours for low wages usually under unsanitary conditions. While sweat shop conditions have been mostly eliminated in the United States because of the union movement and labor legislation, the term is still used informally to refer to various working conditions that employees might find distasteful. For a description of real sweat shops, *see* Leon Stein, ed., *Out of the Sweat Shop: The Struggle for Industrial Democracy* (N.Y.: Quadrangle, 1977).

sweep pay: *see* WELL PAY.

sweetheart agreement, also called SWEETHEART CONTRACT, expressions for any agreement between an employer and a union or union official that benefits them but not the workers. Incidences of employer bribes to labor officials in order to gain their agreement to substandard or "sweetheart" contracts are well known to American labor history.

sweetheart clause, that portion of a union contract that makes a general policy statement about the harmonious manner in which both sides will live up to the spirit and letter of the agreement.

sweetheart contract: *see* SWEETHEART AGREEMENT.

swing shift, extra shift of workers in an organization operating on a continuous or seven-day basis. The swing crew rotates among the various shifts to compensate for those employees who are absent, sick, on vacation, etc.

Sylvis, William H. (1828-1869), credited with "inventing" the union membership card, he led the Iron-Molders' International Union during its most successful period and was a founder and president of the National Labor Union. *See* Jonathan Grossman, *William Sylvis, Pioneer of American Labor: A Study of the Labor Movement During the Era of the Civil War* (New York: Columbia University Press, 1945).

sympathy strike, also called SYMPATHETIC STRIKE, strike by one union undertaken solely to support the aims of another union in an effort to exert indirect pressure upon an employer. The Labor-Management Relations (Taft-Hartley) Act of 1947 made sympathy strikes illegal. *See* Michael H. Boldt, "Design and Manufacturing Corporation: The Multiplant Employer and Sympathy Strikes," *Labor Law Journal* (March 1982); Elvis C. Stephens and Donna Ledgerwood, "Do No-Strike Clauses Prohibit Sympathy Stikes?" *Labor Law Journal* (May 1982).

syndicalism, the theory that trade unions should control the means of production and, ultimately, the government. *Criminal syndicalism* is advocating a crime, sabotage, etc., to take over an industry or affect the government.

synectics, originally a Greek word, meaning the joining together of different and apparently irrelevant elements, it is now used to describe an experimental process of observing and recording the unrestrained exchange of ideas among a group in order to methodically develop new ideas, solve problems and/or make discoveries. As an effort to induce creativity, it is akin to brainstorming. *See* William J. J. Gordon, *Synectics: The Development of Creative Capacity* (N.Y.: Harper & Row, 1961).

synthetic basic-motion times, time standards for fundamental motions and groups of motions.

synthetic seniority: *see* SUPERSENIORITY.

synthetic time study, time study, not dependent upon direct observation, in which time elements are obtained from other sources of time data.

synthetic validity, also called INDIRECT VALIDITY, inferring validity by means of a systematic analysis of a job and its elements, obtaining test validity for the various elements, then combining the elemental validities into a whole synthetic validity. *See* M. J. Balma, "The Development of Processes for Indirect or Synthetic Validity," *Personnel Psychology,* Vol. 12 (1959).

system, any organized collection of parts that is united by prescribed interactions and designed for the accomplishment of a specific goal or general purpose. According to William Exton, Jr., in *The Age of Systems: The Human Dilemma* (N.Y.: American Management Association, 1972), the term system

represents the principle of functional combination of resources to produce intended result of effects. The combination may be great or small, simple or enormously complex, active or poten-

tial, solitary or parallel, new or old, static or dynamic. The intended effect may be fixed or otherwise, unique or repetitive or continuous, geographically or spacially defined or unlimited in territorial scope, physical or symbolic, tangible or intangible.

system, career: *see* CAREER SYSTEM.

System 4, Rensis Likert's term for a participative-democratic managerial style. *See* his *The Human Organization* (N.Y.: McGraw-Hill, 1967).

systemic discrimination, use of employment practices (recruiting methods, selection tests, promotion policies, etc.) that have the unintended effect of excluding or limiting the employment prospects of women and minorities. Because of court interpretations of Title VII of the Civil Rights Act of 1964, all such systemic discrimination despite its "innocence," must be eliminated where it cannot be shown that such action would place an unreasonable burden on the employer or that such practices can not be replaced by other practices which would not have such an adverse effect.

systems analysis, methodologically rigorous collection, manipulation, and evaluation of organizational data in order to determine the best way to improve the functioning of the organization (the system) and to aid a decisionmaker in selecting a preferred choice among alternatives. Ac-

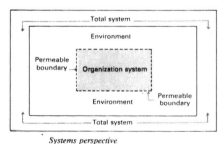

Systems perspective

Source: P. Bryans and T. P. Cronin, Organization Theory (London: Mitchell Beazley, 1983), p. 110.

cording to David I. Cleland and William R. King, in *Management: A Systems Approach* (N.Y.: McGraw-Hill, 1972),

systems analysis is a way of reaching decisions which contrasts with intuition-based and unsystematic approaches; the techniques of systems analysis help to make a complex problem understandable and manageable in the sense of offering possible strategies and solutions and establishing, to the maximum extent practical, criteria for selecting the best solution.

Also see David Easton, *A System Analysis of Political Life*, (New York: John Wiley & Co., 1965); Guy Black, *The Application of Systems Analysis to Government Operations* (New York: Praeger, 1968); E. S. Quade and W. I. Boucher (eds.), *Systems Analysis and Policy Planning* (New York: American Elsevier Publishing Co., 1968); Ida R. Hoos, *Systems Analysis in Public Policy: A Critique* (Berkeley: University of California Press, 1972); David Cleland and William King, *Systems Analysis and Project Management* (New York: McGraw-Hill, 1975); Chris Game and Trish Sarson, *Structured Systems Analysis: Tools and Techniques* (Englewood Cliffs, N.J.: Prentice-Hall, 1979); Hugh J. Miser and Edward S. Quade, eds., *Handbook of Systems Analysis* (New York: Elsevier Science Publishing, 1985).

See also PARETO OPTIMALITY.

systems analyst, specialist in systems analysis.

systems approach, also called SYSTEMS PHILOSOPHY. The systems approach or philosophy can help a manager cope with complex situations by providing an analytical framework which conceives of an enterprise as a set of objects with a given set of relationships and attributes all connected to each other and their environment in such a way as to form an entirety. Because both organizations (as well as the whole world) are constantly changing, approaches to dealing with such systems must necessarily have a corresponding evolution. According to C. West Church-

man, in *The Systems Approach* (N.Y.: Delacorte Press, 1968),

we must admit that the problem—the appropriate approach to systems—is not solved, but this is a very mild way of putting the matter. This is not an unsolved problem in the sense in which certain famous mathematical problems are unsolved. It's not as though we can expect that next year or a decade from now someone will find the correct systems approach and all deception will disappear. This, in my opinion, is not in the nature of systems. What is in the nature of systems is a continuing perception and deception, a continuing re-viewing of the world, of the whole system, and of its components. The essence of the systems approach, therefore, is confusion as well as enlightenment. The two are inseparable aspects of human living.

systems management, according to Richard A. Johnson, Fremont E. Kast and James E. Rosenzweig, in *The Theory and Management of Systems* (N.Y.: McGraw-Hill, 3rd ed., 1973), systems management involves the application of systems theory to managing organizational systems or subsystems. It can refer to management of a particular function or to projects or programs within a larger organization. An important point is that systems theory is a vital ingredient in the managerial process. It involves recognizing a general model of input-transformation-output with identifiable flows of material, energy, and information. It also emphasizes the interrelationships among subsystems as well as the suprasystem to which a function, project, or organization belongs.

systems philosophy: *see* SYSTEMS APPROACH.

systems theory: *see* GENERAL SYSTEMS THEORY.

T

TA: *see* TRANSACTIONAL ANALYSIS.

Taft-Hartley Act: *see* LABOR-MANAGEMENT RELATIONS ACT OF 1947.

take-home pay, also called NET PAY, employee's wages minus deductions that are either required (such as taxes) or requested (such as savings bonds).

tall organization: *see* FLAT ORGANIZATION.

tardiness, reporting to work later than the scheduled time.

target, expected earnings under a piece-rate wage system. The earnings target is usually set at a fixed percentage, 10 to 15 percent, above the base rate.

task, unit of work. A task is created whenever human effort, physical or mental, is exerted to accomplish a specific purpose.

task analysis, identifying the various elements essential to the accomplishment of a task. *See* Ernest J. McCormick, "Job and Task Analysis," in Marvin D. Dunnette, ed., *Handbook of Industrial and Organizational Psychology* (Chicago: Rand McNally, 1976); Frank A. Malinowski, "Job Selection Using Task Analysis," *Personnel Journal* (April 1981); Ricky W. Griffin, *Task Design: An Integrative Approach* (Glenview, Ill.: Scott, Foresman and Co., 1982).

task-and-bonus plan, wage incentive plan paying a specific percent of the base wage rate (in addition to the base wage rate) when a specified level of production is maintained or exceeded for a specified period of time.

task force, also called INTERDISCIPLINARY TEAM, temporary organizational unit charged with accomplishing a specific mission. Committees tend to be chiefly concerned with the assessment of information in order to reach a conclusion. In contrast a task group, task force, or interdisciplinary team is aggressively oriented. According to Lawrence W. Bass, in *Management By Task Forces: A Manual on the Operation of Interdisciplinary Teams* (Mt. Airy, Md.: Lomond Books, 1975), the great benefit of task forces is the great improvement that they bring about in information transfer.

The members develop needed information in their respective spheres. They communicate their findings and conclusions to their colleagues on a timely schedule in order that the others may take them into consideration in carrrying out their own missions. Their contacts are frequent and mutually helpful. They participate in discussions to dovetail their common and individual progress toward main objectives. They are an integrated community.

See also WORK GROUP. *Also see* Robert J. Butler and Lyle Yorks, "A New Appraisal System as Organizational Change: GE's Task Force Approach," *Personnel* (January-February 1984).

task group: *see* WORK GROUP.

TAT: *see* THEMATIC APPERCEPTION TEST.

tax deferred annuity, also called TAX SHELTERED ANNUITY, annuity whose employee contributions are not subject to taxes at the time that the contributions are made. Contributions are later taxed as they are paid out after retirement when the annuitant is presumably in a lower tax bracket.

tax equalization policy, program that has an employer deduct from the salary of employees sent overseas the amount of taxes that would have been due if they had resided in the United States. In return, the employer assumes the total burden of both U.S. and host nation income taxes.

taxes, employment/payroll: *see* EMPLOYMENT TAXES.

Tax Reduction Act Employee Stock Ownership Plan (TRASOP), variant of Employee Stock Ownership Plans (ESOP's) that takes advantage of the Tax Reduction Act of 1975 and the Tax Reform Act of 1976, which sought to stimulate the adoption of ESOP's by offering additional investment tax credit to corporate sponsors. *See* Paul E. Burke, "TRASOPs: The Beautiful Benefit," *Personnel Journal* (March 1978).

tax-reimbursement allowance, additional money paid to an employee assigned overseas to compensate for the additional taxes that must be paid (both U.S. and foreign) in excess of what would have been paid had the employee remained in the United States.

tax sheltered annuity: *see* TAX DEFERRED ANNUITY.

Taylor, Frederick W. (1856–1915), originally an engineer, is now considered the "father of scientific management." He did pioneering work on time-and-motion studies and led the search for the "one best way" of accomplishing any given task. Major works include: *Shop Management* (N.Y.: Harper & Bros., 1903); *The Principles of Scientific Management* (N.Y.: Harper & Bros., 1911). For biographies, *see* Frank Barkley Copley, *Frederick W. Taylor: Father of Scientific Management* (N.Y.: Harper & Bros., 1923; reprinted by Augustus M. Kelley, 1969), 2 volumes; Subhir Kakar, *Frederick Taylor: A Study in Personality and Innovation* (Cambridge, Mass.: M.I.T. Press, 1970). *Also see* Edwin A. Locke, "The Ideas of Frederick W. Taylor: An Evaluation," *Academy of Management Review* (January 1982).
   See also SCIENTIFIC MANAGEMENT.

Taylor Differential Piece-Rate Plan, also DIFFERENTIAL PIECE RATE PLAN, incentive plan where different piece rates are established for substandard, standard, and higher than standard production.

Taylorism, while this term refers to the scientific management teachings of Frederick W. Taylor, it is also used as a general description for the mechanistic and authoritarian style of management so common in American industry.

Taylor Law, in full PUBLIC EMPLOYEES' FAIR EMPLOYMENT ACT, New York State's law governing the unionization of state, county, and municipal employees. It grants all public employees the right to organize and be recognized, provides for a Public Employment Relations Board for the resolution of impasses, prohibits strikes, and provides a schedule of penalties for both striking individuals and their unions. The Taylor Law owes its name to George W. Taylor, a University of Pennsylvania Wharton School professor, who chaired the Governor's Committee on Public Employee Relations that recommended the enacting legislation in 1966. *See* Lynn Zimmer and James B. Jacobs, "Challenging the Taylor Law: Prison Guards on Strike," *Industrial and Labor Relations Review* (July 1981).

tea break: *see* COFFEE BREAK.

Teachers Insurance and Annuity Association (TIAA), manages portable pension plans for professional employees of colleges and universities.
   TIAA
   730 Third Ave.
   New York, N.Y. 10017
   (212) 490-9000

Tead, Ordway (1891–1973), pioneer in applying psychology to industry and co-author of one of the first personnel management texts. Major works include: *Instincts in Industry* (Boston: Houghton Mifflin, 1918); *Personnel Administration: Its Principles and Practice,* with Henry C. Metcalf (N.Y.: McGraw-Hill, 1920); *The Art of Leadership* (N.Y.: McGraw-Hill, 1935); *The Art of Administration* (N.Y.: McGraw-Hill, 1951); *Administration: Its Purpose and Performance* (N.Y.: Harper & Bros., 1959).

team building, any planned and managed change involving a group of people in order to improve communications and working relationships. Team building is most effective when used as a part of a long-range strategy for organizational and personal development. *See* Richard Beckhard, "Optimizing Team-Building Efforts," *Journal of Contemporary Business* (Summer 1972); Thomas H. Patten, Jr., and Lester E. Dorey, "Long-Range Results of a Team Building OD Effort," *Public Personnel Management* (January-February 1977); Patricia Palleschi and Patricia Heim, "The Hidden Barriers to Team Building," *Training and Development Journal* (July 1980).

Teamsters for a Democratic Union, rank-and-file members of the Teamsters who seek to reform the structure and practices of their union.

>Teamsters for a Democratic Union
>P.O. Box 10128
>Detroit, MI 48210
>(313) 842-2600

Teamsters, Local 695* v. *Vogt, 354 U.S. 284 (1957), U.S. Supreme Court case, which held that a state, in enforcing a public policy, may constitutionally enjoin peaceful picketing aimed at preventing effectuation of that policy.

Teamsters* v. *United States: *see* INTERNATIONAL BROTHERHOOD OF TEAMSTERS V. UNITED STATES.

technological unemployment, unemployment that results from the displacement of workers by machinery or by the introduction of more efficient methods of production. *See* Guy Standing, "The Notion of Technological Unemployment," *International Labour Review* (March-April 1984).

technology forecasting, use of techniques, such as surveys of experts or the assessment of a future demand, to anticipate technological developments. *See* Daniel D. Roman, "Technological Forecasting in the Decision Process," *Academy*

of Management Journal (June 1970); James R. Bright, *A Brief Introduction to Technology Forecasting* (Austin, Texas: Permaquid Press, 1972); Joseph P. Martino, *Technology Forecasting for Decision-making* (New York: American Elsevier, 1975).

technology transfer, application of technologies developed in one area of research or endeavor to another, frequently involving a concomitant shift in institutional setting *(e.g.,* from one federal agency to another). Examples include the application of space technology developed under the auspices of NASA to the problems of public transportation or weather prediction.

Temperament Survey, Guilford-Zimmerman: *see* GUILFORD-ZIMMERMAN TEMPERAMENT SURVEY.

temporary appointment: *see* APPOINTMENT.

temporary restraining order: *see* INJUNCTION.

tenure, period of time that one occupies a position. In the academic world and in some government jurisdictions, to have "tenure" means that an individual may continue in his or her position until retirement, subject, of course, to adequate behavior and the continued viability of the organization. *See* T. Michael Bolger and David D. Wilmoth, "Dismissal of Tenured Faculty Members for Reasons of Financial Exigency," *Marquette Law Review* (Spring 1982).

See also PERRY V. SINDERMAN.

term appointment: *see* APPOINTMENT.

terminal arbitration, arbitration that is called for as the final step in a grievance procedure.

terminal earnings formula, a formula that bases pension benefits on average earnings in the final years of credited service—often the last 3 or 5 years.

termination, dismissal from employment. There is no general law which prohibits private employers from discharging employees without good cause. Employers have historically had the right to fire employees at will, unless there was a written contract which protected against it. This broad right to discharge employees at will has been limited by a number of Federal laws which prohibit discrimination based on sex, race, color, religion, national origin, age, physical or mental handicap, union or other protected concerted activities, wage garnishment, and filing complaints or assisting in procedures related to enforcing these laws.

In addition, some States and municipalities have passed laws which prohibit discharge for serving on jury duty, filing workers' compensation claims, refusing to take lie detector tests, or for discrimination based on marital status or sexual orientation. Collective bargaining agreements between employers and unions, and employee complaint procedures, also impose limitations on the absolute right of an employer to fire workers.

Some employees have challenged their discharges in courts, and in a few cases have succeeded in placing additional limitations on employers' right to discharge. Courts in some States have ruled in favor of discharged employees—when the discharge was contrary to public policy, such as refusal to commit perjury or to approve market testing of a possibly harmful drug; when it was not based on good faith and fair dealing, such as discharge for refusal to date a supervisor, or to avoid paying a large commission; or when there was an implied promise of continued employment. An implied promise of continued employment might be demonstrated by the personnel policies or practices of an employer, an employee's length of service, the nature of the job, actions or communications by the employer, and industry practices.

See Stuart A. Youngblood and Gary L. Tidwell, "Termination at Will: Some Changes in the Wind," *Personnel* (May–June, 1981); Stuart R. Korshak, "Arbitrating the Termination of a Union Activist,"
Personnel Journal (January 1982); William J. Holloway and Michael J. Leech, *Employment Termination: Rights and Remedies* (Washington, D.C.: Bureau of National Affairs, Inc., 1985).

Also see
DISMISSAL
EMPLOYMENT AT WILL
FIRE
GET THE SACK

termination contract, agreement between an employer and a new employee that provides for salary continuation for the employee in the event of termination. The length of time that compensation continues to be paid typically varies from six months to two years. *See* Frank R. Beaudine, "The Termination Contract as a Recessionary Employment Tool," *Personnel Journal* (June 1975)

termination pay: *see* SEVERANCE PAY.

term life insurance, temporary insurance that offers protection for a limited number of years and has no cash value.

terms and conditions of employment, the entirety of the environment in which an employee works; all aspects of an employee's relationship with his or her employer and fellow employees, including compensation, fringe benefits, physical environment, work-related rules, work assignments, training and education, and opportunities to serve on committees and decision-making bodies.

test anxiety, nervousness that an examinee experiences before and during the administration of a test. For a study concluding that test anxiety is, except for extremes, inversely correlated with test performance, *see* C. S. Berkely and C. F. Sproule, "Test Anxiety and Test Unsophistication: The Effects and Cures," *Public Personnel Management* (January 1973).

test fidelity, extent to which a test represents the actual duties of a job.

Test of Mental Maturity, California: *see* CALIFORNIA TEST OF MENTAL MATURITY.

Test of Mental Maturity, California Short Form: *see* CALIFORNIA SHORT FORM TEST OF MENTAL MATURITY.

test publishers, are listed in current edition of O. K. Buros (ed.), *The Mental Measurements Yearbook* (Highland Park, N.J.: Gryphon Press) and Richard C. Sweetland, Daniel J. Keyser and William A. O'Connor, editors, *Tests: A Comprehensive Reference for Assessments in Psychology, Education and Business* (Kansas City, MO: Test Corporation of America, 1983).

See also selective listing "TEST PUBLISHERS" in box near this entry.

test-retest reliability, measure of the reliability obtained by giving individuals the same test for a second time after an interval and correlating the sets of scores.

tests and testing: *see* entries listed below (asterisk identifies commercially available tests commonly used in employment selection and placement):
- *ADVANCED PERSONNEL TEST (APT)
- *ADAPTABILITY TEST, THE
- *BENNETT MECHANICAL COMPREHENSION TEST (BMCT)
- *BERNREUTER PERSONALITY INVENTORY
- *CALIFORNIA OCCUPATIONAL PREFERENCE SURVEY (COPSYSTEM)
- *CALIFORNIA PSYCHOLOGICAL INVENTORY
- *CALIFORNIA SHORT FORM TEST OF MENTAL MATURITY (CTMM/SF)
- *CALIFORNIA TEST OF MENTAL MATURITY (CTMM)
- *CATTELL CULTURE FAIR INTELLIGENCE TEST
- *CONCEPT MASTERY TEST (CMR)
- CONFIDENCE TESTING
- *COOPERATIVE SCHOOL AND COLLEGE ABILITY TESTS (SCAT)
- *CRAWFORD SMALL PARTS DEXTERITY TEST
- CREATIVITY TEST
- CRITERION-REFERENCED TEST
- CULTURE-FAIR TEST
- *DAVIS READING TEST
- *DIFFERENTIAL APTITUDE TESTS (DAT)
- DEXTERITY TEST
- DIAGNOSTIC TEST
- *EDWARDS PERSONAL PREFERENCE SCHEDULE (EPPS)
- EMPLOYMENT TESTING
- *EYSENCK PERSONALITY INVENTORY (EPI)
- *FIRO B
- *FLANAGAN APTITUDE CLASSIFICATION TEST (FACT)
- *FLANAGAN INDUSTRIAL TEST (FIT)
- FREE-RESPONSE TEST
- *FUNDAMENTAL ACHIEVEMENT SERIES (FAS)
- *GORDON OCCUPATIONAL CHECK LIST (GOCL)
- *GUILFORD-ZIMMERMAN TEMPERAMENT SURVEY (GZTS)
- *HALL OCCUPATIONAL ORIENTATION INVENTORY (HOOI)
- HANDS-ON TEST
- INDIVIDUAL TEST
- INTELLIGENCE TEST
- INTEREST TEST
- *JOB TESTS PROGRAM
- *KUDER GENERAL INTEREST SURVEY (KGIS)
- *KUDER OCCUPATIONAL INTEREST SURVEY (KOIS)
- *KUDER PREFERENCE RECORD
- *MILLER ANALOGIES TEST (MAT)
- *MINNESOTA CLERICAL TEST (MCT)
- *MINNESOTA MULTIPHASIC PERSONALITY INVENTORY (MMPI)
- *MINNESOTA RATE OF MANIPULATION TEST
- *MINNESOTA SPATIAL RELATIONS TEST
- *MINNESOTA VOCATIONAL INTEREST INVENTORY (MVII)
- *MULTIPLE APTITUDE TESTS (MAT)
- MULTIPLE-CHOICE TEST
- *MYERS-BRIGGS TYPE INDICATOR
- NORM-REFERENCED TEST
- *OHIO VOCATIONAL INTEREST SURVEY (OVIS)
- *OTIS-LENNON MENTAL ABILITY TEST (OLMAT)
- PERFORMANCE TEST
- *PERSONALITY RESEARCH FORM (PRF)
- PERSONALITY TEST
- *PERSONNEL TESTS FOR INDUSTRY (PTI)
- POST-TEST
- POWER TEST
- PRE-TEST

TEST PUBLISHERS

American Guidance Services, Inc.
  Publisher's Building
  Circle Pines, MN 55014
Bobbs-Merrill Company, Inc. (The)
  4300 West 62nd Street
  Indianapolis, IN 46206
California Test Bureau
  CTB/McGraw-Hill
  Del Monte Research Park
  Monterey, CA 93940
Consulting Psychologists Press, Inc.
  577 College Avenue
  Palo Alto, CA 94306
Educational and Industrial Testing Service
  P.O. Box 7234
  San Diego, CA 92107
Follett Educational Corporation
  1010 West Washington Blvd.
  Chicago, IL 60607
Harcourt, Brace, Jovanovich, Inc.
  747 Third Avenue
  New York, NY 10017
Houghton Mifflin Company
  110 Tremont Street
  Boston, MA 02107
Industrial Psychology Inc.
  515 Madison Avenue
  New York, NY 10022
Institute for Personality and Ability
  Testing, Inc.
  P.O. Box 188
  1602 Coronado Drive
  Champaign, IL 61820
McCann Associates, Inc.
  2763 Philmont Avenue
  Huntington Valley, PA 19006

Merit Employment Assessment Services,
  Inc.
  P.O. Box 193
  Flossmoor, IL 60422
Psychological Corporation (The)
  7500 Old Oak Blvd.
  Cleveland, Ohio 44130
Research Psychologists Press, Inc.
  P.O. Box 948
  Port Huron, MI 48060
Science Research Associates, Inc.
  155 North Wacker Drive
  Chicago, IL 60606
Sheridan Psychological Services, Inc.
  P.O. Box 6101
  Orange, CA 92667
Slosson Educational Publications
  P.O. Box 280
  East Aurora, NY 14052
Stanford University Press
  Stanford, CA 94305
William, Lynde, and Williams
  153 East Erie Street
  Painesville, OH 44077
Wonderlic, E.F., and Associates
  Box 7
  Northfield, IL 60093

Texas and New Orleans Railway v. Brotherhood of Railway and Steamship Clerks, 281 U.S. 548 (1930), U.S. Supreme Court case, which denied a company the option of bargaining with its "company union" and required it to bargain with the self-organized union of its employees.

Textile Workers v. Darlington Manufacturing Company, also called DARLINGTON CASE, 380 U.S. 263 (1965), U.S. Supreme Court case, which held that while an employer had an absolute right to terminate his entire business for any reason, he does not have the right to close or move part of his business if he is motivated by anti-union bias. *See* Sherman F. Dallas and Beverly K. Schaffer, "Whatever Happened to the Darlington Case?" *Labor Law Journal* (January 1973); Robert A. Bedolis, "The Supreme Court's Darlington Mills Opinion," *The Conference Board Record* (June 1965).

Textile Workers v. Lincoln Mills, 353 U.S. 448 (1957), U.S. Supreme Court case, which held that the arbitration clause in a collective bargaining agreement is the *quid pro quo* given by the employer in return for the non-strike clause agreed to by a union.

T-Group: *see* LABORATORY TRAINING.

T-Group, family: *see* FAMILY T-GROUP.

Thematic Apperception Test (TAT), projective test that uses a standard set of pictures and calls for the subject to reveal his or her personality by making up stories about them. Variations of the TAT have been successfully used for vocational counseling and executive selection, as well as for determining attitudes toward labor problems, minority groups, and authority. *See* P. C. Cummin, "TAT Correlates of Executive Performance," *Journal of Applied Psychology* (February 1967).

Theory X and Theory Y, contrasting sets of assumptions made by managers about human behavior that Douglas McGregor distilled and labeled in *The Human Side of Enterprise* (N.Y.: McGraw-Hill, 1960).

Theory X holds that:
1. The average human being has an inherent dislike of work and will avoid it if possible.
2. Because of this human characteristic of dislike of work, most people must be coerced, controlled, directed, or threatened with punishment to get them to put forth adequate effort toward the achievement of organizational objectives.
3. The average human being prefers to be directed, wishes to avoid responsibility, has relatively little ambition, wants security above all.

Theory X assumptions are essentially a restatement of the premises of the scientific management movement, not a flattering picture of the average citizen of modern industrial society. While McGregor's portrait can be criticized for implying greater pessimism concerning the nature of man on the part of managers than is perhaps warranted, Theory X is all the more valuable as a memorable theoretical construct because it serves as such a polar opposite of Theory Y. (McGregor would later deny that the theories were polar opposites and assert that they were "simply different cosmologies.")

Theory Y holds that:
1. The expenditure of physical and mental effort in work is as natural as play or rest. The average human being does not inherently dislike work. Depending upon controllable conditions, work may be a source of satisfaction (and will be voluntarily performed) or a source of punishment (and will be avoided if possible).
2. External control and the threat of punishment are not the only means for bringing about effort toward organizational objectives. Men and

women will exercise self-direction and self-control in the service of objectives to which they are committed.

3. Commitment to objectives is a function of the rewards associated with their achievement. The most significant of such rewards *(e.g., the satisfaction of ego and self-actualization needs)* can be direct products of effort directed toward organizational objectives.

4. The average human being learns, under proper conditions, not only to accept but to seek responsibility. Avoidance of responsibility, lack of ambition, and emphasis on security are generally consequences of experience, not inherent human characteristics.

5. The capacity to exercise a relatively high degree of imagination, ingenuity, and creativity in the solution of organizational problems is widely, not narrowly, distributed in the population.

6. Under the conditions of modern industrial life, the intellectual potentialities of the average human being are only partially utilized.

While McGregor admitted that the assumptions of Theory Y were not finally validated, he found them "far more consistent with the existing knowledge in the social sciences than are the assumptions of Theory X." A central motif in both Theory X and Theory Y is control. With Theory X, control comes down from management via strict supervision. Theory Y, on the contrary, assumes that employees will be internally rather than externally controlled. Such internal control presumably comes from an inward motivation to perform effectively.

Theory Z, an approach to management generally associated with the Japanese that emphasizes participative management from employees who are committed to their work through cultural tradition, shared socioeconomic values, and communal forms of decision making. Theory Z personnel policies are characterized by high levels of trust, lifetime or long-term job security, and holistic career planning.

See William Ouchi, *Theory Z: How American Business Can Meet the Japanese Challenge* (Reading, Mass.: Addison-Wesley, 1981); William G. Ouchi, "Organizational Paradigms: A Commentary on Japanese Management and Theory Z Organizations," *Organizational Dynamics* (Spring 1981); Ronald Contino and Robert M. Lorusso, "The Theory Z Turnaround of a Public Agency," *Public Administration Review* (January–February 1982); Grover Starling, "Performance Appraisal in the Z Organization," *Public Personnel Management* (Winter 1982); Stephen P. Robbins, "The Theory Z Organization from a Power-Control Perspective," *California Management Review* (January 1983).

therblig, basic elements of work motions first classified by the "inventor" of motion study, Frank G. Gilbreth. Therbligs (Gilbreth spelled backward) came in 17 varieties and remain the foundation of the science of motion study. The basic therbligs, as modified by the Society for the Advancement of Management, are: search, select, grasp, reach, move, hold, release, position, pre-position, inspect, assemble, disassemble, use, unavoidable delay, avoidable delay, plan, and rest to overcome fatigue.

think tank, colloquial term that refers to an organization or organizational segment whose sole function is research. Some of the better known "think tanks" include: The RAND Corporation, The Hudson Institute, and The Stanford Research Institute. For a complete account, *see* Paul Dickson, *Think Tanks* (N.Y.: Atheneum, 1971).

third-party allegations of discrimination, allegations of discrimination in employment brought by third parties—that is, groups or individuals not alleging discrimination against themselves and not seeking relief on their own behalf. The purpose of third-party procedures is to permit organizations with an interest in furthering equal opportunity to call attention to equal opportunity problems that appear to require correction or remedial action and that are unrelated to individual complaints of discrimination.

third sector, all those organizations that fit neither in the public sector (government) nor the private sector (business). Theodore Levitt, in *The Third Sector: New Tactics for a Responsive Society* (N.Y.: Amacom Press, 1973), defines the third sector as comprising "those organizations which have risen to institutionalize activism in order to meet problems ignored by the other two sectors." For a symposium, *see* Michael E. McGill and Leland M. Wooton (eds.), "Management in the Third Sector," *Public Administration Review* (September-October 1975). *Also see* James T. Evans, "Third Sector Management: The Museum in the Age of Introspection—Survival and Redefinition for the 1980s," *Public Administration Review* (September-October 1982).

Thomas v. *Review Board of the Indiana Employment Security Division,* 67 L.Ed. 2d 624 (1981), U.S. Supreme Court case which held the denial of unemployment compensation to a member of Jehovah's Witnesses, who voluntarily quit his job because of his religious beliefs, was violative of the free exercise clause of the First Amendment.

Thompson, James D. (1919-73), sociologist whose landmark book in organizational analysis and theory, *Organizations in Action* (New York: McGraw-Hill, 1967), found organizations to be primarily open systems. But Thompson suggested that the closed system approach might be more realistic at the technical level of operations. He sought to bridge the gap between open and closed systems by suggesting that organizations deal with the uncertainty of their environment by creating specific elements designed to cope with the outside world while other elements are able to focus on the rational nature of technical operations.

Thompson, Victor A. (1912-   ), one of the most gifted stylists in the literature of administration, Thompson is best known for dealing deftly with bureaucratic interactions and dysfunctions. In his most influential work, *Modern Organization* (New York: Knopf, 1961), he reminds us that "One must not forget that clients are notoriously insensitive to the needs of bureaucrats." Other major works include: *Public Administration,* with Herbert A. Simon and Donald W. Smithburg (New York: Knopf, 1950); *Bureaucracy and Innovation* (University of Alabama Press, 1969); *Without Sympathy or Enthusiasm: The Problem of Administrative Compassion* (University of Alabama Press, 1975); *Bureaucracy and the Modern World* (Morristown, N.J.: General Learning Press, 1976).

Thornhill v. *Alabama: see* PICKETING.

threshold effect, total impression a job applicant makes by his or her bearing, dress, manners, etc., as he or she "comes through the door."

throughput, middle step in data processing or a system's operation; it comes after input and before output.

Thurstone Scale, attitude scale created by Louis L. Thurstone that has judges rate the favorability of statements, then has subjects select those statements with which they agree. *See* L. L. Thurstone and E. J. Chave, *The Measurement of Attitude* (Chicago: University of Chicago Press, 1929).

Thurstone Test of Mental Alertness (TTMA), test of mental ability used in screening personnel applicants in business and industry, particularly sales and clerical jobs. Consists of 126 verbal and quantitative items in alternate order and ascending difficulty. TIME: 20 minutes. AUTHOR: Thelma G. and L. L. Thurstone. PUBLISHER: Science Research Associates, Inc. (*see* TEST PUBLISHERS).

TIAA: *see* TEACHERS INSURANCE AND ANNUITY ASSOCIATION.

tiger team, a task force or work group assigned to solve a specific problem or generate new ideas.

time, broken: *see* BROKEN TIME.

time card, most basic payroll form on which is recorded, either manually or by means of a mechanical time clock, the hours that an employee has worked during a particular pay period. For an analysis, *see* E. B. Helin, "Sophisticating the Antiquated Time Card," *Personnel Journal* (June 1971).

time horizon, that distance into the future to which a planner looks when seeking to evaluate the consequences of a proposed action. *See* Ronald J. Ebert and DeWayne Piehl, "Time Horizon: A Concept for Management," *California Management Review* (Summer 1973).

time-in-grade restriction, requirement intended to prevent excessively rapid promotions in the federal government's General Schedule. Generally, an employee may not be promoted more than two grades within one year to positions up to GS-5. At GS-5 and above, an employee must serve a minimum of one year in grade, and cannot be promoted more than one grade, or two grades if that is the normal progression.

time-sharing, simultaneous use of a central computer by two or more remote users, each of whom has direct and individual use of the central computer through the use of a terminal. The first commercial computer time-sharing services began in 1965.

time study, according to Benjamin W. Niebel, in *Motion and Time Study,* (Homewood, Ill.: Richard D. Irwin, 7th ed., 1982),

time study involves the technique of establishing an allowed time standard to perform a given task, based upon

measurement of the work content of the prescribed method, with due allowance for fatigue and for personal and unavoidable delays. The time study analyst has several techniques that can be used to establish a standard: stopwatch time study, standard data, fundamental motion data, work sampling, and estimates based upon historical data.
See also the following entries:
GILBRETH, FRANK BUNKER AND LILLIAN MOLLER
MOTION STUDY
SYNTHETIC TIME STUDY
THERBLIG
WORK SAMPLING

timetable: *see* GOAL.

time wage rate, any pay structure providing for wage payments in terms of an hourly, weekly, or monthly time interval. This is in contrast to a piece-rate structure where an employee is paid only for the amount that he or she produces.

title, also called CLASS TITLE, the "label" used to officially designate a class. It is descriptive of the work performed and its relative level.

titles, in addition to their use as formal job descriptions, are useful management tools (and cheap, too). The appropriate title can provide incalculable psychic income and a decided advantage when dealing with the outside world. A sales representative may be more effective as a vice president for sales. A secretary may be more effective as an administrative assistant. Some housewives are even slightly more content to be known as domestic engineers. Shakespeare's Juliet was wrong. A rose by any other name would not necessarily smell as sweet; sometimes it smells better!

Title VII, in the context of equal employment opportunity, almost invariably refers to Title VII of the Civil Rights Act of 1964 (as amended)—the backbone of the nation's EEO effort. It prohibits employment discrimination because of race, color, religion, sex, or national origin and created the Equal Employment Opportunity Commission as its enforcement vehicle. The federal courts have relied heavily upon Title VII in mandating remedial action on the part of employers. *See* Paul J. Speigelman, "Bona Fide Seniority Systems and Relief from 'Last Hired, First Fired' Layoffs under Title VII," *Employee Relations Law Journal* (Autumn 1976); Gary L. Lubben, Duane C. Thompson, and Charles R. Klasson, "Performance Appraisal: The Legal Implications of Title VII," *Personnel* (May-June 1980); David G. Karro, "The Importance of Being Earnest: Pleading and Maintaining a Title VII Class Action for the Purpose of Resolving the Claims of Class Members," *Fordham Law Review* (May 1981); Elaine Gale Wrong, "The Social Responsibility of Arbitrators in Title VII Disputes," *Labor Law Journal* (September 1981); Nestor Cruz, "Abuse of Rights in Title VII Cases: The Emerging Doctrine," *Labor Law Journal* (May 1981); Kenneth Kirschner, "The Extraterritorial Application of Title VII of the Civil Rights Act," *Labor Law Journal* (July 1983); Ann W. Hart, "Intent vs. Effect: Title VII Case Law That Could Affect You (Part 1)," *Personnel Journal* (March 1984).

See also the following entries:

title-structure change, elimination of a title by substitution of a more appropriate title without any change in duties or responsibilities of the position involved.

Tobin, Maurice J. (1901-1953), Secretary of Labor from 1948 to 1953.

tokenism, in the context of Equal Employment Opportunity, an insincere EEO effort by which a few minority group members are hired in order to satisfy government affirmative action mandates or the demands of pressure groups.

tool-handling time, that time during the normal work day that the worker devotes to tending to the tools that are the necessary instruments of his or her work.

Torcaso* v. *Watkins, 367 U.S. 488 (1961), U.S. Supreme Court case, which held that a state requirement of a declaration of a belief in God as a qualification for office was unconstitutional because it invades one's freedom of belief and religion guaranteed by the 1st Amendment and protected by the 14th Amendment from infringement by the states.

total compensation comparability, major means of incorporating fringe benefits into overall pay policy. The comparability principle, which holds that public employees should be paid wages comparable to those of similar workers in the economy has not kept pace with changing conditions. Consequently, in some jurisdictions, while actual wages and salaries may be comparable to those of private-sector counterparts, the total package of pay plus fringe benefits often gives the public-sector employee a greater total return than that gained by a private-sector counterpart. In response to this situation jurisdictions are increasingly calling for total compensation comparability. This, in essence, calls for both pay and benefits to be included in comparability surveys, rather than pay alone. This move toward total compensation comparability nicely dovetails with governmental concerns for steadily rising inflation, dwindling fiscal resources, and the mood of taxpayers to hold down governmental spending. *See* Pierre Martel, "A Model of Total Compensation in a Market-Comparability Framework," *Public Personnel Management* (Summer 1982); Bruce R. Eillig, "Total Compensation Design: Elements and Issues," *Personnel* (January–February 1984).

total labor force: *see* LABOR FORCE.

totem-pole ranking, rank ordering of employees, usually for purposes of evaluation, where each is placed above or below another with no more than one individual per rank.

See also LOW MAN ON THE TOTEM POLE.

Totten, Ashley Leopold (1884–1963), one of the founders of the Brotherhood of Sleeping Car Porters in 1925 and secretary-treasurer of that union for more than 30 years. For biographical information, *see* Brailsford R. Brazeral, *The Brotherhood of Sleeping Car Porters: Its Origin and Development* (N.Y.: Harper & Bros., 1946).

tour of duty, hours that an employee is scheduled to work.

Tower Amendment, portion of Title VII of the Civil Rights Act of 1964 that was introduced by Senator John Tower of Texas during Senate debate on the act. The Tower Amendment, Section 703 (h), had the effect of establishing, in legal terms, the right of an employer to give "professionally developed ability tests" as long as they were not intentionally discriminatory. The amendment reads as follows:

Nor shall it be an unlawful employment practice for an employer to give and to act upon the results of any professionally developed ability test provided that such test, its administration or action upon the results is not designed, intended or used to discriminate because of race, color, religion, sex, or national origin.

Towne, Henry Robinson (1844–1924), an early scientific management advocate whose efforts predated and influenced Frederick W. Taylor. His most famous paper, "The Engineer as an Economist" (ASME *Transactions,* Vol. 7, pp. 428–432) presented at the 1886 meeting of the American Society of Mechanical Engineers called on his fellow engineers to become interested in management because "the matter of shop management is of equal importance with that of engineering."

track record, athletic metaphor for an individual's history of performance in any given field or endeavor.

trade-off, either the selection of one of several alternatives, or a concession made in response to the other side's concession.

Trade Union Leadership Council, a group of unionists, primarily black, seeking to advance civil rights issues.
Trade Union Leadership Council
8670 Grand River Ave.
Detroit, MI 48204
(313) 894-0303

Trade Union Women of African Heritage, a group of black women unionists united to advance the interests of blacks and other minorities in the union movement.
Trade Union Women of African Heritage
P.O. Box 459
New York, NY 10003
(212) 652-2074

trade union: *see* CRAFT UNION.

trainee rate: *see* BEGINNER'S RATE.

trainerless laboratory, laboratory training experience conducted by the participants themselves.

training, organized effort to increase the capabilities of individuals and modify their behavior in order to achieve previously determined objectives. For texts, *see* I. L. Goldstein, *Training: Program Develop-*

ment and Design (Monterey, Calif.: Brooks/Cole, 1974); Kenneth T. Byers (ed.), *Employee Training and Development in the Public Sector* (Chicago: International Personnel Management Association, rev. ed., 1974); Robert L. Craig (ed.), *Training and Development Handbook* (N.Y.: McGraw-Hill, 2nd ed., 1976); Dugan Laird, *Approaches to Training and Development* (Reading, Mass.: Addison-Wesley, 1978); Kenneth N. Wexley and Gary P. Latham, *Developing and Training Human Resources in Organizations* (Glenview, Ill.: Scott, Foresman and Co., 1981).

See also the following entries:
AMERICAN SOCIETY FOR TRAINING AND DEVELOPMENT
ASSERTIVENESS TRAINING
COLD-STORAGE TRAINING
COMPREHENSIVE EMPLOYMENT AND TRAINING ACT OF 1973
GOVERNMENT EMPLOYEES TRAINING ACT OF 1958
IN-SERVICE TRAINING
JOINT TRAINING
LABORATORY TRAINING
NATIONAL TRAINING LABORATORIES INSTITUTE FOR APPLIED BEHAVIORAL SCIENCE
POST-ENTRY TRAINING
RADIUS CLAUSE
ROLE
TRANSFER OF TRAINING
VERTICAL TRAINING
VESTIBULE TRAINING
VOCATIONAL TRAINING

Training and Development Journal, monthly journal of the American Society for Training and Development, Inc. Articles written both by practitioners and academics emphasize all phases of training and organization development. Selections tend to be more practical than theoretical.

Training and Development Journal
ASTD, Suite 305
600 Maryland Ave., S.W.
Washington, D.C. 20024

training by objectives, much as a management by objectives system establishes objectives and breaks down all

subordinate activity into subdivisions that contribute to the overall objectives, "training by objectives" allows employees to establish their own developmental goals (compatible with organizational goals) and direct their activities toward these goals. For the most comprehensive treatment of this concept, *see* George S. Odiorne, *Training by Objectives: An Economic Approach To Management Training* (N.Y.: The MacMillan Company, 1970).

training demand, also TRAINING NEED, expressed preferences for training programs by individuals. *Training need* reflects some form of skill deficit that is directly related to job performance. If an organization's sole criterion for initiating a training program is demand, the danger will persist that what is demanded is not necessarily what is needed. *See* Richard A. Morano, "Determining Organizational Training Needs," *Personnel Psychology* (Winter 1973); Richard F. Fraser, John W. Gore and Chester C. Cotton, "A System for Determining Training Needs," *Personnel Journal* (December 1978); Stephen V. Steadham, "Learning to Select a Needs Assessment Strategy," *Training and Development Journal* (January 1980); Ron Zemke, "How To Conduct a Needs Assessment For Computer Literacy Training," *Training* (September 1983); John P. Bucalo, Jr., "An Operational Approach to Needs Analysis," *Training and Development Journal* (April 1984); Vicki S. Kaman and John P. Mohr, "Training Needs Assessment in the Eighties: Five Guideposts," *Personnel Administrator* (October 1984).

training evaluation, also TRAINING MEASUREMENT, determination of the extent to which a training program is justified by its results. *Training measurement* must precede training evaluation, because it reveals the changes that may have occurred as a result of training. The essential question is whether or not a training effort has met its objective. Annual reports frequently boast of the number of employees trained during the preceding year but such "facts" should be looked upon with great suspicion. It is a common mistake to assume that the number of people who have been subjected to training is equal to the number who have been trained. No statement of training accomplishment can confidently be made unless it is supported by sophisticated measures of evaluation. *See* Irwin L. Goldstein, *Training: Program Development and Evaluation* (Monterey, Calif.: Brooks/Cole, 1974); Richard Morano, "Measurement and Evaluation of Training," *Training and Development Journal* (July 1975); Donald Kirkpatrick, *Evaluating Training Programs* (Madison, Wis.: American Society of Training and Development, 1975); John W. Newstrom, "Evaluating the Effectiveness of Training Methods," *The Personnel Administrator* (January 1980); Jonathan S. Monat, "A Perspective on the Evaluation of Training and Development Programs," *Personnel Administrator* (July 1981); J. Kevin Ford and Steven P. Wroten, "Introducing New Methods for Conducting Training Evaluation and for Linking Evaluation to Program Redesign," *Personnel Psychology* (Winter 1984); Darlene Russ-Eft and John H. Zenger, "Common Mistakes in Evaluating Training Effectiveness," *Personnel Administrator* (April 1985).

training measurement: *see* TRAINING EVALUATION.

training need: *see* TRAINING DEMAND.

Training: The Magazine of Human Resources Development, monthly trade magazine dealing with all aspects of training and human resource development. Articles tend to be written by practitioners in order to help managers of training development functions use the behavioral sciences to solve human performance problems.

Training: The Magazine of Human Resources Development
731 Hennepin Avenue
Minneapolis, MN 55403

transactional analysis (TA), approach to psychotherapy first developed by Eric Berne. Transactional analysis defines the basic unit of social intercourse as a "transaction." There are three "ego states" from which transactions emanate—that of a "parent," an "adult," or a "child." The transactions between individuals can be classified as complementary, crossed, simple or ulterior, based upon the response that an individual receives to a "transactional stimulus"—any action that consciously or unconsciously acknowledges the presence of other individuals. The transactional analysis framework has become a popular means of helping managers to assess the nature and effectiveness of their interpersonal behavior. By striving for more adult-to-adult transactions, managers may eliminate many of the "games people play." For the first published account, *see* Eric Berne, "Transactional Analysis: A New and Effective Method of Group Therapy," *American Journal of Psychotherapy* (October 1958). For the best seller that made transactional analysis a household term, *see* Eric Berne, *Games People Play: The Psychology of Human Relationships* (N.Y.: Grove Press, 1964). For a general treatment, *see* Thomas A. Harris, *I'm OK—You're OK* (N.Y.: Harper & Row, 1969). For an application to personnel, *see* A. J. Tasca, "Personnel Management: A T/A Perspective," *Personnel Journal* (November 1974).

transactional avoidance, "management theory" described by Norman A. Parker, in "The Tongue-in-Cheek Approach To Management Theories," *Personnel Journal* (July 1978):

The psychologists have put a lot of time into analyzing relationships between people. They have observed that many of these relationships, or transactions, take place between two people playing combinations of roles as parent, child or adult. The conclusion usually reached is that in a work situation, the optimal transaction is conducted by two people playing the role of adult. This is nice if you can get everyone involved to agree to act like an adult. Unfortunately, such is not always the case. Some days, when the planets are right, two people might interact that way.

Most of the time there is just too much going on to bother. You then have the transactor making a real college try to be "OK," while the transactee is sucking his or her thumb or acting like a wounded parent. What this leads to is ambivalence in the transaction process, and that is bad and almost incurable. Transactional Avoidance, however, neatly side-steps all the pitfalls.

The basic concept of Transactional Avoidance was devised by an exhermit. His thesis is that in any kind of confrontation, somebody usually loses and therefore any avoidance of transaction is a plus. The elements of the technique involve free delegation of everything, and since almost everyone is familiar with the rudiments of delegation, there is no long learning process involved. The originator of this system refuses to teach any classes and little has been published on this promising concept.

transcendental meditation, technique utilizing biofeedback, which seeks to expand an individual's intellectual growth and consciousness. For the methodology, *see* Robert B. Kory, *The Transcendental Meditation Program for Business People* (N.Y.: AMACOM, 1976).

transfer, also called LATERAL TRANSFER, job reassignment in which the employee retains approximately the same pay, status, and responsibility as in his or her previous assignment. *See* Edward J. Bardi and Jack L. Simonetti, "The Game of Management Chess-Policies and Perils of Management Transfers," *Personnel Journal* (April 1977).

transfer of training, theory that knowledge or abilities acquired in one area aids the acquisition of knowledge or abilities in other areas. When prior learning is helpful, it is called *positive transfer*. When prior learning inhibits new learning, it is called *negative transfer*.

Trans World Airlines v. Hardison, 432 U.S. 63 (1977), U.S. Supreme Court case, which ruled

that an employer is not required to arrange Saturdays off for an employee so that he may observe his Sabbath, if in doing so the employer would incur more than minimal costs—such as overtime pay for a replacement. The Court also ruled that, if employees' work schedules are determined on the basis of seniority, an employer is not required to violate the seniority privileges of others so that an employee can observe a Saturday Sabbath.

trashcan hypothesis, assertion that the personnel department is the dumping ground of management. According to Dalton E. McFarland, in *Cooperation and Conflict in Personnel Administration* (New York: American Foundation for Management Research, 1962),

in the assignment of functions to employee relations executives, chief executives or members of organizing committees have no systematic basis for determining the degree of appropriateness of the function for this department. Consequently, they view the personnel department as a dumping ground for a broad array of functions having little to do with the major goals of personnel administration. These decisions have a potential for weakening the performance of major employee relations functions. Personnel executives dislike this extension of their duties and the resulting thinning out of time and available resources.

TRASOP: *see* TAX REDUCTION ACT EMPLOYEE STOCK OWNERSHIP PLAN.

Tree Fruits ruling: *see* NATIONAL LABOR RELATIONS BOARD V. FRUIT PACKERS.

trend projections, the examination and study of the behavioral patterns of both past and present statistical data and also the projecting or predicting of the possible range of that data over a future period of time. Predicting trends consists of using usually quantitative methods for plotting data as a function of time to see what did happen to it in the past and determine if the trend or character of the (plotted) data will continue unchanged for some future period. The three major types of predictions used are:

1. *Cyclic predictions,* which may be based on the principle that history repeats itself. Such data when displayed may show periodic fluctuations such as temperature changes throughout the year or the use of electricity in the same period. This can be used only when you are sure how the periodicity comes about and why.

2. *Trajectory predictions,* which are based on changes that occur in data that remain stable in character (e.g., population growths, gross national product, etc.).

3. *Associative predictions,* which are data from one event that are used to predict a second event. "Cause and effect" relationships must exist to predict these situations (e.g., unemployment vs. increase in the welfare rolls).

Triangle Shirtwaist Factory fire, fire that focused national attention on the need for adequate safety regulations in factories. On March 25, 1911, 146 people died in a fire in the Triangle Shirtwaist Factory "sweatshop." For a history, *see* Leon Stein, *Triangle Fire* (Phila.: J. B. Lippincott Co., 1967).

trickle-down economics, description for government policies that seek to benefit the wealthy in hopes that prosperity, in turn, will "trickle down" to the middle and lower economic classes. The term was first coined by humorist Will Rogers (1879–1935) when he analyzed some of the depression remedies of the Hoover administration and noted that "the money was all appropriated for the top in the hopes it would trickle down to the needy."

See also SUPPLY-SIDE ECONOMICS.

trilogy cases: *see* STEELWORKER'S TRILOGY.

true-false item, test question that calls for the examinee to indicate whether a given statement is true or false.

true score, score entirely free of measurement errors. True scores are hypothetical values never obtained in actual testing, which always involve some measurement error. A true score is sometimes defined as the average score that would result from an infinite series of measurements with the same or exactly equivalent tests, assuming no practice or change in the examinee during the testings.

***Truitt Manufacturing* decision:** *see* NATIONAL LABOR RELATIONS BOARD V. TRUITT MANUFACTURING.

Trumka, Richard (1949–   ), became president of the United Mine Workers in 1982.

trusteeship, also called UNION TRUSTEESHIP, situation whereby a labor organization (usually a national or international union) suspends the authority of a subordinate organization (usually a local union) and takes control of the subordinate organization's assets and administrative apparatus. Trusteeships are commonly authorized by the constitutions of international unions in order to prevent and, if necessary, remedy corruption and mismanagement by local union officials. Title III of the Labor-Management Reporting and Disclosure (Landrum-Griffin) Act of 1959 prescribes the conditions under which union trusteeships may be established and continued. *See* Daniel L. Shneidman, "Union Trusteeships and Section 304 (a) of the Landrum-Griffin Act," *Labor Law Journal* (June 1963).

TTB: *see* TYPING TEST FOR BUSINESS.

TTMA: *see* THURSTONE TEST OF MENTAL ALERTNESS.

tuition aid, also called TUITION REFUND, training program that partially or fully reimburses employees for the expenses of taking job related part-time courses at local colleges or universities. For analyses, *see* Richard A. Kaimann and Daniel Robey, "Tuition Refund—Asset or Liability?" *Personnel Journal* (August 1976); *see also*

Milwaukee Personnel Department Training Unit, "Tuition Reimbursement in Employee Productivity and OD: A Survey," *Public Personnel Management* (May–June 1977).

turkey farm, also called TURKEY OFFICE and TURKEY DIVISION, government office having little work and slight, if any, responsibility. Government managers frequently find it easier to place troublesome or incompetent employees on turkey farms rather than go through the hassle of adverse action proceedings.

turnover, movement of individuals into, through, and out of an organization. Turnover can be statistically defined as the total number (or percentage) of separations that occur over a given time period. The turnover rate is an important indicator of the morale and health of an organization. For analyses of turnover, *see* James L. Price, *The Study of Turnover* (Ames, Iowa: Iowa State University Press, 1977); Barrie O. Pettman (ed.), *Labour Turnover and Retention* (N.Y.: Halsted Press, John Wiley and Sons, 1975); Dan R. Dalton, "Turnover Turned Over: An Expanded and Positive Perspective," *Academy of Management Review* (April 1979); J. Thomas Horrigan, "The Effects of Training on Turnover: A Cost Justification Model," *Training and Development Journal* (July 1979); Catherine Begnoche Smith, "Influence of Internal Opportunity Structure and Sex of Worker on Turnover Patterns," *Administrative Science Quarterly* (September 1979); Leonard Greenhalgh, "A Process Model of Organizational Turnover: The Relationship with Job Security as a Case in Point," *Academy of Management Review* (April 1980); William N. Cooke, "Turnover and Earnings: The Scientist and Engineer Case," *Journal of Human Resources* (Summer 1980); Stephen A. Stumpf and Patricia Kelly Dawley, "Predicting Voluntary and Involuntary Turnover Using Absenteeism and Performance Indices," *Academy of Management Journal* (March 1981); David Krackhardt *et al.,* "Supervisory Behavior and Employee Turnover: A Field Experiment," *Academy of Management Journal* (June 1981); Thomas E. Hall, "How to Estimate Employee Turnover Costs," *Personnel* (July–August 1981); Carol M. Utter, "Labor Turnover in Manufacturing: The Survey in Retrospect," *Monthly Labor Review* (June 1982); John W. Seybolt, "Dealing with Premature Employee Turnover," *California Management Review* (Spring 1983); Ellen F. Jackofsky, "Turnover and Job Performance: An Integrated Process Model," *The Academy of Management Review* (January 1984); Jacob Wolpin and Ronald J. Burke, "Relationships Between Absenteeism and Turnover: A Function of the Measures?" *Personnel Psychology* (Spring 1985).

two-career couple, *see* DUAL-CAREER COUPLE.

Typing Test for Business (TTB), used in employment screening of applicants for typing positions. Five tests measure typing skills in straight copy, letters, revised manuscript, numbers, and tables. A 2-minute practice period is allowed for warmup and machine familiarization. TIME: 30/40 minutes. AUTHORS: J. E. Doppelt, A D. Hartman, F. B. Krawchick. PUBLISHER: Psychological Corporation (*see* TEST PUBLISHERS).

U

UCLEA: *see* UNIVERSITY AND COLLEGE LABOR EDUCATION ASSOCIATION.

unaffiliated union, union not affiliated with the AFL-CIO.

unassembled examination, examination in which applicants are rated solely on their education, experience, and other requisite qualifications as shown in the formal application and on any supporting evidence that may be required.

unauthorized strike: *see* WILDCAT STRIKE.

unclassified positions: *see* EXCEPTED POSITIONS.

underachievement: *see* OVERACHIEVE-MENT.

underemployment, those workers who are involuntarily working less than a normal work week and those who are situated in jobs that do not make efficient use of their skills and educational backgrounds. Examples of the latter would include a Ph. D. driving a taxi or an engineer working as a file clerk. *See* Lewis C. Solmon and others, *Underemployed Ph.D's* (Lexington, Mass.: Lexington Books, 1981); H. G. Kaufman, *Professionals in Search of Work: Coping with the Stress of Job Loss and Underemployment* (New York: Wiley, 1982).

underground economy, the totality of economic activity undertaken in order to evade tax obligations. *See* Richard J. McDonald, "The 'Underground Economy' and BLS Statistical Data," *Monthly Labor Review* (January 1984); Carol S. Carson, "The Underground Economy: An Introduction," *Survey of Current Business* (May 1984).

understudy, individual who is engaged in on-the-job training under the direction of a journey worker or an individual who is specifically hired to replace someone planning to retire.

underutilization, in the context of equal employment opportunity, occurs when there are fewer minorities or women in a particular job classification than would be reasonably expected by their general availability.

undocumented workers: *see* ILLEGAL ALIENS.

unemployed, experienced: *see* EX-PERIENCED UNEMPLOYED.

unemployed, hard-core: *see* HARD-CORE UNEMPLOYED.

unemployed, hidden: *see* DISCOURAGED WORKERS.

unemployment, persons able and willing to work who are actively (but unsuccessfully) seeking to work at the prevailing wage rate are among the unemployed. The unemployment rate is probably the most significant indicator of the health of the economy. U.S. economists tend to consider an unemployment rate of about four percent of the total labor force as "full employment." Unemployment statistics are compiled monthly by the Bureau of Labor Statistics. These figures are obtained by surveys of a sample of all U.S. households. The Bureau of the Census, which actually conducts the surveys, defines an unemployed person as a civilian over sixteen years old who, during a given week, was available to work but had none, and (1) had been actively seeking employment during the past month, or (2) was waiting to be recalled from a layoff, or (3) was waiting to report to a new job within 30 days. For the most comprehensive history on the concept of unemployment, *see* John A Garraty, *Unemployment in History: Economic Thought and Public Policy* (N.Y.: Harper & Row, 1978). *Also see* Philip L. Rones, "Recent Recessions Swell Ranks of the Long Term Unemployed," *Monthly Labor Review* (February 1984).

> *See also* the following entries:
> FRICTIONAL UNEMPLOYMENT
> PHANTOM UNEMPLOYMENT
> PHILLIPS CURVE
> RESIDUAL UNEMPLOYMENT
> SEASONAL UNEMPLOYMENT
> STRUCTURAL UNEMPLOYMENT
> TECHNOLOGICAL UNEMPLOYMENT

unemployment benefits, also called UNEMPLOYMENT COMPENSATION, specific payments available to workers from the various state unemployment insurance programs. Unemployment benefits are available as a matter of right (without a means test) to unemployed workers who have demonstrated their attachment to the labor force by a specified amount of recent work and/or earnings in covered employment. To be eligible for benefits, the worker must be ready, able, and willing to work and must be registered for work at a public employment office. A worker who meets these eligibility conditions may still be denied benefits if he or she is disqualified for an act that would indicate the worker is responsible for his or her own unemployment.

A worker's monetary benefit rights are determined on the basis of employment in covered work over a prior reference period (called the "base period"). Under all state laws, the weekly benefit amount—that is, the amount payable for a week of total unemployment—varies with the worker's past wages within certain minimum and maximum limits. In most of the states, the formula is designed to compensate for a fraction of the usual weekly wage (normally about 50 percent), subject to specified dollar maximums.

The requirements for getting unemployment insurance benefits are generally as follows:

1. The worker must register for work at a public employment office and file a claim for benefits.
2. He or she must have worked previously on a job covered by the state law. This usually includes jobs in factories, mines, offices, or other places of private industry and commerce.
3. He or she must have a prescribed amount of employment or earnings in covered employment during a specified "base period," generally a year, prior to the time benefits are claimed.
4. He or she must be able to work. In general, unemployment insurance benefits are not payable to workers who are sick or unable to work for any other reason, although a few states continue to pay the benefits (within the legal limits) to workers who became ill after they had established their claims, so long as no offer of suitable work is refused.
5. The worker must be available for work and must be ready and will-

ing to take a suitable job if one is offered.

6. The worker must not have:
   a. quit his or her job voluntarily without good cause. (In some states, the law says "without good cause attributable to the employer" or "connected with the work.")
   b. been discharged for misconduct in connection with his or her work.
   c. refused or failed, without good cause, to apply for or accept an offer of suitable work. (What is "suitable" work is generally decided by the state. However, under federal law, no worker may be denied benefits for refusing to accept a new job under substandard labor conditions, where a labor dispute is involved, or where the worker would be required to join a company union or to resign from or refrain from joining any bona fide labor organization.)
   d. become unemployed because of a stoppage of work as the result of a labor dispute, in which he or she is interested or participating, that occurred at the establishment where the worker was last employed.

See Peter S. Saucier and John A Roberts, "Unemployment Compensation: A Growing Concern for Employers," Employee Relations Law Journal (Spring 1984); Joe A. Stone, "The Impact of Unemployment Compensation on the Occupation Decisions of Unemployed Workers," The Journal of Human Resources (Spring 1982).

See also the following entries:

NEW YORK TELEPHONE CO. V. NEW YORK STATE DEPARTMENT OF LABOR
SHERBERT V. VERNER
SUPPLEMENTAL UNEMPLOYMENT BENEFITS
THOMAS V. REVIEW BOARD OF THE INDIANA EMPLOYMENT SECURITY DIVISION

unemployment compensation: *see* UNEMPLOYMENT BENEFITS.

unemployment insurance, programs designed to provide cash benefits to regularly employed members of the labor force who become involuntarily unemployed and who are able and willing to accept suitable jobs.

The first unemployment insurance law in the United States was passed by Wisconsin in 1932 and served as a forerunner for the unemployment insurance provisions of the Social Security Act of 1935. Unlike the old-age provisions of the social security legislation, which are administered by the federal government alone, the unemployment insurance system was made federal-state in character.

The Social Security Act provided an inducement to the states to enact unemployment insurance laws by means of a tax offset. A uniform national tax was imposed on the payrolls of industrial and commercial employers who in 20 weeks or more in a calendar year had eight workers or more. Employers who paid a tax to a state with an approved unemployment insurance law could credit (offset) the state tax against the national tax (up to 90 percent of the federal levy). Thus, employers in states without an unemployment insurance law would not have an advantage in competing with similar businesses in states with such a law, because they would still be subject to the federal payroll tax. Furthermore, their employees would not be eligible for benefits. In addition, the Social Security Act authorized grants to states to meet the full costs of administering the state systems. By July 1937, all 48 states, the territories of Alaska and Hawaii, and the District of Columbia had passed unemployment insurance laws. Much later, Puerto Rico adopted its own unemployment insurance program, which was incorporated into the federal-state system in 1961.

Federal law provides that a state unemployment insurance program has to meet certain requirements if employers are to get their offset against the federal tax and if the state is to receive federal grants for administration. These requirements are intended to assure that a state participating in the program has a sound and genuine unemployment insurance system, fairly administered, and financially secure. One of these requirements is that all contributions collected under the state laws be deposited in the unemployment trust fund in the U.S. Treasury. The fund is invested as a whole, but each state has a separate account to which its deposits and its share of interest on investments are credited. Aside from certain broad federal standards, each state has responsibility for the content and development of its unemployment insurance law. The state itself decides what the amount and duration of benefits shall be and, with minor limitations, what the coverage and contributions rates shall be, and what the eligibility requirements and disqualification provisions shall be. The states also directly administer the laws—collecting contributions, maintaining wage records (where applicable), taking claims, determining eligibility, and paying benefits to unemployed workers. For a history, *see* William Haber & Merrill G. Murray, *Unemployment Insurance in the American Economy: An Historical Review and Analysis* (Homewood, Ill.: Richard D. Irwin, 1966). For critiques, *see* Martin S. Feldstein, "Unemployment Insurance: Time for Reform," *Harvard Business Review* (March–April 1975); Arthur Padilla, "The Unemployment Insurance System: Its Financial Structure," *Monthly Labor Review* (December 1981); Murray Rubin, *Federal-State Relations in Unemployment Insurance: A Balance of Power* (Kalamazoo, Mich.: W. E. Upjohn Institute for Employment Research, 1983); Diana Runner, "Changes in Unemployment Legislation During 1983," *Monthly Labor Review* (February 1984).

unfair labor practices (employers). The National Labor Relations (Wagner) Act of 1935 specifically forbade certain actions—unfair labor practices—by employers. These prohibitions, which serve to protect the right of employees to organize themselves in labor unions, are:

Section 8 (a) (1) forbids an employer "to interfere with, restrain, or coerce employees." Any prohibited interference by an employer with the rights of employees to organize, to form, join, or assist a labor organization, to bargain collectively, or to refrain from any of these activities, constitutes a violation of this section. This is a broad prohibition on employer interference, and an employer violates this section whenever it commits any of the other employer unfair labor practices. In consequence, whenever a violation of Section 8 (a) (2), (3), (4), or (5) is committed, a violation of Section 8 (a) (1) is also found. This is called a "derivative violation" of Section 8 (a) (1). Section 9 concerns representatives and elections.

Section 8(a) (2) makes it unlawful for an employer "to dominate or interfere with the formation or administration of any labor organization or contribute financial or other support to it." This section not only outlaws "company unions" that are dominated by the employer, but also forbids an employer to contribute money to a union it favors or to give a union improper advantages that are denied to rival unions.

Section 8(a) (3) makes it an unfair labor practice for an employer to discriminate against employees "in regard to hire or tenure of employment or any term or condition of employment" for the purpose of encouraging or discouraging membership in a labor organization. In general, the act makes it illegal for an employer to discriminate in employment because of an employee's union or other group activity within the protection of the Act. A banding together of employees, even in the absence of a formal organization, may constitute a labor organization for purposes of Section 8(a) (3). It also prohibits discrimination because an employee has refrained from taking part in such union or group activity except where a valid union-shop agreement is in effect. Discrimination within the meaning of the act would include such action as refusing to hire, discharging, demoting, assigning to a less desirable shift or job, or withholding benefits.

Section 8(a) (4) makes it an unfair labor practice for an employer "to discharge or otherwise discriminate against an employee because he has filed charges or given testimony under this Act." This provision guards the right of employees to seek the protection of the act by using the processes of the NLRB. Like the previous section, it forbids an employer to discharge, lay off, or engage in other forms of discrimination in working conditions against employees who have filed charges with the NLRB, given affidavits to NLRB investigators, or testified at an NLRB hearing. Violations of this section are in most cases also violations of Section 8(a) (3).

Section 8(a) (5) makes it illegal for an employer to refuse to bargain in good faith about wages, hours, and other conditions of employment with the representative selected by a majority of the employees in a unit appropriate for collective bargaining. A bargaining representative seeking to enforce its right concerning an employer under this section must show that it has been designated by a majority of the employees, that the unit is appropriate, and that there has been both a demand that the employer bargain and a refusal by the employer to do so.

See also the following entries:

BOULWAREISM

MASTRO PLASTICS CORP. V. NATIONAL LABOR RELATIONS BOARD

WILLIAM E. ARNOLD CO. V. CARPENTERS DISTRICT COUNCIL OF JACKSONVILLE

unfair labor practices (unions). Twelve years after the passage of the National Labor Relations Act, the Congress became convinced that both employees and employers needed additional legal protections against unfair labor practices of unions. So the Labor-Management Relations (Taft-Hartley) Act of 1947 amended the National Labor Relations Act to include the following major prohibitions:

Section 8(b) (1) (A) forbids a labor organization or its agents "to restrain or

NLRB Unfair Labor Practice Charges Procedures

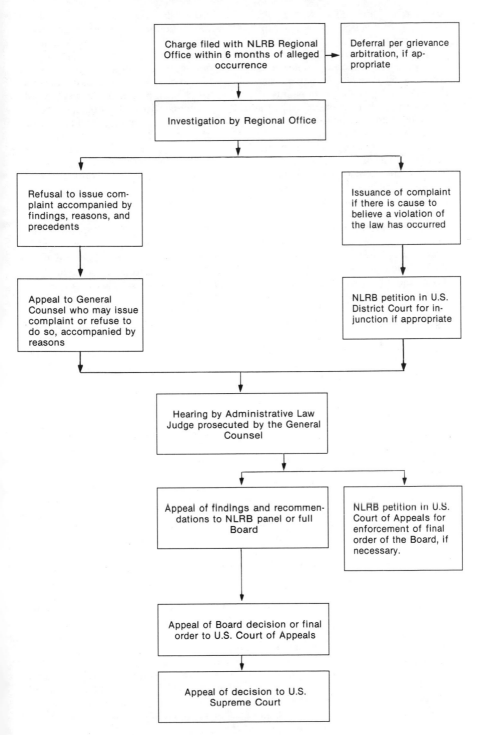

Charge filed with NLRB Regional Office within 6 months of alleged occurrence

Deferral per grievance arbitration, if appropriate

Investigation by Regional Office

Refusal to issue complaint accompanied by findings, reasons, and precedents

Issuance of complaint if there is cause to believe a violation of the law has occurred

Appeal to General Counsel who may issue complaint or refuse to do so, accompanied by reasons

NLRB petition in U.S. District Court for injunction if appropriate

Hearing by Administrative Law Judge prosecuted by the General Counsel

Appeal of findings and recommendations to NLRB panel or full Board

NLRB petition in U.S. Court of Appeals for enforcement of final order of the Board, if necessary.

Appeal of Board decision or final order to U.S. Court of Appeals

Appeal of decision to U.S. Supreme Court

coerce employees." The section also provides that it is not intended to "impair the rights of a labor organization to prescribe its own rules" concerning membership in the labor organization. A union may violate this section by coercive conduct of its officers or agents, of pickets on a picket line endorsed by the union, or of strikers who engage in coercion in the presence of union representatives who do not repudiate the conduct. Unlawful coercion may consist of acts specifically directed at an employee such as physical assaults, threats of violence, and threats to affect an employee's job status. Coercion also includes other forms of pressure against employees such as acts of a union while representing employees as their exclusive bargaining agent. A union that is a statutory bargaining representative owes a duty of fair representation to all the employees it represents. It may exercise a wide range of reasonable discretion in carrying out the representative function, but it violates Section 8(b) (1) (A) if, while acting as the employees' statutory bargaining representative, it takes or withholds action in connection with their employment because of their union activities or for any irrelevant or arbitrary reason such as an employee's race or sex.

Section 8(b) (1) (B) prohibits a labor organization from restraining or coercing an employer in the selection of a bargaining representative. The prohibition applies regardless of whether the labor organization is the majority representative of the employees in the bargaining unit.

Section 8(b) (2) makes it an unfair labor practice for a labor organization to cause an employer to discriminate against an employee. (Section 8 (a) (3) prohibits an employer from discriminating against an employee in regard to wages, hours, and other conditions of employment for the purpose of encouraging or discouraging membership in a labor organization.)

Section 8(b) (3) makes it illegal for a labor organization to refuse to bargain

in good faith with an employer about wages, hours, and other conditions of employment if it is the representative of that employer's employees. This section imposes on labor organizations the same duty to bargain in good faith that is imposed on employers by Section 8(a) (5).

Section 8(b) (4) prohibits a labor organization from engaging in a strike, or to induce or encourage a strike, work stoppage, or a refusal to perform services by "any individual employed by any person engaged in commerce or in an industry affecting commerce" in order to foster a secondary boycott, a strike against certification, a jurisdictional strike, or a "hot cargo" agreement.

Section 8(b) (5) makes it illegal for a union to charge employees covered by an authorized union-security agreement a membership fee in an amount the NLRB "finds excessive or discriminatory under all the circumstances."

Section 8(b) (6) forbids a labor organization "to cause or attempt to cause an employer to pay or deliver or agree to pay or deliver any money or other thing of value, in the nature of an exaction, for services which are not performed or not to be performed."

Section 8(b) (7) prohibits a labor organization that is not currently certified as the employees' representative from picketing or threatening to picket with an object of obtaining recognition by the employer (recognitional picketing) or acceptance by his or her employees as their representative (organizational picketing).

See Myron Roomkin, "A Quantitative Study of Unfair Labor Practice Cases," *Industrial and Labor Relations Review* (January 1981); Howard J. Parker and Harold L. Gilmore, "The Unfair Labor Practice Caseload: An Analysis of Selected Remedies," *Labor Law Journal* (March 1982); William J. Payne and Donald F. Sileo, "Self-Enforcement Under the National Labor Relations Act: Disavowals of Unfair Labor Practice Conduct," *Labor Law Journal* (December 1982); Morris M. Kleiner, "Unionism and Employer Discrimination: Analysis of 8(a)(3) Violations," *Industrial Relations* (Spring 1984). *See also* BOOSTER LODGE NO. 405, MACHINISTS V. NATIONAL LABOR RELATIONS BOARD and WILLIAM E. ARNOLD CO. V. CARPENTERS DISTRICT COUNCIL OF JACKSONVILLE.

unfair list, list of companies (or their products) that a union considers hostile to the interests of labor.

Uniform Guidelines on Employee Selection, guidelines adopted in 1978 by the four federal agencies most concerned with employee selection processes: the Equal Employment Opportunity Commission, the Civil Service Commission, the Department of Justice, and the Department of Labor. The guidelines are designed to assist employers, labor organizations, employment agencies, and licensing and certification boards to comply with requirements of federal law prohibiting employment practices that discriminate on grounds of race, color, religion, sex, or national origin. For the guidelines and clarifying questions and answers, *see Appendices 2 and 3. Also see* William R. Simon, Jr., "A Practical Approach to the Uniform Selection Guidelines," *Personnel Administrator* (November 1979); James Ledvinka, "The Statistical Definition of Fairness in the Federal Selection Guidelines and Its Implications for Minority Employment," *Personnel Psychology* (Autumn 1979); Marilyn Koch Quaintance, "The Impact of the Uniform Selection Guidelines on Public Merit Systems," *Public Personnel Management* (Vol. 9, No. 3, 1980); Alan M. Koral, "Practical Application of the Uniform Guidelines: 'What do do 'Til the Agency Comes,' " *Employee Relations Law Journal* (Spring 1980); Paul S. Greenlaw and John P. Kuhl, "Selection Interviewing and the Uniform Federal Guidelines," *Personnel Administrator* (August 1980); Charles F. Schanie and William L. Holley, "An Interpretive Review of the Federal Uniform Guidelines on Employee Selection Procedures," *The Personnel Administrator* (June 1980); Ad Hoc Group on the Uniform Selections Guidelines, *A Professional and Legal Analysis of the Uniform Guidelines on Employee Selection Procedures* (Berea, Ohio: American Society for Personnel Administration, 1981).

union: *see* list under LABOR ORGANIZATION. *See also* the following entries:
  BONA FIDE UNION
  BREAD-AND-BUTTER UNIONS
  BUSINESS UNIONS
  CENTRAL LABOR UNION
  CLOSED UNION
  COMPANY UNION
  CRAFT UNION
  GENERAL LABOR UNION
  INDEPENDENT UNION
  INDUSTRIAL UNION
  INTERNATIONAL UNION
  LOCAL INDEPENDENT UNION
  LOCAL INDUSTRIAL UNION
  LOCAL UNION
  MULTICRAFT UNION
  NATIONAL UNION
  OPEN UNION
  UNAFFILIATED UNION
  WHITE-COLLAR UNION

union counselors, also called STRIKE COUNSELORS, under ordinary circumstances, a union member who has volunteered to take a training course on the work of his or her community's social agencies. Training completed, the counselor serves as a referral agent in the local union, supplying information about the location, specific services, eligibility requirements, and application procedures to fellow union members who seek help in resolving some personal or family problem. In the event of a strike, the counselor advises strikers how they may best avail themselves of their community's social welfare programs. *See* Armand J. Thiebolt, Jr., and Ronald M. Cowin, *Welfare and Strikes: The Use of Public Funds to Support Strikers* (Philadelphia: The Wharton School of the University of Pennsylvania, 1972).

union dues: *see* DUES.

union hiring hall: *see* HIRING HALL.

unionism, dual: *see* DUAL UNIONISM.

union label, any imprint attached to an item that indicates that it was made by union labor. Unions naturally encourage their members and the public to buy only those products bearing a union label. *See* Monroe M. Bird and James W. Robinson, "The Effectiveness of the Union Label and 'Buy Union' Campaigns," *Industrial and Labor Relations Review* (July 1972).

UNION LABEL

One of the world's most famous union labels is that of the International Ladies Garment Workers Union.

Union Labor Report, information service published by the Bureau of National Affairs, Inc., for union officials at all levels. Covers the rights of unions, shop problems, union administration, equal employment opportunities, organizing, bargaining, elections, NLRB procedures, the rights of strikers, and wages and hours.

union organizer: *see* ORGANIZER.

union scale: *see* JOURNEYMAN PAY.

union security, generally, any agreement between an employer and a union that requires every employee in the bargaining unit, as a condition of employment, to be a member of the union or to pay a specified sum to the union for its bargaining services. *See* Patricia N. Blair, "Union Security Agreement in Public Employment," *Cornell University Law Review* January 1975).

union-security clause, provision in a collective bargaining agreement that seeks to protect the union by providing for a constant flow of funds by any of a variety of means. Union-security clauses typically provide for such things as the checkoff, the closed shop, the union shop, the agency shop, preferential hiring, etc. *See* Thomas R. Haggard, *Compulsory Unionism, the NLRB, and the Courts: A Legal Analysis of Union Security Agreements* (Philadelphia: The Wharton School, University of Pennsylvania, 1977); Glenn A. Zipp, "Rights and Responsibilities of Parties to a Union-Security Agreement," *Labor Law Journal* (April 1982).

union shop, union-security provision found in some collective bargaining agreements that requires all employees to become members of the union within a specified time (usually 30 days) after being hired (or after the provision is negotiated) and to remain members of the union as a condition of employment.
See also MODIFIED UNION SHOP.

union steward: *see* STEWARD.

union trusteeship: *see* TRUSTEESHIP.

unit: *see* BARGAINING UNIT.

unit, employer: *see* EMPLOYER UNIT.

United Airlines v. *Evans,* 431 U.S. 553 (1977), U.S. Supreme Court case that limited an employer's liability for prior violations under Title VII. The court ruled that an employee who was illegally discriminated against after Title VII took effect could lose her right to retroactive seniority if she fails to file charges within the specified period (now 180 days) after the violation occurred. For an analysis, *see* Stephen L. Swanson, "The Effect of the Supreme Court's Seniority Decisions," *Personnel Journal* (December 1977).

United Airlines v. McMann, 434 U.S. 192 (1977), U.S. Supreme Court case, which upheld the Age Discrimination in Employment Act of 1967. The court held that the law, designed to protect the rights of workers age 40 to 65, does not prohibit "bona fide" retirement plans that require involuntary termination before the age of 65. However, the act's 1978 amendments overturned the court's decision.

United Mine Workers v. Pennington, 381 U.S. 657 (1965), U.S. Supreme Court case, which held that pattern bargaining may leave both employers and unions liable for damages under the Sherman Anti-Trust Act of 1890 if it can be shown that the parties who wrote the pattern setting contract conspired to impose it on others. *See* Herman A. Gray, "Pennington and the 'Favored Nation' Clause," *Labor Law Journal* (November 1965).

United Public Workers v. Mitchell: see UNITED STATES CIVIL SERVICE COMMISSION V. NATIONAL ASSOCIATION OF LETTER CARRIERS.

United States Civil Service Commission, the central personnel agency of the United States from 1883 to 1978. It was abolished by the Civil Service Reform Act of 1978.

See also CIVIL SERVICE REFORM ACT OF 1978, OFFICE OF PERSONNEL MANAGEMENT, and MERIT SYSTEMS PROTECTION BOARD.

United States Civil Service Commission v. National Association of Letter Carriers, 413 U.S. 548 (1973), U.S. Supreme Court case, which upheld the Hatch Act's limitations on the political activities of federal employees.

The *Letter Carriers* decision reaffirmed an earlier court ruling, *United Public Workers v. Mitchell,* 330 U.S. 75 (1947), which had held that the ordinary citizen rights of federal employees could be abridged by Congress in the interest of increasing or maintaining the efficiency of the federal service.

In the 1972 case, *National Association of Letter Carriers v. United States Civil Service Commission,* the Court of Appeals for the District of Columbia Circuit declared the Hatch Act to be unconstitutional because its vague and "overboard" language made it impossible to determine what it prohibited. When this case was appealed to the Supreme Court, the court reasoned that, despite some ambiguities, an ordinary person using ordinary common sense could ascertain and comply with the regulations involved. It also argued that its decision did nothing more than to confirm the judgment of history that political neutrality was a desirable, or even essential, feature of public employment in the United States.

United States Code, official lawbooks that contain all federal Laws.

United States Conference of Mayors, an organization of city governments founded in 1933. It is a national forum through which this country's larger cities express their concerns and actively work to meet U.S. urban needs. By limiting membership and participation to the 750 cities with over 30,000 population and by concentrating on questions of federal-city relationships, the Conference seeks to become a focus for urban political leadership.

United States Conference of Mayors
1620 Eye Street, N.W.
Washington, D.C. 20006
(202) 293-7330

United States Court of Appeals: *see* COURT OF APPEALS.

United States District Court: *see* DISTRICT COURT.

United States Employment Service (USES), federal agency within the U.S. Department of Labor, which provides assistance to states and territories in establishing and maintaining a system of over 2,400 local public employment offices. Established by the Wagner-Peyser Act of 1933, the USES is responsible for providing job placement and other employment services to unemployed individuals and other jobseekers, providing employers and workers with job development, placement, recruitment and similar assistance including employment, counseling and special services to youth, women, older workers, and handicapped persons, and related supportive services. The USES is also responsible for the development of state and local information on employment and unemployment, and on occupational demand and supply necessary for the planning and operation of job training and vocational education programs throughout the country.

The USES develops policies and procedures to provide a complete placement service to workers and employers in rural areas. Migrant and seasonal farmworkers receive assistance to help them maintain year-round employment through the federal-state employment services interstate clearance system. The USES is responsible for insuring that, in the interstate recruitment of farm and woods workers, applicable standards and regulations relating to housing, transportation, wages, and other conditions are met.

Other USES services include: certifying aliens who seek to immigrate to the United States for employment; providing employment services and adjustment assistance to U.S. workers adversely affected by foreign imports under the Trade Act of 1974; issuing *Exemplary Rehabilitation Certificates* to qualified persons discharged from the armed services under conditions other than honorable; providing job search guidance and aptitude-testing services to workers; giving specialized recruitment assistance to employers; providing labor market information to other federal or state agencies to meet various program responsibilities and to the public on state and local employment conditions; providing guidance, counseling, referral, and placement in apprenticeship opportunities through *Apprenticeship Information Centers* located in selected state employment service offices; reviewing rural industrialization loan and grant certification applications under the Rural Development Act of 1972; maintaining an occupational research program for the compilation of the *Dictionary of Occupational Titles;* and pro-

viding bonding assistance to individuals who have been unable to obtain it on their own. *See* Henry P. Guzda, "The U.S. Employment Service at 50: It Too Had to Wait Its Turn," *Monthly Labor Review* (June 1983).

United States Reports, official record of cases decided by the U.S. Supreme Court. When cases are cited, *United States Reports* is abbreviated to "U.S." For example, the legal citation for the case of *Pickering* v. *Board of Education* is 391 U.S. 563 (1968). This means that the case will be found on page 563 of volume 391 of the *United States Reports* and that it was decided in 1968.

United States Statutes at Large, bound volumes, issued annually, containing all public and private laws and concurrent resolutions enacted during a session of Congress, reorganization plans, proposed and ratified amendments to the Constitution, and presidential proclamations.

United States v. Allen Kaiser: *see* STRIKE BENEFITS.

United States v. Archie Brown: *see* CLEANSING PERIOD.

United States v. Darby Lumber, 312 U.S. 100 (1941), U.S. Supreme Court case that upheld the Fair Labor Standards Act of 1938, which established minimum wages and maximum hours for workers in businesses engaged in, or producing goods for, interstate commerce.

United States v. Hutcheson, 312 U.S. 219 (1941), U.S. Supreme Court case, which held that criminal liability could not be imposed, under the Sherman Antitrust Act of 1890, on a union that calls for picketing and/or a boycott against an employer because of a jurisdictional dispute with another union.

United States v. Lovett, 328 U.S. 303 (1946), Supreme Court case holding that a congressional effort to dismiss three allegedly "irresponsible, unrepresentative, crackpot, radical bureaucrats" from the executive branch by passing legislation prohibiting the payment of their salaries amounted to an unconstitutional bill of attainder.

United Steelworkers of America v. American Manufacturing Co., 363 U.S. 564 (1960), U.S. Supreme Court case, which held that the role of the federal courts is limited when the parties have agreed to submit all questions of contract interpretation to an arbitrator.

See also STEELWORKERS' TRILOGY.

United Steelworkers of America v. Enterprise Wheel and Car Corp., 363 U.S. 593 (1960), U.S. Supreme Court case, which held that the interpretation of a collective bargaining agreement is a question for an arbitrator and the courts do not have the right to overrule an arbitrator because of his interpretation.

See also STEELWORKERS' TRILOGY.

United Steelworkers of America v. Warrior and Gulf Navigation Co., 363 U.S. 574 (1960), U.S. Supreme Court case, which held that a labor-management dispute could not be judged to be nonarbitrable unless the parties specifically excluded the subject from the arbitration process.

See also ARBITRABILITY and STEELWORKERS' TRILOGY.

United Steelworkers of America v. Weber, et al., 61 L.Ed.2d 480 (1979), decided together with KAISER ALUMINUM & CHEMICAL CORP. V. WEBER, ET AL., U.S. Supreme Court decision that upheld an affirmative action program giving blacks preference in selection of employees for a training program.

In 1974, the United Steelworkers of America and Kaiser Aluminum & Chemical Corporation entered into a master collective bargaining agreement covering terms and conditions of employment at 15 Kaiser plants. The agreement included an affirmative action plan designed to eliminate conspicuous racial imbalances in Kaiser's then almost exclusively white craft work forces. It reserved 50 percent of the openings in in-plant, craft-training programs for blacks until the percentage of black craft workers in a plant became commensurate with the percentage of blacks in the local labor force. This litigation arose from the operation of the affirmative action plan at one of Kaiser's plants, where, prior to 1974, only 1.83 percent of the skilled craft workers were black even though the local work force was approximately 39 percent black. Pursuant to the national agreement, Kaiser, rather than continuing its practice of hiring trained outsiders, established a training program to train its production workers to fill craft openings. Trainees were selected on the basis of seniority, with the proviso that at least 50 percent of the trainees were to be black until the percentage of black skilled craft workers in the plant approximated the percentage of blacks in the local labor force. During the plan's first year of operation, seven black and six white craft trainees were selected from the plant's production work force. The most junior black trainee had less seniority than several white production workers whose bids for admission were rejected. Thereafter, Brian Weber, one of those white production workers, instituted a class action in a federal district court. The suit alleged that because the affirmative action program had resulted in junior black employees receiving training in preference to more senior white employees, Weber and other similarly situated white employees had been discriminated against in violation of Title VII of the Civil Rights Act of 1964 (which makes it unlawful to discriminate because of race in hiring and in the selection of apprentices for training programs).

The district court ruled in favor of Weber. The court of appeals affirmed, holding that all employment preferences based upon race—including those preferences incidental to bona fide affirmative action plans—violated Title VII's prohibition against racial discrimination in employment. The U.S. Supreme Court reversed the lower court rulings. Justice Brennan, in delivering the majority opinion of the court, stated that "the only question before us is the narrow satutory issue of whether Title VII *forbids* private employers and unions from voluntarily agreeing upon bona fide affirmative action plans that accord racial preferences. . . ." The court concluded "that Congress did not intend to limit traditional business freedom to such a degree as to prohibit all voluntary, race-conscious affirmative action." Brennan went on to add that, because Kaiser's preferential scheme was legal, it was unnecessary to "define in detail the line of demarcation between permissible and impermissible affirmative action plans." *See* David H. Rosenbloom, "Kaiser vs. Weber: Perspective From the Public Sector," *Public Personnel Management* (November–December 1979); Andrew J. Ruzicho, "The *Weber* Case—Its Impact on Affirmative Action," *The Personnel Administrator* (June 1980); David E. Robertson and Ronald D. Johnson, "Reverse Discrimination: Did *Weber* Decide the Issue?" *Labor Law Journal* (November 1980); Ronald D. Johnson, "Voluntary Affirmative Action in the Post-*Weber* Era: Issues and Answers," *Labor Law Journal* (September 1981); William A. Simon, Jr., "Voluntary Affirmative Action After *Weber*," *Labor Law Journal* (March 1983).

   See also the following entries:
    AFFIRMATIVE ACTION
    CIVIL RIGHTS ACT OF 1964
    REGENTS OF THE UNIVERSITY OF CALIFORNIA V. ALLAN BAKKE
    REVERSE DISCRIMINATION
    TITLE VII

unit labor cost: *see* LABOR COSTS.

unit seniority: *see* DEPARTMENTAL SENIORITY.

unity of command, concept that each individual in an organization should be accountable to only a single superior.

unity of direction, concept that there should be only one head and one plan for each organizational segment.

universe: *see* POPULATION.

University and College Labor Education Association (UCLEA), an organization founded in 1959 of universities and colleges with regular and continuing programs to provide labor education/labor studies for workers and their organizations.
UCLEA
Richard Z. Hindle
Department of Labor Studies
901 Liberal Arts Tower
Pennsylvania State University
University Park, PA 16802
(814) 865-5425

unobtrusive measures, measures taken without the subject being aware that he or she is being observed. *See* Eugene J. Webb, *et al.*, *Unobtrusive Measures: Nonreactive Research in the Social Sciences* (Chicago: Rand McNally, 1966); Eugene Webb and Karl E. Weick, "Unobtrusive Measures in Organization Theory: A Reminder," *Administrative Science Quarterly* (December 1979).

unpatterned interview: *see* PATTERNED INTERVIEW.

unskilled workers, employees whose jobs are confined to manual operations limited to the performance of relatively simple duties requiring only the slightest exercise of independent judgement.

unstructured role playing, role-play exercise or simulation in which the players are not given specific information on the character of their roles.

Upjohn Institute for Employment Research, private, nonprofit organization founded in 1945 to foster "research into the causes and effects of unemployment and to study and investigate the feasibility and methods of insuring against unemployment and devise ways and means of preventing and alleviating the distress and hardship caused by unemployment."
Upjohn Institute for Employment Research
300 South Westnedge Avenue
Kalamazoo, MI 49007
(616) 343-5541

up-or-out system, career system that terminates individuals who do not qualify themselves for the next higher level of the system within a specified time period. The U.S. military officer corps and Foreign Service are two examples of up-or-out systems.

upward-mobility program, systematic management effort that focuses on the development and implementation of specific career opportunities for lower-level employees who are in positions or occupational series which do not enable them to realize their full work potential. An upward-mobility program is usually just one aspect of an organization's overall EEO effort. *See* Thomas E. Diggin, "Upward Mobility—TECOM puts it all Together," *Public Personnel Management* (May-June 1974); Gary Gemmill, "Reward Mapping and Upward Mobility," *Management of Personnel Quarterly* (Winter 1970); Carlene Jackson, "Upward Mobility in State Government," *Training and Development Journal* (April 1979); William T. McCaffrey, "Career Growth Versus Upward Mobility," *Personnel Administrator* (May 1981).

Urwick, Lyndall F. (1891-1983), one of the pioneers of the classical school of organization theory. Major works include: *Papers on the Science of Administration*, with Luther Gulick (N.Y.: Institute of Public Administration, 1937); *Scientific Principles of Organization* (N.Y.: American Management Association, 1938); *The Elements of Administration* (N.Y.: Harper & Bros., 1944); *The Pattern of Management* (Minneapolis: University of Minnesota Press, 1956); *Staff in Organization*, with Ernest Dale (N.Y.: McGraw-Hill, 1960).

U.S.: *see* UNITED STATES REPORTS

Usery, W.J., Jr. (1923-), Secretary of Labor from 1976 to 1977.

Usery v. Turner Elkhorn Mining Co., 428 U.S. 1 (1976), U.S. Supreme Court case, which upheld that portion of the Federal Coal Mine Health and Safety Act of 1969 making coal mine operators liable for benefits to former miners (and their dependents) who have suffered from black-lung disease (pneumoconiosis).

USES: *see* UNITED STATES EMPLOYMENT SERVICE.

V

vacancy, available position for which an organization is actively seeking to recruit a worker.

vacating an award, court's setting aside an arbitration award.

vacation pay, pay for specified periods of time off work. The vacation or leave time that an employee earns frequently varies with length of service.

valence, in Victor H. Vroom's "Expectancy Theory of Motivation," the value an employee places on an incentive or reward. For a full account of Vroom's theory, *see* his *Work and Motivation* (N.Y.: John Wiley & Sons, 1964). For a test of it, *see* Robert Pritchard, Philip De-Leo, and Clarence VonBergen, Jr., "The Field Experimental Test of Expectancy—Valence Incentive Motivation Techniques," *Organizational Behavior and Human Performance* (April 1976).
See also EXPECTANCY THEORY.

validation, process of investigation by which the validity of a particular type of test use is estimated. What is important here is to identify an ambiguity in the term "to validate," which is responsible for much confusion in the area of employment testing. To validate in ordinary language may mean to mark with an indication of official approval. In this sense, it is also possible to "invalidate" or to indicate official disapproval. In the technical vocabulary of employment testing, to validate is to investigate, to conduct research. Thus, in validating a test (more properly, in validating a use of a test), one is conducting an inquiry. In this context, the term "invalidating" has no meaning at all. *See* Douglas D. Baker and David E. Terpstra, "Employee Selection: Must Every Job Test Be Validated?" *Personnel Journal* (August 1982).

See also the following entries:
CONSENSUAL VALIDATION
CRITERION RELATED VALIDATION
CROSS VALIDATION
DIFFERENTIAL VALIDATION
STATISTICAL VALIDATION
VALIDITY

validity, extent to which a test measures what it is supposed to measure or the accuracy of inferences drawn from test scores.

See also the following entries:
CONCURRENT VALIDITY
CONSTRUCT VALIDITY
CONTENT VALIDITY
CONVERGENT VALIDITY
CURRICULAR VALIDITY
DISCRIMINANT VALIDITY
EMPIRICAL VALIDITY
FACE VALIDITY
ITEM VALIDITY
OPERATIONAL VALIDITY
PREDICTIVE VALIDITY
RATIONAL VALIDITY
SYNTHETIC VALIDITY
VALIDATION

validity coefficient, correlation coefficient that estimates the relationship between scores on a test (or test battery) and the criterion.

Vance v. Bradley, 59 L. Ed. 2d 171 (1979), U.S. Supreme Court case, which held that requiring officers of the U.S. Foreign Service to retire at age 60 did not violate the equal protection component of the due process clause of the Fifth Amendment, even though other federal employees do not face mandatory retirement at such an early age.

variable, any factor or condition subject to measurement, alteration, and/or control.

variable, contextual: *see* CONTEXTUAL VARIABLE.

variable annuity, also called ASSET-LINKED ANNUITY, annuity that varies with the value of assets. In an effort to protect the purchasing power of a pensioner, some pension plans link benefit accruals to the value of an associated asset portfolio. Upon retirement, the pensioner may have the option of continuing to receive asset-linked benefits or to convert total benefits to a conventional fixed-income annuity.

variable life insurance, form of life insurance whose death benefit is dependent upon the performance of investments in a common portfolio.

variance, difference between an expected or standard value and an actual one.

variance analysis: *see* ANALYSIS OF VARIANCE.

velvet ghetto, organizational unit (such as a public relations department) that is overloaded with women in response to an affirmative action program and in compensation for their scarcity in other professional or management categories. For a discussion, *see* "PR: 'The Velvet Ghetto' of Affirmative Action," *Business Week* (May 8, 1978).

vertical communication: *see* COMMUNICATION.

vertical loading: *see* JOB LOADING.

vertical occupational mobility: *see* OCCUPATIONAL MOBILITY.

vertical training, simultaneous training of people who work together, irrespective of their status in the organization.

vertical union: *see* INDUSTRIAL UNION.

vertical work group, work group containing individuals whose positions differ in rank, prestige, and level of skill.

vested benefit: see VESTING.

vestibule training, training that prepares a new employee for an occupation after acceptance for employment but before the assumption of the new job's duties. For example, rookie training for new police.

vesting, granting an employee the right to a pension at normal retirement age even if the employee leaves the organization before the age of normal retirement. Accumulated benefits are "vested" when employees have the nonforfeitable right to receive benefits at retirement, even if they should leave the job before retirement age. Benefits may be partially or fully vested.

Accumulated benefits from the employee's own contributions, if any, must be fully and immediately vested. In order to preserve an employee's right to accumulate benefits contributed by an employer if the employee leaves the job before retiring, ERISA requires that benefits be vested at least as fast as one of three approved schedules. Under any of the approved schedules, an employee must be entitled to at least 50 percent of accumulated benefits after 10 years of service, and to 100 percent after 15 years, regardless of age. Periods of service may be disregarded for vesting purposes under certain circumstances. ERISA has limited the circumstances in which interruption in employment results in the loss of pension benefits earned before the interruption. Plans cannot penalize participants for breaks in service that are shorter than 1 year. The effect of a break for more than 1 year depends on the type of plan, the vesting status of accrued benefits, and the number of years the break lasts, compared to the number of years of service that had been counted for purposes of vesting before the break occurred.

A worker can change jobs after having acquired a vested right to retirement benefits and have the benefits transferred from the pension funds of one employer to that of another, provided the plans allow for it and certain requirements are met. If a person receives a lump sum payout of vested benefits because of leaving before retirement or because the plan is terminated, current taxes can be avoided by depositing the funds in an individual retirement account (IRA).

See also DEFERRED FULL VESTING, DEFERRED GRADED VESTING, PENSION and IMMEDIATE FULL VESTING.

veteran, disabled: see DISABLED VETERAN.

veterans preference. The modern concept of veterans preference dates from 1865, when Congress, toward the end of the Civil War, affirmed that "persons honorably discharged from the military or naval service by reason of disability resulting from wounds or sickness incurred in the line of duty, shall be preferred for appointments to civil offices, provided they are found to possess the business capacity necessary for the proper discharge of the duties of such offices." The 1865 law was superceded in 1919, when preference was extended to all "honorably discharged" veterans, their widows, and to wives of disabled veterans. The Veterans Preference Act of 1944 expanded the scope of veterans preference by providing for a five-point bonus on federal examination scores for all honorably separated veterans (except for those with a service-connected disability who are entitled to a 10 point bonus). Veterans also received other advantages in federal employment (such as protections against arbitrary dismissal and preference in the event of a reduction-in-force).

All states and many other jurisdictions have veterans preference laws of varying intensity. New Jersey, for an extreme example, offers veterans absolute preference: if a veteran passes an entrance examination, he/she must be hired no matter what his/her score before nonveterans can be hired. Veterans competing with each other are rank ordered, and all disabled veterans receive preference over other veterans. Veterans preference laws have

451

been criticized because they have allegedly made it difficult for government agencies to hire and promote more women and minorities. Although the original version of the Civil Service Reform Act of 1978 sought to limit veterans preference in the federal service, the final version contained a variety of new provisions *strengthening* veterans preference. *See* Charles E. Davis, "Veterans' Preference and Civil Service Employment: Issues and Policy Implications," *Review of Public Personnel Administration* (Fall 1982).

See also PERSONNEL ADMINISTRATOR OF MASSACHUSETTS V. FEENEY and MILITARY SERVICE.

Veterans Readjustment Assistance Act of 1974, federal statute that required contractors with federal contracts of $10,000 or more to establish program to take "affirmative action" to employ and advance in employment all disabled veterans (with 30% or more disability) and other veterans for the first 48 months after discharge.

See also LABOR-MANAGEMENT SERVICES ADMINISTRATION.

veterans reemployment rights, reemployment rights program, under provisions of Chapter 43 of Title 38, U.S. Code, for men and women who leave their jobs to perform training or service in the armed forces. The Office of Veterans Reemployment Rights of the Labor-Management Services Administration of the U.S. Department of Labor has responsibility for the program. In general terms, to be entitled to reemployment rights a veteran must leave a position (other than a temporary position) with a private employer, the federal government, or a state or local government for the purpose of entering the armed forces, voluntarily or involuntarily. The employer is generally obligated to reemploy the veteran within a reasonable time after he/she makes application for the position he/she would have occupied if he/she had remained on the job instead of entering military service.

See also FOSTER V. DRAVO CORP.

Vietnam Era Veterans Readjustment

Act of 1974: *see* VETERANS READJUSTMENT ACT OF 1974.

vocational behavior, total realm of human actions and interactions related to the work environment, including preparation for work, participation in the workforce, and retirement. For a text, *see* Donald G. Zytowski, *Vocational Behavior: Readings in Theory and Research* (New York: Holt, Rinehart and Winston, Inc., 1968).

vocational counseling, any professional assistance given to an individual preparing to enter the workforce concerning the choice of occupation.

Vocational Education Act of 1963, federal statute that authorized federal grants to states to assist them to maintain, extend, and improve existing programs of vocational education; to develop new programs of vocational education; and to provide part-time employment for youths who need the earnings from such employment to continue their vocational training on a full-time basis.

See also SMITH-HUGHES ACT OF 1917.

vocational maturity, term, premised upon the belief that vocational behavior is a developmental process, which implies a comparison of an individual's chronological and vocational ages. For a model of vocational maturity, *see* John O. Crites, "Career Development Processes: A Model of Vocational Maturity," Edwin Herr (ed.), *Vocational Guidance and Human Development* (Boston, Houghton Mifflin Co., 1974).

vocational maturity quotient, ratio of vocational maturity to chronological age.

Vocational Preference Inventory (VPI), personality inventory designed to measure a broad range of information about the subject's interpersonal relations, interests, values, self-conception, coping behavior and identification. Consists of 160 occupational titles to which an individual indicates likes or dislikes. TIME: 15/30 minutes. AUTHOR: John L. Holland. PUB-

LISHER: Consulting Psychologists Press, Inc. (*see* TEST PUBLISHERS).

vocational psychology, scientific study of vocational behavior and development. According to John O. Crites, in *Vocational Psychology* (N.Y.: McGraw-Hill, 1969):

Historically the field of vocational psychology grew out of the practice of vocational guidance. It seems desirable to differentiate between them, however, if vocational psychology is to become firmly established as the science of vocational behavior and development—unconfounded with the purposes and procedures of vocational guidance, which is still largely an art. There is one important area of overlap (approximately 10 percent) which should be mentioned. To the extent that vocational guidance, as a stimulus or treatment condition, is functionally related to vocational behavior, then it falls within the purview of vocational psychology as a field of study.

vocational rehabilitation, restoration of the handicapped to the fullest physical, mental, social, vocational and economic usefulness of which they are capable. *See* Ronald W. Conley, *The Economics of Vocational Rehabilitation* (Baltimore: Johns Hopkins Press, 1965).

Vocational Rehabilitation Act of 1973, federal statute that requires federal contractors with contracts in excess of $2,500 to "take affirmative action to employ and advance in employment qualified handicapped individuals." The act also established within the federal government an Interagency Committee on Handicapped Employees whose purpose is "(1) to provide a focus for Federal and other employment of handicapped individuals, and to review, on a periodic basis, in cooperation with the Civil Service Commission [now Office of Personnel Management], the adequacy of hiring, placement, and advancement practices with respect to handicapped individuals, by each department, agency, and instrumentality in the executive branch of Government, and to in-

sure that the special needs of such individuals are being met; and (2) to consult with the Civil Service Commission to assist the Commission to carry out its responsibilities" in implementing affirmative action programs for the handicapped.

vocational training, formal preparation for a particular business or trade. *See* Oscar Corvalan-Vasquez, "Vocational Training of Disadvantaged Youth in the Developing Countries," *International Labour Review* (May-June 1983).

voice stress analyzer: *see* LIE DETECTOR.

voluntary arbitration, arbitration agreed to by two parties in the absence of any legal or contractual requirement.

voluntary bargaining items, those items over which collective bargaining is neither mandatory nor illegal.

voluntary demotion: *see* DEMOTION.

Von Bertalanffy, Ludwig: *see* BERTALANFFY, LUDWIG VON.

VPI: *see* VOCATIONAL PREFERENCE INVENTORY.

Vroom, Victor H. (1932-   ), industrial psychologist and a leading authority on organizational motivation and leadership. His major work on expectancy theory is *Work and Motivation* (N.Y.: John Wiley, 1964).
  See also VALENCE.

vulnerability assessment, an evaluation of the susceptibility of organization functions, programs, or projects in question to future loss of revenues or budgetary reductions.

W

wage, guaranteed annual: *see* GUARANTEED ANNUAL WAGE.

wage, living: *see* LIVING WAGE.

wage and hour laws, the federal and state laws which set minimum wages and maximum hours for workers. *See:* FAIR LABOR STANDARDS ACT.

wage-and-price controls, a government's formal efforts to control inflation by regulating the wages and prices of its economic system. For accounts of the wage-and-price controls of the 1971 to 1974 period, *see* George P. Shultz and Kenneth W. Dam, "Reflections on Wage and Price Controls," *Industrial and Labor Relations Review* (January 1977); Robert A. Kagan, *Regulatory Justice: Implementing a Wage-Price Freeze* (N.Y.: Basic Books, 1978). *Also see* Hugh Rockoff, "Price and Wage Controls in Four Wartime Periods," *Journal of Economic History* (June 1981).

See also FRY V. UNITED STATES.

Wage and Price Stability, Council on: *see* COUNCIL ON WAGE AND PRICE STABILITY.

wage and salary administration, according to Herbert G. Zollitsch and Adolph Langsner, in *Wage and Salary Administration* (Cincinnati, Ohio: South-Western Publishing Co., 2nd ed., 1970), wage and salary administration "may be thought of as the planning, organizing, and controlling of those activities that relate to the direct and indirect payments made to employees for the work they perform or the services they render." *Also see* John D. McMillan and Valerie C. Williams, "the Elements of Effective Salary Administration Programs," *Personnel Journal* (November 1982); Milton L. Rock, editor, *Handbook of Wage and Salary Administration*, 2d ed. (New York: McGraw-Hill Book Co., 1983); Leonard R. Burgess, *Wage and Salary Administration: Pay and Benefits* (Columbus, Ohio: Charles E. Merrill, 1984).

wage and salary survey: *see* WAGE SURVEY.

Wage and Tax Statement: *see* FORM W-2.

wage arbitration, referral of a wage dispute to an arbitrator.

wage area, national and/or regional areas selected on the basis of population size, employment, location, or other criteria for wage surveys. *See* James N. Houff, "Improving Area Wage Survey Indexes," *Monthly Labor Review* (January 1973).

wage assignment, voluntary transfer of earned wages to a third party to pay debts, buy savings bonds, pay union dues, etc.

wage compression: *see* SALARY COMPRESSION.

wage criteria, those external and internal standards or factors that determine the internal pay structure of an organization. According to David W. Belcher, in *Compensation Administration* (Englewood Cliffs, N.J.: Prentice-Hall, 1974),

wage criteria may be used by organizations and unions to rationalize positions taken as well as to arrive at these positions. Also, strictly applying the various criteria would in many situations result in conflicting decisions. For example, if the cost of living is up 10 percent and ability to pay is down 10 percent, comparable wages in the area justify a 5 percent increase, and comparable wages in the industry call for a 5 percent decrease, what change in wage level is justified?

wage differentials, differences in wages paid for identical or similar work that are justified because of differences in work schedules, hazards, cost of living, or other factors. *See* Orel R. Winjum, "Negotiated Wage Rate Differentials," *Personnel Journal* (August 1971); Robert J. Newman, "Dynamic Patterns in Regional Wage Differentials," *Southern Economic Journal* (July 1982).

wage drift, concept that explains the gap between basic wage rates and actual earnings, which tend to be higher because of overtime, bonuses, and other monetary incentives.

Wage Earner Plan, title of Chapter 13 of the Bankruptcy Act, which allows anyone who is employed to get an extension of time to pay off debts in lieu of bankruptcy if the employee submits all earnings to court jurisdiction until all creditors have been paid. For details, see Irving L. Berg, "The Wage Earner Plan as an Alternative to Bankruptcy," *Personnel Journal* (March 1971).

wage floor, minimum wage established by contract or law.

wage increase, deferred: see DEFERRED WAGE INCREASE.

wage inequity: see COGNITIVE DISSONANCE.

wage garnishment: see GARNISHMENT.

wage parity: see PARITY.

wage-price freeze: see WAGE-AND-PRICE CONTROLS.

wage progression, progressively higher wage rates that can be earned in the same job. Progression takes place on the basis of length of service, merit, or other criteria.

wage range: see PAY RANGE.

wage reopener clause: see REOPENER CLAUSE.

wages, also SALARY, as defined by J. D. Dunn and Frank M. Rachel, in *Wage and Salary Administration: Total Compensation Systems* (N.Y.: McGraw-Hill, 1971):

The remuneration (pay) received by an employee (or group of employees) for services rendered during a specific period of time—hour, day, week, or month. Traditionally, the term "wages" has been used to denote the pay of a factory employee or any employee on an hourly rate, and "salary" has been

used to denote the pay of an administrative, professional, clerical, or managerial employee on a weekly, monthly, or annual time basis.

See also the following entries:
BARGAINING THEORY OF WAGES
BOOTLEG WAGES
COMPETITIVE WAGES
GRADUATED WAGES
INDIRECT WAGES
IRON LAW OF WAGES
REAL WAGES
LIVING WAGE
PAY
SALARY

Wages and Hours Act: see FAIR LABOR STANDARDS ACT.

Wage Stabilization Board, federal agency established in 1950; abolished in 1953.

wage survey, also called WAGE AND SALARY SURVEY, and AREA WAGE SURVEY, formal effort to gather data on compensation rates and/or ranges for comparable jobs within an area, industry, or occupation. Wage surveys on both a national and regional basis are available from such organizations as the American Management Association, the International Personnel Management Association, and the International City Management Association. See Bruce R. Ellig, "Salary Surveys: Design to Application," *The Personnel Administrator* (October 1977); James N Houff, "Improving Area Wage Survey Indexes," *Monthly Labor Review* (January 1973); Michael A. Conway, "Salary Surveys: Avoid the Pitfalls," *Personnel Journal* (June 1984); Garry D. Fisher, "Salary Surveys—An Antitrust Perspective," *Personnel Administrator* (April 1985).

See also COMMUNITY WAGE SURVEY.

wage tax, any tax on wages and salaries levied by a government. Many cities have wage taxes that force suburban commuters to help pay for the services provided to the region by the central city.

Wagner Act: *see* NATIONAL LABOR RELATIONS ACT OF 1935.

Wagner Acts, Baby: *see* BABY WAGNER ACTS.

Wagner-Connery Act: *see* NATIONAL LABOR RELATIONS ACT OF 1935.

Wagner-O'Day Act, federal statute, provides that sheltered workshops serving blind and severely handicapped persons shall receive special preference in bidding on federal government contracts for products and services.

Wagner-Peyser Act of 1933, federal statute that established the U.S. Employment Service in the Department of Labor to assist in the development of a cooperative nationwide system of public employment offices.

WAIS: *see* WECHSLER ADULT INTELLIGENCE SCALE.

walk-around pay, pay for workers who "walk around" with federal inspectors. Occupational Safety and Health Administration inspectors must sometimes be accompanied on their plant inspections.

walkout: *see* STRIKE.

Walsh-Healey Public Contracts Act of 1936, federal statute establishing basic labor standards for work done on U.S. government contracts exceeding $10,000 in value.

warm-up effect, adjustment process that takes place at the start of work. The warm-up period is over when the work curve reaches its first peak.

Washington v. Davis, 426 U.S. 229 (1976), U.S. Supreme Court case, which held that although the Due Process Clause of the 5th Amendment prohibits the government from invidious discrimination, it does not follow that a law or other official act is unconstitutional *solely* because it has a racially disproportionate impact. The court ruled that, under the Constitu-

tion (as opposed to Title VII of the Civil Rights Act of 1964), there must be discriminatory purpose or intent—adverse impact alone is insufficient. *See* Carl F. Goodman, "Public Employment and the Supreme Court's 1975-76 Term," *Public Personnel Management* (September-October 1976).

wash up: *see* CLEAN-UP TIME.

Watson-Glaser Critical Thinking Appraisal (WGCT), instrument that provides a measure or analysis of critical thinking abilities. Scores indicate strengths and weaknesses in areas such as inference, assumption, deduction, interpretation, and arguments. Used in a variety of educational assessment situations, selection processes, and research situations. TIME: 50/60 minutes. AUTHORS: Goodwin Watson and Edward M. Glaser. PUBLISHER: Harcourt, Brace, Jovanovich, Inc. (*see* TEST PUBLISHERS).

Watts, Glenn E. (1920-   ), elected president of the Communications Workers of America in 1974.

WBIS: *see* WECHSLER-BELLVUE INTELLIGENCE SCALE.

Weber, Joseph N. (1866-1950), president of the American Federation of Musicians from 1900 to 1940. His union grew from 6,000 to 170,000 members under his leadership.

Weber, Max (1864-1920), German sociologist who produced an analysis of bureaucracy that is still the most influential statement—the point of departure for all further analyses—on the subject. For a biography, *see* Reinhard Bendix, *Max Weber: An Intellectual Portrait* (Garden City, N.Y.: Doubleday, 1960).

Weber decision: *see* UNITED STEELWORKERS OF AMERICA V. WEBER, ET AL.

Wechsler Adult Intelligence Scale (WAIS), widely used test for general intelligence designed for persons ranging in age from 16 to over 75. Consists of six verbal and five performance tests. Revision of Wechsler-Bellvue Intelligence Scale. TIME: 40/60 minutes. AUTHOR: David Wechsler. PUBLISHER: Psychological Corporation (see TEST PUBLISHERS).

Wechsler-Bellvue Intelligence Scale (WBIS), published in 1939, one of the first general intelligence tests designed for adults. Measures general comprehension, arithmetic abilities, vocabulary and other general informational items. Replaced by Wechsler Adult Intelligence Scale (WAIS). TIME: 40/60 minutes. AUTHOR: David Wechsler. PUBLISHER: Psychological Corporation (see TEST PUBLISHERS).

weighted application blank, weights or numeric values can be placed on the varying responses to application blank items. After a job analysis determines the knowledges, skills, and abilities necessary to perform the duties of a position, corresponding personal characteristics can be elicited. Applicants who score highest on the weighted application blank would be given first consideration. See H. M. Trice, "The Weighted Application Blank—A Caution," *The Personnel Administrator* (May–June 1964); Richard D. Scott and Richard W. Johnson, "Use of the Weighted Application Blank in Selecting Unskilled Employees," *Journal of Applied Psychology* (October 1967).

Weingarten decision: see NATIONAL LABOR RELATIONS BOARD V. J. WEINGARTEN, INC.

welfare funds, employer contributions, agreed to during collective bargaining, to a common fund to provide welfare benefits to the employees of all of the contributing employers.

welfare plan, benefits provided for the employees of a single employer.

welfare state, a governing system where it is public policy that government will strive for the maximum economic and social benefits for each of its citizens short of changing the operating premises of the society. The line between an extreme welfare state and socialism is so thin that its existence is debatable. See Edward D. Berkowitz and Kim McQuaid, *Creating the Welfare State: The Political Economy of Twentieth Century Reform* (New York: Praeger, 1980); Roger A. Freeman, *The Wayward Welfare State* (Stanford, Calif.: Stanford University, Hoover Institution Press, 1981); Richard E. Just, Darrell L. Hueth and Andrew Schmitz, *Applied Welfare Economics and Public Policy* (Englewood Cliffs, N. J.: Prentice-Hall, 1982); Bruce R. Scott, "Can Industry Survive the Welfare State," *Harvard Business Review* (September–October 1982).

wellness program, a formal effort on the part of an employer to maintain the mental and physical health of its workforce. See Gordon F. Shea, "Profiting From Wellness Training," *Training and Development Journal* (October 1981); John P. McCann, M.D., "Control Data's 'Staywell' Program," *Training and Development Journal* (October 1981).

well pay, also called SWEEP PAY, incentive payments to workers who are neither "sick" nor late over a specified time period. In some companies, well pay is called "sweep pay" for "Stay at Work, Earn Extra Pay." See Barron H. Harvey, Jerome F. Rogers and Judy A. Schultze, "Sick Pay vs Well Pay: An Analysis of the Impact of Rewarding Employees for Being on the Job," *Public Personnel Management* (Summer 1983).

Wesman Personnel Classification Test (WPCT), general intelligence test used primarily in selection and placement of personnel in business and industry. Composed of verbal and numerical subtests that are summed for a total score. TIME: 25/35 minutes. AUTHOR: Alexander G. Wesman. PUBLISHER: Psychological Corporation (see TEST PUBLISHERS).

West Coast Hotel v. Parrish, 300 U.S. 379 (1937), U.S. Supreme Court case, which upheld the minimum wage law of the State of Washington, by declaring that a minimum wage law did not violate the freedom of contract provided by the Due Process Clause of the 14th Amendment. This case overruled the court's earlier decision, *Adkins* v. *Children's Hospital,* 261 U.S. 525 (1923), which held unconstitutional a federal law establishing minimum wages for women and children in the District of Columbia.

Western Personnel Test, short measure of mental abilities designed for use in business and industry. Measures such things as number series, word meanings, arithmetic reasoning, and sentence arrangement. TIME: 5-10 minutes. AUTHORS: R. L. Gunn and M. P. Manson. PUBLISHER: Psychological Corporation (*see* TEST PUBLISHERS).

W. E. Upjohn Institute for Employment Research: *see* UPJOHN INSTITUTE FOR EMPLOYMENT RESEARCH.

WGCT: *see* WATSON-GLASER CRITICAL THINKING APPRAISAL.

Wharton, Arthur O. (1873-1944), president of the International Association of Machinists from 1926 to 1939. For biographical information, *see* Mark Perlman, *The Machinists: A New Study in American Trade Unionism* (Cambridge, Mass.: Harvard University Press, 1961).

"When in charge, ponder. When in trouble, delegate. When in doubt, mumble.": *see* INTERNATIONAL ASSOCIATION OF PROFESSIONAL BUREAUCRATS.

whipsawing: *see* WHIPSAW STRIKE.

whipsaw strike, strike stratagem that uses one struck employer as an example to others in order to encourage them to accede to union demands without the necessity of additional strikes.

whistle blower, individual who believes the public interest overrides the interests of their organization and publicly "blows the whistle" if the organization is involved in corrupt, illegal, fraudulent or harmful activity. For accounts of famous whistle blowers, *see* Ralph Nader, Peter J. Petkas, and Kate Blackwell (eds.), *Whistle Blowing: The Report of the Conference on Professional Responsibility* (N.Y.: Grossman Publishers, 1972); Charles Peters and Taylor Branch (eds.), *Blowing The Whistle: Dissent in the Public Interest* (N.Y.: Praeger Publishers, 1972). *Also see* Kenneth D. Walters, "Your Employees' Right to Blow the Whistle," *Harvard Business Review* (July-August 1975); James S. Bowman, "Whistle-Blowing in the Public Service: An Overview of the Issue," *Review of Public Personnel Administration* (Fall, 1980); Arthur L. Burnett, "Management's Positive Interest in Accountability Through Whistleblowing," *Bureaucrat* (Summer 1980).

See also FITZGERALD, A. ERNEST.

White Collar Report, weekly report concerning clerical, technical, scientific, professional, and other white collar employees published by the Bureau of National Affairs, Inc. Covers organizing activities, salaries and fringe benefits, collective bargaining, equal employment opportunity activities, court and board decisions.

white-collar unions, general term for a union whose members are more likely to wear street clothes and sit at a desk than wear work clothes and stand at a lathe. *See* Adolf Sturmthal, *White-Collar Trade Unions: Contemporary Developments in Industrialized Societies* (Urbana, Ill.: University of Illinois Press, 1966); George Sayers Bain, *The Growth of White-Collar Unionism* (N.Y.: Oxford University Press, 1970); Everett M. Kassalow, "White-Collar Unions and the Work Humanization Movement," *Monthly Labor Review* (May 1977); Nigel Nicholson, Gill Ursell and Jackie Lubbock, "Membership Participation in a White-Collar Union," *Industrial Relations* (Spring 1981); John G. Kilgour, "Union Organizing Activity Among White-Collar Employees," *Personnel* (March-April 1983). For a house history of the Office and Professional

Employees International Union (OPEIU), see Joseph E. Finley, *White Collar Union: The Story of the OPEIU and Its People* (N.Y.: Octagon Books, 1975).

white-collar workers, employee whose job requires slight physical effort and allows him/her to wear ordinary clothes. *See* C. Wright Mills, *White Collar: The American Middle Class* (N.Y.: Oxford University Press, 1951); J. M. Pennings, "Work Value Systems of White-Collar Workers," *Administrative Science Quarterly* (December 1970); Carl Dean Snyder, *White Collar Workers and the UAW* (Urbana, Ill.: University of Illinois Press, 1973); M. E. Personick, C. B. Barsky, "White-Collar Pay Levels Linked to Corporate Work Force Size," *Monthly Labor Review* (May 1982); C. C. Hoop and J. N. Wolzansky, "Matching White-Collar Skills to the Work," *Harvard Business Review* (November-December 1983); Robert N. Lehrer, ed., *White Collar Productivity* (New York: McGraw-Hill Book Co., 1983).
See also BLUE-COLLAR WORKERS.

Whitney, Alexander Fell (1873-1949), president of the Brotherhood of Railroad Trainmen from 1928 until his death. For biographical information, *see* Joel I. Seidman, *The Brotherhood of Railroad Trainmen: The Internal Political Life of a National Union* (N.Y.: John Wiley, 1962).

Whitten Amendment, amendment to the federal government's Classification Act, which states that most federal employees may only be permanently appointed to one grade within a 52-week period and may be promoted no more than one grade at a time.

whole-job ranking, job evaluation method that simply ranks jobs as a whole. For example, a small organization might rank one person president, another as bookkeeper, two others as stock clerks, etc.

whole-man concept, philosophic attitude that management should be concerned with an employee's physical and mental health both on and off the job.

Whyte, William Foote (1914-   ), sociologist and one of the foremost authorities on human relations in industry. His work has often emphasized the impact of technology upon managerial behavior. Major works include: *Street Corner Society* (Chicago: University of Chicago Press, 1943); *Human Relations in the Restaurant Industry* (N.Y.: McGraw-Hill, 1948); *Pattern for Industrial Peace* (N.Y.: Harper & Row, 1951); *Money and Motivation* (N.Y.: Harper & Row, 1955); *Men at work* (Homewood, Ill.: Richard D. Irwin, 1961).

wildcat strike, also called UNAUTHORIZED STRIKE and OUTLAW STRIKE, work stoppage not sanctioned by union leadership and usually contrary to an existing labor contract. Unless it can be shown unfair employer practices were the direct cause of the wildcat strike, the union could be liable for damages in a breach of contract suit by management. Garth L. Mangum, in "Taming Wildcat Strikes," *Harvard Business Review* (April-May 1960), holds that "wildcat strikes are management's responsibility—they continue as long as the participants find them profitable; cease when management, through disciplinary action, makes them unrewarding." For an analysis of how wildcat strikes are treated by the courts, *see* Evan J. Spelfogel, "Wildcat Strikes and Minority Concerted Activity Discipline, Damage Suits and Injunctions," *Labor Law Journal* (September 1973). *See also* Jeanne M. Brett and Stephen B. Goldberg, "Wildcat Strikes in Bituminous Coal Mining," *Industrial and Labor Relations Review* (July 1979); Steven Rummage, "Union Officers and Wildcat Strikes: Freedom From Discriminatory Discipline," *Industrial Relations Law Journal*, Vol. 4, No. 2 (1981).
See also NONSUABILITY CLAUSE.

Wiley & Sons* v. *Livingston: *see* JOHN WILEY & SONS V. LIVINGSTON.

Williams, Roy L. (19-   ), president of the Teamsters' union from 1981 to 1983.

Williams, Whiting (1878-1975), was the personnel director of a steel company when he quit in order to become a blue-collar "industrial laborer" in order to study working conditions. His subsequent books were the first major studies demonstrating that worker performance was significantly influenced by emotion and attitude. His impressionistic conclusions were later empirically validated by the Hawthorne experiments. Major works include: *What's on the Worker's Mind* (N.Y.: Charles Scribner's Sons, 1920); *Mainsprings of Men* (N.Y.: Charles Scribner's Sons, 1925).

William E. Arnold Co. v. Carpenters District Council of Jacksonville, 417 U.S. 12 (1974), U.S. Supreme Court case, which held that when an activity in question is arguably both an unfair labor practice prohibited by the National Labor Relations Act and a breach of a collective bargaining agreement, the National Labor Relations Board's authority "is not exclusive and does not destroy the jurisdiction" of appropriate courts.

Williams-Steiger Act: *see* OCCUPATIONAL SAFETY AND HEALTH ACT OF 1970.

Wilson, William Bauchop (1862-1934), appointed by President Woodrow Wilson, in 1913 to be the first secretary of the U.S. Department of Labor.

Wilson v. New: see ADAMSON ACT OF 1916.

WIN: *see* WORK INCENTIVE PROGRAM.

wink, unit of time equal to 1/2000 of a minute, which is used in motion-and-time study.

Winpisinger, William W. (1924-   ), president of the International Association of Machinists and Aerospace Workers.

Wirtz, W. Willard (1912-   ), Secretary of Labor from 1962 to 1969.

withholding tax, those federal, state, or local taxes that are withheld by employers from the paychecks of their employees and paid directly to the taxing jurisdiction.

WLW Culture Fair Inventory (CFI), 30-item, nonverbal test that measures reasoning and spatial ability. The test was developed for use in industrial job placement. TIME: 30/45 minutes. AUTHORS: B. O. Murray, L. C. Steckle, R. W. Henderson. PUBLISHER: William, Lynde, and Williams (*see* TEST PUBLISHERS).

WLW Personal Attitude Inventory, 64-item, self-report inventory that measures such factors as emotional stability, friendliness, aggressiveness, humility and insight, reliability and leadership ability. TIME: 20 minutes. AUTHOR: Robert W. Henderson. PUBLISHER: William, Lynde, and Williams (*see* TEST PUBLISHERS).

Wobblies, slang term for members of the Industrial Workers of the World, a radical union that was founded in 1905 and saw its greatest strength before World War I. *See* Patrick Renshaw, *The Wobblies: The Story of Syndicalism in the United States* (Garden City, N.Y.: Doubleday, 1967); Irving Werstein, *Pie in the Sky, An American Struggle: The Wobblies and Their Times* (New York: Delacorte Press, 1969).
    See also INDUSTRIAL WORKERS OF THE WORLD.

Women's Bureau, agency of the U.S. Department of Labor that is responsible for formulating standards and policies to promote the welfare of wage earning women, improve their working conditions, increase their efficiency, advance their opportunities for professional employment, and investigate and report on all matters pertinent of the welfare of women in industry. The Women's Bureau has regional offices established in 10 areas throughout the United States.

Wonderlic Personnel Test (WPT), 50-item timed measure of adult intelligence (an abridged adaptation of the Otis

Self-Administering Test of Mental Ability) used in the screening of individuals for lower-level positions in business and industry (*i.e.*, bookkeeper, cashier, clerk, police, warehouseman, technician, utility lineman). Because performance on this test is closely related to the amount and quality of education an individual has completed, it tends to discriminate against educationally disadvantaged minority group members. This was so noted by the Supreme Court in *Griggs* v. *Duke Power Company*. As a result of this ruling, the Wonderlic Personnel Test now offers separate norms for blacks in areas of education, age, sex, and geographical regions. TIME: 12 minutes. AUTHOR: E. F. Wonderlic. PUBLISHER: E. F. Wonderlic and Associates (*see* TEST PUBLISHERS).

Woodcock, Leonard Freel (1911–   ), president of the United Automobile, Aerospace and Agricultural Implement Workers of America from 1970 until 1977.

Wood v. **Strickland,** 420 U.S. 308 (1975), Supreme Court ruling creating new standards for the immunity of public employees from civil suits for damages. The court held that a school board member (and by implication other public employees) is not immune from liability for damages ". . . if he knew or reasonably should have known that the action he took within his sphere of official responsibility would violate the constitutional rights of the students affected, or if he took the action with the malicious intention to cause a deprivation of constitutional rights or other injury to the student." *See* David H. Rosenbloom, "Public Administrators' Official Immunity and the Supreme Court: Developments During the 1970s," *Public Administration Review* (March–April 1980).

work, according to Mark Twain, in *The Adventures of Tom Sawyer,* "Work consists of whatever a body is obliged to do, and play consists of whatever a body is not obliged to do." For an exhaustive survey of the nature of work, *see* Report of a Special Task Force to the Secretary of HEW, *Work in America* (Cambridge, Mass.: The MIT Press, 1973). *Also see* Irene M. Frank and David M. Brownstone, *The Historical Encyclopedia of Work: The Evolution of Careers, Occupations and Trades from their Origins to the Present* (New York: Facts on File, 1985).

See also the following entries:
 BESPOKE WORK
 DEAD WORK
 FAT WORK
 OUT-OF-TITLE WORK

work-activities centers, centers planned and designed exclusively to provide therapeutic activities for handicapped clients whose physical or mental impairment is so severe as to make their productive capacity inconsequential. The Secretary of Labor is authorized by the Fair Labor Standards Act to allow the employment of handicapped persons in work activities centers at less than the minimum wage.

workaholic, word first used by Wayne Oates, in his *Confessions of a Workaholic: The Facts About Work Addiction* (N.Y.: World Publishing, 1971), to describe the addiction, the compulsion or the uncontrollable need to work incessantly. A workaholic is a person whose involvement in his/her work is so excessive that his/her health, personal happiness, interpersonal relations and social functioning are adversely affected. *See* Wayne E. Oates, *Workaholics, Make Laziness Work for You* (Garden City, N.Y.: Doubleday, 1978); Fernando Bartolome, "The Work Alibi: When It's Harder To Go Home," *Harvard Business Review* (March–April 1983).

work curve, also called OUTPUT CURVE, graphic presentation of an organization's or individual's productivity over a specified period of time.

workday, basic: *see* BASIC WORKDAY.

work design: *see* JOB DESIGN.

work disability: *see* DISABILITY.

461

worker functions, standardized terms used in job analysis to describe a worker's relationship to data, people or things when performing a specific set of tasks. Of the twenty-four defined worker functions, those describing relationships to data and things are arranged in hierarchies according to levels of complexity. A combination of the highest functions (designated by the lowest numbers) which the worker performs in relation to data, people and things expresses the total level of complexity of the job-worker situation. These worker functions are expressed by the 4th, 5th, 6th digits of the DOT code.

Data—Information, knowledge and conceptions related to data, people or things resulting from observation, investigation, interpretation, visualization, and mental creation. Data are intangible and include numbers, words, symbols, ideas, concepts and oral verbalization.

People—Human beings; also animals dealt with on an individual basis as if they were human.

Things—Inanimate objects as distinguished from human beings; substances or materials, machines, tools, equipment, and products. A thing is tangible and has shape, form, and other physical characteristics.

Worker functions (actions)—Identify significant worker functions in the Data, People and Things area:

Data	People
0 - Synthesizing	0 - Mentoring
1 - Coordinating	1 - Negotiating
2 - Analyzing	2 - Instructing
3 - Compiling	3 - Supervising
4 - Computing	4 - Diverting
5 - Copying	5 - Persuading
6 - Comparing	6 - Speaking/ Signaling
	7 - Serving
	8 - Taking Instructions

Things
0 - Setting Up
1 - Precision Working
2 - Operating/Controlling
3 - Driving/Operating
4 - Manipulating
5 - Tending
6 - Feeding/Offbearing
7 - Handling

workers: *see* EMPLOYEE. *See also* following entries:
BLUE-COLLAR WORKERS
DISADVANTAGED WORKERS
DISCOURAGED WORKERS
DISPLACED EMPLOYEE
EXEMPT EMPLOYEE
FULL-TIME WORKERS
GUEST WORKER
HOURLY-RATE WORKERS
ILLEGAL ALIENS
ITINERANT WORKER
PINK-COLLAR JOBS
PRODUCTION WORKERS
SEMISKILLED WORKERS
UNSKILLED WORKERS
WHITE-COLLAR WORKERS

workers' compensation, also called WORKMEN'S COMPENSATION and INDUSTRIAL ACCIDENT INSURANCE, designed to provide cash benefits and medical care when a worker is injured in connection with his/her job and monetary payments to his/her survivors if he/she is killed on the job, was the first form of social insurance to develop widely in the United States. There are now 54 different workers' compensation programs in operation. Each of the 50 states and Puerto Rico has its own workmen's compensation program. In addition, there are three federal workers' compensation programs, covering federal government and private employees in the District of Columbia, and longshoremen and harbor workers throughout the country.

Before the passage of workmen's compensation laws, an injured employee ordinarily had to file suit against his/her employer and prove that the injury was due to the employer's negligence in order to recover damages. The enactment of workmen's compensation laws introduced the principle that a worker incurring an occupational injury would be compensated regardless of fault or blame in the accident and with a minimum of delay and legal formality. In turn, the employer's liability was limited, because workmen's compensation benefits became the exclusive remedy for work-related injuries.

The usual condition for entitlement to benefits is that the injury or death "arises out of and in the course of employment." Most programs exclude injuries due to the employee's intoxication, willful misconduct, or gross negligence. Although virtually limited to injuries or diseases traceable to industrial "accidents" initially, the scope of the laws has broadened over the years to cover occupational diseases as well.

In most states, workers' compensation is paid for entirely by employers who either purchase insurance coverage or self insure —that is, assume total financial liability for the work accidents of their employees.

The Occupational Health and Safety Act of 1970 created the National Commission on State Workmen's Compensation Laws to evaluate the various state workmen's compensation programs. The commission reported that "the evidence compels us to conclude that state workmen's compensation laws are in general neither adequate nor equitable," *Report of the National Commission on State Workman's Compensation Laws* (Washington D.C.: U.S. Government Printing Office, 1972). For critiques of present programs, *see* Daniel M. Kasper, "For a Better Worker's Compensation System," *Harvard Business Review* (March-April 1977); Robert J. Paul, "Workers' Compensation—An Adequate Employee Benefit?" *Academy of Management Review* (October 1976); Mark Reutter, "Workmen's Compensation Doesn't Work or Compensate," *Business and Society Review* (Fall 1980); James R. Chelius, "The Influence of Workers' Compensation on Safety Incentives," *Industrial and Labor Relations Review* (January 1982); U.S. Chamber of Commerce, *Analysis of Workers' Compensation Laws, 1983* (Washington: U.S. Chamber of Commerce, 1983); LaVerne C. Tinsely, "Workers' Compensation: Significant Enactments in 1983," *Monthly Labor Review* (February 1984).

See also MOUNTAIN TIMBER COMPANY V. WASHINGTON and HAWKINS V. BLEAKLY.

workers' councils, also called WORKS COUNCILS, any of a variety of joint labor-management bodies serving as vehicles for the resolution of problems of mutual interest. Workers' councils are usually associated with concepts of industrial democracy and are found mostly in Europe. *See* Erland Waldenstrom, "Works Councils: The Need to be Involved," *Columbia Journal of World Business* (May June 1968).

work ethic: *see* PROTESTANT ETHIC.

workfare, any public welfare program that requires welfare payment recipients to work (work + welfare = workfare) or enroll in a formal job-training program. *See* Linda E. Demkovich, "Does Workfare Work?" *National Journal* (July 4, 1981).

workforce planning, determination by organization management of the numbers, kinds, and costs of the workers needed to carry out each stage of the organization's program plan.

See also HUMAN RESOURCES PLANNING.

work group, also called WORKING GROUP and TASK GROUP, task unit within a larger organizational social system charged with the responsibility for making a specific contribution to the goals of the larger organization. *See* Maxine Bucklow, "A New Role for the Work Group," *Administrative Science Quarterly* (June 1966); J. Stephen Heinen and Eugene Jacobson, "A Model of Task Group Development in Complex Organizations and a Strategy of Implementation," *Academy of Management Review* (October 1976); David G. Bowers and Doris L. Hausser, "Work Group Types and Intervention Effects in Organizational Development," *Administrative Science Quarterly* (March 1977); Panagiotis N. Fotilas, "Semi-Autonomous Work Groups: An Alternative in Organizing Production Work?" *Management Review* (July 1981); Deborah L. Gladstein, "Groups In Context: A Model of

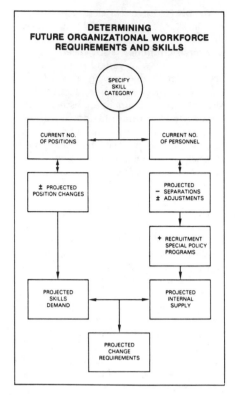

DETERMINING FUTURE ORGANIZATIONAL WORKFORCE REQUIREMENTS AND SKILLS

SOURCE: From Jay M. Shafritz, et al., Personnel Management in Government: Politics and Process (New York: Marcel Dekker, Inc., 1978), p. 85.

Task Group Effectiveness," *Administrative Science Quarterly* (December 1984).
  See also GROUP DYNAMICS

work group, horizontal, *see* HORIZONTAL WORK GROUP.

work-in, form of protest demonstration in which a group of employees report to work as usual but refuse to follow their normal routines.

Work in America Institute, a clearinghouse for information on quality of working life and productivity.
  Work in America Institute
  700 White Plains Road
  Scarsdale, N.Y. 10583
  (914) 472-9600

Work Incentive Program (WIN), federal programs authorized by the Social Security Amendments of 1967 and 1971. It is jointly administered by the Departments of Labor and Health and Human Services and is designed to help persons receiving Aid to Families with Dependent Children (AFDC) become self-supporting. The 1971 amendment shifted the program emphasis from training to immediate employment.

All AFDC applicants and recipients are required (unless exempt by law) to register with the WIN sponsor (usually the state employment agency) for employment and manpower services as a condition of eligibility. WIN utilizes existing employment-related training programs and WIN-funded activities—both directed toward ultimate placements in unsubsidized jobs. In preparation for this, WIN offers such manpower services as on-the-job training for the job-ready, or public service employment arranged by prior agreement with public or private nonprofit organizations for individuals for whom unsubsidized jobs are not available. Manpower services are supplemented by necessary supportive social services, including day care for children, which are provided by or through a separate administrative unit of the welfare agency.

The Revenue Act of 1971 provides employers with an incentive in the form of a tax credit for hiring WIN registrants. As an alternative, a welfare tax credit is also available to employers of WIN registrants under related legislation. *See* Barbara S. Goldman, *Impacts of the Immediate Job Search Assistance Experiment: Louisville WIN Research Laboratory Project* (New York: Manpower Demonstration Research Corp., 1981).

working certificate: *see* WORKING PAPERS.

working class, all who work. When the term is used politically, it tends to exclude managers, professionals, and anyone who is not at the lower end of the educational and economic scales. For an analytical description, *see* Andrew Levison, *The Working-Class Majority* (N.Y.: Coward,

McCann & Geoghegan, Inc., 1974). For a social history of the American working class, *see* Herbert G. Gutman, *Work, Culture, and Society in Industrializing America* (N.Y.: Alfred A. Knopf, 1976). *Also see* Maurice F. Neufeld, Daniel J. Leab and Dorothy Swanson, *American Working Class History: A Representative Bibliography* (New York: R. R. Bowker Co., 1983).

working conditions, those factors, both physical and psychological, which comprise an employee's work environment. Included are such things as arrangement of office and factory equipment, salary or wages, fringe benefits, supervision, work routine, fair employment practices, health and safety precautions, length of work day, and relationship with co-workers. *See* Neal Q. Herrick and Robert P. Quinn, "The Working Conditions Survey as a Source of Social Indicators," *Monthly Labor Review* (April 1971); Robert P. Quinn, *et al.,* "Evaluating Working Conditions in America," *Monthly Labor Review* (November 1973).

working group: *see* WORK GROUP.

working hours, flexible: *see* FLEXI-TIME.

working papers, also called WORKING CERTIFICATE and WORK PERMIT, federal certificate of age showing that a minor is above the oppressive child-labor age applicable to the occupation in which he/she would be employed. Such proof of age is required under the provisions of the Fair Labor Standards Act and the Walsh-Healey Public Contracts Act. Working papers are issued by a designee of the administrator of the Wage and Hour Division of the U.S. Department of Labor.

working permit: *see* WORKING PAPERS.

working poor, employees whose incomes are not adequate enough to pull them out of poverty (defined by the federal government as income below a certain level).

workload, the result expected from an expenditure of any employee's time and energy, performing tasks or functions which can be evaluated in terms of either units produced, yardsticks of progresss, or through judging the application and utilization of his or her effort.

work measurement, any method used to establish an equitable relationship between the volume of work performed and the human resources devoted to its accomplishment. Concerned with both volume and time a work measurement program is basically a means of setting standards to determine just what constitutes a fair day's work. For presentations of methods, *see* Robert I. Stevens and Walter J. Bieber, "Work Measurement Techniques," *Journal of Systems Management* (February 1977); Frank J. Landy and James L. Farr, *The Measurement of Work Performance: Methods, Theory and Applications* (New York: Academic Press, 1983); Paul J. Stonich, "The Performance Measurement and Reward System: Critical to Strategic Management," *Organizational Dynamics* (Winter 1984).

See also MOTION STUDY and TIME STUDY.

work measurement standard, a numerical value applied to the units of work an employee or group can be expected to produce in a given period of time.

workmen's compensation: *see* WORKERS' COMPENSATION.

work motivation: *see* MOTIVATION.

work order, a form used to authorize and control work in a factory.

work permit: *see* WORKING PAPERS.

work premium, also called PREMIUM PAY, extra compensation for work that is considered unpleasant, hazardous, or inconvenient. Overtime is the most obvious example of a work premium. *See* Janice Neipert Hedges, "Long Workweeks and Premium Pay," *Monthly Labor Review* (April 1976).

work preview, also called JOB SAMPLE and JOB PREVIEW, management technique for presenting prospective employees with realistic information about the particular job that they are considering. *See* Michael A. Raphael, "Work Previews Can Reduce Turnover and Improve Performance," *Personnel Journal* (February 1975); John P. Wanous, "A Job Preview Makes Recruiting More Effective," *Harvard Business Review* (September–October 1975); John P. Wanous, "Realistic Job Previews," *Personnel Psychology* (Summer 1978); Bernard L. Dugoni and Daniel R. Ilgen, "Realistic Job Previews and the Adjustment of New Employees," *Academy of Management Journal* (September 1981).

work-ready, term used to describe a handicapped person who, if given employment, would be able to perform adequately on the job without being a burden to others.

Work Related Abstracts, monthly that seeks to abstract the significant and the informative from over 250 management, labor, government, professional, and university periodicals.

> Work Related Abstracts
> Information Coordinators, Inc.
> 1435-37 Randolph Street
> Detroit, MI 48226

work relief: *see* RELIEF.

work restructuring: *see* JOB RESTRUCTURING.

work rules, formal regulations prescribing both on-the-job behavior and working conditions. Work rules are usually incorporated into a collective bargaining agreement at the insistence of the union in order to restrict management's ability to unilaterally set production standards and/or reassign employees. The union's goal is to maximize and protect the jobs available to its members, protect their health and safety, and to maintain stable work assignments for union members. *See* Joseph B. Wollenberger, "Acceptable Work Rules and Penalties: A Company Guide," *Personnel* (July-August 1963).

work sampling, also called JOB SAMPLING, technique used to discover the proportions

of total time devoted to the various components of a job. Data obtained from work sampling can be used to establish allowances applicable to a job, to determine machine utilization, and to provide the criteria for production standards. While this same information can be obtained by time-study procedures, work sampling—dependent as it is upon the laws of probability—will usually provide the information faster and at less cost. For a text on the technique, *see* Ralph M. Barnes, *Work Sampling,* 2nd edition (N.Y.: John Wiley & Sons, 1966).

Work sampling is also used to describe a performance test designed to be a miniature replica of behavior required on-the-job, which attempts to measure how well an employee will perform in the particular occupation. Such tests are considered a more precise device for measuring particular occupational abilities than simple motor skills or verbal ability tests. *See* James J. Asher and James A. Sciarrino, "Realistic Work Sample Tests: A Review," *Personnel Psychology* (Winter 1974); Michael K. Mount, Paul M. Muchinsky, and Lawrence M. Hanser, "The Predictive Validity of a Work Sample: A Laboratory Study," *Personnel Psychology* (Winter 1977); Donald J. Schwartz, "A Job Sampling Approach to Merit System Examining," *Personnel Psychology* (Summer 1977).

works councils: *see* WORKERS' COUNCILS.

worksharing, procedure for dividing the available work (or hours of work) among all eligible employees as an alternative to layoffs during slow periods. Three types of worksharing procedures may be identified—reduction in hours (by far the most common), division of work, and rotation of employment. *Reduction in hours,* as its name implies, requires that weekly hours of work be reduced below normal (nonovertime) schedules, usually within stated limits, to spread the work. The second procedure—*division of work*—is normally found in agreements covering employees on piecework or incentive systems, and emphasizes earnings rather than hours of work (although reduced hours may also occur). All available work is divided equally among eligible employees; under some conditions, faster workers may work somewhat fewer hours than slower ones for the same pay. The last procedure—*rotation of employment* (or layoff)—provides that short, specific periods of layoff be rotated equally among all employees, in contrast to the more common practice of laying off junior employees for longer or indefinite periods. Worksharing provisions are often part of a union contract. *See* Bureau of Labor Statistics, U.S. Department of Labor, *Major Collective Bargaining Agreements: Layoff, Recall and Worksharing Procedures* (Wash., D.C.: U.S. Government Printing Office, Bulletin 1425-13, 1972); Nancy J. McNeff, *et al.,* "Alternatives to Employee Layoffs: Work Sharing and Prelayoff Consultation," *Personnel* (January–February 1978); Maureen E. McCarthy and Gail S. Rosenberg, with Gary Lefkowitz, *Work Sharing: Case Studies* (Kalamazoo, Mich.: W. E. Upjohn Institute for Employment Research, Inc., 1981); Ramelle MaCoy and Martin J. Morand, editors, *Short-Time Compensation: A Formula for Work Sharing* (New York: Pergamon Press, 1984); Martin Nemirow, "Work-Sharing Approaches: Past and Present," *Monthly Labor Review* (September 1984).

See also JOB SHARING.

work simplification, the industrial engineering function which seeks to find the one best way to do each job in a plant, based upon economy of time, material, effort, etc. *See* Alan D. Rowland, "Combining Quality Control Circles and Work Simplification," *Training and Development Journal* (January 1984).

work station, specific location and immediate surrounding area in which a job is performed.

work stoppage, according to both the U.S. Departments of Commerce and Labor, a work stoppage is a concerted and complete withholding of services by employees that lasts for at least one workday or one work shift.

work to rule, work slowdown in which all of the formal work rules are so scrupulously obeyed that productivity suffers considerably. Those working to rule seek to place pressure on management without losing pay by going on strike. Work-to-rule protests are particularly popular in the public sector where most formal strikes are illegal.

work values, importance that employees place on the various aspects of work such as pay, prestige, security, responsibility, etc. *See* Stephen Wollock, et al., "Development of the Survey of Work Values," *Journal of Applied Psychology,* vol. 55, no. 4 (1971); Charles L. Hughes and Vincent S. Flowers, "Shaping Personnel Strategies to Disparate Value Systems," *Personnel* (March–April 1973).

Work Values Inventory (WVI), test used as an aid in understanding the value structure of the individual. Consists of 45 items with 15 scales that include altruism, creativity, independence, security, achievement, prestige, supervisory relations, way of life, etc. TIME: 10-20 minutes. AUTHOR: Donald E. Super. PUBLISHER: Houghton Mifflin Company (*see* TEST PUBLISHERS).

workweek, expected or actual period of employment for a "normal" week, usually expressed in number of hours. According to the Fair Labor Standards Act, a workweek is a period of 168 hours during 7 consecutive 24-hour periods. It may begin on any day of the week and any hour of the day established by the employer. For purposes of minimum wage and overtime payment, each workweek stands alone, and there can be no averaging of two or more workweeks (except for hospital or nursing home employees on an "8-and-80" schedule or seamen on U.S. vessels). Employee coverage, compliance with wage payment requirements, and the application of most exemptions are determined on a work-week basis.

See also the following entries:
BASIC WORKWEEK
4-DAY WORKWEEK
GUARANTEED WORKWEEK

World Federation of Personnel Management Associations, an association of regional personnel management associations whose goal is to establish common positions on matters of concern to the human resources management function. Present members include the Asian Pacific Federation of Personnel Management Associations, the European Association for Personnel Management, the Interamerican Federation of Personnel Administration, and the American Society for Personnel Administration. *See* "The World Federation of Personnel Management Associations," *Personnel Administrator* (July 1984).

WPCT: *see* WESMAN PERSONNEL CLASSIFICATION TEST.

WPT: *see* WONDERLIC PERSONNEL TEST.

wrap-up clause: *see* ZIPPER CLAUSE.

Wright, Carroll Davidson (1840-1909), first head of the U.S. Bureau of Labor; considered the "inventor" of the field of labor statistics. Wright's nonpartisan tone during ten years (1895-1905) as head of the national bureau and his philosophy that supplying facts—and not advocating particular solutions—was the proper function of a labor bureau went far to create the climate that allowed for the eventual creation of the present Department of Labor. He was also the statistical wit who first observed that "figures won't lie, but liars will figure." *See* James Leiby, *Carroll Wright and Labor Reform: The Origin of Labor Statistics* (Cambridge, Mass.: Harvard University Press, 1960); Judson MacLaury, "The Selection of the First U.S. Commissioner of Labor," *Monthly Labor Review* (April 1975).

writ of certiorari: *see* CERTIORARI.

writ of mandamus: *see* MANDAMUS.

W-2 Form: *see* FORM W-2.

Wurf, Jerry (1919-1981), president of the American Federation of State, County, and Municipal Employees (AFSCME) from 1964 to 1981. For biographical accounts, *see* Fred C. Shapiro, "How Jerry Wurf Walks on Water," *The New York Times Magazine* (April 11, 1976); K. Bode, "Crying Wurf," *The New Republic* (July 2, 1977).

WVI: *see* WORK VALUES INVENTORY.

X

x^2: *see* CHI-SQUARE.

X-Theory: *see* THEORY X.

Y

Yablonski, Joseph A. (1910-1969), called JOCK YABLONSKI, unsuccessfully challenged W. A. "Tony" Boyle for the presidency of the United Mine Workers in 1969. Subsequently, Yablonksi, his wife, and daughter were shot by three gunmen hired by Boyle, who was later convicted of three counts of first degree murder. For an account, *see* Brit Hume, *Death and the Mines: Rebellion and Murder in the United Mine Workers* (N.Y.: Grossman, 1971).

Year Book of Labour Statistics, annual summary of the principal labor statistics from about 180 countries or territories that is published by International Labour Office, Geneva, Switzerland.

year-end bonus: *see* NONPRODUCTION BONUS.

yellow-dog contract, any agreement

(written or oral) between an employer and an employee that calls for the employee to resign from, or refrain from joining, a union. In the early part of this century, this was a common tactic used by employers wary of union influences. The Norris-LaGuardia Act of 1932 made yellow-dog contracts illegal.

Yerkes, Robert M. (1876-1956), president of the American Psychological Association in 1918 and one of the team of psychologists who produced the famous Army Alpha and Army Beta intelligence tests first used by the United States Army during World War I.

Yeshiva University decision: see NATIONAL LABOR RELATIONS BOARD V. YESHIVA UNIVERSITY.

Youngstown Sheet and Tube Co. v. Sawyer, 343 U.S. 579 (1952), Supreme Court case involving the constitutionality of President Truman's executive order directing the Secretary of Commerce to take possession of and operate the nation's steel mills in connection with a labor dispute that threatened to disrupt production. By a 6-3 vote, the Supreme Court held that the president exceeded his constitutional powers, although there was no majority opinion. *See* John L. Blackman, Jr., *Presidential Seizure in Labor Disputes* (Cambridge, Mass.: Harvard University Press, 1967).

Z

Zander, Arnold Scheuer (1901-   ), organized and became the first president of the American Federation of State, County, and Municipal Employees. For biographical information, *see* Leo Kramer, *Labor's Paradox: The American Federation of State, County and Municipal*

Employees, AFL-CIO (N.Y.: John Wiley, 1962).

zero-defects program, formal effort at quality assuredness aimed at eliminating human errors during production. *See* George E. Fouch, "Motivation for Quality-Zero Defects Program," *Industrial Quality Control* (November 1965); Gerald V. Barrett and Patrick A. Cabe, "Zero Defects Programs: Their Effects at Different Job Levels," *Personnel* (November-December 1967).

Z score, another way of referring to a standard score.

zipper clause, also called WRAP-UP CLAUSE, portion of a collective bargaining contract that specifically states the written agreement is complete and anything not contained in it is not agreed to. A typical zipper clause might read: "This contract is complete in itself and sets forth all the terms and conditions of the agreement between the parties hereto." The main purpose of the zipper or wrap-up clause is to prevent either party from demanding a renewal of negotiations during the life of the contract. It also serves to limit the freedom of a grievance arbitrator because his rulings must be based solely on the written agreement's contents.

zone of acceptance, also called ACCEPTANCE THEORY OF AUTHORITY, concept that authority stems from the bottom up, based on the extent to which individuals are willing to hold in abeyance their own critical faculties and accept the directives of their organizational superiors. The "zone of acceptance" itself is a theoretical range of tolerance within which organizational members will accept orders without question. A pioneering analysis of this concept is "The Role of Authority," Chapter VII of Herbert Simon's *Administrative Behavior* (N.Y.: The Free Press, 1947). Note that Simon's concept admittedly built upon Chester I. Barnard's concept of the "zone of indifference."

zone of employment, the physical area

(usually the place of employment and surrounding areas controlled by the employer) within which an employee is eligible for workers' compensation benefits when injured, whether or not on the job at the time.

zone of indifference, concept that comes from Chester I. Barnard's *The Functions of the Executive* (Cambridge, Mass.: Harvard University Press, 1938). According to Barnard:

> If all the orders for actions reasonably practicable be arranged in the order of their acceptability to the person affected, it may be conceived that there are a number which are clearly unacceptable, that is, which certainly will not be obeyed; there is another group somewhat more or less on the neutral line, that is, either barely acceptable or barely unacceptable; and a third group unquestionably acceptable. This last group lies within the "zone of indifference." The person affected will accept orders lying within this zone and is relatively indifferent as to what the order is so far as the question of authority is concerned.

zone of uncertainty, range or zone of test scores within which it cannot truly be said that differing scores actually represent differing levels of attainment.

APPENDIX A

OFFICIAL NAMES OF NATIONAL UNIONS WITH
THEIR POPULAR NAMES AND ACRONYMS

The official names of national unions are followed by their popular names and by their acronyms. The popular names are listed alphabetically in appendix B.

Actors' Equity Association, AAAA, AFL-CIO: *Actors Equity* [AEA]

Aluminum, Brick and Glass Workers International Union, AFL-CIO: *Aluminum & Glass Workers* [ABG]

Amalgamated Clothing and Textile Workers Union, AFL-CIO: *Clothing & Textile Workers* [ACTWU]

Amalgamated Lace Operatives of America (Ind.): *Lace Workers* [ALOA]

Amalgamated Transit Union, AFL-CIO: *Transit Union* [ATU]

American Association of University Professors (Ind.): *University Professors* [AAUP]

American Federation of Government Employees, AFL-CIO: *Government Employees* [AFGE]

American Federation of Grain Millers, AFL-CIO: *Grain Millers* [AFGM]

American Federation of Musicians of the United States and Canada, AFL-CIO: *Musicians* [AFM]

American Federation of State, County and Municipal Employees, AFL-CIO: *State County Employees AFSCME* [AFSCME]

American Federation of Teachers, AFL-CIO: *Teachers AFT* [AFT]

American Federation of Television and Radio Artists, AAAA, AFL-CIO: *Television Artists AFTRA* [AFTRA]

American Flint Glass Workers Union, The, AFL-CIO: *Flint Glass Workers* [AFGWU]

American Guild of Musical Artists, AAAA, AFL-CIO: *Musical Artists* [AGMA]

American Guild of Variety Artists, AAAA, AFL-CIO: *Variety Artists* [AGVA]

American Nurses' Association (Ind.): *Nurses ANA* [ANA]

American Postal Workers Union, AFL-CIO: *American Postal Workers* [APWU]

American Soccer League Players Association, AFL-CIO: *Soccer Players American* [ASLPA]

Associated Actors and Artistes of America, AFL-CIO: *Actors & Artists* [AAAA]

Association of Western Pulp and Paper Workers (Ind.): *Pulp & Paper Workers* [AWPPW]

Bakery, Confectionery and Tobacco Workers International Union, AFL-CIO: *Bakery Workers* [BC&T]

Brotherhood of Police and Security Officers (Ind.): *Police & Security Officers* [PSO]
Brotherhood of Railway, Airline and Steamship Clerks, Freight Handlers, Express and
    Station Employees, AFL-CIO: *Railway Clerks* [BRAC]
Brotherhood Railway Carmen of the United States and Canada, AFL-CIO: *Railway
    Carmen* [BRC]
Building and Construction Trades Council, location, AFL-CIO: *Building Trades Council,
    location* (cite, e.g., *Dallas Building Trades Council*)

Communications Workers of America, AFL-CIO: *Communications Workers* [CWA]
Congress of Independent Unions (Ind.): *Independent Union CIU* [CIU]
Coopers International Union of North America, AFL-CIO: *Coopers* [CI]

Distillery, Wine and Allied Workers International Union, AFL-CIO: *Distillery Workers*
    [DWU]

Federation of Professional Athletes, AFL-CIO: *Professional Athletes* [FPA]
Fraternal Association of Special Haulers (Ind.): *Special Haulers* [FASH]

Glass, Pottery, Plastics & Allied Workers International Union, AFL-CIO: *Glass & Pot-
    tery Workers* [GPPAW]
Graphic Communications International Union, AFL-CIO: *Graphic Communications*
    [GCIU]

Hotel Employees & Restaurant Employees International Union, AFL-CIO: *Hotel &
    Restaurant Employees* [HERE]

Independent Union of Plant Protection Employees [Ind.]: *Protection Employees* [IUPPE]
Industrial Union of Marine and Shipbuilding Workers of America, AFL-CIO: *Ship-
    builders* [IUMSWA]
Insurance Workers International Union, AFL-CIO: *Insurance Workers* [IWIU]
International Alliance of Theatrical Stage Employees and Moving Picture Machine
    Operators of the United States and Canada, AFL-CIO: *Stage Employees IATSE*
    [IATSE]
International Association of Bridge, Structural and Ornamental Iron Workers, AFL-
    CIO: *Iron Workers* [IABSOIW]
International Association of Heat and Frost Insulators and Asbestos Workers, AFL-CIO:
    Asbestos Workers [AWI]
International Association of Machinists and Aerospace Workers, AFL-CIO: *Machinists*
    [IAM]
International Brotherhood of Boilermakers, Iron Shipbuilders, Blacksmiths, Forgers and
    Helpers, AFL-CIO: *Boilermakers* [IBB]
International Brotherhood of Electrical Workers, AFL-CIO: *Electrical Workers IBEW*
    [IBEW]
International Brotherhood of Firemen and Oilers, AFL-CIO: *Firemen & Oilers* [IBF&O]
International Brotherhood of Painters and Allied Trades, AFL-CIO: *Painters* [IBPAT]
International Brotherhood of Teamsters, Chauffeurs, Warehousemen and Helpers of
    America (Ind.): *Teamsters* [IBT]
International Chemical Workers Union, AFL-CIO: *Chemical Workers* [ICWU]
International Die Sinkers' Conference (Ind): *Die Sinkers* [DSC]
International Federation of Professional and Technical Engineers, AFL-CIO: *Profes-
    sional Engineers* [IFPTE]
International Guards Union of America (Ind.): *Guards Union* [IGUA]

International Ladies' Garment Workers' Union, AFL-CIO: *Ladies Garment Workers* [ILGWU]

International Leather Goods, Plastics and Novelty Workers' Union, AFL-CIO: *Leather Goods Workers* [ILGPNWU]

International Longshoremen's and Warehousemen's Union (Ind.): *Longshoremen ILWU* [ILWU]

International Longshoremen's Association, AFL-CIO: *Longshoremen ILA* [ILA]

International Molders and Allied Workers Union, AFL-CIO: *Molders* [IM&AWU]

International Organization of Masters, Mates and Pilots, ILA, AFL-CIO: *Masters, Mates & Pilots* [MM&P]

International Plate Printers', Die Stampers' and Engravers' Union of North America, AFL-CIO: *Plate Printers* [PPDSE]

International Typographical Union of North America, AFL-CIO: *Typographical Union* [ITU]

International Union, Allied Industrial Workers of America, AFL-CIO: *Industrial Workers AIW* [AIW]

International Union of Allied, Novelty and Production Workers, AFL-CIO: *Novelty Workers* [IUAN&PW]

International Union of Bricklayers and Allied Craftsmen, AFL-CIO: *Bricklayers* [BAC]

International Union of Electronic, Electrical, Technical, Salaried and Machine Workers, AFL-CIO: *Electronic Workers IUE* [IUE]

International Union of Elevator Constructors, The, AFL-CIO: *Elevator Constructors* [IUEC]

International Union of Operating Engineers, AFL-CIO: *Operating Engineers* [IUOE]

International Union of Petroleum and Industrial Workers, AFL-CIO: *Petroleum Workers* [IUPW]

International Union of Security Officers (Ind.): *Security Officers* [IUSO]

International Union, United Automobile, Aerospace and Agricultural Implement Workers of America (UAW), AFL-CIO: *Auto Workers* [UAW]

International Union, United Plant Guard Workers of America (UPGWA) (Ind.): *Plant Guards* [UPGWA]

International Woodworkers of America, AFL-CIO: *Woodworkers* [IWA]

Laborers' International Union of North America, AFL-CIO: *Laborers* [LIUNA]

Laundry and Dry Cleaning International Union, AFL-CIO: *Laundry Workers* [LDCIU]

Leather Workers International Union, AFL-CIO: *Leather Workers* [LWIU]

Major Indoor Soccer League Players Association, AFL-CIO: *Soccer Players Major Indoor* [MISLPA]

Major League Baseball Players Association (Ind.): *Baseball Players* [MLBPA]

Mechanics Educational Society of America, AFL-CIO: *Mechanics Educational Society* [MESA]

Metal Polishers, Buffers, Platers and Allied Workers International Union, AFL-CIO: *Metal Polishers* [MPIU]

National Alliance of Postal and Federal Employees (Ind.): *Postal & Federal Employees* [NAPFE]

National Association of Broadcast Employees and Technicians, AFL-CIO: *Broadcast Employees NABET* [NABET]

National Association of Letter Carriers of the United States of America, AFL-CIO: *Letter Carriers* [NALC]

National Basketball Players Association (Ind.): *Basketball Players* [NBPA]
National Brotherhood of Packinghouse and Industrial Workers (Ind.): *Packinghouse Workers* [NBP&IW]
National Education Association (Ind.): *National Education Assn.* [NEA]
National Federation of Federal Employees (Ind.): *Federal Employees* [NFFE]
National Federation of Licensed Practical Nurses (Ind.): *Nurses LPN* [LPN]
National Football League Players Association, AFL-CIO: *Football Players* [NFLPA]
National Marine Engineers' Beneficial Association, AFL-CIO: *Marine Engineers* [MEBA]
National Maritime Union of America, AFL-CIO: *Maritime Union* [NMU]
National Plant Protection Association (Ind.): *Plant Protection* [PPA]
National Post Office Mail Handlers, Watchmen, Messengers and Group Leaders Division of the Laborers' International Union of North America, AFL-CIO: *Mail Handlers* [NPOMHU]
National Rural Letter Carriers' Association (Ind.): *Rural Letter Carriers* [RLCA]
National Union of Hospital and Health Care Employees, RWDSU, AFL-CIO: *Hospital Employees* [NUH&HCE]
Newspaper Guild, The, AFL-CIO: *Newspaper Guild* [TNG]
North American Soccer League Players Association, AFL-CIO: *Soccer Players North American* [NASLPA]

Office and Professional Employees International Union, AFL-CIO: *Office Employees* [OPEIU]
Oil, Chemical and Atomic Workers International Union, AFL-CIO: *Oil Workers* [OCAW]
Operative Plasterers' and Cement Masons' International Association of the United States and Canada, AFL-CIO: *Plasterers* [OPCMIA]

Pacific Coast Marine Firemen, Oilers, Watertenders and Wipers Association, AFL-CIO: *Marine Firemen* [MFOW]
Pattern Makers' League of North America, AFL-CIO: *Pattern Makers* [PML]

Retail, Wholesale and Department Store Union, AFL-CIO: *Retail Wholesale Union* [RWDSU]

Sailors' Union of the Pacific, AFL-CIO: *Sailors Union* [SUP]
Screen Actors Guild, AAAA, AFL-CIO: *Screen Actors* [SAG]
Screen Extras Guild, Inc., AAAA, AFL-CIO: *Screen Extras* [SEG]
Seafarers' International Union of North America, AFL-CIO: *Seafarers* [SIU]
Seafarers' International Union of North America, Atlantic, Gulf, Lakes and Inland Waters District, AFL-CIO: *Seafarers Atlantic District* [SIU-A&G]
Seafarers' International Union of North America, Pacific District, AFL-CIO: *Seafarers Pacific District* [SIU-PD]
Service Employees International Union, AFL-CIO: *Service Employees* [SEIU]
Sheet Metal Workers' International Association, AFL-CIO: *Sheet Metal Workers* [SMWIA]
Southern Labor Union (Ind.): *Southern Labor Union* [SLU]
Stove, Furnace and Allied Appliance Workers' International Union of North America, AFL-CIO: *Stove Workers* [SF&AAW]

Textile Processors Service Trades, Health Care, Professional and Technical Employees International Union (Ind.): *Textile Processors* [TPIU]
Tile, Marble, Terrazzo, Finishers & Shopmen International Union, AFL-CIO: *Marble Polishers* [TMTF]

Transport Workers Union of America, AFL–CIO: *Transport Workers* [TWU]

United Association of Journeymen and Apprentices of the Plumbing and Pipe Fitting Industry of the United States and Canada, AFL–CIO: *Plumbers* [UA]
United Brotherhood of Carpenters and Joiners of America, AFL–CIO: *Carpenters* [UBC]
United Cement, Lime, Gypsum, and Allied Workers International Union, AFL–CIO: *Cement Workers* [CLGAW]
United Electrical, Radio and Machine Workers of America (UE) (Ind.): *Electrical Workers UE* [UE]
United Farm Workers of America, AFL–CIO: *Farm Workers* [UFW]
United Food and Commercial Workers International Union, AFL–CIO: *Food & Drug Commercial Workers* [UFCW]
United Furniture Workers of America, AFL–CIO: *Furniture Workers* [UFWA]
United Garment Workers of America, AFL–CIO: *Garment Workers* [UGW]
United Mine Workers of America (Ind.): *Mine Workers* [UMW]
United Paperworkers International Union (UPIU), AFL–CIO: *Paperworkers* [UPIU]
United Rubber, Cork, Linoleum and Plastic Workers of America, AFL–CIO: *Rubber Workers* [URW]
United Steelworkers of America, AFL–CIO: *Steelworkers* [USW]
United Telegraph Workers, The, AFL–CIO: *Telegraph Workers* [UTW]
United Textile Workers of America, AFL–CIO: *Textile Workers UTWA* [UTWA]
United Union of Roofers, Waterproofers and Allied Workers, AFL–CIO: *Roofers* [RW&A]
Upholsterers' International Union of North America, AFL–CIO: *Upholsterers* [UIU]
Utility Workers Union of America, AFL–CIO: *Utility Workers* [UWUA]

Writers Guild of America (Ind.): *Writers Guild* [WGA]

APPENDIX B

POPULAR NAMES OF NATIONAL UNIONS
WITH THEIR OFFICIAL NAMES AND ACRONYMS

Actors & Artists: Associated Actors and Artistes of America, AFL-CIO [AAAA]

Actors Equity: Actors' Equity Association, AAAA, AFL-CIO [AEA]

Aluminum & Glass Workers: Aluminum, Brick and Glass Workers International Union, AFL-CIO [ABG]

American Postal Workers: American Postal Workers Union, AFL-CIO [APWU]

Asbestos Workers: International Association of Heat and Frost Insulators and Asbestos Workers, AFL-CIO [AWI]

Auto Workers: International Union, United Automobile, Aerospace and Agricultural Implement Workers of America (UAW), AFL-CIO [UAW]

Bakery Workers: Bakery, Confectionery and Tobacco Workers International Union, AFL-CIO [BC&T]

Baseball Players: Major League Baseball Players Association (Ind.) [MLBPA]

Basketball Players: National Basketball Players Association (Ind.) [NBPA]

Boilermakers: International Brotherhood of Boilermakers, Iron Shipbuilders, Blacksmiths, Forgers and Helpers, AFL-CIO [IBB]

Bricklayers: International Union of Bricklayers and Allied Craftsmen, AFL-CIO (BAC)

Broadcast Employees NABET: National Association of Broadcast Employees and Technicians, AFL-CIO [NABET]

Building Trades Council, location: Building and Construction Trades Council, location, AFL-CIO (cite, e.g., *Dallas Building Trades Council*)

Carpenters: United Brotherhood of Carpenters and Joiners of America, AFL-CIO [UBC]

Cement Workers: United Cement, Lime, Gypsum, and Allied Workers International Union, AFL-CIO [CLGAW]

Chemical Workers: International Chemical Workers Union, AFL-CIO [ICWU]

Clothing & Textile Workers: Amalgamated Clothing and Textile Workers Union, AFL-CIO [ACTWU]

Communications Workers: Communications Workers of America, AFL-CIO [CWA]

Coopers: Coopers International Union of North America, AFL-CIO [CI]

Die Sinkers: International Die Sinkers' Conference (Ind.) [DSC]

477

Distillery Workers: Distillery, Wine and Allied Workers International Union, AFL-CIO
[DWU]

Electrical Workers IBEW: International Brotherhood of Electrical Workers, AFL-CIO
[IBEW]
Electrical Workers UE: United Electrical, Radio and Machine Workers of America (UE)
(Ind.) [UE]
Electronic Workers IUE: International Union of Electronic, Electrical, Technical, Salaried
and Machine Workers, AFL-CIO [IUE]
Elevator Constructors: The International Union of Elevator Constructors, AFL-CIO
[IUEC]

Farm Workers: United Farm Workers of America, AFL-CIO [UFW]
Federal Employees: National Federation of Federal Employees (Ind.) [NFFE]
Firemen & Oilers: International Brotherhood of Firemen and Oilers, AFL-CIO [IBF&O]
Flint Glass Workers: The American Flint Glass Workers Union, AFL-CIO [AFGWU]
Food & Commercial Workers: United Food and Commercial Workers International
Union, AFL-CIO [UFCW]
Football Players: National Football League Players Association, AFL-CIO [NFLPA]
Furniture Workers: United Furniture Workers of America, AFL-CIO [UFWA]

Garment Workers: United Garment Workers of America, AFL-CIO [UGW)
Glass & Pottery Workers: Glass, Pottery, Plastics & Allied Workers International Union,
AFL-CIO [GPPAW]
Government Employees: American Federation of Government Employees, AFL-CIO
[AFGE]
Grain Millers: American Federation of Grain Millers, AFL-CIO [AFGM]
Graphic Communications: Graphic Communications International Union, AFL-CIO
[GCIU]
Guards Union: International Guards Union of America (Ind.) [IGUA]

Hospital Employees: National Union of Hospital and Health Care Employees, RWDSU,
AFL-CIO [NUH&HCE]
Hotel & Restaurant Employees: Hotel Employees & Restaurant Employees International Union, AFL-CIO [HERE]

Independent Union CIU: Congress of Independent Union (Ind.) [CIU]
Industrial Workers AIW: International Union, Allied Industrial Workers of America,
AFL-CIO [AIW]
Insurance Workers: Insurance Workers International Union, AFL-CIO [IWIU]
Iron Workers: International Association of Bridge, Structural and Ornamental Iron
Workers, AFL-CIO [IABSOIW]

Laborers: Laborers' International Union of North America, AFL-CIO [LIUNA]
Lace Workers: Amalgamated Lace Operatives of America (Ind.) [ALOA]
Ladies Garment Workers: International Ladies' Garment Workers' Union, AFL-CIO
[ILGWU]
Laundry Workers: Laundry and Dry Cleaning International Union, AFL-CIO [LDCIU]
Leather Goods Workers: International Leather Goods, Plastics and Novelty Workers'
Union, AFL-CIO [ILGPNWU]
Leather Workers: Leather Workers International Union, AFL-CIO [LWIU]
Letter Carriers: National Association of Letter Carriers of the United States of America,
AFL-CIO [NALC]

Longshoremen ILA: International Longshoremen's Association, AFL-CIO [ILA]
Longshoremen ILWU: International Longshoremen's and Warehousemen's Union (Ind.) [ILWU)

Machinists: International Association of Machinists and Aerospace Workers, AFL-CIO (IAM]
Mail Handlers: National Post Office Mail Handlers, Watchmen, Messengers and Group Leaders Division of the Laborers' International Union of North America, AFL-CIO [NPOMHU]
Marble Polishers: Tile, Marble, Terrazzo, Finishers & Shopmen International Union, AFL-CIO [TMTF]
Marine Engineers: National Marine Engineers' Beneficial Association, AFL-CIO [MEBA]
Marine Firemen: Pacific Coast Marine Firemen, Oilers, Watertenders and Wipers Association, AFL-CIO [MFOW]
Maritime Union: National Maritime Union of America, AFL-CIO [NMU]
Masters, Mates & Pilots: International Organization of Masters, Mates and Pilots, ILA, AFL-CIO [MM&P]
Mechanics Educational Society: Mechanics Educational Society of America, AFL-CIO [MESA]
Metal Polishers: Metal Polishers, Buffers, Platers and Allied Workers International Union, AFL-CIO [MPIU]
Mine Workers: United Mine Workers of America (Ind.) [UMW]
Molders: International Molders and Allied Workers Union, AFL-CIO [IM&AWU]
Musical Artists: American Guild of Musical Artists, AAAA, AFL-CIO [AGMA]
Musicians: American Federation of Musicians of the United States and Canada, AFL-CIO (AFM]

National Education Assn.: National Education Association (Ind.) [NEA]
Newspaper Guild: The Newspaper Guild, AFL-CIO [TNG]
Novelty Workers: International Union of Allied, Novelty and Production Workers, AFL-CIO [IUAN&PW]
Nurses ANA: American Nurses' Association (Ind.) [ANA]
Nurses LPN: National Federation of Licensed Practical Nurses (Ind.) [LPN]

Office Employees: Office and Professional Employees International Union, AFL-CIO [OPEIU]
Oil Workers: Oil, Chemical and Atomic Workers International Union, AFL-CIO [OCAW]
Operating Engineers: International Union of Operating Engineers, AFL-CIO [IUOE]

Packinghouse Workers: National Brotherhood of Packinghouse and Industrial Workers (Ind.) [NBP&IW]
Painters: International Brotherhood of Painters and Allied Trades, AFL-CIO [IBPAT]
Paperworkers: United Paperworkers International Union (UPIU), AFL-CIO [UPIU]
Pattern Makers: Pattern Makers' League of North America, AFL-CIO [PML]
Petroleum Workers: International Union of Petroleum and Industrial Workers, AFL-CIO [IUPW]
Plant Guards: International Union, United Plant Guard Workers of America (UPGWA) (Ind.) [UPGWA]
Plant Protection: National Plant Protection Association (Ind.) [PPA]
Plasterers: Operative Plasterers' and Cement Masons' International Association of the United States and Canada, AFL-CIO [OPCMIA]

Plate Printers: International Plate Printers', Die Stampers' and Engravers' Union of North America, AFL-CIO [PPDSE]

Plumbers: United Association of Journeymen and Apprentices of the Plumbing and Pipe Fitting Industry of the United States and Canada, AFL-CIO [UA]

Police & Security Officers: Brotherhood of Police and Security Officers (Ind.) [PSO]

Postal & Federal Employees: National Alliance of Postal and Federal Employees (Ind.) [NAPFE]

Professional Athletes: Federation of Professional Athletes, AFL-CIO [FPA]

Professional Engineers: International Federation of Professional and Technical Engineers, AFL-CIO [IFPTE]

Protection Employees: Independent Union of Plant Protection Employees (Ind.) [IUPPE]

Pulp & Paper Workers: Association of Western Pulp and Paper Workers (Ind.) [AWPPW]

Railway Carmen: Brotherhood Railway Carmen of the United States and Canada, AFL-CIO [BRC]

Railway Clerks: Brotherhood of Railway, Airline and Steamship Clerks, Freight Handlers, Express and Station Employees, AFL-CIO ([BRAC]

Retail Wholesale Union: Retail, Wholesale and Department Store Union, AFL-CIO [RWDSU]

Roofers: United Union of Roofers, Waterproofers and Allied Workers, AFL-CIO [RW&A]

Rubber Workers: United Rubber, Cork, Linoleum and Plastic Workers of America, AFL-CIO [URW]

Rural Letter Carriers: National Rural Letter Carriers' Association (Ind.) [RLCA]

Sailors Union: Sailors' Union of the Pacific, AFL-CIO [SUP]

Screen Actors: Screen Actors Guild, AAAA, AFL-CIO [SAG]

Screen Extras: Screen Extras Guild, Inc., AAAA, AFL-CIO [SEG]

Seafarers: Seafarers' International Union of North America, AFL-CIO [SIU]

Seafarers Atlantic District: Seafarers' International Union of North America, Atlantic, Gulf, Lakes and Inland Waters District, AFL-CIO [SIU-A&G]

Seafarers Pacific District: Seafarers' International Union of North America, Pacific District, AFL-CIO [SIU-PD]

Security Officers: International Union of Security Officers (Ind.) [IUSO]

Service Employees: Service Employees International Union, AFL-CIO [SEIU]

Sheet Metal Workers: Sheet Metal Workers' International Association, AFL-CIO [SMWIA]

Shipbuilders: Industrial Union of Marine and Shipbuilding Workers of America, AFL-CIO [IUMSWA]

Soccer Players American: American Soccer League Players Association, AFL-CIO [ASLPA]

Soccer Players Major Indoor: Major Indoor Soccer League Players Association, AFL-CIO [MISLPA]

Soccer Players North American: North American Soccer League Players Association, AFL-CIO [NASLPA]

Southern Labor Union: Southern Labor Union (Ind.) [SLU]

Special Haulers: Fraternal Association of Special Haulers (Ind.) [FASH]

Stage Employees IATSE: International Alliance of Theatrical Stage Employees and Moving Picture Machine Operators of the United States and Canada, AFL-CIO [IATSE]

State County Employees AFSCME: American Federation of State, County and Municipal Employees, AFL-CIO [AFSCME]

Steelworkers: United Steelworkers of America, AFL-CIO [USW]

Stove Workers: Stove, Furnace and Allied Appliance Workers' International Union of North America, AFL-CIO [SF&AAW]

Teachers AFT: American Federation of Teachers, AFL-CIO [AFT]
Teamsters: International Brotherhood of Teamsters, Chauffeurs, Warehousemen and Helpers of America (Ind.) [IBT]
Telegraph Workers: The United Telegraph Workers, AFL-CIO [UTW]
Television Artists AFTRA: American Federation of Television and Radio Artists, AAAA, AFL-CIO [AFTRA]
Textile Processors: Textile Processors Service Trades, Health Care, Professional and Technical Employees International Union (Ind.) [TPIU]
Textile Workers UTWA: United Textile Workers of America, AFL-CIO [UTWA]
Transit Union: Amalgamated Transit Union, AFL-CIO [ATU]
Transport Workers: Transport Workers Union of America, AFL-CIO [TWU]
Typographical Union: International Typographical Union of North America, AFL-CIO [ITU]

University Professors: American Association of University Professors (Ind.) [AAUP]
Upholsterers: Upholsterers' International Union of North America, AFL-CIO [UIU]
Utility Workers: Utility Workers Union of America, AFL-CIO [UWUA]

Variety Artists: American Guild of Variety Artists, AAAA, AFL-CIO [AGVA]

Woodworkers: International Woodworkers of America, AFL-CIO [IWA]
Writers Guild: Writers Guild of America (Ind.) [WGA]

NATIONAL LABOR RELATIONS BOARD

NLRB
STYLE
MANUAL

PREFACE

This *NLRB Style Manual* is largely due to the efforts of Administrative Law Judge Marion C. Ladwig, who freely gave of his own time for months in preparing it as a guide for uniform citations and good usage. Apart from its value as a guide and reference tool, it is expected to result in substantial savings through shortening both Board and judges' decisions. The Board and the General Counsel are pleased to give credit to Judge Ladwig for his outstanding accomplishment.

The manual encourages the use of concise, plain English and provides rules and examples for improving legal writing, without legalese. It adopts a new system of short, standardized case citations and provides authoritative lists of national unions for use in citing unions by popular name.

The manual draws from many sources and reflects original work. It generally follows the *Government Printing Office Style Manual* (rev. ed. 1973), with various Board-approved exceptions. It utilizes or modifies many rules from *A Uniform System of Citation* (13th ed. 1981), the "Blue Book" published by the Harvard Law Review Association, which should be consulted for citations not covered by the manual.

The Board adopts this manual in the hope that its personnel will adhere to the rules and formats and that the rules of citation will be followed by all persons submitting briefs and other documents to the Board and the Division of Judges.

Washington, D.C.
1983

TABLE OF CONTENTS

1. RULES OF CITATION

1.1 CITATION OF THE BOARD
National Labor Relations Board. After the full name is used once, it may be referred to as the Board.

NLRB. Use (without periods or spaces) in Board and court citations.

1.2 CITING BOARD DECISIONS
XYZ Mfg. Co., 260 NLRB 433, 444-445 (1982).
    260 NLRB 433, 444 fns. 2 & 4 (1982). (citing footnotes)
    260 NLRB 433, 444 (1982) (see fn. 6 and cases cited).
    above at 444 (repeating within 2 pages), 260 NLRB at 444 (if beyond 2 pages)
    267 NLRB No. 222, slip op. at 4-5 (Mar. 31, 1983).
    267 NLRB No. 222, JD slip op. at 9 (Mar. 31, 1983).
    Case 16—CA—1432 (1982) (not reported in Board volumes).

1.3 BOARD AND COURT DECISIONS
a. Illustrations. (Always include the year.)
    Stetson Hat Co., 255 NLRB 1 (1981), enfd. mem. 675 F.2d 111 (D.C. Cir. 1982), cert. denied 455 U.S. 900 (1982).
    Hatters Local 11 (Stetson Hat), 255 NLRB 1 (1981), enfd. sub nom. *Roy Bean Co. v. NLRB,* 675 F.2d 1 (3d Cir. 1982).   enfd. per curiam
    NLRB v. Stetson Hat Co., 675 F.2d 1 (6th Cir. 1982), enfg. as modified 255 NLRB 1 (1981).   enfd. in relevant part   enf. denied
    NLRB v. Hatters Local 11, 660 F.2d 1, 4 (11th Cir. 1981) (dissenting opinion) (footnotes omitted), cert. denied 455 U.S. 900 (1982).
    Hatters Local 11 v. NLRB, 455 U.S. 98, 101 (1982), rehearing denied 456 U.S. 924 (1982).
    McLeod v. Hatters Local 11, 545 F.Supp. 500 (S.D.N.Y.1982).
    McLeod v. Stetson Hat Co., 113 LRRM 2525, 94 CCH LC   ¶81,450 (D.Mass.1983).
    NOTE. Insert an abbreviated name of the company (usually a two-word abbreviation) in parentheses after the union name in a Board citation, and also in a court citation if the case is well known by the company name or if the union name is in Spanish (in Puerto Rico). Give the exact date (Mar. 31, 1983) when citing a slip opinion. Use parallel citations when the U.S., F.2d, or F.Supp. citation is not available. In district court citations, give only the district, not the division. (N.D.Ill.1982) (D.D.C.1982). Separate multiple citations with semicolons.

b. Abbreviations used in citing case history.

affd.	(affirmed)	enfd.	(enforced)	revd.	(reversed)
affg.	(affirming)	enfg.	(enforcing)	revg.	(reversing)
cert.	(certiorari)	mem.	(without published	sub nom.	(under the
enf.	(enforcement)		opinion)		name)

but do not abbreviate

appeal	dismissed	granted	motion	relevant
argued	dismissing	grounds	per curiam	remanded
denied	enjoining	modified	petition	vacated
denying	filed	modifying	rehearing	withdrawn

1.4 RUNNING HEAD CASE CITATIONS
a. Running head as guide.
   In citing decisions by the U.S. Supreme Court, lower courts, and the NLRB, use the running head (the case name printed at the top of the page in bound volumes) as a guide. The specific rules are applied to these names.
b. Specific rules.
   (1) Cite the Board as "NLRB."
   (2) Omit the initial "The" (exception: The Ark).
   (3) Use the abbreviations "Assn.," "Bros.," "Co.," "Corp.," "Inc.," "Ltd.," "Mfg.," and "&".
   (4) Omit "Inc." and "Ltd." if the name contains Company, Products, Service, or other clear indication that it is a business firm.
   (5) Omit given names and initials of individuals, and omit "U.S." in names of Federal agencies, e.g., "Postal Service."
   (6) Do not use "et al." or "etc." to indicate omissions.
   (7) For a union, cite first the popular name of the parent union (listed by official names in appendix 1 p. 55 and by popular names in appendix 2 p. 61), then any local, lodge, or district council, e.g., *Auto Workers Local 45.*
c. Additional running head rules.
   The running heads in the future should conform to the specific rules and also to the following additional rules, enabling case citations to be taken directly from the running heads.
   (1) Omit all parties after the first listed on either side.
   (2) Cite the name of the business, omitting "d/b/a" and the preceding name(s).
   (3) Cite only the first company named, even if it is a division.
   (4) Shorten long company names.
   (5) After a union name in the running head of an NLRB case, insert an abbreviation (usually two words) of the company name. (Cite the abbreviated company name in parentheses after the union name in a court case if it is well known by the company name or if the union name is in Spanish, in Puerto Rico.)
d. Examples of court citations.
   (1) *Supreme Court decisions, company names.*
   "NLRB v. Gissel Packing Co.," the Supreme Court's running head for National Labor Relations Board v. Gissel Packing Co., Inc., et al., is cited *NLRB v. Gissel Packing Co.,* 395 U.S. 575 (1969).
   "Labor Board v. Borg-Warner Corp," the running head for National Labor relations Board v. Wooster Division of Borg-Warner Corp., is cited *NLRB v. Borg-Warner Corp.,* 356 U.S. 342 (1958).
   "Pittsburgh Glass Co. v. Labor Board," the running head for Pittsburgh Plate Glass Co. v. National Labor Relations Board, is cited *Pittsburgh Glass Co. v. NLRB,* 313 U.S. 146 (1941).
   "Fibreboard Corp. v. Labor Board," the running head for Fibreboard Paper Products Corp. v. National Labor Relations Board, is cited *Fibreboard Corp. v. NLRB,* 379 U.S. 203 (1964).
   "Labor Board v. Rice Milling Co.," the running head for National Labor Relations Board v. International Rice Milling Co., Inc., et al., is cited *NLRB v. Rice Milling Co.,* 341 U.S. 665 (1951).

(2) *Supreme Court decisions, union names.*

"NLRB v. Longshoremen," the running head for National Labor Relations Board v. International Longshoremen's Assn., AFL-CIO, et al., is cited *NLRB v. Longshoremen ILA,* 447 U.S. 490 (1980).

"Radio Officers v. Labor Board," the running head for Radio Officers' Union of the Commercial Telegraphers Union, AFL v. National Labor Relations Board, is cited *Radio Officers v. NLRB,* 347 U.S. 17 (1954).

"Carpenters' Union v. Labor Board," for Local 1976, United Brotherhood of Carpenters and Joiners of America, A. F. L., et al. v. National Labor Relations Board [the famous *Sand Door* decision, involving Sand Door and Plywood Company], is cited *Carpenters Local 1976 (Sand Door) v. NLRB,* 357 U.S. 93 (1958).

"Electrical Workers v. Labor Board," the running head for International Brotherhood of Electrical Workers et al. v. National Labor Relations Board, is cited *Electrical Workers IBEW Local 501 v. NLRB,* 341 U.S. 694 (1951).

"Electrical Workers v. Labor Board," the running head for Local 761, International Union of Electrical, Radio & Machine Workers, AFL-CIO v. National Labor Relations Board et al., is cited *Electrical Workers IUE Local 761 v. NLRB,* 366 U.S. 667 (1961).

"Labor Board v. Denver Bldg. Council," the running head for National Labor Relations Board v. Denver Building & Construction Trades Council et al., is cited *NLRB v. Denver Building Trades Council,* 341 U.S. 675 (1951).

"Labor Board v. Insurance Agents," the running head for National Labor Relations Board v. Insurance Agents' International Union, AFL-CIO, is cited *NLRB v. Insurance Agents,* 361 U.S. 477 (1960).

(3) *Courts of appeal and district court decisions.*

"N. L. R. B. v. Eldorado Mfg. Corp.," the running head for National Labor Relations Board, Petitioner, v. Eldorado Manufacturing Corporation and United Steelworkers of America, AFL-CIO, Respondents, is cited *NLRB v. Eldorado Mfg. Corp.,* 660 F.2d 1207 (7th Cir. 1981).

"National Labor Relations Bd. v. Industrial Cotton Mills," the running head for National Labor Relations Board v. Industrial Cotton Mills (Division of J. P. Stevens Co.), is cited *NLRB v. Industrial Cotton Mills,* 208 F.2d 87 (4th Cir. 1953), cert. denied 347 U.S. 935 (1954).

"Hinson v. N. L. R. B.," the running head for Harold W. Hinson, d/b/a Hen House Market No. 3, Petitioner, v. National Labor Relations Board, Respondent, is cited *Hinson v. NLRB,* 428 F.2d 133 (8th Cir. 1970).

"N. L. R. B. v. Local Union No. 725, etc.," the running head for National Labor Relations Board, Petitioner, v. Local Union No. 725 of the United Association of Journeymen and Apprentices of the Plumbing and Pipefitting Industry of the United States and Canada, AFL-CIO, Respondent, is cited *NLRB v. Plumbers Local 725,* 572 F.2d 550 (5th Cir. 1978).

"Local 138, Internat'l Un. of Operating Engineers v. N.L.R.B.," the running head for Local 138, International Union of Operating Engineers, AFL-CIO, and its Welfare Fund and Trustees, William C. DeKoning, et al., Petitioners, v. National Labor Relations Board, Respondent, is cited *Operating Engineers Local 138 v. NLRB,* 321 F.2d 130 (2d Cir. 1963).

"N. L. R. B. v. Const. & Bldg. Material Teamsters," the running head for National Labor Relations Board, Petitioner, v. Construction and Building Material

Teamsters Local No. 291, Affiliated with the International Brotherhood of Teamsters, Chauffeurs, Warehousemen and Helpers of America, Respondent, is cited *NLRB v. Teamsters Local 291,* 633 F.2d 1295 (9th Cir. 1980).

"Liquor Salesmen's Union Local 2 v. N. L. R. B.," the running head for Liquor Salesmen's Union Local 2 of the State of New York, Distillery, Rectifying, Wine & Allied Workers' International Union, AFL-CIO, Petitioners, v. National Labor Relations Board, Respondent, is cited *Distillery Workers Local 2 v. NLRB,* 664 F.2d 318 (5th Cir. 1981).

"Morio v. North American Soccer League," the running head for Winifred D. Morio, Regional Director of Region 2 of the National Labor Relations Board, for and on behalf of the National Labor Relations Board, Petitioner, v. The North American Soccer League and its Constituent Member Clubs, Respondents, is cited *Morio v. North American Soccer League,* 501 F.Supp. 633 (S.D.N.Y.1980).

e. Examples of Board citations.

(1) *Company respondents.*

"Greensboro News Co.," the proper running head for The Greensboro News Company, is cited *Greensboro News Co.,* 244 NLRB 689 (1979).

"Justak Brothers and Company," the present running head for Justak Brothers and Company, Inc., would in the future be written and cited *Justak Bros. & Co.,* 253 NLRB 1054 (1981).

"United Contractors Incorporated," the present running head for United Contractors Incorporated, JMCO Trucking Incorporated, Joint Employers, should be *United Contractors,* 244 NLRB 72 (1979).

"Raycor Co.," the proper running head for Raimund Corssen Co., Inc. d/b/a Raycor Co., is cited *Raycor Co.,* 249 NLRB 565 (1980).

"F. W. Woolworth Company," the running head for F. W. Woolworth Company, should be *F. W. Woolworth Co.,* 90 NLRB 289 (1950).

"Kahn's and Company, Division of Consolidated Food Co.," should be cited *Kahn's & Co.,* 253 NLRB 25 (1980).

"Simpson Steel Fabricators," the proper running head for Simpson Steel Fabricators & Erectors, Inc., is cited *Simpson Steel Fabricators,* 249 NLRB 1111 (1980).

Campbell Products Department, Harry T. Campbell Sons Company, Division of Flintkote Company, should be cited *Harry T. Campbell Sons Co.,* 260 NLRB No. 161, JD slip op. at 5 (Mar. 29, 1982).

Nathan Yorke, Trustee in Bankruptcy, Successor in Bankruptcy, or Alter Ego of the Seeburg Corporation and Seeburg Service Parts Co., a Single Employer, is cited *Seeburg Corp.,* 259 NLRB No. 105 (Dec. 28, 1981).

(2) *Union respondent.*

"UAW, Local 1989," the present running head for International Union, United Automobile, Aerospace and Agricultural Implement Workers of America (UAW), Local No. 1989 *and* Caterpillar Tractor Company, would in the future be written and cited *Auto Workers Local 1989 (Caterpillar Tractor),* 249 NLRB 922 (1980).

"Plumbers, Local 412," for United Association of Journeymen and Apprentices of the Plumbing and Pipe Fitting Industry of the United States and Canada, Local Union No. 412, AFL-CIO (Thomas Mechanical, Inc.), should be *Plumbers Local 412 (Thomas Mechanical),* 249 NLRB 714 (1980).

"Sheet Metal Workers, Local 36," the running head for Sheet Metal Workers International Association, Local No. 36, and Harold Tindell, its agent *and* Nothum Manufacturing Company, should be *Sheet Metal Workers Local 36 (Nothum Mfg.)*, 244 NLRB 224 (1979).

"Local 3, IBEW," the running head for Local 3, International Brotherhood of Electrical Workers, AFL-CIO *and* New York Electrical Contractors Association, Inc.; Empire Electrical Contractors Association, Inc.; and Association of the Electrical Contractors, Inc., should be *Electrical Workers IBEW Local 3 (New York Electrical)*, 244 NLRB 357 (1979).

NOTE. If the union is a respondent employer, no company name is inserted in the citation after the union name.

Repeating and Introductory Signals

1.5 *Repeating Signals*
a. Ibid. Use to repeat the immediately preceding citation without any change. Use "ibid." or "id." only when repeating a citation on the same page.
b. Id. Use to repeat the immediately preceding citation except for a different page: Id. at 10.
c. Above "Above" or "supra" is used when the same case is cited a second time within two pages: *Gissel,* above, or *Gissel,* above at 613. Beyond two pages, repeat the full citation or refer to a specific page, 395 U.S. at 613. "Below" or "infra" is used to refer to subsequent matter.

1.6 *Introductory Signals*
a. [No Signal] Indicates direct support.
b. E.g. Indicates that other examples are available. It may also be used with other signals: "See, e.g." or "But see, e.g."
c. Accord Use "Accord:" to cite other directly supporting cases, or cases in another jurisdiction.
d. See Use to cite basic source material supporting the point. It is used instead of "[no signal]" when the point is not explicitly made but follows from it, or is dictum. Cite the initial page and the page where the point is made.
e. See generally Use to cite an authority providing background or relevant considerations, without providing support for the specific point.
f. Compare Use "compare" or "cf." (which means "compare") to cite a case that is to be compared or distinguished on the point. (Add a parenthetic explanation, however brief.) "Compare . . . with . . ." invites a comparison of the authorities cited to support or illustrate a point. (Also explain.)
g. Contra Use "Contra:" to cite a directly opposite holding.
h. But see Suggests a contrary holding. It is used when "see" would be used for support.

1.7 *Order of Citations*
a. Customary order (non-Board material).
   (1) NLRA or other statutes.
   (2) Decisions of the U.S. Supreme Court.
   (3) Decisions of courts of appeals, listing first any decision in the circuit in which the case is pending.
   (4) Decisions of district courts, state courts, or arbitrators if applicable.
   (5) Other authorities or publications.
b. String citations (when they are necessary). Direct holdings are followed by dictum, "contra," and "but see" (omitting the "but" after "contra"). The position of "compare" is governed by its importance.

1.8 *Citation of NLRA, Board's Rules, etc.*
National Labor Relations Act. After the full name is used once, it may be referred to as the Act (or NLRA).
National Labor Relations Act, 29 U.S.C. § 155 et seq.
Labor Management Relations Act, 1947. [LMRA, the Taft-Hartley Act]
Labor-Management Reporting and Disclosure Act of 1959, 29 U.S.C. § 401 et seq. [LMRDA, the Landrum-Griffin Act]
Health care amendment: Pub. L. 93-360 §§ 1-4, July 26, 1974, 88 Stat. 395-397, 29 U.S.C. §§ 152(14), 158(d) and (g), 169, 183.
Postal Service jurisdiction: Postal Reorganization Act, 39 U.S.C. § 1209(a). [PRA]
Board's Rules and Regulations. Also cited as the Board's Rules, or National Labor Relations Board Rules and Regulations and Statements of Procedure.
45 NLRB Annual Report 67 (1980).

1.9 *Frequently Used and Other Citations*
1 Jones, *Evidence* § 3:41 (6th ed. 1972).
McCormick, *Evidence* § 72 at 155 (2d ed. 1972).
2A Moore, *Federal Practice* ¶ 9.02 at 13 fn. 12 (2d ed. 1981).
Morgan, *Basic Problems of Evidence* 215-218 (1962).
2 Sutherland, *Statutory Construction* § 34.08 (4th ed. 1973).
4 Weinstein, *Evidence* ¶ 803 (6) [04] at 803-156 (1979).
3A Wigmore, *Evidence* § 1040 (Chadbourn rev. 1970).
4 Williston, *Contracts* § 618 (3d ed. 1961 & Supp. 1981).
3 Am.Jur.2d, *Agency* § 77 at 1166, 1167 (1972).
Restatement 2d, *Agency* § 103 (1958).
Cox, *Federalism and Individual Rights*, 73 Nw. U.L. Rev. 1 (1978). (Do not close up initials with longer abbreviations in names of law reviews.)
Hart & Wechsler, *The Federal Courts and the Federal System* 921-926 (2d ed. 1973).
Kahn, *Seniority Problems in Business Mergers*, 8 Ind. & Lab. Rel. Rev. 361, 362 (1954).
Note, *A Framework for Preemption Analysis*, 88 Yale L.J. 1335 (1978).
Smith, *Contracts*, 101 U. Pa. L. Rev. 835 (1953).
Washington Post, Jan. 7, 1982 at D11, col. 5.
Fed.R.Evid. 301. [Federal Rules of Evidence, 28 U.S.C.]
Fed.R.Civ.P. 43(c). [Federal Rules of Civil Procedure, 28 U.S.C.]
45 ALR2d 179 (1956). [American Law Reports]
29 CFR § 1604.1 (1980). [Code of Federal Regulations]
45 Fed.Reg. 45259 (1980) (to be codified at 14 CFR § 39.13). [Fed. Register]
44 BNA LA 545 (1965) (Altieri, Arb.). [Labor Arbitration]
24 Lab. L.J. 592 (1973). [Labor Law Journal]
2 Leg. Hist. 2393 (NLRA 1937). [Legislative History]
1 Leg. Hist. 303 (LMRA 1947). [Legislative History]
2 Leg. Hist. 1162 (LMRDA 1959). [Legislative History]
108 LRRM 2001 (1982). [BNA court decisions, labor cases]
92 CCH LC ¶ 12,345 (1982). [CCH Labor Cases, court decisions]
411 P.2d 271 (1966). [Pacific Reporter, 2d series]
5 U.S.C. § 504 *or* 5 U.S.C. § 504 (1976 ed., Supp. V). [official code]
5 U.S.C.A. § 504, 5 USCS § 504. [unofficial editions]
19 L.Ed.2d 32 (1963). [U.S. Supreme Court Reporter, Lawyers' Edition]
84 S.Ct. 1082 (1964). [Supreme Court Reporter]

Miscellaneous

50 U.S.L.W. 2565 (1982). [United States Law Week]
128 Cong.Rec. H1147 (daily ed. Mar. 29, 1982 (remarks of Rep. Wright).
H.R. 2055, 94th Cong., 122 Cong. Rec. 16870 (1976). [House bill]
H.R. Conf. Rep. No. 96-1434 at 26 (1980). [conference report]
Pub. L. 91-190 § 102, 83 Stat. 852, 853 (1970) (before 1975 amendment).
S. 383, 83d Cong., 100 Cong.Rec. 1213 (1954). [Senate bill]
S. Rep. No. 95-797 at 4 (1978). [Senate report after the 91st Congress]
S. Rep. No. 122, 89th Cong. 22 (1965). [Senate report before the 1969-1970 91st
    Congress, when number of Congress was added to S. and H.R. Rep. Nos.; 1st Sess.
    of Cong. in odd-numbered years; 2d Sess. in even-numbered years]
S. Res. 218, 83d Cong., 100 Cong.Rec. 2972 (1954). [Senate resolution]
Administrative Procedure Act, 5 U.S.C. §§ 551-559, 701-706. [APA]
Equal Access to Justice Act, 5 U.S.C. § 504. [EAJA]
Freedom of Information Act, 5 U.S.C. § 552. (FOIA)
GPO Style Manual (or *Government Printing Office Style Manual*) 81.
NOTE. Never use "p." for the page number except in cross-references (e.g., see rule
1.4 p. 2). Use "at" if there is a possibility of confusion. Underscore book titles and
titles of articles in periodicals and newspapers. When the typewriter being used does
not have a key for typing ¶ or §, substitute the abbreviation "par." or "sec." in the
citation. (Leave a space between ¶, ¶¶, §, or §§ and the numeral: ¶ 141, ¶¶ 5-8,
§ 10, §§ 45, 48.) Cite volume numbers in Arabic numerals.

1.10 *Citation of Sections and Articles*
Section 8(a)(3) and (1) *not* Sections 8(a)(3) and (1).
Section 9(c)(1) and Section 2(6) and (7) *or* Sections 9(c) (1) and 2(6) and (7). Note.
    Capitalize sections of NLRA and Board publications.
Section 8(b)(4)(i), (ii)(A) and (B). [for two or more capital letters]
Section 8(b)(4)(i) and (ii)(A). [for a single capital letter]
Section 102.46 of the Board's Rules and Regulations (abbreviated Sec. 102.46 in paren-
    theses, citations in the text, and footnotes).
EAJA, section 504(a)(2), provides [section spelled out in the text]
Compare § 504(a)(2) with . . . [citation in text or footnote]
In article XII, section 3, provision is made [section or article being capitalized only at
    the beginning of sentence]
In section II,B,2,a of his decision, the administrative law judge found [commas and
    no spaces]
The Company deleted section III(B)(2) of the contract.
Section III,B,1(a) and (b) of the agreement provided
Subchapter II of chapter 5 of title 5 of the United States Code codified the Administrative
    Procedure Act on authority of Pub. L. 89-554, Sept. 6, 1966, 80 Stat. 381, which
    enacted Title 5, Government Organization and Employees.
U.S. Const., Art. I, § 9, cl. 2.

2. ABBREVIATIONS

2.1 *List of Abbreviations. See GPO Style Manual 156.*

2.2 *Abbreviate*

a. Geographic terms.
   (1) *United States*, except when used as a separate noun or part of an official title.

     U.S. Attorney   U.S. economy   U.S. Senate
     U.S. district court   U.S. Government   U.S. Supreme Court
     but
     foreign policy of the United States The Supreme Court of the United States

   (2) *States.* The Board uses the Postal Service two-letter abbreviations in headings and addresses, but spells out the names of States in the text. The traditional abbreviations, which are used in district court citations, are listed with the Postal Service abbreviations.

Ala.	AL	Ky.	KY	N.Y.	NY
Alaska	AK	La.	LA	Ohio	OH
Ariz.	AZ	Mass.	MA	Okla.	OK
Ark.	AR	Md.	MD	Ore.	OR
Cal.	CA	Me.	ME	Pa.	PA
Colo.	CO	Mich.	MI	R.I.	RI
Conn.	CT	Minn.	MN	S.C.	SC
D.C.	DC	Miss.	MS	S.D.	SD
Del.	DE	Mo.	MO	Tenn.	TN
Fla.	FL	Mont.	MT	Tex.	TX
Ga.	GA	N.C.	NC	Utah	UT
Hawaii	HI	N.D.	ND	Va.	VA
Idaho	ID	Neb.	NE	Vt.	VT
Ill.	IL	Nev.	NV	Wash.	WA
Ind.	IN	N.H.	NH	Wis.	WI
Iowa	IA	N.J.	NJ	W.Va.	WV
Kan.	KS	N.M.	NM	Wyo.	WY

   (3) *Addresses.* (In parentheses and footnotes)
     St. Ave. Blvd. Cir. Ct. Dr. Hwy. Pkwy. Rd.   Rte.   Ter.
     NW SW NE SE   St. Louis   1400 I St. NW
     but
     North South East West Fort Mount Place Plaza Point Port Square
     14th Street Bridge   Ninth Avenue Building

b. Standard abbreviations.
   et al.   etc.   et seq.   ibid.   id. at 53   p. pp.
   a.m.   p.m.   e.g.   i.e.   ¶ ¶¶(paragraph(s))   § §§ (section(s))

c. Abbreviations used in parentheses, citations in text, and footnotes.

C.P. Exh.	app. apps.	fig. figs.	sec. secs.	L. LL. (line(s))
Emp. Exh.	art. arts.	fn. fns.	vol. vols.	f. ff. (and
G.C. Exh.	bull. bulls.	No. Nos.	subch. subchs.	following
P. Exh.	ch. chs.	par. pars.	subpar. subpars.	page(s))
R. Exh.	col. cols.	pl. pls.	subsec. subsecs.	Tr. (transcript)
U. Exhs.	ed. eds.	pt. pts.	supp. supps.	

Jan. Feb. Mar. Apr. Aug. Sept. Oct. Nov. Dec. *but* May June July

Abbreviations

d. Abbreviations in names.

Carl Brown Jr.	Charles White Sr.	Ed Ray, Esq.	Dr. Irene Brown
John Smith III	White Senior	Anne Roe, Esq.	Irene Brown, MD

NOTE. *Mr., Mrs., Ms.,* and *Miss* are not used in the text except in quoted matter. The comma is omitted before *Jr.* and *Sr.* (which are restrictive—not parenthetic, requiring commas—see rule 8.4,a(4) p. 28 below), but follow individual usage. In the absence of a gender-free term or a feminine counterpart, the traditional term "Esq." is used for both men and women attorneys.

e. Abbreviations in case citations.

affd.	mem.	NLRB	Assn.	Mfg.
affg.	revd.	F.2d	Bros.	&
cert.	revg.	F.Supp.	Co.	d/b/a
enf.	sub. nom.	U.S.	Corp.	No.
enfd.	fn.	Cir.	Inc.	slip op.
enfg.	fns.	D.	Ltd.	JD slip op.

3. CAPITALIZATION

3.1 *Guide to Capitalization. See List, GPO Style Manual 33-60.*

3.2 *Capitalization Used at NLRB*

Act (NLRB)
Administrative Law Judge John Doe (otherwise lowercase)
Advisory Opinion
Agency (referring to NLRB)
Board (NLRB)
Board Agent John Doe (*but* a Board agent)
Board Member
Chairman John Doe
Charging Party (in the case)
Company (the company involved in the case *but* lowercase as modifier)
Conclusions of Law (in the decision)
Consent Election Agreement
Court (U.S. Supreme Court *but* lowercase for other courts)
Decision (judge's)
Decision and Determination of Dispute
Decision and Order
Decision, Order, and Direction of Election
Decision on Review
Employer (in the case)
Executive Secretary
General Counsel
Hearing Officer John Doe (otherwise lowercase)
Intervenor (in the case)

Judge John Doe (otherwise lowercase)
Local 561
Member (of the Board)
Motion for Summary Judgment
Notice to Show Cause
Objection 4
Officer in Charge John Doe (otherwise lowercase)
Order (in the case)
Petitioner (in the case)
recomended Order (note lowercase *r*)
Region (of the Board)
Region 5
Regional Attorney John Doe (otherwise lowercase)
Regional Director
Regional Office
Report on Challenges
Report on Objections
Resident Office
Respondent (in the case)
Rules and Regulations *or* Board's Rules
Section 8(a)(1) (*but* the section)
Stipulated Election Agreement
Subregional Office
Supplemental Decision and Order
Remedy (*but* the remedy section)
Union (the union involved *but* lowercase as modifier)

Do not capitalize

agent	field examiner	order
agreement	judge	petition
answer	local	report (Regional
charge	motion to dismiss	Director's)
complaint	notice of hearing	request for review
court (any lower court)	panel	tally of ballots
decision	objection	telegraphic order

3.3 *General Rules*

a. Capitalize proper names but not derivatives with common meaning.

John Macadam	Macadam family	Paris	Venetian
but			
macadamized	plaster of paris	venetian blinds	

Capitalization

b. Capitalize such particles as d', de, della, du, van, and von in foreign names unless preceded by a forename or title (but follow individual usage).
Du Pont *but* E. I. du Pont de Nemours & Co.   Von Braun *but* Wernher von Braun

c. Capitalize common nouns used as proper names.
Cape of Good Hope   Seventh and I Streets SE   the District (D.C.)

d. Lowercase article "the" in names of newspapers, periodicals, vessels, and firm names.
the Washington Post   the *Mermaid*   the Key Company   *but*   The Hague

e. Governmental and other units.
United States: The Government, Federal, Federal Government
U.S. Senate   the Congress   the Senate   the House
U.S. Supreme Court: the Court   the court of appeals: the court
United States Court of Appeals for the Fifth Circuit: the Fifth Circuit *but* legislative, executive, and judicial departments
a Representative (U.S. Congress)   a Republican (party member)
    but a representative of a group   a republican form of government
a State, the State, New York State, State Attorney *but* out-of-state outflow, state name, state road, church and state, statewide, state's evidence

f. Capitalize names of regions, localities, and geographic features when used as proper names.
East Side (of city)   the North   the Southwest
the Deep South   the Pacific Coast   the West
the Middle West   the Panhandle   *but* the port of New York

g. Capitalize names of events and holidays
Battle of Lexington   Fourth of July: the Fourth   New Year's Eve

h. Lowercase seasons, directions, and descriptive positions.
spring   winter   north   north-central region   southern California
eastern   northerly   northern   north-northeast   oriental

i. Lowercase these dockside terms even when used with names or numbers.
Hudson dock   dry dock   lock   pier 32   *but*   Fisherman's Wharf

j. Capitalize title preceding name of official or supervisor.
Director Morgan   Floorlady Bowman   Foreman Jones   Supervisor Smith
Chief Peters   Superintendent Brown   Vice President-General Manager Roe
Chairman Smith   Judge Harris   Member Martin
but
employee Jones, company witness Joe Ray, General Counsel witness Jean East

NOTE. A person is referred to by his given name and surname the first time he is mentioned in the text, and thereafter by his surname. A member of the bargaining unit may be identified by his general designation (carpenter Joan Hughes, painter Charles White), and a member of management by his title (Supervisor John Smith, Foreman Anne Brown). The designation or title may be repeated with the surname (carpenter Hughes, Supervisor Smith), particularly in subsequent paragraphs, when needed to assist the reader in recalling the person's identity.

k. Capitalize titles immediately following the name of a person of preeminence or distinction, or used alone as a substitute.
Ronald Reagan, President of the United States: the President
Harry Hughes, Governor of Maryland: the Governor
John R. Van de Water, Chairman: the Chairman
John H. Fanning, Board Member: Board Member

William A. Lubbers, General Counsel: the General Counsel
but
William Doe, president: the president
Henry Jones, foreman: the foreman
Joseph Brown, chairman: the chairman
John Smith, field examiner: the field examiner

l.   Capitalize the first and all other words in titles and headings except articles (*a, an,* and *the*), conjunctions (*and, as, both, but, if, nor, or, than, that,* and *when*), and prepositions (*at, by, for, from, in, into, like, of, off, on, over, to, up, upon,* and *with*) of four letters or less, and the abbreviation *etc.*

m. Lowercase such references as the following.

| abstract B | amendment 5 | appendix C | article I, section 2 | book II |
| exhibit 6 | figure 7 | page 2 | paragraph 4 | rule 2.1 | title IV | volume 10 |

4. COMPOUND WORDS

A compound word, with or without a hyphen, "conveys a unit idea that is not as clearly or quickly conveyed" by the separate words. "Word forms constantly undergo modification. Two-word forms often acquire the hyphen first, are printed as one word later, and not infrequently the transition is from the two- to the one-word form, bypassing the hyphen stage." *GPO Style Manual* 73. See "Guide to Compounding," id. at 81-130.

4.1 *Solid Compounds*

a. One-word compounds frequently used in NLRB work.

antiunion	dressmaker	newsprint	runoff*
backpay	drywall	nighttime	salesman
biweekly	engineroom	nonunion	saleswoman
blacklist	evenhanded	nonworking	sawmill
blueprint	floorlady	offset	semiofficial
bookkeeper	forklift	outpatient	setup*
bookseller	hairnet	papermill	shopwork
bookstore	handyman	patternmaker	shutdown*
breakdown*	holdup*	paycheck	storeroom
breaktime	housekeeper	payroll	storewide
bylaws	hydroelectric	percent	strawboss
catchall	industrywide	pickup*	subregion
checkoff*	interstate	piecework	subregional
checkout*	intrastate	plantwide	superseniority
coffeebreak	jobsite	postdecision	timecard
coffeetime	layoff*	postelection	timesheet
commonsense (adj.)	locksmith	postpetition	timewasting
(common sense, n.)	longstanding	powerhouse	toolmaker
companywide	longtime	powerplant	truckdriver (dump
counterman	lumberyard	preelection	truck driver)
counteroffer	lunchbreak	preemployment	turnover
counterproposal	lunchtime	preexisting	warehouseman
courthouse	markup*	pretrial	workplace
coworker	meatcutter	pricelist	worksheet
(*but* cross-examine)	meatpacker	procompany	worktable
(cross-reference)	millwork	prounion	worktime
deemphasis	millyard	racetrack	workweek (*but*
diemaker	multiemployer	recordkeeping	work force)
diesinker	nationwide	rulemaking	wrongdoer

* Two words as verb.

b. Suffixes.
The following <u>underlined suffixes</u> are usually written solid, but a hyphen is used with proper names and to avoid tripling a consonant.

give<u>away</u>	movie<u>goer</u>	inner<u>most</u>	home<u>stead</u>
show<u>down</u>	kilo<u>gram</u>	cut<u>off</u>	wind<u>up</u>
twenty<u>fold</u>	man<u>hood</u>	blow<u>out</u>	area<u>wide</u>

spoon<u>ful</u>	life<u>like</u>	left<u>over</u>	clock<u>wise</u>

but

Florida-like	Truman-like	bell-like	brass-smith

c. Prefixes.

(1) The following underlined prefixes are usually written solid.

<u>a</u>moral	<u>electro</u>magnet	<u>mid</u>summer	<u>pseudo</u>nym
<u>after</u>care	<u>ex</u>communicate	<u>mis</u>state	<u>re</u>unite
<u>Anglo</u>mania	<u>extra</u>hazardous	<u>mono</u>gram	<u>retro</u>spect
<u>ante</u>date	<u>fore</u>finger	<u>multi</u>color	<u>semi</u>annual
<u>anti</u>trust	<u>hydro</u>electric	<u>neo</u>phyte	<u>step</u>father
<u>bi</u>annual	<u>hyper</u>tension	<u>non</u>neutral	<u>sub</u>human
<u>by</u>pass	<u>hypo</u>tension	<u>off</u>shore	<u>super</u>market
<u>circum</u>navigate	<u>in</u>bound	<u>on</u>stage	<u>thermo</u>couple
<u>co</u>exist	<u>infra</u>red	<u>out</u>model	<u>trans</u>oceanic
<u>contra</u>band	<u>inter</u>com	<u>over</u>compensate	<u>tri</u>color
<u>counter</u>sink	<u>intra</u>union	<u>para</u>medic	<u>ultra</u>sonic
<u>desa</u>linize	<u>intro</u>vert	<u>poly</u>ester	<u>un</u>cap
<u>demi</u>tasse	<u>iso</u>metric	<u>post</u>war	<u>under</u>productive
<u>dis</u>embark	<u>mal</u>practice	<u>pre</u>arranged	<u>uni</u>lingual
<u>down</u>hearted	<u>micro</u>phone	<u>pro</u>rate	<u>up</u>date

(2) Exceptions. (a) Capitalized words. Use a hyphen with capitalized words unless the combined form has acquired independent meaning.

ante-Norman   anti-Arab   anti-Semitic   (*but* Antichrist)   inter-American mid-April non-Communist non-Government (*but* nongovernmental) Pan-American post-World War   pre-Columbian   trans-Canadian   (*but* transatlantic)   un-American

(b) Double vowels. Use a hyphen to avoid doubling vowels, except after certain short prefixes (*co, de, pre, re*).

anti-inflation   co-op   co-owner   (*but* cooperate coordinate)   (deenergize deescalate)   electro-optics   extra allowance   micro-organisms   pre-engineered (*but* preemergence preeminent preempt preexist)   (reemploy reenact reenter) semi-idleness   semi-indirect   ultra-ambitious

(c) Other examples. by and large   by-election   by-product   down-to-earth   extra-large (adj.)   extra-long (adj.)   extra-strong (adj.)   in-between   in-law   mid-1982 non-civil-service   non sequitur   non-taxpaid   off-color   off-season   off-the-record   on-and-off   on-the-job   out-of-doors   out-of-pocket   out-of-the-way part-time   pre-impasse   pre-interview   pro forma   re-create   re-cross-examination   re-redirect   second-guess   sub rosa (adv.)   sub-rosa (adj.)   tractor-trailer   up-and-coming   up-to-date (adj.)   well-being

d. Personal pronouns and certain pronouns and adverbs.

herself	itself	ourselves	yourself
himself	myself	themselves	yourselves
anybody	everybody	nobody	somebody
anyone*	everyone*	no one	someone*
anything	everything	nothing	something
anywhere	everywhere	nowhere	somewhere

* Two words if a single or particular person or thing is indicated.

Compound Words

4.2 *Hyphenated Compounds*

a. Modifiers preceding noun.

above-mentioned company
above-named union
agreed-upon method
arm's-length agreement
Board-conducted election
cease-and-desist order
closed-shop provisions
collective-bargaining agreement
common-law right
contested-election cases
contract-bar issues
decision-making process
dues-checkoff provision
far-reaching effects
full-time, part-time employees
  (employed full time, part-time)
good-faith doubt
grievance-arbitration procedure

in-plant committee
law-abiding citizen
left-hand side
loose-leaf services
maintenance-of-membership clause
most-favored-nation clause
night-shift employees
old-fashioned style
rank-and-file employees
right-to-work law
secret-ballot election
single-store unit
time-and-a-half wage rate
tool-and-die maker
union-security clause
union-shop agreement
well-known supporter
work-for-word report

b. Prepositional-phrase compound noun consisting of three or more words.

case-by-case	5-to-4 decision	mother-in-law	right-of-way
case-in-chief	grant-in-aid	mother-of-pearl	step-by-step

but

attorney at law	heir at law	leaves of absence	next of kin

c. Joined capital letter and certain prefixes.

I-beam	all-round	no-show	self-government
T-shirt	ex-Governor	no-trump	wide-awake
V-necked	ex-repairman	quasi-contractual (an adjective)	
X-raying	ex-vice-president	*but* quasi appointment	
		(part of noun)	

but

exfoliate	ex post facto	wide gauge	widemouthed

d. Element of title.

President-elect   Vice-President-elect   vice-presidency   (*but* Vice President)

e. Compound verb.

blue-pencil   cold-shoulder   cross-file   soft-pedal

f. Compounds having a common basic element.

English- or Spanish-speaking men   long- and short-term money rates
but
American owned and managed firms   twofold or threefold

g. Compound numbers from twenty-one to ninety-nine (when spelled out), and spelled-out fractions (two-thirds full), see Rule 6.4,a p. 21.

4.3 *Omit the Hyphen*

a. When the meaning is clear and readability is not aided.

atomic energy project	high school student	production credit loan
bargaining unit em-	income tax form	public utility plant
ployees	interstate commerce law	real estate tax
child welfare plan	land bank loan	running head citations
civil rights case	land use program	social security program

civil service examination life insurance company   soil conservation
due process law   parol evidence rule   measures
durable goods industry   per capita tax   special delivery mail
flood control study   portland cement plant   speech correction class
free enterprise system   *but* no-hyphen rule

b. When the last element of a predicate adjective is a present or past participle.
   The area was used for beet growing   The area is drought stricken.
   The effects were far reaching.   The boy is freckle faced.

c. When the first element of a two-word modifier is an adverb ending in *ly* or the
   first two elements of a three-word modifier are adverbs.

   eagerly awaited moment   unusually well preserved specimen
   wholly owned subsidiary   longer than usual lunch period
   but
   ever-normal granary   still-lingering doubt   well-kept farm
   ever-rising flood   still-new car   well-known lawyer

d. When the first element of a two-word modifier is a comparative or superlative.
   better drained soil   higher level decision   better paying job
   best liked books   larger sized dress   lower income group
   but
   bestseller (noun)   undercoverman   uppercase, lowercase type
   low-paying job   uppercrust society   upperclassman

e. When modifier consists of a foreign phrase.
   ante bellum days   ex officio member   per diem employee
   bona fide transaction per capita tax   prima facie evidence

f. In all titles except to indicate combined offices.
   assistant professor   editor in chief   secretary-treasurer
   attorney general   officer in charge   vice president

g. In proper nouns used as modifiers unless the first one ends in *o* or unless they
   designate joint relationship.
   Italian American area   Latin American trip   South Dakota roads
   but
   Italo-American   Afro-American   French-Irish descent

5. FOOTNOTES

5.1 *Excessive Footnotes Discouraged.* An excessive use of footnotes, requiring the reader to read at two levels on the page, makes the material less readable and constitutes an imposition on many parties who are not familiar with law-review writing. Although some footnotes are necessary, many could easily be avoided. They often contain relevant facts and circumstances, explanatory remarks, various parenthetic matters, and citations that could well be placed in the text (in parentheses if preferred).

5.2 *General Rules.* Each footnote ends with a period. Essential discussion must be placed in the text, not in footnotes. If a footnote must be carried over to the next page, it is continued there after the text, without repeating the footnote number. If matter is quoted in a footnote (instead of in the text) and placed in a block (indented) quotation, it is preceded by an introductory statement; if not in a block quotation, it is placed in quotation marks and typed flush as any other footnote.

---

[2] The Company filed a reply brief and submitted a motion to strike certain

---

matter from the General Counsel's (next page)

---

[3] Jones testified:
>   Q. Where did you go?
>   A. I went to the back of the storage room and talked to the union steward.
> Then I went with the steward to the front office. Mr. Jones was waiting for us.

---

[3] "I went to the back of the storage room and talked to the union steward. Then I went with the steward to the front office."

Note. Footnotes in a block quotation are typed, indented, at the end of the quotation. The General Counsel would exclude all 10 on the ground that 3 of them are supervisors and the other 7 are employed principally in grocery work, and the extent of their (part-time) employment in meat department work is insufficient to warrant their inclusion.[4]

---

    [4] In determining the eligibility of these dual-function employees, the governing case is *Berea Publishing Co.*, 140 NLRB 516 (1963).

5.3 *Placement of Footnote References.* A footnote reference should be placed on the same page as the footnote. It should be placed at the end of a sentence or clause, immediately after the quotation or statement to which it refers. It may appear after any punctuation mark except a dash. It is placed before a closing parenthesis if the footnote related only to matter within the parentheses.

given to him."[1]   series [2] and

given to him.)[1]   (if footnote refers to matter both inside and outside the parentheses)

given to him.[1]   (if footnote refers to matter inside the parentheses)

of that union.[2] [3]

of that union[2] or its representative.[3] (preferred)

NOTE. Footnote references should not be placed in the caption or appearances of a judge's Decision because that part of the JD is not published.

5.4 *Numbering Footnotes*. Footnotes are numbered consecutively (beginning with [1]) except quoted footnotes, which bear their own numbers. Footnotes in a separate opinion or attached appendix are numbered separately.

6. NUMERALS

6.1 *General Rules*

a. Nine-and-under rule. Spell out numbers one through nine and use figures for numbers 10 and higher, whether they are cardinal numbers (one, two . . . 10, 11 . . .) or ordinal numbers (first, second . . . 10th, 11th . . .).

b. Numbers in series. Use figures if one of a group of two or more related numbers in a sentence is 10 or higher, but write out single and related numbers at the beginning of a sentence.

The man had one suit, two pairs of shoes, and one hat.

The man had 1 suit, 2 pairs of shoes, and 15 pairs of socks for the trip.

From the First to the Ninth Congress. From the 1st to the 82d Congress.

Forty were killed.   Seventy-eight or seventy-nine passengers died.

c. Cardinal and ordinal numbers. When appearing in the same sentence, cardinal and ordinal numbers are treated as if they were in separate sentences.

The third group contained nine items. The third group contained 10 items.

The 9th group contained three items and the 10th group contained four.

6.2 *When to Use Figures: Measurement and Time*

Units of measurement and time, actual or implied, are expressed in figures. They do not affect the use of figures for other numbers in a sentence.

a. Age.

| 6 years old | age 70 | at the age of 3 | *but* | his third birthday |

The 70-year-old had only one suit, two pairs of shoes, and one hat.

b. Clock time.

| 10 o'clock | 10 p.m. | 12 noon | 12 midnight |
| 4:30 p.m. | half past 4 | this p.m. | 5 minutes till 9 |

c. Dates.

June 29, 1982	29 June 1982; 15 July (in NLRB decisions)	
May 1 to June 1, 1982	June and July 1982	May, June, and July 1982
1980, 1982	1981–1982	1970–1982
A.D. 1066; 429 B.C.	from 1981 to 1982	between 1970 and 1982
the 1st [day] of the month	*but*	the first [part] of October
4th of July (the date)	*but*	Fourth of July (the holiday)

d. Decimals.

| .25 inch | 1.25 inches | .30 caliber | 3.5 times |

e. Measurements.

about 6 acres	6 pounds 3 ounces	6 feet 1 inch tall	6 degrees
8½ × 11 paper	8 by 12 inches	1½ (*or* 1-1/2) miles	6 below zero
500 meters	8-by-12 inch ad	5-inch ad	2 feet by 1 foot 8 inches

but

| two dozen | one gross | zero miles | three-ply | six votes |

(See rule 6.4,b below for spelling out numbers in indefinite expressions.)

f. Money.

$3	$3.65	76 cents	50-cent-an-hour increase	$600	$1200
$5665	$56,651	$560,000	$2,700,000	$2½ (*or* $2-1/2) million
$5—$6 billion	5 to 10 million dollars' worth	4 million in assets

g. Percentages.

12 percent	25.5 percent	.5 percent	*or*	one-half percent

h. Time.

8 days	3 fiscal years	7 minutes	1 month
6 hours 8 minutes 20 seconds		10 years 3 months 29 days	

but

four afternoons	three decades	three quarters (9 months)
fourth century	in a year or two	statistics of any one year

i. Unit modifiers

5-day week	½-inch pipe	6-by-9 foot rug	5-foot-6 girl
10-foot pole	7½-percent raise	5-foot-wide rug	*but* a girl 5 feet 6

6.3 *Other Figures*

a. In serial numbers.

Bulletin 725	¶ 2	§ 55	pages 352–357	Matthew 2:6
chapter 2	lines 5 and 6	paragraph 1	1721–1723 P Street NW	

b. In addresses—but use the nine-and-under rule for street names. (See rule 2.2,a(3) p. 9 for abbreviations in parentheses and footnotes.)

7 First Street NW	4711 Fifth Avenue	20 North First Street
7 51st Street SE	810 West 12th Street	51–53 62d Avenue North

6.4 *When to Spell Out*

a. Fractions below one, except when used as a modifier.

one-half inch	one-third of a lifetime	one one-hundredth inch
half an inch	three-fourths of an inch	50 one-hundredths inch

but

½-inch-diameter pipe	3½ (or 3-1/2) times	½ to 1½ pages

b. Indefinite expressions—but *about, approximately, around, nearly,* etc., do not constitute indefinite expressions.

a thousand and one reasons	in his midthirties, in his seventies
one hundred percent wrong	in the early eighties, in the eighties
temperature in the thirties	hundredfold, twentyfold to thirtyfold

but

about 200, 1 to 3 million,
90-odd persons, 40-plus,
mid-1951, early 1980s

c. Formal language.

threescore years and ten	millions for defense but not one cent for tribute
the Thirteen Original States	in the year nineteen hundred and eighty-two

d. Figures of speech.

Air Force One	Gay Nineties	number one choice
Ten Commandments		

e. Numbers of less than 100 preceding a compound modifier containing a figure.

two ½-inch boards	ninety-nine 6-inch guns	*but*	120 8-inch boards

6.5 *Roman Numerals*

Roman numerals should be used sparingly, and only in lower numbers.

6.6 *Punctuation of Numerals*

a. In modifiers containing figures, hyphenate the compound.

6-foot-4 man	3-pound roast	50-gram dose	10-page decision

Numerals

b. Use apostrophes for omissions and the plural of single figures, but not for the plural of multiple figures. (See rules 7.1,k and 8.1,b below.)

class of '82   cross out the 6's   the 1980s

c. In numbers containing five or more digits, use commas to separate groups of three digits, but do not use commas in addresses, phone numbers, and serial numbers. (Do not use *No.* or # before a number unless required to identify it as a number.)

1000   1333   9000   10,000   200,000   4,333,000

but

17445 P Street NW   212-555-1212   Case 2-CA-13675

45 Fed.Reg. 45259 (1980)   122 Cong.Rec. 16870 (1976)

7. PLURALS

7.1 General Rules

a. Most plurals are formed by adding s.

b. Add es to nouns ending in s, z, x, ch, and sh.

buses	buzzes	foxes	torches	bushes
Joneses	Schmitzes	Essexes	(but Bachs)	Bushes

c. Add es and change y to i when nouns end in consonant-plus-y, except proper names.

cities	skies	but	Marys	Januarys	Kansas Citys

d. Add s to nouns ending in vowel-plus-y, except nouns ending in quy.

attorneys	chimneys	moneys	but	soliloquies

e. Add s to nouns ending in vowel-plus-o.

cameos	portfolios	radios	studios	trios

f. Add es to most nouns ending in consonant-plus-o.

echoes	heroes	tomatoes	torpedoes	vetoes

but

albinos	dynamos	kimonos	photos	solos
armadillos	Eskimos	lassos	pianos	tobaccos
autos	falsettos	magnetos	piccolos	twos
avocados	ghettos	mementos	provisos	virtuosos
banjos	halos	memos	salvos	zeros

g. Use the English plurals of words borrowed from foreign languages, except foreign plurals in common usage.

adieus	beaus	formulas	minimums	sanitariums
agendas	cactuses	geniuses	opuses	stadiums
antennas	dogmas	indexes	plateaus	styluses
aquariums	equilibriums	insignias	podiums	syllabuses
automatons	focuses	maximums	sanatoriums	tableaus

but

addenda	curricula	fungi	memoranda	radii
alumni	data*	larvae	minutiae	referenda
appendices	desiderata	media	nuclei	stimuli
criteria	errata	matrices	phenomena	strata

* Both singular and plural.

h. Change i to e to form the plural.

analysis analyses	ellipsis ellipses	synopsis synopses
basis bases	hypothesis hypotheses	thesis theses
crisis crises	parenthesis parentheses	but chassis (sing. & pl.)

i. Add s to nouns ending in ful.

cupfuls	handfuls	teaspoonfuls

j. Add s or es to form the plural of spelled-out numbers, words containing an apostrophe, and words referred to as words (but 's if required to avoid difficulty in reading).

twos, threes, sevens	the pros and cons		yeses and noes
can'ts and won'ts	whereases and	but	do's and don'ts
ifs, ands, or buts	wherefores		which's and that's

Plurals

k. Add *s* to form the plural of numbers or abbreviations consisting of multiple figures or capital letters (see rule 8.1,b p. 26 for using an apostrophe to form the plural of symbols, single figures and letters, and lowercase abbreviations).
    B52s '80s 1980s ABCs CPAs JDs LPNs MDs PhDs YMCAs

7.2 *Compound Terms.* The significant word takes the plural form.

a. Significant word first.

attorneys at law	courts-martial	postmasters general
attorneys general	heirs at law	presidents-elect
bills of fare	leaves of absence	prisoners of war
brothers-in-law	mothers-in-law	rights-of-way
conflicts of interest	notaries public	sergeants at arms

b. Significant word in middle.

assistant attorneys general	assistant comptrollers general
assistant chiefs of staff	deputy surgeons general

c. Significant word last.

assistant attorneys	general counsels	trade unions
deputy sheriffs	*but* counsel (sing. & pl.)	vice chairmen

d. Both nouns of equal significance: both take the plural form.

coats of arms	men employees	women advisers
men buyers	secretaries-treasurers	women writers

e. No word significant in itself: the last word takes the plural form.

also-rans	go-betweens	jack-in-the-pulpits
come-ons	hand-me-downs	run-ins

f. When a noun is hyphenated with an adverb or preposition, the plural is formed on the noun.

goings-on	hangers-on	listeners-in	passersby

8. PUNCTUATION

"Punctuation should aid in reading and prevent misreading." *GPO Style Manual* 131.

8.1 *Apostrophe*
a. Possessives.
   (1) *General rule.* Add *'s* to a singular or plural noun not ending in *s;* add *'* (apostrophe) to a singular or plural noun ending in *s* or an *s* sound.

man's, men's	hostess', hostesses'	Jones', Joneses'
Congress'	prince's, princes'	Lopez', Lopezes'
Corps'	princess', princesses'	*but* Essex's, Essexes'

   (2) *Compound nouns.* Add *'* or *'s* to the last noun.

attorney at law's fee	John White Jr.'s account
attorney general's appointments	Mr. Brown of Massachusetts' motion
comptroller general's decision	secretary-treasurer's appointment

   (3) *Joint or separate possession.* Add *'* or *'s* to the last noun for joint possession, to each noun for individual or alternative possession.

Brown & Nelson's store	men's and women's clothing
soldiers and sailors' home	Mrs. Smith's and Mrs. Allen's children
John's, Thomas', and Henry's ratings	St. Michael's Men's Club

   (4) *Indefinite or impersonal pronouns.* Add *'* or *'s* to form possessive.

each other's books	one's mortgage	somebody's proposal
others' homes	someone's typewriter	*but* somebody else's pen

   (5) *General terms.* The singular possessive case is used for such general terms as the following.

arm's length	printer's ink	writer's cramp	author's alterations

   (6) *Idiomatic phrases.* Use the possessive case even though there is no actual ownership.

a stone's throw	1 day's labor	2 hours' traveltime
for pity's sake	2 weeks' allowance	6 billion dollars' worth

   (7) *Nouns ending in "ce."* For euphony, add only *'* to form the possessive of these nouns when followed by a word beginning with *s.*

for acquaintance' sake	for appearance' sake	for conscience' sake

   (8) *Noun used as adjective.* A possessive noun used in an adjective sense requires the addition of *'* or *'s.*

He is a friend of John's and mine.	Stern's is running a sale.
She drives her brother Francis' car.	

   (9) *Noun before gerund.* Should be in possessive case.

in the event of Mary's leaving	the ship's hovering nearby

b. Other uses of apostrophe. Add *'* or *'s* to indicate contractions, the omission of figures or letters, and the plural of symbols, single figures and letters, and lowercase abbreviations. (For plurals of multiple figures and capital letters, see rule 7.1,k p. 24 above.)

don't, I've, o'clock	49'ers, 4-H'ers	#'s, 7's
it's (it is)	MC'ing, TV'ers	a's, A's, U's
spirit of '76	the three R's	c.o.d.'s, mph's

509

c. The apostrophe is not used
   (1) *In possessive personal pronouns*

hers	its	ours	theirs	yours

   (2) *After words more descriptive than possessive (not indicating personal posses-sion)* except when the plural does not end in s, and *after names of countries and other organized bodies ending in s.*

editors handbook	Teamsters Union	United States control
merchants exchange	technicians guide	*but* women's votes
nurses aide	Congress attitude	children's hospital
teachers college	Massachusetts laws	workmen's compensation

   (3) *In abbreviations and shortened forms of certain words.*

assn.	enfd.	phone	Sgt.	till

   (4) *In plurals of spelled-out numbers, and words as words,* except to avoid difficulty in reading.

sevens	ins and outs	whereases	ifs, ands, or buts
twos, threes	ups and downs	yeses and noes	*but* do's and don'ts

8.2 *Brackets*

a. Their function. Brackets are used to indicate that the original copy has been changed or added to.
   (1) *Emphasis added and information supplied.* Brackets are used to enclose the words "emphasis added" when placed inside a quoted sentence or at the end of an indented (block) quotation, and to enclose interpolations and words inserted in the quoted matter. ("Emphasis added" is placed in parentheses after nonindented quotations (see rule 9.3 p. 36).)
   "Smith was *not* [emphasis added] in the room with us."
   the *primary* result. [Emphasis added.]   (at end of block quotation)
   "The president pro tem [Arnold] spoke briefly."
   "The witness tried [evidently without success] to convince the court."
   "Mr. Adams [arrived] late."
   (2) *Corrections and notations of error.* Significant errors may be corrected, or merely noted.
   "He arrived at 13 [12] o'clock."
   "The statue [sic] was on the statute books."
   (3) *Change in type.* When a lowercase letter is changed to uppercase or vice versa, the letter is enclosed in brackets.
   "[T]he other four were present."
b. Multiple paragraphs. When matter in brackets makes more than one paragraph, start each paragraph with a bracket and place the closing bracket at the end of the last paragraph.

8.3 *Colon*

"A colon tells the reader that what follows is closely related to the preceding clauses. The colon has more effect than the comma, less power to separate than the semicolon, and more formality than the dash." Strunk & White, *The Elements of Style* 7 (3d ed. 1979).

a. The colon is used
   (1) *List or amplify.* After an independent clause, to introduce a list of particulars, an amplification, or an illustrative quotation.

He produced several items in his defense: a compilation of dates, 10 daily production records, and a sample of his work.

Give up conveniences; do not demand special privileges; do not stop work: these are necessary while we are at war.

The squalor of the streets reminded him of a line from Oscar Wilde: "We are all in the gutter, but some of us are looking at the stars."

(2) *Introduce formally.* To introduce formally any matter that forms a complete sentence, question, or quotation (the first word after the colon being capitalized).

The court said: "The underlying purpose of this statute is industrial peace. This conduct is not conducive to that end."

The following question came up for discussion: What policy should be adopted?

(3) *Salutation and time.* After a formal salutation and to express time.

Dear Sir: Ladies and Gentlemen: To Whom It May Concern: 2:40 p.m.

b. The colon is not used to separate a verb or preposition from its object (no punctuation being needed).

The language should be as follows: *or*   The language should be
Wisdom grows from experience. . .   *but*   Wisdom grows from:

8.4 *Comma*

a. The comma is used

(1) *Series.* Before the conjunctions *and, or,* and *nor* in series of three or more terms, except that when the conjunction (or *which*) precedes parenthetic matter set off with commas, omit the comma before the conjunction (or *which*).

red, white, and blue   a, b, and c   neither snow, rain, nor heat

It is sold by the bolt, by the yard or, when on hand, in remnants. (phrases)

He sold his business, rented his house, gave up his car, paid off his creditors, and set off for Africa. (short clauses)

It is ordered to cease and desist, to bargain on request and, if an agreement is reached, to embody the understanding in a signed agreement.

It is a valuable contribution which, if utilized, would be most helpful.

(2) *Short quotation.* Before a direct quotation of a few words following an introductory phrase, or before a quotation grammatically in apposition (see rule 8.3,a(1) and (2) p. 27 for using a colon after an independent clause and to formally introduce matter).

He said, "John arrived several hours after the others."

I am reminded of the advice of my neighbor, "Never worry about your heart till it stops beating."

(3) *Modifiers.* To separate a series of modifiers unless the final modifier is considered part of the noun modified. Use the comma only when "and" could be substituted.

It is a young, eager, intelligent group.   *but*   He is a clever young man.

(4) *Parenthetic matter* To set off parenthetic words and phrases.

It is obvious, however, that this is no solution.

The employee, ignoring the time, continued to work through the lunch period.

The restriction is laid down in title IX, chapter 8, section 15, of the code.

His only son, John, went with him.

but His daughter Mary was in college. (restrictive, not parenthetic)

(5) *Nonrestrictive clause.* To set off nonrestrictive, parenthetic clauses which, like restrictive clauses, are relative clauses (beginning with *that, when, where, which, who,* or *whom*). Nonrestrictive clauses, which are set off by commas, are merely descriptive or additive (do not identify or define), and could be omitted without changing the meaning of the main clause. Restrictive clauses, which are never set off by commas, are essential to the meaning of the sentence. Usually, *which* introduces a nonrestrictive clause and *that* introduces a restrictive clause; *who* may introduce either.

(nonrestrictive) The atomic bomb, which we developed, was first used by us.
Union Steward Clark, who participated in the strike, was promoted.
Dallas, where he was born, is a thriving metropolis.
(restrictive) The dam that gave way was poorly constructed.
All employees who participated in the strike were summarily discharged.

(6) *Explanatory words and abbreviations.* To set off explanatory words or abbreviations.

There are many exceptions, namely, silk, cotton, nylon, and wool.
The Company produces many items, e.g., electrical and mechanical equipment.

(7) *Compound sentence.* To separate independent clauses joined by a conjunction, except that the comma may be omitted between short independent clauses.

We have not carried that model for some time, but we expect to restock it.
but He ran but he missed the train.

(8) *Single subject.* When the subject for two clauses is the same, a comma is used if the connective is *but*, but is not used if the connective is *and*.

I have heard his arguments, but am still not convinced.
He has had several years' experience and is thoroughly competent.

(9) *Interjections and transitional words.* To set off interjections and such transitional words as *oh, yes, no, well, moreover,* and *incidentally* at the beginning of a sentence. (See rule 8.4,b(3) p. 30 for exceptions.)

Yes, they are coming.   No, she isn't here.   Moreover, they are not.

(10) *Clarification.* To separate two words or figures that might otherwise be misunderstood.

In 1980, 400 men were dismissed.   As you would expect, Brown did.
Instead of 20, 50 came.   What the difficulty is, is not known.

(11) *Abbreviations, degrees, States.* Before and after *Esq., etc., i.e., e.g., et al.,* academic degrees, and States when preceded by names of cities and except when used as modifiers. A comma is not required after *Inc.* or *Ltd.*

Thomas Brown, Esq.,   See, e.g.,   Douglas Smith, PhD,
good example, i.e.,   Reed, Black, et al.,   Dallas, Texas,
but
Dayton, Ohio suburbs   Dallas, Texas facility   May 4, 1982
                                                                discharge
TRW, Inc. recently built a new assembly plant in the city.

(12) *Omission.* To indicate the omission of a word or words.

Then we had much; now, nothing.

(13) *Interrogative clause.* After an interrogative clause, followed by a direct question.

You are sure, are you not?

(14) *Titles.* Between the title of a person and the name of an organization in the absence of the words *of* and *of the*.

president, the Key Company   Member, National Labor Relations Board

15) *Numbers.* To separate large numbers, but *not* in addresses, decimals, or case, serial, telephone, ZIP code, or executive order numbers.

| 10,000 | 44,230 | 530,491 | 1,250,000 |

but

14500 Ninth Avenue 1.0947 Case 16-CA-14590 motor No. 189463
202-633-0500   Washington, DC 20570   Executive Order 11240

b. Do not use the comma
   (1) *Between month and year* in dates.
   June 1982 22d of May 1982 February and March 1982 Labor Day 1982
   January, February, and March 1982   *but*   September 11, 1982
   (2) *To separate two nouns,* one of which identifies the other.
   the heading "Collective Bargaining"   the painter Van Gogh
   (3) *To set off* short *transitional* or introductory *expressions,* unless one would normally tend to pause in speaking at that point (see rule 8.4,a(9)).
   They had indeed gone.   Obviously she had no intention of going.
   but
   Meanwhile, the president left.
   (4) *After a question mark.*
   He asked her, "What are you doing?" and she told him her plans.
   (5) *To set off Jr., Sr.* (which are restrictive-not parenthetic, requiring commas-see rule 8.4,a(1) p. 28 above), but follow individual usage.
   Charles White Sr.   Jack Brown Jr.   Smith Senior

NOTE: When only the last name is used, *Junior* and *Senior* are spelled out.

   (6) *Between superior figures in footnote references.*
   Numerous instances may be cited,[1] [2]   (should be avoided if possible)

8.5 Dash

"A dash is a mark of separation stronger than a comma, less formal than a colon, and more relaxed than parentheses." Strunk & White, *The Elements of Style* 9 (3d ed. 1979).

a. The em dash is used   (—)
   (1) *Abrupt break.* To set off an abrupt break or interruption.
   He said—and no one contradicted him—"The battle is lost."
   If the bill should pass—which God forbid—the service will be wrecked.
   (2) *Summary.* Before a final clause that summarizes a series of ideas (see rule 8.3,a(1) p. 27 for using a colon after an independent clause to list particulars or amplify preceding matter).
   Freedom of speech, freedom of worship, freedom from want, freedom from fear—these are the fundamentals of moral world order.
   (3) *Emphasis.* To set off nonrestrictive appositives or other words for emphasis.
   Only one person—the chairman—voted against the proposal.
   If you don't know how to spell a word—look it up.
   (4) *Letters deleted.* Replace with dash or hyphens.
   Where the h— is he?   that son of a b—   G— d—
   (5) *After question mark.* After a question mark (but not immediately after a comma, colon, or semicolon).
   How can you explain this?—"Fee paid, $5."
   (6) *Credit line.* To precede a credit line.
   Every man's work shall be made manifest.—I Corinthians 3:13.

b. The en dash is used   (-)
    (1) *Combinations.* In a combination of figures, letters, and certain words.

Case 26-CA-4219	AFL-CIO	1981-1983
$100-$200	4-H Club	May-October
301-942-8367	WTOP-TV	Monday-Friday

    (2) *Titles.* In compound titles or positions when needed for clarity.
       painter-door builder Jones   Vice President-General Manager Brown

c. The en dash is not used to replace *to* or *and* when the word *from* or *between* precedes the first of two related figures or expressions.

From January 1 to June 30, 1982	*not*	from January 1-June 30, 1982
Between 1980 and 1982	*not*	between 1980-1982

8.6 *Ellipsis* (see rules 9.4 and 9.5 pp. 36-37)

8.7 *Exclamation Point*
The exclamation point is used to mark surprise, incredulity, admiration, appeal, or other strong emotion, which may be expressed even in a declarative or interrogative sentence. It should be used sparingly.

"Great!" he shouted.	What!
He acknowledged the error!	Who shouted, "All aboard!" (no
How beautiful!	question mark used)

8.8 *Hyphen* (see "Compound Words" pp. 14-17)
A "hyphen joins, in contrast to the dash, whose job is to separate."
Copperud, *American Usage and Style: The Consensus* 188 (1980).

8.9 *Parentheses*
a. Parentheses are used
    (1) *Parenthetic matter.* To set off words or sentences not intended to be part of the main thought or statement, yet important enough to be included (and placed in the text in preference to footnotes).
      This 1980 case (447 U.S. 490) is not relevant.
      The United States is the principal purchaser (by value) of these exports (23 percent in 1980 and 19 percent in 1981).
      The foreman saw him at the timeclock and directed him to the office. (Smith had never been late before. Many others had been.) They met the steward.
    (2) *Subsequent acronym or usage and explanatory words.* To indicate subsequent use of an acronym or shortened name, and to enclose an explanatory word.
      Baskin-Robbins Ice Cream Company (BRICO) utilized a three-level franchise plan.
      R. M. Conway Co. (Conway)   *or*   against the Company, the Respondent,   Portland (Ore.) Chamber of Commerce   *but*   Washington, D. C. schools
    (3) *Items in series or in the alternative.* To enclose letters or numbers designating items in a series, or the singular or plural.
      You will observe that the sword is (1) old fashioned, (2) still sharp, and (3) unusually light for its size.
      Paragraph 7(b)(1)(a) will be found on page 6.   exceptions and brief(s)
    (4) *References.* To enclose references inside or at the end of sentences. Parentheses enclosing a reference at the end of a sentence are placed before the closing period unless the reference relates to more than one preceding sentence.

He admitted having heard a rumor in the plant (Tr. 76).
The agreement (G.C. Exh. 2) was never signed (Tr. 26–27).
It included a bargaining order. It also included a broad order. (Tr. 11, 12.)
(He testified, "It was news to me" (Tr. 54), but later admitted, "I heard about it the day before" (Tr. 57).)

b. Multiple paragraphs. When matter in parentheses makes more than one paragraph, start each paragraph with a parenthesis and place the closing parenthesis at the end of the last paragraph.

8.10 Period

The period is used

(1) *Sentence.* After a declarative sentence that is not exclamatory, and after an imperative sentence, an indirect question, or a rhetorical question.

Do not be late.   Tell me how he did it.   May we ask prompt payment.

(2) *Abbreviations.* In most lowercase and capital-lowercase abbreviations, but omit periods in most uppercase abbreviations.

a.m.   c.o.d.   e.s.t.   i.e.   ibid.   Assn.   Ave.   Blvd.   D.C.   U.S.
but
mph   rpm   AT&T   CBS   FBI   HUD   IRS   ITT   LPN
NAACP   NLRB   SMU   UAW   USDA

(3) *Ellipsis.* To indicate ellipsis. (See rule 9.4 p. 36 for using three periods to indicate an omission within a sentence, and four periods at the end of a sentence. See rule 9.5 p. 37 for inserting and indenting four periods as an ellipsis signal to show a deletion of one or more paragraphs.)

(4) *Items in series.* In place of parenthesis after a letter or number denoting a series.

a. Bread well baked.   1. Punctuate moderately.
b. Meat cooked rare.   2. Compound sparingly.
c. Cubed apples stewed.   3. Index thoroughly.

8.11 Quotation Marks

a. Quotation marks are used

(1) *Entitled, etc.* To enclose any matter following the terms *entitled, the term, the word, classified, designated, endorsed, marked, named,* or *signed;* but are not used to enclose expressions following the term *known as, called,* and *so-called* unless the expressions are misnomers or slang.

entitled "The Harbor Act"   After the word "man," insert a dash.
but
It was known as glucinium.   The so-called investigative body.

(2) *Titles, headings.* To enclose titles of addresses, captions, chapter and part headings, editorials, essays, headings, headlines, motion pictures and plays, TV and radio programs, short poems, reports, songs, subheadings, subjects, and themes.

(3) *Emphasis.* To give greater emphasis to a word or phrase—but this use should be kept to a minimum.

(4) *Slang, nicknames, etc.* To enclose misnomers, slang expressions, jargon, nicknames, and ordinary words used in an arbitrary way.

the "lameduck" amendment   George Herman "Babe" Ruth
the "drop a footnote" habit   It was a "gentlemen's agreement."

b. Quotation marks are not used

(1) To enclose *block (indented) quotations.*

(2) To enclose article titles in periodicals and newspapers *and book titles,* which are underscored instead (see rule 1.9 p. 7 for examples).

    (3) *With indirect quotations, paraphrasing, tallies.*
        He told her yes.   She said Jones was a born liar.
        He said that no he would not.   The vote was 77 yes and 9 no.

c. Placement of punctuation.
    (1) *General rule.* A comma or final period is placed inside, and a colon or semi-colon outside, the quotation marks; other punctuation is placed inside only if a part of the quoted matter (see rule 9.1 p. 36 for examples).
    (2) *Amendments.* In work showing amendments, the punctuation mark is placed outside the quotation marks when not a part of the quoted matter.
        Insert the following: "and the Universal Military Training Act,".

d. Single and double. Quotation marks are limited to three sets (double, single, double).
    The answer is "Maybe."   He reported, "Smith said 'No sale.' "
    "The question is, 'Can he become a "bona fide" citizen of the country?' "

8.12 *Word Division.* Avoid all word divisions in decisions. Carry over to the next line the whole word (including hyphenated words).

8.13 *Semicolon*
a. The semicolon is used
    (1) *To separate clauses containing commas,* and listed items, some of which contain commas.
    (2) *To separate clauses* in a compound sentence *with no connective.*
        The sketches have been submitted; we await their approval.
        It is true in peace; it is true in war.
    (3) *To separate multiple citations.*
        Section 8(a)(5) of NLRA; *NLRB v. Gissel Packing Co.*, 395 U.S. 575 (1969).
b. The semicolon should be avoided when a comma suffices.

9. QUOTATIONS

9.1 *Short Quotations.* A quotation of three lines or less is usually placed in the text, in quotation marks. A comma or final period is placed inside the quotation marks, a colon or semicolon is placed outside, and a question mark or exclamation point is placed inside only if it is part of the matter quoted.

"The President," he said, "will veto the bill."

He told the employee, "That's right"; he then changed his mind.

Why call it a "gentlemen's agreement"?

He asked, "Have you an appointment?"

The trainman shouted, "All aboard!"

NOTE. The citation is placed before or immediately after a short quotation.

9.2 *Block Quotations.* Four or more lines of quoted matter are usually written as a block quotation, indented 10 spaces from the margin (without quotation marks). Further indent if the quoted matter begins a new paragraph; otherwise type the first line flush, capitalizing the first word as follows if the beginning of the sentence has been omitted.

> [I]t is clear from all the facts that the dispute between the Union and the Company was concerned solely with the proper interpretation and application of their contract, and that the parties had so viewed the dispute from the beginning.

NOTE. Unless placed before the indented quotation, the citation should be the first nonindented matter after it. ("Emphasis added" and "Tr.___" may be placed in brackets at the end of the block quotation, see Rules 9.3 and 9.5.)

9.3 *Emphasis Added.* When the words "emphasis added" are inserted in a quoted sentence or placed at the end of a block quotation, they are enclosed in brackets. When the words are placed at the end of a short, nonindented quotation, they are enclosed in parentheses and placed outside the quotation marks (after any citation of the source quoted).

Jones claimed, "Smith was *not* [emphasis added] in the room," but four other witnesses testified positively that both Jones and Smith *were* present.

the *primary* results. [Emphasis added.] (at end of block quotation)

The Board found that "the striker was *lawfully* discharged during the strike and *is not entitled* to reinstatement." (265 NLRB at 9, emphasis added.)

He claimed, "I was *not* present." (Emphasis added.)

9.4 *Omissions*

a. Use of ellipsis. An ellipsis signal of three periods indicates an omission within a quoted sentence. A signal of four periods is used to indicate an omission of the last part of a quoted sentence or an omission of matter between that sentence and the remainder of the quotation. (If the omission occurs at the end of the sentence, three periods are added to the period closing the sentence; if the last part of the sentence is omitted, four periods are inserted, beginning one space after the last quoted word.)

When the quotation continues after the four periods, the ellipsis signal may indicate the omission of either the first part of the next sentence or a whole sentence or more, including the intervening punctuation.

He called . . . and left . . . . When he returned the
He called . . . and . . . . he returned.
b. Ellipsis rules. An ellipsis signal is not used when quoting a complete sentence or
    an obviously incomplete sentence. An ellipsis signal should never be used to begin
    a quotation. If the quotation follows a colon or stands by itself as a full sentence,
    but the beginning of the original sentence has been omitted, capitalize the first
    letter (if not already capitalized) and place it in brackets without any ellipsis signal.
    When omitting part of a sentence, be sure the words following the omission agree
    in number, gender, and tense.
"As he watches, they arriv[e] in a truck and the violence resumes."
The violence resumed shortly after "he arrive[d] in his truck."
"[H]e arrived in his truck and the violence resumed."
"They had stopped work . . . and [had gone] to the office."

9.5 *Deleted Paragraph.* When deleting one or more entire paragraphs, insert and in-
     dent four periods as the ellipsis signal.
        Q. What was the first time you heard that a union was trying to organize?
        A. I heard some talk in the shop.
        Q. When was the first time?
        . . . .
        Q. When was the first time?
        A. The last week in May. [Tr. 57.]
On June 15, John Doe replaced Robert Smith as general manager of the Company. Doe had been employed since 1959.
    . . . .
    . . . [O]n June 15 or 16, Doe visited Smith in Smith's office.
NOTE. An ellipsis signal is not used at the beginning or end of either quotation. When
   deleting language that would otherwise be indented to form the beginning of the
   second or subsequent paragraph (as in the second illustration above), indent and
   insert the ellipsis signal. Do not indicate the deletion of matter after the period concluding the final quoted sentence.

9.6 *Alterations.* Any changes or corrections in quoted matter, and any notation of
     a significant mistake, are shown in brackets.
"It is not unreasonable to assume that [the Union] will engage in strike violence again."
"It occurred during the first shift at 12 [noon]."
"The times [sic] was 4 p.m."

10. SPELLING

10.1 Frequently Misspelled Words

abridgment
absence
accede
accommodate
acknowledgment
adjuster
adviser
align
all right
all-round
analogous
anomalous
benefited
buses
calendar
canceled
cancellation
candor
cannot
catalog
channeled
commingle
consummate
converter
conveyor
corollary
counseled
counselor
countervailing
credence
credible
credulity
credulous
decision making
defendant
dependent
descendant

diminutive
discernible
disingenuous
egregious
enclose
endorse
enforceable
enroll
ensure
excel
exhibitor
extant
feasible
flammable
forbade
forbear
forgo (abstain)
fulfill
gauge
goodbye
gray
gruesome
guarantee
harass
hierarchy
homogeneous
imminent
imprimatur
inadmissible
inadvertence
incumbent
inferable
innocuous
innuendo
inquiry
insistence
instill

interfered
interfering
intervenor
irrelevant
judgment
labeled
lengthwise
leveled
liaison
libelant
likable
liquefy
maneuver
marshaled
mediocre
memoranda
mileage
milieu
minuscule
mischievous
misspell
modeled
mold
moneys
movable
mustache
nickel
occurrence
offense
outrageous
pastime
percent
pleaded
prerogative
proffer
programmer
programming

prologue
questionnaire
readable
recurrence
referable
referred
relevant
rescission
resistant
reviser
salable
scurrilous
seize
sizable
skillful
specious
spiel
stupefy
subtlety
supersede
surreptitious
surveillance
T-shirt
threshold
totaled
trafficking
transferable
transferred
transshipment
traveled
union animus
untrammeled
usable
vicissitude
vilify
willful
withhold

10.2 Endings "ise" and "ize"
The following words use ise. Others in this class use ize (agonize, etc.).

advertise
advise
apprise
arise
chastise
circumcise
comprise
compromise

demise
despise
devise
disfranchise
disguise
enfranchise
enterprise
excise

exercise
exorcise
franchise
improvise
incise
merchandise
misadvise
revise

rise
supervise
surmise
surprise
televise

519

Spelling

10.3 Endings "ible" and "able"

The following words end in *ible*. Other common, familiar words in this class end in *able* (as manageable, regrettable, unmistakable).

accessible	edible	incorrodible	irreversible
addible	educible	incorruptible	legible
admissible	eligible	incredible	negligible
apprehensible	erodible	indefeasible	omissible
audible	exemptible	indefensible	ostensible
coercible	exhaustible	indelible	perceptible
cohesible	expansible	indestructible	perfectible
collapsible	expressible	indigestible	permissible
collectible	fallible	indiscernible	persuasible
combustible	feasible	indivertible	pervertible
commonsensible	flexible	indivisible	plausible
compatible	forcible	inducible	possible
comprehensible	fungible	ineligible	producible
compressible	fusible	inexhaustible	protectible
contemptible	gullible	inexpressible	reducible
controvertible	horrible	infallible	reprehensible
convertible	illegible	infeasible	repressible
convincible	immersible	inflexible	reproducible
corrigible	imperceptible	infusible	resistible
corrodible	impermissible	insensible	responsible
corruptible	impersuasible	instructible	reversible
credible	implausible	insuppressible	revertible
crucible	impossible	insusceptible	seducible
deducible	impressible	intangible	sensible
deductible	inaccessible	intelligible	submersible
defeasible	inadmissible	interruptible	suggestible
defensible	inapprehensible	invertible	supersensible
descendible	inaudible	invincible	suppressible
destructible	incoercible	invisible	susceptible
diffusible	incombustible	irascible	tangible
digestible	incompatible	irreducible	terrible
discernible	incomprehensible	irremissible	transmissible
discussible	incontrovertible	irreprehensible	unintelligible
distractible	inconvertible	irrepressible	unsusceptible
divestible	inconvincible	irresistible	vincible
divisible	incorrigible	irresponsible	visible

10.4 i-Before-e Rule

Write *i* before *e* in words pronounced with an *ee* sound, but write *ei* after *c* and in words pronounced with an *eye* or long *a* sound.

ee sound:	believe	grievous	niece	relief	relieve	siege
after *c*:	ceiling	conceit	deceive	perceive	receipt	receive
exceptions:	either	leisure	neither	seize	sheik	weird
eye sound:	feisty	Geiger counter	height	Meistersingers	stein	
long *a*:	deign feign heinous	neighbor reign reindeer seine weigh				
others:	deity	financier	foreign	forfeit	friend	heir
	piety	science	siesta	sieve	specie	

10.5 *Endings "cede," "ceed," and "sede."* Only one word ends in *sede* (supersede); only three end in *ceed* (exceed, proceed, succeed); all other words of this class end in *cede* (precede, etc.).

10.6 *Suffix Rules.*
a. Doubling final consonant. If a one-syllable word or a word with primary stress on the last syllable ends with a single consonant after a single vowel, double the consonant before a suffix beginning with a vowel (but not before a consonant). Do not double the final consonant if primary stress is not on the last syllable, or if the primary shifts from the last syllable.

bag, bagging baggage   occur, occurred occurrence   *but* total, totaled
get, getting   transfer, transferred transferring   *but* travel, traveled
commit, committal committed comitee committing *but* commitment (consonant)
prefer, preferring   *but*   preference (stress shifted to the first syllable)
exceptions
chagrin, chagrined   transfer, transferal transference transferor
b. Silent *e*. In words ending in a silent *e*, drop the *e* before a suffix beginning with a vowel.

interfere, interfering   sale, salable   *but*   dye, dyeing
force, forcible   true, truism   mile, mileage
c. Words ending in *ce* or *ge*. Retain the *e* before any suffix not beginning with *e* or *i*, thus preserving the softness of the *c* or *g*.

notice, noticeable   change, changeable changeless changing
peace, peaceably   courage, courageous encouraged en-
                         couraging
d. Words with *d* preceding *ge*. The *d* acts as a preserver of the soft sound and permits the dropping of the *e*.

abridge, abridgment   acknowledge, acknowledgment   judge, judgment
e. Consonant-plus-*y*. Change *y* to *i* unless the suffix begins with *i*.

defy, defiance defied defying   liquefy, liquefied liquefying

10.7 *Indefinite Articles.* Use *a* before consonants, aspirated *h*, long *u*, and *o* pronounced as *one*; use *an* before other vowels and silent *h*.
a man, a historic event, a eulogy (long *u* sound), a one-way ticket, a union
an aunt, an event, an onion, an unusual one (short *u*), miles an hour
Use *an* before groups of initials beginning with vowels *a, e, i,* and *o*, and vowel-sounding consonants *f, h, l, m, n, r, s,* and *x*; use *a* before *u* and *y* and the remaining consonants.

an AFL-CIO study   an NLRB (en) decision   an FDA (ef) finding
a UNESCO project   a TWA schedule   a WMAL program

11. UNDERSCORING

11.1 *Foreign Expressions*

a. Underscoring unnecessary. The trend is no longer to underscore or italicize foreign
    words and expressions when used in legal writing.

a fortiori	With stronger reason, all the more
alter ego	Other self
amicus curiae	Friend of the court
arguendo	In arguing, for the sake of argument
de facto	In fact, existing without lawful authority
de jure	By right, according to law
de minimis	Very small, trifling
de novo	Anew, over again
en banc	On the bench, before entire membership of the court
ex parte	On or from one side only
fait accompli	A thing accomplished and presumably irreversible
ibid.	In the same place, same citation at same page
id.	Same, same citation but different page
in camera	In chambers, in private
in haec verba	In these words, in the same words
in toto	In all, totally (preferred)
infra	Below (preferred)
inter alia	Among other things, among others
ipso facto	By the fact itself
per curiam	By the court
per se	By itself, taken alone
pro forma	As a matter of form, without consideration of its merits
quid pro quo	Something for something else
seriatim	In a series, in turn (preferred)
[sic]	So, such, as written
sine qua non	Without which not, without which the thing cannot be
status quo ante	The state of things before
sua sponte	On its own motion (preferred)
sub nom.	Under the name or title of
subpoena ad testificandum	Subpoena to testify
subpoena duces tecum	Subpoena to produce documents
supra	Above (preferred)
vel non	Or not (preferred)
voir dire	Preliminary examination

NOTE. More common, understandable English words can often be substituted. The
trend in legal writing is away from the use of foreign words, which are incomprehensi-
ble to many or most parties.

b. Do not underscore

ad hoc	caveat	certiorari	e.g.	et seq.
bona fide	cf.	dictim	et al.	etc.

ex officio	non sequitur	pro rata	subpoena
i.e.	per capita	res judicata	verbatim
imprimatur	per diem	situs	vice versa
mandamus	prima facie	status quo	

11.2 *Underscore Titles (Including "v.") in Case Citations*
F. W. Woolworth Co., 90 NLRB 289 (1950).
Plumbers Local 412 (Thomas Mechanical), 249 NLRB 714 (1980).
NLRB v. Teamsters Local 291, 633 F.2d 1295 (9th Cir. 1980).
NLRB v. Gissel Packing Co., 395 U.S. 575 (1969).
Carpenters Local 1976 (Sand Door) v. NLRB, 357 U.S. 93 (1958).
American Potash rule   *Moore Dry Dock* criteria   *Tree Fruits* decision

11.3 *Underscore Book and Article Titles.* In citations, underscore book titles and the titles of articles that appear in periodicals and newspapers. Do not underscore authors' surnames and the titles of periodicals and newspapers. (See rule 1.9 p. 7 for examples.)

11.4 *Underscore Names of Vessels,* Aircraft, and Spacecraft

NS *Savannah*   SS *America*   USS *Nautilus*   *Freedom 7*

11.5 *Underscore Certain Letters.* For clarity, underscore the letter "1" when cited as a subdivision. Also underscore capital letters used to represent names of hypothetical parties or places.

§ 23(*1*)
Employee *A* reported to Foreman *B* in department *X.*

523

12. GOOD USAGE

Strunk & White, *The Elements of Style* (3d ed. 1979) ("the little book") contains such crisp rules (with examples) as "Use the active voice" (rule 14), "Put statements in positive form" (rule 15), and "Omit needless words" (rule 17, stating "Vigorous writing is concise. A sentence should contain no unnecessary words, a paragraph no unnecessary sentences . . . . This requires not that the writer make his sentences short . . . but that every word tell"). Its brief rules of usage and principles of composition are recommended reading.

12.1 Avoid Legalese

Make a conscious effort to avoid using *said, such, aforecited, aforementioned,* and *aforesaid* (in place of *the, this,* or *these*), *and/or, duly, respective* (when *the* suffices), *respectively* (when avoidable), *same* and *such* (in place of *it* or *them*), inexact words *forthwith, herein,* and *herewith,* and the legal jargon *hereby, hereinafter, hereto, therefor, therefrom, therein, thereof, therewith, to wit, unto, vis-a-vis, viz, whereby,* and *wherein* (omitting or replacing them with plain words in common usage).

12.2 Avoid Wordy Phrases

Along the line of *(like)*
As far as I am concerned *(as for me)*
At all times *(always)*
At about, at approximately *(about)*
At such time as *(when)*
At the present time *(now)*
By means of *(by, with)*
By the name of *(named)*
Despite the fact that *(although)*
Due to the fact that *(because)*
During such time *(while)*
During the course of *(during)*
During the time that *(during)*
Each and every one *(each)*
For the purpose of *(for, to)*
In advance of *(before)*
In connection with *(in, concerning)*
In regard to *(regarding, concerning)*
In a manner similar to *(like)*
In a negligent manner *(negligently)*
In a position to *(can)*
Inasmuch as *(because, as, for)*
In excess of *(over)*
In lieu thereof *(instead)*
In many cases *(often)*
In order to *(to)*
In respect to *(about, concerning)*

In some cases *(sometimes)*
In spite of the fact *(despite)*
In the amount of *(for)*
In the case of *(if)*
In the course of *(during)*
In the event of *(if)*
In the immediate vicinity of *(near)*
In the last analysis *(delete)*
In the matter of *(in, concerning)*
In the near future *(soon)*
In the neighborhood of *(near, about)*
In the not too distant future *(soon)*
In this day and age *(today)*
In view of *(because)*
In view of the fact that *(because,
    considering that)*
Notwithstanding the fact *(although)*
Of an indefinite nature *(indefinite)*
Of an unusual kind *(unusual)*
Of great importance *(important)*
On or about *(about)*
On the ground that *(because)*
On the order of *(about)*
On the part of *(by)*
Owing to the fact that *(because)*
Prior to *(before)*
The fact that *(delete)*

The present time (now)

There can be no question that
(unquestionably)

Surrounding circumstances
(circumstances)

Subsequent to (after)

Until such time as (until)

With the exception of (except for)

Whether or not (omit not when
possible)

With reference to (about, concerning)

With regard to (regarding, concerning)

12.3 The Right Word

According to (according to company witness Edward Jones) and **claimed** (union witness John Smith claimed that) both imply doubt of veracity. Other terms in attribution are *acknowledged, added, admitted, announced, argued, asserted, commented, concealed, conceded, continued, declared, denied, disclosed, explained, mentioned, observed, pointed out, recounted, revealed, said, stated, swore,* and *testified.* They should be used for their specific meaning, not interchangeably merely for variety.

Adverb A verb may be split by an adverb. (They will soon go.) But an adverb should not intervene between a verb and its object. (They completed the negotiations satisfactorily—*not* completed satisfactorily the negotiations.

All of is correct before a pronoun (all of us), but not otherwise (all the money). The same rule applies to **both of.**

Allude to Someone or something that is identified is not *alluded to,* but *referred to.* An allusion is an indirect reference.

Although is preferable at the beginning of a sentence. **Though,** which is less formal, is preferable for introducing phrases and short clauses. (He was careless, though not intentionally.)

Alumnus, executor, sculptor now refer to women as well as men. The Postal Service designates both men and women "postmasters." If a gender-free term or feminine counterpart is not in common use, traditional terms may be used even though not literally accurate (Jane Smith, Esq.).

Among is used with more than two persons or things. (The money was divided among the four players.) When more than two are considered individually, however, **between** is preferred. (An agreement between the six heirs.)

As to is often superfluous (there was a question whether—*not* as to whether—they won) or misused as a preposition (there was a doubt about—*not* as to—proper conduct for the occasion; he was instructed on—*not* as to—the correct operating procedure).

Balance should not be used in place of *rest* or *remainder.* (The rest of them—*not* the balance of them—said nothing.)

Because is the most specific causal conjunction. (Because the remaining ballots were not determinative, he found it unnecessary to . . .) **Since,** which means "from a definite past time until now," may be used as a causal conjunction, but it is less definite, more casual, and more characteristic of easy speech than of writing. It should be avoided as a conjunction when it leaves the reader in suspense whether it is used in the temporal or causal sense.

As and **for** (after a comma) are also used as causal conjunctions.

Beside means "at the side." (We stood beside the river.)

Besides means "in addition to." (Besides the lecture there was a concert.)

Bid is past tense and the participle, in the sense of *an offer* (he has bid on the job); but **bade** and **bidden** are, in the sense of *direct, command.*

Case is often used unnecessarily. (It has rarely been the case that any mistake has been made.) Such sentences should be rewritten. (Few mistakes have been made.)

Connote, denote "What a word denotes is what it specifically means; what it connotes is what it suggests." Copperud, *American Usage and Style: The Consensus* 86 (1980).

During means "through the course of" (during the workweek).

When refers to a moment (when stepping off the curb).

While refers to a period of time (while crossing the street).

Ensure, insure, assure *Ensure* means "to make certain." *Insure* means "to provide insurance." *Assure* means "to remove worry or uncertainty." (Events are ensured; objects or lives are insured; persons are assured.)

Farther serves as a distance word. (You walk farther than he does.)

Further serves as a time or quantity word. (Pursue the subject further.)

Fewer, less Although *fewer* is used with countable units (fewer cars, houses, ships) and *less* is used otherwise (less gasoline, opportunity, sugar, time, weight), *less* is also used with plurals that indicate a unit such as distance (less than 150 miles), periods of time (less than 20 minutes), sums of money (less than $200), and weight (less than 50 pounds).

Former, latter are objectionable because they often make the reader look back and figure out which is which. Also, when referring back to a noun, *latter* should not displace a pronoun. (The new law concerns the government official. It is not clear whether he—not the latter—realizes it.)

He (Smith) If *he* alone is ambiguous, substitute *Smith;* never use both.

However should not be used at the beginning of a sentence unless it is intended to mean "in whatever way" or "to whatever extent." (However discouraging the prospects, he never lost heart.)

In, into *In* denotes location. (They met in the office.) *Into* denotes motion. (He went into the office.)

Include is not an all-inclusive word like *belong to, comprise, consist of,* or *be composed of.* It indicates that some members are omitted. (His group includes only three of the fast workers.) *Are* or *comprise* is preferable to introduce the all-inclusive. (Members of the group are . . . ; the group comprises all the factions.)

Incredulous applies only to people and means unwilling to accept what is offered as true. (The testimony was given with conviction, but the judge was obviously incredulous.

Incredible may apply to people, but usually applies to statements and means "unbelievable." (His story was incredible.)

Like, as *Like* is a preposition, meaning "similar to." It is correctly used before a noun or pronoun. (He looks like a happy person.) *As* is correctly used as a conjunction before a phrase or clause. (She looks happy, as in the old days.)

Male, female are not suitable for referring to a man or woman.

On is superfluous in stating days and dates (he arrived Tuesday), except at the beginning of a clause or sentence (on May 2, the Board . . .).

On, upon *On* is preferred when appropriate.

Oral, verbal Oral means "by mouth"; verbal means "in words," either spoken or written. "Oral agreement" is more precise than "verbal agreement."

Partially is best used in the sense of "to a certain degree" (partially resigned to it, partially blind). **Partly** carries the idea of a part as distinct from the whole (partly luck, partly skill, a log partly submerged).

Parameter means "general boundary" or "characteristic element."

Perimeter means "outer boundary of a two-dimensional figure."

People is used to refer to a segment of humanity (people of Paris).

Persons is used with a numeral (27 persons arrested).

Per annum is preferably replaced by *a year.*

Plus means "increased by." It does not have the conjunctive force of *and.* Consequently, a verb that follows it may be singular or plural, depending on the number of the subject. (Two plus two equals four; his ability plus his connections puts him in a good position.)

Profanity is irreverent or blasphemous, or swearing.

Obscenity is offensive to decency.

Vulgarity offends good taste and embraces both profanity and obscenity.

Reasons why is redundant. (The reason—*not* the reason why—he opposed it; *or* why he opposed it.)

Some time, sometime, sometimes *Some time* is an adverbial phrase meaning "an interval or period." (He stayed some time.) *Sometime* is an adverb indicating an indefinite occasion. (He will come sometime.) *Sometimes* means "occasionally" or "at one time or another." (Sometimes it rains.)

That introduces a restrictive clause and does not take commas. (The bridge that fell was 50 years old.)

Which introduces a nonrestrictive clause and takes commas. (The bridge, which was over 50 years old, was an asset to the community.) (See rule 8.4,a(5) p. 28 above.)

Various is preferable to **different** to indicate diversity without emphasizing unlikeness. (Various—*not* different—actors have performed.)

Watch A standard meaning of *watch* is "to keep under surveillance."

Where, when, in which, if *Where* indicates place (States where the rule is followed) and **is not a substitute for** *when* (when—*not* where—he refused to go to the office), *in which* (cases in which—*not* where—objections were filed), **or** *if* (if—*not* where— the evidence fails to show union animus; if—*not* where—a case involves no real issues).

While should be used only with strict literalness, in the sense of "during the time that," not in place of *and, but,* or *although.*

Whose may refer to things. (The tree whose leaves were falling.)

12.4 Rules for Singular and Plural

a. Affirmative.   When one subject is affirmative and the other is negative, the verb agrees with the affirmative. (Your honesty, not your pleas, causes me to relent.)

b. Agreement with subject.   The number of the verb agrees with the subject. (The trouble with truth is its many varieties. Houses are a commodity.)

c. Collective nouns.   Such nouns as *audience, majority, number, staff,* and *pair* (as well as the pronoun *some*) require singular or plural verbs, depending on whether they are used in a singular or plural sense. (A slim majority was for it; a majority of the votes were no. The number of accidents is great; a number of men were hurt.)

d. Compound subject.   Two or more nouns joined by *and* take a plural verb, except that a singular verb is used when the sense is a single idea. (Bread and butter was all he had. Every window, picture, and mirror was smashed.)

e. Either . . . or. If one subject is singular and the other is plural, the verb agrees with the nearer subject. (Either food or drinks are needed.)

f. Indefinite pronouns. *Anyone, anybody, each, either, everyone, everybody, neither, nobody, no one, one, somebody,* and *someone* usually take a singular verb. (Everyone takes off his coat.)

g. Money, time, distance. An amount of money, a space of time, or a unit of measurement takes a singular verb. (Fifty cents is the price. Twenty years is a long time. Five miles is a long way to walk.)

h. None takes a singular verb when it means "no one" or "not one." (None of us is perfect.) It takes a plural verb when it suggests more than one. (None are so fallible as those who are sure they are right.)

i. Plenty of. If *abundance, plenty, rest,* or *a fraction* is modified by a phrase introduced by *of,* the verb agrees with the noun in the phrase. (Plenty of potatoes are grown. One-fifth of the boats were lost.)

j. Relative clause. A plural is used in a relative clause following *one of.* (One of those people who are never on time.)

k. Words joined to subject. When other words are joined to a singular subject with *along with, as long as, as well as, besides, except, in addition to, including, like, no less than, not alone, together with,* or *with,* a singular verb is used. (His speech as well as his manner is objectionable.)

12.5 *The Right Preposition*

Errors are often made in choosing the right preposition to convey the intended meaning. Sometimes an unabridged dictionary must be consulted, because a desk dictionary may not be detailed enough to be helpful.

aberration: *from* his usual course, *of* mind
abhorrent: *of* compromises, *to* reason
ability: *at* painting, *with* paints
abut: *against* the cliff, *on* the line he surveyed
accessory: *after* (or *before*) the fact, *to* a crime
accommodate: *to* the inconvenience, *with* a loan
accompanied: *by* their dog, *with* a smile
accord: *between* the two, *of* interest, *with* the rest
accountable: *for* a trust, *to* an employer
acquiesce: *in* the ruling
acquit: *of* a crime, *with* credit
adapted: *for* seating many, *from* a model, *to* heavy weather
adept: *at* good newswriting, *in* handicrafts
adequate: *for* the purpose, *to* the need
advantage: gained *by* skillful maneuvering, *in* the air, *of* birth, *over* me
advise: *of* his coming, *with* his friends
advocate: *for* his chief, *of* air power
affinity: *between* them, *with* their surroundings
agree: *on* a plan, *to* a proposal, *with* a person
aggression: *upon* a country
aided: *by* running sales, *in* the attempt
alien: *from* the one intended, *to* the topic, *under* consideration
alienation: *between* the classes, *from* such ideas, *of* affections

allegiance: *from* the people, *to* the government
ally: *against* the enemy, *by* economic agreements, *of* the student, *with* Greece
aloof: *from* success, *in* choosing loneliness
alternate: *along* the route, *between* study and working, *in* the leading role, *with* each
    other
ambition: *for* him to succeed, *of* returning to work
amity: *between* nations, *of* one nation *with* another
amplify: *by* illustrative remarks, *on* his remarks
amused: *at* (or *by*) his antics, us *with* his antics
analogy: *between* things, *by* metaphor, *to* their own works, *with* another
anesthetize: *by* ether
anger: *at* an insult or injustice, *toward* the insulter or offender
angry: *at* an action, *with* a person
annoyed: feel annoyed *at* (or *with*), be annoyed *by*
antipathy: *against* (or *to*) a thing, *between* persons, *toward* a person
anxiety: *about* the future, *to* succeed
anxious: *about* a problem, *for* our happiness, *to* ameliorate the condition
apathy: *of* feeling, *toward* action
appreciation: *for* the help, *of* fine shades of meaning, *of* his work
apprehensive: *for* another's safety, *of* danger
approximation: *of* one type *to* another, *to* the truth
apropos: *of* the preceding statement
argue: *about* a question, *for* a proposition, *with* a person
arrive: *at* a small town, *in* a large city
arrogate: *for* another, *to* oneself
attest: *to* the truth
augmentation: *of* our numbers *by* enlistments
augmented: *by* reinforcements
auger: *from* signs, *of* success, *for* a cause
aversion: *to* (or *for*) persons or things, *from* exercise

basis: *for* and argument, *of* conjecture
beguile: *by* a sham, *with* an entertaining book
behalf: (formal representative) *on* behalf of, *in* behalf of a cause
break: away *from* the narrowness, *in* relations, *with* precedent

capacity: *for* work, *of* 10 gallons, *to* sign a document
careless: *about* dress, *in* one's work, *of* the feeling of others
cause: *for* alarm, *of* trouble
chagrin: *at* losing the opportunity
circumstances: *in* reduced circumstances, *under* the circumstances
cleared: my mind *about* the arrangement, *at* a loss, *for* top-secret work, snow *from*
    the walk, *of* all suspicion, *through* our committee, *up* after the rain, *with* the
    committee
coalesce: *for* the final thrust, *into* one, *on* a candidate
colliding: a car colliding *with* a truck (both in motion), waves colliding *with* the rocks
compare: *to* or *with* (now interchangeable)
compatible: *with* black and white sets
compete: *for* a prize, *with* others
complacent (satisfied): *toward* his situation
complaisant (obliging): *toward* all leaders
complement: *of* his extensive training

complementary: *to* his experience
compliment: *on* her outfit
concentration: *of* attention, *on* a problem
concerned: *about* the welfare of a friend, *by* the confusion, *for* somebody in trouble, *in* intrigues, not *to* disappoint the child, *with* business
concur: *in* a decision, *with* others
confided: *in* our discretion, his savings *to* me
conform: this regulation *to* existing practices, *with* the forested area
conformity: *to* his duty, *with* his ideals
congenial: *to* the spirit, *with* reason
congratulate: *for* keeping a cool head, *on* finding a job, his son *upon* his graduation
connect: *by* good roads *with* Hicksville
connive: *at* the violation of a law, *with* the officials
conscious: *during* the operation, *of* one's faults
consequent: *on* the growth of nationalism, *to* a rise in production
consist: *in* respecting the opinion of others, *of* two parts
consistent: *in* everything we do, *with* her former statement
consonant: *with* his character
contact: *among* many, *between* two, *of* the mind, *with* literature
contend: *against* an obstacle, *for* what he believed was right, *with* his superior
contiguous: *to* a road
contingent: *on* the weather, *on* his presence
contrast: *between* this and that, *of* three to one, *to* his dark hair, *with* a brilliant student, words contrasted *with* his behavior
convenient: *for* a purpose or use, *to* a place
conversant: *with* his story
correlation: *between* two comparable entities, *of* the three items
correlative: *with* the other
correspond: *to* reality, *with* me regularly
culminate: *in* a fight

debar: *from* taking his position
decide: *in* his favor, *on* their verdict
defect: *in* a machine, *of* judgment or character
defend: *from* harm, *against* intruders
deficiency: *in* intelligence, *of* food
defile: *by* an act, *with* a substance
depend: *on* the accuracy, *on* their parents, *upon* effort and ability
derogate: *from* his authority
derogation: *from* his book, *of* his influence
desirous: *of* learning, *to* ask his help
desist: *from* trying, *in* his efforts
destined: *for* the Orient, *to* be elected
destructive: *of* health, *to* young trees
devolve: *from* the emperor *upon* the subjects, *in* the strict order of seniority
differ: *about* (or *over*) its success (a question), *from* his brother in taste, *with* you
differentiate: *among* many, *between* two, this *from* that
disappointed: *in* a person, plan, hope, result, *with* a thing
disdain: *for* his actions, *to* reply
disgusted: *at* an action, *by* a quality or habit, *with* a person
dislike: *of* hard work, *for* Bach

dispense: *from* your promise, *with* formalities, the law *without* bias
displace: *by* force, *from* his country, position
displeased: *at* a thing, *with* a person
dispossess: *from* his land, *of* his property
disqualify: *for* citizenship, *from* competition
dissension: *among* friends, *between* friends, *with* the world
dissimilar: *from* those defending him, *to* the others
distill: *from* grain, *out* the impurities
distinguished: *by* talent, *for* honesty, *from* another person or thing
distrustful: *of* coincidences
diverted: *by* the child's playfulness, funds *from* the treasury *to* his own use
divest: oneself *of* responsibility
divide: *by* cutting, *into* parts
divorce: *between* thought and action, *from* society
dominant: *in* power or manner, *over* others
dominate: *by* religion, *over* everyone
drenched: *in* folklore, *with* sunlight, a drench *of* rain

eager: *for* success, *to* succeed
educated: *concerning* the needs of life, *for* living, *in* liberal arts
eligible: *for* the presidency, *to* the office
embark: *in* a new venture (to engage or invest), *on* a trip or new career (to make a start)
emigrate: *from* a country
employ: *at* a suitable wage, *in* a gainful pursuit
enamored: *of* a person, *with* a scene
encouraged: *by* success, another *in* his work
encroach: *on* their rights
endowed: *with* ability
enraged: *against* (or *with*) a person, *at* an action
enter: *by* the window, items *in* a ledger, *into* the spirit of it
entertained: *by* persons, *with* their doings
entrusted: *to* me, *with* the money
equal: *in* qualities, *to* a task
equivalent (adj.): *in* volume, *to* saying no; (n.) *of* two doses
essential: *in* study, *to* (or *for*) success, essentials *of* mathematics
estrangement: *from* bourgeois life, *of* her son
example: *from* history, *of* the split infinitive, *to* you
excuse (n.): *for* an action; (v.) *from* an obligation
expect: *profit* from investments, *honesty* of a person
experience: *for* oneself, *in* (or *of*) travel
expert: *at* chess, *with* knitting needles

faced: *by* alternatives, *with* ruin
familiar: *to* us, *with* another person
fascinated: *by* the results, *with* the furnishings
favorable: *for* skating, *to* his proposal
fear: *of* water, *for* another
flinch: *at* the thought, *from* making the attempt
forbid: him *to* go
freedom: *from* incarceration, *of* our country, *to* speak

friend: a friend *of* mine, a friend *to* the boy's club
frighten: *at* something threatening, *away* pigeons, *by* a sudden noise
frightened: *of* the dark

grieve: *after* mourning, *at* the funeral, *for* her mother
guard: *against* peril, *from* a person

honored: *by* your invitation, *for* his honesty, *with* an invitation
hope: *for* better times, *of* heaven

identical: *with* past experiments
identify: *by* credentials, *to* the police, *with* the man known to be innocent
immerse: *in* hot water
immigrate: *to* the United States
impatient: *at* action, *with* persons
impose: *on* (or *upon*) the guests
impress: *into* service, a duty *upon* a child, wax *with* a die
impressed: *by* her performance, *with* clarity
improve: *in* hardiness, *by* grating, *upon* that plan
improvement: *in* health, *upon* that
incentive: *for* employees, *to* work fast
indulge: *in* fattening foods, *with* the wrong crowds
indulgent: *of* bad habits, *to* gambling activities
infiltrate: *into* organized crime
infiltration: *of* the area *by* the guerrillas
influence (v.): *by* actions, *for* good
influence (n.): *of* a good man over others, exercise influence *upon* others
inimical: *to* the king, *toward* the enemy
initiate: *into* action
innate: *in* all qualities
inquire: *into* causes, *of* a person
inquiry: *about* (or *concerning*) any destination, *of* a bystander
inroad: *into* a battle
inseparable: *from* birth
insert: a change *in* a manuscript, bands of lace *on* the blouse
insight: *into* the future
inspire: *by* example, *with* courage
instill: *in* a child, *into* beliefs
intent: *on* pursuing, *upon* graduation
intention: *of* the burglar, *to* steal the goods
intercede: *for* a culprit, *with* a judge
intermediary: *between* persons, *in* a dispute
intervene: *between* sides, *in* the fight
intimacy: *of* association, *with* persons
introduce: *to* the judge, *into* evidence
intrude: *into* the house, *on* all those busy people, *upon* her uninvited
inundate: *by* letters, *with* pain
invest: *in* stocks and bonds, *with* great power

jealous: *of* a person, *of* one's good name, *for* their welfare
justified: *in* the murder

labor: *as* a miner, *at* a task, *for* a cause, *on* the new treaty, *through* the foreign dictionary, *under* a handicap, *up* one flight of stairs, *with* tools

laugh: *at* the clown, *away* our troubles, him *into* some manners, *off* the threats as being baseless, caused him to laugh *on* the wrong side of his mouth, him *out* of town

level: a gun *at*, building leveled *to* the ground, *with* you, line level *with* the horizon, leveled *against* the leaders, differences leveled *down*, trails leveled *out*

liable: *for* illegal acts, *to* prosecution

liberal: *in* his views, *with* praise

live: *at* a place, *in* a town, honor lives *among* men, *by* peddling, *for* science, on *through* his deeds, *to* a ripe age, *up* to that standard, *with* gusto, *with* the band leader

martyr: *to* rheumatism, martyred *for* his beliefs

mastery: *in* the field, *of* a craft, *of* the great artists, *over* his enemies

meddle: *in* his affairs, *with* my things

militate: *against* his promotion, *in* favor of progress

mock: *at* a person, him *for* showing fear, be mocked *with* vain desires

negligent: *about* traffic regulations, *in* her support, *of* attention

oblivious: *of* past slights, *to* the risks he runs

overlaid: *by* folklore, *with* a thick veneer

overrun: *by* rats, *with* weeds

overwhelm: *by* demands, *with* bills

parallel: *in* history, *to* the edge, cases parallel *with* each other

part: *from* a person, *with* a thing

persevere: *against* opposition, *in* a pursuit

persist: *against* objection, *for* 2000 years, *in* an action, *through* generations

piqued: *at* something done to us, *by* ridicule, him *to* violent efforts

plunge: road plunges *along* the slope, *into* debt, *into* the water, *through* a crowd

possessed: *by* a passion, *of* a strong back, *with* a desire for money

practice: *at* smoking, *in* penmanship, *of* a profession

precedent: *for* subversive action, *in* organizing the group, *of* paying only himself

predestined: *for* the ministry, *to* die

preface: his speech *with* a vow, *of* the manuscript, *to* a great discovery

pregnant: *by* her lover, *with* meaning

prejudice: *against* alcoholics, *for* drinking, *in* favor *of* nonalcoholics

prejudiced: *against* the appeal, *by* campaigning

prerequisite: *for* voting, *of* a surgeon, *to* join

prevail: *against* force, *in* the carpet's colors, *over* enemies, *with* her to go

prevailed: silence prevailed *along* the funeral route, *upon* her to sing, *with* youthful skill

prohibit: them *from* striking

protest: in protest *against* (or *to*)—not *of*

provide: *against* disaster, *for* your college, *with* food and clothes

put: *across* his point, *aside* (or *away*) the book, the time *at* 5 o'clock, plants put *forth* leaves, *in* one's opinion, *in* (or *into*) use, *in* (or *into*) water, *on* the table, a tax *on* cigarettes, wrong impressions *on* events, minds *to* it, *to* work, *upon* by his friends, *up* with

replaced: *by* an understandable English phrase, to replace *it* a larger one repugnance: *between* versions of testimony, *of* a person *against* another, *to* a deed or duty

resemblance: *of* one thing to another

revenge: *for* a hurt, *on* one's enemies

sanction: *for* an act, *of* the law

solicitous: *about* the crime rate, *for* her life, *of* the esteem of others, *to* please

strive: *against* drawbacks, *for* excellence, *to* achieve, *with* no regrets

sympathetic: *to* their needs, *toward* the dying, *with* the patients

sympathize: *in* another's mood, *with* a friend in trouble

sympathy: *for* another, *in* his sorrow, *with* his desires

talk: *to* (speak to) one or more persons, *with* (converse with) one or more persons in a discussion

taste: *for* simplicity, *in* house furnishings, *of* honey

thrill: *at* the song of a thrush, *with* pleasure

tolerance: *for* sugar, *of* a diseased heart, *to* antibiotics

tormented: *by* shyness, *with* severe headaches

umbrage: take umbrage *at* one's rudeness, gave umbrage *to* someone by not sending an invitation

unequal: *in* qualities, *to* a task

unfavorable: *for* a new enterprise, *to* a calm discussion

vary: *from* a rule, *with* the seasons

vest: power is vested *in* a man, a man is vested *with* power

vexed: *at* a thing, *with* a person

wait: *for* something to happen, *on* people at a table, *until* 6 o'clock

worthy: *of* note, *to* be called

yearn: *for* a loved one, *with* compassion

yield: *of* authority, *to* a sign